Victorian Arch

Original Plans for Cottages, Small Estates, and Commerce

Foreword by Tina Skinner

4880 Lower Valley Road, Atglen, PA 19310 USA

Front matter layout by Mark David Bowyer
Type set in Korinna BT/Korinna BT

ISBN: 0-7643-1969-8
Printed in China

Published by Schiffer Publishing Ltd.
4880 Lower Valley Road
Atglen, PA 19310
Phone: (610) 593-1777; Fax: (610) 593-2002
E-mail: Info@schifferbooks.com
Please visit our web site catalog at **www.schifferbooks.com**
We are always looking for people to write books on new and related subjects. If you have an idea for a book, please contact us at the above address.

This book may be purchased from the publisher.
Include $3.95 for shipping.
Please try your bookstore first.
You may write for a free catalog.

In Europe, Schiffer books are distributed by
Bushwood Books
6 Marksbury Avenue
Kew Gardens
Surrey TW9 4JF England
Phone: 44 (0) 20 8392 8585
Fax: 44 (0) 20 8392 9876
E-mail: Bushwd@aol.com
Free postage in the UK. Europe: air mail at cost.

Foreword

Late in the 1800s, architects began to publish plan books, very much like those that are so popular in bookstores and home design centers today. In these books, customers get the opportunity peruse pretty pictures of homes, and to study floor plans in order to choose a home that suits them. They then can order the complete plans and hire a contractor to build their "custom" home. The idea was quite novel at the turn of the century, born largely on the fact that printing costs allowed such dissemination of information.

With such resources available, more common citizens were able to commission architect-designed houses, and to pool local labor and resources to have them built. Previously, a home builder either paid an architect a much more exorbitant fee for an original design, or they simply scratched together a home working from a square-box plan, the results of which varied as greatly as the talents of those undertaking the project.

Thus "carpenter-built" was born as a term for "fancy" homes, and second homes, that were springing up everywhere. The movement hit at a prosperous time for the nation, when seaside resorts were mushrooming at the far reaches of new roads and train tracks, and the West was being won, and settled. Historic accounts of architecture in the Western states are peppered with the term "carpenter-built," documenting a trend among newly wealthy settlers to imitate the architectural styles they fondly recalled from back east. In resort towns, cottages or bungalows, were being built as summer havens.

This is one of the earlier books published that helped spawn the growth of "carpenter-built." It features more than 250 Victorian buildings pooled from the Co-operative Building Plan Association of architects in New York City and published in 1890. The book includes dozens of examples of architecture popular at the turn of the century, including bungalow, stick-style, Gothic revival, chateau style, Queen Anne, and Eastlake influenced designs.

The book was intended as a complete guide to the new homebuilder, and includes essays meant to gently instruct them in the skill of decorating and furnishing their new homes, as well as craft projects to satisfy the decorative urges of housewives. An essay in the book extols the virtues of Medieval Scandinavian architecture, a nod to the stick-style designs that predominate this volume. Further, the homeowner is instructed with a series of "desirable" finishes and "Rules of Color."

Should the reader consider cutting corners and simply decide to make improvements to their current dwelling, an essay on remodeling an old house advises strongly against such notions, as the "cost of remodeling and thoroughly improving an old house equals, if it does not exceed the cost of building a new one of superior accommodations and better appearance."

Much text is devoted to furnishing and decorating summer cottages, as seaside resorts are springing up to accommodate the disposable income of a rising middle class. In all, over 800 illustrations include artist renderings and photographs of front and side views, and floor plans complete with dimensions. Written descriptions include general dimensions, suggestions for interior finishes, color schemes, and cost estimates.

Beginning with humble cottages and working its way up to expansive residences, the book is presented in terms of cost – from homes that were intended to cost less than $1,000 to build, to homes that would run over $10,000; thus a broad range is represented. There are also several row houses. Commercial building plans include a hotel, bank, church or meeting hall, a boathouse, and a seven-room school plan. There are plans for a carriage house and nine stables, plus design tips for an ice house, greenhouse, a cistern, and hints on heating and ventilation, removal of household waste, plumbing and drainage, and landscape gardening. There's even a charming children's playhouse.

Chas. Hart. Lith. 36 Vesey St. N.Y.

Example of colors (as shown on cover) for a frame cottage.

Selected Designs

FROM

Shoppell's ∴ Modern ∴ Houses,

WITH

FULL DESCRIPTIONS AND ESTIMATES OF COST.

A WORK OF PRACTICAL ASSISTANCE

TO

Owners and Builders.

OVER 800 ILLUSTRATIONS.

PUBLISHED BY

THE CO-OPERATIVE BUILDING PLAN ASSOCIATION, ARCHITECTS,

63 Broadway, New York.

PREFACE AND GENERAL INDEX.

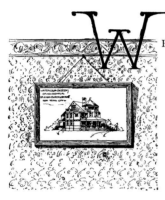

WHEN workmen finish a good building on which they bestowed unusual care and exercised their utmost skill, they are apt to present it to the owner with but few words ; they know it will speak for itself. With much the same feeling the "workmen" who prepared this volume present it to the reader. All we desire to say in a commendatory way is this : the two hundred and sixty designs selected for this volume are the best—"the survival of the fittest," so to speak—of more than six hundred designs made by this Association.

Long tables of contents and lists of illustrations which usually cover many pages of a work of this character are not given here, for the reason that the arrangement of contents is simplicity itself. The first part of the volume contains the miscellaneous matter, and the latter part the designs which succeed each other in the order of cost.

The following concise index is considered sufficient for all practical purposes :

SCANDINAVIAN DWELLINGS

—— OF THE ——

MIDDLE AGES

AS DESCRIBED

BY VIOLLET-LE-DUC.

*   *   *   *   *   *   *   *

Like their Aryan ancestors, it is their custom to build a great hall in their dwellings, in which they assemble their equals and retainers. There they deliberate, settle differences, and give banquets which are prolonged for several days and nights, and which frequently issue in brawls.

If an expedition to a neighboring territory promises great results, they select, as we said above, some unfrequented beach, commanded by a promontory or peninsula at the mouth of the river, and there fortify themselves so as to have a place of refuge and defense in the event of a failure, until another expedition comes to their relief: hence they are very careful always to keep themselves in communication with the sea, which secures them and their booty from all pursuit; for no other people is so inured to a maritime life, or capable of crossing the sea so rapidly, as these men of the North.

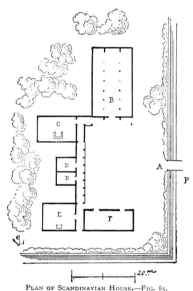

PLAN OF SCANDINAVIAN HOUSE.—FIG. 85.

The habitations of persons of distinction among them consist of a group of buildings of various dimensions and uses, arranged without symmetry, but with reference to the convenience of each. The most extensive of them resemble villages; for each apartment—or nearly so—is a house, small or large, according to the requirements. These houses are either in juxtaposition, just touching at one point, or apart, in which case they communicate by very low wooden passages.

Roofed with pine shingles or slabs of schist, these dwellings are of one floor only, and are often even partly sunk in the ground to secure the inhabitants more effectually from the cold. Palisading, hedges, and ditches surround the dwelling, for the men of this country are very tenacious of their independence; and even the towns rather resemble an agglomeration of establishments, each with its inclosure, than a collection of houses in juxtaposition along the highway. To prevent the accumulation of snow upon the roofs, they are made very steep.

The Scandinavians breed horses, and are good riders. The broad meadows of their country supply forage for these animals, which are, moreover, inured to hardship.

In their maritime expeditions they do not hesitate to take their horses with them in their capacious boats, and they carry off those which they meet with in the country they invade; thus they readily form bands of formidable cavalry, falling unawares upon the hamlets they pillage, and then retiring and rejoining the main body of their armed force.

Figure 85 gives the plan of one of the above-mentioned detached habitations. At A is the entrance, a foot-bridge across a fosse, on whose escarpment is planted a quickset hedge. At B, is the great hall, whose roof is supported by a double row of posts.

A wooden porch gives access to a hall c, in the middle of which a hearth is constructed. It is there that the family stay in winter, and the viands are prepared. The inhabitants even sleep in these apartments during the severe cold. At D, are the living rooms of the family during the temperate season. At E, the hall reserved for the servants and for strangers. At F, a large stable and barn for forage.

Figure 86 presents the view of this habitation from the point P. The openings which light the apartments are filled in with perforated wood, presenting fanciful designs. To prevent draughts, sheets of talc, in the dwellings of the wealthy, or of asses' skin in those of the poor, are fastened on the insides of these openings, admitting a dim light.

The smoke escapes through wide openings left in the roof, and sheltered by a kind of movable louvre, which is lowered at pleasure to close the orifice.

As previously mentioned, the roofs are covered with shingles of pine-wood overlapping like scales, or in some districts with large slaty stones.

VIEW OF SCANDINAVIAN HOUSE.—FIG. 86.

The timbers are painted in very lively colors forming interlacings. The elders among the Scandinavians assert that the dwellings of their forefathers were circular.

The Scandinavians have a great regard for trees, and their habitations are surrounded by them.

Planning a Modern House.

I. THE INTERIOR.

The points to be decided first are the number and sizes of the rooms; then their arrangement with the objects in view of obtaining the greatest convenience, the free communication between the different rooms and parts of the house, and the proper lighting, heating and ventilating of each separate room.

A well planned house should provide passages from the main hall to the kitchen portion and to any other part of the house. That is, the hall should be so arranged as to command all the rooms, but in doing this space should not be wasted nor rooms cramped or distorted, as the nearer to square the rooms are kept, the better the result.

The doors and windows should be so placed as to allow sufficient room for furniture; doors should be swung so that they cannot possibly "clash" with each other.

The kitchen portion should be isolated as completely as practicable from the main or living parts of the house. This is best accomplished by an arrangement that makes it necessary to pass *two doors* in going from the main part to the kitchen and by so arranging the butler's pantry that communication between the dining-room and kitchen will be through it.

By these precautions the odors of the kitchen are kept within bounds.

Ample pantry room should be provided in the kitchen; the cellar stairway should be in direct communication with the kitchen. If a servants' stairway is desired, it should be so placed as to be accessible from or near the kitchen and should land in a hall or corridor in the second story; the object being to allow the servants to pass from the first to second story without having to enter the main part of the house.

The relative positions of the different rooms in the main house depend greatly upon the conditions of the site, points of the compass, etc.

If the problem will admit it, a large, well-lighted hall, with an open fire-place, should be decided upon as it gives an impression of cheerfulness, comfort and room that is painfully lacking in the narrow and gloomy halls so often found in houses that in other respects are well-arranged. A large hall also answers the purpose of a sitting-room or a reception-room, and thus saves the expense of one room. The main hall should be entered if possible through a vestibule, particularly in cold climates.

The dining-room should have a southern exposure.

The library may be partially isolated, if desired, for greater privacy.

The parlor should have the most direct communication with the main hall and should command the best view.

In planning these rooms the fire-places should be so placed as to economize in chimney stacks as much as possible, making one stack answer for two or more fire-places.

VIEW OF AN ATTRACTIVE HALL.

The positions and sizes of the verandas and porches depend upon the conditions of the site and the exterior design of the house.

The arrangement of rooms in the second story should allow direct communication from halls to all bedrooms, bath-room, main and servants' stairs.

Each bedroom should have ample closets and a large linen closet should be provided, accessible from the hall.

If the height of the roof permits, it is well to plainly finish a number of bedrooms in the attic designed for the use of servants.

The finish and decoration of the several parts of the house depend of course upon the amount of money the owner wishes to expend.

It is always desirable to finish with hard wood as many of the principal rooms in the first story as the limit of cost will allow.

The main hall and vestibule should be finished alike and both should have wainscoting about four feet high, either paneled or staved as the cost admits. The wainscoting should continue up the main stairway to the second story hall and stop at any convenient point.

The main staircase should be of the same materials as the hall finish, and should be as elaborate and graceful as consistent with the general design of the interior.

A stationary seat in the main hall, either at the fire-place or near the stairs is desirable ; when neatly upholstered it has a very pleasing effect and it is very useful.

By means of a neat plaster cornice and a picture moulding placed at such a distance below it as the general proportions of the hall demand, and a plaster centre piece, a pleasing and inexpensive finish is devised. The walls may be left plain or can be papered or tinted. An economical and beautiful method of decorating the walls is by tinting, which is done by mixing kalsomine colors with the finishing coat of plaster. Almost any color can be obtained in this manner, the favorites being yellows, pinks and blues. The frieze between the cornice and picture moulding may be very effectively treated with a stenciled border of some foliating design. The effect thus obtained is artistic while the cost is comparatively slight. The ceilings may be tinted in the same manner in some color that will blend well with the walls, or they may be left white. The same effect can be obtained by kalsomining but is not so lasting. If the walls are papered the same general scheme is retained. This mode of decorating the walls and

ceilings may be carried out for the other principal rooms, using different tints if desired.

If the owner does not mind the extra expense it is advisable to finish the main hall and vestibule with an open timber ceiling, as the richness of effect thus obtained more than justifies the extra outlay. The beams are false beams boxed with ⅞ inch stuff, with a moulding run at the intersection of the beams with the ceiling. The spaces between the beams may be plastered, but the best effect is obtained by filling them in with narrow tongued and grooved ceiling stuff.

The parlor should have a neatly moulded base, picture moulding, plaster cornice and centre piece. The same general treatment of walls and ceilings may be carried out as is used in the main hall.

The dining-room should be wainscoted, if not too expensive. In case wainscoting is not used a neat moulded chair rail should be used which, with a moulded base, picture moulding, plaster cornice and centre piece, completes the finish.

The other principal rooms should have the same general treatment omitting the wainscot or chair rail.

The kitchen should have staved wainscoting about three feet six inches high with moulded cap and floor strip. The sink should be supported on turned wooden legs and the space beneath it left open with the plumbing exposed.

MANTEL AND FIRE-PLACE.

The butler's pantry should be wainscoted the same as the kitchen, and fitted up with sink and dresser with sliding glass doors and shelves in the upper portion, and with counter shelf and drawers underneath.

The principal bedrooms may have moulded base, plaster cornice, picture moulding and centre piece, if the owner desires. If not, they should be finished with a neatly moulded base and picture moulding only.

The bath-room should have staved wainscoting three feet six inches high, with moulded cap and floor strip. The fixtures may be encased in staved casing to correspond with the wainscot or may have paneled casing. The top of the bath tub and the seat and flap of water closet should be of hard wood; the wash basin should have a small door underneath.

The mantels throughout the house should correspond in design and finish with the general finish of the rooms in which they are placed, and as they are the principal features in the rooms they should be as well finished and as elaborate as the cost of the house will allow.

The hearths and facing of fire-places may be tiled, if not too costly, or may be of marble or slate. An economical, and at the same time effective mode of treating the facings of fire-places is with enameled brick or red or buff-colored pressed brick, with joints neatly pointed.

The style of trim may be varied according to the owner's taste. In the principal rooms the trim of the windows should run to the floor and finish on a base block the same as the door trim; the windows should have panel backs to correspond with the doors. Portiere openings may be trimmed the same as doors and, if desired, can be elaborated by a turned or twisted wooden transom grille. The portiere poles should be of the same material as the finish of the rooms in which they are placed and should be supported on suitable wooden or brass brackets.

DESIGN No. 471. PERSPECTIVE VIEW OF THE HALL AND STAIRCASE

AXIOMS AND RULES OF COLOR

The following, prepared by Dr. Dresser, form an admirable compend for the guidance of persons interested or engaged in the decoration of houses.

1. Regarded from an art point of view, there are but three colors, namely: blue, red and yellow.
2. Blue, red and yellow have been termed primary colors; they cannot be formed by the admixture of any other colors.
3. All colors other than blue, red and yellow result from the admixture of the primary colors.
4. By the admixture of blue and red, purple is formed; by the admixture of red and yellow, orange is formed; and by the admixture of yellow and blue, green is formed.
5. Colors resulting from the admixture of two primary colors are termed secondary; hence purple, orange and green are secondary colors.
6. By the admixture of two secondary colors a tertiary color is formed; thus, purple and orange produce russet (the red tertiary); orange and green produce citrine (the yellow tertiary); and green and purple, olive (the blue tertiary); russet, citrine and olive are the three tertiary colors.
7. When a light color is juxtaposed to a dark color, the light color appears lighter than it is and the dark color darker.
8. When colors are juxtaposed, they become influenced as to their hue. Thus, when red and green are placed side by side, the red appears redder than it actually is, and the green greener; and when blue and black are juxtaposed, the blue manifests but little alteration, while the black assumes an orange tint or becomes "rusty."
9. No one color can be viewed by the eye without another being created. Thus, if red be viewed, the eye creates for itself green, and this green is cast upon whatever is near. If it views green, red is in like manner created and cast upon adjacent objects; thus, if red and green are juxtaposed, each creates the other in the eye, and the red created by the green is cast upon the red, and the green created by the red is cast upon the green; and the red and the green become improved by being juxtaposed. The eye also demands the presence of the three primary colors, either in their purity or in combination; and if these are not present, whatever is deficient will be created in the eye, and this induced color will be cast upon whatever is near. Thus, when we view blue, orange, which is a mixture of red and yellow, is created in the eye, and this color is cast upon whatever is near; if black is in juxtaposition with the blue, this orange is cast upon it, and gives to it an orange tint, thus causing it to look "rusty."
10. In like manner, if we look upon red, green is formed in the eye, and is cast upon adjacent colors; or if we look upon yellow, purple is formed.
11. Harmony results from an agreeable contrast.
12. Colors which perfectly harmonize improve one another to the utmost.

13. In order to perfect harmony, the three colors are necessary, either in their purity or in combination.
14. Red and green combine to yield a harmony. Red is a primary color, and green, which is a secondary color, consists of blue and yellow — the other two primary colors. Blue and orange also produce a harmony, and yellow and purple, for in each case the three primary colors are present.
15. It has been found that the primary colors in perfect purity produce exact harmonies in the proportions of 8 parts of blue, 5 of red, and 3 of yellow; that the secondary colors harmonize in the proportions of 13 of purple, 11 of green, and 8 of orange; and that the tertiary colors harmonize in the proportions of olive 24, russet 21, and citrine 19.
16. There are, however, subtleties of harmony which it is difficult to understand,
17. The rarest harmonies frequently lie close on the verge of discord.
18. Harmony of color is, in many respects, analagous to harmony of musical sounds.
19. Blue is a cold color, and appears to recede from the eye.
20. Red is a warm color, and is exciting; it remains stationary as to distance.
21. Yellow is the color most nearly allied to light; it appears to advance toward the spectator.
22. At twilight blue appears much lighter than it is, red much darker, and yellow slightly darker. By ordinary gaslight blue becomes darker, red brighter, and yellow lighter. By this artificial light a pure yellow appears lighter than white itself when viewed in contrast with certain other colors.
23. By certain combinations, color may make glad or depress, convey the idea of purity, richness or poverty, or may affect the mind in any desired manner, as does music.
24. When a color is placed on a gold ground, it should be outlined with a darker shade of its own color.
25. When a gold ornament falls on a colored ground, it should be outlined with black.
26. When an ornament falls on a ground which is in direct harmony with it, it must be outlined with a lighter tint of its own color. Thus, when a red ornament falls on a green ground, the ornament must be outlined with a lighter red.
27. When the ornament and the ground are in two tints of the same color, if the ornament is darker than the ground, it will require outlining with a still darker tint of the same color; but if lighter than the ground no outline will be required.

VIEW OF AN INTERIOR WITH PORTIÈRES

A PLEA FOR PORTIÈRES

ITHIN a comparatively few years the portière has been working its way into popular notice and favor.

At first in public places, in lecture halls
and theatres, the little curtains were found
to be an improvement upon noisily swinging doors or treacherous screens; then
their beauty and utility began to be
appreciated in private houses, till at last
they have won a recognized position in
the household economy of thousands of
home-loving people.

The day of the angular, hard and
noisy door, with its unyielding habits
and unfortunate trick of being always in
the way, is nearly numbered, except for
principal passageways. People are finding out that a portière does
not get ajar and take one unexpectedly between the eyes at night;
the portière does not slam with every sudden gust of wind and
disturb every one within ear-shot as a cannon or a dynamite blast
would; the portière is not liable to be left open when it should be
closed and closed when it should be open by thoughtless children
or careless domestics. It is noiseless, inexpensive, inviting, convenient, comfortable.

But many people will object that by the use of the portière one
is subject to sudden draughts or unwelcome incursions. This is not
the case, however. When properly hung a light curtain will admit
air, yet exclude draughts, better than a door: with the door it is
always a feast or a famine—either all draught or no air, but its softer
substitute checks the direct current and admits only the pleasant
coolness.

As we have already suggested, no one would dream of closing a
hallway or entrance to a detached suite of rooms by a portière;
propriety will dictate where it should be used. Between apartments

naturally connected, as between parlor and library, or nursery or
alcove, for study or boudoir or music room, no other means of sepa-
ration is so good because it separates without disconnecting.

In the old times, when one "living room" was superheated and
the rest of the house left at an Arctic temperature, it was wise to
have solid doors to seal an apartment hermetically. Now when the
aim of modern heating appliances is to give an even temperature to
the whole house, the old-time freezing hall and passages are things
of the past and we no longer need tight fitting doors to inside rooms.

And now the question comes up, "how shall we hang our
portières?" It is a query very quickly and easily answered. A rod
of brass or wood or whatever material one cares to use is placed over
the door and supported by brackets on each end. This is the first
step. We do not insist upon the material of either rod or brackets,
because that is always a matter for individual taste to settle. Along
the rod are strung a number of loosely fitting rings, and from these
rings depends the curtain, which may be of any suitable fabric. We
have seen cretonne, heavy curtain stuff, Persian fabrics and decorated sail cloth in use, sometimes plain and unadorned and again
covered with embroidery or ornaments of brass, old coins, Japanese
figures, or any of the thousand and one fashionable adornments of
the day. Sometimes one curtain is used, swinging across the
entire length of the rod, and sometimes two, leaving the aperture
in the middle. At the floor curtains should touch, but not drag.

Æsthetically considered portières supply much needed color
and beauty. They are, in themselves, highly decorative and if they
had no other value this should commend them to people of taste
and refinement. From an economical standpoint it is sufficient to
say that they are cheaper than good doors—much cheaper if the
ladies are left to manage it, as their knowledge of beautiful but
inexpensive stuffs, their skill in lining thin materials, their good
taste in adapting materials already on hand, brought forth from
chests or store-rooms, not only secure economy, but give an in-
dividuality to the rooms which is invaluable.

VIEW OF A HALL AND STAIRCASE

THE HALL AND STAIRCASE

THE narrow, cold and cheerless staircase hall will soon be a thing of the past. The hall is now made a useful and beautiful feature of every good design.

It should be square rather than long and narrow, thus making it a room rather than a passage.

It should have a fireplace, not only for the sake of comfort and beauty, but for the reason that a fireplace in the lower hall ventilates the whole house, more or less. The impoverished air from adjoining rooms and from the upper floors (bad air is heavy and descends) is attracted to it and carried off.

It should have a beautiful staircase (not necessarily expensive), with risers not over seven inches, treads not less than ten inches, and at least one platform to afford a rest and make the ascent easy. Winding steps should never be built where they can be possibly avoided.

It should display some stained glass, if stained glass is wanted. The hall does not require full light; a subdued light is better.

It should have a hat and coat closet.

It should be protected from cold and draughts by a vestibule or storm doors during the winter season.

THE OLD HOUSE.

THE REMODELED HOUSE.

REMODELING AN OLD HOUSE.

ADVICE to people about to remodel old houses :—*Don't*. Generally speaking, the cost of remodeling and thoroughly improving an old house equals, if it does not exceed the cost of building a new one of superior accommodations and better appearance. Labor is the largest item of expense. In remodeling, much of the labor is expended in tearing down before the work of building up commences.

For the sake of " old association " is not a good reason for remodeling, because the " old association " features are usually destroyed. When the heights of stories must be changed the waste of labor is so great that the purpose of remodeling should be dismissed at once.

Where practicable, the most satisfactory disposition of the old house is to build a new house in front of it, using the old house as a rear extension. Inexpensive changes of its exterior will sufficiently assimilate the styles of the old and the new.

But there are plenty of exceptions to the general advice given above : One is when the owner has a Colonial house of good design, he may be advised to repair and enlarge it, improving the interior with modern plumbing and conveniences, even elaborating some of the exterior and interior ornamental features, always being careful to preserve the original spirit or style of the design. This is called restoring and enlarging rather than remodeling.

An exterior that is profusely ornamented about the cornices with gig-saw work copied from pantalet patterns may be vastly improved by removing the cheap stuff and substituting solid verge boards with molded edges.

An interior first floor with narrow doorways from the hall and between the rooms may be greatly improved by widening the doorways, excepting those which connect with the kitchen.

To improve a first floor that is too near the ground the entire frame of the house may be raised and new under-pinning may be introduced from the grade line to the sill, without much expense.

A narrow veranda is a nuisance that may be abated by simply building out the floor to any width desired, covering the newly-made open veranda with an awning.

Bay windows are effective and useful improvements. A bay gives to a room, often, the slight enlargement that is needed to make it comfortable.

The cuts given herewith illustrate remodeling that was fairly successful. All the conditions were unusually favorable: the old frame was as good as new, the foundation walls were perfect and of sufficient height, the arrangement of rooms was satisfactory, and

very little in the way of new trim and decoration was required for the interior.

The only new wall built was for a wing on the right side, indicated on the floor plan by black lines. As shown by the plan, the wing provided for a square hall, a staircase with landings, and a library.

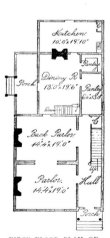

FIRST FLOOR PLAN OF OLD HOUSE.

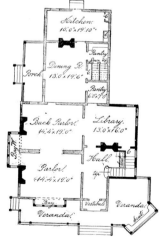

FIRST FLOOR PLAN OF REMODELED HOUSE.

But the intelligent student of plans will note all the changes readily. It seems necessary to say, only, that the wing, the veranda, the bays and the high slated roof which provided for four new bedrooms, supplied the additional accommodations required, and that the owner was satisfied with the new exterior and with the amount expended.

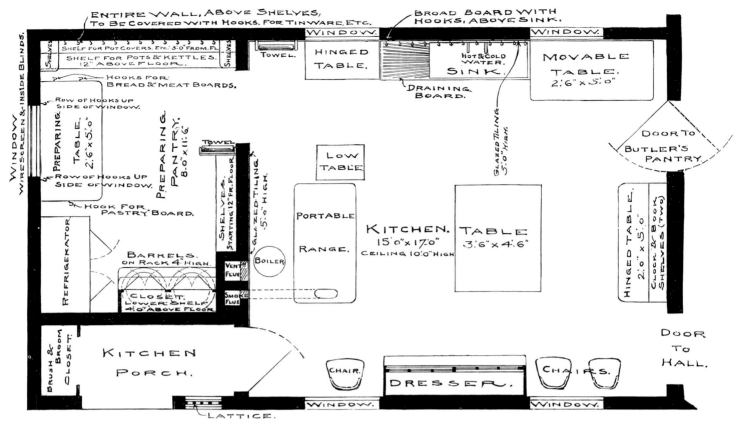

MARIA PARLOA'S PLAN FOR A MODEL KITCHEN

*A MODEL KITCHEN

BY MARIA PARLOA

NO room in the house requires more thought and care for its construction than the kitchen. The aim should be to arrange it simply, and yet so conveniently that work may be done with the fewest steps and the least loss of time. There is such a thing as having so many improvements that the whole machinery becomes complicated, and a great deal of time and labor is needed to keep it in order.

The size of the kitchen is an important matter. Although the room should be spacious enough to contain sink, range, table, dresser and chairs, and to give ample opportunity for free movements, it should not be so large as to oblige one to make many steps to and from sink, table, range or pantry. A good size is 15 x 17.

The ventilation is a prominent factor of the comfort of not only those who work in the kitchen, but of the entire household. If the room lack good ventilation, the strength of those who work in it will become exhausted sooner than it should, and they will become unnecessarily irritated. Besides, the odors of cooking, which should pass to the open air, will instead escape to all parts of the house.

The room should be high, with large windows that can be dropped from the top. When the kitchen is located in a one-story extension the ventilation may be made almost perfect by means of a skylight or ventilator in the roof. In any case a ventilator may be arranged in the chimney. No matter how excellent the room may be in all other respects, it will be a failure unless there be light in plenty and good ventilation. Let these matters be among the first that are taken into consideration. There should not be a part of the kitchen or its closets which the light of day does not reach. Health and cleanliness demand this. When a house is small and

economy must be rigorously observed, the kitchen chimney will be used also for other rooms, but when expense need not be taken into account, it will be well to have the kitchen chimney entirely separate. This is one of the best ways to prevent all the odors of cooking from reaching other rooms.

Every part of the kitchen, pantry and closet, except the ceiling, should be finished in such a way that it may be washed. Nothing is better for the flooring than hard wood. If the floors are to be covered, no better material than lignum can be used. It is soft, clean and durable. Oilcloth is very cold and is the cause of a great deal of rheumatism.

It is well to have the wood-work such as to require oiling only, and the walls should be painted a rather light color. When possible, the walls about the sink, tables and range should be tiled. Tiles seem to be rather expensive at the outset, but in the long run it is true economy to use them, as they will last as long as the house. They may be easily kept bright and clean. The time will come when few people will think of finishing a kitchen without them. The English or Dutch tiles should be used, and blue and white should predominate.

Lack of table room is a drawback met with in most kitchens. There ought to be an abundance of such room, so that when a meal is being prepared or served there need be no crowding or confusion, and it may be obtained by having two or three swinging tables in the room. When they are not in use they may be dropped.

The sink should be large,—there is nothing better than iron,— with a sloping and grooved shelf at one end, on which to drain dishes. It should not be enclosed. Every dark, enclosed place in a

kitchen is a source of temptation to the slovenly. Let the light reach every part of the room. At the right hand of the sink have a long, narrow table containing two drawers for towels. Unless the walls above, below and at the sides of the sink be tiled, they should be finished with hard wood. If tiles be used, have a broad capping of hard wood extend across the upper edge of the top row, in which to put hooks for various small utensils that are in frequent use about the sink. Under the sink have more hooks for dish-pans, dish-cloth, etc.

There should be a door between the kitchen and the china closet or butler's pantry. This should be near the sink and the pantry. On the opposite side of the kitchen a dresser should be built between the windows. Here can be kept the kitchen table-ware and various utensils. The shelves each should have a groove, in order that platters and other dishes may be placed on edge. There should be two drawers, and below the drawers, two closets with shelves. The doors of the upper part of the dresser should be made in part of glass, and should slide.

In the centre of the kitchen have another table about 3½ x 4½ feet. This should contain a drawer for knives, forks, spoons and other utensils that are in frequent use in that part of the kitchen. Have a small table also, about the height of the range. This is for use as a resting place for utensils used when griddle-cakes, omelets, waffles, etc., are made. When not in use it may be moved aside. Between the door to the hall and that to the china-closet have a swinging table or a settee table; the latter being that kind which serves as a seat when not in use for ironing or other purposes. Above the table have two shelves for cook-books and other books, and a clock.

Now comes the question of a range. Which shall it be—a set or a portable range? There are points in favor of each. Set ranges occupy less room, permit of roasting and broiling before the fire, and insure a constant supply of hot water. But there are disadvantages; they do not respond quickly to checks and draughts, they consume a large amount of coal, the brick hearth becomes very hot and uncomfortable to stand upon, and there is only one side to approach, which necessitates considerable lifting and moving of utensils.

A portable range can be so placed that it will be possible to walk all around it. It can be run with about half the quantity of coal required for a set range. It responds quickly to the opening or shutting-off of a draught. One's feet do not become heated by standing near it. There are no dark corners. It does away with the necessity of much lifting of heavy utensils. And it can be so managed that there shall be a hot oven at any time of the day.

But with a portable range the supply of hot water is limited, the roasting must be done in the oven and the broiling over the coals.

The window seats should be broad, that a few pots of flowers or herbs may be placed on them. There is no other room in the house where plants will grow so well.

Convenient to the range and sink there should be a large pantry—about 12 ft. x 8 ft. The window should have a wire screen and inside blinds. A large, strong table, with two drawers, should be placed before this window. Have hooks on the ends of the table on which to hang the pastry-board, the board on which cold meats are cut, and that on which bread and cake are cut. The rolling-pin, cutters, knives and various small utensils may be kept in one drawer, and spices, flavoring extracts, baking-powders, etc., in the other.

The wall at one end of the room should be covered with hooks on which to hang saucepans and other utensils. About one foot from the floor there should be a strong, broad shelf, on which to place heavy pots and kettles. Two feet above it there should be a narrow shelf for the covers of the pots and saucepans. By this arrangement all of these utensils may be kept together and always in sight, and no time need be lost in searching for any of the articles.

A number of shelves may be placed between the window and this end of the room, on which to keep materials used very frequently, such as sugar, salt, rice, tapioca, etc.

In the frame of the window, but within easy reach, put hooks, on which to hang spoons and an egg-beater.

At the lower end of the room have wall-closets built about four feet from the floor. The shelves within them should be about twenty inches wide and the doors should be supplied with locks. Under the closets have a strong rack, four inches high, on which to keep barrels. The rack secures a free circulation of air under the barrels, thus keeping their contents sweet.

On one side, running the length of the room, have shelves, beginning a foot from the floor and running as high as the top of the wall-closets. On the lower shelves may be kept buckets and jugs, while the upper ones will accommodate mixing bowls, measuring cups, baking and mixing pans, and, indeed, all of the utensils for which space has not already been provided.

At the end of this row of shelves have a place for a towel, so as to avoid the trouble of going to the kitchen whenever the hands require wiping.

With this arrangement of the kitchen and pantry the cooking and the washing of dishes can be done in a small space, steps and time can be saved, and half of the kitchen will generally be unused and ready for the servants' table or any other purpose. The points kept in view throughout are—concentration of work, good light and ventilation, ample table room, cleanliness, and the giving of an attractive appearance.

It is understood that there is a cellar or cold room convenient to the kitchen.

FURNISHING AND DECORATING A SUMMER COTTAGE

By Adelia B. Beard

NO one wishes to expend a large amount in furnishing a cottage which is inhabited only a few months each summer, and for the rest of the year is left to take care of itself. Indeed, expensive furniture is decidedly inappropriate and out of place in such a house, but at the same time there is no reason why the little summer home need be barren of all decoration, nor why it should be furnished, as it so often is, without regard to taste or the eternal fitness of things.

It requires but a trifling expense to make of the cottage a pretty and inviting retreat, containing all of the necessaries, many of the comforts, and not a few of the beauties of a home.

Some hints were given in a previous article in this magazine on how to treat a seaside cottage. The following suggestions will be found appropriate for the furnishing and decorating of a cottage among the mountains. The majority of these houses, or "boxes" as they are sometimes called, are small, and it has been my endeavor to adapt the furnishing to their limited space as well as to their peculiarities of structure.

The first illustration shows an original design for a dressing-stand. It is made of two plain pine shelves, two segar boxes, two small brackets and an ordinary mirror. The shelves are fastened to the wall with braces or brackets made of pine. The larger shelf is covered with cretonne, and has a plaiting of the same around the edge. On each end of this shelf is tacked or screwed a segar box, used for holding brushes and combs. These boxes, as well as the upper shelf and small side brackets, are painted the prevailing color of the cretonne. The larger shelf reaches across, and is fastened to the two upright wall joists, while the smaller one fits in between the joists, and is fastened to the wall. The mirror is hung over the small shelf and rests upon it. Small squares of pine board are used for the side brackets, and they, like the shelves, rest upon wooden braces.

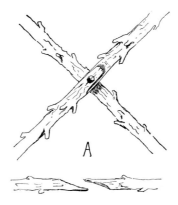

A Dressing-Stand

The second picture shows a wash-stand, simple in the extreme, yet not unattractive in its simplicity; one that occupies but little space and requires but a short time to construct.

A wide shelf fitting in between the upright joists, supported by strong braces, forms the wash-stand proper. This shelf has a round hole directly in the centre, which is large enough to admit the lower half of a wash-basin, and is covered with marbleized enamel cloth. The edge of the cloth is cut in points, then turned over and tacked to the edge of the shelf. The brackets on either side of the shelf are also covered with the enamel cloth. Two broomsticks fastened together and hung by a heavy cord form the towel rack. The top stick is a trifle shorter than the other, but both are long enough to reach across and rest against the two joists. This allows space at the back and gives plenty of room for the towels.

A Wash-Stand

A convenient form of corner clothes-press or closet is shown in the third illustration, which will, perhaps, be appreciated by those who, while domiciled in a summer cottage, have felt the woeful need of some place to hang their clothes where they will be out of sight and free from dust.

This clothes-press is simply constructed, as the plan shows. Two boards about four feet long and one wide are placed across the corner of the room, one near the ceiling, the other resting on the floor. They are secured by hooks, which are fastened at each corner of the boards, and rings screwed in the wall. A corner shelf resting upon cleats nailed to the wall, or on braces, is fastened in the corner; under this, flat against the wall, fitting into the corner, is a row of hooks. Hooks are also fastened to the edge of the shelf. The drapery of cretonne or canton flannel is fastened on the inner edge of the top board, and falls to the floor inside of the lower board. Both of the boards are covered with a box-plaited quilling of the material used for the drapery. The curtains, although parted in the illustration to show the interior of the press, should be full enough to fall together and enclose the opening.

Only some pine twigs, a piece of bamboo fishing rod, two yards of cheese cloth and a dozen brass rings are necessary to dress a

window like that in our fourth illustration. It is a pretty and suitable window decoration for a mountain cottage and anyone can manage it. The twigs for the lattice work

Rustic Dressing of a Window.

are tacked together where they cross, and, as they must necessarily be short ones, they are joined at these points, as shown in diagram letter A. The lattice is made entire before it is fitted to the window, and requires to be tacked to the window-frame only at the corners. This allows of its being removed when the window is washed. The bamboo rod from which the short Dutch curtain is suspended rests upon two brass hooks, screwed into the window-frame on either side of the window.

The curtains, made of cheese cloth, are hemstitched at top and bottom.

The same kind of lattice work as that used for the window may be used as a transom in a doorway just above the portiere. An alpenstock or mountain staff should be used for the pole, held in place by bands of birch bark tacked to the door jamb. The portiere to be made of momie cloth or canton flannel.

Although I might continue this subject to the filling of many pages, limited space necessarily restricts me to the few items given, but they will serve as examples of what may be done with little expenditure of either time, labor or money. Taste and ingenuity is the capital upon which to draw when furnishing and decorating a summer cottage.

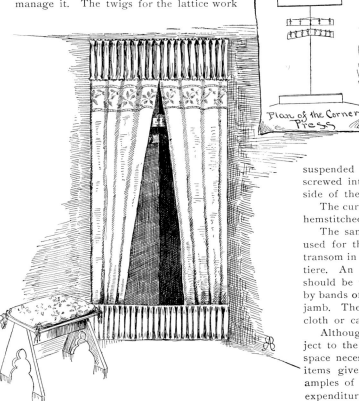

A Clothes-Press.

GREENHOUSE AND HOTBEDS.

THE foundation walls should be built of the best hard burned brick, laid in cement mortar. The bricks will crumble after a time unless of good quality. The topping out of the foundation

Perspective View of Greenhouse and Hotbeds.

wall should be of cement, with a sufficient wash so that water will not be retained on top of the walls, thus preventing the rotting of the timbers on which the sashes rest.

The section of sash muntin shows clearly how any condensation on the under side of the glass is carried down to the wall by the little grooves or gutters in the sides of the muntin. This does away with the unpleasant dripping that would otherwise occur.

The building should extend north and south, and may be of any desired length ; the building shown is 30 feet long and 12 feet wide, inside dimensions. When it is impossible to run the building north and south it should have the ridge tree near one side, with almost the entire sash exposure sloping to the south, so as to obtain the greatest sun exposure.

The hotbeds are formed by posts set in the ground, at short intervals, with planking (coated with tar or other good preservative) spiked to the posts to form the sides, and ordinary hotbed sash placed thereon.

Several good heating apparatuses are in use. The best results are obtained by using hot water circulating in pipes. Steam cools off too rapidly.

The ventilation may be secured by using iron bars, having a saw tooth edge, hinged to the lower end of the ventilation sash. This will hold the sash at any desired angle by having the saw tooth edge fit into suitable stops.

The pathway through the centre should be of concrete. In this design it is somewhat wider than ordinary, but is none too wide when it is desired to exhibit the plants, etc., to visitors.

The benches for flower pots should be just wide enough to reach all the plants handily from the walk, and as high as convenient.

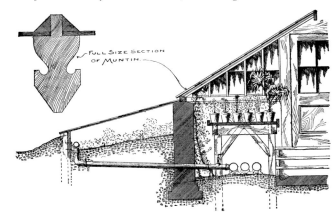

Cross Sectional View of Greenhouse and Hotbeds.

The top of benches should be made of narrow planks, laid with spaces between, so that water can not accumulate on them and surround the bases of the pots.

The cost of the greenhouse shown is estimated at $315, exclusive of heating apparatus and patent sash openers. Flower benches are included. Cost of the hotbed, $35.

ABOUT PICTURE HANGING AND PICTURE FRAMES

IF the owner of a home is fortunate enough to possess many good pictures, the problem of covering and decorating the wall spaces is simple. All there is to do is to paint, paper, or distemper the walls with such a tint as shall form a good background for the pictures. A rich brownish green will be found one of the best tints for this purpose.

Whenever elaborate and expensive wall decorations are proposed for a residence we feel that we must advise against it. Why? Because however fine they may be they scarcely excite a momentary feeling of interest and pleasure. In the place of elaborate decorations we suggest pictures—plenty of good pictures. Plain walls are the best to display pictures and the inexpensiveness of plain walls provides a fund, so to speak, to spend on art.

The arrangement of pictures symmetrically so as to produce a sort of uniformity in size and disposition is always pleasing, as is all true symmetry. In a small room the eye takes in the whole of the picture at a glance and rests with content upon such a disposition of parts. On the other hand, if the pictures are of all sizes and hung without any regard to this principle, they look incongruous, as if they were not worth the trouble of arranging properly. It is not always that our stock of pictures will be sufficiently near in size to enable us to distribute them equally. Still, if they are judiciously arranged, we may do away with the objection in a great measure. If it is engravings alone we have to hang, it is an easy matter to get them in pairs of a uniform size. With a mixture of oil paintings and engravings this cannot well be done, but with care and good taste even these may be so arranged that they will not clash with one another.

The practice of hanging pictures so that they shall project forward at their tops is a question of position as to light. When the light falls full upon a picture, whether a varnished oil painting or a framed engraving or water-color, there is a glare or brightness which prevents the whole of the picture from being seen. This is a common case, and the only means of avoiding it is to let the picture hang out from the top so that we can see the whole of it from any part of the room without this objectionable light upon its surface. This is effected by placing the rings of the frame low enough down to cause the picture to have the desired inclination. It is a good plan, when about hanging a room with pictures, to make a sketch of the proposed arrangement previous to commencing hanging. This saves much after-labor and vexation. The largest picture should always have a central position, so that those of a less size can be symmetrically grouped around it. The eye will be satisfied by such an arrangement. The character and form of the frames is a very important factor in the question. Engravings and water-color paintings should always have a broad margin to the mount and a narrow light frame. The margin serves to isolate the painting or engraving, and thus enables us to see its beauties to a much greater advantage. This is more especially the case if the wall upon which they are hung has a pattern upon it. These frames should be alike in make and breadth as far as possible.

Fig I.

Oil paintings require a different and much heavier frame than water-colors and engravings. The principal object in both cases is to display the painting to the best advantage. The broad margin does this with water-colors, but the oil painting having no plain margin we must depend upon the frame to effect its isolation. In our opinion a great mistake is often made in having these frames too elaborately ornamented, although some pictures will bear more ornamental frames than others. It is not the frame we want to exhibit but the picture.

In the hanging of pictures there are several points necessary to be attended to in order that they may be safe and easily adjusted. A picture molding firmly secured to the wall just underneath the cornice or frieze, upon which hooks are made to slide along, not only affords a firm support, but is an addition to the decoration of a room. This molding may be made and fixed by any ordinary joiner, or may be bought at most of the paper-hanging establishments, in gilt, black, or in various woods in combination with gilt beads. The hooks also may be procured from the same source. Brass rods have been much used for hanging pictures from, but they are not so serviceable or neat-looking as a picture molding, they are also soon spoiled by the action of the gas and moisture in the room, which eats into and destroys the lacquer. They are now but little used.

Strong wire, cord or line, both "gold" and "silver," is now made, of different thicknesses, for hanging pictures, and is admirably adapted for the purpose, being very thin but capable of bearing great weights. All picture cords of whatever kind should be as near the color of the wall upon which they are put as possible, in order to cause them to be but little seen. Too many cords are always objectionable. It is better to hang the picture with straight cords, that is to loop the cord onto two hooks so that it shall be perpendicular at each side of the picture, and not looped onto a single hook or nail. When one picture is hung beneath another the bottom one should be hung from the one above and not from the top; we thus avoid multiplying the cords, which is always objectionable. Pictures may also be hung without any cords showing by crossing the cord through the rings at the back of the picture, and looping this into a nail or hook; neither cord or hook will then be seen. When picture moldings are not fixed, strong nails may be used having earthenware, china, or brass heads on them. These screw onto the head of the nail, so that the nail may be knocked into its place and the head screwed on afterward. These are very neat and have a good appearance, and always clean up well.

Pictures of all kinds should be kept free from dust at the back, for where this accumulates injury is sure to result. To effect this two pieces of cork at the bottom edge of the frame will keep the frame from the wall, relieve the pressure, and allow the dust to a great degree to fall down and be cleared away. Gold frames should never be dusted with anything but a feather brush, and when they become dirty, servants or inexperienced persons should not be allowed to attempt to clean them, as they will be sure to spoil them. In cleaning the glass of water-color paintings and engravings, the greatest

care should be used to avoid rubbing the frames. They never should be wetted with the sponge or leather, or they will soon be spoiled.

We will conclude this article with a contribution by Miss Adelia B. Beard, which shows very plainly that we need not always patronize the dealers for our frames :

A picture frame as a rule, is quite an expensive article, but with a little ingenuity and good taste, almost any art student may manufacture frames, if not of equal finish, at least as durable and quite as artistic as any the dealer can produce.

The cost? The cost is the price of a wooden stretcher and a bottle of gold paint.

The first sketch shown here (figure 1.) will give some idea of the appearance of a frame decorated appropriately for a marine picture. The articles necessary for this frame are a stretcher, some rope,

a piece of fish net, several dried star fish and gold paint. Dent's gold paint is the best for the purpose. The stretcher must first be gilded, then the rope, upon which the fish net has been strung, should be fastened with small tacks around the outer edge, joining it at the corner, where the star fish will hide the ends. The net must be large enough to drape gracefully across one corner, along the top, and fall a short distance down the other side of the frame. When the star fish, graduating in size, are tacked around the draped corner and they, as well as the rope and net, are given a coat of gilt, a pretty, unique and substantial frame is the result If star

Fig. 2.

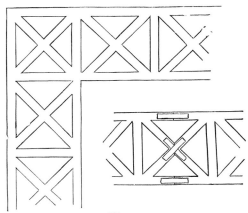

Fig. 3.

fish are not to be had, sea shells may be used instead (these of course will have to be glued in place), and if fish net is also out of reach, a piece of fine netted hammock can be used as a substitute.

For the benefit of those who spend their summers at the seashore where such things are obtainable, I would advise that a small collection be made of these quaint and pretty products of the place, as they will be found useful in various ways for decorative purposes. In drying star fish, wash them first in fresh water and then spread on a board in a dry place (not in the sun), and leave them undisturbed for a few days.

The next sketch (figure 2) shows a corner section of frame especially appropriate for a flower piece. The open lattice-like border is cut with a sharp penknife from stiff pasteboard and tacked along the edge of the frame.

The pattern shown in diagram is simple, quite easily made, and well suited for a border, though other and more elaborate ones may be used. This border must, of course, be made in sections. The edges to be connected should be cut to fit exactly, then after tacking them upon the frame the whole may be laid upon a table, face downward, and strips of paper pasted across the joints (see figure 3), which will hold them securely together. If the work is neatly done, when the gilt is applied all traces of the joints will disappear. The decorations of this frame consist of a spray of artificial rosebuds and leaves, gilded and tacked on the upper left hand corner. A few scattered rosebuds look well upon the lower part of the frame near the right-hand side.

The last sketch, figure 4, is the section of a frame which will look well on almost any kind of picture. It is made by tacking a small rope around the inside edge and then covering it and the frame with crumpled tin-foil, which, after it is pressed to fit the rope, is brought around and tacked on the wrong side of the frame, joining that edge which is turned over the top. Care should be taken while handling

Fig. 4.

the tin-foil not to flatten it, as its beauty depends upon its roughness. The pieces are joined by simply lapping one edge over the other, the uneven surface hiding all seams. This frame like the others must be gilded.

A very effective rough surface on a frame can be produced by dabbing on it with a palette knife the scrapings of the palette. Of course this frame cannot be made in a day, but if every time the palette is cleaned the paint is used in this way, it will not be long before the surface is covered and ready for gilding.

There are as many ways of decorating frames as there are individual tastes. The descriptions given here are offered more as suggestions which an inventive mind may take hold of and alter to suit its own purpose, than as fixed styles which cannot be changed.

SEA-SIDE COTTAGE DECORATION

By Adelia B. Beard

SEA-SIDE cottages are peculiarly well adapted to amateur decoration. Their ceiled walls offer plain, even, flat tinted surfaces for any kind of ornamentation, and the absence of plaster makes it possible to drive nails wherever it is desirable to have them.

During a summer spent in one of these cottages on the coast of Maine, its many possibilities in the way of decoration were revealed, and personal experience has demonstrated that even the plainest of these temporary abiding places is capable of being greatly beautified in a short time, and with materials usually close at hand, being obtainable from the fishermen and from the sea itself.

The windows first claim our attention in any house and our little cottage is no exception to the rule. With, or without, the regulation shades, windows should always be draped; the formality of their straight lines and angles can be subdued in no other way.

Light, airy curtains are suitable for summer, and the prettiest, most graceful window drapery imaginable can be made of ordinary fish net. An oar for a pole; rings made of rope (Fig. 2); the looping formed of a rope tied in a sailor's knot; and a wooden hoop, such as is used to attach the sail to the mast on a sail-boat (Fig. 1), are all that are necessary for the completion of this nautical curtain. Small rings screwed into the oar, with corresponding hooks in the window frame just above the window, will hold the oar securely in place. The looping should hang

A FISH NET CURTAIN

from a hook fastened in the wall near the window. The illustration given here will aid the imagination in picturing the effect of a window treated in this simple manner.

Another pretty curtain may be made of unbleached cotton, with bands of blue at top and bottom, covered with the ever decorative fish net.

Gray linen curtains, with strips of the net set in as insertion at top and bottom, will also be found extremely pretty and serviceable; or they may be composed of strips of linen and net, of equal width, running the length of the curtain. Made up in either way the effect is excellent.

From window drapery we will turn to that suitable for the doorways. Portieres in a room where the prevailing tints are gray and light wood color, should not present too violent a con-

trast to those subdued tones. A curtain of wood brown, neither too dark nor too light, will give the needed strength and decision, without destroying the harmonious coloring. One can be quickly and easily made of brown canton flannel and decorated with dried star-fish—as shown in the illustration. The star-fish are soft enough to admit of being sewed to the curtain, and they should be placed with the underside out, as that is much prettier than the back, showing as it does two shades of color. A heavy rope with a knot at each end, stretched taut across the doorway and held in place with two hooks, will answer for a pole, and the drapery can be hung from it with iron rings. If the rope is very heavy the ends will have to be parted into strands before the knots can be tied. Figs. 3 and 4 show the manner of tying the knot and fastening the end of a moderately heavy rope.

Bookshelves made of half of a flat-bottomed row-boat is not only an appropriate piece of furniture for a cottage by the sea, but also a very useful one. The fact of its shape allowing it to occupy a corner makes it a welcome addition to the furnishing, since there are so few things adapted to fill that angle. Fig. 5 shows half of boat with cleats nailed on to hold the shelves, which must be made to fit the boat. The shelves, when resting on the cleats, are secure enough and need not be fastened in any other way. If the bookshelves, when finished, are painted black, unvarnished, they will have the appearance of being ebonized.

The hat rack, which our drawing represents, makes an excellent and convenient hall decoration. The materials used in its construction are a small mirror, which can be procured at any country store; four boards, whose length and breadth depend upon the size of the mirror; two oars, with one-third of each handle sawed off; one dozen large-sized nails, or small spikes, and a piece of rope about twelve feet long. The frame is easily made by nailing the boards together as shown in illustration, placing

Fig. 1

Fig. 2

the end boards on top. The opening left in the centre should be one inch smaller than the **mirror**. When eight of the spikes have been driven into the frame at regular distances the mirror must be fastened on the back with strips of leather or sail-cloth, as shown in diagram (Fig. 6). The diagram also shows how the oars are held in place and the rope attached. The knot in

A CANTON FLANNEL PORTIERE

which the rope is tied is called a true-lover's knot, and can readily be fashioned by studying the diagram. Small nails driven through the rope where it crosses the back of the oar will keep the loops from slipping out of place. The remaining four spikes are to suspend the hat rack from, and must be driven into the wall so that two will hold the top loops, and the others the extreme upper corners of the side loops.

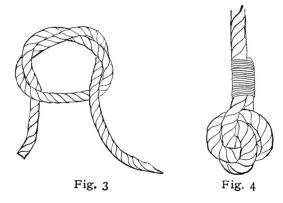

Fig. 3   Fig. 4

The frame and oars may be painted black and the spikes and ropes gilded, or the whole will look well painted yellow or brown.

A handsome screen, adding not a little to our decorations can

be made in the following manner: Procure a nice, firm clothes-horse, saw off the legs close to the bottom cross piece, then cover the whole neatly, on both sides, with dark green cambric. Next tack smoothly on one side of each fold light brown wrapping paper, which comes quite wide, and may be bought by the yard. For the border use dark green canton flannel cut in strips eight inches wide. Tack this around each fold of the screen with gimp tacks, and paste the inside edges smoothly over the paper.

The decorations of the screens shown in the illustration are composed entirely of products of the sea.

Two panels are shown. One is dec orated with sea-weed, star-fish and shells. Sea-weed and shells also are used on the other, but a group of horseshoe crabs take the place of the star-fish.

Sea-weed of various kinds suitable for this use can be found along the coast, and they may be gathered and dried in this way: Loosen the sea-weed from whatever it is attached to, and while still in the water slip a piece of stiff paper beneath it and lift it out. Quite a number can be carried on the same paper, but they snould be taken home as soon as possible and placed in a tub of fresh water. The tub will give the larger kinds room to spread out, when a smaller vessel would cramp and rumple them. On

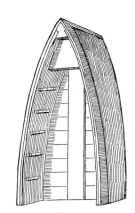

Fig. 5

BOOKSHELVES MADE FROM HALF OF A ROW-BOAT

sheets of paper, of the kind used for the screen, carefully lift each sea-weed out of the water, and with a long pin gently straighten the parts that are too much folded, and separate those that lie too close together. Should the plant be very much crumpled when taken out, quickly replace it in the water and try again.

When they have all been satisfactorily spread on the paper and have become partially dry, they must be pressed by laying

them between sheets of newspapers spread on a table or floor, with a board on top. On the board place some kind of weight, not too heavy. When the sea-weed is quite dry it will be found that some varieties will cling closely to the paper on which it has been spread, while others can readily be removed. Do not try to separate the first-mentioned kind from the paper, but with sharp scissors neatly trim off the edges around the

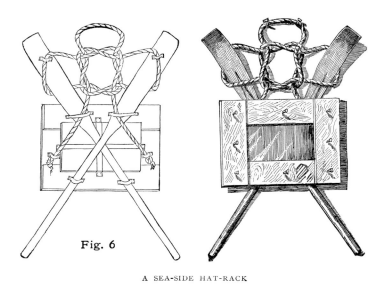

Fig. 6

A SEA-SIDE HAT-RACK

SCREEN DECORATED WITH SEA PRODUCTS

sea-weed. As the paper underneath is the same as that of the screen on which it is to be pasted it will not show. The other sea-weed can be taken from the paper and fastened to the screen with mucilage.

Before commencing the decoration some idea of the design, or the effect to be produced, should be decided upon, then with deft fingers the articles used can be glued in place. When the glue is

dry the whole must be given a coat of white varnish. This will help to hold things in place, and will also keep the sea-weed from chipping off.

THE CISTERN

The cistern should be located within easy reach of the laundry and kitchen and *outside* of the house. When located inside of the house it is difficult to ventilate it ; if not well ventilated, and if not often and thoroughly cleaned, it is a positive source of danger to health.

A cistern built in a circular form (see Fig. 1), is the cheapest, as a much lighter wall will keep the earth from caving in, than would a wall built in any other form.

Fig 1.

The wall should be built of hard brick, laid in cement mortar, and thoroughly coated on the inside with Portland cement. This coating should be run to a smooth surface, in order that it may be easily cleaned.

The next step is to build a curved wall of porous brick across the cistern, dividing the cistern vertically into two compartments.

A curved wall should be built to insure strength.

Turning the water into the larger chamber (*a* Fig. 1), it presses against the curved wall, and percolates through to the smaller chamber (*b* Fig. 1), leaving the greater part of its impurities in the larger chamber and in the wall.

Other impurities (if there be any) should be retained by means of a charcoal filter attached to the pump supply pipe, so that when the water comes to the surface it should be pure.

A dome shaped cover and man hole should be provided so that both chambers can be easily reached and often cleaned. The man hole cover should be perforated to secure ventilation. A fine wire screen secured to the under side of the man hole cover will prevent bugs, dirt, etc., from falling in.

The objection to this plan is that, in time, the porous partition wall may become fouled, requiring its removal and rebuilding with new brick.

Another good plan is to build the cistern in a circular and dome covered form, as described above, and at one side build a separate filtering receiver as shown in Fig. 2.

The water is received in the reservoir *a*, and is relieved of its impurities by passing underneath a dividing partition and through layers of gravel and charcoal, rising in the compartment *b* to the level of the outlet leading directly to the cistern proper (*c*)

The objection to this plan is that a heavy and rapid rain fall is apt to force the water so rapidly through the filtering layers that impurities may be carried into the cistern.

By combining the best features of the two plans described above the best cistern is secured, in our opinion. To do this make the partition in Fig. 1 of hard burned brick ; lay the same in Portland cement, and coat each side of the partition with cement the same as walls, so that water can not percolate through the bricks from "*a*" to "*b*." At the floor of the cistern a row of holes about 4 inches square and 16 inches apart, should be left to allow the water to pass through. In the bottom of each chamber place a layer of gravel about 12 inches deep, on this a layer of charcoal 6 inches deep, and on this again a layer of sand about 6 inches deep. This gives the water a double filtration before it reaches the pump, which should have a charcoal filter attached to the base of the supply pipe.

This arrangement of the layers makes it an easy task to clean the cistern ; by removing the layer of the sand in the chamber "*a*," the matter most likely to decompose and breed disease, can be taken up with the sand, and a fresh layer put in. When the charcoal and gravel become foul, they may be easily replaced in a like manner. The one man hole as shown in Fig. 1 answers for the two chambers.

At the bottom of the leader from the roof there should be two pipes, one leading to the cistern and the other to the sewer or the ground. A damper arrangement is placed at the junction of these pipes for the purpose of turning the first part of a rainfall and with it all the dust, leaves, bird excrement, etc., into the sewer or on to the ground. This attachment can be procured, ready made, and is supplied by roofers.

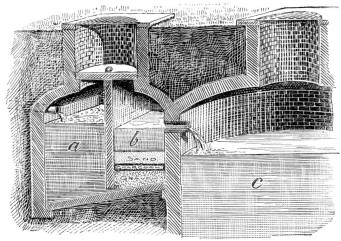

Fig 2.

HINTS ON HEATING AND VENTILATION

By CHAS. F. WINGATE, Sanitary Engineer.

TO warm an ordinary dwelling, the householder of moderate means may choose between open fires, stoves and furnaces. Steam and hot water apparatus are excellent for large buildings, but they are costly as compared with the other methods. Hot water heating is the ideal method, as the temperature is kept at a uniform degree, and on mild or muggy days one is not made uncomfortable by excess.

Open fires are very delightful from the æsthetic standpoint, and are excellent as an adjunct, but they are not sufficient alone to warm large rooms. Most of the heat is wasted and goes up the chimney, while there are apt to be drafts along the floor which annoy delicate persons and cause cold feet. Yet, every house should have one or more open fires, both for comfort and to assist ventilation.

Close stoves supply ample heat, but they "burn" the air and make the atmosphere of a room unfit for breathing. A Franklin stove with an open grate is the best form of stove, as it serves for ventilation as well as for warming. What is known as the Fire on the Hearth stove is a good example of this form of apparatus, and is commended by all sanitarians. A simple plan to overcome the defects of ordinary stoves is to surround them with a jacket of sheet iron, such as is shown by Figure 1, and to connect this at the bottom with a pipe running outdoors, so that a supply of fresh air can be brought in and warmed by striking against the heated base of the stove, when it rises and is diffused throughout the room. This avoids all chance of draft, and the supply can be regulated by a damper on the pipe A, according to the state of the weather. Some prefer to extend the jacket around only a part of the stove, and leave the door uncovered ; or the jacket may stop at the bottom of the stove and be made fast to the latter at that point. The arrangement is equivalent to a "portable furnace," such as is usually placed in a cellar or a basement hall.

The same results will be gained by placing the stove directly in front of a window with a movable metal screen on the opposite side (see Figure 2). On opening the window sash cold air will enter and, quickly warmed by contact with the stove, will be diffused through the room without creating any draft.

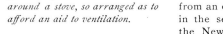

Fig. 1.—*A Jacket or Metal Screen around a stove, so arranged as to afford an aid to ventilation.*

These illustrations are taken from an essay on School Hygiene in the second annual report of the New York State Board of Health, prepared by Dr. D. F. Lincoln, an accepted authority on the subject.

Figure 3 shows air brought in so as to be warmed by contact with a stove pipe. The inlet flue is enlarged and runs up with the stove pipe like a jacket, for some distance.

Figure 4 shows how a stove pipe may assist in removing injurious air. The diagram represents a two-story house with a chimney which comes down to only a very short distance from the roof. The opening into the chimney for the stove pipe is enlarged so as to receive a much larger pipe, which encircles the stove pipe like a jacket. This jacket may stop short at the floor level or may be carried through to the floor level of the first story. It will secure a draft from either story, as may be arranged. A chimney into which a smoke flue discharges may be opened at any point below, and not too near the point where the smoke enters Many rooms, for instance, have chimneys which reach to the floor, while the stove pipe enters near the ceiling. Such chimneys ought to lend their powers to the task of ventilating the room, by an opening near the floor. The latter ought to be closed when the fire is making.

But such devices will not serve in large houses, and a good furnace will prove far more satisfactory in the end. A furnace is simply a large stove placed in the cellar, so as to form a central reservoir of heat. Fresh air is brought in through a cold air box and, being warmed by contact with the hot chamber, it rises through flues and registers into living rooms. To work satisfactorily, a furnace should be big enough to supply ample warmth on the coldest days without heating it red hot. It should be near the centre of the house, so that the hot air will not have too far to travel. The flues should rise straight

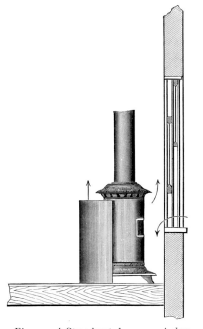

Fig. 2.—*A Stove located near a window, and a semi-circular Screen of Metal so placed as to inclose the stove, except the side toward the window.*

from the top and not run too near wood-work for fear of a fire. Cellar air should not be taken in, but fresh air from outdoors through a tight box.

Cold air supply boxes for furnaces are usually made of unseasoned wood, which soon warps and admits cellar instead of atmospheric air. Such boxes should be constructed of galvanized iron, or of well-seasoned wood, with joints made tight with white lead, putty or paper, and the whole well painted. They should not terminate at the street front of the house, if possible, as a purer supply may be obtained from the back yard. Most of the street air in our cities is largely made up of what Prof. Chandler calls "roasted manure," and the dirt which is found in cold air boxes is apt to be largely composed of organic matter. When exposed to fire it gives off an odor like burnt feathers. The ends of cold air boxes should not open just above a dark area, or under a veranda or stoop, where dust, decayed leaves, etc., abound. In Dr. John Hall's church, in New York, the supply of fresh air for the heating apparatus is brought from the top of the steeple, and is thoroughly purified by being passed through a spray of water before entering the furnace. By extending these

boxes in dwellings a few feet above the ground, the chances of drawing in damp ground air are greatly lessened.

Where there is a northern exposure, such an arrangement is specially advantageous, as it prevents too strong an inward draft, such as is often complained of. The ends of all cold air boxes should be closed by wire netting, preferably of brass wire, which can be readily removed and cleaned, as they soon clog up with dust. Cats, rats and other animals have a special liking for such receptacles as abiding places, and their remains are often found in them, and prove a source of very foul odors. A furnace should never be started without thorough examination and cleansing to prevent such accidents.

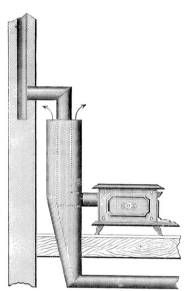

Fig. 3.—An arrangement for bringing air in so as to warm it by contact with the stove pipe.

Furnace cold air boxes are built often with but three sides, and fastened against the ceiling which forms the top. This is a very bad arrangement, as they are sure to sag in time and leave large openings along the sides for cellar air to enter.

Furnace air, *per se*, is not so unwholesome, but it is the absence of ventilation which makes it so. If a furnace is of sufficient size to warm a building without opening every draft and heating the fire pot red hot, and if the fresh air supply is taken from a proper source and not from a damp area or unclean cellar, and furthermore, if there are sufficient openings at the top of the house, to allow the impure air which rises to that point to escape and thus cause a constant circulation of sufficiently warmed but not overheated air through the house ; under these conditions a furnace is unobjectionable.

Every person requires a sufficient supply of air. A man can live forty days without ordinary food, but not half forty minutes without lung food. One foot of fresh air per second for each person is considered a sufficient supply. Very few living rooms make any such provision for fresh air, and we are content to breathe the same supply over and over again in a most unwholesome and disgusting manner. The Italian scavenger raking up garbage to eat is no whit worse than our nice people seated in a crowded theatre or concert room, or in a reeking street car in rainy weather with all the doors and windows closed.

Ventilation is one of the lost arts—if, indeed, it ever was discovered. The almost universal prevalence of catarrh, and the worn-out, wearied look of Americans which Herbert Spencer noted, may be justly charged to the bad ventilation of our houses. The chief difficulty about ventilating most dwelling-houses is that there are not sufficient means of carrying off the foul and heated air. If provision is supplied for doing this, then plenty of fresh air will leak in through window casings and cracks, as most of our houses are not tightly built. It is perfectly easy to prevent a draft by raising the sash a few inches and placing a narrow board in the space below, so that the cold air will enter between the upper and lower sash and be deflected toward the ceiling, without causing any annoyance to persons in the room. There are a number of patented devices for the same purpose, but the arrangement here described can be made by any one at the cost of a few cents.

People cannot understand that a circulation of air is necessary both for warming and for ventilation. When it is proposed to open skylights at the roof of a house, it will be complained : "Why, we shall feel too cold, as all the heat will escape." In reality, furnaces and stoves will act all the more briskly because of the escaping foul air, and the house will be warmer instead of colder, provided the ventilating cowl is of the proper construction and does not permit a down draft. I have found the Wing Ventilator well adapted for this purpose.

In hundreds of dwellings a skylight will be found on the roof over the main stairway without any opening into the air, or where there is an opening, the stained glass sash in the ceiling above the stairway will be closed tight, and thus the air contaminated by gas-lights, odors of cooking and washing, and by other impurities, will have no chance to escape, but will stagnate on the upper floors which are occupied as sleeping rooms. By raising the stained glass sash on small wooden blocks at each corner, this air will have a chance to escape through the opening in the skylight, and much relief will thus be afforded without any annoyance from snow or rain beating in. It is surprising how many houses are defective in this respect, although the remedy will cost only a trifle. In large dwelling-houses which have separate back stairs for the servants, running from the basement to the roof, the latter may be used as a ventilating shaft to advantage. The growing practice of placing galvanized iron flues with lanterns in them to ventilate water closets is a great step in advance. So also is the custom of providing flues in new houses for ventilating gas-jets. The cost of these is not great, while the benefits are remarkable.

Most ventilating flues are entirely too small and are badly built. They should be of ample size, made smooth on the inside, with the fewest possible bends or obstructions, and with a clean inlet and outlet. If there are a number of flues from different rooms ending in an attic, they should be joined together and protected from cold with an outlet above the roof, away from chimneys or side walls, which may cause a down draft.

Dr. Lincoln remarks : "How can we be sure that air will not come down flues instead of going up as desired ?" First, the flues must be warmed ; if this is not done there may be trouble. Second, a cap should be put over them, of some pattern suited to prevent the wind from descending. Third, inasmuch as air will not pass up these pipes unless there is air to pass, it is advisable to have a constant free supply of warmed air coming into the room.

It is not worth while to place dependence upon any cap, cowl or hood, for the purpose of increasing the discharge of air from a ventilator. The safe thing to rely upon is the ascensional force of warm air in a flue.

Fig. 4.—A Stove Pipe so arranged that it will assist in removing bad air.

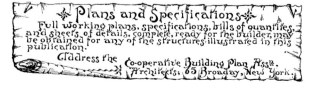

THE REMOVAL OF HOUSE SLOPS, &c.

By CHAS. F. WINGATE, Sanitary Engineer.

WHERE householders have no interior plumbing, but are content with outdoor privies or earth closets, it is not necessary to provide any very elaborate arrangements for getting rid of the house slops. Under no circumstances, however, should they be thrown upon the ground near the house, as mischief will surely follow this nasty and uncleanly practice. Hundreds of cases of diphtheria and typhoid fever have developed from thus saturating the ground near to dwellings with slops. Instead of this reprehensible practice, let the householder provide an empty kerosene barrel on wheels which can stand near the back door entrance way and receive domestic slops, and afterwards be rolled to a safe distance and emptied at brief intervals. Such a barrel, if painted within and without, will not become an eye-sore or cause offense.

The accompanying sketch, Fig. 1, shows a simple plan of arranging a drain from a kitchen to receive waste water from a pump, and to act as a receptacle for kitchen slops. It is important that the tile drain should be laid close to the surface, with open joints, and have a good fall, and that the sink opening should be ample to prevent saturating the ground about it. A wire strainer should also be placed over the opening to exclude rags and other articles which might stop up the pipe. Such drains are common in many houses, but they are generally constructed of rough plank laid with little fall, and hence they accumulate slime and other refuse and become noisome. If they are let discharge into a stagnant ditch or muck heap or slough, they may breed dangerous odors, especially if they are not trapped, and the end terminates just inside the kitchen. It is therefore better to make such drains of smooth earthen pipe and have a clear outfall

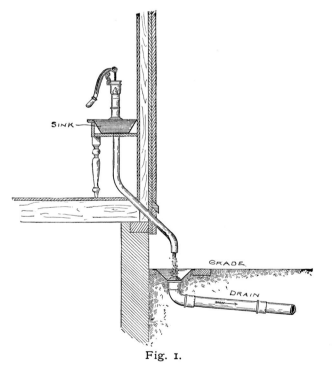

SINK

GRADE

DRAIN

Fig. 1.

above ground, if possible, which may be in the barn yard or pig pen. The joints on this drain may be left open, and the fluid contents allowed to soak through them into the soil if it is sufficiently porous.

A good plan is to make a square wooden trough, raised above the ground, with a good slant, and running from the kitchen sink to the stable or other safe place. This can be covered with a board to keep out the sun and snow, and occasionally during a sharp rainfall this can be taken off and the drain scoured thoroughly.

The chief practical question in arranging to drain an ordinary dwelling is to avoid having superfluous fixtures in the basement or cellar, so that the main drain can be kept as near to the surface of the ground as possible, and the cess-pool thus be as shallow as practicable. If the drain could start from the house at the ground level, then supposing the cess-pool was fifty feet distant, and that the drain had a fall of even one in twenty-five, the drain would connect with it not more than two feet below the surface, and the outlet would be at the same level. The cess-pool need not in that case be more than six feet deep at the most, while any overflow would be distributed close to the surface of the ground, where the roots of the grass and trees would have a chance to absorb it, and the air would penetrate through the soil and oxidize it. But if, as is often the case, the house owner insists on having a set of wash tubs or other fixtures in his cellar, then the house drain must start at this lower level, and by the time it reaches the cess-pool it will be five or six feet below the surface if the ground is level. This requires digging an unusually deep and expensive cess-pool, while the overflow will be at such a depth that but little benefit can be derived from it.

In the majority of houses a cess-pool is the only available means for disposing of domestic drainage. As ordinarily constructed, it is merely a hole roughly dug in the ground with stone or brick sides and arched top, the whole covered with soil and sods so as to be hidden from view. If the soil is very porous the fluid contents of the cess-pool, or "soak" pool as it was originally called, will leach away, and on opening it there will be little solid material left to remove. But even in gravelly soil the ground directly under the cess-pool will in time become clogged with grease and other solids, and the liquids will be retained until the hole is filled up and then it will have to be abandoned and another one dug near by. It is common to find half a dozen such receptacles filled and thus left fermenting to be a source of possible danger. Too often it is only discovered that the cess-pool is full when its contents back up through the house drain, saturating the ground about the foundations and forcing its way into the cellar. More than one outbreak of sickness has been traced to this cause.

If the cess-pool is dug in clay or other tough soil, it will soon fill up and have to be cleaned out, often at great expense and annoyance. The drain connecting with the house is also liable to choke with grease, and must be taken up and cleaned periodically. The longer and the larger such a drain is, the quicker it will choke, especially if it has little fall, so that the flow is sluggish and the grease readily chills. I have taken up a thousand feet of five-inch drain almost closed with grease from this cause, and I have known similar lengths of pipe to require taking up every year at great cost.

It is therefore wise and economical to keep the grease out of the drain by providing a grease trap which will retain it where it can be easily got at and removed. Such an appliance as that shown in the annexed cut, Fig. 2, is good for the purpose and is not expensive. It will serve also to keep the cess-pool free from grease and thus assist soakage and cleansing. Bear in mind that the decomposing grease creates the worst stench, and that a kitchen drain or cess-pool smells viler than any vault or closet.

So long as pan water-closets with an insignificant flush were used, in most dwellings cess-pools were less liable to be filled up, but with

the modern improved water-closets, consuming a couple of gallons of water every time they are used, there is greater chance of cess-pools overflowing and their contents backing up through drains. Under such conditions the volume of sewage will be largely fluid, and hence can be easily pumped out and spread upon a garden. It therefore

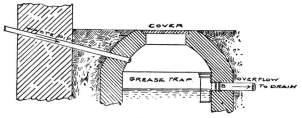

Fig. 2.

seems as if there was no alternative, and that either a cess-pool must be made large, and hence costly to construct, that it should have ample means of overflow, or that it should be frequently cleaned. This last remedy is expensive, and a householder may well object to spending $100 or more every year to clean his cess-pool, when by a little more outlay he might abolish it altogether.

The risks from cess-pools are threefold. First : from the creating of foul and dangerous gases which have no escape except into the house. Second : from their contents overflowing and backing up, especially if rainfall is admitted into them and percolating into wells and cellars. Third : from permanent soil saturation, resulting through the constant pollution of the earth around. All these are grave, important dangers, worthy of serious consideration. The common belief that kitchen slops are entirely harmless, either in a cess-pool or when emptied on the ground, is a great mistake. Such refuse, as already stated, when putrid, is no less offensive than water-closet waste; and quite as much, if not more, care is therefore to be taken in disposing of it.

It is hardly necessary to warn householders of the danger of placing cess-pools near wells, in any soil and especially in a porous one. Even at a distance of fifty feet there is risk of pollution especially if the well is very deep and the soil below the cess-pool contains rifts or cracks through which its contents may seep into the well.

The overflows of cess-pools are often badly contrived. It will not do to allow the superabundant sewage to lie upon the ground, exposed to the sun, and polluting the atmosphere. Nor is a shallow ditch, without fall or flushing current, much better. Such arrangments are certain to cause trouble in time. So long as the material is spread over a sufficient area to be quickly and freely absorbed by the soil, and to be sucked up by the roots of grass and other vegetation, no fault can be found; but what is specially objectionable is to allow the surplus sewage to remain exposed over a limited space, where it cannot be absorbed and where it must stagnate and breed miasma. Some persons throw stable manure under their cess-pool overflow and compost the material. This is not a bad arrangement if it is looked after carefully, but such material is not very absorbent and must be frequently replaced.

As to the ventilation of cess-pools there seems to be a difference of opinion. Most persons pile planks and stone and sods carefully over them, and thus prevent any escape of air excepting through the drains leading from their houses. Colonel Waring says that sometimes ventilated cess-pools give offense, and E. S. Philbrick remarks that there may be a down draft in the ventilator. It seems to me that the whole question depends upon the amount of ventilation, and that, if sufficient openings are made to admit the air freely, all foul gases will be oxidized and their offensive properties destroyed. Again, persons are very apt to fancy that they perceive an unpleasant smell if there is an opening from a cess-pool in sight. The imagination has much to do with these things. In ventilating cess-pools one opening will not suffice, as may be illustrated by the following simple experiment: Close a common wide-mouthed pickle bottle with a bung. Into this put a piece of tubing of any kind, about a foot long. Fill the bottle with smoke from a pipe stem or glass tube. Then blow across the top of the pipe, and it will not clear the bottle of its smoke. Now, repeat the experiment, but previous to doing so, make a hole in the bung, into which place another short piece of pipe, then blow across the

upper opening, and the bottle will be cleared of smoke as if by magic.

Where, as is common, a cess-pool is covered with a piece of flagging, I usually advise having the latter raised a few inches by placing a brick under each corner, so as to allow the air to escape around the sides, where foul odors may be partly absorbed by the vegetation, and this has generally been found satisfactory. If the soil-pipe of a house is carried up to the roof and has few openings upon it, it may do to ventilate the cess-pool through this pipe, provided there is a large grating at the top of the latter, but it is always preferable to have a trap on the main drain between the house and the cess-pool, with an air inlet opening at some convenient point. This is to avoid the chance of cess-pool air being drawn through traps or possible leaks into living rooms, a possibihty at all times with our highly heated houses, and it is best to avoid the risk. Mr. J. C. Bayles recommends covering cess-pools with a flagstone, having a hole about eight inches square in it, containing a wooden chimney six feet high, into which wire screens covered with charcoal as a deodorizing material may be placed. The chimney should have a cover open at all sides to exclude rain and to keep the charcoal dry, and one side should be hinged like a door to give free access, so as to remove the wire screens from time to time. This arrangement seems feasible, though I do not know if it has been practically carried out.

In many thousands of towns and villages where the expense of sewering is too great for the resources of the property owners, or where the latter are not sufficiently intelligent to appreciate the benefit of such outlay, some other method of drainage must be provided. Their is a large field for experiment in this direction. Often sewers are impracticable from the difficulty of obtaining an out fall. Again, the ground may be too level to secure a proper grade, notably at the sea-shore ; while the risk of causing a dangerous nuisance forbids discharging sewers into ponds, streams, or even into the ocean in the neighborhood of occupied houses or bathing places. Some other method of drainage must therefore be employed. The cess-pool system may do with modifications. Irrigation farms have been constructed to dispose of the drainage of many European towns, but it is not always possible to obtain land that is suitably located, or that is cheap enough for the purpose. Neighboring residents will object to living near a sewerage farm, and will insist that it is a nuisance and dangerous to health. If it is placed far away from thickly settled centres, then the cost of reaching will be heavy, and there are other difficulties to be overcome. Of some of these methods of domestic sewage disposal I shall speak on another occasion.

PRIVIES

No water, garbage, ashes, house slops or other refuse should be thrown into a privy vault. By excluding such material and keeping the vault dry and well ventilated, the annoyance from flies, mosquitoes and spiders will be greatly reduced. The contrast between a privy that is well cared for and one that is not is surprising.

By planting quick-growing vines around an out-house it may be hidden from view and thus the important requisite of privacy will be secured. It will also be shielded from the hot sun; the vegetation will assist in purifying the air, and the roots will suck up the valuable fertilizing material from the soil. A wind-break of evergreens should also be provided to shield the place in winter and an arbor to keep off the rain, while a board or gravel walk will be a valuable addition. If we must have these outdoor necessities let us at least see that they are as little objectionable to the eye and other senses as possible.

EARTH CLOSETS

In every country house where there are no plumbing conveniences, an earth closet should be provided for the use of invalids and delicate persons and for women and children in severe weather. This appliance was first recommended for modern use by the Rev. Mr. Moule, an Englishman, and it has been extensively introduced with excellent results. Its simplicity, economy, and convenience are readily apparent. Its features are briefly as follows: A cemented box or vault which can be readily cleaned or removed, with a supply of dry earth or sifted ashes,—say a barrelful for an ordinary household—a portion

of which is daily deposited over the contents of the vault. The effect of this slight covering is to deodorize the material, absorb all liquids, and render the whole innoxious, as well as to preserve its full value as manure. There is thus no waste in economy, no risk to health, and no source of offense to the senses. If the earth closet is situated conveniently, yet not too near to living-rooms, and is promptly cleaned, it is a wholesome arrangement in private dwellings. A number of patented devices of this kind have been introduced and are to be had, but they are expensive, and while claiming to be automatic are very liable to get out of order. Sometimes the deodorizing material will hang suspended in the reservoir, and has to be jarred down before the discharging apparatus will work. But the principal difficulty is that it is seldom thrown where it is most needed, and that the dust is inconveniently deposited on the seat.

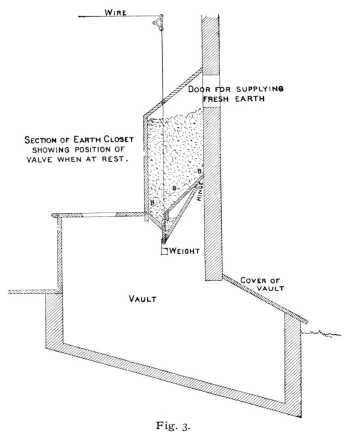

Fig. 3.

Figure 3 shows a somewhat elaborate design for an earth closet but it can also be made by an ordinary mechanic. The multiplication of such devices would effect a vast improvement.

The reservoir or hopper is filled from the outside. A lid of plain boards is hinged to the back of the hopper. When at rest the weight of the earth holds the lid back, the opening being closed by a slide. By pushing in a lever, pulling a cord, or other means, the inverted lid is thrown forward and the slide raised, shutting off the descent of earth, but throwing the portion already contained in it over the vault in a uniform sheet. On the relaxing of the impulse the weight draws the slide back and supplies the measurer with a fresh dose. By regulating the front edge of the measurer the sheet of earth may be directed as required. B B B is a sheet of wire netting fixed in the hopper, which serves to sift the earth and to prevent it from packing so firmly in the bottom as to impede the movement of the measurer. The jar communicated to the apparatus shakes down the earth, a matter of some importance. The vault may consist of tight plank boxes on wheels, so as to be easily rolled out. Otherwise a shallow pit lined with 8-inch brick, with sloping bottom of bricks on edge, also laid in cement, is necessary.

Figure 4 shows a simple form of earth closet devised by Mr. J. C. Bayles, which can be made by any one who has any skill at carpentry and at trifling cost. The inventor says:

The body is a plain pine box. Its sides are not over 14 inches high; its depth is 18 inches (measuring from front to back), and in length about 30 inches. It is divided into two compartments, one 18 x 18 inches and the other 18 x 12 inches. The larger of these compartments has no bottom; the smaller has a tight bottom. On top I

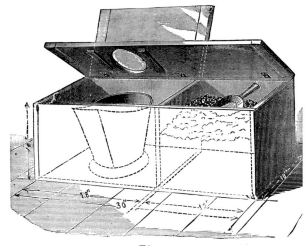

Fig. 4.

have two covers. The lower cover, hinged to the upper edge of the back, extends all the way across both compartments. In this is cut the seat, of usual pattern, over the centre of the larger compartment. The upper cover is hinged to the lower one, and may be raised independently. It is made the size of the larger compartment only, both covers having a little overhanging to facilitate lifting them. The material in, and work on, such a box will cost anywhere from two to three dollars, according to the amount of finish put on it by the carpenter. The receiving vessel is a galvanized iron coal hod as large as will stand in the larger compartment with the covers down. The smaller compartment is filled with dry earth, ashes, peat dust, or whatever else is used as deodorizer, and a little hand shovel or scoop is laid in. The closet is then ready for use, which should be preceded by throwing into the coal hod as much of the dry material as is needed to cover its bottom one inch deep. When used the upper cover is raised, exposing the seat. After use the lower cover is also raised, uncovering both compartments. A small quantity of the dry material is then taken in the scoop and sprinkled over the contents of the hod. A quart is usually more than sufficient. This operation is repeated whenever the closet is used, until the hod is full, when, of course, it must be emptied. Its contents will turn out as a solid mass, inoffensive to sight and smell. Even the most fastidious person, with strength enough to carry the full hod out of doors, would make no objection to emptying it. Occasionally, it is well to air and sun the hod after emptying. I have never known one to require other cleansing. It is better not to use an earth closet as an urinal, but so much of such use as is incidental to its employment as a stool in no respect interferes with its satisfactory workings. In my own house I have placed no restrictions whatever upon its use for any purpose for which any one with sense would consider it adapted. The best material for use in an earth closet is the fine siftings of anthracite coal ashes. Ashes from bituminous coal are not adapted to the purpose. Dry, loamy earth, or leaf mold will answer very well, but it is troublesome to dry and store it. It cannot be had dry enough out of doors, even in midsummer. Sand is useless.

Discreetly and decently used, an earth closet gives very little trouble. If ashes are thrown in after each use, it will not require any attention until the receiving vessel is full. After an absence of about three weeks, during the hottest part of the summer, I returned home to find, notwithstanding the fact that the earth closet had been locked up in a close room, not a trace of disagreeable odor could be detected. The object of leaving the larger compartment bottomless is to facilitate cleaning. More or less ashes will be spilled around the hod, and this should be swept out frequently. By raising one end of the box, the floor under it can be swept much cleaner than the bottom of a box could be without turning it over.

ABOUT PLUMBING AND DRAINAGE

By CHAS. F. WINGATE, Sanitary Engineer.

IN considering how to arrange the plumbing of an ordinary house, it is first necessary to decide how many fixtures will be required, and what amount of work has to be done. This will depend upon the size of the building, the number of inmates, and the length of the owner's purse.

In an ordinary household, numbering six or eight persons, occupying an average dwelling, there will usually be a single bath-room, two water closets, one upstairs and one for the use of domestics, a kitchen sink and hot water boiler, wash trays, butler's pantry sink, and from one to five stationary wash basins, while if the water pressure is deficient in the city, or if in the country the roof water is stored for family consumption, a tank or cistern will be required. In such a dwelling a four-inch soil pipe will be ample for the drainage from the principal fixtures, and a two-inch cast iron waste pipe from the basins, if any are located at a distance from the main lines. There will also be need for a two-inch waste from the kitchen fixtures, together with a five-inch rain leader, and connections from surface cess-pools in the front and back yards. All these pipes will discharge into a five-inch main drain leading to the sewer or cess-pool. To plumb a house of this grade will cost in the neighborhood of three hundred dollars.

The first consideration in planning the plumbing for any house is to concentrate the fixtures as much as possible and to strive to have everything compact and accessible. I am strongly opposed to scattering plumbing helter skelter all over a building with no system, and with the necessity of carrying pipes in places where they are liable to freeze or where they are quite inaccessible, so that in case of accident they cannot be got at without great damage to walls and ceilings and much outlay of money.

Previous to the sewer gas scare, householders had become inordinately fond of having plumbing, and they placed no check upon its amount. I have heard of a dozen water closets being in a house occupied by three persons, and still the owner was not satisfied, but like Oliver Twist, he asked for "more." The present tendency to do away with fixed basins in sleeping rooms is to be encouraged, and householders should learn to get along without such superfluities. It seems absurd to talk of isolating plumbing when one sees the number of fixtures demanded by wealthy householders in their houses. In a Fifth avenue residence, recently completed, there are eight water closets, twenty-four basins, eight baths, six sitz baths, and six sinks, besides other fixtures. Again, it is so common to find plumbing fixtures in out of the way rooms, intended for the use of guests or for occasional visitors, which have traps with no water in them, that I should strongly advise never to leave a fixture where it will not have constant surveillance.

It is a good plan in order to secure complete isolation of plumbing, to place the principal fixtures in an extension away from living rooms, and in a line directly over each other. This is economical and is now being largely followed.

The second consideration in plumbing a house should be to employ nothing but the very best materials, and the most substantial and tried appliances and fixtures. There is no economy in using cheap materials.

The soil pipe and main drain should be of extra heavy cast iron pipe, tarred inside and outside, and carefully examined and tested to insure that it is of uniform thickness. The days of using light weight pipe have passed, and it is a wonder that such pipe has so long been countenanced by architects and plumbers, as it is liable to be full of sand holes and flaws. It is easily cracked and on that account it is difficult to make a tight joint.

While it is desirable that pipe of extra heavy weight should always be employed, particularly if it is to be laid underground, yet where economy is to be studied, ordinary pipe may be employed, provided it is made by a reputable firm and stamped with its tested weight. There is so much poor pipe on the market that no other guarantee can be accepted. Tarring the pipe is not sufficient security as there may be sand holes, cracks, and other flaws which will be covered up by the tar and thus concealed from view. Poor pipe is brittle, and hard to cut without splitting.

The best extra heavy pipe is made from special patterns and not by shaving off the core from which ordinary pipe is made, which reduces the interior diameter, and it should be full size inside. Testing with a hammer will reveal flaws. Good pipe when examined with the eye should be perfectly straight end from end, and not be sprung at any point so as to create depressions. On examining the cut edge of a piece of inferior pipe it will be seen to have a steely crystalline hue and not the dull gray color of good iron.

The drain within the house should under all circumstances be of cast iron. The weight of opinion among sanitarians and intelligent plumbers seems to be that no other material should be employed. In the first place it is desirable in all cases to carry the main drain along the side wall of the cellar or suspend it from the ceiling so as to be in full view. Of course tile pipe could not be exposed in this way. Even where the main drain has to be laid underground on account of special conditions, it is preferable to use cast iron pipe rather than tile within doors owing to the greater risk of the latter being damaged in some way. Tile pipe is brittle and may be easily crushed or cracked by the house settling or by other causes. The lengths are shorter and there are hence more joints in a given distance than with iron pipe. The joints also being made with cement may give way or be injured by rats, and in case of any such contingency, from the fact that the pipes are hidden from view, the consequences of any accident might prove serious before the evil was discovered. The final objection to employing tile pipe within doors is that such pipe is in most cases carelessly laid, and is constantly imperfect and leaky. In my whole experience in sanitary work I have scarcely ever found such an earthenware house drain properly laid, and I invariably distrust them and insist upon testing their condition before passing upon them. The same opinion is expressed by most plumbers, architects and health inspectors whom I have met, so that I have no doubt that as far as indoor drainage is concerned tile pipe must be abandoned for cast iron in all good work. And yet no one denies that tile pipes are excellent from their smoothness, cheapness and non-corrosiveness by acids. If they could be securely laid they would be preferable to iron.

Some plumbers prefer to cover drain pipes entirely with cement; others lay them so that the cement reaches up to the middle of the pipe. It seems preferable to expose the drain as much as possible to view and not to cover it entirely.

If a drain is not laid with a proper fall, it is not possible to make the joints secure, as the ends of the lengths of pipe will not fit tightly. In laying drains so as to secure the proper fall, first measure the distance from the cess-pool, or from the front wall to the rear of the house where the soil pipe or leader is to join, and having calculated the distance and depth of the cess-pool inlet it is easy to find out how much fall is possible. For example, suppose that the drain within the house is fifteen feet long, and that from the rear of the house to the cess-pool in the yard is sixty feet; this makes just sixty-five feet in all. Suppose the bottom of the cellar is seven feet below the surface of the ground, and that the top of the drain must end at this point to accommodate a servant's closet or other fixture at the rear. This would give a fall of five feet in sixty-five, or say roughly, one in twelve. By cutting a piece of wood so as to be two inches high, and laying this under the end of a two-foot spirit level upon each length of drain pipe as it is laid, the proper fall can be obtained.

The workmen should begin at the cess-pool and work upwards with the drain; a running trap should be placed close to the front wall, enclosed in a brick manhole with a wooden cover, so as to be convenient of access. The trap itself should be placed on a level, and should have a cleaning-out hole and a branch for the air inlet or foot ventilation.

Tree roots often enter the joints of drains and cause trouble. To guard against this chance, where drains must be laid near trees, the pipes should be bedded in concrete.

LANDSCAPE GARDENING—BY S. B. PARSONS

I.—PLANTING A SMALL PLOT FACING SOUTH

THE principles of landscape art are few and simple; the application of them is as wide as the variety of plants and the combinations of them which can be made by the skillful artist. These combinations require not only a quick eye for the possibilities which are given by earth and sky, by the houses and plants which are already located, but they require also a reasonable knowledge of trees and shrubs.

The charm of nature is its infinite variety of expression; no two trees, no two leaves, no two petals are precisely alike; each one has its own form, its own shading, and its own curl; no one has its fellow. This infinite variety may not be apparent to the casual observer, but, it is there, and the landscape artist of the future will be the man or woman who can see the largest part of these variations, and seeing them freely, will combine knowledge with taste and produce scenes which may never equal but will nearly approach the wild perfection of nature. He may do more, and as the highest art is the idealizing of nature, he may succeed in throwing an ideal charm over his work in presenting more clearly to our limited conceptions, the infinite variations and combinations of beauty which are hidden from all but the careful observer. He may be, in comparison with others of his profession what Thoreau was and Burroughs is, in comparision with ordinary observers. Yet the ideal is based upon the actual, which for landscape adornment is a knowledge of trees, shrubs and plants. Without this knowledge there cannot be success, and with it there cannot be entire failure.

For our present purpose the highest art is not needed, for the size of the lot treated forbids the use of large trees; only shrubs or perhaps a few trees of the smallest class can be employed. There is needed no reaching for sky effects nor for deep shadows. Judicious grouping and grading of plants, with a careful eye to color, will give us all we desire.

There is a decided advantage in shrubs, they can be removed readily if study would favor a change of position, and therefore, for immediate effect they can be planted closely. They can be pruned freely if they interfere with eaeh other. They give pleasure by their flowers as well as their foliage, and leave uninjured the turf which is often destroyed by the exhausting roots of large trees. It is rarely justifiable to plant large trees in a moderate sized town lot. The trees upon the sidewalk are enough for the front and it is not just to a neighbor to plant trees at the side which may become large and thus overshadow and exhaust his ground. There should be a law to prevent a man from covering his neighbors ground with a tree as there is now one to prevent his covering it with a part of his house. The golden rule is a good one, but it does not operate with all men.

On the next page will be found a list of shrubs which can be planted eighteen inches from the east and west lines and four feet apart. This distance will be sufficient for some years, after which they can be pruned to keep them as separate plants, or they can be allowed to grow together as a belt. If immediate effect is desired the list can be doubled and they can be planted two feet apart, to be removed when growing too thickly. These shrubs are located for a lot one hundred feet wide and one hundred and fifty feet deep, fronting south. If fronting north, west or east, the location of certain kinds would be different.

The walks are as few as possible. A walk should be made for utility only, as it requires labor to keep it clean. The smooth dry turf is pleasanter to walk upon. With this idea the western walk might be spared, but it balances well and is useful for promenading when the grass is wet.

The first shrub on the list for the side lines should be planted three feet from the front and eighteen inches from the side. The others should be continued in a straight line, according to the list, eighteen inches from the side, and four feet apart. The stiffness of a straight line will be broken by other shrubs to be planted against them.

The lines on the east and west side being planted, those on the list designated as second can be planted two to four feet inside the others. It is difficult to locate these without seeing the ground, for they will not be in a straight line but must be grouped at the side or in front of the others to produce the general effect which is sought to be designated on the plan. It should be borne in mind to keep the plants with colored leaves on the outside as much as possible, that they may be seen from the house.

The front line may now receive consideration. There trees may be admissible and should be evergreen. Let Abies Alcockiana be six feet from the west side line and ten feet from the front; Abies Polita twenty feet distant and seven feet from the front; Picea Japonica twenty feet distant and seven feet from the front, and Abies Pungens twenty feet distant and ten feet from the front. Between these will be for some years vacant spaces in which can be placed without formality a Golden Oak, a Japan Judas Tree, a Japan Weeping Cherry, and a White Fringe, then for further filling, Fraxinus Atrovirens, Andromeda arborea, Retinospora squarrosa, Evergreen Thorn, American Holly. Between these again can be placed any of the evergreens of which we give a list, some of which can also be in front of some of the projections on the side lines. The vacant spaces between the large evergreens can be filled up with shrubs, evergreens, roses, etc., as may be preferred.

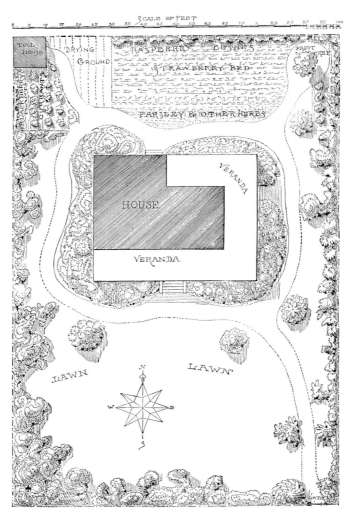

PLAN OF A PLOT 100 x 150 FEET, FACING SOUTH

These can be removed after some years when the growth of the large trees shall encroach upon them.

The centre of the clump on the front lawn at the southwest of the house should be a Weeping Sophora planted six feet from the walk; the next opposite the southeast corner of the house should be Salisburia, planted five feet from the walk; the third should be Chinese Cypress also five feet from the walk. Nearly opposite the Salisburia and on the side lawn opposite the path in front of the house should be a Weeping Hemlock, planted five feet from the path. The leading shoots of the Sophora and Hemlock should be trained to a stake until they are eight feet high and then allowed to fall. If desired they can be carried twenty feet. On the west side of the front gate can be a group of eight Rhododendrons and on the east side a group of four Kalmias. At the corners of the house should be planted four Salisburias; with their long branches covered only with leaves, they make the very best ornament for training under the eaves. The Japanese Ampelopsis can be planted three feet apart around the house if it is desired to cover it with foliage. They are very beautiful, cling to wood or stone, require no training and the leaves hang over each other making a sort of thatch which protects the house from rain.

The ground between the paths and the house should be turfed after there is grouped in it the low-growing shrubs and evergreens, such as Spiræa crispifolia, Mahonia aquifolium, Biota elegantissima, Biota semper aurescens, Thuya Columbia, Thuya aurea, Thuya Vervæneana, Silver Japan Juniper, Golden Japan Juniper, Picea Hudsonica, Golden Sun-ray Pine, Golden Retinospora filifera, Dwarf R. obtusa, Weeping R. obtusa, Golden R. plumosa, Golden Yew, Andromeda Catesbaei, Azalea amœna, Daphne Cneorum, Tea Roses, Geraniums, &c. A Tamarix Indica should go in the middle of the plot, south of the house, five feet from it, and west of the front steps, and an African tamarix in the middle of the plot, on the east side of the house, and north of the side steps a tree box can be planted each side of the front steps. Six Japan Maples could also be grouped together on the east side. A group of Taxus can be made on the south side of house. Limonia trifoliata trained on its south wall is very effective.

It is important that the soil immediately around the house and between it and the paths should be of the very best quality. Therefore, when the excavation is made for the house let the black soil be placed on one side, and with other black soil be used for grading from the house to the path.

It should be borne in mind that these shrubs being of nursery size, will be small enough for several years to leave space around them for the planting of all the roses and summer flowers that may be needed.

We have provided nothing for the outside of the sidewalk. If the lot faced west we should advise the Salisburia. It is always de-sirable to keep open the view of the western sky and the remarkable sunsets of our climate; as the public requirement will not allow the absence of street trees, some sort must be placed there, and there is no tree like the Salisburia for giving broad glimpses between its leaf-clothed arms.

For a southern exposure, however, there is nothing so charming as the Schwerdler Maple; its rich tints in May and June cannot be surpassed. These should be planted on the outside of the sidewalk, those at the end twelve feet from the continuation of the lot lines and three others twenty-five feet apart.

Over the tool-house, in the northwest corner, can be planted vines of Akebia, Aristolochia, Halleana and variegated Honeysuckles, and on the south side Tecoma grandiflora. On the west fence near the tool-house can be planted five Early Wilson Blackberries, and between these and the walk six White Grape Currant and six Fay's Currant. On the east fence, opposite the last, can be planted five Kittatinny Blackberries, and near them six Downing Gooseberries. All these berry plants should be four feet apart. A Stump Peach tree can go in the centre of the path near the north fence, and after planting there may be found room for two more Peach trees— George IV and Old Mixon. The vacant space on the back fence will hold something less than two hundred Charles Downing Strawberries which should be planted in rows three feet apart, with plants in the rows fifteen inches apart. These should be allowed to make runners in the rows, but all young plants between the rows should be kept cut off. In odd places room can be found for half a dozen plants of Liemaen's Rhubarb, with, perhaps, a frame for early Lettuce.

Around the drying ground will be required high posts to hold the wires. On these can be placed grapevines, the best six of which are El Dorado, Golden Gem, Berckmans, Martha, Niagara and Miles. There are many other fine varieties which mildew and other causes make uncertain. For many reasons the autumn is the best time for planting deciduous things and the spring for evergreens. When everything is ready, however, in the spring, planting should not be delayed.

We think that our plan, if reasonably followed, will give pleasure and the interest in it will grow with its growth. Every plan, however needs additional touches after the main planting is finished, as the true sculptor uses his chisel after the statue has come from the hands of his workman. This can be done year by year as growth shows the need of it. Our chief object now is to furnish a ground-work, every individual of which will give pleasure, for after all it is the individual element in material things that gives the enjoyment which the distant observer finds in masses. In a future number we will treat a larger space of ground where room can be found for many large growing trees which produce the sky and shadow effects that constitute the charm of ample and well planted grounds.

PLANTS FOR WEST SIDE, NEXT TO THE FENCE

Lilac President Massart
" Common White
" Josikæ
" Chinese White
Euonymus Europæus
" latifolius
" alatus
Eleagnus longipes
Colutea halepica
Calycanthus floridus
Cornus alba sanguinea
Viburnum oxycoccus
" japonicum latifolium
" plicatum
Lonicera fragrantissima
Spiræa prunifolia flore pleno
" Reevesiana flore pleno
Exochorda grandiflora
Forsythia viridissima
Rhodotypus kerrioides
Hydrangea paniculata grandiflora
" nivea

Weigela rosea
" Lavellee

Sambucus laciniata
Berberis atropurpurea
Deutzia candidissima flore pleno albo
Symphoricarpos racemosus
Celastrus orixa
Clethra alnifolia
Cydonia japonica Mallardii
" " simplex alba
" " Moerlosii
Spiræa opulifolia aurea
" Douglasi
Ribes Gordonianum
Philadelphus coronarius
Prunus triloba

PLANTS FOR EAST SIDE, NEXT TO THE FENCE

Double Carmine Peach
" White "
Paul's Hawthorn
Malus Halleana
Red Flowering Dogwood
Magnolia Thompsoniana
" atropurpurea   Magnolia stellata
Stuartia   Rose Acacia

PLANTS FOR EAST SIDE, SECOND ROW

Golden Elder
Prinos verticillata
Hydrangea quercifolia
Hypericum aureum
Dwarf, Double White Almond
" " Red "
Deutzia gracilis
Viburnum nana
Weigeleanana variegata
Spiræa Thunbergii

PLANTS FOR WEST SIDE, SECOND ROW

Golden Leaved Syringo
Californian Privet
Berberis Thunbergii
Euonymus nanus erectus
Itea Virginica
Cydonia japonica tricolor
Daphne Genkwa   Daphne Mezereum

PLANTS FOR FRONT LINE

Abies Alcockiana
" polita
Picea japonica
Abies pungens

PLANTS FOR FRONT LAWN

Weeping Japan Cherry   Japan Judas Tree
Golden Oak   White Fringe
Retinospora squarros   Evergreen Thorn
Audromeda arborea   American Holly
Fraxinus atrovirens   Weeping Sophora
5 Salisburia   Chinese Cypress
Weeping Hemlock   4 Kalmias
Weeping Silver Fir   8 Rhododendrons
Weeping Norway Spruce   10 Hardy Azaleas
Hemlock macrophylla   10 Hardy Roses
Dwarf Black Spruce

BETWEEN PATHS AND HOUSE

Tamarix indica   Tamarix africana
Spiræa crispifolia   Mahonia aquifolia
Biota elegantissima
Biota semper aurescens
Thuya Columbia
" Aurea
" Vervæneana
2 Tree Box

PLANTS BETWEEN PATHS AND HOUSE

Silver Japanese Juniper
Golden " "
Picea Hudsonica
Golden Sun-ray Pine
Golden Retinospora filifera
" " plumosa

Dwarf Retinospora obtusa
Weeping " "
Golden Yew
Andromeda Catesbaei
Azalea amœna
Daphne cneorum
18 Japan Ampelopsis
Limonia trifoliata
Washington Yew
6 Japan Maples—east of path
Tree Pæony

PLANTS FOR STREET

4 Schwerdler Maple

PLANTS FOR THE TOOL-HOUSE

Akebia
Aristolochia
Honeysuckle Halleana
" variegated
Tecoma grandiflora

FRUIT PLANTS

5 Early Wilson Blackberry
5 Kittatinny "
6 White Grape Currant
6 Fay's Red Currant
6 Downing Gooseberries
15 Cuthbert Raspberries
200 Charles Downing Strawberries
3 Peach Trees
6 Linnaeus Rhubarb
6 Grapevines—El Dorado, Miles, Golden Gem, Berckmans, Niagara, Martha

The Estimated Cost of the Plants in the foregoing list is $175

LANDSCAPE GARDENING—BY S. B. PARSONS

II.—Planting a plot 300 x 480 facing south

A PLAN illustrating landscape art on grounds unknown or unvisited can never be an entire success. Planting adapted to a northern exposure would be entirely unsuited to a southern, and so with each point of the compass. It would be useless to aim at sky effects when an old forest of tall trees is a next neighbor. A level surface requires a different treatment from a broken one. Vistas cannot be opened unless the artist knows the end of the vista. For these things there is nothing like a personal inspection of the ground.

This publication, however, is for those who cannot have professional aid or who desire to plant for themselves.

We have, therefore, made our plan for a level piece of ground, fronting south, with a width of 300 feet and a depth of 480 feet. It can be changed to any point of the compass, only bearing in mind that the evergreen trees and shrubs should be on the north and west sides.

For speedy effect, the trees are not placed at the distance from each other that would be proper for an avenue, and the shrubs can be always kept from crowding each other by judicious pruning after the flowering.

The walks and drives are those only which utility requires. Others require labor and are not so pleasant for walking as the shaved turf. These walks and drives should be made, if possible, with a substratum of twelve to eighteen inches of rough stone covered with the coarser and then the finer sifting of the brown Red Hook gravel, which is used in Central Park. Failing this, any other good gravel will answer. After being made they should be well rolled in wet weather. It will be noticed that to keep open a view of the western sky the evergreens west of the house are those of a lower growing character. Trees on the adjoining property may render this useless, but a sunset view is very desirable.

Below will be found a list of the best trees and shrubs, appended to each of which is a number corresponding with a similar number on the plan. This will greatly aid the planter. These numbers are sometimes the same for different classes but the symbol on the map will show where they belong.

A prominent feature in the plan is the avenue of Weeping Beeches on the east side (No. 34). The first of these should be planted twenty feet distant from the front fence and from the east line and continue to the stable twenty feet apart and twenty feet from the east line. As these grow the inside branches can be cut away leaving only a shell. This will make, in time, a foliage covered way, close at the top, close at the sides, with irregularity of top outline. This covered way does not, we think, yet exist either in Europe or America, and will thus be unique in its beauty. A similar effect for narrow walks can be made with Cerasus japonicum roseum, which like the Weeping Beech grows upward while it droops. A similar effect can also be obtained with the Weeping Hemlock by training up a leading stem for ten feet and trimming out the inside. So also with the Japan Sophora.

A Salisburia should be planted at each corner of the house to be trained along its eaves. To fill the vacant space between the Weeping Beeches and the fence, a line of Peach Trees can be planted until the Beeches encroach upon them. The vines will go on the east fence. Limonia trifoliata should be trained against the south or east side of the house. The carriage-house should be covered with Ampelopsis Veitchii.

For the edge of the walk in the front street Tilia Sulphurea and Acer Schwerdlerii will be striking and very ornamental. They should be planted alternately and thirty feet apart. If, after planting, the trees or shrubs seem too far apart for immediate effect others can be temporarily placed between them. The circle near the *Porte Cochere* can be left in grass with the Weeping Hemlock in its centre.

The American Holly hedge around the drying ground will be a charming novelty, and by using small plants from pots, will be a success.

That as well as the Golden Yew and Golden Retinospora should be set two feet farther from the walk than shown on the plan.

The vinery for foreign grapes is essential to every gentleman's place. The fences on the north and west lines of the fruit and kitchen garden should be tight, and on them should be trained the stone fruits ; these trees will escape the curculio only by being covered with mosquito netting.

They should be planted not less than ten feet apart.

The best time for planting is, Spring for Evergreens, Autumn for Deciduous.

EVERGREEN TREES AND SHRUBS

1 Abies alba
2 " alcockiana
3 " canadensis
4 " " atrovireus
5 " " macrophylla
6 " " weeping
7 " excelsa
8 " " conica
9 " " elata
10 " " Gregoriana
11 " " inverta
12 " nigra pumila
13 " orientalis
14 " polita
15 " pungens
16 Biota elegantissima
17 " orientalis, golden
18 Juniperus canadensis
19 " hibernica
20 " japonica, silver
21 " " golden
22 " oblonga pendula
23 " sinensis variegata
24 " suecica
25 " " nana
26 " sabina
27 " virginiana glauca
28 " venusta
29 Picea cilicica
30 " concolor
31 " japonica
32 " Hudsonica
33 " nobilis
34 " nordmaniana
35 " pectinata compacta
36 " " pendula
37 " pichta
38 Pinus austriaca
39 " densiflora
40 " excelsa
41 " mandschurica
42 " massoniana

43 Pinus massoniana aurea
44 " " variegata
45 " monticola
46 " mughus compacta
47 " resinosa
48 " strobus
49 " " compacta
50 " sylvestris
51 " " pumila
52 Retinospora filifera
53 " " aurea
54 " obtusa
55 " " nana
56 " " pendula
57 " pisifera
58 " plumosa aurea
59 " squarrosa
60 Taxus aurea
61 " cuspidata
62 " Jacksoni
63 " repandeus
64 " Washingtonii
65 Thuya Brinckerhoffi
66 " compacta
67 " Hoveyii
68 " occidentalis, golden
69 " pyramidalis
70 " siberica
71 " Vervaenana, golden
72 " Columbia
73 Thuiopsis Standishii

DECIDUOUS TREES

1 Acer cucullatum
2 " rubrum
3 " Schwerdlerii
4 " saccharinum
5 Aesculus hippocastanum, double white
6 " hippocastanum, red flowering
7 Alnus imperialis, cut leaf
8 Aralia spinosa
9 Betula atropurpurea

10 Betula fastigiata
11 " laciniata
12 Carpinus betulus
13 Castanea Americana
14 " japonica
15 Catalpa aurea
16 Celtis occidentalis
17 Cerasus avium, dbl white
18 " japonicum, weeping
19 Cercis canadensis
20 " japonica
21 Chionanthus virginica
22 Cornus Florida
23 " " red flower'g
24 " " weeping
25 Cratægus arbutifolia
26 " double white
27 " Paul's dbl. red
28 Cytisus laburnum
29 Diospyros virginica
30 Fagus atropurpurea
31 " cuprea
32 " ferruginea
33 " laciniata
34 " pendula
35 " sylvatica
36 Fraxinus aurea
37 Fraxinus concavaefolia
38 " juglandifolia
39 Gleditschia sinensis
40 Gymnocladus
41 Halesia
42 Kolreuteria
43 Larix Europæa
44 " pendula
45 " leptolepsis
46 Liquidambar
47 Liriodendron
48 Magnolia conspicua
49 " cordata
50 " hypoleuca
51 " Lennei
52 " macrophylla
53 " stellata

54 Magnolia Thompsoniana
55 Malus coronaria, double
56 " Halleana
57 " spectabilis
58 Persica camelliæflora
59 " double white
60 " purple leaved
61 Phellodendron amurense
62 Populus golden
63 Prunus Pissardi
64 Quercus cerris
65 " concordia
66 " Daimio
67 " fastigiata
68 " nigricans
69 " phellos
70 " palustris
71 " rubra
72 Rhus cotinus
73 " osbeckii
74 Robinia hispida
75 Salisburia
76 Salix laurifolia
77 Sophora, weeping
78 Sorbus Americana
79 Staphylea bumalda
80 Tamarix indica
81 Taxodium sinensis
82 Tilia Americana
83 " alba pendula
84 " argentea
85 " laciniata rubra
86 " sulphurea
87 Ulmus fulva pendula
88 " purpurea
89 Virgilia lutea

SHRUBS—EVERGREEN

1 Andromeda catesbæi
2 Azalea amœna
3 Buxus rotundifolia
4 Cotoneaster microphylla
5 Cratægus pyrancantha
6 Daphne cneorum

7 Ilex opaca
8 Kalmia latifolia
9 Limonia trifoliata
10 Mahonia aquifolia
11 Rhododendron, assort'd

SHRUBS—DECIDUOUS

12 Aesculus macrostachya
13 Amelanchier botryapium
14 Andromeda arborea
15 Amorpha fruticosa
16 Berberis atropurpureum
17 " Hakodate
18 " Thunbergii
19 " vulgaris
20 Callicarpa Americana
21 Calycanthus floridus
22 Caragana altagana
23 " argentea
24 Caragana chamlagu
25 Celastrus orixa
26 Cephalanthus occidentalis
27 Clethra alnifolia
28 Colutea halepica
29 Cornus alba sanguinea
30 " mascula
31 " paniculata
32 Corylus avellana, purple
33 Cotoneaster Simonsii
34 Cydonia japonica, double [scarlet
35 " " aurora
36 " " mallardii
37 " " moerlosii
38 " " simplex [alba
39 " " tricolor
40 Cytisus nigricans
41 Daphne Genkwa
42 " mezereum
43 Deutzia crenata, dbl. white
44 " " " purple
45 " gracilis
46 " scabra

47 Eleagnus hortensis
48 " longipes
49 Euonymus alata
50 " Americanus
51 " Europeus
52 " " purple [leaved
53 " " nanus [erectus
54 " latifolius
55 Exochorda
56 Forsythia Fortunii
57 " suspensa
58 " viridissima
59 Hibiscus Syriacus
60 " compacta
61 " Buist's
62 " tota alba
63 Hydrangea nivea
64 " grandiflora
65 " quercifolia
66 " radiata
67 Hypericum kalmianum
68 " prolificum
69 " aureum
70 Itea virginica
71 Kerria japonica
72 " variegated [leaf
73 Ligustrum ovalifolium
74 Lonicera fragrantissima
75 " Standishii
76 " tartarica
77 " xylosteum
78 Pæonia moutan
79 Philadelphus coronarius
80 " golden leaved
81 " Gordonianus
82 " grandiflorus
83 Potentilla fruticosa
84 Prinos verticillata
85 Prunus maritima
86 " sinensis, dbl. white
87 " " " rose

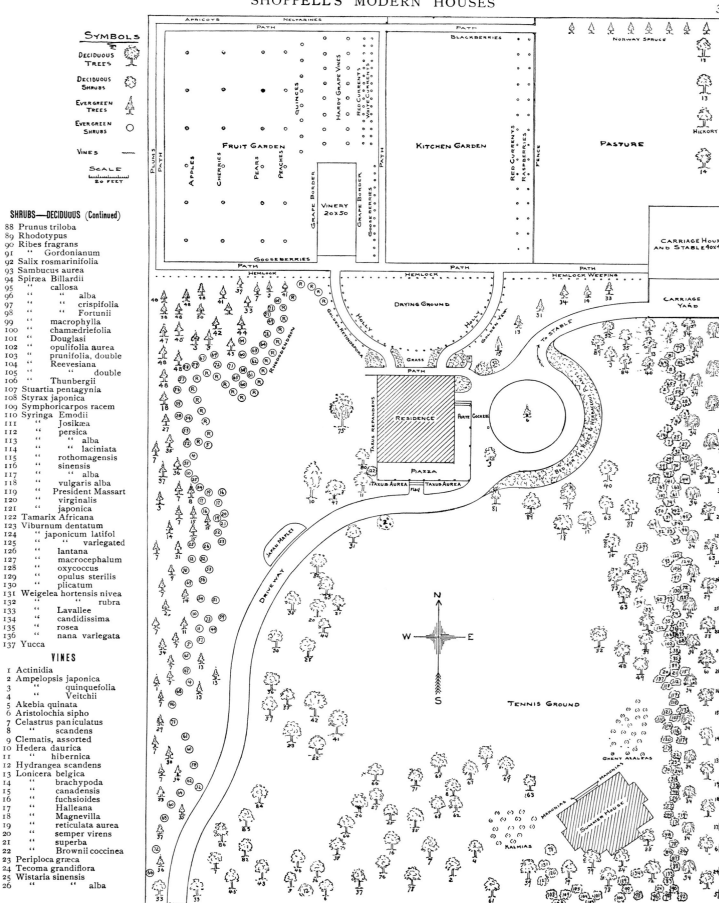

SYMBOLS

DECIDUOUS TREES

DECIDUOUS SHRUBS

EVERGREEN TREES

EVERGREEN SHRUBS

VINES ———

SCALE
20 FEET

SHRUBS—DECIDUOUS (Continued)

88 Prunus triloba
89 Rhodotypus
90 Ribes fragrans
91   "   Gordonianum
92 Salix rosmarinifolia
93 Sambucus aurea
94 Spiræa Billardii
95   "   callosa
96   "   "   alba
97   "   "   crispifolia
98   "   "   Fortunii
99   "   macrophylla
100   "   chamædriefolia
101   "   Douglasi
102   "   opulifolia aurea
103   "   prunifolia, double
104   "   Reevesiana
105   "   "   double
106   "   Thunbergii
107 Stuartia pentagynia
108 Styrax japonica
109 Symphoricarpos racem
110 Syringa Emodii
111   "   Josikæa
112   "   persica
113   "   "   alba
114   "   "   laciniata
115   "   rothomagensis
116   "   sinensis
117   "   "   alba
118   "   vulgaris alba
119   "   President Massart
120   "   virginalis
121   "   japonica
122 Tamarix Africana
123 Viburnum dentatum
124   "   japonicum latifol
125   "   "   variegated
126   "   lantana
127   "   macrocephalum
128   "   oxycoccus
129   "   opulus sterilis
130   "   plicatum
131 Weigelea hortensis nivea
132   "   rubra
133   "   Lavallee
134   "   candidissima
135   "   rosea
136   "   nana variegata
137 Yucca

VINES

1 Actinidia
2 Ampelopsis japonica
3   "   quinquefolia
4   "   Veitchii
5 Akebia quinata
6 Aristolochia sipho
7 Celastrus paniculatus
8   "   scandens
9 Clematis, assorted
10 Hedera daurica
11   "   hibernica
12 Hydrangea scandens
13 Lonicera belgica
14   "   brachypoda
15   "   canadensis
16   "   fuchsioides
17   "   Halleana
18   "   Magnevilla
19   "   reticulata aurea
20   "   semper virens
21   "   superba
22   "   Brownii coccinea
23 Periploca græca
24 Tecoma grandiflora
25 Wistaria sinensis
26   "   "   alba

PLAN OF A PLOT 300 x 480 FEET—FACING SOUTH

CHILDREN'S PLAY HOUSE

TO our children the possession of a play house affords as much delight as the ownership of a fine mansion gives to the parents. We build the fine mansion, indeed, for them, yet they have but little feeling of ownership in it. The play house they will consider theirs—guaranteed, in fee simple, and by every other right that the minds of youth can imagine.

We give elevations and a plan, shown to quarter scale, of a simple design for a play house. The cost to build, of spruce dressed, is $90. Painting, $10. Built of hemlock, all rough, except plates and posts, $75.

This house appears very well placed against some other structure, which a limited playground may sometimes require. In this case leave off the brackets and projecting roof from one end. A play house is practically useful in relieving the residence of a good many traps which are valuable and amusing to the young people, but which

Front View

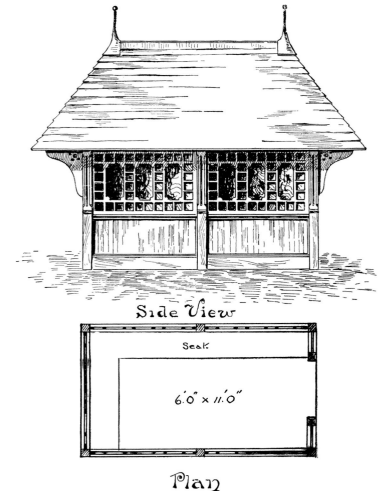

Side View

Seat

6'.0" x 11'.0"

Plan

are not ornamental and cause no end of trouble to a nice housekeeper.

This play house design answers very well for a summer house. Used for this purpose it should have entrances at both ends and seats on each of the long sides. The entrances should be higher. For the playhouse the entrance is but 5 ft., 6 ins. high.

HOW WE SHOULD PLACE OUR HOUSES

IT was Karl Vogt, the eminent scientist of Geneva, Switzerland, who, by experiment, established the fact that, leaving the north side of a building out of the question, the south side is found during the summer months to be always the coolest, the east side following next in degree of temperature, while the west side he found to be the warmest. The direct effect of the solar rays upon the eastern and western walls of a house he found to be greatly stronger than upon the southern walls, this difference being accounted for by the different angles of incidence of the solar rays falling upon the walls. On the east and west sides, the said angle reaches its maximum size of ninety degrees, while the south walls are struck at an acute angle, hence the effect is much slighter. Vogt for the first time called attention to the problem of computing scientifically how our dwelling houses should be placed to insure for them a sufficient quantity of solar heat and light. Although the idea would not seem to be of much practical value, when applied to our customary city dwellings, surrounded as they are, by other buildings, it must be conceded, that in its application to detached dwellings, it is deserving of careful consideration at the hands of the professional architect.

As long as nineteen hundred years ago, Vitruvius, the Roman architect, laid stress on the principle that, in planning cities the streets must not be laid parallel with the direction of the prevailing atmospherical currents. In Germany, the prevailing currents are north-east and south-west ; hence her towns if laid out on the rectangular plan, should have streets running from east to west and from north to south. This plan has actually been followed in a number of cases, for instance, the cities of Mannheim, Darmstadt and others. Supposing a house so placed, it is evident that the prevailing north east winds must strike the sides of the house at angles of incidence averaging forty-five degrees. Other winds striking the walls squarely or nearly so, are usually of short duration, blowing only for a few hours at one time.

It will be observed that, if we locate our houses on the principle advocated by Vitruvius, we are, at the same time, fulfilling the requirements demanded by Professor Vogt. During the summer months, the sun rising in the north-east and setting in the north-west, the east and west walls of a house will be heated to a greater, and the south wall to a lesser degree, since the rays of the sun then being at its great declination, fall more obliquely upon the latter than they do upon the former. On the other hand, during the winter months, the sun rising in the south-east and setting in the south-west, it is the south wall which is exposed to rays thrown upon it almost at right angles by the sun which then is at its minimum declination, whilst both east and west walls receive oblique rays only. Hence, if your house is so planned that one side greatly exceeds in length the other, place its long side on a line running from east to west to insure for the same greater warmth in winter and less heat in summer, whilst the short side can better afford to be the cooler side in winter and the hotter one in summer, just because it is the shorter side

It may be objected that, as there will be a long side combining the advantages of its southward position in hot and cold weather, so will there be a correspondingly long northern side receiving no sun during any time of the year, besides offering an extended surface to cold north-easterly winds. To this we answer, that it is impracticable to devise a plan that will combine all the advantages sought. By placing a rectangular house with its long side running from south to north, a more uniform distribution of the heating effect of the solar rays, and the different sides, may perhaps be obtained in winter, but—and here we have to touch upon another important factor governing the designing architect—the long side of the building, so placed would then receive a much smaller amount of light than it would get by facing south.

It is, therefore, the desire to obtain the greatest possible amount of sunlight which causes men to place the long sides of their houses so as to face the south, and thus to instinctively obey the law discovered by the scientist. In one class of buildings, the noblest one—churches, this rule has from olden times been recognized and strictly adhered to. Since man began to erect houses to God, up to the churches of the present day, it has been the favorite plan to build these edifices running from east to west.—*Translation from the Deutsche Bauzeitung in the American Architect.*

AN ICE HOUSE AND COLD ROOM

THE foundation of this combined ice house and cold room should be started sufficiently deep to avoid the action of the frost, may be made of either brick or stone and should be carried up to the under side of the sill. The sill is 4 x 8-inch yellow pine, and should be set in cement, weathered. Upon the sill rests the 3 x 4-inch hemlock studding and 4 x 6-inch hemlock corner posts.

PERSPECTIVE VIEW

The lower floor joists of the ice chamber also rest upon the sill and should be spiked to the studding, which is to be set 12 inches on centres. The upper floor joists are to be carried on a heavy girt, 2 x 6 inches, laid on top of the furring strips, which form the air passage.

The entire exterior walls to be sheathed on the outside with ⅞-inch hemlock sheathing laid horizontally, covered with rosin-sized sheathing paper, well tacked on, and finished with clapboards or novelty siding, with bands, casings and mouldings. All to be of good quality white pine, free from defects. The walls to be sheathed inside with matched ⅞-inch hemlock, laid diagonally. The air space around the ice-chamber is made by nailing 2 x 2-inch furring strips against the inner sheathing and directly over studs, and then covering with 1½-inch yellow pine tongued and grooved boards laid closely.

The space between outer and inner sheathing to be filled in with mineral wool or some good non-conductor. The rafters to be ceiled on the under side, and the space between rafters left open at the eaves, to admit a free passage of air through and out at the ventilator.

CROSS SECTION

The doors to be constructed in the same manner as the walls, to have beveled edges and to be hung on strong hinges, fastened with hasps and padlocks.

The floor above the high part of the cold room to be covered with any suitable and durable material, and carried up back of inner lining of the ice chamber, and made perfectly water-tight to avoid dripping.

The lower floor of ice chamber is made of 2-inch planks, 6 inches wide, laid about a half inch apart, so as to allow the water and cold air to descend to the cold chamber. As cold air always has a downward tendency, by this means the cold chamber gets the full benefit of the ice used, and is further assisted by the ventilation of the chamber, which allows the upper and warmer air to escape. The water running in the gutters on the cold room floor (so arranged as to make water traverse the distance several times before leaving the building) also helps to reduce the temperature.

The shelving to be perfectly plain, supported on cleats against the wall at one end and hung at the other end by ¾-inch iron rod. Hooks to any desired number to be placed at the side of the shelving for hanging meats, etc.

The floor of entire cold chamber to be made of concrete, covered with a coating of cement, made smooth and

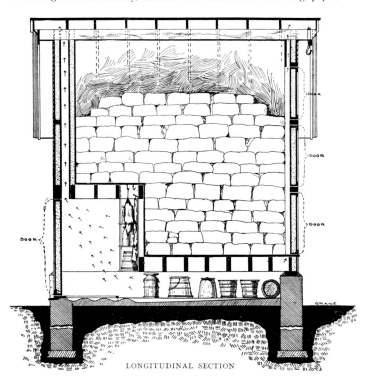

LONGITUDINAL SECTION

PLAN

so arranged as to have the water run in the direction of the arrows and discharge through trapped pipe to outside of building. Lay a wooden grating where necessary to walk upon.

The scale of the drawings is 3-16-inch = 1 foot.

DESCRIPTION OF DESIGN NUMBER 508

A SCHOOL BUILDING

IN the planning, designing and construction of a school building the controlling considerations should be safety in case of fire or panic, perfect sanitary arrangement, thorough ventilation and heating and good light.

If not wholly fire-proof, the stairways should be fireproof, they should have short runs and should not be too wide. Wide stairways, having long runs are almost sure to cause falling and jambing in case of a panic.

The ventilation of all parts of the building is effected by means of the vent flues shown on the plan. A draught is created by the heat the vent flues receive from the smoke pipes. The heating may be by hot air or steam. A portion of the cellar or basement is designed for the heating apparatus and for coal; the remainder may be used for gymnasium, or for a playroom in stormy weather.

The light of a schoolroom should not only be unobstructed, but it should fall so that it will not cast shadows. A glance at the floor plan will explain this. As the pupils sit facing towards the front the light falls from the windows on their left directly upon their desks, without a shadow being cast by their right hands when writing.

The building shown is so arranged that the classes may be assembled or dismissed without interfering with each other, and at a moment's notice the class rooms may be transformed into an assembly room, by opening the large sliding doors between the rooms.

The clothes closets or wardrobes which are of ample size, have passages through them, so that pupils can file through and hang up their clothes when assembling and file through and get their clothes when dismissed. These wardrobes are open at the top, the enclosing partition on the hall side not being carried to the top of the hall ceiling. This provides thorough ventilation for the wardrobes, any bad odors arising from the clothing being carried into the hall. Wire netting should piece out the partition at the top, to prevent some of the merry youngsters from throwing the hats of other merry youngsters over the partition into the hall. By this arrangement the wardrobe can be under the direct care of the teacher.

This design is susceptible of enlargement or reduction. If the front portion,

having three or four rooms on each floor, fill present requirements, the addition of a section of one or more rooms on each floor at any future time may easily be accomplished.

The attic over the front portion may be used for a laboratory, for lecture rooms or for janitor's quarters. It is generally preferable to have the janitor and his assistants live in a separate building. The roof may be flat, which would be less imposing but much cheaper.

The building is designed with a view to separating, according to primary and grammar grades or by sexes. Each grade or sex, as the case may be, to occupy separate floors.

The front is designed to be built of red stretcher brick laid in red mortar. The sides and back to be of common hard brick laid in white mortar. Blackboards are placed in the panels of the sliding doors as well as upon the space of the side walls.

THE COST of the building, without school furniture and heating apparatus, is roughly estimated at $28,000 to $30,000. No closely figured estimate has been made.

NO. 508, SCHOOL BUILDING, FRONT ELEVATION

SCHOOL BUILDING, FIRST FLOOR, NO. 508

A COUNTRY PARLOR

A PARLOR in a country house has been made pretty at very little expense by the inmates thereof. The floor is stained an olive green and polished. A large Chinese cotton rug, of white ground, with an arabesque border and medallion of pink and pale olive green, is laid in the centre, showing a border a yard wide, of the stained floor. The walls are tinted a shrimp pink color, and have a paper frieze of pink ground, with a pattern of deep pink peonies with olive green foliage. A green bronze picture rail separates the frieze from the wall. The old-fashioned marble mantel and hearth are painted green and the mantel is decorated with panels of Lincrusta-Walton which are painted a green bronze color. The mantel draperies are of cream-colored cheese cloth, painted with gold and bronze disks. An over mantel of railed shelves has a mirror background, and is decorated with bits of artistic pottery. Simple curtains of cheese cloth, with frieze band, painted similarly to the mantel drapery, hang from the windows, and there are inner or sash curtains, of cheese cloth, with a trimming of cream white tassel fringe. A pretty cane sofa is stained a dark olive green, and has back and seat cushions of golden olive plush, tied with two shades of green ribbons. Two or three bamboo chairs, painted olive green, have cushions of pink plush. A hanging cabinet and several prettily framed water color sketches and engravings are upon the walls. * * The decorations and furniture of this room are of the simplest, yet a look of quiet refinement reigns over all.—*Art Age.*

DESCRIPTION OF DESIGN NUMBER 509

A SMALL BANK BUILDING

SIZE OF STRUCTURE: Front, 25 ft. Side, 48 ft.

HEIGHT OF STORIES: Cellar, 8 ft.; First Story, 12 ft.; Second Story, 10 ft., 6 ins.

MATERIALS: Foundations, stone walls; walls above foundation, brick; Roof, tin.

COST: $4,900, complete.

SPECIAL FEATURES: Designed for a bank and office building, but can be used for store or altogether for offices by a different arrangement of the partitions on ground floor, and the omission of the vault. Cellar under the front part, extending as far back as the partition wall of the directors' room.

The vault has a double brick wall with an air space between, with a heavy stone foundation.

The banking rooms are finished with hardwood; the offices with pine. The estimate of cost includes the fitting up of the banking room with partitions and counters.

The fireplace in the directors' room has a mantel of the value of $50.

The middle offices on the second floor are lighted by sashes from the front and rear rooms. There is a skylight over the hall.

The floors are of hard Southern pine, which makes a very durable and handsome floor.

All windows in the front are glazed with plate glass.

The front wall is faced with the best press brick. The upper work of the main cornice, and the balustrade above it is of galvanized iron.

Many a small but rapidly growing town in the western or southern part of this country feels the need of just such buildings as this. The walls are thick enough to carry another story, which would increase the revenue derived from the building very considerably.

An excellent way to finish the interior of a building of this kind is to ceil the walls and ceilings with narrow matched and beaded yellow pine. A small wood moulding in the angle formed by the wall and the ceiling will cover any rough joints and make the effect of a cornice. In most localities this finish will cost a little more than plastering but the effect is better. The wood should be well oiled. After it has stood for some little time it will have a depth of color that is very pleasing.

We do not advocate this finish for dwellings, as it is not as warm as plastering, and offers a hiding place for vermin; it conveys

sounds, also, from one room to another more than plastered walls. But for a summer cottage, where warmth is not a requisite, it makes an excellent finish and is quite in keeping with the character and purposes of the building.

In some sections poplar is plentiful and very inexpensive. This wood makes a good finish for walls as above described, and should be stained to make it a little darker than its natural color. Ash, oak, maple and birch can be used for the same purpose.

It is quite permissible, and the effect is very pretty, to plaster the side walls of the rooms, and cover the ceiling with any of the woods mentioned, hiding the junction at the angle with a wood moulding. The strips can be laid diagonally so as to make square or lozenge shaped figures. These ceilings do away with the danger of falling plaster.

MODERN CARPENTRY

A HUNDRED years ago all the woodwork of a house was got out by hand labor. The timbers were hewn with axe and adze from trees felled on the spot where the house was to stand, or in the neighboring forest. The boards covering the exterior walls were split in short lengths, the full width of the log, and smoothed with the broad axe or adze, or else the walls were covered by long split shingles. The flooring was laboriously sawed by hand from the logs and nailed down with nails made by the village blacksmith. All mouldings were "stuck" by hand, that is, the plane or iron of the desired shape was worked by hand. In short the whole of the woodwork was cut and put together by one man or one set of men.

The method now is very different. The timber is felled a thousand miles away, perhaps, and is sawed to the desired dimensions by a gang saw which cuts up a large log into inch boards in a few minutes—work that required two men a week or more by the old method of hand sawing. All planing and moulding is done with machines, which for accuracy of work and rapidity are truly wonderful. Sashes, doors and blinds are made by the million. The sandpapering, even, is done on a large wheel revolved by steam or other power. Very little remains for the modern carpenter to do but the putting together of the various parts which the mill has made.

The result has been the building of thousands of houses and this wholesale making of homes may justify the means. But there are serious drawbacks, one of which is that first-class joiners are scarce, the result of their getting so little experience with the finer work.

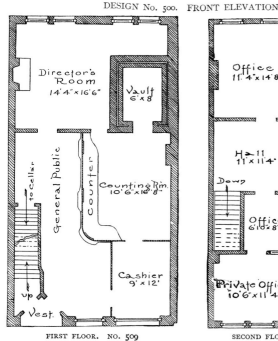

DESIGN No. 500. FRONT ELEVATION

FIRST FLOOR. NO. 509

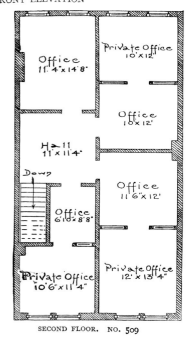

SECOND FLOOR. NO. 509

DESCRIPTION OF DESIGN NUMBER 533.

SIZE OF STRUCTURE: Front width, 25 ft. Side depth, 42 ft., not including the front bay, the veranda, nor the pantry at the rear.

MATERIALS EMPLOYED: Exterior—Foundations, stone and brick; First Story, clapboards; Second Story, clapboards; Mansard Roof, slate and tin. Interior—Cemented cellar floor; finish throughout with soft woods, except stairway which is cherry.

ACCOMMODATIONS: The principal rooms, closets, etc., are shown by the floor plans given here. Beside these there is a cellar under the whole house, and the third floor has four rooms, a store-room and a large hall.

COST: $2,500 to $4,000, according to the prevailing prices for materials and labor in different localities. All complete, except heating and mantels.

THE "OLD WAY" AND THE NEW.

The "old way" of proceeding to build was to go to a carpenter or builder and in some imperfect manner come to an understanding with him *about* what kind of a structure it should be, make a contract with him and order him to go ahead. From beginning to end there was trouble. The owner had to fight for good materials and workmanship, and for *his* understanding of this, that, and the other thing, during the whole progress of the work, unless, indeed, he did not know his rights, or was so meek-spirited that he would not assert them. With this way of doing business there could be but one result —dissatisfaction. Even if the owner succeeded in getting the best materials and workmanship, and in having *his* understanding carried out, there would remain the faults of arrangement and the common-place appearance which seem to be characteristics of every house built by the "old way."

The "new way," and by far the better way, is for the owner to supply himself first with accurate Working Plans, Specifications, etc., prepared by competent architects. These aids serve five important purposes: First, the arrangement of rooms, the exterior appearance and every part of the design are the results of professional skill; second, these aids thoroughly acquaint the owner with all the requirements before the work is undertaken; third, they enable the owner to invite competition and thus to secure the lowest contract; fourth, they are made the basis of the contract between the owner and contractor and, being full and explicit, they will settle every dispute and misunderstanding that may arise; fifth, they guide the workmen at every step in the construction of the house.

Why any intelligent man will undertake the building of a house, however small, without these aids is hard to understand. They certainly *save money* as well as secure peace of mind. In times past, when competent architectural services cost from 4 to 5 per cent. of the cost of the structure, there was some excuse, but that objection is now met by The Co-operative Building

FRONT ELEVATION OF DESIGN NUMBER 533.

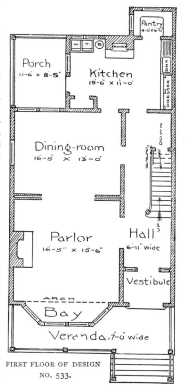

FIRST FLOOR OF DESIGN NO. 533.

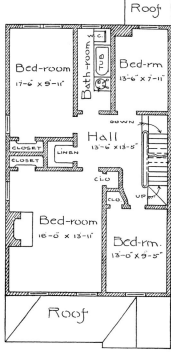

SECOND FLOOR OF DESIGN NO. 533.

Plan Association, whose charges are about 1 per cent. Another and serious objection was the owner's fears that he could not contract at the architect's estimate and that the result would be the loss of the amount paid for Plans, etc., or the expenditure of a larger sum for building than he intended. This objection is most effectually met by the guaranteed estimates of the Association.

BATH-ROOMS AND FIRE-PLACES IN HOUSES OF LOW AND MODER-ATE COST.

Now and then an extremely practical man exclaims, "Why, there are too many bath-rooms and fire-places in your designs. They cost money and are unnecessary."

Our answer is, omit them if you prefer; make closets out of the bath-room, or enlarge it and make it a bedroom, or add it to the space of an adjoining room; build up the chimneys, leaving only stove-pipe holes.

But we advise against these omissions. Plumbing is not the mysterious and expensive matter that it was years ago. It is simpler, better, stronger, and the materials are cheaper. So simple, indeed, is some of the best designed plumbing, that it scarcely requires expert labor to put it in place.

It is not necessary to have a plumber and two or three helpers standing around in each other's way, prolonging the job at $10 to $15 a day.

The owner should study the plumbing design—it is easily understood— then go and have a look at the materials required and learn their cost. He can then estimate closely the labor required, and he will probably not allow himself to be victimized.

Regarding fire-places, they are called for in our designs, not so much for heating purposes as for ventilating. They are the least effective for heating, seventy to eighty per cent. of the heat going up the chimney; but they are the best and most economical of ventilating arrangements. Beside they help to furnish the room: nothing is more cheerful than a fire-place and nothing prettier than a well-designed mantel. In building an ordinary fire-place instead of a flue, the cost of extra labor and bricks required does not exceed $5. The grate, including setting, and the fender will cost from $10 to $30, according to style wanted; the mantel from $8 to $75. The lowest prices named secure good materials, not lacking in ornamental features. Especially is this the case regarding mantels. Some of the cheapest are among the prettiest.

Do not omit the bath-room and the fire-places, for they are essential to good health, and therefore conducive of good looks, cheerfulness of spirits, vigorous work and absence of doctors' bills.

Speculative builders — those who build houses to rent or to sell — are naturally desirous of keeping the cost down, but they certainly make a mistake when they omit the requirements demanded by health and comfort. Ordinarily, larger rentals are produced by houses which have "modern improvements."

George H. Bonte, Esq., Cincinnati, Ohio, says:

"The Plans were satisfactory in all respects. Your estimate of cost was very close. I have the finest, prettiest and best built house in South Norwood, and many parties say within many miles of it, and that is saying a great deal; it is acknowledged to be the finest and best of the three or four hundred houses that are in the neighborhood."

DESCRIPTION OF DESIGN NUMBER 546.

A BANK.

SIZE OF STRUCTURE: Front width, 30 ft. Side depth, 70 ft.

MATERIALS EMPLOYED: Exterior—Foundations, stone; First Story, brick; Second Story, brick; Roof, metallic shingles. Interior—Cellar floor cemented; First Story finished with cherry, stained mahogany; Second Story, with white pine; stairway, from first to second story, cherry, stained mahogany.

ACCOMMODATIONS: The principal rooms, closets, etc., are shown by the floor plans given here. Beside these there is a cellar, 26 ft. by 33 ft., and an attic story unfinished.

COST: $7,500 to $10,000, according to the prevailing prices for materials and labor in different localities. All complete, except vault, bank counter and railings.

BUILD A MODERN HOUSE.

The desirability of building modern houses, especially those of moderate cost, to rent, to sell or to live in, is now very well understood. But there are many who have given the subject no serious attention, although they have the means with which to build. Such persons make a serious mistake, and they will realize some day with regret that they have paid out for rent more than sufficient to have built desirable houses. There are no real difficulties in the way of building, even by those of no experience whatever, when our drawings, specifications and directions are followed.

There are many others whose savings will *partly* pay for building. If such a one will call upon some wise friend for advice (perhaps the head of the firm or an officer of the company that employs him) he will probably learn that it is wholly practicable to build, say, for instance, a $2,500 house with $1,000—perhaps even with a less amount. There is not

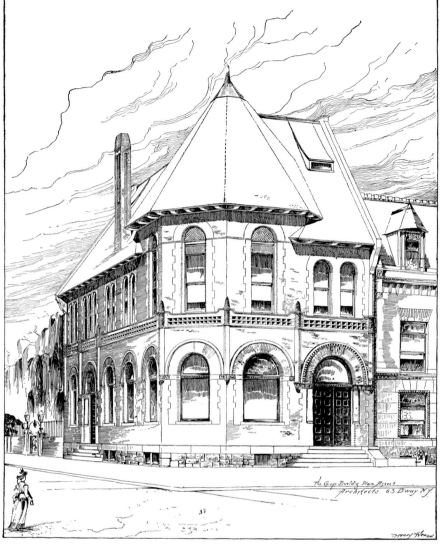

A BANK. PERSPECTIVE VIEW OF DESIGN NUMBER 546.

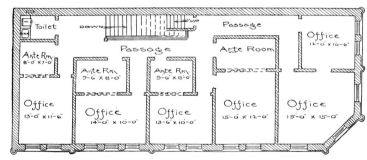

SECOND FLOOR OF DESIGN NO. 546.

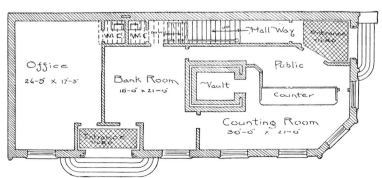

FIRST FLOOR OF DESIGN NO. 546

space here to explain this to apply to individual cases, but the general plan is as follows: Fully pay for the lot and make the first and, perhaps, the second payment to the contractor; the capitalist who furnishes the balance of the money to make the remaining payments as they become due, taking a mortgage as his security. In the course of a few years the increased value of the property may more than equal the mortgage and provide for its removal.

Do not buy a house that is already built. It never thoroughly satisfies, and it costs more than to build one. It is generally said that the only way to get a handsome and convenient modern house is to build it. Remember that, until recently, nearly all the houses of moderate cost were built after one common-place and ill-arranged style. Do not become the owner of one of these, when for the same investment, or for less, a really beautiful and convenient house can be built.

A very simple preparation enables any one to realize the sizes of the houses and the rooms, which are very plainly marked on the plans in this book: procure a tape measure, yard-stick or "ten foot pole," measure the heights, lengths and breadths of some familiar rooms, those at present occupied, for instance. This gives a basis for comparisons, and very accurately brings to mind the sizes described. The comparison can be applied to the exterior width and depth also.

"'SHOPPELL'S MODERN HOUSES' is a publication devoted to domestic architecture, and is so full of common sense, practical suggestions and valuable advice, that it ought to be in the hands of every person who has any desire to build a house. Its aim is high, and it is evident that its authors are capable of the grandest work, but we are glad to see that they show a predilection for demonstrating how houses of low and moderate cost may have beauty and elegance of design and convenience of arrangement, such as people of cultivation and good taste require."—*New York Daily World.*

CONCERNING FENCES.

A PUBLIC-spirited citizen of a village near New York—one of the villages that are so ambitious to attract permanent residents from the city—recently submitted to the architect a number of photographic views of the principal streets, with a request for suggestions of plans for improving the appearance of the village. The request was very specific in one particular, the expense must be small.

"For," he said, "although my neighbors and myself have long agreed that concerted effort and a small fund would make our village another Garden of Eden, the only concert we have been able to organize has been too entirely vocal. We realize that we must have an instrumental accompaniment — some jingling of cash. But we cannot jingle very loudly at the start."

The photographic views showed vistas of old, but rather pretty detached cottages, well set back from the streets, with yards in front somewhat overgrown with shrubbery and long grass, and with fences high enough and strong enough to impede the progress of a drove of buffaloes. For the most part the fences were of the commonplace board and "sappling" or "picket" variety, but each differed in design from the others, as if to call attention to the extreme narrowness of some of the lots. In their full height and strength these fences extended back between the lots, shutting off views and interfering with air currents ; but, evidently, very handy in case of war. Great battles have been fought and won behind barricades less substantial than one of these fences.

The architect tacked one of the photographs to a drawing board, covered it with a bit of tracing paper, and in a few minutes made an exact copy of the view, with these exceptions : in place of the high and irregular fences his sketch showed a uniform style of fence, like that designated as costing 40 cents a foot, extending in front of and between all the cottages ; his sketch also showed less shrubbery and shorter grass ; also a few of the lower branches of some trees fopped off, and the sidewalk improved by simply filling up some holes that had been washed out.

"That's wonderful !" exclaimed the citizen, when the photograph and the sketch were placed side by side; "but what will it cost ?"

"Next to nothing," answered the architect, "for it is quite possible that the old fences can be sold for an amount equal to the cost of the new fence. At any rate, the old fence materials can be used for chicken yards."

In the most elegant communities there are no fences whatever. Each resident respects his neighbor's bounds, and does not intrude upon them without invitation, and all enjoy enlarged prospects, better air, and more beautiful views by reason of their absence The laws of the land and the rules of good-breeding amply guard every man's "castle."

For those who must have fences, the following are submitted as approved designs, with the recommendation that the least elaborate of them, and the cheapest, are the best.

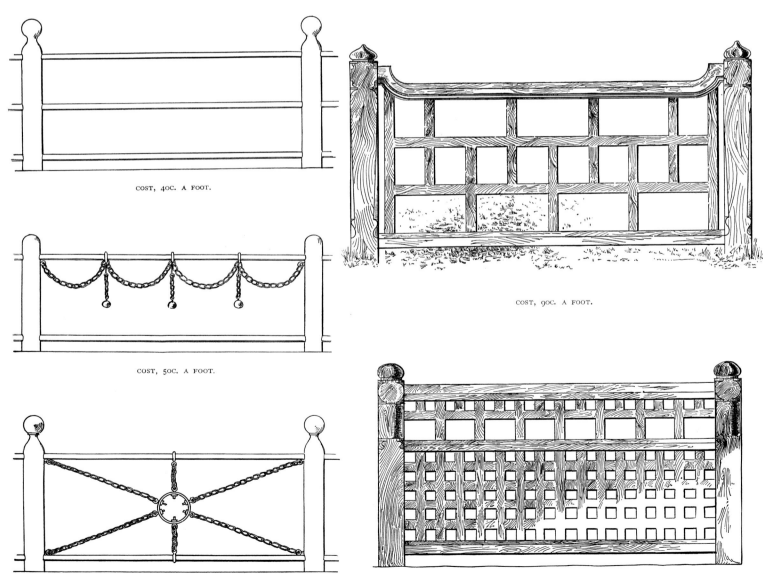

COST, 40C. A FOOT.

COST, 90C. A FOOT.

COST, 50C. A FOOT.

COST, 60C. A FOOT.

COST, $1.00 A FOOT.

FENCES—Continued.

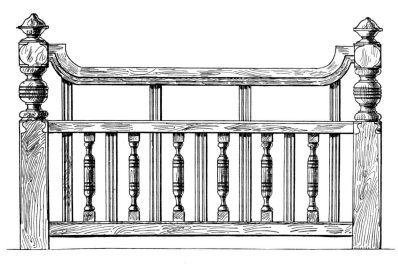

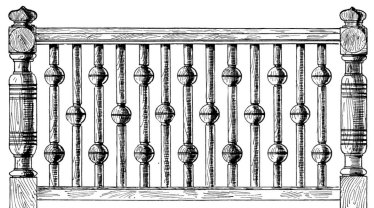

A Complete and Economical System of Aids for the Building of a House.

See the " Testimony of those who have Built" on the following pages.

SELECTING THE DESIGN.

It may be fairly claimed that the building designs published and prepared by this Association, and known as Shoppell's Modern Houses, are the best—best in arrangement, in appearance and in construction, and that they are perfectly reliable as to estimates. Our estimates result from careful and laborious calculation of every item of material and every hour of labor required for each design. We exhibit our own confidence in them by guaranteeing their correctness, under penalty of charging nothing for our services if they are found to be incorrect.

If the intending builder finds a design in this book that "fills the bill," that answers his requirements fully, or that will answer them with slight alterations, his best course is to adopt it.

Do not insist on having a very odd or a peculiar house ; the owner himself is likely to tire of it, and if ever he is desirous of selling it, he will find a purchaser with difficulty. The best house is one whose exterior and interior are generally approved by people of good taste. On the other hand the house should not be too plain, such as a carpenter would design, for then it will be commonplace. It is believed that our publications are the most reliable guides in avoiding the extremes referred to.

IMPORTANCE OF PERFECT WORKING PLANS, SPECIFICATIONS, ETC.

With proper aids it is an easy matter to build a good house; without them the most intelligent owner has a "world of trouble," and usually fails in getting satisfactory work.

Too often the owner is content with imperfect drawings and specifications. Sometimes he simply contracts for a duplicate of some other house, not knowing that the contractor can duplicate the appearance without duplicating the value. Sometimes he allows the contractor to make the drawings and specifications, which is far from being the part of wisdom. Suppose, during the progress of the work, the owner discovers that the contractor is not carrying out the true spirit of the drawings and specifications. There is no help for the owner, because the contractor will be regarded as the best interpreter of the drawings and specifications. If they had been prepared by the architect, the architect's version would decide disputed points.

A COMPLETE SET OF PLANS, SPECIFICATIONS, Etc.

The following is a full and complete list of architectural aids for the building of a house. Our charges for these aids are about one-quarter of the charges usually made by other architects :

WORKING PLANS of the foundation, floors, roofs and elevations, figured and drawn to a scale one-fourth inch to the foot.

DETAIL DRAWINGS of the Cornices, Verandas, Windows, Doors, Gables, Staircases, Trim, etc., large scale and full size.

SPECIFICATIONS minutely describing the qualities of material and workmanship throughout, including the painting and plumbing.

COLOR SHEET giving examples of elevations properly colored, with directions for mixing and applying the paints.

SUPPLEMENT SHEET (A), containing drawings and descriptions of approved methods of building a cistern, the best plan for removing house slops, and the construction and management of earth closets and privies.

SUPPLEMENT SHEET (B), containing a number of designs for fences, with estimates of cost.

AGREEMENTS, in duplicate, with the proper times indicated for making the several payments to the contractor, ready for use.

CONSULTATIONS. At all times the client is entitled to full and free consultations before commencing, during the progress and at the completion of the work.

BILL OF MATERIALS, giving the true quantities in detail of all the materials required.

†† The bill of materials is needed by the owner only in case of his intention to purchase the materials.

THE FIRST STEP.

After the design has been selected, the first step is to order a complete set of Working Plans, Specifications, etc. When they arrive, which will be almost by return mail or express (charges prepaid), give them a close examination. After this examination the owner is often convinced that the alterations which he may have contemplated will not improve the design.

However, after examination, if alterations and modifications are wanted, write us fully about them and we will advise as to their practicability and as to their effect on the cost. We will make, also, the changes on the drawings

and in the specifications, if requested to do so, charging a small fee (seldom exceeding five dollars) for the work.

Or, after examination and study, if the owner prefers some other design, we will allow him to exchange, by his returning to us all the drawings and specifications unused and allowing us twenty per cent. of their cost to cover the extra expenses involved.

THE SECOND STEP.

When the Plans and Specifications finally represent just what is wanted invite bids from builders and award the contract to the lowest approved bidder.   Competition among builders, which is made possible only by having complete Working Plans and Specifications, is the only way to get the contract price down to the right figure. When there is no competition a builder studies the owner, trying to estimate how big a price he will stand ; when there is competition the builder studies the plans and specifications trying to estimate how low he can do the work to get the contract.

When the contract has been awarded send us the name of the contractor, the amount, the time for completion and a memorandum of any extras or omissions agreed upon. We will then write out the Agreement in proper form, dividing up the amount into several payments, each to become due at certain stages of the work. State the number of payments the contractor wants. The Agreement is a very important matter and should be properly prepared, the principal care being that at no payment shall the contractor be overpaid. We make no charge for preparing the Agreement.

* OUR DESIGNS PATENTED.

It often happens that when an owner has completed a handsome and convenient house, it is taken as a pattern, and similar houses spring up all over the neighborhood. This is annoying to many. In order to limit and control this duplication we take out patents for our designs, which enables us to require that owners and builders who use them, or who use the principal features of them, must have licenses to do so from us.

We charge nothing for a license. It is sent free for any design, when the Working Plans, Specifications, etc., of that design are ordered. *We respectfully warn all unauthorized persons that we intend to fully protect our rights in this matter.*

‡ NEW YORK PRICES FOR MATERIALS AND LABOR.

The cost of structures given in this book are based on prices for materials and labor as given below. By comparing with prices which prevail in his own neighborhood, the intending builder can judge whether our estimates would run over or under, in his locality.

Excavations, per cubic yard.............. ....$0 25	Clear pine trim, reeded or moulded ⅞ x 5 in.
Rough stone work below grade laid up complete, all materials furnished by contractor, per perch of 25 cubic feet...................4 25	per lineal foot,.......................$0 03
	Novelty siding, per 1000 feet .... $30 00 to 35 00
Stone wall finished above grade, 25c. per foot, or per perch........... .... 6 25	Mouldings per sq. inch of section, per 100 lineal feet.............................. 65
Brick work laid in the wall, per M....15 00 to 16 00	Moulded base, 8 in. high, ⅞ in. thick, per
Plastering, per yard................... 30 to 35	lineal foot................................ 05
Spruce timber, per 1000 feet 20 00	Glazed window sash, 2 ft. 7 in. x 5 ft. 6 in. x
Hemlock timber, per 1000 feet.... ....14 00	1½ in., two lights, per pair...... .... 2 00
Hemlock Sheathing Boards, per 1000 feet.....15 00	Doors, four panels, moulded both sides, 2 ft.
Pine shingles, per 1000 ....4 50 to 5 00	8 in. x 7 ft. x 1½ in., each........ .... 2 60
Pine flooring, merchantable, per 1000 feet ...26 00	Blinds will average all round per window...... 1 50
Clear pine clapboards, per 1000 feet 25 00 to 30 00	Tinning, per square of 100 square feet...... 6 00
NOTE.—For some sections of the country where other woods are used in place of spruce, hemlock and pine, we modify the specifications to conform.	Painting, including materials and labor, per square yard, each coat............. 06
	Carpenters' labor, per day.......... 2 50 to 3 00
	Masons' and plasterers', per day......3 00 to 3 50

† ESTIMATES NOT INCLUDING MANTELS, RANGE AND HEATER.

Mantels are not included because they may cost as low as $10 each, or as high as $100, or even higher, according to the owner's taste or his wishes as to expense. Many low-cost mantels are beautiful in design. The size and kind of range and its cost depend largely on the size of the family and their requirements as to cooking. Cost is from $25 upward. The heating apparatus and its cost depend on climate principally. For a hot-air heater cost is from $125 upward. For a steam or hot-water heater cost is from $225 upward. After learning his requirements, we advise the owner of the best appliances to suit his purposes.

SUMMARY.

The advantages offered to the intending builder by this Association may be summarized as follows :

1. The owner is supplied with a large number of the most approved designs from which to make a selection.

2. The estimates are thoroughly reliable.

3. The designs are patented and the owner is protected from unauthorized duplication of the house he builds.

4. Alterations of the design selected are made for the owner until they fully suit his requirements, or an exchange of design is permitted at small cost.

5. A properly written Agreement with the contractor is prepared without charge.

6. At all times the owner has full and free consultations before commencing, during the progress and at the completion of the work.

REBATE.

From the price of Working Plans, Specifications, etc., the owner may deduct the amount he has paid us for books to the extent of five dollars.

CONCLUDING WORD.

In the limited space of a page many of the advantages of our system must be left unsaid ; but we would like intending patrons to feel—as we believe every one of our numerous patrons does feel—that our dealings are characterized by a liberal spirit ; that the most painstaking efforts are always made to please them and to serve their best interests.

Respectfully,

THE CO-OPERATIVE BUILDING PLAN ASSOCIATION, ARCHITECTS,

63 BROADWAY, NEW YORK.

TESTIMONY OF THOSE WHO HAVE BUILT

ONE OR MORE OF SHOPPELL'S MODERN HOUSES WITH THE AID OF WORKING PLANS, SPECIFICATIONS, ETC. FURNISHED BY THE CO-OPERATIVE BUILDING PLAN ASSOCIATION, ARCHITECTS, 63 BROADWAY, NEW YORK.

Are Shoppell's Designs well-planned?
Are the Estimates reliable?
Are the Drawings and Specifications perfect?
Are the patrons of the Association treated with fairness and consideration?

The questions opposite are such as a new patron naturally asks. We respectfully submit that these questions are fully and favorably answered in the following pages.

CALIFORNIA.

Office of J. A. INGRAHAM & Co.
OAKLAND, CAL., Dec. 16th, 1889.

* * *

Your plans were received with promptness and given in charge of my contractor. The result is a beautiful house admired by all in our fair city.

Allow me to compliment you upon your methods of doing business, and state that I would most cheerfully recommend your Association to any one.

Yours most truly, G. A. PENNIMAN.
Director Peoples' Building and Loan Association, Oakland, Cal.

SELMA, FRESNO CO. CAL., Dec. 10th 1889.

* * *

The house I built from your plans is admired by every one. Its arrangement of rooms is compact, cosy and convenient. Would cheerfully recommend your plans to all intending builders.

Truly, GEORGE B OTIS.

COLORADO.

CANON CITY, COLO., Nov. 28th, 1889.

* * *

I secured a thoroughly good house, handsome without, tasteful and very convenient within, by using your plans. I am more and more struck with its good points when I see houses built "home-made." A crucial test of a good design is the arrangement of closets, stairways and chimneys. Mine are perfect. I consider the small outlay for your plans repaid many times over by the satisfaction we daily have in the beauty and comfort of our home; and were I to build again, would first consult you. If I might say more, it would be that the less builders went by their own ideas, and the more they employed the experience and talent of educated architects, the more money would be saved, the greater comforts would be enjoyed, and the more attractive would our dwellings be. You are doing a good work and I wish you all success.

Very truly yours, (REV.) G. M. DU BOIS.

CONNECTICUT.

TUTTLE & WHITTEMORE Co. Malleable Iron Castings,
NAUGATUCK, CONN., Nov. 25th, 1889.

* * *

I was well pleased with the plans I bought from you, and cheerfully recommend your work to all who contemplate building.

Very truly, L. D. WARNER, Secretary.

OAKVILLE, CONN., Dec. 2d, 1889.

* * *

Have completed my house built from your plans, and have been living in it about ten months, and like it very much. It is greatly admired by all who see it, both as to exterior appearance and interior arrangement. It is quite different from any around here, which makes it still more attractive.

Your business treatment of me has been entirely satisfactory. Yours, etc.

C. W. COOPER.

Office of A. N. CLARK, Manufacturer,
PLAINVILLE, CONN., Nov. 25th, 1889.

* * *

The modern house which I built at Rockledge, Indian River, Fla., for a winter home, from plans furnished by your firm proved quite satisfactory. The house when completed had a finer appearance than the building design represented.

Many have expressed their admiration of it and it induced others to build similar places.

I take pleasure in recommending your designs to others. Yours truly,

A. N. CLARK.

RIVERSIDE, CONN.

* * *

I have built eleven houses in this place, some from designs by architects to whom I have paid very high prices; but none have pleased me so much as the last house, which I built from your plans. In future I shall use them; they are cheaper, and I consider them more practical than others.

E. A. SKELDING.

THOMPSONVILLE, CONN., Nov. 26th, 1889.

* * *

I have often thought I would write and let yoll know how much I thank you, for by the aid and ass stance of your plans I have one of the best and, I think, the finest looking house of its size in the village.

The drawings and specifications saved me a great deal of trouble. I had very little knowledge about building.

Your estimate was about right. I am perfectly satisfied, and thank you very much for the efficient help you have rendered me.

Yours truly, WILLIAM PICKENS.

FLORIDA.

JACKSONVILLE, FLA.

* * *

I am very much pleased with the house built from your plans.

JULIUS HAYDEN,
Superintendent Jacksonville & Atlantic R.R.

OCALA, FLA., Nov. 26th, 1889.

* * *

I will state that my house, built according to plans furnished by you, is in every respect satisfactory.

I am satisfied that at least five hundred dollars was saved to me by having the plans, specifications, drawings, etc., furnished by you. Your business treatment of me was in every respect honest and prompt. Yours respectfully,

R. L. ANDERSON.

Office of A. E. DELOUEST, Dealer in General Hardware,
OCALA, FLA., Nov. 26th, 1889.

* * *

About two years ago you furnished me with plans and specifications for a cottage, and it affords me great pleasure to say that our house is shown to strangers as the prettiest building in the town.

I found your detail plans very exact. The specification was well drawn up, and with a few alterations to meet our market, I have erected a beautiful house. Yours respectfully,

A. E. DELOUEST.

PENSACOLA, FLA., Dec. 4th, 1889.

* * *

My house is now nearing completion and I am more and more pleased, as the work progresses, with the development of your plans They make a pretty house, very satisfactorily complete in every detail. I consider that your plans have saved me already more than their cost, besides helping me to realize a more convenient and complete house than I could otherwise have obtained. With thanks for the very prompt, obliging and businesslike manner with which you have conducted all the transactions and correspondence between us,

I am, yours very truly,
C. R. OGLESBY, M.D.

ROCKLEDGE, BREVARD CO., FLA., Dec. 9th, 1889.

* * *

I have recently built a house from plans and specifications furnished by the Co-operative Building Plan Association and am well pleased. Many of our friends and visitors have expressed admiration for the house. To the surprise of the mechanics here, the plans and specifications furnished all the details and information necessary for its complete erection. The Co-operative Building Plan Association treated me fairly and in a very satisfactory manner. Yours truly,

E. M. LREESE.

TAMPA, FLA, Dec. 9th, 1889.

* * *

I am pleased to say that I am very well satisfied with my dwelling built after your plans. It is well arranged and comfortable, and it is pronounced one of the most attractive houses in the city.

I am well satisfied with the business relations had with your firm. Yours respectfully,

THOS. E. JACKSON, Mayor.

GEORGIA.

N. H. HAND, Dealer in General Merchandise,
H. D. INGERSOLL, Manager.
DAHLONEGA, GA., Nov. 26th, 1889.

* * *

I built a house from your plans last year and I have just now finished a stable from your stable plans. I can truly say that they are the best and cheapest plans in the world. The house plans cost me $40, and I saved at least $200 by using them; they were so plain and simple that any workman could build from them. The stable plans cost $20, and I estimate I saved $100 on that work. Every one that has seen the house and stable is well pleased with them.

You were prompt and honest in all the dealings I had with you, and if I were to build a house that would cost $50,000 I should use your plans.

Very respectfully yours,
(Capt.) H. D. INGERSOLL, Postmaster,
Dahlonega, Ga.

CENTRAL RAILROAD & BANKING CO OF GEORGIA,
MACON, GA., Dec. 3d, 1889.

* * *

Replying to your favor of recent date I will say the plans you furnished for my residence were quite concise and complete. The build ng has, I believe, been generally admired. Several amusing attempts to copy the architecture have been made by our local builders.

I am confident that it is much cheaper and more satisfactory to secure full and complete plans and specifications, even for the most ordinary class of buildings, and my experience with you justifies a favorable opinion of your work.

Very truly yours,
C. E. MARVIN, Road Master.

THE JETER & BOARDMAN GAS & WATER ASSOCIATION
MACON, GA., Dec. 13th, 1889.

* * *

The building plan which I purchased of you last year was very complete in detail and design. Now that the building is erected it is much admired, and as it is situated in a sparsely settled country, Western North Carolina, it has attracted considerable attention. Although most of my material had to be hauled in wagons some twenty miles I succeeded in erecting the structure within a close margin of the estimated cost as given by you. Hoping to have future dealings with you, and as satisfactory as in the past, I remain, Yours respectfully,

A. E. BOARDMAN, Sec. and Treas.

Office of "MORNING NEWS,"
SAVANNAH, GA., Nov. 25th, 1889.

* * *

I think your work of furnishing architectural designs and building plans at reasonable prices has greatly improved the character of American houses, making them comfortable and picturesque, and at the same time at less cost than would have been entailed upon the builders had they built in the old, ugly style. You are also helping architects by educating people up to a proper appreciation of their work. I think you are entitled to a niche in the temple of fame as one who has contributed to the comfort and happiness of his fellow creatures. Yours truly,

(Col.) J. H. ESTILL.

ILLINOIS.

SUTTER BROS., Leaf Tobacco,
CHICAGO, Nov. 25th, 1889.

* * *

The plans I received from you for my summer residence at Lake Delavan, Wis., proved very satisfactory in every respect. I am more than pleased, and certainly recommend your plans to all my friends. Yours, etc.

LOUIS P. SUTTER.

MERCHANTS NATIONAL BANK,
CHICAGO, Dec. 6th, 1889.

* * *

I built a house from one of your plans and by your specifications about three and one-half years ago. It has been very satisfactory, and is generally liked by my friends.

I regard your dealings with myself as thoroughly honorable in every respect, and am very sure your charges are much cheaper than those of architects in general. I regard your work as inferior to none.

Respectfully,
WM. T. BARR.

BAEDER, ADAMSON & Co. Manufacturers of Glue Curled Hair and Flint Paper,
CHICAGO, Dec. 10th, 1889.

* * *

Our new house built from your design is pronounced by every one who has seen it, the model for comfort, light, saving of room, and everything else that goes to make up a cheerful home. I found your estimate correct. I cannot recommend your system too highly to anyone who wishes to build a residence. Yours very truly,

EDWARD P. MARTIN.

THE SAWYER-GOODMAN Co., Lumber,
CHICAGO, ILL.

* * *

I shall take pleasure in recommending your plans whenever opportunity occurs. The house which I built attracts attention, and I am asked frequently where I got the plans.

J. A. NOURSE.

CHICAGO, ILL

* * *

We believe your work to be of inestimable advantage to those contemplating building.

R. S. DICKIE.

DECATUR BREWING CO.,
DECATUR, ILL. Nov. 25th, 1889.

* * *

My wife and myself have had no occasion to regret having used your plans. Our house just suits us and we would not have a single alteration. It is much admired by our friends for its convenient internal arrangement. I can truly say that all your dealings with me have been entirely satisfactory.

Yours truly, FRANK SHLAUDEMAN,
Vice-President.

EUREKA COLLEGE,
EUREKA, ILL., Nov. 26th 1889.

* * *

The plan that I purchased from you two years ago has given entire satisfaction.

We have been living in the house nearly two years and like it better every day. It is as handsome and certainly as convenient a house as there is in our city. The cost of the house was about what you estimated. Respectfully,

CARL JOHANN, LL.D.,
President of Eureka College.

EAST ST. LOUIS, ILL., Dec. 3d, 1889.

* * *

I do not wish to withdraw anything I have said in regard to your grand work in giving the builder so much information for so little money. I have built two houses since my first trial, and must still say your work is good. Respectfully,

E. A. THOMAS.

Clerk's Office APPELLATE COURT OF ILLINOIS,
OTTAWA, ILL, Nov. 25th, 1889.

* * *

I am well pleased with the houses, four in number, which I built from your plans.

I have found the plans true to the pictures and in every way satisfactory.

People have said that the community owes me a vote of thanks for erecting so fine a looking row of houses. I tell them the vote of thanks must be for you. Yours respectfully,

(Hon.) J. R. COMBS, Clerk of Court.

PEORIA, ILL

* * *

You got up for me one of the nicest plans I ever saw I have recommended three or four to you for plans.

CHAS. B. HALL, Grain Merchant.

INDIANA.

Office of UDELL WOODENWARE WORKS,
NORTH INDIANAPOLIS, IND., Nov. 26th, 1889

* * *

My house, which I built some two years ago from plans bought from you, has given perfect satisfaction, and is much admired by all who see it. The cost of building was something within the figures as given by you. To those contemplating building I would heartily recommend your plans.

Yours respectfully,
WM. C. BENNEY.

KNIGHTSTOWN, Nov. 24th, 1889.

* * *

The plans for my house worked out perfectly. The building of it has been worth several thousand dollars to the county as it has given others new ideas of how to build.

We have no fault to find with the house and cannot find any alteration to make.

I have recommended your plans to every one who has paid my house a visit.

Very respectfully,
JAMES M. WOODS.

SWEETSERS BANK, MARION, IND.

* * *

Everybody wonders where we got so much room in our house. We have entertained sixty people on several occasions, seating them all, and had room for half as many more.

You have permission to refer to me in any manner you see proper. I have a handsome and very convenient dwelling, made from your plans, and I was well pleased with your promptness in furnishing plans, details, etc.

GEO. WEBSTER, JR. Cashior.

IOWA.

Office of C. M. DOXSEE, Abstracter, Real Estate and Loan Broker,
ALGONA, IOWA, Nov. 26th, 1889.

* * *

I take pleasure in assuring you that I am more than pleased with the house I built in the fall of 1888, both with the general appearance and convenient arrangement of rooms. For the cost it cannot be excelled in style and beauty in this town.

I can heartily recommend your designs to any one contemplating building a modern house.

Respectfully,
C. M. DOXSEE.

BOOR & BENJAMIN,
Lumber, Coal, Wood, Grain and Live Stock,
ASHTON, IOWA, Nov. 26th, 1889.

* * *

I found the plans that I bought of you two years ago very complete, and should try them again if I were to build another house.

Yours respectfully,
W. L. BENJAMIN.

DES MOINES, IOWA, Dec. 2d, 1889.

* * *

I have built several houses from your plans Have found them in every instance satisfactory both to me as an investment and to the buyers as homes. In all our business relations I have found you prompt and honorable, and can only add that I wish you every success.

Very cordially yours, JOHN D. KEELER.

DECORAH, IOWA.

* * *

I can most heartily recommend your Association as filling the bill complete, so far as I am concerned.

JAS. ALEXANDER LEONARD.

ELDORA, IOWA

* * *

I would feel satisfied if I had paid double the price for the plans.

A. ANDERSON.

H. F. WELLS, Lumber and Coal,
ESTHERVILLE, IOWA, Nov. 28th, 1889.

* * *

My house is about completed, and we are very much pleased with it. Every one that looks it over praises it very highly. It has a handsome exterior, and the interior is convenient and compact.

It was built very close to a house that cost much more than mine, but, almost invariably, people express themselves as liking my house the best, both for design and convenience. It certainly does not suffer by the contrast.

I will take pleasure in referring parties to you who intend building. Respectfully,

H F. WELLS.

POTTSVILLE, IOWA.

* * *

I can heartily recommend your plans and your Company for fair dealing.

G. W. HANKS.

KANSAS.

CAWKER CITY, KAN.

* * *

I am well satisfied with the arrangement and appearance of my house I would advise all who contemplate building to first secure working plans It is economy and a saving of much vexation.

A. W. SMITH.

COUNCIL GROVE, KAN. Dec. 3d, 1889.

* * *

In nothing am I more sincere than in recommending your plans. The complete arrangement of every room from cellar to attic is a source of daily enjoyment. My friends all say: 'You have a beautiful home." I ask no better until I go to the house with "many mansions."

With gratitude,
MRS. E. D. M'COLLOM.

SCHILLING & ATEN Bankers,
HIAWATHA, KAN., Nov. 29th, 1889.

* * *

Intending to build a dwelling, I examined a large number of plans, finally deciding on one of yours. I then procured from you the working plans, specifications and bill of quantities. During the summer of 1888 I built my house and we are entirely satisfied with it. For economy of room and comfort the inside arrangement is perfectly satisfactory. The outside appearance is artistic. It also affords me pleasure to say that from first to last I found your business treatment efficient, honest and satisfactory. Very truly yours

HENRY J. ATEN.

* * * All of the above letters were addressed either to the C.-O. B. P. Ass'n or to Mr. Shoppell, Pres. of the Ass'n. Repetitions of the addresses are omitted to save space.

TESTIMONY OF THOSE WHO HAVE BUILT (Continued)

ONE OR MORE OF SHOPPELL'S MODERN HOUSES WITH THE AID OF WORKING PLANS, SPECIFICATIONS, ETC. FURNISHED BY THE CO-OPERATIVE BUILDING PLAN ASSOCIATION, ARCHITECTS, 63 BROADWAY, NEW YORK.

Office of GEO. C. EATON & Co., Real Estate and Loan Brokers,
KANSAS CITY, KAN., Nov. 30th, 1889.

* * *

We have used your plans and were well pleased—found no trouble in working with them. We expect to order a set of plans selected from the $3000 class, but will not start the work until spring; then you may expect to hear from us.
Very truly yours,
GEO. C. EATON.

DRIGGS MANUFACTURING COMPANY,
KANSAS CITY, KAN., Nov. 26th, 1889.

* * *

The plans and specifications purchased of you for my dwelling house were in every respect satisfactory. The house is very attractive and I am well pleased with it. Yours truly,
T. C. DRIGGS, President.

KINGMAN ABSTRACT COMPANY,
KINGMAN, KAN., Nov. 30th, 1889.

* * *

The plans and specifications which you prepared for me for a dwelling and stable were in every respect satisfactory and the estimates as to cost correct; in fact, I managed to have the place put up for $52 less than your figures. This I found the greatest advantage of dealing with you. My previous experience with architects having been that their estimates and contractors' estimates usually vary about 30 per cent. and that a house the architect tells you will cost $2000 will really cost $3000 before you are through with it.

In conclusion I would say that if I ever have occasion to build again I should most assuredly avail myself of your experience in preference to any other architect for the sake of economy and final satisfaction. Your truly,
CHAS. ENGELMAN, Pres't.

LAWRENCE, KAN., Nov. 27th, 1889.

* * *

I built after plans and specifications furnished by you. My house attracts much attention and receives very favorable comment. It is a beautiful house outside and inside, very convenient, admirably adapted to our requirements, and cost less than estimated. Other houses, not as large, convenient or well finished, built the same season, cost several hundred dollars more. Your plans are worth much more than their cost to any one wishing to build. Very respectfully yours,
(Gen'l) H. S. HALL.

SOUTHWICK BROS., Publishers,
RILEY, KAN., Dec. 12th, 1889.

* * *

We are well pleased with the plans obtained from you and with the cottage built therefrom. As far as your business treatment of us is concerned will say that we have found your house prompt, obliging and reliable. Any houses we may build in the future will be built from plans furnished by you.
Very truly yours,
SOUTHWICK BROS.

Office of J. R. BROWN, Register of Deeds, Sedgwick County, Kansas.
WICHITA, KAN., Nov. 23th, 1889.

* * *

After having built four houses of your designs I wish to say that I am fully satisfied with them in every respect. As to your estimates I think they are full and complete. The carpenters found your plans to fit each other, *i.e.* they worked out, which was not the case with plans obtained from......... at a greater comparative expense.

In the future if I conclude to build more houses I shall certainly call upon you for my plans and estimates. Very truly,
H. W. STEWART.

KENTUCKY.

CLAY CITY, KY., Nov. 25th, 1889.

* * *

We have built several houses from plans furnished by your Company and are more than pleased with them. In fact, they are fully up, if not better, than your recommendation to us. The cottages here, erected from the plans, are very much admired. Yours truly,
KENTUCKY UNION LAND CO.,
Per M. A. CASBY, Sup't.

UNITED STATES POST OFFICE,
DANVILLE, KY., Dec 10th, 1889.

* * *

The plans and specifications you sent me for a Queen Anne cottage were all that I expected. I built from them, without any trouble, a very beautiful, cosy place, which has been greatly admired. Respectfully,
JAS. R. MARRS, P. M.

HOPKINSVILLE, KY., Nov. 26th, 1889.

* * *

In August, 1888, after looking over your book of designs, my wife and I concluded to order plans and specifications. We built our house accordingly, Messrs. Forbes & Bro., of this city being the contractors; and I have no hesitancy in saying that your plans are admirable, your specifications being intelligible to any one, and your estimates exceedingly accurate. While of course we feel a great pride in our own little home, I do not think that I am saying too much when I say that on account of its unique architectural design, its compactness, and its conveniences, it has attracted more favorable comment than any house ever built in this city. Several gentlemen from a distance as well as here have asked me for the plans, and one gentleman was so much taken with it that he built himself a similar one at Greenville, Ky.

I regard my investment with you as the best I ever made. To a young man, like myself, who gets married and begins to look around him for a house, I have the advice to give: look over Shoppell's designs before building.
Very truly yours,
JOHN FELAND, JR.

LOUISIANA.

LAKE CHARLES, LA., Nov. 28th, 1889.

* * *

I am much pleased with the plan and specifications of the two-story dwelling you made for me, and recommend you cheerfully to all who intend to build. The house makes a handsome appearance and is much admired. Very respectfully,
A. ALBERT.

MONROE, LA.

* * *

It affords me pleasure to unite with your other customers in commending you to the public for your artistic manner of getting up building plans.
D. C. MORGAN, Attorney.

MAINE.

BAR HARBOR, ME., Nov. 26th, 1889.

* * *

I built a house from your plans in Bar Harbor in the fall of 1887. I found the estimates and drawings of great assistance and worth several times their cost. Am still living in the house and am perfectly satisfied with it.

My business relations with you were very satisfactory. Yours truly,
W. P. FOSTER,
Attorney and Counsellor-at-Law.

E. & I. K. STETSON, Ship Builders and Repairers,
BANGOR, ME., Nov. 28th, 1889.

* * *

It is with pleasure that I write recommending your plans to any possible builder, for they are so complete that any carpenter can easily construct a house from them. Both of my head workmen say they never had more complete plans. The house has been greatly admired, and a gentleman from New Jersey sent his builder to look at it, being so well pleased with its style and details. The ladies are especially pleased on account of all the conveniences, and all say that they never saw a house with so much room for its size. Sincerely yours,
ISAIAH K. STETSON.

HALLOWELL, ME., Dec. 1st, 1889.

* * *

The plan I purchased of you gave satisfaction in every respect. There were thirty or forty houses built within three miles of mine the same season planned by other architects, and everybody says that mine is the best looking house in the whole lot; some of them cost twice as much as mine.
Yours respectfully,
G. H. SEAVEY.

YORK HARBOR, ME., Dec. 9th, 1889.

* * *

I was so well pleased with plans of the cottage you furnished me that I am now erecting another after the same plans. Yours truly,
J. H. VARRELL.

MARYLAND.

Office of JESSE KRIEG, Manufacturer of all kinds of Buggies, Carriages, Wagons, Carts, etc.
ADAMSTOWN, MD., Dec. 3d, 1889.

* * *

I can safely say that your plans and specifications are correct. From your plans any man who can handle tools can build. I am a carriage builder and superintended the work, and I am pleased to know that I have one of the most complete houses in Frederick County. People have come from a distance to look at it, and everybody says it is the finest house in the village. As for dealings you are square and prompt. Yours very truly,
JESSE KRIEG.

ACCOKEEK, MD., Nov. 1889.

* * *

I consider that dealing with you has saved me several hundred dollars. I built from your design and the cost was less than your estimate. Without your specifications and bill of materials I could not possibly have prevented the contractor from cheating me. Very truly yours,
L. R. C. TOWLES, M.D.

AMMENDALE, MD., Dec. 7th, 1889.

* * *

In reply to your inquiry I have to say that I am entirely satisfied with your plan and estimates furnished me, and with the cottage I built. It is thought very well of, and I consider your business treatment valuable, honest and straightforward. I would not build again without availing myself of your aid. Very truly yours,
DAN'L AMMEN.

REUTER & MALLORY, Railroad, Steamboat and Machinists' Supplies,
BALTIMORE, MD., Dec. 2d, 1889.

* * *

Your plans were of great use to me, and saved me $450 on my house. J. D. MALLORY.

BALTIMORE, MD., Dec. 7th, 1889.

* * *

The house built by me from plans obtained from you is very satisfactory and pleases all who see it. I did not succeed in placing contract at figure at which you said the house could be built, but at a figure $250 higher. The estimate as to cost placed upon the house, however, by those who see it, is always from $500 to $1000 higher than its actual cost. I am very well satisfied.
Very truly, C. G. WOODALL.

C. W. KENNARD & Co., Manufacturers of and Dealers in Fertilizers, Chemicals, etc.
CHESTERTOWN, MD., Dec. 2d, 1889.

* * *

It is with pleasure I repeat what I formerly wrote you, after building my house from your plans. I am just as proud of it as ever, and know that its beauty and low cost have brought you a number of customers, and many admirers. It has now been built three years. Very respectfully,
C. W. KENNARD.

B. G. & J. C. SMITH, Manufacturers of Flint and Feldspar,
CONOWINGO, CECIL CO. MD., Nov. 25th, 1889.

* * *

We found that the plans were all correct, the carpenter following them out in every detail as specified. Your estimate of cost was also as nearly correct as could be, the carpenter's contracting price being but $100 in excess of your estimate. After living in the house two years we are more than pleased with its convenience, economy of room, and neat and tasteful appearance. I can cheerfully and truthfully recommend your plans to any one desiring the full worth of their money.
Very truly, EDW. S. EDGE.

ELKTON, MD., Dec. 24th, 1889.

* * *

Last year desiring to build myself a house, I was induced to get my plans for the same from your company. I found them complete and satisfactory in every particular, so much so, that an ordinary contractor could build the house according to the plans and specifications without any difficulty. I am very much pleased with my house, which is much admired by all competent judges. The small amount I paid you was one of the best investments I have ever made. I found your estimates of quantities of materials and cost of house to be much more reliable than is generally the case with architects. My dealings with you have been so satisfactory that I shall recommend any one intending to build, even the smallest house, to use your plans.
Yours truly, JOHN S. WIRT.

MISSISSIPPI.

WILDER COTTON COMPANY, Cotton Buyers,
GRENADA, MISS., Nov. 30th, 1889.

* * *

I can cheerfully add my testimony to the value and usefulness of your efforts in placing before the public in the way you do, an opportunity to study the appearance and construction of neat and convenient buildings at a cost which enables anyone to have the services of good architects and working plans. I built a small house from your plans some three years ago and am so well pleased that I assure you I would not attempt the erection of any kind of a building without first supplying myself with a full set of plans and specifications.

Heretofore the cost of employing an architect has kept many from securing their services, but your method has changed that.

Hoping you may continue to have the success which your efforts deserve, I am,
Yours truly, C. L. WILDER.

FIRST NATIONAL BANK,
GREENVILLE, MISS., Dec. 19th, 1889.

* * *

I have built my residence by your plans and specifications, and take great pleasure in assuring you that I am highly gratified with the result. The house is elegant and homelike and gives me continued satisfaction.

I always tell my friends that you saved me three hundred to four hundred dollars, and saved me much annoyance in avoiding disputes with contractors. Yours truly,
THOMAS MOUNT, Cashier.

MASSACHUSETTS.

"MOUNTAIN VIEW,"
ADAMS, MASS., Nov. 25th, 1889.

* * *

In the spring of '87 I procured of you plans for a cottage, and in August of same year it was completed and occupied by my family.

As the name I gave my place indicates, we are located upon an elevation among the Berkshire Hills which commands a view of mountains north, south and west, "Old Graylock" being directly in front. In such a location it was fitting that we should have, if not an expensive house, a tasteful one, and this we were fortunate to secure by procuring from you the design and working plans.

Our builder said they were complete in every detail, and our friends compliment us on our good taste in the erection of so pretty a house. Were I to build again I should call on you for design and plans. Respectfully yours,
GEO. F. BARDEN.

JOS. W. CREASEY, Dealer in Drugs, Medicines, Books and Stationery,
AMESBURY, MASS., Nov. 25th, 1889.

* * *

I have examined a great many house designs from nearly every source but I find none of them where every conceivable space is so utilized as in your plans. Every one who has examined my new house admires the arrangement and expresses surprise at the amount of room. One gentleman from Washington, D.C., examined my plans and since then has purchased one of your designs.

The contractor took the job at your figures, although I added $500 to the finish. If I can help you any by referring any one to me I will show them in a few minutes how they can save money and be dealt with in an honest and straightforward manner. Yours truly,
J. W. CREASEY.

1045½ WASHINGTON STREET,
BOSTON, MASS., Jan. 21st, 1889

* * *

Having purchased of you plans for dwelling house some two years ago and being well pleased with the way I was treated and also with the plans I write asking if you have any book showing different styles of church edifices. I am a member of the standing committee of the Society that are going to erect a church of the description named.
I remain, yours respectfully,
JOHN M. BIRD.

BOSTON, MASS., Dec. 18th, 1889.

* * *

Last year I built a house from plans furnished by you and they gave entire satisfaction.

My carpenter informed me that everything fitted to a charm, and he did not have to make a single alteration.

I like my house and so do my neighbors. You did by me just what you agreed to.

If I build another house I shall apply to you for the plans. I remain, yours truly,
GEORGE P. DESHER.

ST. ANDREWS LAND CO. AND CHAMCOOK WATER CO.
BOSTON, MASS Nov. 27th, 1889.

* * *

From seeing your portfolios of building designs, we were last year led to get the plans of a frame summer villa, and a brick and granite business building, for erection at St. Andrews, N. B., a seaside resort we have under development. The result, after completion, satisfied us that the plans, specifications, and material lists, were made by people who knew their business. The cost of both buildings was approximately what you estimated. Our faith in your methods is such that we have recommended parties who contemplate locating their summer homes at St. Andrews, to patronize you.
Yours truly,
ST. ANDREWS LAND CO.,
Per ROBERT S. GARDINER, Vice-President.

BOSTON, MASS., Nov. 30th, 1889.

* * *

Am more than satisfied with the house built from plans and specifications furnished by you. Your business treatment was all that could be desired, and I have recommended several of my friends to examine your plans and specifications before deciding upon the style of building to be erected.
Very sincerely yours,
(Capt.) JOSEPH A. MOORE,
State Inspector of Factories and Public Buildings.

CHELSEA, MASS., Nov. 25th, 1889.

* * *

We are very much pleased with the house built from your plan. It is a model of comfort and convenience, and we enjoy every moment of time spent in it. Every one who visits us exclaims, "What a pretty house you have got!"

We had many opportunities for selling it while we were building, and had we wished to dispose of it could have easily done so to our entire satisfaction, but having located it upon a desirable spot we could not be induced to part with it.

Our business relations with your firm were fully as satisfactory as the house built from your plan. We heartily recommend you to all who wish to procure plans for building purposes.
Respectfully yours,
MR. AND MRS. S. B. KNOWLTON.

COTTAGE CITY, MASS., Dec. 2d, 1889

* * *

In answer to your letter will say that I built a two-story Queen Anne house at Mansfield, Mass. after plans and specifications from your Association, and that I found them very simple and easily understood; what was of the most value they were correct and minute in all details. Was very much pleased with the house, especially the way it was specified in regard to painting which brought the different parts out so well. Respectfully yours,
H. J. GREENE.

GREENFIELD, MASS., Dec. 2d, 1889.

* * *

We are now occupying the house, for the beauty and convenience of which we feel greatly indebted to you. In its architecture you have produced a beautiful combination of the Colonial with the Queen Anne, that delights the eye of all who see it, while for all other conditions of real home comfort it cannot be improved. We thank you for making it so easy to accomplish our desires in these respects, as well as for your honorable and prompt business methods. Wishing you may make many more hearts satisfied in the same way,
I remain sincerely,
W. S. CLARK.

Office of B. B. NOYES & Co.
Manufacturers of Hardware and Trimmings,
GREENFIELD, MASS., Nov. 27, 1889.

* * *

I beg to state that I am very well satisfied with the plans I had of you and with the house I built from them. The expressions of admiration I hear from those who visit my house are remarkable.
Very truly yours,
B. B. NOYES.

Office of "MANCHESTER CRICKET,"
MANCHESTER, MASS., Dec. 18th, 1889.

* * *

I have completed the building of a very fine residence, the plans for which were furnished by you. I wish to say that the plans and specifications were very accurate, and embodied many modern ideas. Mine was the first house built from your plans in this town, and I think it will prove a good advertisement for you. One other party here has built from your plans after seeing mine and others will probably follow. Yours truly,
I. M. MARSHALL, Editor.

PITTSFIELD, MASS., Nov. 20th, 1889.

* * *

The house I built from your plan is much admired, especially the interior, being so convenient, no waste room and everything in keeping. If I were to build again I should use your plans, specifications, etc. I heartily recommend them to all who contemplate building. Yours truly,
C. H. CHAPIN.

SOUTH EASTON, MASS., Dec. 9th, 1889.

* * *

My house has been called the best looking building in the vicinity. Your business treatment of me has been satisfactory. Yours truly,
HERBERT FRENCH.

TAUNTON, MASS., Nov. 23d, 1889.

* * *

I am glad to state that I have been more than pleased with the several plans and specifications which you have furnished me. I have found you prompt, efficient and businesslike in every instance. Your estimates of cost have always exceeded the estimates of local builders.
Faithfully yours, J. M. HAYWARD, M.D.

WEST ROXBURY, MASS., Dec. 7th, 1889.

* * *

Nearly three years ago I purchased a plan of you which was built from, and I am glad to say that the house is entirely satisfactory to the family who occupy it. They consider it as convenient as a house of its size can be. I am no novice in building and expect soon to build another house, probably from one of your plans. I should never hesitate to recommend highly your plans to any one contemplating building a house for themselves. One of your houses was built on a lot of land which I sold in West Roxbury and is entirely satisfactory. I consider your ideas regarding colors as especially good, and I do not recollect that I ever discovered any architectural error in your plans. I see no reason why your plans do not furnish all that an intending builder needs. Your methods of doing business, I consider as thoroughly satisfactory and liberal, and I am glad to say so.
Yours truly, CHAS. M. SEAVER.

* * * All of the above letters were addressed either to the C.-O. B. P. Ass'n or to Mr. Shoppell, Pres. of the Ass'n. Repetitions of the addresses are omitted to save space.

TESTIMONY OF THOSE WHO HAVE BUILT (Continued)

ONE OR MORE OF SHOPPELL'S MODERN HOUSES WITH THE AID OF WORKING PLANS, SPECIFICATIONS, ETC. FURNISHED BY THE CO-OPERATIVE BUILDING PLAN ASSOCIATION, ARCHITECTS, 63 BROADWAY, NEW YORK.

WOODS HOLL, MASS., Nov. 30th, 1889.

* * *

I think very highly of your house plans, and am very well pleased with the house you designed for me. It is a neat house and a cheap one and people say so, too. I have always found you fair and honest, and all your dealings with me have been square and above-board. The supervision of the work on the part of your representative was equally satisfactory. You deserve support.

Very truly yours,
C. MAC SWEENEY, Catholic Priest.

MICHIGAN.

Office of BEACH & ALGER,
Dealers in Hardware and Stoves,
ALPENA, MICH., Nov. 26th, 1889.

* * *

Would say the plans I received from you which I used in building my house in 1887 were all that I expected them to be—correct in every detail. The design was so different from anything that had been built here, up to that time, that everybody watched it closely until finished. Since, there have been several houses built after that style. I can recommend any one contemplating building to get your plans and specifications. Yours,
H. G. BEACH.

BAD AXE, MICH.

* * *

I consider the plans, specifications, etc., purchased from you to be one of the best investments I ever made. WM. M. LOGAN.

ISHPEMING NATIONAL BANK,
ISHPEMING, MICH., Dec. 3d, 1889.

* * *

In the year 1888 I procured from you a design and full detail drawings for a winter residence, to be built at Lake Maitland, Fla. The design and working plans were placed in the hands of a builder, who experienced no difficulty in completing the work to my full satisfaction. The house is a model of neatness and is admired by all. It gives me pleasure to testify to the worth of your designs and to the accuracy of your working plans.

C. H. HALL,
President of Bank and Mayor of Ishpeming.

THREE RIVERS, MICH., Nov. 26th, 1889.

* * *

The plans you furnished me proved very satisfactory indeed. With them I built myself what I regard one of the prettiest houses in the vicinity.

The house is admired by all who examine it. The treatment received by me from the Co-operative Building Plan Association was satisfactory in every particular. Yours very truly,
A. C. TITUS, Attorney-at-Law.

MINNESOTA.

MERCHANTS' NATIONAL BANK,
DULUTH, MINN.

* * *

I have just completed a house from the plans you sent me. They have given the best of satisfaction. The mechanic in charge tells me they are quite accurate and intelligible to work from.

H. A. SMITH, Cashier.

JOHNSON & BICKNELL,
Real Estate, Law, Loans and Insurance,
MORRIS, MINN., Nov. 26th, 1889.

* * *

The plans are worth all they cost. I should not think of building another house without plans and specifications by some competent architect. I do not know of any one better able to furnish what is wanted at a reasonable price than yourselves.

Yours truly,
J. A. JOHNSON.

MISSOURI.

BOWLING GREEN, MO.

* * *

I built from your designs, and have the "slickest" house in town. I think I saved three to four hundred dollars by having your plans and specifications.

L. M. EDWARDS.

CAPE GIRARDEAU, MO.

* * *

We are more than satisfied with your work. I do not hesitate to refer to you any parties in this vicinity who contemplate building.

J. A. MATTESON.

CHILLICOTHE, MO., Nov. 30th, 1889.

* * *

We are well satisfied, for the house is very convenient. There have been several who took the plans and tried to improve upon them, but according to my judgment they have not succeeded. If, at any future time I should build I shall send for your plans. Yours truly,
JOS. BILLINGHAM.

THE DOE RUN LEAD COMPANY,
DOE RUN, MO., Nov. 25th, 1889.

* * *

The plans you sent me proved very satisfactory. I built a very neat and stylish cottage, and found no trouble in working from the plans. We are well pleased with the house, and it has had the effect of introducing an entirely new style of architecture in this vicinity. Several new cottages have been built in similar style, taken from these plans.

Yours truly, F. P. GRAVES,
Sec. Doe Run Lead Co.

KANSAS CITY, MO., Nov. 27th, 1889.

* * *

I built a house in the southern part of this city after your plan, and am heartily glad I did so. My contractor's bid was $2200, just your estimate.

The plans were perfect and completely detailed. I am proud of my home, and it is greatly admired by our friends and all who happen to see it.

Was pleased with your treatment of me, and shall not hesitate to recommend your plans to any possible builder. Yours truly,
LEE K. MOONEY.

COBURN & EWING,
KANSAS CITY, MO., Nov. 26th, 1889.

* * *

Without knowing a great deal about your Association, I built a house something more than two years ago by one of your plans, and having lived in it for most of the time since I built it am qualified to express an opinion on the subject.

As to the accuracy of detail, will say that I had no complaint whatever from the contractor who built the house. Some of the bids I received upon the plans were less than the estimated amount given by your Association.

I do not know of any higher recommendation I can give than to say that were I to build again I should certainly build from one of your plans.

I am, very truly yours, J. M. COBURN.

A. LESCHEN & SONS' ROPE CO.
Manufacturers of Wire Rope,
ST LOUIS, Nov. 26th, 1889.

* * *

I was well pleased with your plans, and I like my house very much. Everybody praises it.

Respectfully yours, EDW. M. VOSSLER,
Vice-President.

MONTANA.

THE MONTANA COMPANY,
MARYSVILLE, MONT., Nov. 29th, 1889.

* * *

I am in a position to testify to the completeness of your designs and accuracy of details furnished by your Company, as I have recently constructed in the city of Helena, Montana, two houses from plans obtained from you. Your business treatment has been all that anyone could desire; in fact you have kindly placed additional information in my hands without compensation that I have found to be entirely reliable, and the information has saved me both time and expense.

The houses are very neat and the interior arrangement is all that could be desired. I do not now see that any modification of them would be an improvement. Respectfully,
G. H. ROBINSON.

NEBRASKA.

ALMA, NEB., Dec. 1st, 1889.

* * *

I have used plans I obtained from you, having just completed a residence therefrom, and beg to say I consider your business treatment efficient, honest and straightforward. The plans and detailed drawings I find were accurate, and the general plan of the building very good. The estimate of prices furnished by you was within the limit of your guaranty. Yours respectfully,
(Hon.) C. C. FLANSBURG.

ARAPAHOE, NEB.

* * *

I am very well satisfied. The house is a daisy—looks nicer than it did in the engraving.

GEO. J. BURGESS.

GRAND ISLAND, NEB., Dec. 21st, 1889.

* * *

I was well satisfied with the plans, and heartily recommend your plans to any one contemplating the erection of a nice, convenient residence.

Yours truly,
JOHN P. VOITLE.

KEARNEY, NEB., Nov. 26th, 1889.

* * *

In regard to the plans you furnished me they turned out just as represented and figured up all right from the brick work in the foundation to the shingles on the roof. I am well satisfied with my house, and it is well liked by all who see it.

Courteously yours,
J. D. HAWTHORNE, Jeweler.

LINCOLN, NEB., Dec. 4th, 1889

* * *

The plans prepared by your Association for my new residence have been very satisfactory in every particular. The details fit with an admirable nicety. They were very comprehensive and complete. With an intelligent carpenter as foreman I had no trouble whatever in producing from your plans one of the cosiest homes in our city. So far as I can judge it is much admired. It is very convenient, comfortable and satisfactory to us.

Very truly yours.
R. H. OAKLEY,
President Board Trade.

M. A. UPTON COMPANY,
General Real Estate Dealers—Investment Bankers,
OMAHA, NEB., Nov. 29th, 1889.

* * *

I am well pleased with my house which was built by your plans. I think I have about as complete a house as any in the neighborhood, and everyone who sees it admires it; the plans were accurate. I have no reason to find fault in any particular.

Yours truly,
M. A. UPTON.

PENDER, NEB.

* * *

I take great pleasure in saying that I used one of your plans, and I am more than satisfied with the result. I have a beautiful dwelling, costing not more than an ordinary building, but worth twice as much, either to sell or live in, on account of its convenient interior and its beautiful exterior.

W. E. PEEBLES, Banker.

VAIL & GREENE, Boots and Shoes,
YORK, NEB., Nov. 27th, 1889.

* * *

I wish to express my entire satisfaction with the plans bought of you, and can recommend them to any one wishing to build a house.

My builder informed me that they were the only set of plans he had ever worked by and found every detail correct. Very respectfully,
WARREN GREENE.

NEW HAMPSHIRE.

EXETER, N. H., Dec. 7th, 1889.

* * *

Have lived in my new house since July, '88, and am satisfied that I have the sunniest and most convenient house in town, though by no means the most expensive. It is cool in summer and easily warmed in winter. I think I got from you a much more satisfactory plan than I could have hoped to obtain from another architect for twice the price. Your estimate of the cost of building was very fair indeed. Your dealings with me were characterized by the utmost fairness and honesty, and if I were to build again I should certainly endeavor to get the plans from you. Yours truly,
ARTHUR O. FULLER, Counselor-at-Law.

NEW JERSEY.

BUTLER, N. J., Nov. 27th, 1889.

* * *

Your plans are accurate and reliable. The builder had no trouble in working from them and expressed himself as well pleased. Our house is much admired for its great utility of space—not a foot of waste room in it, and the exterior shows off beautifully for a house costing so moderately. The interior is as cosy, homelike and compact as a house could be arranged.

In our business correspondence and personal interviews we found you courteous, and we take pleasure in recommending your Association.

Yours truly,
WM. ROOME, Civil Engineer.

30 GILES ST., BRIDGETON, N. J., Dec. 2d, 1889.

* * *

I am quite willing you should keep my name on your list for reference, as I do at all times most heartily endorse your plans. My house is in every way satisfactory. Have lived in it now for three years; it is still quite the prettiest small house in the town. Very respectfully yours,
SARA H. BUCK.

Office of FLORENCE IRON WORKS,
FLORENCE, N. J., Nov. 28th, 1889.

* * *

It gives me pleasure to express my hearty commendation of your plans for building houses and your ways of doing business. We found the plans and estimates and quantities all correct. The house is admired by every one who sees it. We consider the cost of the plans, etc. as money well spent.

Resp'y, W. F. THACHER, Manager.

IRVINGTON, N. J., Dec. 15th, 1889.

* * *

It gives me pleasure to state that we have been living in the house built from your designs for nearly a year, and that we are even more pleased with it than we anticipated. Of some half a dozen new houses lately erected in the near vicinity it is, for its size and cost, much the prettiest in our estimation and in the estimation of a majority of our friends. Your estimate of its cost was $2300. It was built by contract for $2000. We consider all of your designs exceedingly neat, tasteful, and original. Your treatment of us was thoroughly businesslike and courteous. I am,
Yours truly, MRS. G. F. BIDEWELL.

JAMESBURG, N. J., Nov. 26th, 1889.

* * *

It affords me pleasure to say that your plans and specifications are all that you claim for them.

Your figures held out to within a few dollars of cost. My house gives me great satisfaction. The builder was so taken with the plans that he purchased them from me. Should I build another house I would not think of undertaking it without your plans, etc. to go by. I remain, yours resp'y,
J. H. ENRIGHT.

JERSEY CITY HEIGHTS, N. J., Dec. 9th, 1889.

* * *

I have employed a number of architects during the past four years with the following results:

1st. I consider your form of specifications superior to any I have ever seen.

2d. Your work was done promptly as promised.

3d. You were very courteous in making any changes in drawings or specifications that I requested.

4th. Your floor plans, elevations, details and specifications were all well done.

5th. Your charges were very much lower than any I have ever had for the same work.

In consideration of above facts I may say I am entirely satisfied with all the dealings I have had with your Company. Yours truly,
GEORGE GIFFORD.

LITTLE FALLS, N. J.

* * *

Have built ten cottages from your plans, and they are all very satisfactory.

R. BEATTIE,
Pres. Beattie Manufacturing Co.

MADISON, N. J., Dec. 10th, 1889.

* * *

I will say that I regard the Co-operative Building Plan Association superior to ordinary architects. The plans drawn for me were correct in all measurements. My carpenter tells me that the timbers cut by your measurements always come out right. My house built by your plans, both outside and inside, has been greatly admired, and has been pronounced the prettiest in our town; no waste room inside and right proportion outside. When I build again, if I ever do, the Co-operative Building Plan Association will be my architects.

Respectfully yours,
EDWARD MILLER.

RUTGERS COLLEGE, NEW BRUNSWICK, N. J.

* * *

After receiving the house plans, I made arrangements which necessitated a change of residence, and I sold the plans to the contractors, Messrs. A. & O. Burdick, who completed the house, and I understand were well pleased; as well they might be, for they were able to sell the house at a good profit, even before it was completed.

PROF. A. A. TITSWORTH.

PALMYRA, N. J.

* * *

While sitting in my cosy library looking at the storm, I am reminded of what appears to me a duty, viz., to make my acknowledgments to you for some of the comforts I am enjoying. Have had a five months' trial of the house, and am more and more pleased with the arrangement every day, and, what is unusual, have not discovered anything that could be changed for the better. The appearance and shape outside also is all that I could wish. It is the handsomest house in this place—is so acknowledged—and many have come quite a distance to see it.

L. B. BLYDENBURG.

PATERSON, N. J., Dec. 12th, 1889.

* * *

My house at Broadway and 23d Street, Paterson, N. J., built from your plans, is very satisfactory to us. I judge it is liked by others, as it has been copied largely. Yours truly,
E. W. PAIGE.

ANCIENT ORDER UNITED WORKMEN,
Rahway Lodge, No. 25.
RAHWAY, N. J., Nov. 27th, 1889.

* * *

I selected the design for my new house and received from you a full set of working plans, specifications, etc., within thirty-six hours; they were so complete and detailed that not a question was necessary to be asked.

Your estimates of cost I consider exact, as they will not vary $50 either way.

The plan and appearance of my house has been commented upon very freely, and is unanimously pronounced "truly a model house," especially as to the best use of every inch of room in the floor plans.

I have no hesitancy in recommending your Association to any of my friends, as I consider your business treatment efficient, honest, courteous, and straightforward. Yours truly,
W. E. HAVERSTICK,
Recorder of the Lodge.

RIVERTON, N. J, Dec. 2d, 1889.

* * *

The house I built from your plans has been pronounced by over sixty persons, who have inspected it, as perfect in every detail. It is considered the most comfortable and complete house in Riverton or Palmyra. All of which I lay to your plans and specifications and to a good builder. Had I to build again I would not think of doing so without your aid. The builder says he never saw a more complete set of plans in all his life. Yours,
MRS. F. W. HAND.

SADDLE RIVER, N. J., Nov. 29th, 1889.

* * *

I built my house from plans drawn by the Co-operative Building Plan Association. I am perfectly satisfied with it, and consider your business treatment honest and efficient in every particular. I hope your business will be generally understood and used by those anticipating building a house.

Yours respectfully,
H. MAXWELL.

A. W. BOSTWICK,
Shipping Agent Westmoreland Coal Company,
SOUTH AMBOY, N. J., Dec. 2d, 1889.

* * *

I shall be happy to give you my name as a reference as to completeness of the work you do. I have often spoken to friends who contemplated building of the full and complete plans, etc. you give. Yours truly,
A. W. BOSTWICK.

SPARTA, N. J., Nov. 28th, 1889.

* * *

I am well pleased with your building plans, and should I ever build again I would patronize none other but your Association. I consider your business treatment honest and straightforward in all respects. Yours very truly,
HENRY FOLK, Merchant Miller.

NEW YORK.

THE MERCANTILE AGENCY—R. G. DUN & CO.
ALBANY, N. Y., Nov. 29th, 1889.

* * *

The house I built from your plans is one which is very much admired, both as to its convenience inside and its architectural beauty outside. There is one other house on our avenue built from your designs. Yours respectfully,
ALFRED GREEN.

NO. 183 FRANKLIN AVE.
BROOKLYN, N. Y., Nov. 27th, 1889.

* * *

I cannot find words to express the satisfaction I have experienced in the plans of my house so ably drawn in your office. The simplest details were so perfectly drawn and explained that to make a mistake in its erection was an impossibility.

I shall do my utmost to encourage the patronage you so well deserve. With respect,
LILLIE WESTERN.

FIRE MARSHAL'S OFFICE,
BROOKLYN, N. Y. Nov. 25th, 1889.

* * *

The plans which you furnished me together with specifications I found to be correct in every particular. I built the cottage at Pleasant Lake, Sullivan County, New York. To those who contemplate building I cheerfully recommend them to your Company for good plans and honest treatment.

Yours very truly, BENJAMIN LEWIS.

J. S. BULL & CO.
Dealers in Fine Shingles,
CORTLAND, N. Y., Nov. 25th, 1889.

* * *

We recently built a house from plans furnished by you It is considered the best house in this section for the cost. It attracts a great deal of attention and is well liked. Respectfully,
J. S. BULL & CO.

CORONA, L. I., Nov. 28th, 1889.

* * *

It is with pleasure that I write you of the high esteem in which I hold your plans, and of your excellent methods of doing business. In the estimation of "people who know" my house is considered the prettiest and best house on Long Island.

To intending builders I would say that I know of nothing that will save them so much time and money as selecting and building a house from Shoppell's plans. When I need the services of an architect again, you will be the first to know it.

Wishing you the success you merit, I remain,
Very respectfully, P. O'NEILL.

* * * All of the above letters were addressed either to the C.-O. B. P. Ass'n or to Mr. Shoppell, Pres. of the Ass'n. Repetitions of the addresses are omitted to save space.

TESTIMONY OF THOSE WHO HAVE BUILT (Continued)

ONE OR MORE OF SHOPPELL'S MODERN HOUSES WITH THE AID OF WORKING PLANS, SPECIFICATIONS, ETC. FURNISHED BY THE CO-OPERATIVE BUILDING PLAN ASSOCIATION, ARCHITECTS, 63 BROADWAY, NEW YORK.

TACK-A-POUSHA HOUSE,
FAR ROCKAWAY, L.I., N.Y., Nov. 24th, 1889.

* * *

I consider myself very fortunate in selecting you to draw the plans for my hotel.

It is considered by all my patrons to be one of the best laid out buildings for hotel purposes on the coast. Its construction and architectural design speaks for itself.

I have sent many friends to you who desired plans for cottages, and they made their selection from your designs and built their houses satisfactorily.

Very respectfully yours,
DAVID ROCHE.

FONDA, N. Y., Dec. 2d, 1889.

* * *

I have built several houses after your plans. I like them very much, and the people generally seem well pleased with them.

Your estimate as to material required and cost was very correct, and your treatment of me efficient, honest and straightforward. I will soon require your services again. Respectfully yours
ISAAC A. ROSA,
Late Sheriff of Montgomery Co.

Office of WILLIAMS & HOLMES,
Owners of Patents of Oren Williams' Snow Plow,
GOUVERNEUR, N. Y., Dec. 16th, 1889.

* * *

The house you made drawings and plans for pleases me very much. My foreman says the drawings were very plain and correct and easy to work from. The house is admired and many traveling men call it the prettiest house in Northern New York. If I were to build again I would send to you for plans and drawings. I paid you $90, and my foreman says it was a good investment; he claims I saved $300, besides I got a better proportioned house than any of our contractors could get up. A. J. HOLMES.

HOOSAC, N. Y., Nov. 25th, 1889.

* * *

My house, built from one of your designs, is in every way satisfactory. It is considered the handsomest house in the village. The cost varied but little from your estimate. Yours very truly,
WARREN E. PUTNAM, M. D.

KIDDER'S FERRY, N. Y., Dec. 2d, 1889.

* * *

I like your plans, and am well satisfied with the house. I contracted with a builder here for less than your figures and had hardwood floors on the lower floor. The people here think it quite an addition to the summer cottages on the lake.

Very resp'y yours, FRED'K WYER.

No. 5 BEEKMAN ST, N. Y., Dec. 23d, 1889.

* * *

I have been living for over two years in a house built according to plans purchased from you. If I should build another house I would certainly patronize you. Your plans are free from the inaccuracies that make building a difficult undertaking. I have recommended you to others and shall continue to do so. I have met many others who have built from your plans and they all testify satisfaction. EDWARD P. THOMPSON,
Patent Att'y and M. E.

36 WASHINGTON SQUARE, N. Y., Nov. 27th, 1889.

* * *

The working plans of the cottage built after one of your designs, were both complete and satisfactory. JOS. P. NORRIS.

NEW YORK, Nov. 26th, 1889

* * *

I have used your plans for the erection of three houses at Rockaway Beach, L. I., and am greatly pleased to say that I have found them to be p rfect in every respect. Yours etc.,
MAURICE LEVY, 223 East Broadway.

J. M. NOYES & Co.
Bankers & Brokers, 53 Exchange Place,
NEW YORK, Nov. 26th, 1889

* * *

It affords me pleasure to say that the plans for my house and stable, which I purchased of you last September, have fully come up to my expectation. I am more than satisfied with the results. My stable is all completed and my house is now enclosed and ready for the inside work. I can say that there is not another house anywhere in the vicinity that pleases me as well as mine. I gladly recommend your plans to anyone contemplating building. Yours truly,
CHARLES P. NOYES.

EDWIN H. BROWN,
Counselor-at-Law and Solicitor of Patents,
32 Park Place,
NEW YORK, Nov. 25th, 1889.

* * *

I have used your plans and found them very satisfactory. I expect to call upon you for some in the near future. Yours truly,
EDWIN H. BROWN.

Office of WM H. LYON & Co., 483 & 485 Broadway,
NEW YORK, Nov. 29th, 1889.

* * *

The plans of my house have proved very satisfactory in style and arrangement. Since building I h ve been very much interested in architectural plans and have taken notice of other buildings in the country surrounding New York City, but so far have failed to find any I like better. I may say to those who have never built that, with your plans, specifications and list of building materials, they will be able to figure with contractors as thoroughly as if that were their business.

Yours respectfully,
WILLIS GAYLORD, JR.

ALEXANDER D. WILSON,
Dealer in Diamonds, Watches, Jewelry, Clocks and Optical Goods, 1307 Broadway,
NEW YORK, Dec. 4th, 1889.

* * *

It affords me pleasure to say that the plans I had from you, and from which I built a house at Big Indian, Ulster Co., N.Y., were very satisfactory. The contractor said that they were the best working plans he had seen. The "New York Times," in its Catskill news, reported the cottage being built by me as the prettiest building erected this year. In every way it has been a success.

Respectfully yours,
A. D. WILSON.

16 CATHARINE ST., NEW YORK, Nov. 30th, 1889.

* * *

The plans furnished by you for our house at Woodbourne, Sullivan Co., gave entire satisfaction. All who have seen the house think it the most commodious and best planned of any in that section of the country. Yours, etc.,
JAMES Y. WATKINS.

MISSION ROOMS, METHODIST EPISCOPAL CHURCH,
805 Broadway,
NEW YORK, Dec. 4th, 1889.

* * *

You are filling the land with beautiful homes. I meet them everywhere. These plans are all you claim for them. The cheapest houses may be beautifully and tastefully built.

Yours,
REV. C. C. McCABE.

Law Office of PHILO CHASE, 58 William Street,
NEW YORK, D c. 2d, 1889.

* * *

Your house plans I have used with very great satisfaction. They have many important advantages: among others, they enable one to build a house of handsome and modern design, to select the design best adapted to one's purse and taste, to know of just what material the house will be made, how the work will be done, what it will cost, and how it will look and be when it is done.

My builder remarked to me that your details worked perfectly, that everything came together just right, without any loss of time or waste of material.

You are doing a good work in improving the house architecture of the country.

Truly yours,
PHILO CHASE.

PORT JERVIS, N Y., Nov. 27th, 1889.

* * *

It affords me much pleasure to inform you of my complete and entire satisfaction with the dwelling which I have lately constructed (and am now occupying) from plans and specifications furnished by you.

I am more than pleased with its attractive appearance and its convenient interior arrangement.

Your estimate of the entire cost varied but a trifle from the exact amount expended. I cheerfully recommend an examination of your plans to all who may contemplate building. Your efficient manner of transacting business afforded great satisfaction and saved much trouble.

Yours respectfully,
S. M. SINGSEN.

MERRITT & COLVILL,
Dealers in Stoves, Tinware, etc.
MILLBROOK, DUTCHESS CO. N. Y., Nov. 26th, 1889.

* * *

I am very much pleased with the house I built after your plans. It is very much admired by the people of this village. I am often asked how I came to build such a house and where I got the plans.

I will be happy to answer any question in regard to the house at any time, as I am very much pleased with it. Yours respectfully,
WM. A. COLVILL.

MOUNT VERNON, N. Y., Dec. 2d, 1889.

* * *

I consider your business of furnishing good, desirable plans worthy of patronage by all desiring cheap, durable and beautiful homes, and I do not hesitate to recommend them to all who are contemplating building.

I am in the wood working business and I see and work from a number of your plans in the course of a year. Respectfully,
ALBERT S. BURTIS.

NEW ROCHELLE, N. Y., Nov. 29th, 1889.

* * *

The plans and specifications I received from you are very satisfactory. The builder had no trouble in working from them. The house is now completed, and I think is the best arranged country house I ever was in, and it is so acknowledged by those who have been through it.

Respectfully yours, JAMES GIBSON, JR.

NEW ROCHELLE, N. Y., Nov. 27th, 1889.

* * *

My most sanguine expectations are more than realized in the completion of my residence after the plans and specifications furnished by your Company. The exterior is very attractive, and excites general admiration, while the interior is unusually convenient and economically arranged, not an inch of space being wasted.

Being my first experience in building, your information and suggestions were of great service to me, and to your efficiency and correctness and the honesty of my carpenter I am indebted for a prettier and better house than many built in the village "under supervision" at from three to four times the expense for special architects.

I have taken great pleasure in recommend ng several of my friends to your careful consideration.

Truly yours, C. M. BOWLES.

PORT RICHMOND,
STATEN ISLAND, N. Y., Dec. 9th, 1889.

* * *

I built a house after one of your plans, was well satisfied with it. Every one who sees it remarks "what a pretty house." As to the working plans, specifications, etc., the carpenters and myself were perfectly well pleased. Your treatment of me regarding this house was all I could desire, perfectly straightforward, honest and gentlemanly. Should I build another house would come to you again for plans. Very truly,
MRS E. C. MUNDY.

PORT RICHMOND (S. I.), N. Y.

* * *

I built my house for the price named in your book. Everybody likes it.

WM. A. SLOAN.

ROCKVILLE CENTRE, N. Y., Dec. 11th, 1889.

* * *

I have no reason to regret having used your plans for building my house last year at this place.

Architecturally it is an ornament to the neighborhood, and it is well adapted to its surroundings. The economy of space in the arrangement of the rooms and halls is admirable. If I build again it will probably be from your plans and designs.

Yours very truly, HERMAN E. STREET.

MORRIS PARK, L. I. (Richmond Hill P. O.), N. Y.

* * *

I shall always consider myself fortunate in having purchased from you the plans for the house which I have lately built and now occupy The exterior is beautiful while the interior is just the pink of convenience. To those who may be interested I cannot commend your work too highly.

HENRY C. BEEBE.

Office of ECKERMANN & WILL,
Wax Bleachers and Refiners and Man'f's of Candles,
SYRACUSE, N. Y., Dec. 4th, 1889.

* * *

I built from a design furnished by you, and am pleased to say, to my entire satisfaction. I sh ll feel it my duty to recommend your Association whenever chance permits.

Very truly yours, ANTHONY WILL.

SCHENECTADY ELEVATOR, SCHENECTADY, N. Y.

* * *

I am much pleased; there are houses in my immediate neighborhood that have cost much more money, but they do not disparage mine in the least; it stands there and speaks for itself.

A. AUSTIN, Supt.

THE THOMSON PULP & PAPER CO.
THOMSON'S MILLS, N. Y., Dec. 14th, 1889.

* * *

I cheerfully state that the plans and specifications you furnished are comprehensive and perfectly satisfactory in every respect. The design elicits most favorable comment from those who are acqua nted with artistic houses both here and abroad.

Your business methods are as gratifying, and it will always be a pleasure to recommend your services to any one who contemplates build ng.

Very truly yours, JOHN A. DIX.

WALDEN, ORANGE CO., N. Y., Dec. 19th, 1889.

* * *

I have just finished two houses built from the plans furnished by you, and I am very much pleased with them. All who have examined the houses admire the plans. Every inch of space has been utilized. The working plans were all right; the builders found no difficulty in working from them.

Your business treatment of me has been entirely satisfactory. Yours truly, MARK WILD.

Office of WILLIAM A. SAXE, Lumber Dealer,
WATERFORD, N. Y., Nov. 25th, 1889.

* * *

Your style of buildings I much admire, and your plans are concise and practical. The detail drawings furnished for outside and inside trim are of value in giving style and finish to the house. The specifications for the painting add to the value of your plans. I was well satisfied with the plans furnished me. Respectfully,
WM. A. SAXE.

NORTH CAROLINA.

HANFORD N. LOCKWOOD,
Wholesale Jobber of Bristle Goods,
ASHEVILLE, N. C., Nov. 27th, 1889.

* * *

I have just completed a dwelling from your designs, and am well pleased in all particulars. The plans and details were accurate, and your estimate fully covered the cost.

My plans were destroyed by a local fire, but were speedily replaced by your kin ness. It affords me pleasure to indorse your Association.

Respectfully.
HANFORD N. LOCKWOOD.

CLERK'S OFFICE OF THE SUPERIOR COURT,
ASHBORO, N. C., Nov. 27th, 1889.

* * *

I am pleased to testify that my house, in every appointment and detail, is highly satisfactory, and evokes commendation from every observer. I am further pleased to endorse and commend your efficiency, honesty and fair dealing.

Very truly,
HON. G. S. BRADSHAW.

THE NATIONAL BANK OF GREENSBORO,
GREENSBORO, N. C., Dec. 3d, 1889.

* * *

It gives me pleasure to say that the plans and specifications furnished by you for our banking house proved in all respects satisfactory. The house is conveniently arranged, well adapted to our business, presents a very handsome appearance, and is generally admired by all who see it.

Very truly yours,
JULIUS A. GRAY, President.

NORTH DAKOTA.

GEORGE A. McCREA,
Dealer in Shelf and Heavy Hardware, Stoves
Tinware, Iron, Steel and Nails,
DRAYTON, NORTH DAK., Nov. 26th, 1889.

* * *

I have intended writing you before this to tell you that I was very well satisfied with the plans and specifications which I got of you for my house. I found that everything came out all right, and I did not find it necessary to make any changes, and when the building was completed it looked first-class.

I made an estimate from the bill of materials furnished, and knew just what it was going to cost before I commenced building, and when everything was finished I found your bill of materials was correct. I do considerable contract work myself, and have had occasion to use plans from several architects, but I am much better satisfied with yours than any of the others, and would cheerfully recommend your plans to any one.

Yours truly,
GEO. A. McCREA.

OHIO

U. S. MARINE HOSPITAL SERVICE--SURGEON'S OFFICE,
District of the Great Lakes,
ASHTABULA O., Dec. 24th, 1889.

* * *

We like our house, built after your plans. Your business with us was honest and straightforward.

Hastily,
H. W. DORMAN, M.D.

BELLAIRE WINDOW GLASS WORKS,
BELLAIRE O., Nov. 30th, 1889.

* * *

Two years since I purchased plans of you for a dwelling house in which I have been living for over a year. The plans suited me in every way. The house is a model for convenience. After living in it for the length of time referred to, we see no changes we would care to make in order to fit it better to our use.

Respectfully yours,
S. S. WOODBRIDGE, Secretary.

CIRCLEVILLE, O., Dec. 18th, 1889.

* * *

The plans were perfectly satisfactory and the cottage has been much admired. What is better I have no trouble to get a tenant for same at a paying figure. Yours truly,
A. C. WILKES.

CINCINNATI, OHIO.

* * *

The plans were satisfactory in all respects. Your estimate of cost was very close. I have the finest, prettiest and best built house in South Norwood and many parties say within many miles of it, and that is saying a great deal. It is acknowledged to be the finest and best of the three or four hundred houses that are in the neighborhood.

GEO. H. BONTE.

CANTON, OHIO.

* * *

You are at liberty to use my name. I built two houses from your plans, and they give excellent satisfaction.

NORMAN C. RAFF.

FINDLAY, OHIO.

* * *

I shall always deem it a pleasure to impart information to all who make inquiries conc rning your Association, with whom I have had the pleasure of doing business, and the prompt manner in which you responded to my recent order.

WM. M. LOWTHER.

DR. BEELER & BRO., Pharmacists,
HAMILTON, O., Nov. 25th, 1889.

* * *

We have completed the house for which you furnished the plans, etc. and are well pleased with the result. The contract was let for somewhat less than your estimate. We are well satisfied with your plans and pleased with your methods and manner of doing business. Yours truly.
BEELER & BRO.

KENNEDY, O., Dec. 3d, 1889.

* * *

In reference to the plans purchased from you, will say that I liked them very well, had no trouble at all with them, they were easily understood by all the contractors who bid on the work. The estimate you made as to the cost of building was only a few dollars over the lowest bidder. Should I have occasion to use any more plans you will certainly hear from me. Meanwhile I remain,

Very truly yours,
N. T. HORTON.

LIMA, O., Nov. 25th, 1889.

* * *

Am well pleased in every particular. House admired by everyone. No deception in anything. Estimate close.

If I were building a hundred houses would not look further. WM. OWENS.

OREGON.

UNITED STATES ENGINEER'S OFFICE,
PORTLAND, ORE., Dec. 6th, 1889.

* * *

My house was built exactly to the specifications, and I can confidently say that there is not a house of its size in Portland that is more comfortable, substantially built, or artistic in appearance, both inside and out. Every one who has seen the house has expressed admiration of the whole building. The house was built for less than your estimate. I am so well satisfied with your method of doing business and with the excellence of your designs, that I hope in the near future to call on you for two other sets of plans for other houses I propose erecting. You are at liberty to refer to me if I can serve you. Yours truly,
WM. C. STEVENS, Chief Clerk.

PENNSYLVANIA.

Office of PUSEY & KERR,
Wall Paper, Carpets and Curtains,
ALLEGHENY, PA., Nov 27th, 1889.

* * *

Having used one of your plans for a residence, I hereby testify to your prompt and honest method of dealing. I am much pleased with the house that I built, as are all who see it. Everything worked out according to the plans, there being no miscalculations whatever.

Yours very truly,
J H. PERMAR.

KEASBEY & MATTISON,
Manufacturers of Chemical Products,
AMBLER, PA., Nov. 27th, 1889.

* * *

I have used your plans and know of others who have used them, and must congratulate you upon your enterprise in placing such complete details of economic house building before the public. I expect to build several additional houses soon, and shall of course want more of your various detailed plans, as those which I have had thus far have proven very satisfactory.

Respectfully,
RICHARD V. MATTISON, M.D.,
Pres. Ambler Real Estate and Improvement Co.

* * * All of the above letters were addressed either to the C.-O. B. P. Ass'n or to Mr. Shoppell, Pres. of the Ass'n. Repetitions of the addresses are omitted to save space.

TESTIMONY OF THOSE WHO HAVE BUILT (Continued)

ONE OR MORE OF SHOPPELL'S MODERN HOUSES WITH THE AID OF WORKING PLANS, SPECIFICATIONS, ETC. FURNISHED BY THE CO-OPERATIVE BUILDING PLAN ASSOCIATION, 63 BROADWAY, NEW YORK.

Law and Land Office of F. W. KNOX & SON, COUDERSPORT, PA., Dec. 1st, 1889.

* * *

Am pleased to say that I built here a very handsome residence from specifications and detail drawings furnished from your office. It is *the admired* house of this village. I heard no complaint from the carpenters. Certainly you furnished the needed information much *cheaper* than any architect that I have had any business with. My son completed a handsome house selected from your plans. All my dealings with you have been honorable, prompt and entirely satisfactory.

F. W. KNOX, President of the C. & P. A. Railroad Co.

CLEARFIELD, PA., Nov. 25th, 1889.

* * *

The house built by me, and for which you furnished plans, specifications, details and blank contracts, is a model of neatness and comfort. It was so planned as to utilize every inch of space, and there is an abundance of light in every part. In external appearance the house is unlike any building I have seen. All who see it are much pleased. The plans and details, etc., went together like clockwork. If I were building a dozen houses I certainly would endeavor to secure my plans from you. I have no complaints to make.

Very truly, FRANK G. HARRIS, Attorney-at-Law.

JOHNSTON, BUCK & CO., Bankers, EBENSBURG, PA., Dec. 14th, 1889.

* * *

I take very great pleasure in assuring you that I am more than pleased with my house, and further have to assure you that your treatment has, in every way, been entirely satisfactory and business like. The house I built, while not the most expensive, is considered by far the handsomest in our town, and excites the admiration and praise of our people, all of which I attribute to your excellent skill. You are at perfect liberty to refer to me as often as you see proper.

Yours very truly, A. W. BUCK.

ELMHURST, PA., Nov. 27th, 1889.

* * *

I have used your plans with entire satisfaction as to estimates, measurements, etc. The appearance of the buildings after completion do not disappoint me, and elicit favorable comments from others. The economy of your plans with your painstaking and satisfactory business methods should commend your work to every one. I expect to use other of your plans in the up-building of Elmhurst.

Very respectfully yours, (Col.) U. G. SCHOONMAKER.

GWYNEDD, PA., Nov. 25th, 1889.

* * *

In answer to your letter of inquiry I have to say: *Firstly:* I have found the plans and specifications furnished by you for my house at Gwynedd, Pa., complete in every respect.

Secondly: The estimate of cost given me for this locality proved to be reasonably accurate.

Thirdly: The house—built on your plans and at a price closely approximating to your estimate—is, in my opinion, as substantial, convenient, and tasteful as could be gotten here within the limits of its cost.

Fourthly: It gives me pleasure to say that your treatment of me has been thoroughly courteous, efficient and straightforward.

I am, very truly yours, W. L. CATHCART.

Law Offices of GOBIN & GRUMBINE, LEBANON, PA., Dec. 24th, 1889.

* * *

The plans and specifications were full, correct, reliable, complete, and in every way satisfactory. The house is equally satisfactory. My business takes me to many towns and cities in this and neighboring States, and I haven't seen the house of equal cost and similar character for which I would exchange mine. *It perfectly suits my family*, and that is the main point. It is greatly admired also by others. In this case it would not be fair to say "as pretty as a picture." It is handsomer than the picture.

It gives me pleasure to testify to the fair dealing, the honest and straightforward business treatment and the courteous and accommodating disposition of "The Co-operative Building Plan Association, Architects." Very respectfully,

LEE L. GRUMBINE.

LOWER MERION, MONTGOMERY CO., PA. Nov. 27th, 1889.

* * *

Your plans were very satisfactory, and were easily followed by the workmen in the construction of what is unmistakably the finest house in our place (Merion Square). It affords me pleasure to testify to your fair dealing. Yours,

H. A. ARNOLD, M.D.

PENN. BOLT & NUT CO., LEBANON, PA.

* * *

Your plans, details, etc., were very full and concise—in fact, entirely satisfactory

H. V. L. MEIGS, Supt.

NANTICOKE, PA.

* * *

Your work for me has given the best of satisfaction, and I can cheerfully recommend the same to those who contemplate building.

J. C. BRADER.

MARKELSVILLE, PERRY CO., PA., Nov. 25th, 1889.

* * *

I have now been living in my house (the designs and specifications for which I obtained from you) for over two years, and I am more than pleased with it in every particular. It is, without exception, the best planned and most convenient house in this part of the country. Should I ever conclude to build again, I shall certainly apply to you.

Very respectfully, W. MIFFLIN SMITH.

CHELTENHAM ACADEMY, OGONTZ, PA., Nov. 26th, 1889.

* * *

I write to say that the cottage plan which you furnished me proved entirely satisfactory, and to thank you for your readiness in furnishing me with all information I desired in reference to the plans and specifications. The plans were beautifully drawn, and the cottage is handsomer even than we had expected it would be. We are much pleased with it, and we are told it is considered one of the handsomest of the smaller cottages on Lake Keuka.

The specifications were done with great carefulness and neatness, and were correct even to the smallest detail. Sincerely yours,

SAM'L M. OTTO, Instructor in Greek.

PITTSBURGH, Dec. 28th, 1889.

* * *

I write to say that I have been using your Modern House Designs for some time, and have built a number of houses according to your plans and specifications. I like your plans very much, and the houses and cottages built according to your designs have been much admired. I have found your estimates accurate and your plans reliable.

Yours truly, GEORGE C. BURGWIN, Attorney-at-Law.

JOS. M. SHOEMAKER, Banker and Broker, PHILADELPHIA, Nov. 26th, 1889.

* * *

The house I had built last year at Prout's Neck, Me., from your plans is thoroughly satisfactory, and is certainly very neat, attractive and comfortable. The plans, specifications, etc., were complete, and any carpenter should be able to build from them. I furnish this testimonial cheerfully, and you can use it as you deem proper. Very truly yours,

JOS. M. SHOEMAKER.

ROCKHILL FURNACE, PA., Nov. 25th, 1889.

* * *

We are satisfied in every particular with your plans and your business treatment of us. Our School House is about completed. Cost about $8000.

It is generally conceded that we have the finest looking building in our county, although some of them cost three or four times as much.

If this be any good to you you can use it in any way you wish or refer to us at any time. We will certainly say a good word for the Co-operative Building Plan Association. Yours truly,

T. J. C. RIPPLE, Sec'y School Board.

SUNBURY, PA., Nov. 28th, 1889.

* * *

I take great pleasure in stating that the house I erected at Wildwood Beach in accordance with plans furnished by you has proved very satisfactory. I found the plans all that any builder needed to complete the building in accordance with design selected from your books. I can heartily recommend any one who intends building to you for designs and plans.

Very respectfully yours, S. P. WOLVERTON, Attorney-at-Law.

HUNTINGDON FURNACE, GEO. D. BLAIR, Manager. SPRUCE CREEK, PA., Nov. 26th, 1889.

* * *

I have built several houses from your plans and specifications, and have found them very reliable and satisfactory.

Yours truly, GEO. D. BLAIR.

UPLAND, DEL. CO., PA.

* * *

Your architectural work for me has been very satisfactory not only to me, but to others who saw my house in the course of erection. One of the largest property owners said to me: "I have been through your house from cellar to attic and think it very complete; it must have cost a deal of thought to arrange everything so well. It is an ornament to our town."

BENJAMIN CROWTHER.

WARREN, PA., Nov. 25th, 1889.

* * *

The plans of the house I built proved very satisfactory, and worked out in detail very correctly. The house is a very handsome house, is entirely satisfactory, and is generally admired. Your business treatment of me in our correspondence was efficient, honest and straightforward.

Yours truly, FRANCIS HENRY.

Established 1850.

THE DINGEE & CONRAD CO., Growers and Importers WEST GROVE, PA., Nov. 26th 1889.

* * *

The house is very much admired by all who see it and is very satisfactory to me. I am thankful that I employed you. After we got the working plans we did not have occasion to ask you a single question, every part went together like a charm. My builder, a man of large experience, said he never had anything to do with plans that worked out so nicely. Your charges were just what you agreed to, no extras. I was more than pleased both with your work and your prompt and very generous treatment. I advise all my friends who contemplate building before they engage an architect to give you a call.

Yours truly, CHAS. DINGEE.

Office of DANIEL H. LEVAN, Millwright, Contractor and Builder, WHITE HAVEN, PA., Nov. 27th, 1889.

* * *

I am more than pleased with the house I built from plans furnished by you. The cost as put down by you is correct unless great changes take place. I am glad to recommend your plans to any one wishing to build for themselves a house.

If I were to build fifty houses I would not do a thing without first consulting the C. B. P. A.

I remain, yours truly D. H. LEVAN.

RHODE ISLAND.

WOONSOCKET, R. I., Nov. 29th, 1889.

* * *

The plans and specifications were duly received. I found a wide difference in the estimates made by the different contractors, but I was able to let the contract at about your estimate. The house is admired by all who see it.

Very truly yours, OSCAR J. MORSE.

SOUTH CAROLINA.

Office of FOSTER, WILKINS & CO., General Merchants, UNION, S. C., Nov. 26th, 1889.

* * *

The house you planned for me last summer was completed about one month ago, and it fills my want exactly. It is considered one of the most modern and convenient dwellings in the town. The actual cost exceeded your estimate only $4.18. Your framing bill was very close, and there was comparatively little waste in cutting the timbers. The plastering was thirty yards less than you estimated. I can recommend your work to all who desire comfortable and convenient residences at reasonable cost.

Yours truly, B. F. ARTHUR.

TENNESSEE.

MCMINNVILLE, TENN.

* * *

I am delighted with my house. It has received many flattering praises.

L. F. JEANMAIRE.

UNION CITY, TENN.

* * *

I was well pleased with the plans, and consider their cost as money well spent. I have the handsomest and best business house in this city. I take pleasure in referring to your Association all parties here that I find are going to build.

JAMES F. LUKENS.

TEXAS.

BRYAN, TEXAS, Nov. 28th, 1889.

* * *

Your plans and prices are the things for this country. My house is one of the most convenient of any of the modern houses of this city. All who see it are pleased. Yours truly,

CLIFF A. ADAMS. Mayor of Bryan, Texas.

DALLAS, TEXAS, Nov. 29th, 1889.

* * *

I take pleasure in saying that by using plans and specifications furnished by you I made no mistake. My house is liked by all whom I have heard express themselves in regard to it, and we like it splendidly. It has the appearance of being a much more expensive house than it really is. So far as your business treatment is concerned I have no fault to find, as everything came up exactly as represented. You may use my name in anyway that you see proper toward extending your business, for I feel that were I to build again you would be consulted before any definite plans were decided upon.

Yours most truly, WM. M. ROBINSON.

THE COMMERCIAL NATIONAL BANK, HOUSTON, TEXAS, Nov. 27th, 1889.

* * *

I owe you an apology for not acknowledging my obligation to you sooner. The fact is, I am so well pleased with the result of my venture in using your plans, etc., that I actually forgot to write you to that effect. Had anything proved unsatisfactory you may rest assured you would have heard from me immediately. I unhesitatingly endorse your Association and recommend its methods. I consider that your form f contract and specifications saved me in "extras" at least $200, and I enlarged the plan very considerably, and still came within your estimate. I think of building another and larger house and you may confidently expect to hear from me when that time arrives.

Very truly yours, (Capt.) G. L. PRICE.

VERMONT.

SMITH & HUNT, Manufacturers of Children's Carriages, BRATTLEBORO, VT., Nov. 29th, 1889.

* * *

Our house, built from one of your plans, is very satisfactory, and was put up for some less than your estimated cost. All dealings with you were perfectly satisfactory, and I should recommend your plans to any one contemplating building.

Very respectfully yours, FRANK L. HUNT.

BRATTLEBORO, VT.

* * *

The plans you supplied for my house have been more than satisfactory in every respect. I have been the means of your getting three orders in this town, and shall be glad to have you refer to me at any time. ROSS WHITE.

WATERBURY, VT., Dec. 11th, 1889.

* * *

I can heartily recommend you as to promptness and business principles, and think your plan saved me more than twice the cost of it.

Yours, W. F. MINARD, M.D.

VIRGINIA.

MCMENAMIN & CO., Hermetically Sealed Goods, HAMPTON, VA., Nov. 28th, 1889.

* * *

It gives me pleasure to express the satisfaction I feel at having a cottage built after your plans. I have not only a pleasing and convenient structure, but a solid one as well. It was built entirely within your estimate. I am sure it could not have been built as cheaply without your plans. At its completion we wondered at the small amount of wastage. Its dimensions were calculated to fit the standard sizes of lumber of all kinds so exactly that four wheel-barrows would have held all the pieces that were left over.

This is a point that is rarely taken into consideration by intending builders, who think they can get along without an architect.

Very truly yours JAMES McMENAMIN.

CARSON & SON, Makers of Lime, Brick, etc. RIVERTON, VA.

* * *

We regard your Association as doing a work of great value to the public, and you can use our name as a reference. We have used one of your plans. It is the most noticed house in the village, and it is as good as it is attractive.

CARSON & SON.

WEST VIRGINIA.

SHATTUCK & JACKSON, Wholesale Grocers and Jobbers of Teas and Tobaccos, PARKERSBURG, W. VA., Nov. 26th, 1889.

* * *

I like your plans for building houses. As you know, I have built three, all expensive ones. They are among the nicest of our city. I have had no trouble with the plans, and the builders say they are the most correct, and therefore the easiest to work after. Were I going to build more, would have you make plans for all.

Respectfully, J. M. JACKSON, JR.

WASHINGTON.

Office of HOQUIAM MILLS, HOQUIAM, WASH., Dec. 4th, 1889.

* * *

Have built a cottage after your design which has given satisfaction in every particular and detail.

It was the first Queen Anne on Gray's Harbor, and has received many compliments on its appearance by visitors and residents. Yours truly,

(HON.) JOHN F. SOULE.

MONTESANO, WASH., Nov. 24th, 1889.

* * *

The plan for cottage received last summer gave full satisfaction and is a little beauty.

Respectfully, GEO. W. BOYINGTON.

SPOKANE FALLS, WASH., Nov. 26th, 1889.

* * *

I take great pleasure in saying that I have built after your plans and specifications, and have found them reliable and accurate. You do all you promise, and at a saving of four-fifths of the cost over local architects' prices.

My residence, built last year, after the plans, drawings and specifications furnished by you is noted as one of the most complete buildings of its kind in the city. It has been examined by parties contemplating building. Last, but not least by any means, I erected it *within* your estimate of cost.

Cheerfully recommending you to those contemplating building, I am, yours truly,

(JUDGE) W. A. LEWIS.

WISCONSIN.

JACKSON COUNTY BANK, BLACK RIVER FALLS, WIS., Nov. 26th, 1889.

* * *

The plans and specifications I had of you for which I paid twenty dollars, are more satisfactory than anything I could have procured here for three times that amount. Yours truly,

W. R. O'HEARN, Cashier.

FIRST NATIONAL BANK, HUDSON, WIS., Nov. 26th, 1889.

* * *

I can with pleasure recommend to those contemplating building, your plans and specifications. I am much pleased with the house in Spokane Falls built after your plans. It has the commendation of all who see it and gives entire satisfaction.

Very truly yours, A. E. JEFFERSON, Cashier.

PLATTEVILLE, WIS., Dec. 8th, 1889.

* * *

We were perfectly satisfied in every respect, with regard to our business with you, and take pleasure in recommending you to others, who contemplate building.

As to how we like our house, I will say without hesitation, that I am really proud of it. It has been an object of admiration for those living in our city. Several have remarked to me that it is the most modern and handsomest house around Platteville. Since its erection others are building similar to it. I could write much more of our appreciation of the house and the flattering remarks of strangers regarding its general appearance, but will stop for fear you will think I have written many unnecessary remarks already. Very respectfully,

(MISS) JULIA IVEY.

SHAWANO, WIS.

* * *

The plans we received from you we used for a parsonage, and I must, in justice, say that they gave entire satisfaction in every particular.

J. A. ALLEN.

WYOMING TERRITORY.

BUFFALO, WYO. T., Nov. 29th, 1889.

* * *

We are highly pleased with the house we built in 1888, and would recommend all who intend to build to deal with you. Think they would save ten times the cost of plans and specifications.

Yours truly, R. S. HOPKINS.

CANADA.

BANK OF BRITISH NORTH AMERICA, MONTREAL, Nov. 25th, 1889.

* * *

I have much pleasure in expressing my satisfaction with the house just erected, plans furnished by you. The details are especially pleasing, and my builder informs me that in all his experience he has met with no plans so complete and true in every sense. I am, yours truly,

J. PENFOLD.

NEEPAWA, MANITOBA, CAN.

* * *

You can use our name. We found everything exactly as required in the plans sent us—drawings and specifications all perfect.

F. & J. SKELDING.

PELLETIER FILS & CIE, RIVIERE DU LOUP, Nov. 27th, 1889.

* * *

I built two cottages from plans furnished by The Co-operative Building Plan Association. Both cottages are amongst the nicest ever built in Riviere du Loup and Cacouna. People appreciate them very much, and I am greatly obliged to you.

Yours faithfully, NARC. GEO. PELLETIER, Mayor Riviere du Loup.

* * * All of the above letters were addressed either to the C.-O. B. P. Ass'n or to Mr. Shoppell, Pres. of the Ass'n. Repetitions of the addresses are omitted to save space.

THE CO-OPERATIVE BUILDING PLAN ASSOCIATION, ARCHITECTS, 63 BROADWAY, NEW YORK.

*Shoppell's Modern Houses—*Designs Patented.*   *Cottage, Design No. 629*

PERSPECTIVE.

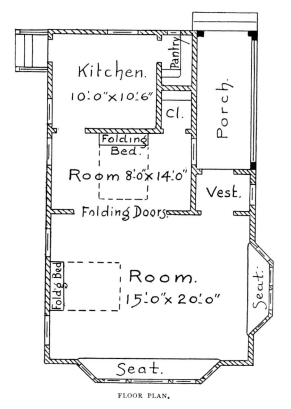

FLOOR PLAN.

DESCRIPTION.

For explanation of all symbols (* † etc.) see page 42.

SIZE OF STRUCTURE : Width, 23 ft.; depth, 36 ft. 6 in.

MATERIALS FOR EXTERIOR : Foundations, posts or piers; side walls and roof, shingles.

HEIGHT OF STORY : 10 ft.

INTERIOR FINISH : Smoothed and chamfered studding and ceiling joists to be left exposed. Walls between studding and ceiling joists to be papered. Flooring and all trim of windows and doors to be of white pine or other soft wood. All doors and sashes of manufactured stock sizes. The windows that command fine views should be glazed with plate glass; all other windows with double thick glass. All interior wood work to be varnished, showing natural colors.

EXTERIOR COLORS : All side shingling, cream. All trim, mouldings and veranda rails, dark red. Veranda posts and balusters, cream. Outside blinds and doors, roof and chimneys, dark red. Underside of roof overhang, cream. Porch floor and ceiling oiled, showing natural color of wood.

ACCOMMODATIONS : All of the rooms are shown by the floor plan. The attic is floored and is reached by a step-ladder. No cellar is provided, as this cottage, built as described, is intended for summer occupancy only. To fit it for winter use a cellar under the whole house should be built, at an additional cost of about $200; and the interior walls of the cottage should be plastered, at an additional cost of $75.

SPECIAL FEATURES : The large bays may be said to give character to the exterior of this design as well as to provide attractive features within. With cushions provided for the bay-window seats the sitting room is indeed a comfortable place. The overhanging roof gives an appearance of large size. The chimneys (one over the kitchen and one over the sitting room) are simple and inexpensive, but substantial, built of terra-cotta resting on the ceiling joists.

COST : In all localities where the prices for labor and materials are about the same as those of ‡ New York City, $500.

Price for working plans, specifications and * license to build,   - $15.00

Price for †† bill of materials,   -   -   -   -   -   5.00

Address, THE CO-OPERATIVE BUILDING PLAN ASSOCIATION, Architects, 63 Broadway, New York.

49

THE CO-OPERATIVE BUILDING PLAN ASSOCIATION, ARCHITECTS, 63 BROADWAY, NEW YORK.

*Shoppell's Modern Houses—*Designs Patented.* *Cottage, Design No. 630*

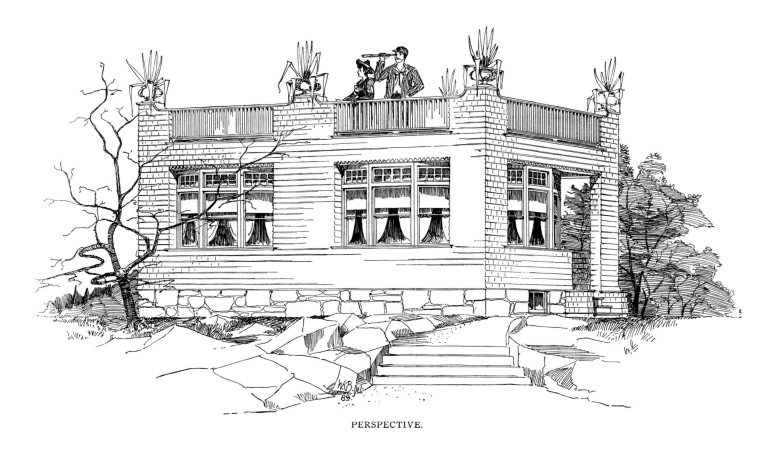

PERSPECTIVE.

DESCRIPTION.

For explanation of all symbols (* † etc.) see page 42.

GENERAL DIMENSIONS: Width, 21 ft.; depth, 31 ft. 6 in. Height of story, 9 ft.

EXTERIOR MATERIALS: Foundations, stone; first story, shingles; roof, tin, with an independent flooring laid over the tin.

INTERIOR FINISH: No plaster. All studding and joists are dressed and varnished to show, the spaces between being covered by heavy paper secured to the sheathing. Trim, flooring and stairs to roof, white pine varnished and left natural color.

COLORS: Stone work neatly pointed with red mortar. All shingles, silver stain. Trim, rail and balusters, dark drab. Sashes, green. Porch floor and ceiling varnished.

ACCOMMODATIONS: All the rooms are shown by the floor plan. There are closets under the bay windows. Stairway to roof is covered by a hinged hatch door. The independent flooring on roof saves the tin from wear, and forms air spaces that protect the rooms from over-heating. For the kitchen flue a terra-cotta pipe is carried through the roof to a height of five feet or more and is properly stayed by iron rods. All interior doorways (except that of the kitchen) are intended for curtains, but doors can be hung if preferred. If the flower urns are omitted, turned balls should be substituted. This design would make a good annex cottage for a seaside or summer hotel.

COST: $500. The estimate is based on ‡ New York prices for materials and labor.

Price for working plans, specifications and * license to build,   - - $15.00

Price for †† bill of materials, - - - - - - - - - - - 5.00

Address, THE CO-OPERATIVE BUILDING PLAN ASSOCIATION, Architects, 63 Broadway, New York.

FEASIBLE MODIFICATIONS: Height of story, sizes of rooms, materials and colors may be changed. A hipped or gabled roof may be planned, providing a second story with two rooms. The interior may be plastered and a cellar may be built under the whole house.

The price of working plans, specifications, etc. for a modified design varies according to the alterations required, and will be made known upon application to the Architects.

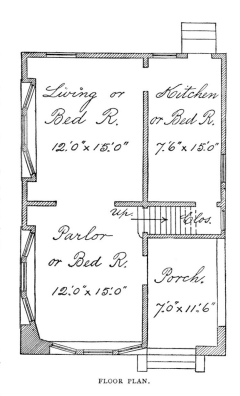

FLOOR PLAN.

50

THE CO-OPERATIVE BUILDING PLAN ASSOCIATION, ARCHITECTS, 63 BROADWAY, NEW YORK.

*Shoppell's Modern Houses—*Designs Patented.*   *Cottage or Lodge Design, No. 591*

PERSPECTIVE.

DESCRIPTION.

For explanation of all symbols († * etc.) see page 42.

GENERAL DIMENSIONS : Width, 24 ft.; depth, 39 ft. 7 in., including front porch. Heights of stories : Cellar, 6 ft.; first story, 10 ft. 6 in.

EXTERIOR MATERIALS : Foundation, posts ; first story, clapboards and shingles ; roof and dormers, shingles.

INTERIOR FINISH : Plastered walls and ceilings. Soft wood trim and flooring.

COLORS : Clapboards, light brown. Trim and blinds, dark brown. Outside doors, panels light brown ; framing of panels dark brown. Sashes, dark red. Porch floors, brown. Porch ceiling, oiled. Conductors and tin gutters, dark red. Wall shingles, oiled. Roof shingles left unfinished.

ACCOMMODATIONS : The principal rooms and their sizes, etc., are shown by the plan. Cellar with outside entrance and with brick wall, under kitchen. Attic floored but unfinished ; space for two rooms besides storage space. Flues for dining room and kitchen stoves.

COST : $600. The estimate is based on ‡ New York prices for materials and labor. In many sections of the country the cost should be less.

Price for working plans, specifications and * license to build, - - - $15.00
Price for †† bill of materials, - - - - - - - - - 5.00

Address : THE CO-OPERATIVE BUILDING PLAN ASSOCIATION, Architects, 63 Broadway, New York.

FEASIBLE MODIFICATIONS : Height of story, sizes of rooms, materials and colors may be changed. Cellar may be enlarged or omitted. Veranda or porch may be indefinitely extended to suit climate. Terra cotta or brick flues may be built to serve stoves in every room.

The price of working plans, specifications, etc., for a modified design varies according to the alterations required, and will be made known upon application to the Architects.

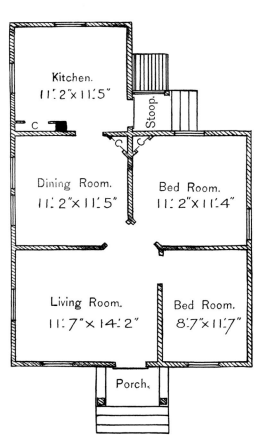

Kitchen.
11' 2" x 11' 5"

Stoop.

Dining Room.
11' 2" x 11' 5"

Bed Room.
11' 2" x 11' 4"

Living Room.
11' 7" x 14' 2"

Bed Room.
8' 7" x 11' 7"

Porch.

FIRST FLOOR.

51

THE CO-OPERATIVE BUILDING PLAN ASSOCIATION, ARCHITECTS, 63 BROADWAY, NEW YORK.

*Shoppell's Modern Houses—*Designs Patented.* *Lodge or Cottage, Design No. 631*

PERSPECTIVE.

FLOOR PLAN.

DESCRIPTION.

For explanation of all symbols (* † etc.) see page 42.

GENERAL DIMENSIONS: Width, 31 ft.; depth, including veranda, 31 ft. 6 in. Height of story, 9 ft.

EXTERIOR MATERIALS: Foundations, stone; first story, clapboards; gables and main roofs, shingles; roofs of bays, tin.

INTERIOR FINISH: Flooring and trim, white pine. No plaster. The studs and joists are dressed and varnished; wall and ceiling spaces between timbers are filled with heavy paper secured to the sheathing. The under side of the attic floor is dressed and varnished; the first floor is varnished, intended for the use of rugs.

COLORS: Clapboards, gable shingles and panels of bays painted Colonial yellow. Trim, facia of cornice, stiles and rails of bay paneling, veranda posts and balusters, painted white. Mouldings, veranda rails, post caps and bases and ball terminals of bays, painted dark yellow. Roofs, red. Veranda, floor and ceiling, oiled.

ACCOMMODATIONS: All the rooms and their sizes are shown by the floor plan. No cellar and no attic finish. All interior doorways (except the opening to kitchen) intended for curtains. Folding beds are recommended for all small houses.

COST: $600. The estimate is based on ‡ New York prices for materials and labor.
Price for working plans, specifications and * license to build, - - - $15.00
Price for †† bill of materials, - - - - - - - - - 5.00
Address, THE CO-OPERATIVE BUILDING PLAN ASSOCIATION, Architects, 63 Broadway, New York.

FEASIBLE MODIFICATIONS: Height of story, sizes of rooms, materials and colors, all may be changed. Bay windows may be omitted. Walls and ceilings may be plastered. The bed-room may connect with the parlor and the space at rear of the hall added to the kitchen or pantry. Posts may be used for foundations and terra-cotta for the chimney; this would do away with all mason work. Stained glass may be introduced in front door and in upper sashes.

The price of working plans, specifications, etc. for a modified design varies according to the alterations required, and will be made known upon application to the Architects.

52

THE CO-OPERATIVE BUILDING PLAN ASSOCIATION, ARCHITECTS, 63 BROADWAY, NEW YORK.

Shoppell's Modern Houses—*Designs Patented.   *Lodge or Cottage, Design No. 632*

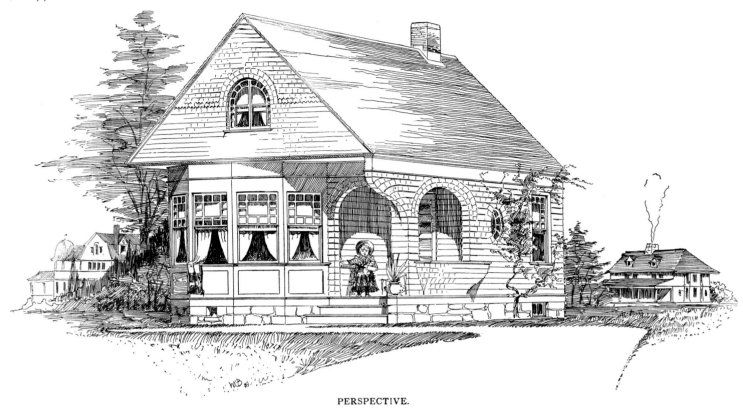

PERSPECTIVE.

DESCRIPTION.

For explanation of all symbols (* † etc.) see page 42.

GENERAL DIMENSIONS: Width, 22 ft. 6 in.; depth, 36 ft. 6 in. Heights of stories: Cellar, 6 ft.; first story, 8 ft. 6 in.; second story, 8 ft.

EXTERIOR MATERIALS: Foundations, stone; side walls, gables and roof, shingles.

INTERIOR FINISH: Two coats of plaster and paper. Trim, staircase and flooring, white pine (or other soft wood), hard finished in first story and painted in second story.

COLORS: Roof, shingles, stained red; all other shingles stained sienna. Trim and outside doors painted green; panels on bay and facia of main cornice, lighter green. Sashes, red. Porch floor and ceiling, and brick work of chimney, oiled. Stone work pointed with red mortar.

ACCOMMODATIONS: The principal rooms and their sizes are shown by the floor plans. There is a small cellar under the kitchen with an outside entrance to same.

COST: $800.

The estimate is based on ‡ New York prices for materials and labor. In many sections of the country the cost should be less.

Price for working plans, specifications and * license
    to build, - - - - - - - - $15.00
Price for †† bill of materials, - - - - 5.00

Address, THE CO-OPERATIVE BUILDING PLAN ASSOCIATION, Architects, 63 Broadway, New York.

FEASIBLE MODIFICATIONS: Heights of stories, colors, sizes of rooms, and kinds of materials may be changed. Cellar may extend under whole house. Porch seat may be omitted. A veranda may extend across the front carrying the gable forward to cover the same; this would enlarge the second story.

The price of working plans, specifications, etc. for a modified design varies according to the alterations required, and will be made known upon application to the Architects.

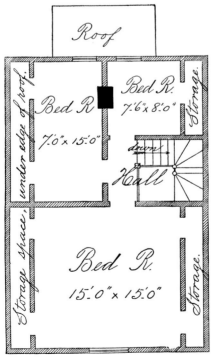

SECOND FLOOR.

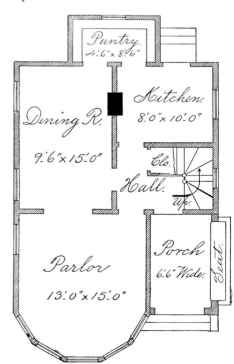

FIRST FLOOR.

THE CO-OPERATIVE BUILDING PLAN ASSOCIATION, ARCHITECTS, 63 BROADWAY, NEW YORK.

*Shoppell's Modern Houses—*Designs Patented.   *Cottage, Design No. 633*

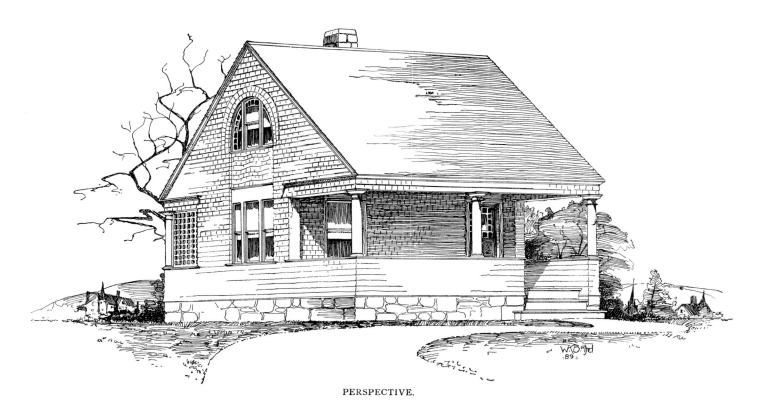

PERSPECTIVE.

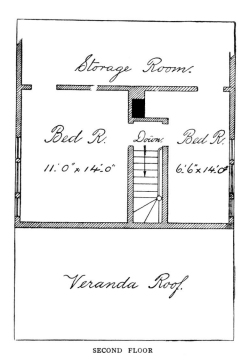

SECOND FLOOR

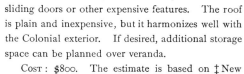

FIRST FLOOR.

DESCRIPTION.

For explanation of all symbols (* † etc.) see page 42.

GENERAL DIMENSIONS: Width, 22 ft. 6 in.; depth, 34 ft. Heights of stories: First story, 8 ft. 6 in.; second story, 8 ft.

EXTERIOR MATERIALS: Foundations, stone; first story, gables, veranda rails and roof, shingles.

COLORS: All shingles, including roof, stained silver. All trim, veranda, posts and risers, painted white. Sashes, outer doors and lattice work, painted dark green. Veranda floor and ceiling, oiled.

ACCOMMODATIONS: All the rooms and their sizes are shown by the floor plans. No fire-places, mantels, sliding doors or other expensive features. The roof is plain and inexpensive, but it harmonizes well with the Colonial exterior. If desired, additional storage space can be planned over veranda.

COST: $800. The estimate is based on ‡ New York prices for materials and labor. In many sections of the country the cost should be less.

Price for working plans, specifications and * license to build, - - - - - - $15.00
Price for †† bill of materials, - - - 5.00

Address, THE CO-OPERATIVE BUILDING PLAN ASSOCIATION, Architects, 63 Broadway, New York.

FEASIBLE MODIFICATIONS: Heights of stories, kinds of materials, sizes of rooms and colors, may be changed. Cellar may be built. By building a gable at the rear another bed-room may be planned. Veranda may be extended around either side or both sides. The veranda enclosure may be open balusters and rails, but the solid enclosure is more in keeping with the design.

The price of working plans, specifications, etc. for a modified design varies according to the alterations required, and will be made known upon application to the Architects.

THE CO-OPERATIVE BUILDING PLAN ASSOCIATION, ARCHITECTS, 63 BROADWAY, NEW YORK.

*Shoppell's Modern Houses—*Designs Patented.*

Cottage, Design No. 370

PERSPECTIVE.

DESCRIPTION.

For explanation of all symbols (* † etc.) see page 42.

GENERAL DIMENSIONS: Width, 29 ft. 8 in.; depth, 28 ft. Heights of stories: First story, 9 ft. 3 in.; second story, 8 ft.

EXTERIOR MATERIALS: Foundation, posts; first story, clapboards; second story and roof, shingles.

INTERIOR FINISH: Soft wood flooring, trim and stairway. Interior walls are not plastered, but are finished with red building paper; studding and all wood-work is dressed and exposed to view, and finished with varnish.

COLORS: Clapboards, front door panels and piazza floor, light brown. Trim and front door framing for panels, dark brown. Roof shingles dipped and brush coated with dark red paint. Sashes, dark red. Rafters and ceiling of piazza varnished. Wall shingles of tower and gables dipped and brush coated with sienna stain.

ACCOMMODATIONS: The principal rooms and their sizes are shown by the plans. There is no cellar. Ceiling in tower room is full height. Stairway leads up to a gallery at side of living room; living room is open to roof. The fireplace, with brick mantel and wood shelf of quaint design, is artistic, and yet simple enough to be made by an ordinary mechanic; its cost is included in the estimate. An appropriate design for a fishing camp, shooting lodge or summer residence.

COST: $861. The estimate is based on ‡ New York prices for materials and labor. In many sections of the country the cost should be less.

Price for working plans, specifications and * license to build, $12.00.

Price for † † bill of materials, - - - - - $3.00

Address, THE CO-OPERATIVE BUILDING PLAN ASSOCIATION, Architects, 63 Broadway, New York.

FEASIBLE MODIFICATIONS: Heights of stories, colors, sizes of rooms and kinds of materials may be changed. Cellar may be put under a part or the whole of house. Veranda may be reduced or extended.

The price of working plans, specifications, etc. for a modified design varies according to the alterations required, and will be made known upon application to the Architects.

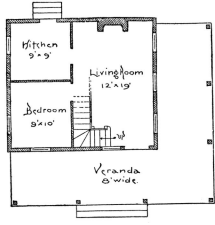

FIRST FLOOR.

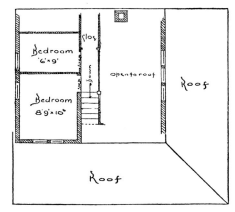

SECOND FLOOR.

THE CO-OPERATIVE BUILDING PLAN ASSOCIATION, ARCHITECTS, 63 BROADWAY, NEW YORK.

Shoppell's Modern Houses—*Designs Patented.　　　　　　　　　*Cottage, Design No. 246*

PERSPECTIVE.

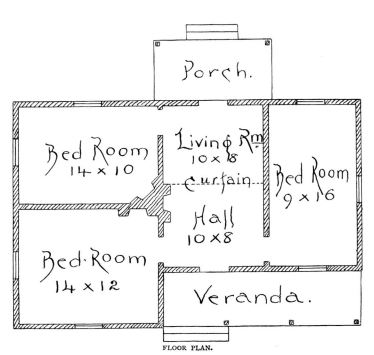

FLOOR PLAN.

DESCRIPTION.

For explanation of all symbols (* † etc.) see page 42.

GENERAL DIMENSIONS: Width, 35 ft.; depth, 23 ft. 6 in. Height of first story, 10 ft.

EXTERIOR MATERIALS: Foundations, brick piers; first story, vertical siding and shingles; roof and gables, shingles.

INTERIOR FINISH: Hard white plaster. Soft wood floor and trim. Interior wood-work, painted colors to suit owner.

COLORS: Vertical siding, blinds, and piazza rafters, light olive green. All shingles to be dipped and brush coated with reddish stain. Trim, outside doors and veranda floor, dark green. Veranda ceiling, light drab. Sashes, dark red.

ACCOMMODATIONS: The principal rooms and their sizes are shown by the floor plan. No cellar. House is designed for summer occupancy or a southern climate, and to be used in connection with detached kitchen. Three fireplaces with mantels are included in the estimate.

COST: $794. The estimate is based on ‡ New York prices for materials and labor. In many sections of the country the cost should be less.

Price for working plans, specifications and * license to build, $10.00

Price for † † bill of materials, - - - - - 2.00

Address, THE CO-OPERATIVE BUILDING PLAN ASSOCIATION, Architects, 63 Broadway, New York.

FEASIBLE MODIFICATIONS: Height of story, colors, sizes of rooms and kinds of materials may be changed. Cellar may be placed under a portion or the whole of house. Veranda may be widened and extended indefinitely. Fireplace heater may be used in hall, and fireplaces and mantels in bedrooms omitted. A kitchen and pantry extension may be placed at rear, and one of the present bedrooms used as a dining room.

The price of working plans, specifications, etc., for a modified design varies according to the alterations required, and will be made known upon application to the Architects.

56

THE CO-OPERATIVE BUILDING PLAN ASSOCIATION, ARCHITECTS, 63 BROADWAY, NEW YORK.

*Shoppell's Modern Houses—*Designs Patented.*   *Cottage, Design No. 512*

PERSPECTIVE.

DESCRIPTION.

For explanation of all symbols (* † etc.) see page 42.

GENERAL DIMENSIONS: Width, 22 ft.; depth, 28 ft., not including porch. Heights of stories: First story, 8 ft. 6 in.; second story, 8 ft.

EXTERIOR MATERIALS: Foundation, wood posts; side walls, siding or clapboards; gables, panels and shingles; dormers and roofs, shingles.

INTERIOR FINISH: No plaster; walls are wainscoted and papered. Terra cotta chimney. Trim, flooring and stairway, soft wood.

COLORS: Clapboards and veranda floor, dark slate color. Trim, outside doors, blinds and rain conductors, blue stone color. Sashes, Pompeian red. Veranda ceiling, oiled. Gable and dormer wall shingles dipped and brush coated buff stain. Roof shingles left natural color.

ACCOMMODATIONS: The principal rooms, and their sizes, closets, etc., are shown by the floor plans. No cellar. Loft over second story floored, and may serve for storage or air space.

COST: $806. The estimate is based on ‡ New York prices for materials and labor. In many sections of the country the cost should be less.

Price for working plans, specifications and * license to build, - - - - - - - - - - - - $12.00

Price for †† bill of materials, - - - - - $3.00

Address, THE CO-OPERATIVE BUILDING PLAN ASSOCIATION Architects, 63 Broadway, New York.

FEASIBLE MODIFICATIONS: Heights of stories, colors, sizes of rooms and kinds of materials may be changed. Cellar may be planned under a portion or the whole of house. Porch may be extended across entire front. Side porch may be omitted and entrance to kitchen made at rear. The hallway may extend through from front door to kitchen by omitting earth closet, coal box, passage and porch. Bathroom may be omitted entirely and space given to small rear bedroom, or it may serve as a large storage closet. If the earth closet be omitted in first story a water closet may be placed in bathroom. A one-story kitchen may be added at rear, and dining room extend across the entire house. The roof may be raised so as to give full height to second story.

The price of working plans, specifications, etc., for a modified design varies according to the alterations required, and will be made known upon application to the Architects.

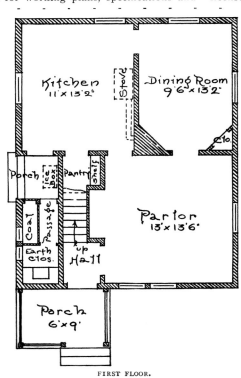

FIRST FLOOR.

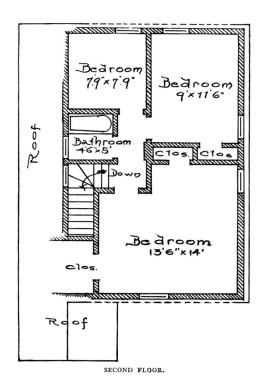

SECOND FLOOR.

THE CO-OPERATIVE BUILDING PLAN ASSOCIATION, ARCHITECTS, 63 BROADWAY, NEW YORK.

*Shoppell's Modern Houses—*Designs Patented.*   *Cottage, Design No. 634*

PERSPECTIVE.

DESCRIPTION.

For explanation of all symbols (* † etc.) see page 42.

GENERAL DIMENSIONS: Width, 17 ft.; depth, 34 ft. 6 in. Heights of stories: Cellar, 6 ft.; first story, 9 ft.; second story, 8 ft.

EXTERIOR MATERIALS: Foundations, first story, veranda, posts and rails, and chimney top, rock-faced stone, pointed with red mortar. The stone to be even in color, all newly broken or all old surfaces. Gables, panels and shingles. Roof, shingles.

INTERIOR FINISH: Two-coat plaster and paper. White pine or other soft woods, for flooring, trim and stairway, all stained and finished in hard oil to imitate hard woods.

COLORS: Trim, sashes and outer doors, dark green; facia between first and second stories, and panels in gables, a lighter green. Roof, dark red stain. Veranda floor and ceiling, oiled.

ACCOMMODATIONS: All the rooms are shown by the floor plans. There is a small cellar. A good fire in the living room will send a good deal of heat up the stairway to warm the rooms above. The closet off the second story hall is large and is intended to serve for both bed-rooms.

COST: $900, † not including mantels, range and heater. The estimate is based on ‡ New York prices for materials and labor, and can be built for above amount only in localities where the stone costs little or nothing. In many localities there is suitable stone on the place, without cost except the small expense of a short haul to the building site.

Price for working plans, specifications and * license to build, $15.00
Price for †† bill of materials, - - - - - - 5.00

Address, THE CO-OPERATIVE BUILDING PLAN ASSOCIATION, Architects, 63 Broadway, New York.

FEASIBLE MODIFICATIONS: Heights of stories, colors and kinds of materials may be changed. Bay window may be built straight. Veranda posts and railing may be built of wood if designed to harmonize with the general exterior. Cellar may be omitted or extended under the whole house.

The price of working plans, specifications, etc. for a modified design varies according to the alterations required, and will be made known upon application to the Architects.

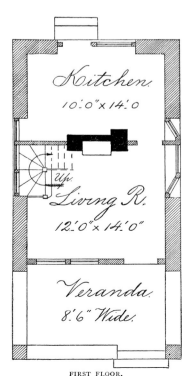

FIRST FLOOR.

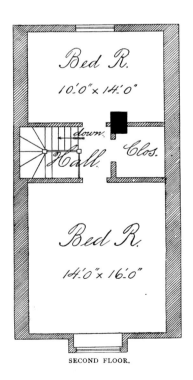

SECOND FLOOR.

58

THE CO-OPERATIVE BUILDING PLAN ASSOCIATION, ARCHITECTS, 63 BROADWAY, NEW YORK.

Shoppell's Modern Houses—*Designs Patented.　　　　　　　*Cottage, Design No. 570*

PHOTOGRAPHIC VIEW.

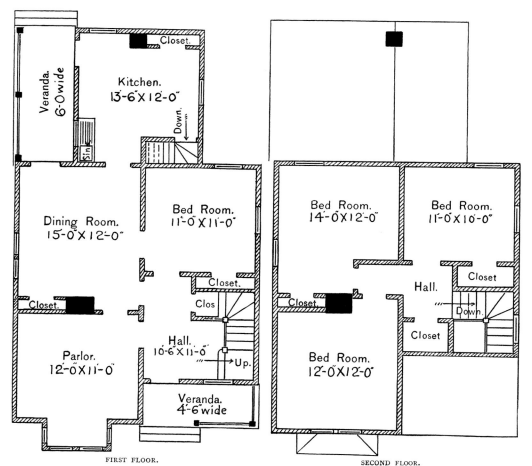

FIRST FLOOR.　　　　　　SECOND FLOOR.

DESCRIPTION.

For explanation of all symbols (* † etc.) see page 42.

GENERAL DIMENSIONS: Width, 24 ft. 6 in.; depth over all, 44 ft. 6 in. Heights of stories: Cellar, 6 ft. 6 in.; first story, 8 ft. 6 in.; second story, 8 ft.

EXTERIOR MATERIALS: Foundations, stone; first story, clapboards; second story, clapboards and shingles; gables and roof, shingles. Outside blinds to all windows, except those of the cellar.

INTERIOR FINISH: Hard white plaster. Soft wood trim, stairs and flooring.

COLORS: All clapboards in first story light yellow. All clapboards and shingles in second story and gables, dark yellow. Trim, sashes, veranda posts, rails and balusters and all cornices, white. Outside doors and blinds, dark green. Veranda floors and ceilings, oiled.

ACCOMMODATIONS: The principal rooms and their sizes, closets, etc., are shown by the plans. Cellar under kitchen only. No attic; loft floored for storage. Fair sized house at low cost.

COST: $1,000, † not including mantels, range and heater. The estimate is based on ‡ New York prices for materials and labor. In many sections of the country the cost should be less.

Price for working plans, specifications and * license to build, $20.00.

Price for †† bill of materials, $5.00

Address, THE CO-OPERATIVE BUILDING PLAN ASSOCIATION, Architects, 63 Broadway, New York.

FEASIBLE MODIFICATIONS: Heights of stories, sizes of rooms, materials and colors may be changed. Cellar may extend under whole house. Front chimney may be omitted if heating apparatus be used.

The price of working plans, specifications, etc., for a modified design varies according to the alterations required, and will be made known upon application to the Architects.

59

THE CO-OPERATIVE BUILDING PLAN ASSOCIATION, ARCHITECTS, 63 BROADWAY, NEW YORK.

*Shoppell's Modern Houses—*Designs Patented.*   *Cottage, Design No. 571*

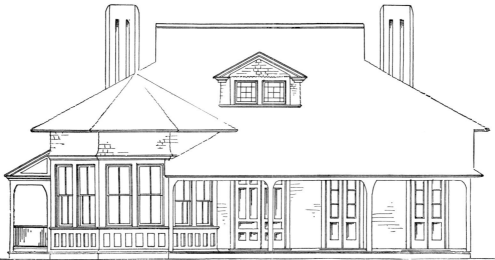

FRONT ELEVATION.

DESCRIPTION.

For explanation of all symbols (* † etc.) see page 42.

GENERAL DIMENSIONS : Width over all, 46 ft.; depth, 41 ft. 6 in., including veranda. Height of first story, 11 ft.

EXTERIOR MATERIALS : Foundation, stone ; first story, clapboards ; second story, roofs, dormer and gables, shingles. Outside blinds to all windows of first story.

INTERIOR FINISH : Hard white plaster. Soft wood flooring and trim. Chair rail in dining room ; all finished in hard oil.

COLORS : All clapboards, light brown. Trim, brown. Outside doors, panels tan color ; framing of panels brown. Blinds, sashes and rain conductors, red. Veranda floor, tan. Veranda ceiling, buff. Wall shingles dipped and brush coated in oil. Roof shingles left unfinished.

ACCOMMODATIONS : The principal rooms and their sizes are shown by the plan. No cellar. Attic floored but unfinished, and reached by scuttle and step-ladder. Four fireplaces and mantels.

COST : $1,000, † not including mantels, range and heater. The estimate is based on ‡ New York prices for materials and labor. In many sections of the country the cost should be less.

Price for working plans, specifications and * license to build, - - - - - - - - - - - $20.00

Price for †† bill of materials, - - - - - 5.00

Address, THE CO-OPERATIVE BUILDING PLAN ASSOCIATION, Architects, 63 Broadway, New York.

FEASIBLE MODIFICATIONS : Height of story, sizes of rooms, materials and colors may be changed. Cellar may be placed under a part or the whole of house. Two rooms and a hallway may be finished in second story. One chimney may be omitted if heating apparatus be used. Ordinary windows may be substituted for those which extend to floor.

The price of working plans, specifications, etc., for a modified design varies according to the alterations required, and will be made known upon application to the Architects.

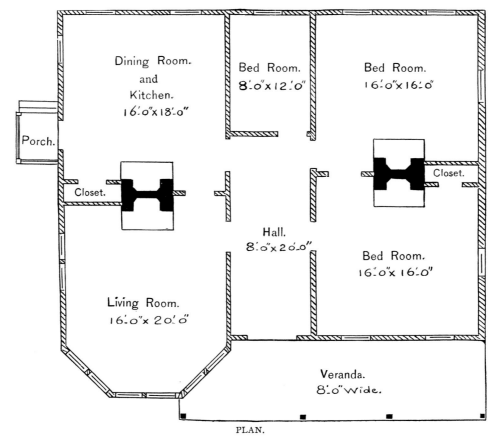

PLAN.

THE CO-OPERATIVE BUILDING PLAN ASSOCIATION, ARCHITECTS, 63 BROADWAY, NEW YORK.

*Shoppell's Modern Houses—*Designs Patented.* Cottage Design, No. 245

PERSPECTIVE.

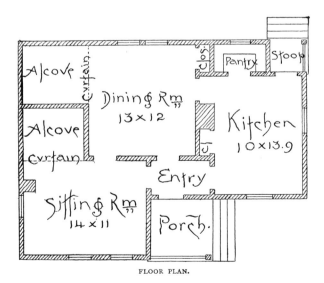

FLOOR PLAN.

FEASIBLE MODIFICATIONS : Height of story, colors, sizes of rooms, and kinds of materials may be changed. Cellar may be omitted or built under the whole house. Porch may be extended indefinitely. The two alcoves may be combined to form one bed-room. Sitting room chimney may be omitted.

The price of working plans, specifications, etc., for a modified design varies according to the alterations required, and will be made known upon application to the Architects.

DESCRIPTION.

For explanation of all symbols (* † etc.) see page 42.

GENERAL DIMENSIONS : Width, 32 ft. 6 in.; depth, 25 ft. 6 in. Heights of stories : Cellar, 6 ft.; first story, 9 ft. 6 in.

EXTERIOR MATERIALS : Foundation, posts ; first story, clapboards ; gables and roof, shingles.

INTERIOR FINISH : Hard white plaster. Soft wood flooring and trim. Interior wood-work painted colors to suit owner.

COLORS : Clapboards, light olive drab. Trim and cornices, light olive green. Porch ceiling, light gray. Porch floors, yellow stone color. Sashes, dark red. Wall shingles dipped in and brush coated with sienna stain. Outside doors, bronze green. Roof shingles dipped in and brush coated with red stain.

ACCOMMODATIONS : The principal rooms, and their sizes, are shown by the plan. There is a cellar under kitchen with brick walls and outside entrance. Space over rooms is floored for storage. Alcoves off dining and sitting rooms may be screened by curtains during the day, concealing beds.

COST : $913. The estimate is based on ‡ New York prices for materials and labor. In many sections of the country the cost should be less.

Price for working plans, specifications and * license to build, - - - - - - - - - - - $10.00
Price for † † bill of materials, - - - - - - 2.00

Address, THE CO-OPERATIVE BUILDING PLAN ASSOCIATION, Architects, 63 Broadway, New York.

61

THE CO-OPERATIVE BUILDING PLAN ASSOCIATION, ARCHITECTS, 63 BROADWAY, NEW YORK.

Shoppell's Modern Houses—*Designs Patented. *Cottage, Design No. 169*

FRONT ELEVATION.

FIRST FLOOR.

SECOND FLOOR.

DESCRIPTION.

For explanation of all symbols (* † etc.) see page 42.

GENERAL DIMENSIONS: Width, 20 ft. 8 in.; depth, 24 ft. Heights of stories: Cellar, 6 ft. 6 in.; first story, 8 ft. 8 in.; second story, 8 ft.

EXTERIOR MATERIALS: Foundation, brick walls and piers or wood posts set in concrete; first story, clapboards; second story, gables and roof, shingles.

INTERIOR FINISH: Hard white plaster. Flooring, stairs and trim, soft wood finished in hard oil.

COLORS: Clapboards, drab. Trim, cornices and porch floor, olive green. Porch ceiling, light stone color. Blinds and sashes, Pompeian red. Outside doors, bronze green. All shingles dipped in and brush coated with red paint.

ACCOMMODATIONS: The principal rooms and their sizes, closets, etc., are shown by the floor plans. Cellar under living room. Mantel in parlor is included in estimate. By using a fireplace heater in parlor two upper rooms may be warmed. Large vestibule protects house from cold and dust.

COST: $971. The estimate is based on ‡ New York prices for materials and labor. In many sections of the country the cost should be less.

Price for working plans, specifications, and * license to build, - - - - - - - - - - - - - - - $12.00

Price for †† bill of materials, - - - - - 3.00

Address, THE CO-OPERATIVE BUILDING PLAN ASSOCIATION, Architects, 63 Broadway, New York.

FEASIBLE MODIFICATIONS: Heights of stories, colors, sizes of rooms and kinds of materials may be changed. Cellar may extend under whole house or be omitted entirely. Seat in vestibule may be omitted. Porch may be extended indefinitely.

The price of working plans, specifications, etc., for a modified design varies according to the alterations required, and will be made known upon application to the Architects.

62

THE CO-OPERATIVE BUILDING PLAN ASSOCIATION, ARCHITECTS, 63 BROADWAY, NEW YORK.

*Shoppell's Modern Houses—*Designs Patented.* *Cottage, Design No. 552A*

PERSPECTIVE.

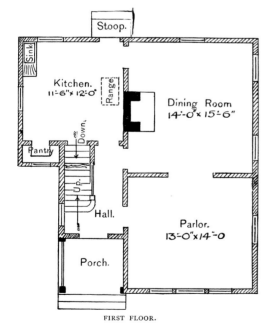

FIRST FLOOR.

SECOND FLOOR.

DESCRIPTION.

For explanation of all symbols (* † etc.) see page 42.

GENERAL DIMENSIONS: Width over all, 27 ft.; depth, 30 ft. Heights of stories: Cellar, 6 ft. 6 in.; first story, 8 ft. 6 in.; second story, 8 ft.

EXTERIOR MATERIALS: Foundations, stone; first story, clapboards; second story, gables and roofs, shingles.

INTERIOR FINISH: Hard white plaster. Trim, stairs and floors, soft wood painted colors to suit owner.

COLORS: Clapboards and porch post, pale green. Trim, porch rail and balusters, and outlookers on front gable, dark green. Shingles on gables dipped and brush coated reddish stain. Roof shingles dipped and brush coated brown stain. Sashes Pompeian red. Outside doors and blinds, dark green. Porch floor and ceiling oiled.

ACCOMMODATIONS: The principal rooms and their sizes, closets, etc., are shown by the plans. Cellar under hall and parlor. Loft over second story floored and ventilated at each end by small windows.

COST: $900, † not including mantel, range and heater. The estimate is based on ‡ New York prices for materials and labor. In many sections of the country the cost should be less.

Price for working plans, specifications and * license to build, - - - - - - - - - - - $15.00
Price for † † bill of materials, - - - - - 10.00

Address, THE CO-OPERATIVE BUILDING PLAN ASSOCIATION, Architects, 63 Broadway, New York.

FEASIBLE MODIFICATIONS: Heights of stories, sizes of rooms, materials and colors may be changed. Cellar may extend under whole house or may be omitted entirely. Dining room fireplace and mantel may be omitted. Sliding doors may connect parlor, dining room and hall.

The price of working plans, specifications, etc., for a modified design varies according to the alterations required, and will be made known upon application to the Architects.

63

THE CO-OPERATIVE BUILDING PLAN ASSOCIATION, ARCHITECTS, 63 BROADWAY, NEW YORK.

*Shoppell's Modern Houses—*Designs Patented.*

Cottage, Design No. 551

PERSPECTIVE.

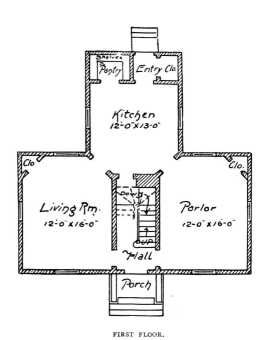

FIRST FLOOR.

SECOND FLOOR.

DESCRIPTION.

For explanation of all symbols (* † etc.) see page 42.

GENERAL DIMENSIONS: Width, 32 ft.; depth, 31 ft., not including porches. Height of stories: Cellar, 6 ft. 6 in.; first story, 8 ft. 6 in.; second story, 8 ft.

EXTERIOR MATERIALS: Foundations, stone; first story, clapboards; second story, roof and dormers, shingles.

INTERIOR FINISH: Two coat plaster. Soft wood trim, flooring and stairway, painted colors to suit owner.

COLORS: Roof shingles stained red; all other shingles stained sienna. Clapboards, light green. Trim and outside doors painted green. Sashes, red. Porch floor and ceiling and brick-work, oiled. Stone-work pointed with red mortar.

ACCOMMODATIONS: The principal rooms and their sizes are shown by the floor plans. Cellar under main house.

COST: $1,000, † not including range and heater. The estimate is based on ‡ New York prices for materials and labor. In many sections of the country the cost should be less.

Price for working plans, specifications and * license to build, - - - - - - - - - - $15.00.
    Price for † † bill of materials, - - - - - 10.00
    Address, THE CO-OPERATIVE BUILDING PLAN ASSOCIATION, Architects, 63 Broadway, New York.

FEASIBLE MODIFICATIONS: Heights of stories, sizes of rooms, colors, and kinds of materials may be changed. Cellar may extend under whole house. Porch may be widened into a veranda and extended indefinitely.

The price of working plans, specifications, etc., for a modified design varies according to the alterations required, and will be made known upon application to the Architects.

64

THE CO-OPERATIVE BUILDING PLAN ASSOCIATION, ARCHITECTS, 63 BROADWAY, NEW YORK.

*Shoppell's Modern Houses—*Designs Patented.*   *Cottage, Design No. 371.*

PERSPECTIVE.

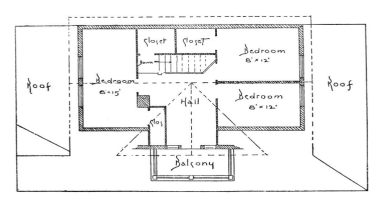

SECOND FLOOR.

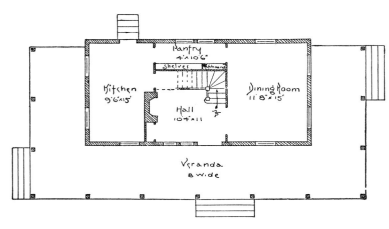

FIRST FLOOR.

DESCRIPTION.

For explanation of all symbols (* † etc.) see page 42.

GENERAL DIMENSIONS: Width, 49 ft., including veranda; depth, 24 ft., including veranda. Heights of stories: First story, 10 ft.; second story, 9 ft.

EXTERIOR MATERIALS: Foundation, wood posts; first story, clapboards; second story, clapboards and shingles; roof, shingles.

INTERIOR FINISH: Interior is not plastered, but is finished with heavy red paper; the wood-work is exposed to view and varnished. This pretty and inexpensive finish is very suitable for a summer cottage. Soft wood is used throughout for stairs, flooring and trim, all varnished the same as the other exposed wood-work.

COLORS: Clapboards and piazza floor, light brown. All trim, and front door, dark brown. Sashes, dark red. Rafters and ceiling of piazza, varnished. Roof shingles dipped in and brush coated with dark red paint. Wall shingles dipped in and brush coated with sienna stain.

ACCOMMODATIONS: The principal rooms and their sizes are shown by the floor plans. No cellar. Open fireplace and mantel in hall included in estimate. Designed for a seaside or mountain cottage. Suitable also for shooting lodge or "box." Balcony in second story affords pleasant outlook.

COST: $1,194. The estimate is based on ‡ New York prices for materials and labor. In many sections of the country the cost should be less.

Price for working plans, specifications and * license to build, - - - - - - - - - - $14.00
Price for † † bill of materials, - - - - 4.00

Address, THE CO-OPERATIVE BUILDING PLAN ASSOCIATION, Architects, 63 Broadway, New York.

FEASIBLE MODIFICATIONS: Heights of stories, colors, sizes of rooms and kinds of materials may be changed. Cellar may be placed under the whole or a part of the house. Veranda may be reduced or extended. Bedrooms over dining room may be united to form one large room.

The price of working plans, specifications, etc., for a modified design varies according to the alterations required, and will be made known upon application to the Architects.

65

THE CO-OPERATIVE BUILDING PLAN ASSOCIATION, ARCHITECTS, 63 BROADWAY, NEW YORK.

*Shoppell's Modern Houses—*Designs Patented.* *Cottage, Design No. 372*

PERSPECTIVE.

DESCRIPTION.

For explanation of all symbols (* † etc.) see page 42.

GENERAL DIMENSIONS: Width, 43 ft. 6 in., including veranda; depth, 23 ft. 6 in., including veranda. Heights of stories: First story, 9 ft.; second story, 8 ft.

EXTERIOR MATERIALS: Foundation, brick piers; first story, clapboards; second story, gables and roofs, shingles.

INTERIOR FINISH: Two coat plaster for papering. Floors, trim and stairway, soft wood, finished in hard oil.

COLORS: Clapboards, sashes and blinds, light brown. All trim and doors, dark brown. Wall shingles dipped in and brush coated with buff stain. Roof shingles left natural color.

ACCOMMODATIONS: The principal rooms and their sizes are shown by the floor plans. No cellar.

COST: $1,128. The estimate is based on ‡ New York prices for materials and labor. In many sections of the country the cost should be less.

Price for working plans, specifications and * license to build, - - - - - - - - - - - - $15.00

Price for † † bill of materials, - - - - 5.00

Address, THE CO-OPERATIVE BUILDING PLAN ASSOCIATION, Architects, 63 Broadway, New York.

FEASIBLE MODIFICATIONS: Heights of stories, colors, sizes of rooms and kinds of materials may be changed. Second story may have level ceilings throughout by raising roof. Veranda may be extended or reduced; the uncovered portion may be covered. The kitchen space may be added to the dining room and a new kitchen built at rear.

The price of working plans, specifications, etc., for a modified design varies according to the alterations required, and will be made known upon application to the Architects.

NOTE.—On the second floor plan a window at the rear of hall should be shown; omitted by mistake.

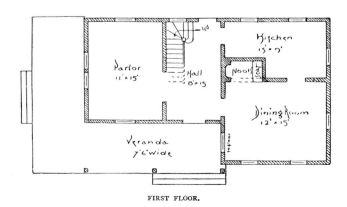

FIRST FLOOR.

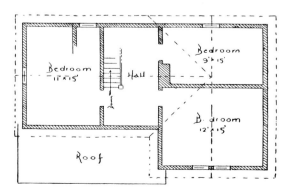

SECOND FLOOR.

66

THE CO-OPERATIVE BUILDING PLAN ASSOCIATION, ARCHITECTS, 63 BROADWAY, NEW YORK.

Shoppell's Modern Houses—*Designs Patented.   *Cottage, Design No. 312*

PERSPECTIVE.

DESCRIPTION.

For explanation of all symbols (* † etc.) see page 42.

GENERAL DIMENSIONS: Width, 24 ft. 2 in.; depth, 30 ft. 5 in., including verandas. Heights of stories: First story, 9 ft.; second story, 8 ft.

EXTERIOR MATERIALS: Foundation, posts; first story, clapboards; second story and roof, shingles.

INTERIOR FINISH: Hard white plaster. Flooring, trim and stairway, soft wood finished in hard oil.

COLORS: Clapboards, outside door framing for panels, and sashes. light brown. Trim, outside door panels, veranda ceiling, and rain water conductors, dark brown. Veranda floor, oiled. Wall shingles, sienna stain. Roof shingles, unpainted.

ACCOMMODATIONS: The principal rooms and their sizes are shown by the floor plans. No cellar. If built with plank construction and the interior finished with paper in place of plaster, the cost should be somewhat less than our estimate.

COST: $1,132. The estimate is based on ‡ New York prices for materials and labor. In many sections of the country the cost should be less.

Price for working plans, specifications and * license to build, - - - - - - - - - - - $12.00
Price for † † bill of materials, - - - - - - - 3.00

Address, THE CO-OPERATIVE BUILDING PLAN ASSOCIATION, Architects, 63 Broadway, New York.

FEASIBLE MODIFICATIONS: Heights of stories, colors, sizes of rooms and kinds of materials may be changed. Cellar may be placed under a portion of or under the whole house. Veranda may be extended across front and sides.

The price of working plans, specifications, etc., for a a modified design varies according to the alterations required, and will be made known upon application to the Architects.

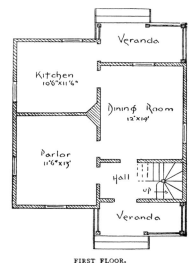

FIRST FLOOR.

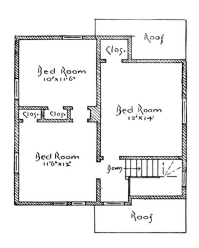

SECOND FLOOR.

67

THE CO-OPERATIVE BUILDING PLAN ASSOCIATION, ARCHITECTS, 63 BROADWAY, NEW YORK.

Shoppell's Modern Houses—*Designs Patented. *Cottage Design, No. 592*

PERSPECTIVE.

DESCRIPTION.

For explanation of all symbols (* † etc.) see page 42.

GENERAL DIMENSIONS: Width, including verandas, 48 ft.; depth, including verandas, 35 ft. Heights of stories: First story, 11 ft.; second story, 10 ft.

EXTERIOR MATERIALS: Foundation, posts; first story, clapboards; second story, shingles and panels; roof, shingled.

INTERIOR FINISH: No plastering; partitions all wood covered with plaster board. Flooring, trim and stairway, soft woods finished in hard oil, stained to suit owner. Fireplace and hearth of pressed brick in hall.

COLORS: Clapboards and second story shingles, light brown. All trim, cornices, piazza posts, balcony rail and balusters, dark brown. Sashes, dark red. Front door, dark brown with light brown panels. Veranda floors, oiled. Rafters and ceiling of veranda, varnished. Roof shingles, dark red.

ACCOMMODATIONS: The principal rooms and their sizes, closets, etc., are shown by the plans. No cellar; the house is designed for summer occupancy. Loft over second story floored for storage space.

COST: $1,200. The estimate is based on ‡ New York prices for materials and labor. In many sections of the country the cost should be less.

Price for working plans, specifications and * license to build, - $15.00.
Price for †† bill of materials, - - - - - - - - 5.00.

Address, THE CO-OPERATIVE BUILDING PLAN ASSOCIATION, Architects, 63 Broadway, New York.

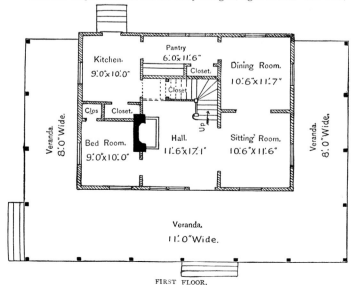

FIRST FLOOR.

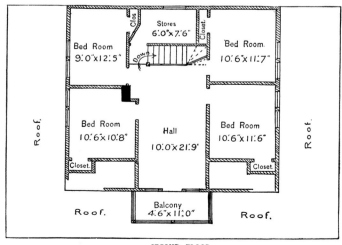

SECOND FLOOR.

68

THE CO-OPERATIVE BUILDING PLAN ASSOCIATION, ARCHITECTS, 63 BROADWAY, NEW YORK.

*Shoppell's Modern Houses—*Designs Patented.*

Cottage, Design No. 549

PERSPECTIVE.

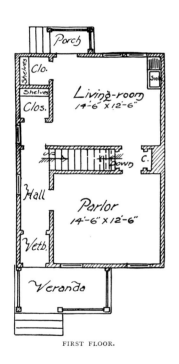

FIRST FLOOR.

DESIGN NO. 549, AS A DOUBLE COTTAGE.

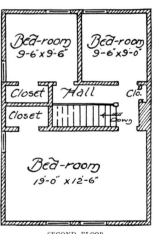

SECOND FLOOR.

DESCRIPTION.

For explanation of all symbols (* † etc.) see page 42.

GENERAL DIMENSIONS: Width, 20 ft.; depth, 40 ft., including veranda and porch. Heights of stories: Cellar, 6 ft. 6 in.; first story, 8 ft. 6 in.; second story, 8 ft.

EXTERIOR MATERIALS: Foundations, stone; first story, clapboards; second story, gables and roof, shingles.

INTERIOR FINISH: Two coats of plaster for papering Trim, staircase and flooring, soft wood; hard finish in first story, painted in second story.

COLORS: Clapboards, sashes, and veranda floor, light brown. Trim, outside doors and blinds, dark brown. Wall shingles dipped and brush coated buff stain. Roof shingles left natural. Chimney painted Indian red. Veranda ceiling, yellow stone color.

ACCOMMODATIONS: The principal rooms and their sizes, closets, etc., are shown by the floor plans. Cellar under the whole house. Loft over second story floored for storage.

COST: $1,300. The estimate is based on ‡ New York prices for materials and labor. In many sections of the country the cost should be less.

Price for working plans, specifications and * license to build, - - - - - - - - - $15.00
Price for †† bill of materials, - - - - - 10.00

Address, THE CO-OPERATIVE BUILDING PLAN ASSOCIATION, Architects, 63 Broadway, New York.

FEASIBLE MODIFICATIONS: Heights of stories, colors, sizes of rooms and kinds of materials may be changed. Cellar may be reduced in size or omitted. Veranda may be extended across the front and on sides. House may be doubled, as shown by the small perspective.

The price of working plans, specifications, etc., for a modified design varies according to the alterations required, and will be made known upon application to the Architects.

THE CO-OPERATIVE BUILDING PLAN ASSOCIATION, ARCHITECTS, 63 BROADWAY, NEW YORK.

*Shoppell's Modern Houses—*Designs Patented.*

Residence, Design No. 177

PERSPECTIVE.

DESCRIPTION.

For explanation of all symbols (* † etc.) see page 42.

GENERAL DIMENSIONS: Width, 20 ft.; depth, 25 ft. Heights of stories: Cellar, 7 ft.; first story, 8 ft. 6 in.; second story, 8 ft.

EXTERIOR MATERIALS: Foundations, stone; first story, clapboards; second story and roof, shingles; gables, paneled.

INTERIOR FINISH: Hard white plaster. Soft wood flooring and trim. Ash stairway. Interior wood-work finished in hard oil.

COLORS: Clapboards, veranda floor and ceiling, olive. Trim, cornices, blinds and sashes, dark brown. Brick-work, Indian red. Outside doors, dark green. All shingles dipped in red stain and brush coated.

ACCOMMODATIONS: The principal rooms and their sizes, closets, etc., are shown by the plans. Cellar under whole house. No attic, but floored storage space.

COST: $1,335, † not including mantels, range and heater. The estimate is based on ‡ New York prices for materials and labor. In many sections of the country the cost should be less.

Price for working plans, specifications and * license to build, - - - - - - - - - - $15.00

Price for † † bill of materials, - - - 5.00

Address, THE CO-OPERATIVE BUILDING PLAN ASSOCIATION, Architects, 63 Broadway, New York.

FEASIBLE MODIFICATIONS: Heights of stories, colors, sizes of rooms and kinds of materials may be changed. Cellar may be reduced in size or omitted entirely. Porch or veranda may be extended indefinitely. All sashes, doors, blinds and trim may be factory made, which reduces cost. Gables may be shingled instead of paneled. Fireplaces and mantels may be introduced. One fireplace heater in first story may be arranged to heat two rooms in second story.

The price of working plans, specifications, etc., for a modified design varies according to the alterations required, and will be made known upon application to the Architects.

70

THE CO-OPERATIVE BUILDING PLAN ASSOCIATION, ARCHITECTS, 63 BROADWAY, NEW YORK.

*Shoppell's Modern Houses—*Designs Patented.*   *Cottage, Design No. 313*

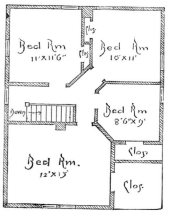

PERSPECTIVE.

DESCRIPTION.

For explanation of all symbols (* † etc.) see page 42.

GENERAL DIMENSIONS: Width, 23 ft.; depth, 30 ft., not including rear porch. Heights of stories: Cellar, 6 ft. 6 in.; first story, 9 ft.; second story, 8 ft.

EXTERIOR MATERIALS: Foundation, posts; first story, clapboards; second story and roof, shingles; gables, shingles and panels.

INTERIOR FINISH: Hard white plaster. Flooring, trim and stairway, soft wood, finished in hard oil.

COLORS: Clapboards, outside door framing for panels, and sashes, light brown. Trim, outside door panels, veranda ceiling and rain-water conductors, dark brown. Veranda floor, oiled. Wall shingles dipped in and brush coated with sienna stain. Roof shingles unpainted.

ACCOMMODATIONS: The principal rooms and their sizes, closets, etc., are shown by the floor plans. There is a cellar 10x10 ft., with plank walls, and a stairway to same from the dining room. There are four gables. A good seaside or mountain cottage.

COST: $1,287. The estimate is based on ‡ New York prices for materials and labor. In many sections of the country the cost should be less.

Price for working plans, specifications and * license to build, - - - - - - - - - - - $14.00
Price for †† bill of materials, - - - - - - - 4.00
Address, THE CO-OPERATIVE BUILDING PLAN ASSOCIATION, Architects, 63 Broadway, New York.

FEASIBLE MODIFICATIONS: Heights of stories, colors, sizes of rooms and kinds of materials may be changed. Cellar may extend under whole house or be omitted entirely. Porch may be extended across front. May be built with plank construction and paper on interior instead of plaster, at somewhat lower cost than our estimate. Estimate is for balloon frame.

The price of working plans, specifications, etc., for a modified design varies according to the alterations required, and will be made known upon application to the Architects.

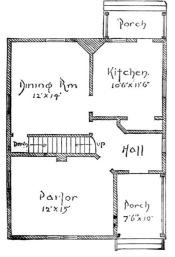

FIRST FLOOR.

SECOND FLOOR.

THE CO-OPERATIVE BUILDING PLAN ASSOCIATION, ARCHITECTS, 63 BROADWAY, NEW YORK.

*Shoppell's Modern Houses—*Designs Patented.*   *Cottage, Design No. 320*

PERSPECTIVE.

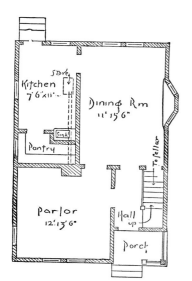

FIRST FLOOR.

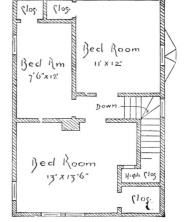

SECOND FLOOR.

DESCRIPTION.

For explanation of all symbols (* † etc.) see page 42.

GENERAL DIMENSIONS : Width, 20 ft.; depth, 30 ft. Height of stories: Cellar, 6 ft. 6 in.; first story, 9 ft.; second story, 8 ft.

EXTERIOR MATERIALS : Foundation, brick; first story, clapboards; second story and roof, shingles; gables, panels and shingles.

INTERIOR FINISH : Hard white plaster. Soft wood flooring and trim. Ash staircase. All interior wood-work finished in hard oil.

COLORS : Clapboards, veranda posts, rail and balusters, light chocolate. Trim, outside doors, sashes and rain conductors, maroon. Veranda floor, oiled. Wall shingles dipped and brush coated with oil. Roof shingles left natural color.

ACCOMMODATIONS : The principal rooms and their sizes, closets, etc., are shown by the floor plans. There is a cellar under the front portion of the house. There is space above the second story ceiling for storage. Sink in kitchen is placed in recess to economize space. Dining room has a small bay window with a window seat. May be built on a 25 foot lot and still leave passage at side. Chimney centrally located and accessible to most of the rooms.

COST : $1,356, † not including mantels, range and heater. The estimate is based on ‡ New York prices for materials and labor. In many sections of the country the cost should be less.

Price for working plans, specifications and * license to build, $15.00

Price for †† bill of materials, - - - - - - - 5.00

Address, THE CO-OPERATIVE BUILDING PLAN ASSOCIATION, Architects, 63 Broadway, New York.

FEASIBLE MODIFICATIONS : Heights of stories, colors, sizes of rooms and kinds of materials may be changed. Cellar may extend under the whole house, or be omitted entirely. The veranda may extend across the front.

The price of working plans, specifications, etc., for a modified design varies according to the alterations required, and will be made known upon application to the Architects.

72

THE CO-OPERATIVE BUILDING PLAN ASSOCIATION, ARCHITECTS, 63 BROADWAY, NEW YORK.

*Shoppell's Modern Houses—*Designs Patented.*   *Cottage, Design No. 611*

PERSPECTIVE.

DESCRIPTION.

For explanation of all symbols (* † etc.) see page 42.

GENERAL DIMENSIONS: Width, 22 ft., including bay; depth, 30 ft. 6 in. Heights of stories: Cellar, 6 ft. 6 in.; first story, 9 ft.; second story, 8 ft.

EXTERIOR MATERIALS: Foundations, brick; first story, clapboards; second story, gables and roof, shingles.

INTERIOR FINISH: Hard white plaster. Soft wood trim. Stairway ash. All interior wood-work of first story finished in hard oil, and in second story painted colors to suit owner. Stained glass in front door and staircase window.

COLORS: All clapboards, porch floor, rails, balusters and post, light brown. Trim, outside doors, brackets and cornices, medium dark brown. Veranda ceiling oiled natural color. Shingles in second story and gables dipped in and brush coated with greenish stain. Roof shingles dipped in and brush coated with silver stain.

ACCOMMODATIONS: The principal rooms and their sizes, closets, etc., are shown by the plans. Cellar under whole house. Loft floored for storage. Bay and overhang give character to the design and increase room in both stories.

COST: $1,300. The estimate is based on ‡ New York prices for materials and labor. In many sections of the country the cost should be less.

Price for working plans, specifications and * license to build, - - - - - - - - - - $15.00
Price for † † bill of materials, - - - - - 10.00

Address, THE CO-OPERATIVE BUILDING PLAN ASSOCIATION, Architects, 63 Broadway, New York.

FEASIBLE MODIFICATIONS: Heights of stories, colors, sizes of rooms and kinds of materials may be changed. Cellar may be reduced or omitted. Veranda may extend across the front. Slide to pass dishes may be placed between pantry and dining room. Fireplaces may be introduced in parlor and front bedroom.

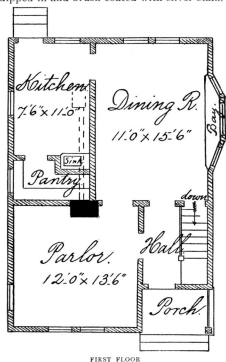

FIRST FLOOR

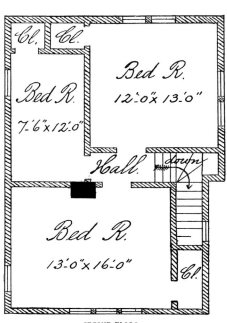

SECOND FLOOR

73

THE CO-OPERATIVE BUILDING PLAN ASSOCIATION, ARCHITECTS, 63 BROADWAY, NEW YORK.

Shoppell's Modern Houses—*Designs Patented.   *Cottage, Design No. 610*

PERSPECTIVE.

DESCRIPTION.

For explanation of all symbols (* † etc.) see page 42.

GENERAL DIMENSIONS: Width, 24 ft. 6 in.; depth, including rear porch, 35 ft. 6 in. Heights of stories: Cellar, 6 ft. 6 in.; first story, 9 ft.; second story, 8 ft.

EXTERIOR MATERIALS: Foundation, posts; first story, clapboards; second story and roofs, shingles.

INTERIOR FINISH: Hard white plaster. Trim, staircase and flooring, soft woods.

COLORS: Woodwork of foundation, including water table, dark red. Clapboards, medium light green. Trim, outside doors, sashes, porch posts, rails and balusters, dark green. Wall shingles stained and brush coated with red. Roof shingles stained and brush coated with dark brown. Brickwork painted red. Porch ceilings and floors, oiled.

ACCOMMODATIONS: The principal rooms and their sizes are shown by the floor plans. Circular cellar 10 ft. in diameter with inside entrance. Loft floored for storage. Overhang of second story gives variety and interest to the design and increases the size of the second story. All rooms may be heated by stoves. Hard wood mantel in parlor included in estimate.

COST: $1,300. The estimate is based on ‡ New York prices for materials and labor. In many sections of the country the cost should be less.

Price for working plans, specifications and * license to build, - - $15.00
Price for †† bill of materials, - - 10.00

Address, THE CO-OPERATIVE BUILDING PLAN ASSOCIATION, Architects, 63 Broadway, New York.

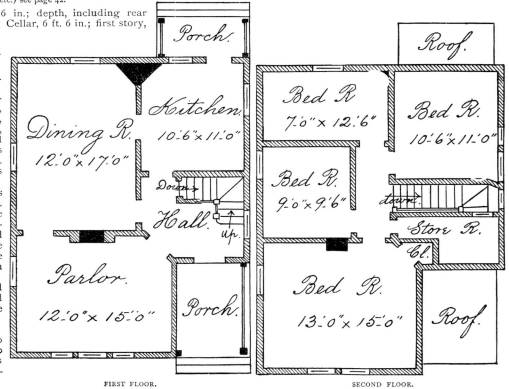

FIRST FLOOR.   SECOND FLOOR.

74

THE CO-OPERATIVE BUILDING PLAN ASSOCIATION, ARCHITECTS, 63 BROADWAY, NEW YORK.

Shoppell's Modern Houses—*Designs Patented.   *Cottage, Design No. 427*

PERSPECTIVE.

DESCRIPTION.

For explanation of all symbols (* † etc.) see page 42.

GENERAL DIMENSIONS: Width, including veranda, 28 ft.; depth, including veranda, 33 ft. 6 in. Heights of stories: first story, 9 ft.; second story, 8 ft.

EXTERIOR MATERIALS: Foundation, brick piers; first story, clapboards; second story, clapboards and shingles; gables and roofs, shingles.

INTERIOR FINISH: Hard white plaster. Flooring, trim and stairs, soft wood finished in hard oil.

COLORS: Clapboards, panels of outside doors, and sashes, light brown. Trim, framing for panels of outside doors, veranda ceiling, and rain water conductors, dark brown. Veranda floor, oiled. Brick-work, cleaned with acid. Wall shingles dipped and brush coated with sienna stain. Roof shingles left unpainted.

ACCOMMODATIONS: The principal rooms and their sizes, closets, etc., are shown by the plans. There is no cellar nor attic. The central chimney provides flues for most of the rooms in first and second stories.

COST: $1,317. The estimate is based on ‡ New York prices for materials and labor. In many sections of the country the cost should be less.

Price for working plans, specifications and * license to build, - - - - - - - - - - - $15.00

Price for †† bill of materials, - - - - - 5.00

Address, THE CO-OPERATIVE BUILDING PLAN ASSOCIATION, Architects, 63 Broadway, New York.

FEASIBLE MODIFICATIONS: Heights of stories, colors, sizes of rooms and kinds of materials may be changed. Cellar may be placed under a part or the whole of house. Size of porch may be reduced. Hallway from the front door to the kitchen may be planned by omitting the living room closet.

The price of working plans, specifications, etc., for a modified design varies according to the alterations required, and will be made known upon application to the Architects.

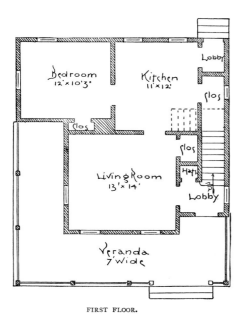

FIRST FLOOR.

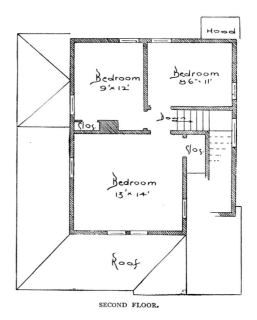

SECOND FLOOR.

75

THE CO-OPERATIVE BUILDING PLAN ASSOCIATION, ARCHITECTS, 63 BROADWAY, NEW YORK.

Shoppell's Modern Houses—*Designs Patented.   *Residence, Design No. 425*

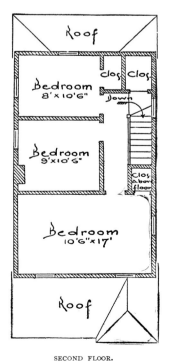

SIDE ELEVATION.

PERSPECTIVE.

DESCRIPTION.

For explanation of all symbols (* † etc.) see page 42.

GENERAL DIMENSIONS: Width, 18 ft.; depth, 41 ft. 6 in. over all. Heights of stories: Cellar, 6 ft.; first story, 8 ft. 6 in.; second story, 8 ft.

EXTERIOR MATERIALS: Foundation, brick; first story, clapboards; second story, gables, dormer and roofs, shingles.

INTERIOR FINISH: Hard white plaster. Flooring, trim and stairs, soft wood finished in hard oil.

COLORS: Clapboards, yellow stone color. Trim, outside doors, blinds, and rain conductors, bronze green. Sashes, dark red. Veranda floor, brown stone color. Veranda ceiling, oiled. Wall shingles dipped and brush coated with sienna stain. Roof shingles left unfinished.

ACCOMMODATIONS: The principal rooms and their sizes, closets, etc., are shown by the floor plans. Cellar under parlor. Fireplace in parlor with mantel included in estimate. A heater placed in parlor fireplace will heat two bedrooms in second story. There is an arch between parlor and stairway, where a curtain may be hung with good effect. The attic is floored but otherwise unfinished; it has space for two small rooms.

COST: $1,404, † not including range and heating apparatus. The estimate is based on ‡ New York prices for materials and labor. In many sections of the country the cost should be less.

Price for working plans, specifications and * license to build, - - - - - - - - - - - - - - $15.00

Price for † † bill of materials, - - - - - 5.00

Address, THE CO-OPERATIVE BUILDING PLAN ASSOCIATION, Architects, 63 Broadway, New York.

FEASIBLE MODIFICATIONS: Heights of stories, colors, sizes of rooms and kinds of materials may be changed. Cellar may extend under whole house or may be omitted. A bath-room with partial or full plumbing may be placed where two closets are shown in second story. Parlor fireplace and mantel may be omitted.

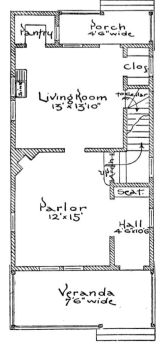

FIRST FLOOR.

SECOND FLOOR.

The price of working plans, specifications, etc., for a modified design varies according to the alterations required, and will be made known upon application to the Architects.

THE CO-OPERATIVE BUILDING PLAN ASSOCIATION, ARCHITECTS, 63 BROADWAY, NEW YORK.

Shoppell's Modern Houses—*Designs Patented.   *Cottage, Design No. 514*

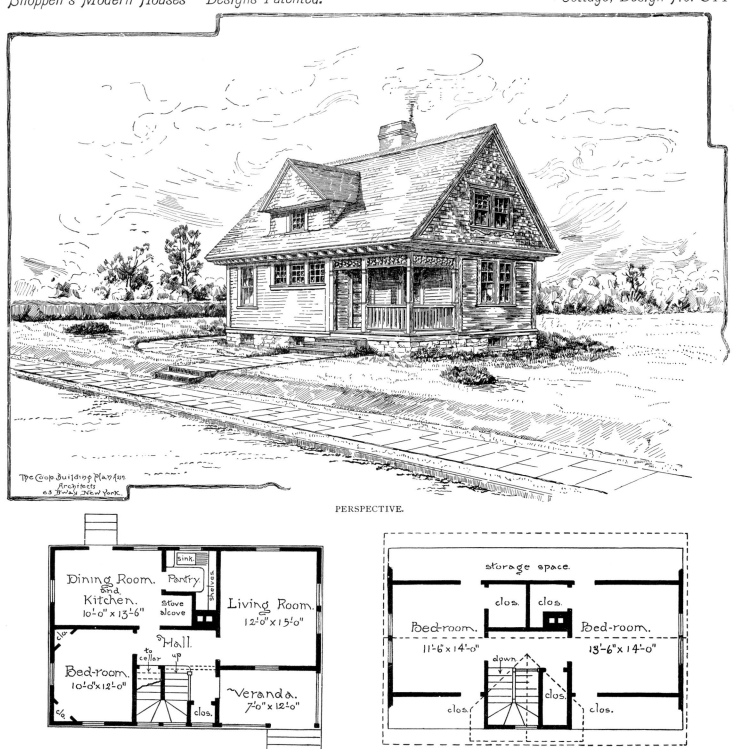

PERSPECTIVE.

FIRST FLOOR.   SECOND FLOOR.

DESCRIPTION.

For explanation of all symbols (* † etc.) see page 42.

GENERAL DIMENSIONS: Width, 34 ft.; depth, 23 ft. 6 in. Heights of stories: Cellar, 6 ft. 8 in.; first story, 9 ft.; second story, 8 ft.

EXTERIOR MATERIALS: Foundations, stone; first story, clapboards; second story gables and roof, shingles. Outside blinds.

INTERIOR FINISH: Two coat hard white plaster. Soft wood flooring, trim and stairs. Interior wood-work painted colors to suit owner. Stairs finished in hard oil.

COLORS: Clapboards, Colonial yellow. Trim, veranda posts, rails, balusters and spindles, and all cornices and other mouldings, seal brown. Outlookers under roof, red. All shingles dipped and brush coated red stain. Outside doors finished in hard oil. Sashes, red. Blinds, light seal brown. Brick-work, red. Veranda floor and ceiling, oiled.

ACCOMMODATIONS: The principal rooms and their sizes, closets, etc., are shown by the plans. Cellar under kitchen.

COST: $1,450, † not including range. The estimate is based on ‡ New York prices for materials and labor. In many sections of the country the cost should be less.

Price for working plans, specifications and * license to build, - - - - - - - - - - - - $12.00

Price for † † bill of materials, - - - - - - 3.00

Address, THE CO-OPERATIVE BUILDING PLAN ASSOCIATION, Architects, 63 Broadway, New York.

FEASIBLE MODIFICATIONS: Heights of stories, colors, sizes of rooms and kinds of materials may be changed. Cellar may be extended under whole house. Kitchen extension may be added at rear, and back stairway and bath-room introduced. Front entrance may have vestibule. Fireplaces and mantels may be introduced in living room and bedroom over same.

77

THE CO-OPERATIVE BUILDING PLAN ASSOCIATION, ARCHITECTS, 63 BROADWAY, NEW YORK.

*Shoppell's Modern Houses—*Designs Patented.*   *Cottage, Design No. 609*

PERSPECTIVE.

DESCRIPTION.

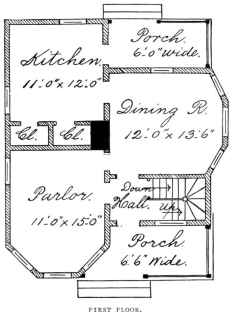

FIRST FLOOR.

For explanation of all symbols (* † etc.) see page 42.

GENERAL DIMENSIONS: Extreme width, 26 ft.; depth, 31 ft. 6 in. Heights of stories: Cellar, 7 ft.; first story, 9 ft.; second story, 8 ft.

EXTERIOR MATERIALS: Foundations, stone; first story, clapboards; second story and roof, shingles. Outside blinds to all windows except those of the cellar.

INTERIOR FINISH: Hard white plaster. Soft wood trim. Staircase, newels, rails and balusters, hard wood; all finished in hard oil. Flooring throughout, soft wood.

COLORS: Clapboards, pale yellow. Casings of doors and windows, corner boards, water table, cornices, bands, porch posts, porch rails and floors, white. Shingling on side walls and roof, silver stain. Outside doors, white with yellow panels. Blinds, white with yellow slats. Sashes, dark green. Brick-work red. Porch ceilings, finished in oil.

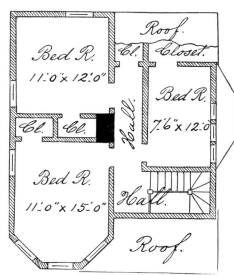

SECOND FLOOR.

ACCOMMODATIONS: The principal rooms, and their sizes, closets, etc., are shown by the plans. Cellar under the whole house. Garret loft floored for storage room. The swell front and side enlarge the important rooms, and add much to the exterior appearance. The front parapet is roofed with tin level with its top at the sides, rising a little in the center to carry off rain or snow. This parapet has the appearance of a balcony.

COST: $1,500. The estimate is based on ‡ New York prices for materials and labor. In many sections of the country the cost should be less.

Price for working plans, specifications and * license to build, - - - - - - - - - - - - - - - $15.00

Price for †† bill of materials, - - - - - - $10.00

Address, THE CO-OPERATIVE BUILDING PLAN ASSOCIATION, Architects, 63 Broadway, New York.

FEASIBLE MODIFICATIONS: Heights of stories, colors, sizes of rooms and kinds of materials may be changed. Cellar may be reduced in size or omitted. Porch may be extended around dining room side and widened. A one-story kitchen extension may be added to rear at a cost of about $150, and the present rear porch enclosed, to serve as a pantry. The present kitchen may be changed to a sitting room and connected with the parlor.

78

THE CO-OPERATIVE BUILDING PLAN ASSOCIATION, ARCHITECTS, 63 BROADWAY, NEW YORK.

*Shoppell's Modern Houses—*Designs Patented.*   *Cottage, Design No. 525*

PERSPECTIVE.

DESCRIPTION.

For explanation of all symbols (* † etc.) see page 42.

GENERAL DIMENSIONS : Width, 59 ft., including veranda; depth, 44 ft. over all. Height of first story, 11 ft.

EXTERIOR MATERIALS : Foundation, posts; first story, vertical boards; roof and gables, shingles.

INTERIOR FINISH : Walls covered with plaster board. Soft wood trim and floors. Loft floored for storage. Interior wood-work painted colors to suit owner.

COLORS : Body of first story and shingles in gables, light brown. Trim, veranda posts, cornices, sashes and blinds, dark seal brown. Outside doors, dark brown with light brown panels. Roof shingles dipped and brush coated silver stain.

ACCOMMODATIONS : The principal rooms and their sizes, closets, etc., are shown by the floor plan. There is no cellar nor attic. Designed for a warm climate or for summer occupancy. Fireplaces and mantels in hall and dining room included in estimate.

COST : $1,500, † not including range. The estimate is based on ‡ New York prices for materials and labor. In many sections of the country the cost should be less.

Price for working plans, specifications and * license to build, - - - - - - - - - - - - - - - $10.00

Price for †† bill of materials, - - - - - 5.00

Address, THE CO-OPERATIVE BUILDING PLAN ASSOCIATION, Architects, 63 Broadway, New York.

FEASIBLE MODIFICATIONS : Height of story, colors, sizes of rooms and kinds of materials may be changed. Cellar may be placed under a part or whole of house. Veranda may be reduced in size. Hollow square formed by inside veranda may be glazed on top and at rear to form a conservatory. Bath tub may be placed at end of wash trays, allowing laundry and kitchen to be connected by a door.

The price of working plans, specifications, etc., for a modified design varies according to the alterations required, and will be made known upon application to the Architects.

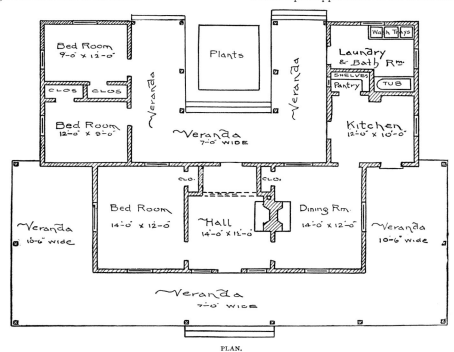

PLAN.

79

THE CO-OPERATIVE BUILDING PLAN ASSOCIATION, ARCHITECTS, 63 BROADWAY, NEW YORK.

Shoppell's Modern Houses—*Designs Patented.　　　*City Residence, Design No. 574*

FRONT ELEVATION.　　　　　SIDE ELEVATION.

DESCRIPTION.

For explanation of all symbols (* † etc.) see page 42.

GENERAL DIMENSIONS : Width, 20 ft., not including side porch ; depth, 45 ft. 6 in., including veranda and porch. Heights of stories : Cellar, 8 ft.; first story, 11 ft.; second story, 9 ft. 6 in.

EXTERIOR MATERIALS : Foundations, brick ; first and second stories, clapboards ; main roof, tin ; veranda and porch roofs, shingles.

INTERIOR FINISH : Hard white plaster. Soft wood flooring and trim. Walnut staircase. All finished in hard oil.

COLORS : All clapboards and sashes, ecru. Trim, veranda floor, and rain conductors, golden brown. Outside doors and blinds, seal brown. Veranda ceiling, buff. Brick-work, oiled. Shingle roofs, oiled ; tin roof, painted dark red.

ACCOMMODATIONS : The principal rooms and their sizes, closets, etc., are shown by the plans. Bath-room on first story with cold water supply.

COST : $1,500, † not including mantels, range and heater. The estimate is based on ‡ New York prices for materials and labor. In many sections of the country the cost should be less.

Price for working plans, specifications, and * license to build, - - - - - - - - - - - $20.00
Price for † † bill of materials, - - - - - 5.00

Address, THE CO-OPERATIVE BUILDING PLAN ASSOCIATION, Architects, 63 Broadway, New York.

FEASIBLE MODIFICATIONS : Heights of stories, sizes of rooms, materials and colors may be changed. Dining room may be placed in first story and bath-room planned as a butler's pantry with dumb waiter to basement. Full plumbing may be introduced in bathroom. Sliding door may be omitted. Size of veranda may be reduced.

The price of working plans, specifications, etc., for a modified design varies according to the alterations required, and will be made known upon application to the Architects.

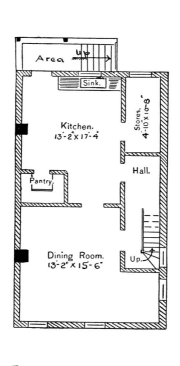

BASEMENT FLOOR.

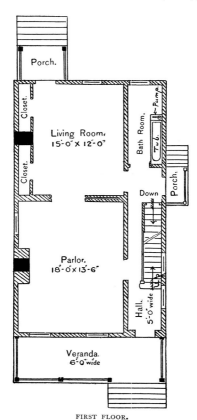

FIRST FLOOR.

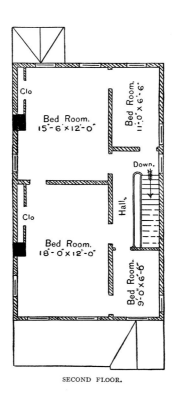

SECOND FLOOR.

80

THE CO-OPERATIVE BUILDING PLAN ASSOCIATION, ARCHITECTS, 63 BROADWAY, NEW YORK.

*Shoppell's Modern Houses—*Designs Patented.* *Cottage, Design No.* 374

PERSPECTIVE.

DESCRIPTION.

For explanation of all symbols (* † etc.) see page 42.

GENERAL DIMENSIONS: Extreme width, 28 ft. 6 in.; depth, 28 ft. 6 in., not including porches. Heights of stories: Cellar, 6 ft. 6 in.; first story, 9 ft.; second story, 8 ft.

EXTERIOR MATERIALS: Foundation, brick; first story, clapboards; second story and roof, shingles.

INTERIOR FINISH: Hard white plaster for ceilings; side walls plastered for papering. Flooring, trim and stairs, soft wood; all finished in hard oil.

COLORS: Clapboards, lattice work in front gable, sashes and piazza floor, light brown. Siding below window sills in first story, all trim, and doors, dark brown. Brick-work, dark red. Wall shingles dipped in buff stain and brush coated. Roof shingles left natural.

ACCOMMODATIONS: The principal rooms and their sizes, closets, etc., are shown by the floor plans. Cellar under dining room and hall.

COST: $1,519, † including mantel in the parlor. The estimate is based on ‡ New York prices for materials and labor. In many sections of the country the cost should be less.

Price for working plans, specifications and * license to build, - - - - - - - - - - - $15.00
Price for ‡‡ bill of materials, - - - - - 5.00
Address, THE CO-OPERATIVE BUILDING PLAN ASSOCIATION, Architects, 63 Broadway, New York.

FEASIBLE MODIFICATIONS: Heights of stories, colors, sizes of rooms and kinds of materials may be changed. Cellar may extend under whole house or be omitted entirely. Porch may be extended across front.

The price of working plans, specifications, etc., for a modified design varies according to the alterations required, and will be made known upon application to the Architects.

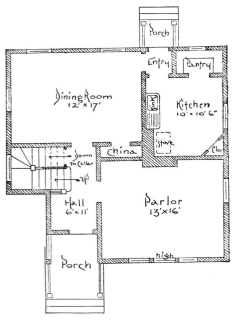

FIRST FLOOR.

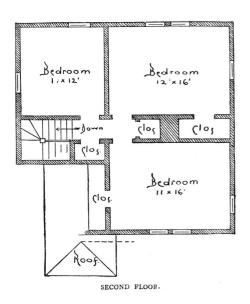

SECOND FLOOR.

81

THE CO-OPERATIVE BUILDING PLAN ASSOCIATION, ARCHITECTS, 63 BROADWAY, NEW YORK.

*Shoppell's Modern Houses—*Designs Patented.* *Cottage, Design No. 375A*

The exterior appearance of this design is the same as shown by the Perspective of No. 374, on opposite page.

DESCRIPTION.

For explanation of all symbols (* † etc.) see page 42.

GENERAL DIMENSIONS: Width, 28 ft. 6 in.; depth, including veranda, 50 ft. 10 in. Heights of stories: First story, 9 ft.; second story, 8 ft.

EXTERIOR MATERIALS: Foundation, brick piers; first story, clapboards; second story and roof, shingles.

INTERIOR FINISH: Hard white plaster ceilings; walls plastered for papering. Floors, trim and stairs, soft wood, finished in hard oil.

COLORS: Same as those specified for No. 374, on opposite page.

ACCOMMODATIONS: The principal rooms and their sizes, closets, etc., are shown by the plans. No cellar. Bath-room over kitchen.

COST: $1,888, † including mantels in parlor and library. The estimate is based on ‡ New York prices for materials and labor. In many sections of the country the cost should be less.

Price for working plans, specifications and * license to build, - - $20.00
Price for † † bill of materials, - 5.00

Address, THE CO-OPERATIVE BUILDING PLAN ASSOCIATION, Architects, 63 Broadway, New York.

FEASIBLE MODIFICATIONS: Heights of stories, sizes of rooms, colors and materials may be changed. Cellar may be placed under a part or whole of house. Veranda may be reduced. A portion or all of the plumbing may be omitted. If heating apparatus be used one chimney will suffice.

The price of working plans, specifications, etc., for a modified design varies according to the alterations required, and will be made known upon application to the Architects.

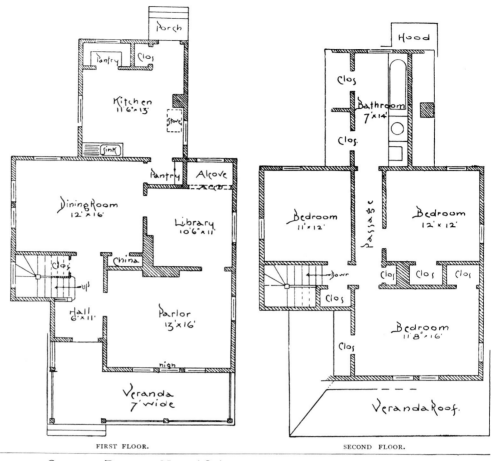

FIRST FLOOR.　　SECOND FLOOR.

Cottage Design, No. 494.

The exterior appearance of this design is the same as shown by the Perspective of No. 374, on opposite page.

DESCRIPTION.

GENERAL DIMENSIONS: Extreme width, 28 ft. 6 in.; depth, 36 ft. 4 in., including porch and stoop. Heights of stories: Cellar, 6 ft. 6 in.; first story, 9 ft.; second story, 8 ft.

EXTERIOR MATERIALS: Foundation, brick; first story, clapboards; second story, shingles; gables, panels, brackets and shingles; roof, shingles.

INTERIOR FINISH: Hard white plaster. Soft wood flooring, trim and stairway, finished in hard oil.

COLORS: Clapboards, outside door panels and outside blind slats, yellow stone color. Trim, framing of panels of outside doors

and blinds, rain conductors, and veranda floor, light brown. Veranda ceiling, buff. Brick-work, dark red. Wall shingles dipped and brush coated terra cotta stain. Roof shingles, oiled.

ACCOMMODATIONS: The principal rooms and their sizes, closets, etc., are shown by the plans. Cellar under hall, kitchen and dining room. Open fireplaces in parlor and dining room with wood mantels.

COST: $1,535, † not including mantels, range and heater. The estimate is based on ‡ New York prices for materials and labor. In many sections of the country the cost should be less.

Price for working plans, specifications and * license to build, - - - - - - - - - - - $12.00
Price for † † bill of materials, - - - - - 3.50

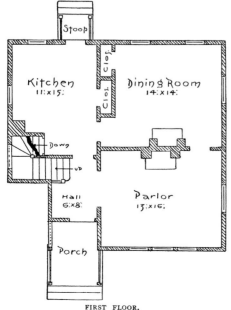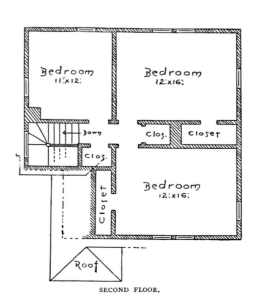

FIRST FLOOR.　　SECOND FLOOR.

82

THE CO-OPERATIVE BUILDING PLAN ASSOCIATION, ARCHITECTS, 63 BROADWAY, NEW YORK.

*Shoppell's Modern Houses—*Designs Patented.* *Cottage, Design No. 430*

PERSPECTIVE.

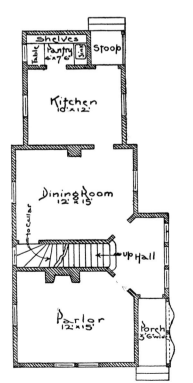

FIRST FLOOR.

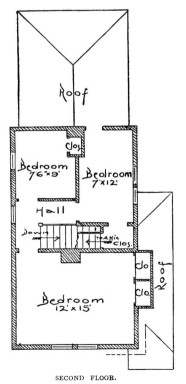

SECOND FLOOR.

Address, THE CO-OPERATIVE BUILDING PLAN ASSOCIATION, Architects, 63 Broadway, New York.

FEASIBLE MODIFICATIONS : Heights of stories, colors, sizes of rooms and kinds of materials may be changed. Cellar may extend under whole house or may be omitted entirely. Clapboards with mitred corners may be used in place of shingles. Porch may be carried across front. Kitchen extension may be two stories high.

DESCRIPTION.

For explanation of all symbols (* † etc.) see page 42.

GENERAL DIMENSIONS : Width, 20 ft.; depth, 44 ft. Heights of stories : Cellar, 6 ft. 6 in.; first story, 8 ft. 6 in.; second story, 8 ft.

EXTERIOR MATERIALS : Foundations, stone and brick ; first and second stories, veranda gables, and roofs, shingles.

INTERIOR FINISH : Hard white plaster ceilings ; side walls plastered for papering. Floors, trim and stairs, soft wood, stained with colors to suit owner, and varnished.

COLORS : Cornices, mouldings, window frames, sashes and rails, and framing for panels of front door, light brown. Door panels and panel between hall windows, dark brown. All wall shingles dipped and brush coated silver stain. Roof shingles left natural color. Porch floors and steps, dark brown. Porch ceilings, varnished.

ACCOMMODATIONS : The principal rooms and their sizes are shown by the floor plans. Cellar under the dining room. Storage space over second story and over kitchen. Fireplace and mantel in parlor included in estimate. Size and shape of this design suitable for a 25 foot lot.

COST : $1,562, † not including range and heater. The estimate is based on ‡ New York prices for materials and labor. In many sections of the country the cost should be less.

Price for working plans, specifications and * license to build, - - - - - - - - - - - - $15.00
Price for †† bill of materials, - - - - - 5.00

Second story ceilings may be made full height, in which case the attic would be available for small rooms. If heater be used one chimney will suffice.

The price for working plans, specifications, etc., for a modified design varies according to the alterations required, and will be made known upon application to the Architects.

83

THE CO-OPERATIVE BUILDING PLAN ASSOCIATION, ARCHITECTS, 63 BROADWAY, NEW YORK.

Shoppell's Modern Houses—*Designs Patented.   *Residence, Design No. 192*

PERSPECTIVE.

DESCRIPTION.

For explanation of all symbols (* † etc.) see page 42.

GENERAL DIMENSIONS: Width, 25 ft. over all; depth, 42 ft. 6 in., including veranda. Heights of stories: Cellar, 6 ft.; first story, 8 ft. 8 in.; second story, 8 ft.

EXTERIOR MATERIALS: Foundation, posts; first and second stories, clapboards; gables, upper portion of staircase annex, and roof, shingles.

INTERIOR FINISH: Hard white plaster. Soft wood floors and trim. Hard wood stairs. Kitchen wainscoted. Interior wood-work finished in hard oil.

COLORS: Clapboards, blinds and sashes, bronze green. Trim, outside doors, veranda floor, and rain conductors, seal brown. Veranda ceiling, chrome yellow. Brick-work, Indian red. Wall shingles dipped and brush coated sienna stain. Roof shingles dipped and brush coated Indian red stain.

ACCOMMODATIONS: The principal rooms and their sizes, closets, etc., are shown by the plans. Small cellar with plank walls under kitchen. Attic floored, but unfinished; space for two rooms. Two fireplaces with hard wood mantels are included in estimate. A Baltimore or fireplace heater placed in the dining room or parlor will warm two of the bedrooms and hall in second story. Stained glass in staircase windows is included in estimate.

COST: $1,646, † not including range and heater. The estimate is based on ‡ New York prices for materials and labor. In many sections of the country the cost should be less.

Price for working plans, specifications, and * license to build, - - - - - - - $20.00

Price for †† bill of materials, - - - - 5.00

Address, THE CO-OPERATIVE BUILDING PLAN ASSOCIATION, Architects, 63 Broadway, New York.

FEASIBLE MODIFICATIONS: Heights of stories, colors, sizes of rooms and kinds of materials may be changed. Cellar may extend under whole house, with brick or stone walls. Veranda may be

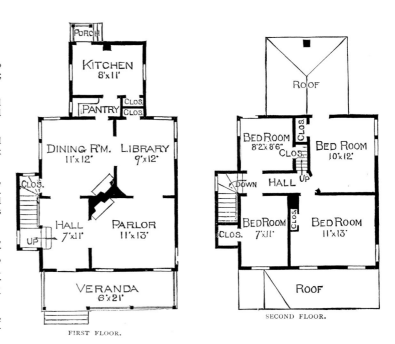

FIRST FLOOR.

SECOND FLOOR.

extended indefinitely or may be reduced to a mere porch. Bath-room may be placed in second story or attic. Kitchen extension may be made two stories high and back stairway introduced. Fireplaces and mantels may be omitted, and if heating apparatus be used one chimney will suffice. The dining room may be enlarged by omitting library.

The price of working plans, specifications, etc., for a modified design varies according to the alterations required, and will be made known upon application to the Architects.

Shoppell's Modern Houses—*Designs Patented.

Cottage, Design No. 526

PERSPECTIVE.

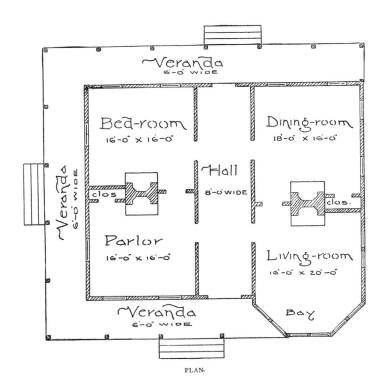

PLAN.

The price of working plans, specifications, etc., for a modified design varies according to the alterations required, and will be made known upon application to the Architects.

DESCRIPTION.

For explanation of all **symbols** (* † etc.) see page 42.

GENERAL DIMENSIONS: Width, 48 ft., including veranda ; depth, 45 ft. 6 in., including veranda. Height of first story, 12 ft.

EXTERIOR MATERIALS: Foundation, posts ; first story, clapboards and shingles ; roof, shingles.

INTERIOR FINISH: Hard white plaster. Soft wood floors and trim, finished in hard oil.

COLORS: Clapboards, yellow drab. Trim, dark drab. Outside doors and blinds, olive drab. Sashes, rain conductors and brickwork Pompeian red. Veranda floor, light drab. Veranda ceiling and rafters, light blue. Wall shingles dipped and brush coated in oil without stain. Roof shingles left unfinished.

ACCOMMODATIONS: The principal rooms and their sizes are shown by the floor plan. No cellar. Attic floored but unfinished, reached by trap-door and step-ladder ; space for two rooms. Ceiling very high. The windows above the veranda afford perfect ventilation, and if glazed with stained glass produce beautiful effect. Kitchen to be in a detached building.

COST: $1,600, † not including mantels. The estimate is based on ‡ New York prices for materials and labor. In many sections of the country the cost should be less.

Price for working plans, specifications and * license to
build, - - - - - - - - - - - - - - - $15.00
Price for †† bill of materials, - - - - - - 10.00
Address, THE CO-OPERATIVE BUILDING PLAN ASSOCIATION, Architects, 63 Broadway, New York.

FEASIBLE MODIFICATIONS: Height of story, sizes of rooms, materials and colors may be changed. Cellar may be introduced under a portion or the whole of house. Kitchen and pantries may be added at rear of dining room. Bath-room with full or partial plumbing may be planned. Fireplaces and mantels may be omitted. If house be heated by furnace one chimney will suffice.

THE CO-OPERATIVE BUILDING PLAN ASSOCIATION, ARCHITECTS, 63 BROADWAY, NEW YORK.

*Shoppell's Modern Houses—*Designs Patented.*   *Residence, Design No. 428*

PERSPECTIVE.

DESCRIPTION.

For explanation of all symbols (* † etc.) see page 42.

GENERAL DIMENSIONS: Width, 24 ft.; depth, 31 ft. Height of stories: Cellar, 6 ft.; first story, 9 ft.; second story, 8 ft.

EXTERIOR MATERIAL: Foundation brick; first story, clapboards; second story, panels and shingles; gables, panels; roof, shingles.

INTERIOR FINISH: Hard white plaster. Soft wood flooring and trim. Ash stairs. Interior wood-work finished in hard oil.

COLORS: Clapboards, outside door panels, and sashes, light brown. Trim, outside door framing for panels, blinds, veranda ceiling, and rain conductors, dark brown. Veranda floor, oiled. Wall shingles dipped and brush coated light sienna stain. Roof shingles, oiled.

ACCOMMODATIONS: The principal rooms and their sizes, closets, etc., are shown by the plans. Cellar under the kitchen, entered from outside. Space above second story is unfinished but is floored for storage. Sliding door between dining room and parlor. Cost of fireplace and mantel in dining room included in estimate.

COST: $1,657. † not including range and heater. The estimate is based on ‡ New York prices for materials and labor. In many sections of the country the cost should be less.

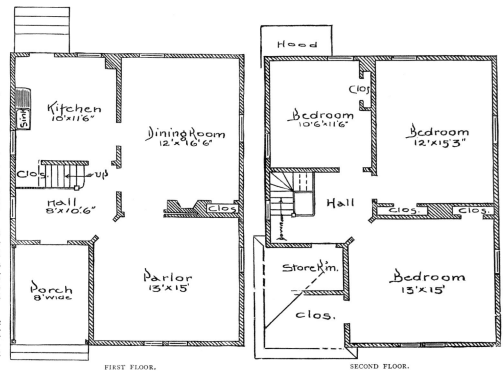

FIRST FLOOR.   SECOND FLOOR.

Price for working plans, specifications and * license to build, $18.00.

Price for †† bill of materials, $4.00.

Address, THE CO-OPERATIVE BUILDING PLAN ASSOCIATION, Architects, 63 Broadway, New York.

FEASIBLE MODIFICATIONS: Height of stories, sizes of rooms, colors and materials may be changed. Size of cellar may be enlarged. Bathroom may be introduced in second story with full or partial plumbing. Sliding door, fireplace and mantel may be omitted. If heating apparatus be used one chimney will suffice. Inside entrance to cellar may be placed under main stairway.

The price of working plans, specifications, etc. for a modified design varies according to the alterations required, and will be made known upon application to the Architects.

86

THE CO-OPERATIVE BUILDING PLAN ASSOCIATION, ARCHITECTS, 63 BROADWAY, NEW YORK.

*Shoppell's Modern Houses—*Designs Patented.*

Cottage, Design No. 423

PERSPECTIVE

ELEVATION OF RIGHT SIDE

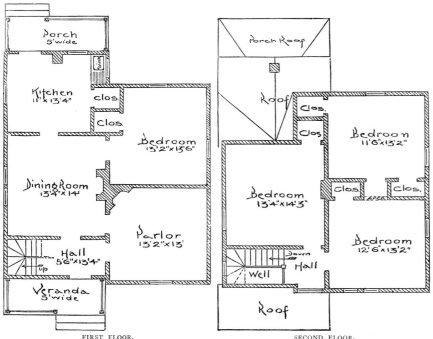

FIRST FLOOR.

SECOND FLOOR.

DESCRIPTION.

For explanation of all symbols (* † etc.) see page 42.

GENERAL DIMENSIONS: Width, 28 ft.; depth, 41 ft. 10 in. Heights of stories: First story, 9 ft.; second story, 8 ft.

EXTERIOR MATERIALS: Foundation, posts; first story, clapboards; second story, gables and roofs, shingles.

INTERIOR FINISH: Hard white plaster. Floor, trim and stairs, soft wood finished in hard oil.

COLORS: Clapboards, panels of outside doors, and sashes, light brown. Trim, blinds, framing for panels of outside doors, veranda ceiling and rain water conductors, dark brown. Veranda floor, oiled. Wall shingles dipped and brush coated sienna stain. Roof shingles natural color.

ACCOMMODATIONS: The principal rooms and their sizes. closets, etc., are shown by the plans. No cellar. No attic, but space over second story is floored for storage and is reached by a trap door. Fireplaces with mantels in dining room and parlor included in estimate. Heater placed in one of the fireplaces will warm upper story.

COST : $1,678. The estimate is based on ‡ New York prices for materials and labor. In many sections of the country the cost should be less.

Price for working plans, specifications and * license to build, - - - - - - - - - - $15.00
Price for † † bill of materials, - - - - 5.00
Address, THE CO-OPERATIVE BUILDING PLAN ASSOCIATION, Architects, 63 Broadway, New York.

FEASIBLE MODIFICATIONS: Heights of stories, sizes of rooms, colors and kinds of materials may be changed. Cellar with stone or brick walls, may be built under a portion or whole of house. Bath-room with full or partial plumbing may be planned. Fire-places and mantels may be omitted, or number reduced, If heating apparatus be used one chimney less would answer. First story bed-room may be connected with parlor and used as a library. Passage to give direct access to rear bedroom may be planned.

87

THE CO-OPERATIVE BUILDING PLAN ASSOCIATION, ARCHITECTS, 63 BROADWAY, NEW YORK.

Shoppell's Modern Houses—*Designs Patented.   *Residence, Design No. 176*

PERSPECTIVE.

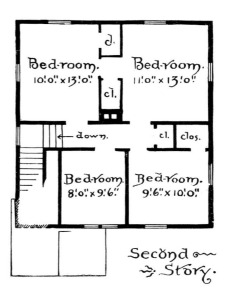

First Story.

Second Story.

DESCRIPTION.

For explanation of all symbols (* † etc.) see page 42.

GENERAL DIMENSIONS: Width, 25 ft.; depth, 27 ft. 6 in., not including veranda. Heights of stories: Cellar, 7 ft.; first story, 9 ft.; second story, 8 ft.

EXTERIOR MATERIALS: Foundations, stone; first story, clapboards; second story and roof, shingles; gables, paneled.

INTERIOR FINISH: Hard white plaster. Soft wood floor (spruce) and trim (white pine). Ash stairway. Interior wood-work finished in hard oil.

COLORS: Clapboards, framing of panels in gables, dark olive drab. Trim, veranda floor and rain-water conductors, bronze green. Outside doors, dark green. Sashes, and body of panels in gables, dark red. Veranda ceiling, varnished. Wall shingles dipped and brush coated in oil without stain. Roof shingles dipped and brush coated dark red stain.

ACCOMMODATIONS: The principal rooms and their sizes, closets, etc., are shown by the plans. Cellar under whole house. Attic floored for storage; space for two small rooms. Parlor fireplace with hard wood mantel included in estimate. Platform stairway of neat design.

COST: $1,707, † not including range and heater. The estimate is based on ‡ New York prices for materials and labor.

Price for working plans, specifications and * license to build, - - - - - - - $20.00
Price for †† bill of materials, - - - - - 5.00
Address, THE CO-OPERATIVE BUILDING PLAN ASSOCIATION, Architects, 63 Broadway, New York.

FEASIBLE MODIFICATIONS: Heights of stories, sizes of rooms, colors and materials may be changed. Hall may be enlarged by omitting hat closet. A vestibule may be added. Wide openings with either folding or sliding doors may connect parlor with hall and dining room. A bath-room may be introduced in second story small bedroom, in which case the adjoining bedroom may be enlarged. Veranda may be widened and extended indefinitely. The front bedrooms may be combined, making one large room.

88

THE CO-OPERATIVE BUILDING PLAN ASSOCIATION, ARCHITECTS, 63 BROADWAY, NEW YORK.

*Shoppell's Modern Houses—*Designs Patented.*   *Cottage, Design No. 573*

PERSPECTIVE.

DESCRIPTION.

For explanation of all symbols (* † etc.) see page 42.

GENERAL DIMENSIONS: Width, 33 ft.; depth, including veranda and porch, 40 ft. 6 in. Heights of stories: Cellar, 6 ft. 6 in.; first story, 9 ft.; second story, 8 ft.

EXTERIOR MATERIALS: Foundations, stone; first story, clapboards; second story, clapboards mitred at corners to produce shingling effect; gables, clapboards; roofs and dormer, shingles.

INTERIOR FINISH: Two coat plaster tinted to suit owner. Flooring in first story, maple, with diagonal under floor of hemlock covered with tarred paper. Second story flooring, white pine. Interior trim, white pine. Stairs, ash. Chair rail in kitchen. Interior wood-work finished in hard oil.

COLORS: All clapboards and body of panels in pediment, light brown. All trim and stiles and rails of panels in pediment, maroon. Outside doors, sashes, and rain conductors, olive. Veranda floor, tan. Veranda ceiling, Tuscan yellow. All shingles dipped and brush coated with slate-colored stain.

FIRST FLOOR.

Porch. Passage. Kitchen. 12'-0"x12'-0". Bed Room. 12'-0"x12'-0". Hall. Clos. Arch. Dining Room. 12'-0"x17'-0". Reception Hall. 19'-6"x12'-0". Veranda. 12'-0" wide.

SECOND FLOOR.

Landing. Bed Room. 12'-0"x12'-0". Bed Room 12'-0"x12'-0". Hall. Closet. Bed Room. 17'-0"x12'-0". Clos. Clos. Bed Room. 12'-0"x16'-0".

ACCOMMODATIONS: The principal rooms and their sizes, closets, etc., are shown by the floor plans. Cellar under kitchen only, remainder of house on piers. Loft over second story floored for storage. Fireplaces and mantels in dining room and reception hall included in estimate. Large veranda. Quaint and attractive design.

COST: $1,800, † not including heater and range. The estimate is based on ‡ New York prices for materials and labor. In many sections of the country the cost should be less.

Price for working plans, specifications and * license to build, - - - - - - - - - $20.00

Price for †† bill of materials, - - - - $5.00

Address, THE CO-OPERATIVE BUILDING PLAN ASSOCIATION, Architects, 63 Broadway, New York.

FEASIBLE MODIFICATIONS: Heights of stories, sizes of rooms, materials and colors may be changed. Cellar may be enlarged. Fireplaces and mantels may be omitted. One chimney will serve if heating apparatus be used. Staircase hall may be partitioned from the reception hall, and the stairway re-arranged. Bath-room may be introduced in second story. Veranda may be extended.

THE CO-OPERATIVE BUILDING PLAN ASSOCIATION, ARCHITECTS, 63 BROADWAY, NEW YORK.

*Shoppell's Modern Houses—*Designs Patented.*   *Cottage, Design No. 595*

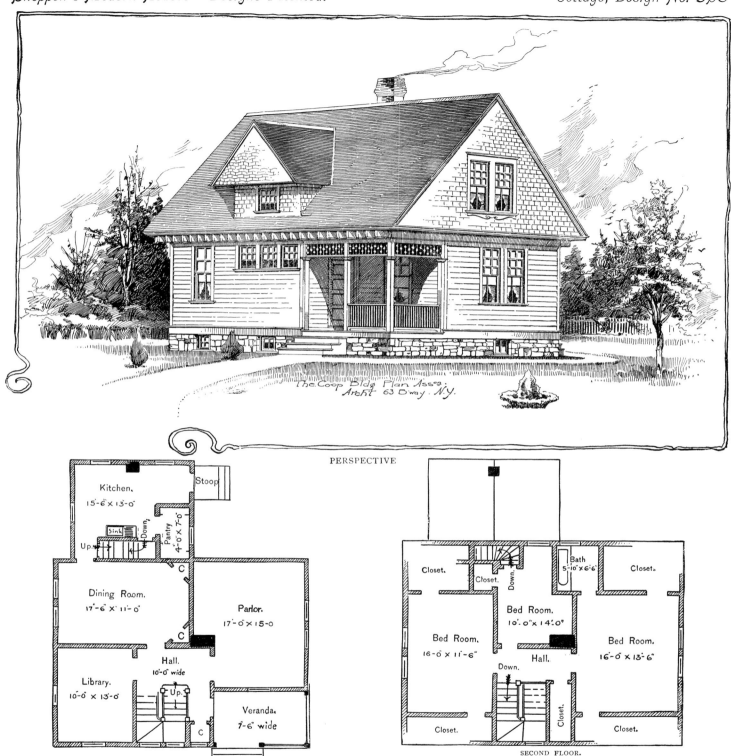

PERSPECTIVE

FIRST FLOOR.

SECOND FLOOR.

DESCRIPTION.

For explanation of all symbols (* † etc.) see page 42.

GENERAL DIMENSIONS: Width, 34 ft.; depth, 39 ft. Heights of stories: Cellar, 6 ft. 6 in.; first story, 9 ft. 6 in.; second story, 8 ft. 6 in.

EXTERIOR MATERIALS: Foundations, stone; first story, clapboards; second story and roof, shingles. Outside blinds to all windows except those of the cellar.

INTERIOR FINISH: White pine trim. Hard white plaster. Main stairway, ash. Interior wood-work finished in hard oil.

COLORS: Clapboards, outside door and blind panels, veranda ceiling, soffit under main cornice, shingles of dormers, spindles, and balusters of veranda, yellow stone color. Trim, rain-water conductors, frame of outside doors and blinds, and veranda floor, brown stone color. Brick-work stained dark red, and oiled. Outlookers or brackets under main cornice, and roof shingles, dark terra cotta. Gable shingles, Tuscan yellow.

ACCOMMODATIONS: The principal rooms and their sizes, closets, etc., are shown by the plans. Cellar under all except kitchen. Bath-room has tub with cold water supply. Stained glass in the stairway windows is included in the estimate.

COST: $1,800, † not including mantels, range and heater. The estimate is based on ‡ New York prices for materials and labor. In many sections of the country the cost should be less.

Price for working plans, specifications and * license to build, - - - - - - - - - - $20.00
Price for †† bill of materials, - - - - 10.00
Address, THE CO-OPERATIVE BUILDING PLAN ASSOCIATION, Architects, 63 Broadway, New York.

FEASIBLE MODIFICATIONS: Heights of stories, sizes of rooms, materials and colors may be changed. Cellar may be enlarged or reduced. Fireplaces and mantels may be introduced in parlor and dining room. The dining room may be connected with the parlor or library by sliding or folding doors or portiere. Full plumbing may be introduced or plumbing be entirely omitted. If heating apparatus be used one chimney will suffice. Stained glass may be omitted.

90

THE CO-OPERATIVE BUILDING PLAN ASSOCIATION, ARCHITECTS, 63 BROADWAY, NEW YORK.

*Shoppell's Modern Houses—*Designs Patented.*   *Residence, Design No. 180*

PERSPECTIVE.

DESCRIPTION.

For explanation of all symbols (* † etc.) see page 42.

GENERAL DIMENSIONS: Width, 22 ft. 6 in.; depth, 39 ft. 6 in. Heights of stories: Cellar, 6 ft. 6 in.; first story, 9 ft.; second story, 8 ft. 4 in.

EXTERIOR MATERIALS: Foundation, brick; first story, clapboards; second story, shingles; gables, shingles and panels; roof, shingles.

INTERIOR FINISH: Hard white plaster. Soft wood floor and trim. Ash stairs. All wood-work painted in colors to suit owner.

COLORS: Clapboards, olive green. Trim, cornices, and veranda floor, bronze green. Veranda ceiling, light stone color. Blinds and sashes, dark red. Outside doors, dark green. All shingles dipped and brush coated in red paint.

ACCOMMODATIONS: The principal rooms and their sizes, closets, etc., are shown by the plans. Cellar under part of house. Attic floored but unfinished; space for two small rooms. Principal rooms on first story connected by wide openings. Fireplaces with mantels in parlor, dining room and library included in estimate.

COST: $1,810, † not including range and heating apparatus. The estimate is based on ‡ New York prices for materials and labor. In many sections of the country the cost should be less.

Price for working plans, specifications and * license to build, - - - - - - - - - - - - - - $20.00

Price for †† bill of materials, - - - - - 5.00

Address, THE CO-OPERATIVE BUILDING PLAN ASSOCIATION, Architects, 63 Broadway, New York.

FEASIBLE MODIFICATIONS: Heights of stories, sizes of rooms, colors and materials may be changed. Cellar may be enlarged or omitted. Bath-room may be planned with partial or full plumbing. Number of fireplaces and mantels may be reduced. If heating apparatus be used one chimney will suffice. Sliding doors may be introduced.

FIRST FLOOR.   SECOND FLOOR.

The price of working plans, specifications, etc., for a modified design varies according to the alterations required, and will be made known upon application to the Architects.

91

THE CO-OPERATIVE BUILDING PLAN ASSOCIATION, ARCHITECTS, 63 BROADWAY, NEW YORK.

*Shoppell's Modern Houses—*Designs Patented.*   *Cottage, Design No. 593*

The Co-operative Building Plan Assocⁿ Architects, New York.

FRONT ELEVATION.

DESCRIPTION.

For explanation of all symbols (* † etc.) see page 42.

GENERAL DIMENSIONS: Width, 25 ft. 6 in.; depth, 45 ft. 6 in. Heights of stories: Cellar, 6 ft. 6 in.; first story, 9 ft.; second story, 8 ft. 4 in.

EXTERIOR MATERIALS: Foundation, brick; first story, clapboards; second story, gables, dormers and roofs, shingles. Outside blinds.

INTERIOR FINISH: Hard white plaster. White pine trim and ash stairs; all finished in hard oil. Spruce flooring. House piped for gas.

COLORS: All clapboards, spindle work on porch, body of all panels, including front door, light brown. Trim, blinds, framing of all panels, including front door, brown. Sashes, maroon. Veranda floor, tan color. Veranda ceiling, oiled. Wall shingles dipped and brush coated sienna stain. Roof shingles dipped and brush coated dark red stain.

ACCOMMODATIONS: The principal rooms and their sizes, closets, etc., are shown by the plans. Cellar under whole house, with entrance thereto from porch. House designed for one or two families. Rear stairway running from second story to cellar. Sinks and boilers in both kitchens, wash basin in bedroom of first story. Space in garret for two small rooms. Parlor mantel and fireplace with rubbed slate hearth included in estimate.

COST: $1,800, † not including ranges and heater. The estimate is based on ‡ New York prices for materials and labor. In many sections of the country the cost should be less.

Price for working plans, specifications and * license to build, - - - - - - - - - - - - - - $20.00
Price for ‡‡ bill of materials, - - - - - 10.00
Address, THE CO-OPERATIVE BUILDING PLAN ASSOCIATION, Architects, 63 Broadway, New York.

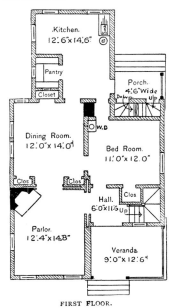

FIRST FLOOR.

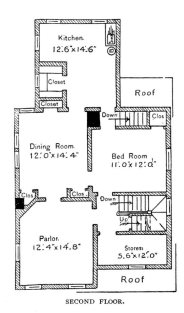

SECOND FLOOR.

FEASIBLE MODIFICATIONS: Heights of stories, sizes of rooms, materials and colors may be changed. Cellar may be reduced in size. Fireplace, sliding doors and all plumbing may be omitted. If heating apparatus be used the front chimney may be omitted.

The price of working plans, specifications, etc., for a modified design varies according to the alterations required, and will be made known upon application to the Architects.

92

THE CO-OPERATIVE BUILDING PLAN ASSOCIATION, ARCHITECTS, 63 BROADWAY, NEW YORK.

Shoppell's Modern Houses—*Designs Patented. *Residence, Design No. 255*

PERSPECTIVE

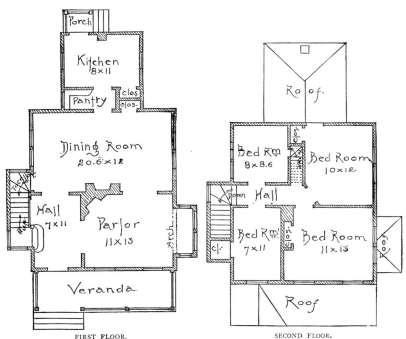

FIRST FLOOR.   SECOND FLOOR.

DESCRIPTION.

For explanation of all symbols (* † etc.) see page 42.

GENERAL DIMENSIONS: Width, 28 ft. over all; depth, 42 ft. 6 in. including veranda. Heights of stories: Cellar, 6 ft. 6 in., first story, 9 ft.; second story, 8 ft. 4 in.

EXTERIOR MATERIALS: Foundation, stone and brick; first story, clapboards; second story, clapboards and shingles; gables, panels and shingles; roof, shingles. Outside blinds to all windows except those of cellar and attic.

INTERIOR FINISH: Hard white plaster. Soft wood floor and trim. Ash staircase. Panels under dining room and parlor windows. Wainscoting in kitchen and pantry. Interior wood-work finished in hard oil.

COLORS: All clapboards, dark olive drab. Trim, sashes and outside doors, bronze green. Blinds, seal brown. Veranda floor, medium drab. Veranda ceiling, dark red. Wall shingles dipped and brush coated sienna stain. Roof shingles dipped and brush coated red stain.

ACCOMMODATIONS: The principal rooms and their sizes, closets, etc., are shown by the plans. Cellar under the main house. Attic floored; space for two rooms but none finished. The large central chimney economizes heat. Large dining room with windows at each end. Two fireplaces with mantels included in estimate.

COST: $1,952, † not including range and heater. The estimate is based on ‡ New York prices for materials and labor. In many sections of the country the cost should be less.

Price for working plans, specifications and * license to build, - - - - - - - - - - - $20.00
Price for †† bill of materials, - - - - 5.00

Address, THE CO-OPERATIVE BUILDING PLAN ASSOCIATION, Architects, 63 Broadway, New York.

FEASIBLE MODIFICATIONS: Heights of stories, sizes of rooms, colors and materials may be changed. Cellar may be enlarged or reduced. Bathroom with full or partial plumbing, may be placed in second story or attic.

The price of working plans, specifications, etc. for a modified design varies according to the alterations required, and will be made known upon application to the Architects.

93

THE CO-OPERATIVE BUILDING PLAN ASSOCIATION, ARCHITECTS, 63 BROADWAY, NEW YORK.

Shoppell's Modern Houses—*Designs Patented.

Cottage, Design No. 556

PHOTOGRAPHIC VIEW.

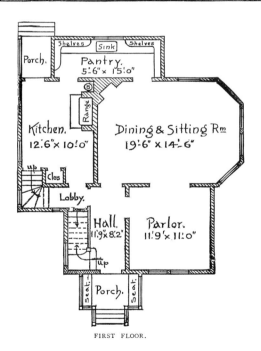

FIRST FLOOR.

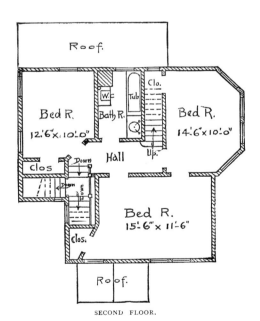

SECOND FLOOR.

DESCRIPTION.

For explanation of all symbols (* † etc.) see page 42.

GENERAL DIMENSIONS: Width through dining room and kitchen, 31 ft.; depth, including porch and pantry, 38 ft. 9 in. Heights of stories: Cellar, 8 ft.; first story, 9 ft.; second story, 8 ft.

EXTERIOR MATERIALS: Foundations, stone and brick; first story, clapboards; second story, gables and roof, shingles.

INTERIOR FINISH: Walls and ceilings covered with plaster board. Soft wood flooring and trim. Ash stairway. Kitchen and bath-room wainscoted. Interior wood-work finished natural color.

COLORS: Clapboards and veranda ceiling, light green. Trim and outside doors, bronze green. Blinds, veranda floor, and rain conductors, dark green. Sashes, Pompeian red. Brick-work, painted Indian red. Wall shingles dipped and brush coated sienna stain. Roof shingles dipped and brush coated Indian red stain.

ACCOMMODATIONS: The principal rooms and their sizes, closets, etc., are shown by the floor plans. Cellar under whole house. Attic floored but unfinished; space for one good room. Dining room fireplace with mantel included in estimate. Combined front and back stairway economizes space.

COST: $2,000, † not including range and heater. The estimate is based on ‡ New York prices for materials and labor. In many sections of the country the cost should be less.

Price for working plans, specifications and * license to build, - - - - - - - - - - $15.00
Price for † † bill of materials, - - - - - 10.00

Address, THE CO-OPERATIVE BUILDING PLAN ASSOCIATION, Architects, 63 Broadway, New York.

FEASIBLE MODIFICATIONS: Heights of stories, sizes of rooms, colors and kinds of materials may be changed. Cellar may be reduced in size, or omitted entirely. Fireplace, mantel, and a part or all of plumbing may be omitted. Sliding doors may connect parlor, hall and dining room. If plumbing be omitted the bath-room will form another bedroom, or its space may enlarge the adjoining bedroom.

THE CO-OPERATIVE BUILDING PLAN ASSOCIATION, ARCHITECTS, 63 BROADWAY, NEW YORK.

*Shoppell's Modern Houses—*Designs Patented.*   *Cottage, Design No. 635*

PERSPECTIVE.

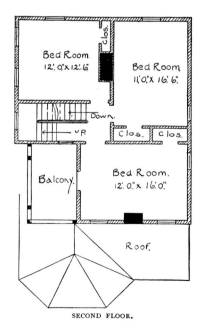

SECOND FLOOR.

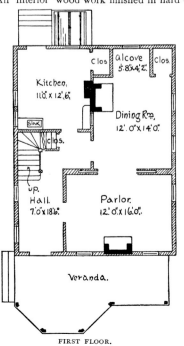

FIRST FLOOR.

DESCRIPTION.

For explanation of all symbols (* † etc.) see page 42.

GENERAL DIMENSIONS: Width, 24 ft. 8 in.; depth, including veranda, 44 ft. 8 in. Heights of stories Cellar, 7 ft.; first story, 9 ft. 6 in.; second story, 9 ft.

EXTERIOR MATERIALS: Foundations, stone; first story, clapboards; second story, shingles; gables, shingles and panels; roof, shingles.

INTERIOR FINISH: Hard white plaster throughout. Flooring and trim, white pine. Staircase, whitewood. All interior wood work finished in hard oil.

COLORS: Clapboards, sashes and veranda floor, painted light brown. Outside doors and blinds, dark brown. Shingles on walls and gables, stained buff; shingles on roofs left natural. Brick work painted Indian red. Veranda ceiling, painted yellow stone color.

ACCOMMODATIONS: The principal rooms and their sizes, closets, etc., are shown by the floor plans. In addition there is a cellar under the whole house and one finished room in the attic. There is a convenient slide for passing dishes, etc., from the kitchen to the dining room.

COST: $2000, † not including mantels, range and heater. The estimate is based on ‡ New York prices for materials and labor. In many sections of the country the cost should be less.

Price for working plans, specifications and * license to build, $20.00
Price for †† bill of materials, - - - - - 10.00

Address, THE CO-OPERATIVE BUILDING PLAN ASSOCIATION, Architects, 63 Broadway, New York.

FEASIBLE MODIFICATIONS: Heights of stories, sizes of rooms, exterior materials, interior finish, and colors, all may be changed. A room may be planned in place of the balcony. Front chimney, one or all fire-places, and sliding doors, may be omitted. Vestibule can be planned. Clapboards may be used throughout and retain the same general exterior appearance.

The price of working plans, specifications, etc. for a modified design varies according to the alterations required, and will be made known upon application to the Architects.

95

THE CO-OPERATIVE BUILDING PLAN ASSOCIATION, ARCHITECTS, 63 BROADWAY, NEW YORK.

Shoppell's Modern Houses—*Designs Patented.   *Cottage, Design No. 373*

The exterior appearance of this design is the same as that shown by the Perspective of Design No. 635.

DESCRIPTION.

For explanation of all symbols (* † etc.) see page 42.

GENERAL DIMENSIONS: Width, including veranda, 24 ft. 6 in.; depth, 43 ft., including veranda. Heights of stories: first story, 10 ft.; second story, 9 ft.

EXTERIOR MATERIALS: Foundation, brick piers; first story, clapboards; second story and roof, shingles; gables, paneled.

INTERIOR FINISH: Plastered for papering. Floor, trim and stairs, all soft wood. Interior wood-work finished in hard oil, natural color.

COLORS: Clapboards, sasnes, blinds, and panel work in front gable, light brown. Trim and outside doors, dark brown. Veranda floor and ceiling, oiled. Brick-work, painted Indian red. Wall shingles dipped and brush coated buff stain. Roof shingles left natural.

ACCOMMODATIONS: The principal rooms and their sizes, closets, etc., are shown by the plans. Attic is floored but unfinished. Fireplace and mantel included in estimate. ·

COST: $1,803, † not including range. The estimate is based on ‡ New York prices for materials and labor. In many sections of the country the cost should be less.

Price for working plans, specifications and * license to build, - - - - - - - - - $20.00
Price for † † bill of materials, - - - 5.00

Address, THE CO-OPERATIVE BUILDING PLAN ASSOCIATION, Architects, 63 Broadway, New York.

FEASIBLE MODIFICATIONS: Heights of stories, sizes of rooms, materials and colors may be changed. Cellar, with brick or stone walls, may be planned under a part or the whole of house. Bath-room with full or partial plumbing may be introduced. Stairway may be partitioned off from hall or may be re-arranged as in Design No. 635. Front chimney and fireplace may be omitted. Clapboards may be used throughout without changing general appearance. Veranda may be reduced in size.

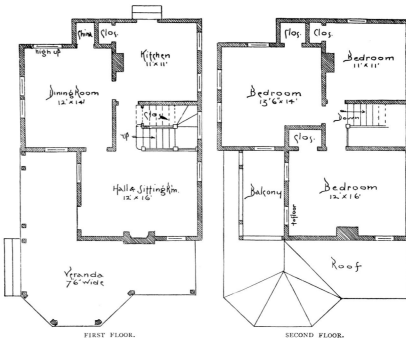

FIRST FLOOR.   SECOND FLOOR.

The price of working plans, specifications, etc., for a modified design varies according to the alterations required, and will be made known upon application to the Architects.

Cottage, Design No. 529.

The exterior appearance of this design is the same as that shown by the Perspective of Design No. 635.

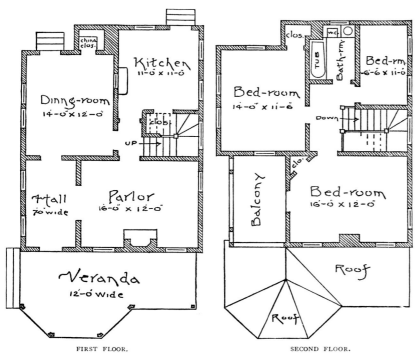

FIRST FLOOR.   SECOND FLOOR.

DESCRIPTION.

For explanation of all symbols (* † etc.) see page 42.

GENERAL DIMENSIONS: Width, 24 ft. 6 in.; depth, including veranda, 43 ft. Heights of stories: First story, 10 ft.; second story, 9 ft.

EXTERIOR MATERIALS: Foundation, brick piers; first story, clapboards; second story and roof, shingles; gables, panels and shingles. Outside blinds to all windows except those of the attic.

INTERIOR FINISH: Hard white plaster. Flooring, trim and stairway, soft wood all finished in hard oil. Bath-room wainscoted.

COLORS: Clapboards, sashes and veranda floor, light brown. Trim, outside doors, blinds, and rain conductors, dark brown. Veranda ceiling, yellow stone color. Brick-work, Indian red. Wall shingles dipped and brush coated buff stain. Roof shingles left natural.

ACCOMMODATIONS: The principal rooms and their sizes, closets, etc., are shown by the plans. Attic floored but unfinished. Fireplace with mantel in parlor. Slide for passing dishes from kitchen to dining room.

COST: $2,000, † not including range. The estimate is based on ‡ New York prices for materials and labor. In many sections of the country the cost should be less.

Price for working plans, specifications and * license to build, - - - - - - - - - $20.00
Price for † † bill of materials, - - - 10.00

Address, THE CO-OPERATIVE BUILDING PLAN ASSOCIATION, Architects, 63 Broadway, New York.

FEASIBLE MODIFICATIONS: Heights of stories, size of rooms, exterior materials, interior finish, and colors may be changed. A room may be planned in the place of balcony. Front chimney and fireplace may be omitted. A vestibule can be planned. Cellar may be placed under the whole or a part of the house.

The price of working plans, specifications, etc., for a modified design varies according to the alterations required, and will be made known upon application to the Architects.

THE CO-OPERATIVE BUILDING PLAN ASSOCIATION, ARCHITECTS, 63 BROADWAY, NEW YORK.

*Shoppell's Modern Houses—*Designs Patented.*   *Cottage, Design No. 186*

PERSPECTIVE.

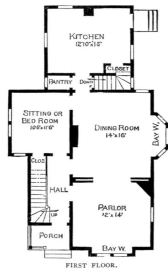

FIRST FLOOR.

SECOND FLOOR.

DESCRIPTION.

For explanation of all symbols (* † etc.) see page 42.

GENERAL DIMENSIONS: Width, 28 ft. 11 in.; depth, 47 ft. Heights of stories: Cellar, 6 ft. 6 in.; first story, 9 ft. 6 in.; second story, 9 ft.

EXTERIOR MATERIALS: Foundations, stone; first story, clapboards; second story, clapboards and shingles; roof, shingles.

INTERIOR FINISH: Sand finish plaster. Soft wood flooring (double in first story) and trim. Hard pine stairs. Interior woodwork painted in tints to suit owner and hard wood finished in hard oil.

COLORS: Clapboards of first and second stories, light brown. Trim, cornices, and porch floor, dark brown. Porch ceiling, outside doors, and sashes, olive. Shingles dipped and brush coated olive stain.

ACCOMMODATIONS: The principal rooms and their sizes, closets, etc., are shown by the plans. Cellar under rear half of house. No attic but loft is floored and ventilated. Sliding doors connect parlor and dining room. No open fireplaces, but two mantels are included in estimate.

COST: $2,000, † not including range and heater. The estimate is based on ‡ New York prices for materials and labor. In many sections of the country the cost should be less.

Price for working plans, specifications and * license to build, - - - - - - - - - - - - - - $20.00
Price for † † bill of materials, - - - - - - 5.00

Address, THE CO-OPERATIVE BUILDING PLAN ASSOCIATION, Architects, 63 Broadway, New York.

FEASIBLE MODIFICATIONS: Heights of stories, colors, sizes of rooms and kinds of materials may be changed. Cellar may be enlarged or omitted. Sliding doors and mantels may be omitted. If heating apparatus be used number of chimneys may be reduced. Bath-room with partial or full plumbing may be introduced. Either or both bay windows may be omitted. Back stairway may be introduced and kitchen extension raised another story. Porch may extend across the entire front.

The price of working plans, specifications, etc., for a modified design varies according to the alterations required, and will be made known upon application to the Architects.

THE CO-OPERATIVE BUILDING PLAN ASSOCIATION, ARCHITECTS, 63 BROADWAY, NEW YORK.

Shoppell's Modern Houses—*Designs Patented.   *Cottage, Design No. 199*

PERSPECTIVE.

DESCRIPTION.

For explanation of all symbols (* † etc.) see page 42.

GENERAL DIMENSIONS: Width, 31 ft. 6 in., including veranda; depth, 33 ft. over all. Heights of stories: Cellar, 6 ft. 6 in.; first story, 9 ft. 2 in.; second story, 9 ft.

EXTERIOR MATERIALS: Foundations, stone and brick; first story, clapboards; second story and roofs, shingles; gables, panels and shingles. Outside blinds to all windows except those of the cellar and attic.

INTERIOR FINISH: Sand finished plaster. Hard wood floor (yellow pine) in first story; soft wood floors elsewhere. Hard wood staircase and trim. Inside Venetian blinds in first story bay window. Interior wood-work finished in hard oil.

COLORS: Clapboards, piazza rafters, blinds, sashes, and panels of outside doors, olive green. Trim, cornices, and framing for panels of outside doors, bronze yellow. All shingles dipped in and brush coated with brown stain.

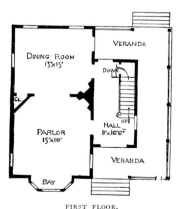

FIRST FLOOR.

SECOND FLOOR.

ACCOMMODATIONS: The principal rooms and their sizes, closets, etc., are shown by the plans. Basement under whole house with kitchen at the rear. Attic is floored, but otherwise unfinished; space for two rooms. In bedroom over hall a closet with raised floor gives stairway head room. Two fireplaces and two mantels are included in estimate.

COST: $2,030, † not including range and heater. The estimate is based on † New York prices for materials and labor. In many sections of the country the cost should be less.

Price for working plans, specifications and * license to build, - - - - - - - - - - - $24.00

Price for †† bill of materials, - - - - $4.00

Address, THE CO-OPERATIVE BUILDING PLAN ASSOCIATION, Architects, 63 Broadway, New York.

FEASIBLE MODIFICATIONS: Heights of stories, sizes of rooms, colors and kinds of materials may be changed. Cellar may be omitted. Kitchen extension may be added, connecting it with dining room by a pantry at rear of hall. Side veranda may be omitted. Bath-room with partial or full plumbing may be planned.

The price of working plans, specifications, etc., for a modified design varies according to the alterations required, and will be made known upon application to the Architects.

Shoppell's Modern Houses—*Designs Patented. *Cottage, Design No. 434*

PERSPECTIVE.

DESCRIPTION.

For explanation of all symbols (* † etc.) see page 42.

GENERAL DIMENSIONS : Width, 27 ft. 6 in.; depth, 30 ft. 6 in. Heights of stories : Cellar, 6 ft. 6 in.; first story, 9 ft.; second story, 8 ft.

EXTERIOR MATERIALS : Foundations, stone; first story, clapboards; second story, gables, dormers and roofs, shingles. Outside blinds to all windows except those of the cellar and attic.

INTERIOR FINISH : Hard white plaster. Soft wood flooring and trim. Hard wood stairs (ash). Kitchen wainscoted. Interior wood-work finished in hard oil.

COLORS : Clapboards and veranda floor, dark olive drab. Trim, and rain water conductors, bronze green. Outside doors and blinds, dark green. Sashes, bright red. Veranda ceiling, varnished. Wall shingles dipped in oil. Roof shingles left natural color.

ACCOMMODATIONS : The principal rooms and their sizes, closets, etc., are shown by the plans. Cellar under whole house with inside and outside entrances. Attic floored for storage ; space for small room, if desired. Combination front and back stairway economizes space. Open fireplaces with mantels in hall, parlor and dining room are included in estimate.

COST : $2,062 † not including range and heater. The estimate is based on ‡ New York prices for materials and labor.

Price for working plans, specifications and * license to build, - - - - - - $20.00
Price for †† bill of materials, - - - - - $5.00

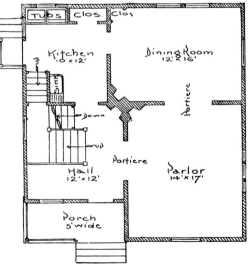

FIRST FLOOR.

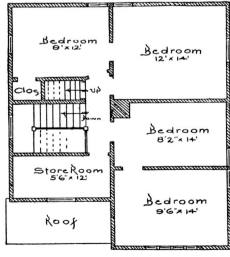

SECOND FLOOR.

Address, THE CO-OPERATIVE BUILDING PLAN ASSOCIATION, Architects, 63 Broadway, New York.

FEASIBLE MODIFICATIONS : Heights of stories, sizes of rooms, kinds of materials and colors may be changed. Fireplaces and mantels may be reduced in number or omitted altogether. The three bedrooms over parlor and dining room may be arranged to form two large bedrooms with ample closets.

99

THE CO-OPERATIVE BUILDING PLAN ASSOCIATION, ARCHITECTS, 63 BROADWAY, NEW YORK.

Shoppell's Modern Houses—*Designs Patented.　　　　　　　　　　*Residence, Design No. 258*

PERSPECTIVE.

DESCRIPTION.

For explanation of all symbols (* † etc.) see page 42.

GENERAL DIMENSIONS: Width, 24 ft. 6 in.; depth, 47 ft. 6 in. Heights of stories: Cellar, 7 ft.; first story, 9 ft.; second story, 8 ft. 6 in.

EXTERIOR MATERIALS: Foundations, stone; first story, clapboards; second story and roof, shingles; gables, panels and shingles. Outside blinds to all windows except those of the cellar and the small casements.

INTERIOR FINISH: Hard white plaster with plaster cornices and centers in hall, parlor and dining room. Soft wood floor and trim. Ash stairs. Interior wood-work, hard oil finish.

COLORS: Clapboards, brown stone color. Trim, cornices and blinds, light brown. Piazza floors, dark olive drab. Piazza ceiling, light drab. Sashes, maroon. Brick-work, Indian red. Outside doors, bronze green. Wall shingles dipped and brush coated umber stain. Roof shingles dipped and brush coated red stain.

ACCOMMODATIONS: The principal rooms and their sizes, closets, etc., are shown by the plans. Cellar under the dining room only. Attic space suitable only for storage. Dressing rooms in first and second stories. Parlor fireplace with mantel included in estimate.

COST: $2,200, † not including range and heater. The estimate is based on ‡ New York prices for materials and labor. In many sections of the country the cost should be less.

Price for working plans, specifications and * license to build, - - - - - - - - - - - - - $23.00
Price for †† bill of materials, - - - - - - 5.00
Address, THE CO-OPERATIVE BUILDING PLAN ASSOCIATION, Architects, 63 Broadway, New York.

FEASIBLE MODIFICATIONS: Heights of stories, sizes of rooms, materials and colors may be changed. Size of cellar may be enlarged. Dressing rooms may be omitted and the space thus gained thrown into hallways or used for closets. Bath-room with full or partial plumbing may be introduced in second story where dressing room is now shown.

The price of working plans, specifications, etc., for a modified design varies according to the alterations required, and will be made known upon application to the Architects.

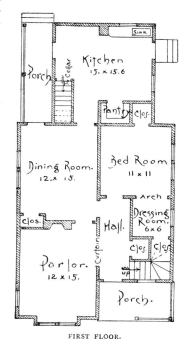

FIRST FLOOR.

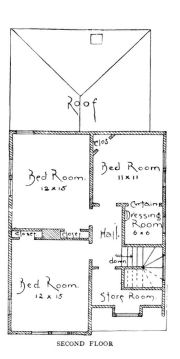

SECOND FLOOR

100

THE CO-OPERATIVE BUILDING PLAN ASSOCIATION, ARCHITECTS, 63 BROADWAY, NEW YORK.

*Shoppell's Modern Houses—*Designs Patented.*   *Residence, Design No. 579*

PHOTOGRAPHIC VIEW.

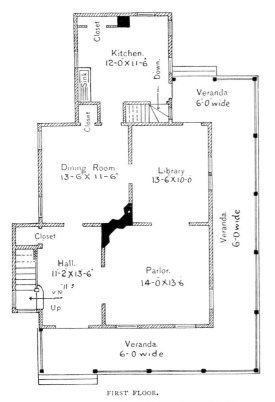

FIRST FLOOR.

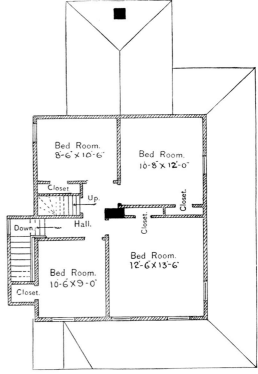

SECOND FLOOR.

DESCRIPTION.

For explanation of all symbols (* † etc.) see page 42.

GENERAL DIMENSIONS: Width over all, 32 ft. 8 in.; depth, including front veranda, 49 ft. 6 in. Heights of stories: Cellar, 6 ft. 6 in.; first story, 8 ft. 8 in.; second story, 8 ft.

EXTERIOR MATERIALS: Foundations, stone; first and second stories, clapboards; second story front and roof, shingles; gables, panels and shingles.

INTERIOR FINISH: Hard white plaster. Soft wood flooring and trim. Ash stairway. Kitchen wainscoted. Wood-work finished in hard oil.

COLORS: All clapboards, blinds and sashes, bronze green. Trim, outside doors, veranda floor, and rain water conductors, seal brown. Veranda ceiling, chrome yellow. Brick-work, Indian red. Wall shingles dipped and brush coated sienna stain. Roof shingles, dipped and brush coated Indian red stain.

ACCOMMODATIONS: The principal rooms and their sizes, closets, etc., are shown by the plans. Cellar under the kitchen. Attic floored but not finished. Two fireplaces and two mantels included in estimate. Extensive veranda.

COST: $2,200, † not including range and heater. The estimate is based on ‡ New York prices for materials and labor. In many sections of the country the cost should be less.

Price for working plans, specifications and * license to build, - - - - - - - - - - - $25.00
Price for †† bill of materials, - - - - - - 5.00

Address, THE CO-OPERATIVE BUILDING PLAN ASSOCIATION, Architects, 63 Broadway, New York.

FEASIBLE MODIFICATIONS: Heights of stories, sizes of rooms, materials and colors may be changed. Cellar may be increased in size. Fireplaces and mantels may be omitted. One chimney will suffice if heating apparatus be used. Sliding doors may be introduced. Bathroom with all necessary plumbing may be introduced in second story.

101

THE CO-OPERATIVE BUILDING PLAN ASSOCIATION, ARCHITECTS, 63 BROADWAY, NEW YORK.

Shoppell's Modern Houses—*Designs Patented.   *Cottage, Design No. 500*

_ SIDE ELEVATION _

PERSPECTIVE.

DESCRIPTION.

For explanation of all symbols (* † etc.) see page 42.

GENERAL DIMENSIONS : Width, 27 ft.; depth, 48 ft. over all. Heights of stories : Cellar, 6 ft. 6 in.; first story, 9 ft.; second story, 8 ft.

EXTERIOR MATERIALS : Foundations, stone walls ; first story, clapboards ; second story, gables and roofs, shingles. Outside blinds to all except cellar and attic windows.

INTERIOR FINISH : Sand-finished plaster. Flooring, trim and stairs, soft wood finished in hard oil.

COLORS : Clapboards, blinds, panels of outside doors, and rain conductors, maroon. Trim, framing for panels of outside doors, sashes and veranda floor, light brown. Veranda ceiling, varnished. Brick-work, Indian red. Wall shingles dipped in and brush coated with Indian red. Roof shingles left natural.

ACCOMMODATIONS : The principal rooms and their sizes, closets, etc., are shown by the floor plans. Cellar under the kitchen. Attic floored, but otherwise unfinished. Stationary tubs and earth closet in wash room. There are four gables. A good seaside or mountain cottage.

COST : $2,216. The estimate is based on ‡ New York prices for materials and labor. In many sections of the country the cost should be less.

Price for working plans, specifications and * license to build,   -   -   - $20.00

Price for † † bill of materials,   -   3.00

Address : THE CO-OPERATIVE BUILDING PLAN ASSOCIATION, Architects, 63 Broadway, New York.

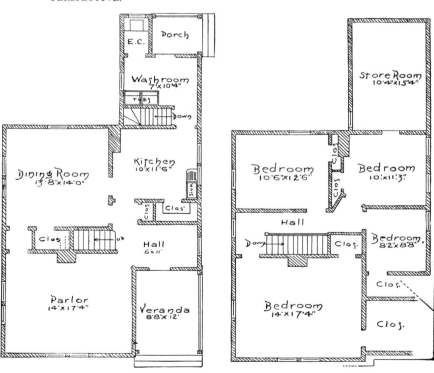

FIRST FLOOR.   SECOND FLOOR.

FEASIBLE MODIFICATIONS : Heights of stories, colors, sizes of rooms and kinds of materials may be changed. Cellar may extend under whole house, or be omitted entirely. Porch, earth closet and wash room may be omitted. Veranda may extend across the front. May be built with plank construction and paper on interior instead of plastering, at somewhat lower cost than our estimate ; estimate is for balloon frame. For a smaller house of this style see Design 313, page 70.

The price of working plans, specifications, etc., for a modified design varies according to the alterations required, and will be made known upon application to the Architects.

102

THE CO-OPERATIVE BUILDING PLAN ASSOCIATION, ARCHITECTS, 63 BROADWAY, NEW YORK.

Shoppell's Modern Houses--*Designs Patented.   *Residence, Design No. 613*

PERSPECTIVE.

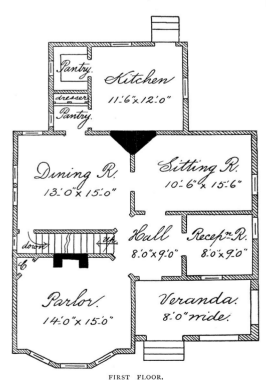

FIRST FLOOR.

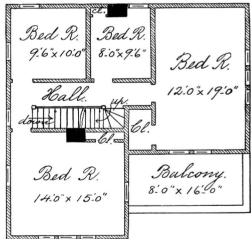

SECOND FLOOR.

DESCRIPTION.

For explanation of all symbols (* † etc.) see page 42.

GENERAL DIMENSIONS: Width, 32 ft.; depth over all, 44 ft. Heights of stories: Cellar, 7 ft.; first story, 9 ft.; second story, 8 ft.

EXTERIOR MATERIALS: Foundations, stone; first story, clapboards and shingles; second story, gables and roofs, shingles.

INTERIOR FINISH: Hard white plaster. Soft wood trim and stairway; all finished in hard oil, stained to suit owner.

COLORS: Entire body and gables painted Colonial (medium shade of) yellow. All trim, all mouldings, brackets, window and door frames, white. Outside doors treated with wood filler and finished with oil, showing natural colors. Roof shingles, oiled. Veranda ceiling and floor oiled and finished natural.

ACCOMMODATIONS: The principal rooms and their sizes, closets, etc., are shown by the plans. Cellar under main house with inside and outside entrances. Garret floored for storage. Balcony tinned and top floored. Parlor mantel included in estimate. The exterior is a combination of the Colonial and Romanesque, unusual and striking in appearance.

COST: $2,200, † not including range and heater. The estimate is based on ‡ New York prices for materials and labor. In many sections of the country the cost should be less.

Price for working plans, specifications and * license to build, - - - - - - - - - - $20.00
Price for †† bill of materials, - - - - - - 10.00

Address, THE CO-OPERATIVE BUILDING PLAN ASSOCIATION, Architects, 63 Broadway, New York.

FEASIBLE MODIFICATIONS: Heights of stories, sizes of rooms, colors and materials may be changed. Cellar may be enlarged or reduced in size. The hall may be enlarged by including the reception room. The sitting room may be used as a bedroom, the reception room serving as a dressing room. The small bedroom in second story may be converted into a bath-room.

103

THE CO-OPERATIVE BUILDING PLAN ASSOCIATION, ARCHITECTS, 63 BROADWAY, NEW YORK.

*Shoppell's Modern Houses—*Designs Patented.*   *Residence, Design No. 612*

PERSPECTIVE.

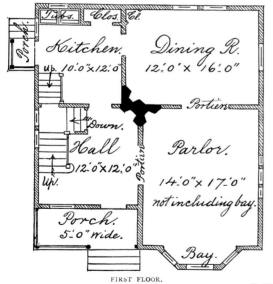

FIRST FLOOR.

SECOND FLOOR.

DESCRIPTION.

For explanation of all symbols (* † etc.) see page 42.

GENERAL DIMENSIONS : Width, including side porch, 30 ft. 6 in.; depth over all, 33 ft. Heights of stories : Cellar, 6 ft. 6 in.; first story, 9 ft.; second story, 8 ft.; attic, 7 ft. 6 in.

EXTERIOR MATERIALS : Foundations, brick ; first story, clapboards ; second story, gables, dormers and roofs, shingles.

INTERIOR FINISH : First and second stories, hard white plaster; two coat plaster in attic. Soft wood trim. Hard wood staircase. Hard wood mantels in hall, parlor and dining room. All interior wood-work stained to suit owner, and finished in hard oil.

COLORS : Clapboards, light seal brown. Trim, veranda posts, outside doors and blinds, darker seal brown. Wall shingles in second story, gables and cheeks of dormers dipped and brush coated light brown stain. Roof shingles dipped and brush coated red stain. Sashes, dark green. Brick-work, oiled. Porch floor and ceiling oiled natural color.

ACCOMMODATIONS : The principal rooms and their sizes, closets, etc., are shown by the plans. Cellar with cemented floor under whole house. One room finished in attic ; remainder of attic floored for storage. All plumbing good and substantial, but plain. Combination front and back stairway economizes space. The exterior is Colonial in style and regarded as very pleasing.

COST : $2,200, † not including range and heater. The estimate is based on ‡ New York prices for materials and labor. In many sections of the country the cost should be less.

Price for working plans, specifications and * license to build, - - - - - - - - - - $20.00
Price for †† bill of materials, - - - - 10.00
Address, THE CO-OPERATIVE BUILDING PLAN ASSOCIATION, Architects, 63 Broadway, New York.

FEASIBLE MODIFICATIONS : Heights of stories, sizes of rooms, materials and colors may be changed. Cellar may be reduced in size. Fireplaces and a part or all of the plumbing may be omitted.

104

THE CO-OPERATIVE BUILDING PLAN ASSOCIATION, ARCHITECTS, 63 BROADWAY, NEW YORK.

*Shoppell's Modern Houses—*Designs Patented.*　　　　　　　　　*Cottage, Design No. 386*

PERSPECTIVE.

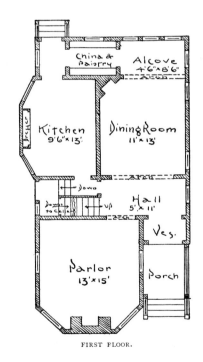

FIRST FLOOR.　　　　　　　　　SECOND FLOOR.

DESCRIPTION.

For explanation of all symbols (* † etc.) see page 42.

GENERAL DIMENSIONS: Width through dining room and kitchen, 22 ft.; depth, 40 ft. Heights of stories: Cellar, 7 ft.; first story, 9 ft.; second story, 8 ft.

EXTERIOR MATERIALS: Foundation, brick; first story, clap-boards; second story, gables, and roof, shingles. Outside blinds to all windows except front windows in parlor and cellar and attic windows.

INTERIOR FINISH: Hard white plaster; plaster cornices and centers in parlor, hall and dining room. Soft wood flooring and trim; ash stairs; all finished in hard oil.

COLORS: Clapboards and body of all paneling, Nile green. Trim, framing for panels of outside doors and other paneling, blinds and rain-water conductors, greenish drab. Sashes and brick-work, Indian red. Veranda floor, maroon. Veranda ceiling, buff. Wall shingles oiled. Roof shingles dipped in and brush coated with Indian red.

ACCOMMODATIONS: The principal rooms and their sizes, closets, etc., are shown by the plans. Cellar under hall, dining room and kitchen. Attic is floored for storage. Suitable design for 25 foot lot. A wide doorway practically makes the hall a part of the dining room. Side entrance and kitchen are directly accessible from front hall. Open fireplace in parlor, dining room and one bedroom. The kitchen and bath-room are wainscoted. Dining room alcove is a good place for plants in winter.

COST: $2,300, † not including mantels, range and heater. The estimate is based on ‡ New York prices for materials and labor. In many sections of the country the cost should be less.

Price for working plans, specifications and * license to build, - - - - - - - - - - - - $25.00
Price for † † bill of materials, - - - - - 5.00

Address, THE CO-OPERATIVE BUILDING PLAN ASSOCIATION, Architects, 63 Broadway, New York.

FEASIBLE MODIFICATIONS: Heights of stories, sizes of rooms, colors and kinds of materials may be changed. Cellar may be enlarged, reduced, or omitted entirely. Water closet may be introduced, or all plumbing omitted. Fireplaces and mantels may be omitted.

105

THE CO-OPERATIVE BUILDING PLAN ASSOCIATION, ARCHITECTS, 63 BROADWAY, NEW YORK.

Shoppell's Modern Houses—*Designs Patented.   *Residence, Design No.* 323

PERSPECTIVE.

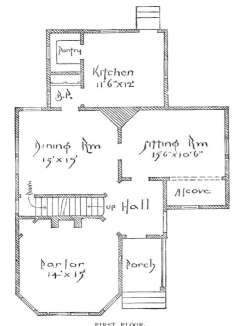

FIRST FLOOR.

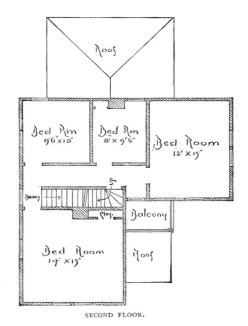

SECOND FLOOR.

DESCRIPTION.

For explanation of all symbols (* † etc.) see page 42.

GENERAL DIMENSIONS: Width through dining and sitting rooms, 32 ft.; depth over all, 44 ft. Heights of stories: Cellar, 6 ft. 6 in.; first story, 9 ft.; second story, 8 ft.

EXTERIOR MATERIALS: Foundation, brick; first story, clapboards; second story, gables and roofs, shingles. Outside blinds to all except cellar and attic windows.

INTERIOR FINISH: Hard white plaster. Soft wood floors (spruce) and trim (white pine.) Stairways, hard wood steps and risers, cherry hand rail. Interior wood-work finished in hard oil.

COLORS: Clapboards, gray stone color. Trim, outside doors, and rain conductors, dark green. Blinds, olive. Sashes, dark red. Veranda floor, gray. Veranda ceiling, varnished. Wall shingles dipped in and brush coated with red stain. Roof shingles, oiled.

ACCOMMODATIONS: The principal rooms and their sizes, closets, etc., are shown by the plans. Cellar under dining room. Attic floored but unfinished. Three hard wood mantels included in estimate. Open fireplace in parlor only.

COST: $2,216, † not including range and heater. The estimate is based on ‡ New York prices for materials and labor. In many sections of the country the cost should be less.

Price for working plans, specifications and * license to build, - - - - - - - - - - $20.00

Price for †† bill of materials, - - - - - 5.00

Address, THE CO-OPERATIVE BUILDING PLAN ASSOCIATION, Architects, 63 Broadway, New York.

FEASIBLE MODIFICATIONS: Heights of stories, colors, sizes of rooms and kinds of materials may be changed. Cellar may be enlarged or omitted entirely. A bath-room may be introduced with partial or full plumbing. Fireplaces may be planned for all rooms of first story. Kitchen extension may be made two stories.

The price of working plans, specifications, etc., for a modified design varies according to the alterations required, and will be made known upon application to the Architects.

106

THE CO-OPERATIVE BUILDING PLAN ASSOCIATION, ARCHITECTS, 63 BROADWAY, NEW YORK.

*Shoppell's Modern Houses—*Designs Patented.*

Cottage, Design No. 482

PERSPECTIVE.

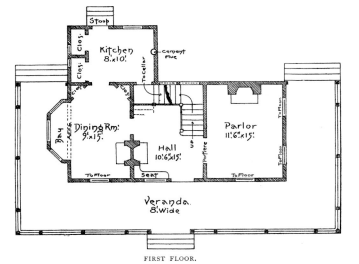

FIRST FLOOR.

SECOND FLOOR.

DESCRIPTION.

For explanation of all symbols (* † etc.) see page 42.

GENERAL DIMENSIONS: Width, including veranda, 49 ft.; depth, including veranda and kitchen, 32 ft. 6 in. Heights of stories · Cellar, 6 ft. 6 in.; first story, 10 ft.; second story, 8 ft.

EXTERIOR MATERIALS: Foundation, brick walls and piers; first story, clapboards; second story and roof, shingles; gables, shingles and lattice. Outside blinds to all windows.

INTERIOR FINISH: Hard white plaster. Soft wood flooring (spruce) and trim (white pine). Ash stairway. Interior wood-work finished in hard oil.

COLORS: Clapboards, panels of outside doors, veranda floor, and blinds, light brown. Trim, framing for panels of outside doors, and rain conductors, dark brown. Sashes, dark red. Veranda ceiling, varnished. Brick work, Indian red. Wall shingles dipped and brush coated, sienna stain. Roof shingles dipped and brush coated, dark red paint.

ACCOMMODATIONS: The principal rooms and their sizes are shown by the floor plans. Cellar under hall and dining room.

Square hall with large open fireplace. Dutch door to hall, with stained glass in upper half. Three mantels included in the estimate.

COST: $2,385, † not including range and heater. The estimate is based on ‡ New York prices for materials and labor. In many sections of the country the cost should be less.

Price for working plans, specifications and * license to build, - - - - - - - - - - - $20.00
Price for † † bill of materials, - - - - - 3.85
Address, THE CO-OPERATIVE BUILDING PLAN ASSOCIATION, Architects, 63 Broadway, New York.

FEASIBLE MODIFICATIONS: Heights of stories, colors, sizes of rooms and kinds of materials may be changed. Cellar may be enlarged, or omitted entirely. House may be placed on posts or piers. A bath-room with partial or full plumbing may be introduced.

The price of working plans, specifications, etc., for a modified design varies according to the alterations required, and will be made known upon application to the Architects.

*Shoppell's Modern Houses—*Designs Patented.*   *Residence, Design No. 594*

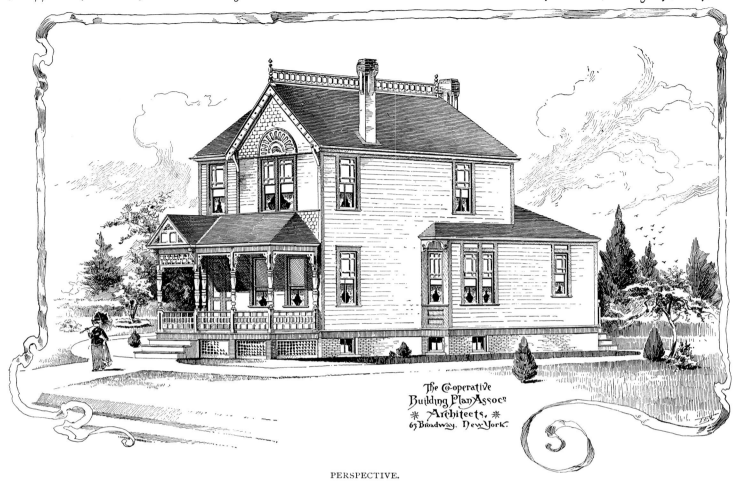

PERSPECTIVE.

DESCRIPTION.

For explanation of all symbols (* † etc.) see page 42.

GENERAL DIMENSIONS: Width, through living and bedrooms, 21 ft. 6 in.; depth, including veranda, 52 ft. 6 in. Heights of stories: Cellar, 7 ft.; first story, 10 ft.; second story, 9 ft.

EXTERIOR MATERIALS: Foundations, brick; first and second stories, clapboards; roofs, shingles. Outside blinds to all windows except those of the cellar.

INTERIOR FINISH: Plaster for papering. Trim, stairway and flooring, white pine. Kitchen wainscoted. All interior wood-work finished in hard oil.

COLORS: Clapboards, pale buff. Trim, outside doors, blinds, and rain conductors, dark green. Sashes, body of panels in gable, Tuscan yellow. Veranda floor, brown. Veranda ceiling, oiled. Framing for gable panels, buff. All shingles dipped and brush coated dark red stain.

ACCOMMODATIONS: The principal rooms and their sizes, closets, etc., are shown by the plans. Cellar under main part of house. All plumbing concentrated in or near kitchen. No fireplaces, but mantels in parlor and living room. Attic unfinished, but floored for storage. Sliding doors connect principal rooms and hall of first story.

COST: $2,300, † not including heater and range The estimate is based on ‡ New York prices for materials and labor. In many sections of the country the cost should be less.

Price for working plans, specifications and * license to build,   - - - - - - - - - - - $25.00

Price for ‡‡ bill of materials,   - - - - - 10.00

Address, THE CO-OPERATIVE BUILDING PLAN ASSOCIATION, Architects, 63 Broadway, New York.

FEASIBLE MODIFICATIONS: Heights of stories, sizes of rooms, materials and colors may be changed. Cellar may be reduced or enlarged. Sliding doors and a part or all of the plumbing may be omitted. If heating apparatus be used front chimney may be omitted. Kitchen extension may be made two stories.

The price of working plans, specifications, etc., for a modified design varies according to the alterations required, and will be made known upon application to the Architects.

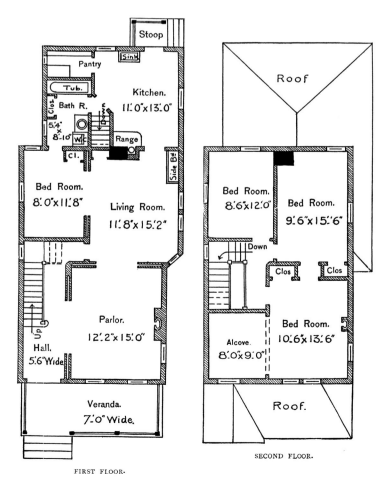

FIRST FLOOR.

SECOND FLOOR.

108

THE CO-OPERATIVE BUILDING PLAN ASSOCIATION, ARCHITECTS, 63 BROADWAY, NEW YORK.

*Shoppell's Modern Houses—*Designs Patented.*

Residence, Design No. 435

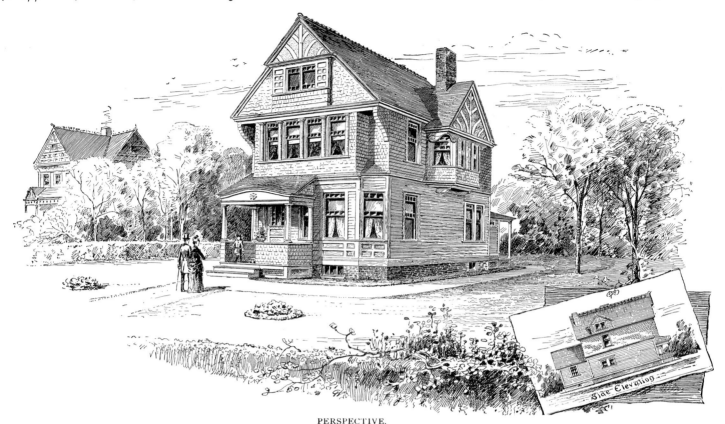

PERSPECTIVE.

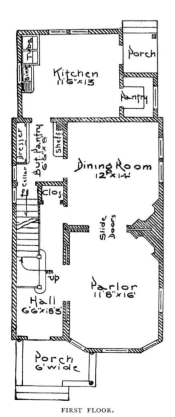

FIRST FLOOR.

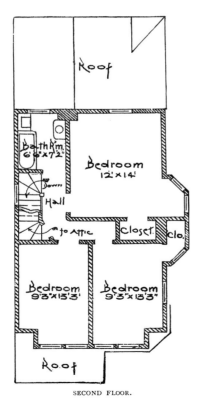

SECOND FLOOR.

The price of working plans, specifications, etc., for a modified design varies according to the alterations required, and will be made known upon application to the Architects.

DESCRIPTION.

For explanation of all symbols (* † etc.) see page 42.

GENERAL DIMENSIONS : Width, 20 ft.; depth, including veranda, 49 ft. Heights of stories : Cellar, 6 ft. 8 in.; first story, 9 ft.; second story, 8 ft. 6 in.; attic, 7 ft. 6 in.

EXTERIOR MATERIALS : Foundations, stone and brick ; first story, clapboards · second story and roof, shingles ; gables, panels and shingles.

INTERIOR FINISH : Hard white plaster ; plaster cornices and centers in parlor, dining room and hall. Soft wood flooring (white pine) and trim (white pine). Stairs, ash. All interior wood-work finished in hard oil. Bath-room and kitchen wainscoted.

COLORS : Clapboards, drark olive drab. Trim, outside doors, and sashes, bronze green. Blinds, seal brown. Veranda floor, medium drab. Veranda ceiling, dark red. Wall shingles dipped and brush coated reddish stain. Roof shingles left natural.

ACCOMMODATIONS : The principal rooms and their sizes, closets, etc., are shown by the plans. Cellar under main house. Bath-room, with tub, water closet and wash bowl, in second story. Two hard wood mantels included in estimate.

COST : $2,475, † not including range and heater. The estimate is based on ‡ New York prices for materials and labor. In many sections of the country the cost should be less.

Price for working plans, specifications and * license to build, - - - - - - - - - - - $25.00
Price for †† bill of materials, - - - - - 5.00

Address, THE CO-OPERATIVE BUILDING PLAN ASSOCIATION, Architects, 63 Broadway, New York.

FEASIBLE MODIFICATIONS : Heights of stories, sizes of rooms, colors and materials may be changed. Fireplaces and mantels and a part or all of the plumbing may be omitted. Cellar may be reduced in size or extended under entire house. If heating apparatus be used, the kitchen chimney will suffice. Porch may be extended across entire front.

109

THE CO-OPERATIVE BUILDING PLAN ASSOCIATION, ARCHITECTS, 63 BROADWAY, NEW YORK.

*Shoppell's Modern Houses—*Designs Patented.*   *Residence, Design No. 264*

PERSPECTIVE.

DESCRIPTION.

For explanation of all symbols (* † etc.) see page 42.

GENERAL DIMENSIONS: Extreme width, 32 ft.; depth, including veranda, 35 ft. Heights of stories: Cellar, 6 ft. 6 in.; first story, 9 ft.; second story, 8 ft. 3 in.

EXTERIOR MATERIALS: Foundations, stone; first story, clapboards; second story, roofs and dormers, shingles; gables, paneled and shingled. Outside blinds to all windows except those of the attic, cellar and staircase.

INTERIOR FINISH: Hard white plaster. Spruce flooring and white pine trim. Stairs, ash. Bath-room and kitchen wainscoted. All interior wood-work finished in hard oil.

COLORS: Clapboards, Oriental drab. Trim and rain conductors, olive green. Outside doors, bronze green. Blinds and sashes, dark red. Veranda floor, light drab. Veranda ceiling, varnished. Wall shingles dipped in and brush coated with reddish stain. Roof shingles dipped in and brush coated with dark red stain.

ACCOMMODATIONS: The principal rooms and their sizes, closets, etc., are shown by the plans. Cellar under the whole house. Two rooms and hall finished in attic. Stained glass in front door and staircase windows included in estimate. First story hall connects with all rooms. Two hard wood mantels included in estimate.

COST: $2,451, † not including range and heater. The estimate is based on ‡ New York prices for materials and labor. In many sections of the country the cost should be less.

Price for working plans, specifications, and * license to build, - - - - - - - - - - - $23.00

Price for †† bill of materials, - - - - - 5.00

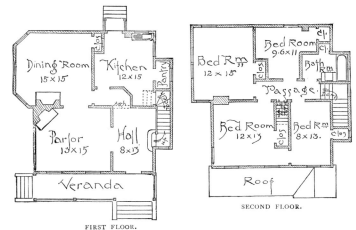

FIRST FLOOR.

SECOND FLOOR.

Address, THE CO-OPERATIVE BUILDING PLAN ASSOCIATION, Architects, 63 Broadway, New York.

FEASIBLE MODIFICATIONS: Heights of stories, sizes of rooms, colors, and kinds of materials may be changed. Cellar may be reduced or omitted. Fireplaces, plumbing and mantels may be omitted. If heating apparatus be used one chimney will suffice. Stained glass may be omitted. Veranda may be enlarged or reduced.

The price of working plans, specifications, etc., for a modified design varies according to the alterations required, and will be made known upon application to the Architects.

THE CO-OPERATIVE BUILDING PLAN ASSOCIATION, ARCHITECTS, 63 BROADWAY, NEW YORK.

*Shoppell's Modern Houses—*Designs Patented.*   Residence, Design No. 618

PERSPECTIVE.

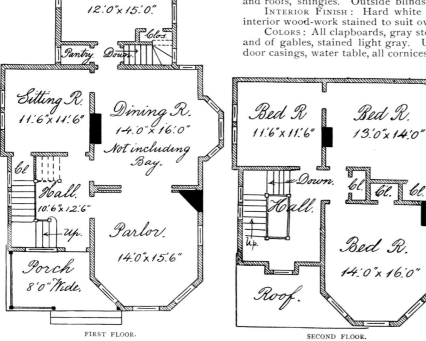

Kitchen.
12'0" x 15'0"

Clos.

Pantry.   Down.

Sitting R.
11'6" x 11'6"

Dining R.
14'0" x 16'0"
Not including
Bay.

Cl.

Hall.
10'6" x 12'6"

up.

Parlor.
14'0" x 15'6"

Porch
8'0" Wide.

FIRST FLOOR.

Bed R.
11'6" x 11'6"

Bed R.
13'0" x 14'0"

Down.

Cl.   Cl.   Cl.

Hall.

up.

Bed R.
14'0" x 16'0"

Roof.

SECOND FLOOR.

DESCRIPTION.

For explanation of all symbols (* † etc.) see page 42.

GENERAL DIMENSIONS : Width, including bay window, 30 ft.; depth, 49 ft. Heights of stories : Cellar, 7 ft.; first story, 9 ft. 6 in.; second story, 9 ft.; attic, 8 ft.

EXTERIOR MATERIALS : Foundation, brick ; first story, clapboards ; second story, gables and roofs, shingles. Outside blinds to all windows except cellar and stairway windows.

INTERIOR FINISH : Hard white plaster. Soft wood trim. Hard wood staircase. All interior wood-work stained to suit owner and finished in hard oil.

COLORS : All clapboards, gray stone color. Shingles of second story and tower up to roof, and of gables, stained light gray. Under side of gable overhang, corner boards, window and door casings, water table, all cornices and belts, medium dark drab. Doors and blinds, medium dark drab, with lighter shade of drab for panels and slats. Sashes, white. Roofs and roof ridges stained light green. Foundation walls and chimneys, red.

ACCOMMODATIONS : The principal rooms and their sizes, closets, etc. are shown by the plans. Cellar under the whole house. Two rooms and a hall finished in attic. Balcony arranged to be enclosed with glass when desired. Quaint leaded panes in hall windows. Sliding doors between parlor and dining room. If preferred, stairway may start up from rear of the hall instead of from the front.

COST : $2,500, † not including mantels, range and heater. The estimate is based on ‡ New York prices for materials and labor. In many sections of the country the cost should be less.

Price for working plans, specifications and * license to build,   - - - $20.00
Price for †† bill of materials,   10.00

Address, THE CO-OPERATIVE BUILDING PLAN ASSOCIATION, Architects, 63 Broadway, New York.

FEASIBLE MODIFICATIONS : Heights of stories, sizes of rooms, materials and colors may be changed. Sliding doors and balcony may be omitted. Two chimneys less will answer if heating apparatus be used.

THE CO-OPERATIVE BUILDING PLAN ASSOCIATION, ARCHITECTS, 63 BROADWAY, NEW YORK.

*Shoppell's Modern Houses—*Designs Patented.*   *Cottage, Design No. 636*

PERSPECTIVE.

DESCRIPTION.

For explanation of all symbols (* † etc.) see page 42.

GENERAL DIMENSIONS: Front, including veranda, 27 ft. 7 in.; depth, 44 ft. 6 in. Heights of stories: Cellar, 7 ft.; first story, 9 ft. 6 in.; second story, 8 ft. 6 in.

EXTERIOR MATERIALS: Foundations, stone; first story, clapboards; second story and gables, shingles; roofs, slate.

INTERIOR FINISH: Ceilings, hard white plaster; side walls, "plastico." Plaster cornices and centres in parlor and dining room. All floors spruce, intended for carpets. Trim throughout and stairs of soft woods stained and finished in imitation of hard woods.

COLORS: All clapboards, buff. Trim, outside doors and blinds, dark bronze green. Sashes, mahogany brown. Veranda floor, brown; veranda ceiling, oiled. Side wall and gable shingles, oiled.

ACCOMMODATIONS: The principal rooms and their sizes, closets, etc., are shown by the plans. There is a cellar under the whole house. The attic is a floored open garret, reached by a ladder through a trap door.

COST: $2500, † not including mantels, range and heater. Estimate is based on ‡ New York prices for materials and labor. In many sections of the country the cost should be less.

Price for working plans, specifications and * license to build, - $25.00
Price for †† bill of materials,   - - - - - 10.00

Address, THE CO-OPERATIVE BUILDING PLAN ASSOCIATION, Architects, 63 Broadway, New York.

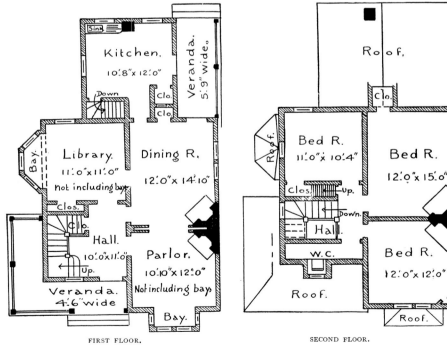

FIRST FLOOR.   SECOND FLOOR.

FEASIBLE MODIFICATIONS: Heights of stories, sizes of rooms, colors and kinds of materials may be changed. Size of cellar may be reduced and brick used for walls in place of stone. W. C. and fire-places, particularly those in second story, may be omitted.

The price of working plans, specifications, etc. for a modified design varies according to the alterations required, and will be made known upon application to the Architects.

112

THE CO-OPERATIVE BUILDING PLAN ASSOCIATION, ARCHITECTS, 63 BROADWAY, NEW YORK.

*Shoppell's Modern Houses—*Designs Patented.*　　　　　*Cottage, Design No. 555*

Evans . PHOTO'S .　　　　　HIAWATHA, KANS .

PHOTOGRAPHIC VIEW.

DESCRIPTION.

For explanation of all symbols (* † etc.) see page 42.

GENERAL DIMENSIONS : Width, 28 ft.; depth, including veranda, 49 ft. 10 in. Heights of stories : Cellar, 7 ft.; first story, 10 ft.; second story, 8 ft.

EXTERIOR MATERIALS : Foundations, stone ; first story, brick veneer ; second story, shingles ; gables, ornamental panels and shingles ; roof, slate. Outside blinds to all windows except those of the cellar and attic.

INTERIOR FINISH : Hard white plaster. Flooring in kitchen and bath-room, yellow pine ; remainder of flooring, white pine. Trim throughout, white pine. Stairway, ash. Bath-room and kitchen wainscoted. Interior wood-work finished in hard oil.

COLORS : Brick-work left natural color but cleaned down thoroughly at completion. Trim, outside doors, sashes and rain conductors, dark green. Veranda floor, dark olive drab. Veranda ceiling, light olive drab. Blinds, and veranda posts, rail and balusters, bronze green. Shingles dipped and brush coated with brownish stain.

ACCOMMODATIONS : The principal rooms and their sizes, closets, etc., are shown by the plans. Cellar under whole house. Attic floored for storage. First story is veneered on outside with 4 inches of brick-work securely fastened to sheathing and studding. Two fireplaces with hard wood mantels included in estimate. Bath-room off kitchen economizes plumbing.

COST : $2,500, † not including range and heater. The estimate is based on ‡ New York prices for materials and labor. In many sections of the country the cost should be less.

Price for working plans, specifications, and *license to build, - - - - - - $30.00
Price for † † bill of materials, - - 10.00

Address, THE CO-OPERATIVE BUILDING PLAN ASSOCIATION, Architects, 63 Broadway, New York.

FEASIBLE MODIFICATIONS : Heights of stories, sizes of rooms, colors and kinds of materials may be changed. Cellar may be reduced in size or omitted entirely. Bath-room may be changed to second story or may be omitted entirely. Fireplaces and mantels may be omitted. Sliding doors may be introduced.

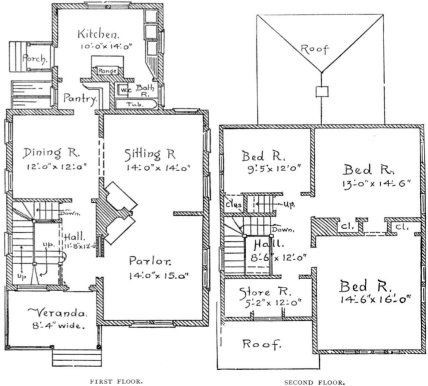

FIRST FLOOR.　　　　　SECOND FLOOR.

The price of working plans, specifications, etc., for a modified design varies according to the alterations required, and will be made known upon application to the Architects.

113

THE CO-OPERATIVE BUILDING PLAN ASSOCIATION, ARCHITECTS, 63 BROADWAY, NEW YORK.

*Shoppell's Modern Houses—*Designs Patented.*   *Residence, Design No. 628*

PERSPECTIVE

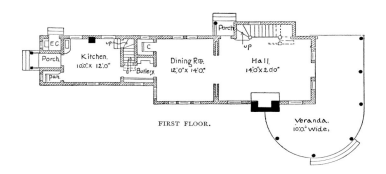

FIRST FLOOR.

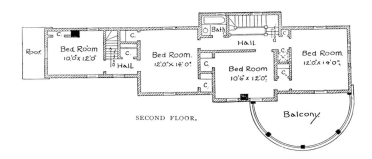

SECOND FLOOR.

DESCRIPTION.

For explanation of all symbols (* † etc.) see page 42.

GENERAL DIMENSIONS: Front (width) 17 ft. 9 in., not including veranda; depth, 56 ft. 9 in., including veranda. Heights of stories: Cellar 6 ft. 6 in.; first story, 8 ft. 6 in.; second story, 8 ft.

EXTERIOR MATERIALS: Foundations, stone; first story, clapboards; second story and gables, square butt shingles; roof, shingles.

EXTERIOR COLORS: All clapboards and shingles on side walls and gables, gray; all trim white; roof shingles, oiled. Veranda floor and ceiling, oiled.

INTERIOR FINISH: Rough brown plaster tinted, and yellow pine trim.

ACCOMMODATIONS: All the rooms and their sizes, closets, etc. are shown by the plans given herewith. Beside these there is a cellar under the whole house and storage-room in the attic. All city house conveniences are provided. Open timber ceiling in hall and dining room. A more descriptive name for the hall would be living room. Every room may have the most thorough ventilation.

Cost, with "plank" frame, $2000; with balloon frame, $2500.

"Plank" frame requires somewhat less material and labor; in appearance it is quite equal to balloon frame.

ESTIMATE is based on ‡ New York prices for materials and labor. In many sections of the country the cost should be less.

Price for working plans, specifications and * license to build, - $20.00
Price for †† bill of materials, - - - - - - 10.00

Address, THE CO-OPERATIVE BUILDING PLAN ASSOCIATION, Architects, 63 Broadway, New York.

FEASIBLE MODIFICATIONS: Heights of stories, sizes of rooms, kinds of materials, and colors may be changed. Part or all of the plumbing, the sliding doors and the earth closet may be omitted. May leave off the present kitchen and use the present dining room as a kitchen, and the present hall as a dining room.

The price of working plans, specifications, etc. for a modified design varies according to the alterations required, and will be made known upon application to the Architects.

114

THE CO-OPERATIVE BUILDING PLAN ASSOCIATION, ARCHITECTS, 63 BROADWAY, NEW YORK.

*Shoppell's Modern Houses—*Designs Patented.*   *Cottage, Design No. 331*

PERSPECTIVE.

FIRST FLOOR.   SECOND FLOOR.

DESCRIPTION.

For explanation of all symbols (* † etc.)
see page 42.

GENERAL DIMENSIONS: Extreme width, 33 ft. 6 in.; depth, 47 ft. Heights of stories: Cellar, 7 ft.; first story, 9 ft. 6 in.; second story, 9 ft.

EXTERIOR MATERIALS: Foundations, stone; first story, clapboards; second story, clapboards and shingles; roof, shingles. Outside blinds to all except attic and cellar windows.

INTERIOR FINISH: Hard white plaster; plaster cornices and centers in parlor, hall and dining room. Soft wood (white pine) flooring and trim. Ash stairs. Windows in parlor and dining room have panels below. Chair rail in dining room. Wainscot in bath-room and kitchen. Interior wood-work finished in hard oil. Two fireplaces and mantels included in estimate.

COLORS: Clapboards in first story, olive green; in second story painted to match shingles. Trim, blinds, and rain conductors, bronze green. Veranda floor, medium drab. Veranda ceiling finished in hard oil. Brick-work, Indian red. Wall shingles dipped and brush coated sienna stain. Roof shingles dipped and brush coated dark red stain.

ACCOMMODATIONS: The principal rooms and their sizes, closets, etc., are shown by the plans. Cellar with concrete floor under the whole house.

Attic floored for storage. Sliding doors connect dining room with parlor. Bath-room with tub and water-closet between kitchen and bedroom.

COST: $2,527, † not including range and heater. The estimate is based on ‡ New York prices for materials and labor. In many sections of the country the cost should be less.

Price for working plans, specifications and * license to build, - $25.00
Price for † † bill of materials,   -   -   -   -   -   -   -   -   5.00

Address, THE CO-OPERATIVE BUILDING PLAN ASSOCIATION, Architects, 63 Broadway, New York.

FEASIBLE MODIFICATIONS: Heights of stories, sizes of rooms, colors, and kinds of materials may be changed. Cellar may be reduced in size or omitted entirely. Bath-room may be placed in second story or omitted. Fireplaces and mantels may be omitted. If heating apparatus be used one chimney will suffice. Second story may be made full height, in which case there would be space for three good rooms in attic. Sliding doors may be omitted, or others introduced. Bay window may be omitted, or others added.

115

THE CO-OPERATIVE BUILDING PLAN ASSOCIATION, ARCHITECTS, 63 BROADWAY, NEW YORK.

Shoppell's Modern Houses—*Designs Patented.   *Cottage, Design No. 516*

PERSPECTIVE.

DESCRIPTION.

For explanation of all symbols (* † etc.) see page 42.

GENERAL DIMENSIONS: Width, 22 ft.; depth over all, 37 ft. 6 in. Heights of stories: Cellar, 7 ft.; first story, 9 ft.; second story, 8 ft. 4 in.

EXTERIOR MATERIALS: Foundations, stone and brick; first story, clapboards; second story and roof, shingles; gables, panels and shingles. Outside blinds to all windows except those of the parlor, cellar and attic.

INTERIOR FINISH: Hard white plaster; plaster cornices and centers in parlor, hall and dining room. Soft wood flooring and trim. Ash stairway. Panels under parlor and dining room windows. Wainscot in kitchen. All interior wood-work finished in hard oil.

COLORS: Clapboards, light chocolate. Trim, outside doors, blinds, sashes and rain conductors, maroon. Veranda floor, brown stone color. Veranda ceiling, cream color. Wall shingles dipped and brush coated sienna stain. Roof shingles dipped and brush coated dark slate stain.

ACCOMMODATIONS: The principal rooms and their sizes, closets, etc., are shown by the plans. Cellar under the whole house. Piping for furnace and necessary registers throughout the house are included in the estimate. Sliding doors connect parlor and dining room. Attic is floored for storage; there is space for two rooms if desired. Stained glass in front door and windows at side of same, also two hard wood mantels, included in the estimate.

COST: $2,529, † not including range and heater. The estimate is based on ‡ New York prices for materials and labor. In many sections of the country the cost should be less.

Price for working plans, specifications and * license to build, - - - $15.00
Price for † † bill of materials, - 4.50

Address, THE CO-OPERATIVE BUILDING PLAN ASSOCIATION, Architects, 63 Broadway, New York.

FEASIBLE MODIFICATIONS: Heights of stories, sizes of rooms, colors and kinds of materials may be changed. Cellar may be reduced in size or omitted. If heating apparatus be used one chimney will suffice. Mantels, fireplaces, sliding doors and stained glass may be omitted. Bath-room with tub and hot and cold water supply may be placed in the attic, and a water-closet in second story; or bath-room with full or partial plumbing may be placed in the second story.

The price of working plans, specifications, etc., for a modified design varies according to the alterations required, and will be made known upon application to the Architects.

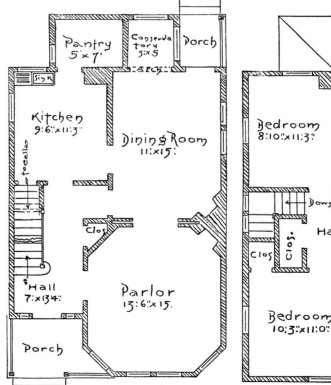

FIRST FLOOR.

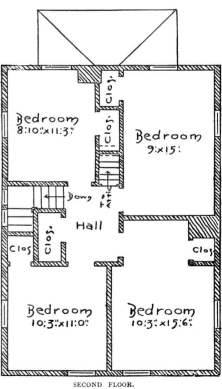

SECOND FLOOR.

THE CO-OPERATIVE BUILDING PLAN ASSOCIATION, ARCHITECTS, 63 BROADWAY, NEW YORK.

Shoppell's Modern Houses—*Designs Patented.   *Cottage, Design No. 380*

PERSPECTIVE.

DESCRIPTION.

For explanation of all symbols (* † etc.) see page 42.

GENERAL DIMENSIONS: Width over all, 32 ft.; depth, including veranda, 55 ft. 8 in. Heights of stories: Cellar, 6 ft. 6 in.; first story, 9 ft. 6 in.; second story, 9 ft.

EXTERIOR MATERIALS: Foundations, stone and brick; first story, clapboards; second story and roof, shingles; gables, shingles and panels. Outside blinds to all windows except those of the attic and cellar.

INTERIOR FINISH: Hard white plaster; plaster cornices and centers in hall, parlor, dining and sitting rooms. Soft wood flooring and trim. Ash stairway. Kitchen wainscoted. Interior wood-work finished in hard oil.

COLORS: Clapboards, Oriental drab. Trim and rain conductors, light olive green. Outside doors and framing of panels, Oriental drab; panels, light olive green. Blinds and sashes, dark red. Veranda floor, light stone color. Veranda ceiling, lilac. Brick-work, Indian red. Wall shingles dipped and brush coated sienna stain. Roof shingles dipped and brush coated dark red stain.

ACCOMMODATIONS: The principal rooms and their sizes, closets, etc., are shown by the plans. Cellar with concrete floor under kitchen, dining and sitting rooms. Attic floored for storage. Sliding doors between parlor and dining room. No plumbing except sink in kitchen. Hat and coat closet in hall. Ample head room throughout second story. Mantel shelves for parlor and dining room.

COST: $2,534, † not including range and heater. The estimate is based on ‡ New York prices for materials and labor. In many sections of the country the cost should be less.

Price for working plans, specifications, and
* license to build, - - - - - - $30.00
Price for †† bill of materials, - - - 5.00

Address, THE CO-OPERATIVE BUILDING PLAN ASSOCIATION, Architects, 63 Broadway, New York.

FEASIBLE MODIFICATIONS: Heights of stories, sizes of rooms, colors, and kinds of materials may be changed. Cellar may be reduced or enlarged; concrete floor may be omitted. Fireplaces may be introduced in principal rooms of first and second stories. Bath-room may be introduced with full or partial plumbing. Bay window may be omitted or extended up through all stories.

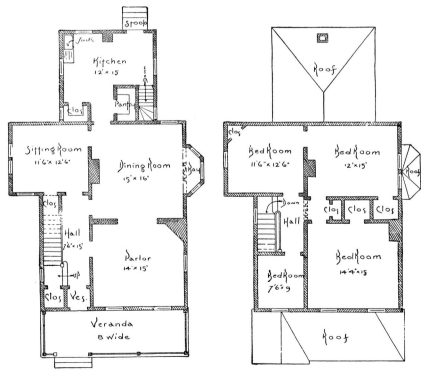

FIRST FLOOR.   SECOND FLOOR.

The price of working plans, specifications, etc., for a modified design varies according to the alterations required, and will be made known upon application to the Architects.

117

THE CO-OPERATIVE BUILDING PLAN ASSOCIATION, ARCHITECTS, 63 BROADWAY, NEW YORK.

*Shoppell's Modern Houses—*Designs Patented.*

Cottage, Design No. 442

PERSPECTIVE.

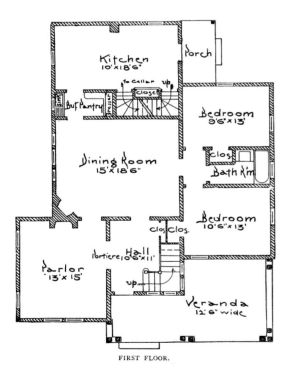

FIRST FLOOR.

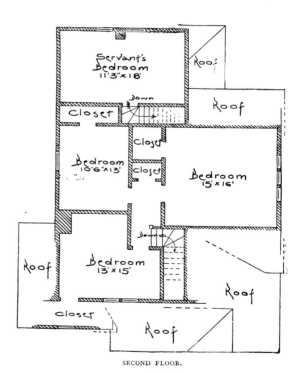

SECOND FLOOR.

DESCRIPTION.

For explanation of all symbols (* † etc.) see page 42.

GENERAL DIMENSIONS: Width, 38 ft. 6 in.; depth, 49 ft., including veranda. Heights of stories: Cellar, 6 ft. 6 in.; first story, 9 ft. 6 in.; second story, 9 ft.

EXTERIOR MATERIALS: Foundations, stone; first story, clapboards; second story and roof, shingles. Outside blinds to all windows except those of the cellar.

INTERIOR FINISH: Hard white plaster. Soft wood flooring and trim. Ash stairway. Kitchen, butler's pantry and bath-room wainscoted. Chair rail in dining room. All interior wood-work finished in hard oil.

COLORS: Clapboards, veranda floor and ceiling, brown stone color. Trim and rain conductors, medium drab. Outside doors and blinds, light brown. Sashes, Pompeian red. Wall shingles dipped and brush coated brownish stain. Roof shingles dipped and brush coated dark red stain.

ACCOMMODATIONS: The principal rooms and their sizes, closets, etc., are shown by the plans. Quaint design having a broad base

and good roof lines, well suited for a hill-top or any exposed position. Two fireplaces with wood mantels are included in estimate.

COST: $2,562, † not including range and heater. The estimate is based on ‡ New York prices for materials and labor. In many sections of the country the cost should be less.

Price for working plans, specifications and * license to build, - - - - - - - - - - $30.00
Price for †† bill of materials, - - - - - 5.00

Address, THE CO-OPERATIVE BUILDING PLAN ASSOCIATION, Architects, 63 Broadway, New York.

FEASIBLE MODIFICATIONS: Heights of stories, colors, sizes of rooms, and kinds of materials may be changed. Cellar may be enlarged, or omitted entirely. Bath-room may be transferred to second story. A part or all of plumbing may be omitted. Fireplaces and mantels may be omitted or more may be introduced. Second story hallway may be continued to connect with servant's bedroom.

118

THE CO-OPERATIVE BUILDING PLAN ASSOCIATION ARCHITECTS, 63 BROADWAY, NEW YORK.

Shoppell's Modern Houses—*Designs Patented.   *Cottage, Design No. 378*

Side Elevation

PERSPECTIVE.

DESCRIPTION.

For explanation of all symbols (* † etc.) see page 42.

GENERAL DIMENSIONS: Width, 23 ft. 6 in.; depth, 43 ft. 6 in. Heights of stories: Cellar, 6 ft. 6 in.; first story, 9 ft.; second story, 8 ft.

EXTERIOR MATERIALS: Foundations, stone and brick; first story, clapboards; second story and roof, shingles; gables, panels and shingles. Outside blinds to all windows except those of the cellar, attic and small casements.

INTERIOR FINISH: Hard white plaster. Soft wood flooring and trim. Ash staircase. Bath-room and kitchen wainscoted. Interior wood-work hard finished.

COLORS: Clapboards, olive green. Trim and rain conductors, bronze green. Outside doors, dark green. Blinds, sashes, and bands in gables, dark red. Veranda floor, yellow stone color. Veranda ceiling, light stone color. Wall shingles, oiled. Roof shingles dipped and brush coated in red stain.

ACCOMMODATIONS: The principal rooms and their sizes, closets, etc., are shown by the plans. Cellar under whole house. Attic floored, but unfinished. Heater pipes and registers are set ready for connection with furnace. Compact house with a large number of rooms. Open fireplaces with mantels in parlor, dining room and library.

COST: $2,585, † not including range and heater. The estimate is based on ‡ New York prices for materials and labor. In many sections of the country the cost should be less.

Price for working plans, specifications and * license to build, - - - - - - - - - - - - - $30.00
Price for † † bill of materials, - - - - - 5.00

Address, THE CO-OPERATIVE BUILDING PLAN ASSOCIATION, Architects, 63 Broadway, New York.

FEASIBLE MODIFICATIONS: Heights of stories, colors, sizes of rooms and kinds of materials may be changed. Cellar may be reduced in size. Heater pipes, registers, fireplaces and mantels may be omitted. If heating apparatus be used the rear chimney will suffice.

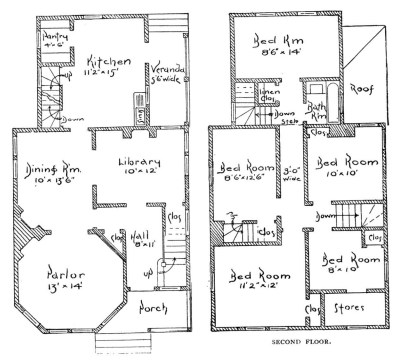

FIRST FLOOR.

SECOND FLOOR.

The price of working plans, specifications, etc., for a modified design varies according to the alterations required, and will be made known upon application to the Architects.

THE CO-OPERATIVE BUILDING PLAN ASSOCIATION, ARCHITECTS, 63 BROADWAY, NEW YORK.

*Shoppell's Modern Houses—*Designs Patented.*

Residence, Design No. 515

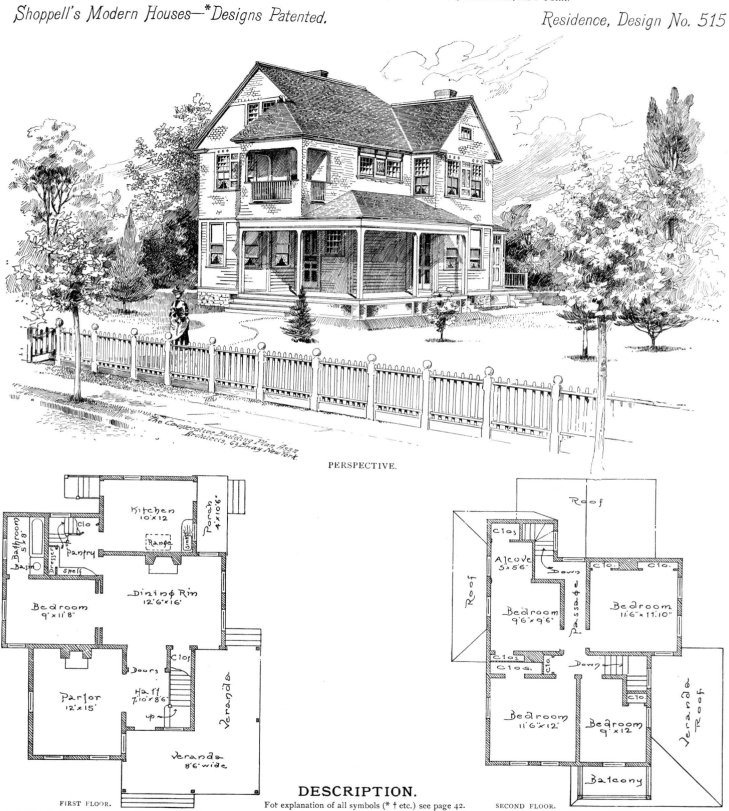

PERSPECTIVE.

FIRST FLOOR.

SECOND FLOOR.

DESCRIPTION.

For explanation of all symbols (* † etc.) see page 42.

GENERAL DIMENSIONS: Extreme width, 34 ft.; depth, 44 ft., including veranda. Heights of stories: Cellar, 6 ft. 6 in.; first story, 9 ft.; second story, 8 ft.

EXTERIOR MATERIALS: Foundations, stone walls; first story, clapboards; second story, gables, and roof, shingles. Outside blinds to all windows except those of the attic and cellar.

INTERIOR FINISH: Hard white plaster. Hard wood (ash and hard pine) flooring in first and second stories. Soft wood (white pine) trim. Ash stairs. Bath-room and kitchen wainscoted. Interior wood-work finished in hard oil.

COLORS: Clapboards, yellow drab. Trim, outside doors, blinds, and body of panels, brown stone color. Sashes and framing of panels, blue stone color. Veranda floor, medium drab. Veranda ceiling, yellow stone color. Brick-work painted Indian red. Wall shingles dipped and brush coated reddish stain. Roof shingles dipped and brush coated with dark slate color stain.

ACCOMMODATIONS: The principal rooms and their sizes, closets, etc., are shown by the plans. Cellar with inside and outside entrances and concrete floor, under dining room and kitchen. Attic is unfinished, but floored, with space for two small rooms. Open fireplaces in parlor and dining room. Front and back stairways; well lighted hall in second story.

COST: $2,600, † not including mantels, range and heater. The estimate is based on ‡ New York prices for materials and labor. In many sections of the country the cost should be less.

Price for working plans, specifications and * license to build, - $21.00
Price for † † bill of materials, - - - - - - - - 5.00

Address, THE CO-OPERATIVE BUILDING PLAN ASSOCIATION, Architects, 63 Broadway, New York.

FEASIBLE MODIFICATIONS: Heights of stories, sizes of rooms, materials and colors may be changed. Cellar may be enlarged, or omitted entirely. Front balcony may be omitted. Veranda may extend across entire front. Bath-room may be transferred to second story. Water-closet may be introduced. First story bedroom and bath-room may be used as library and study. Sliding doors, fireplaces and mantels may be omitted. If heating apparatus be used, rear chimney will be sufficient. Front chimney may be placed at outer rear corner of parlor, permitting bedroom and parlor to be connected by sliding or folding doors.

THE CO-OPERATIVE BUILDING PLAN ASSOCIATION, ARCHITECTS, 63 BROADWAY, NEW YORK.

*Shoppell's Modern Houses—*Designs Patented.*

Residence, Design No. 327

View of Rear and other Side.

PERSPECTIVE.

FIRST FLOOR.

SECOND FLOOR.

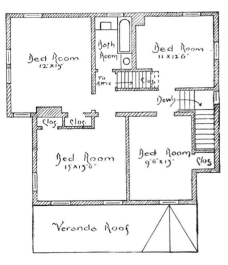

DESCRIPTION.

For explanation of all symbols (* † etc.) see page 42.

GENERAL DIMENSIONS : Extreme width, 32 ft.; depth, including veranda, 36 ft. 6 in. Heights of stories : Cellar, 6 ft. 6 in.; first story, 9 ft.; second story, 8 ft. 3 in.

EXTERIOR MATERIALS : Foundations, stone and brick ; first story, clapboards ; second story and roof, shingles ; gables, panels and shingles. Outside blinds to all windows except those of the cellar and attic.

INTERIOR FINISH : Hard white plaster ; plaster cornices and centers in hall, parlor and dining room. Soft wood flooring and trim. Ash stairs. Bath-room and kitchen wainscoted. All interior wood-work finished in hard oil.

COLORS : Clapboards, seal brown. Trim, outside doors, blinds, and veranda floor, maroon. Sashes and rain conductors, dark green. Brick-work, Indian red. Cement cornice on front, oiled. Panels in front gables, seal brown, with maroon for the frames of panels. Wall shingles dipped and brush coated light sienna stain. Roof shingles dipped and brush coated Indian red stain.

ACCOMMODATIONS : The principal rooms and their sizes, closets, etc., are shown by the plans. Cellar under hall and parlor. Attic floored, but unfinished ; space for two good rooms. Parlor and dining room directly accessible from main hall. Kitchen shut off from main part by two doors and a pantry. Bath-room centrally located and pipes well protected against freezing. Fireplaces with hard wood mantels in parlor and dining room. Slide between kitchen closet and dining room for passing dishes. Fireplace heater will warm two bedrooms of second story.

COST ; $2,604, † not including range and heater. The estimate is based on ‡ New York prices for materials and labor. In many sections of the country the cost should be less.

Price for working plans, specifications and * license to build, - $25.00
Price for †† bill of materials, - - - - - - - - - 5.00

Address, THE CO-OPERATIVE BUILDING PLAN ASSOCIATION, Architects, 63 Broadway, New York.

FEASIBLE MODIFICATIONS : Heights of stories, sizes of rooms, materials and colors may be changed. Cellar may be extended under whole house or omitted entirely. Set range may be placed in kitchen. A part or all of plumbing may be omitted. If heating apparatus be used in cellar one chimney will suffice.

121

THE CO-OPERATIVE BUILDING PLAN ASSOCIATION, ARCHITECTS, 63 BROADWAY, NEW YORK.

*Shoppell's Modern Houses—*Designs Patented.*   *Residence, Design No. 328*

The exterior appearance of this design is the same as that of No. 327, shown on the opposite page.

DESCRIPTION.

For explanation of all symbols (* † etc.) see page 42.

GENERAL DIMENSIONS: Extreme width, 32 ft.; depth, 52 ft., including veranda. Heights of stories: Cellar, 6 ft. 6 in.; first story, 9 ft.; second story, 8 ft. 3 in.

EXTERIOR MATERIALS: Foundations, stone and brick; first story, clapboards; second story and roof, shingles; gables, panels and shingles. Outside blinds to all windows except those of attic and cellar.

INTERIOR FINISH: Hard white plaster; plaster cornices and centers in hall, parlor, library and dining room. Soft wood flooring and trim. Ash stairs. Bath-room and kitchen wainscoted. Interior wood-work finished in hard oil.

COLORS; Clapboards, seal brown. Trim, outside doors, blinds, and veranda floor, maroon. Sashes and rain conductors, dark green. Brick-work, Indian red. Cement cornice on front, oiled. Panels in front gable seal brown, with maroon framing around panels. Wall shingles dipped and brush coated light sienna stain. Roof shingles dipped and brush coated Indian red stain.

ACCOMMODATIONS: The principal rooms and their sizes, closets, etc., are shown by the plans. Cellar under whole house. Attic floored, but unfinished; space for three rooms and storage. Open fireplaces in dining room and parlor with hard wood mantels.

COST: $3,362, † not including range and heater. The estimate is based on ‡ New York prices for materials and labor. In many sections of the country the cost should be less.

Price for working plans, specifications and
* license to build, - - - - . - $30.00
Price for †† bill of materials, - - - 5.00
Address, THE CO-OPERATIVE BUILDING PLAN ASSOCIATION, Architects, 63 Broadway, New York.

FEASIBLE MODIFICATIONS: Heights of stories, sizes of rooms, colors and kinds of materials may be changed. Cellar may be reduced or omitted entirely. If heating apparatus be used front chimney may be omitted. Hall and dining room may be connected, omitting the hall closet. Parlor chimney may be placed in outer rear corner of parlor, to allow a wide opening between parlor and dining room. Rear stairway may be introduced. Library may be enlarged by a bay and be used as dining room; present dining room could then be used as a library, a sitting room or a bedroom.

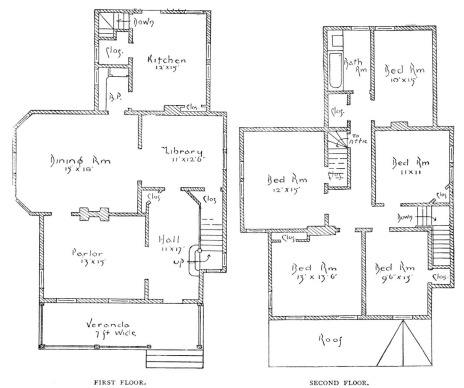

FIRST FLOOR.   SECOND FLOOR.

The price of working plans, specifications, etc., for a modified design varies according to the alterations required, and will be made known upon application to the Architects.

A Paper Model of Design No. 327.

DIRECTIONS FOR PUTTING IT TOGETHER.

AT the first glance the diagrams may appear intricate, but by commencing at No. 1 of the directions and by following the directions carefully in detail, the operation will be found to be simplicity itself, a child of ten years of age being fully competent, with ordinary care, to construct it. Of course, like everything else that is worth doing at all, it is worth doing well. The plans are accurately drawn on a scale of 3-16 of an inch to the foot. Each piece will be found to be a perfect fit if carefully adjusted according to directions.

The first requirement is a perfectly firm and level base. To secure this, cut out the ground plan and paste or gum it carefully on a block of wood of the proper size, or on thick pasteboard. The wood is preferable, as it overcomes all tendency to warping.

Use a sharp-pointed knife to score the pieces on the *dotted* lines, being careful to pass the point as nearly through the center of the dotted lines as possible. Do not cut too deep, merely enough so that on bending the paper it will make a sharp, clean angle. This should be tried first on a margin of the paper. After scoring all the dotted lines of a piece (using a straight-edge or ruler), bend all the portions so scored into perfect shape before attempting to gum them. This will give at once a clear idea of the form of the part and where and how it fits.

In some cases (for instance the base of the roofs), the colors run inside the dotted lines. This is simply to prevent raw edges of white appearing if roof pieces do not fit accurately. If proper care is used everything will fit accurately.

The gum should be as thick as possible—like pitch—so that the parts will adhere quickly and not warp. To secure this, get five cents' worth of *powdered* gum arabic at the nearest drug store and pour it into any bottle of common mucilage, stirring it thoroughly. This is necessary for rapid work and a satisfactory result.

The cornices may puzzle the beginner at first; it is simply necessary, after scoring all the dotted lines of a piece, to bend the parts so scored one under the other until they are in this position ▿, then gum the two upper horizontal surfaces together and hold them in position until they adhere firmly. The eaves of the gables of the main roof assume this form ▿. All the moldings or cornices of a piece should be firmly gummed (making them take as little room as possible) before attaching the pieces in place.

In setting up the four walls of the main building and the walls of the projections, care should be taken that they come accurately to the lines on the ground plan, as a poor beginning makes a worse ending.

Perspective views of the cottage as it appears when completed are shown as follows:

The different parts go together in the following order:
1.—A. & B.   Front and one Side Wall.
" 1.—C.   Side Wall.
" 1.—D.   Rear Wall.

NOTE.—It is better to attach these four walls together before fastening them to the ground plan; taking care to adjust the end of No. 1.—C and No. 1.—B marked "X" to the points on No. 1.—D marked "XX" as No. 1.—D projects beyond the others at both ends.

No. 2.—A.   Base of Projection (octagonal), on Wall No. 1.—B.
" 2.—B.   Piece forming brackets and base of upper portion of projection.
" 2.—C.   Walls of upper portion of projection (rectangular).
" 2.—D.   Portion of roof of same with cornices.

NOTE.—Wherever cornices or moldings occur they should be bent and gummed in shape before attaching the piece of which they are a part, in its place.

No. 3.—A.   Walls of Projection on side No. 1.—C.
" 3.—B.   Piece forming cornice and base of Roof of same.
" 3.—C.   Piece forming cornice and base of gable of same.
" 3.—D.   Part of Gable Roof. } Put these together and then fasten
3.—E.   Gable Piece. { in place.

NOTE.—Where brackets occur in this explanation the pieces enclosed by them are to be fastened together before attaching to building.

No. 3.—F.   Roof on lower portion of projection. }
" 3.—G.   Gable end of same. }

No. 4.—A.   Front and sides of Piazza. }
" 4.—B.   Floor of Piazza. }
" 4.—C.   Piece forming cornice and base of Roof.
" 4.—D.   Roof of Piazza. }
" 4.—E.   Gable end of Roof. }
" 4.—F.   Gable end of Roof. }
" 4.—G.   Gable Roof over Entrance. }
" 4.—H.   Gable Front over Entrance. }
No. 5.—   Main Roof.

NOTE.—Care should be taken that all the cornices and moldings on this piece should be firmly and *accurately* fastened before putting it in place; and it should not be fastened in position till all the walls, piazza, etc., are firmly adjusted.

No. 6.—A.   Front Gable Roof.
" 6.—B.   Gable Piece showing ornaments at lower corners. }
" 6.—C.   Front Gable Piece with ogee at bottom. }

NOTE.—The curves of the ogee to be got with back of knife blade—curling the strid lightly, back and front, until it comes to its place.

No. 6.—D.   Brackets under eaves at corners.
" 7.—   Front steps to Piazza.

NOTE.—The dotted lines on stairs marked "X" are to be slightly scored from *back* of paper, so as to bend an opposite direction.

No. 8.—A.   Platform and steps at Rear Door.
" 8.—B.   Railing to same.

No. 9.—A.   Chimney on Rear of Roof.
" 9.—B.   Chimney on Ridge of Roof.
" 10.—   Ornament on Ridge of Front Gable.

THE CO-OPERATIVE BUILDING PLAN ASSOCIATION, ARCHITECTS, 63 BROADWAY, NEW YORK.

*Shoppell's Modern Houses—*Designs Patented.*   *Cottage, Design No. 495*

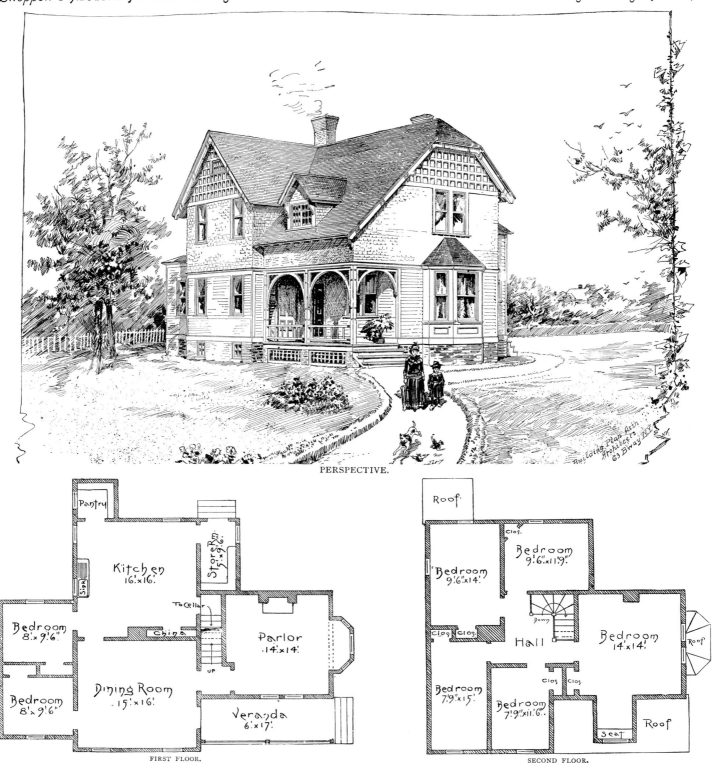

PERSPECTIVE.

FIRST FLOOR.

SECOND FLOOR.

DESCRIPTION.

For explanation of all symbols (* † etc.) see page 42.

GENERAL DIMENSIONS: Extreme width, through dining room, kitchen and pantry, 38 ft.; depth, including bay window, 48 ft. Heights of stories: Cellar, 6 ft. 6 in.; first story, 9 ft.; second story, 9 ft.

EXTERIOR MATERIALS: Foundations, stone walls under main part, wooden posts under one-story extension; first story, clapboards; second story, clapboards and shingles; gables, paneled; roof, shingled. Outside blinds to all windows.

INTERIOR FINISH: Hard white plaster. Soft wood floors and trim. Ash staircase. Kitchen wainscoted. Interior wood-work finished in hard oil.

COLORS: Clapboards, yellow tan. Trim and blinds, Tuscan yellow. Outside doors, panels, yellow tan; framing of panels, Tuscan yellow. Sashes and rain conductors, red. Veranda floor, light brown. Veranda ceiling, oiled. Wall shingles dipped and brush coated yellow stain. Roof shingles left natural.

ACCOMMODATIONS: The principal rooms and their sizes, closets, etc., are shown by the plans. Cellar with cemented floor and inside and outside entrances, under parlor, dining room and kitchen. Attic floored for storage. Fireplace and mantel in parlor included in estimate.

COST: $2,626, † not including range and heater. The estimate is based on ‡ New York prices for materials and labor. In many sections of the country the cost should be less.

Price for working plans, specifications and * license to build, - - - - - - - - - - - - - - $21.25
Price for †† bill of materials, - - - - - - 5.00

Address, THE CO-OPERATIVE BUILDING PLAN ASSOCIATION, Architects, 63 Broadway, New York.

FEASIBLE MODIFICATIONS: Heights of stories, colors, sizes of rooms and kinds of materials may be changed. Cellar may be enlarged, reduced or omitted.

123

THE CO-OPERATIVE BUILDING PLAN ASSOCIATION, ARCHITECTS, 63 BROADWAY, NEW YORK.

Shoppell's Modern Houses—*Designs Patented.   *Cottage, Design No. 379*

PERSPECTIVE.

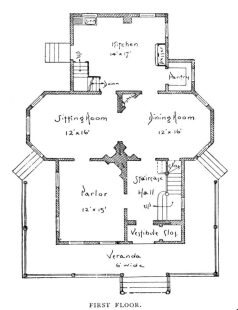

FIRST FLOOR.

SECOND FLOOR.

DESCRIPTION.

For explanation of all symbols (* † etc.) see page 42.

GENERAL DIMENSIONS: Extreme width, including veranda, 35 ft. 6 in.; depth, including veranda, 49 ft. Heights of stories: Cellar, 6 ft. 6 in.; first story, 8 ft. 10 in.; second story, 8 ft. 4 in.

EXTERIOR MATERIALS: Foundation, brick; first story, clapboards; second story, gables, dormers and roofs, shingles. Outside blinds to all windows except those of cellar.

INTERIOR FINISH: Hard white plaster. Soft wood flooring and trim. Ash staircase. Kitchen wainscoted. Panels under windows in parlor. Interior wood-work finished in hard oil.

COLORS: Clapboards, dark green. Trim, outside doors, blinds, and rain conductors, bronze green. Sashes, dark red. Veranda floor, dark olive drab. Veranda ceiling, varnished. Brick-work, Indian red. Wall shingles dipped and brush coated Venetian red stain; roof shingles dipped and brush coated with a darker red stain.

ACCOMMODATIONS: The principal rooms and their sizes, closets, etc., are shown by the plans. Cellar under kitchen, with concrete floor. Attic available only for storage purposes. Open fireplaces in parlor, sitting and dining rooms, mantels included in estimate.

Vestibule door is made to slide, to avoid interference with passage to stairway. Sliding doors connect sitting and dining rooms. Back stairway to second story.

COST: $2,687, † not including range and heater. The estimate is based on ‡ New York prices for materials and labor. In many sections of the country the cost should be less.

Price for working plans, specifications and * license to build, - - - - - - - - - $30.00
Price for †† bill of materials, - - - - - 5.00

Address, THE CO-OPERATIVE BUILDING PLAN ASSOCIATION, Architects, 63 Broadway, New York.

FEASIBLE MODIFICATIONS: Heights of stories, sizes of rooms, colors and kinds of materials may be changed. Cellar may extend under whole house, or be omitted entirely. Sliding doors, fireplaces and mantels and part of veranda may be omitted. Bath-room with partial or full plumbing may be introduced.

The price of working plans, specifications, etc., for a modified design varies according to the alterations required, and will be made known upon application to the Architects.

124

THE CO-OPERATIVE BUILDING PLAN ASSOCIATION, ARCHITECTS, 63 BROADWAY, NEW YORK.

*Shoppell's Modern Houses—*Designs Patented.*   *Residence, Design No. 598*

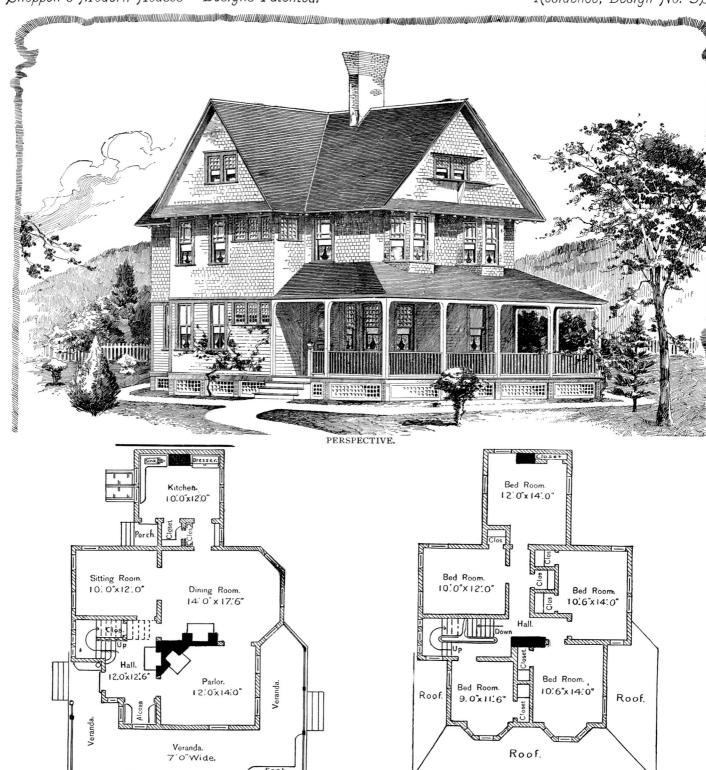

PERSPECTIVE.

FIRST FLOOR.   SECOND FLOOR.

DESCRIPTION.

For explanation of all symbols (* † etc.) see page 42.

GENERAL DIMENSIONS: Width, 34 ft. 6 in., including veranda; depth, 49 ft., including veranda. Heights of stories: Cellar, 6 ft. 6 in.; first story, 9 ft.; second story, 8 ft. 6 in.

EXTERIOR MATERIALS: Foundation, posts; first story, clapboards; second story, gables, and roofs, shingles. Outside blinds to all windows except those of the cellar.

INTERIOR FINISH: Hard white plaster. Hard wood staircase and white pine trim finished in hard oil. Soft wood flooring throughout.

COLORS: All clapboards, tan color. Trim, light brown. Veranda posts, rails, etc., brown. Outside doors, blinds, sashes and rain conductors, brownish red. Veranda floor, light brown. Veranda ceiling, buff. Wall shingles dipped in and brush coated with sienna stain. Roof shingles left natural color.

ACCOMMODATIONS: The principal rooms and their sizes, closets, etc., are shown by the plans. Cellar with plank walls under kitchen. Attic floored, but not finished; space for three rooms and storage. Cosy alcove with seats in front hall.

COST: $2,600, † not including mantels, range and heater. The estimate is based on ‡ New York prices for materials and labor. In many sections of the country the cost should be less.

Price for working plans, specifications and * license to build, - $25.00
Price for †† bill of materials, - - - - - - 10.00

Address, THE CO-OPERATIVE BUILDING PLAN ASSOCIATION, Architects, 63 Broadway, New York.

FEASIBLE MODIFICATIONS. Heights of stories, sizes of rooms, materials and colors may be changed. Cellar may be enlarged. Sliding doors may be introduced. A bath-room with all plumbing fixtures may be planned for second story. A window may be substituted for the front entrance and new entrance planned to open into the alcove. If heating apparatus be used one chimney will suffice.

THE CO-OPERATIVE BUILDING PLAN ASSOCIATION, ARCHITECTS, 63 BROADWAY, NEW YORK.

*Shoppell's Modern Houses—*Designs Patented.*   *Residence, Design No. 619*

PERSPECTIVE.

DESCRIPTION.

For explanation of all symbols (* † etc.) see page 42.

GENERAL DIMENSIONS: Width, through dining room and kitchen, 24 ft.; depth over all, 46 ft. Heights of stories: Cellar, 8 ft.; first story, 10 ft.; second story, 9 ft. 6 in.; attic, 7 ft. 6 in.

EXTERIOR MATERIALS: Foundations: brick; first story, clapboards; second story, gables, dormers and roofs, shingles. Solid shutters for cellar windows; for all other windows, outside blinds.

INTERIOR FINISH: Hard white plaster. Soft wood trim and floors. Hard wood staircase. Bathroom and kitchen wainscoted. House piped for gas.

COLORS: All clapboards, light tan. Trim and outside doors, dark tan. Blinds, sashes, veranda floor, and rain conductors, seal brown. Veranda ceiling, buff. Brick-work painted red. Wall shingles dipped in and coated with deep buff paint.

ACCOMMODATIONS: The principal rooms and their sizes, closets, etc., are shown by the plans. Cellar under whole house. Laundry with two stationary tubs and servants' W. C. in cellar. Dumb waiter from cellar to first and second stories. One room finished in attic with space for another if desired. Two hard wood mantels included in estimate. Sliding doors connect all rooms of first story.

COST: $2,700, † not including heater and range. The estimate is based on ‡ New York prices for materials and labor. In many sections of the country the cost should be less.

Price for working plans, specifications and * license to build, - - - - - - - - $25.00
Price for †† bill of materials, - - - - - 10.00

FEASIBLE MODIFICATIONS: Heights of stories, sizes of rooms, materials and colors, all may be changed. Cellar may be reduced in size. Fireplaces, sliding doors and a part or all of the plumbing may be omitted. Front chimney may be omitted if a heating apparatus be used. The side porch may have a door leading to main hall, and a window in kitchen in place of the present door. If built on a narrow lot all the side windows in kitchen wing may be omitted.

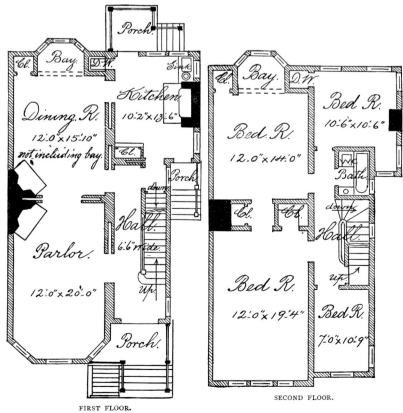

FIRST FLOOR.

SECOND FLOOR.

126

THE CO-OPERATIVE BUILDING PLAN ASSOCIATION, ARCHITECTS, 63 BROADWAY, NEW YORK.

Shoppell's Modern Houses—*Designs Patented.   *Residence, Design No. 431*

PERSPECTIVE.

DESCRIPTION.

For explanation of all symbols (* † etc.) see page 42.

GENERAL DIMENSIONS: Width, 22 ft.; depth, including porch, 50 ft. Heights of stories: Cellar, 6 ft. 6 in.; first story, 9 ft.; second story, 8 ft. 6 in.

EXTERIOR MATERIALS: Foundations, stone; first story, clapboards; second story and roof, shingles; gables, panels and shingles. Outside blinds to all windows.

INTERIOR FINISH: Hard white plaster. Soft wood flooring and trim. Ash stairs. Kitchen and bath-room wainscoted. Interior wood-work of kitchen, pantry and attic, painted tints to suit owner, and other wood-work finished in hard oil.

COLORS: Clapboards, Oriental drab. Trim, and rain conductors, light olive green. Outside doors, a mixture of Oriental drab and light olive green. Blinds and sashes, dark red. Veranda floor, light stone color. Veranda ceiling, lilac. Wall shingles dipped and brush coated sienna stain. Roof shingles dipped and brush coated red stain.

ACCOMMODATIONS: The principal rooms and their sizes, closets, etc., are shown by the plans. Cellar with inside and outside entrances and concrete floor, under whole of main house. Two bedrooms and hallway finished in attic. Design well suited for a 25 foot lot, allowing room for passage at side. Large openings connect all first floor rooms. Two bedrooms may be heated by a fireplace heater in the parlor or dining room. Three hard-wood mantels included in estimate.

COST: $2,720, † not including range and heater. The estimate is based on ‡ New York prices for materials and labor. In many sections of the country the cost should be less.

Price for working plans, specifications and * license to build, - - - - - - - - - - - - - - - $25.00

Price for † † bill of materials, - - - - - 5.00

Address, THE CO-OPERATIVE BUILDING PLAN ASSOCIATION, Architects, 63 Broadway, New York.

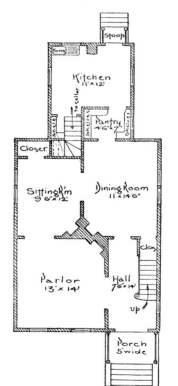

FIRST FLOOR.

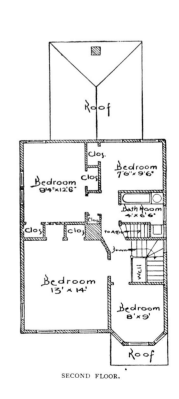

SECOND FLOOR.

FEASIBLE MODIFICATIONS: Heights of stories, colors, sizes of rooms and kinds of materials may be changed. Cellar may be enlarged, reduced, or omitted entirely. Concrete floor may be omitted. Fireplaces and mantels may be omitted. If heating apparatus be used one chimney will be sufficient. A part or all plumbing and attic finish may be omitted.

The price of working plans, specifications, etc., for a modified design varies according to the alterations required, and will be made known upon application to the Architects.

127

THE CO-OPERATIVE BUILDING PLAN ASSOCIATION, ARCHITECTS, 63 BROADWAY, NEW YORK.

Shoppell's Modern Houses—*Designs Patented.   *Cottage, Design No. 534*

PERSPECTIVE.

FIRST FLOOR.

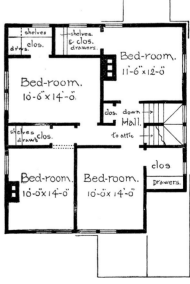

SECOND FLOOR.

DESCRIPTION.

For explanation of all symbols (* † etc.) see page 42.

GENERAL DIMENSIONS: Width, 27 ft. 6 in.; depth, including veranda, 42 ft. Heights of stories: Cellar, 6 ft. 6 in.; first story, 10 ft.; second story, 9 ft.; third story, 8 ft.

EXTERIOR MATERIALS: Foundations, stone; first story, clapboards; second story, gables and roof, shingles.

INTERIOR FINISH: Hard white plaster. Soft wood flooring and trim. Ash staircase. Interior wood-work finished in hard oil.

COLORS: Clapboards, pale green. Trim, rain conductors, veranda posts, rail and balusters, dark green. Front door finished in hard oil natural color; other outside doors painted dark green, with pale green panels. Sashes, Pompeian red. Soffit of roof overhang, painted pale green. Brick-work, dark red. Wall shingles in second story and gables dipped and brush coated with light colored moss green stain. Roof shingles dipped and brush coated same as wall shingles, but of darker shade.

ACCOMMODATIONS: The principal rooms and their sizes, closets, etc., are shown by the plans. Cellar under whole house. Two rooms and hall finished in attic. Fireplaces in parlor and dining room. Place for set range in kitchen. Large closets throughout.

COST: $2,700, † not including mantels, range and heater. The estimate is based on ‡ New York prices for materials and labor. In many sections of the country the cost should be less.

Price for working plans, specifications and * license to build, - - - - - - - - - - - - - - - - $25.00
Price for †† bill of materials, - - - - - - - - 10.00
Address, THE CO-OPERATIVE BUILDING PLAN ASSOCIATION, Architects, 63 Broadway, New York.

FEASIBLE MODIFICATIONS: Heights of stories, colors, sizes of rooms and kinds of materials may be changed. Cellar may be reduced in size, or omitted. Bath-room with full or partial plumbing may be introduced. If heating apparatus be used kitchen chimney will suffice. Mantels and fireplaces and sliding doors may be omitted. Veranda may extend across the front.

The price of working plans, specifications, etc., for a modified design varies according to the alterations required, and will be made known upon application to the Architects.

128

THE CO-OPERATIVE BUILDING PLAN ASSOCIATION, ARCHITECTS, 63 BROADWAY, NEW YORK.

Shoppell's Modern Houses—*Designs Patented.   *Residence, Design No. 343*

PERSPECTIVE.

DESCRIPTION.

For explanation of all symbols (* † etc.) see page 42.

GENERAL DIMENSIONS: Extreme width, 34 ft. 6 in.; depth, including veranda, 49 ft. 6 in. Heights of stories: First story, 9 ft.; second story, 8 ft. 6 in.; attic, 7 ft. 6 in.

EXTERIOR MATERIALS: Foundation, brick piers; first story, clapboards; second story, gables and roofs, shingles. Outside blinds.

INTERIOR FINISH: Hard white plaster; plaster cornices and centers in hall, parlor and dining room. Soft wood flooring and trim. Ash stairway. Panels under windows in parlor and dining room. Kitchen wainscoted. Interior wood-work finished in hard oil.

COLORS: Clapboards and veranda floor, light drab. Trim, and rain conductors, seal brown. Outside doors, blinds and sashes, bronze green. Veranda ceiling, lilac. Brick-work, Indian red. Wall shingles dipped and brush coated sienna stain. Roof shingles dipped and brush coated reddish stain.

ACCOMMODATIONS: The principal rooms and their sizes, closets, etc., are shown by the plans. No cellar. Attic floored, but otherwise unfinished. Fireplaces in parlor and dining room, with mantels, included in estimate. Balcony at front of second story.

COST: $2,752, † not including range. The estimate is based on ‡ New York prices for materials and labor. In many sections of the country the cost should be less.

Price for working plans, specifications and * license to build, - - - - - - - - - - - - $35.00

Price for † † bill of materials, - - - - 5.00

Address, THE CO-OPERATIVE BUILDING PLAN ASSOCIATION, Architects, 63 Broadway, New York.

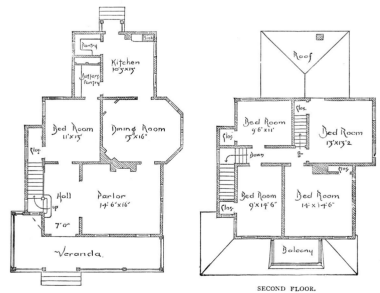

FIRST FLOOR.

SECOND FLOOR.

FEASIBLE MODIFICATIONS: Heights of stories, colors, sizes of rooms and kinds of materials may be changed. Cellar may be placed under a part or the whole of building, with stone, brick or plank walls. Bath-room with partial or full plumbing may be introduced, either in second or attic story.

The price of working plans, specifications, etc., for a modified design varies according to the alterations required, and will be made known upon application to the Architects.

129

THE CO-OPERATIVE BUILDING PLAN ASSOCIATION, ARCHITECTS, 63 BROADWAY, NEW YORK.

Shoppell's Modern Houses—*Designs Patented.

Residence, Design No. 342

PERSPECTIVE.

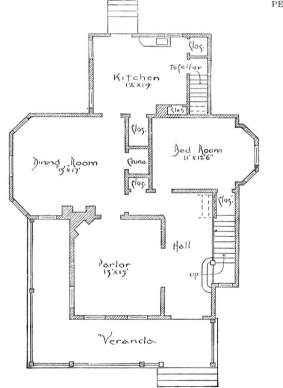

FIRST FLOOR.

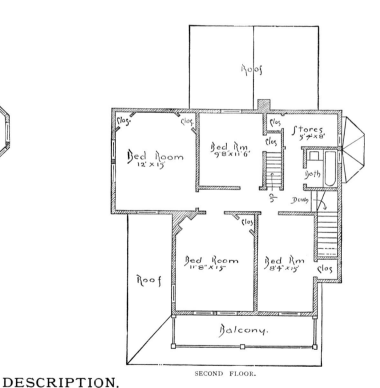

SECOND FLOOR.

DESCRIPTION.

For explanation of all symbols (* † etc.) see page 42.

GENERAL DIMENSIONS. Extreme width, 37 ft.; depth, including veranda, 52 ft. Heights of stories: Cellar, 6 ft. 6 in.; first story, 9 ft. 6 in.; second story, 9 ft.

EXTERIOR MATERIALS: Foundations, stone and brick; first story, clapboards; second story and roof, shingles; gables, panels and shingles. Outside blinds to all windows except those of cellar.

INTERIOR FINISH: Hard white plaster; plaster cornices and centers in hall, parlor and dining room. Soft wood flooring and trim. Ash stairway. Bath-room and kitchen wainscoted. Interior wood-work finished in hard oil.

COLORS: Clapboards, dark drab. Trim, outside doors, and rain conductors, bronze green. Blinds and sashes, dark red. Veranda floor, light drab. Veranda ceiling, varnished. Wall shingles dipped and brush coated red stain; roof shingles dipped and brush coated darker red stain.

ACCOMMODATIONS: The principal rooms and their sizes, closets, etc.,

are shown by the plans. Cellar under kitchen only. Attic floored, but unfinished; space for two good rooms. Fine large balcony. Ample veranda. Fireplaces in parlor, dining room and one bedroom, with hard wood mantels, included in estimate.

COST: $3,458, † not including range. The estimate is based on ‡ New York prices for materials and labor. In many sections of the country the cost should be less.

Price for working plans, specifications and * license to build, - $30.00
Price for †† bill of materials, - - - - - 5.00
Address, THE CO-OPERATIVE BUILDING PLAN ASSOCIATION, Architects, 63 Broadway, New York.

FEASIBLE MODIFICATIONS: Heights of stories, colors, sizes of rooms and kinds of materials may be changed. Cellar may be enlarged. Fireplaces and mantels may be omitted. Kitchen extension may be made two stories high and back stairway introduced.

*Shoppell's Modern Houses—*Designs Patented.*

Residence, Design No. 332

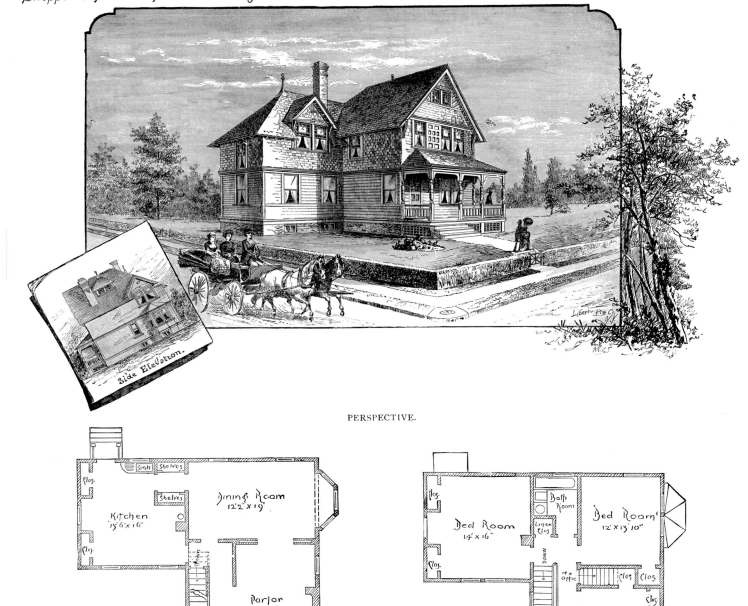

PERSPECTIVE.

FIRST FLOOR.

SECOND FLOOR.

DESCRIPTION.

For explanation of all symbols (* † etc.) see page 42.

GENERAL DIMENSIONS: Extreme width, including bay window, 39 ft.; depth, including veranda, 38 ft. 6 in. Heights of stories: Cellar, 6 ft. 6 in.; first story, 9 ft.; second story, 8 ft. 6 in.; attic, 7 ft.

EXTERIOR MATERIALS: Foundations, stone and brick; first story, clapboards; second story and roof, shingles; gables, panels and shingles. Outside blinds.

INTERIOR FINISH: Hard white plaster. Soft wood flooring and trim. Ash stairs. Kitchen and bath-room wainscoted. Interior wood-work finished in hard oil.

COLORS: Clapboards, light olive green. Trim, and rain conductors, bronze green. Outside doors, dark green. Blinds and sashes, dark red. Veranda floor, light stone color. Veranda ceiling, French gray. Brick-work, Indian red. Wall shingles dipped and brush coated sienna stain. Roof shingles dipped and brush coated dark red stain.

ACCOMMODATIONS: The principal rooms and their sizes, closets, etc., are shown by the plans. Cellar under the whole house. One room finished in the attic. Sliding doors between parlor and dining room. Pantry between dining room and kitchen. One fireplace with mantel included in estimate.

COST: $2,765, † not including range and heater. The estimate is based on ‡ New York prices for materials and labor. In many sections of the country the cost should be less.

Price for working plans, specifications and * license to build, - - - - - - - - - - $20.00

Price for †† bill of materials, - - - - 5.00

Address, THE CO-OPERATIVE BUILDING PLAN ASSOCIATION, Architects, 63 Broadway, New York.

FEASIBLE MODIFICATIONS: Heights of stories, colors, sizes of rooms and kinds of materials may be changed. Size of cellar may be reduced. Attic may be left unfinished. Bay window, sliding doors, fireplaces, mantels, and a part or all plumbing may be omitted. If heating apparatus be used one chimney will suffice.

131

THE CO-OPERATIVE BUILDING PLAN ASSOCIATION, ARCHITECTS, 63 BROADWAY, NEW YORK.

Shoppell's Modern Houses—*Designs Patented.   *Design No. 438*

PERSPECTIVE.

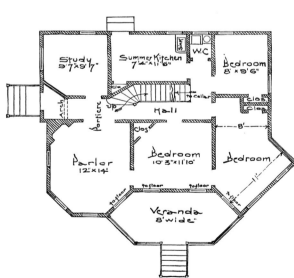

FIRST FLOOR.

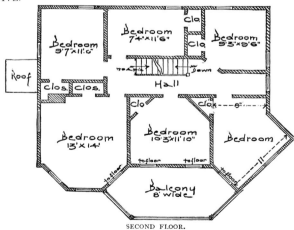

SECOND FLOOR.

DESCRIPTION.

For explanation of all symbols (* † etc.) see page 42.

GENERAL DIMENSIONS : Width, 38 ft. 10 in.; depth, including veranda, 33 ft. Heights of stories : Cellar, 6 ft. 8 in.; first story, 9 ft.; second story, 8 ft. 6 in.

EXTERIOR MATERIALS : Foundations, stone walls and brick piers; first story, clapboards ; second story, gables and roofs, shingles.

INTERIOR FINISH : Hard white plaster ; plaster cornices in parlor and hall. Soft wood flooring and trim. Second story floor deafened. Stairs, yellow pine. Kitchen wainscoted. Interior wood-work finished in hard oil. Inside folding blinds in first and second stories.

COLORS : Clapboards and panels of outside doors, olive. Trim, framing of panels of outside doors, and rain conductors, dark green.

Sashes, Pompeian red. Brick-work and veranda floor, oiled. Veranda ceiling, light drab. Wall shingles dipped and brush coated with stain slightly darker than the natural color of wood. Roof shingles left natural.

ACCOMMODATIONS : The principal rooms and their sizes, closets, etc., are shown by the plans. Cellar under the parlor. Designed for erection near a hotel where meals are supplied ; the small kitchen to serve in case of emergency. Fireplace with mantel in parlor included in estimate. Water-closet, sink and wash-bowl in first story; no other plumbing. Attic floored, but unfinished; space for three rooms.

COST : $2,792. The estimate is based on ‡ New York prices for materials and labor. In many sections of the country the cost should be less.

Price for working plans, specifications and * license to build, - - - - - - - - - - - - $30.00
Price for †† bill of materials, - - - - - - 5.00
Address, THE CO-OPERATIVE BUILDING PLAN ASSOCIATION, Architects, 63 Broadway, New York.

132

THE CO-OPERATIVE BUILDING PLAN ASSOCIATION ARCHITECTS, 63 BROADWAY, NEW YORK.

Shoppell's Modern Houses—*Designs Patented.   *Cottage, Design No. 537*

The Coöp Building Plan Assn Architects'
63 Broadway New York

PERSPECTIVE.

DESCRIPTION.

For explanation of all symbols (* † etc.) see page 42.

GENERAL DIMENSIONS: Width, including veranda, 34 ft. 2 in.; depth over all, 46 ft. 6 in. Heights of stories: Cellar, 7 ft.; first story, 9 ft.; second story, 8 ft. 6 in.

EXTERIOR MATERIALS: Foundations, stone; first story, clapboards; second story and roof, shingles; gables, panels and shingles. Outside blinds to all windows except those of the cellar.

INTERIOR FINISH: Hard white plaster. Flooring of hall, dining room and kitchen, quartered yellow pine. All other flooring soft wood. Double floors throughout entire first story. Trim, yellow pine. Stairway, cherry with yellow pine steps and risers. Bath-room, dining room, hall and kitchen wainscoted. Interior wood-work finished in hard oil.

COLORS: Clapboards, seal brown. Trim, Tuscan yellow. Outside doors, blinds, sashes, and rain conductors, dark green. Veranda floor, yellow stone color. Veranda ceiling, varnished. Wall shingles dipped and brush coated yellow stain. Roof shingles dipped and brush coated red stain.

ACCOMMODATIONS: The principal rooms and their sizes, closets, etc., are shown by the plans. Cellar under whole house. No finish in attic except flooring; space for two rooms. Bath-room supplied with basin, tub and water-closet. Pantry connecting kitchen with dining room shuts off odors and heat.

COST: $2,800, † not including mantels, range and heater. The estimate is based on ‡ New York prices for materials and labor. In many sections of the country the cost should be less.

Price for working plans, specifications and * license to build, - - - - - - - - - - - - - - - - $30.00

Price for † † bill of materials, - - - - - 10.00

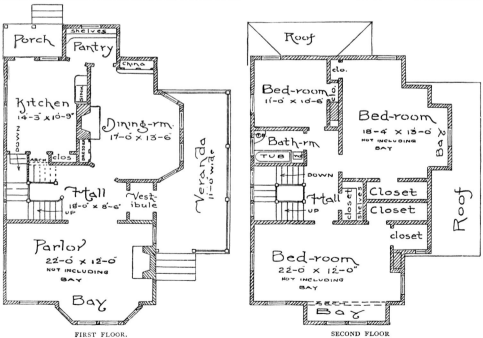

FIRST FLOOR.

SECOND FLOOR.

Address, THE CO-OPERATIVE BUILDING PLAN ASSOCIATION, Architects, 63 Broadway, New York.

FEASIBLE MODIFICATIONS: Heights of stories, colors, sizes of rooms and kinds of materials may be changed. Cellar may be reduced or omitted. Sliding doors may connect parlor with hall. If heating apparatus be used parlor chimney may be omitted. A part or all plumbing may be omitted. By a re-arrangement of closets in second story, another small bedroom may be planned.

133

THE CO-OPERATIVE BUILDING PLAN ASSOCIATION, ARCHITECTS, 63 BROADWAY, NEW YORK.

*Shoppell's Modern Houses—*Designs Patented.*   *Residence, Design No. 210*

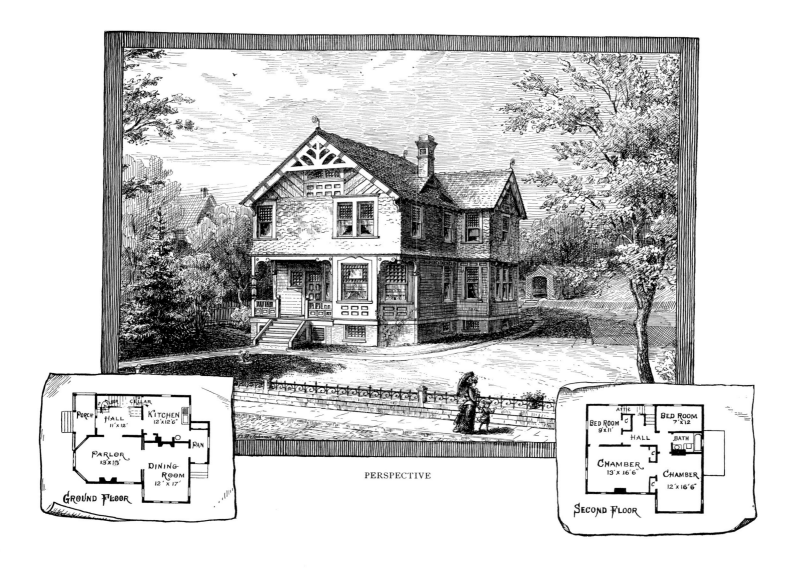

PERSPECTIVE

DESCRIPTION.

For explanation of all symbols (* † etc.) see page 42.

GENERAL DIMENSIONS. Width through dining room and kitchen, 31 ft.; extreme depth, 37 ft. Heights of stories: Cellar, 7 ft.; first story, 9 ft. 6 in.; second story, 8 ft. 6 in.

EXTERIOR MATERIALS: Foundations, stone and brick; first story, clapboards; second story and roof, shingles; gables, panels imitating open timber work. Outside blinds to all windows except those of the cellar and attic.

INTERIOR FINISH: Hard white plaster; plaster cornices and centers in hall, parlor and dining room. Soft wood flooring and trim. Ash stairway. Panels under parlor and dining room windows. Bath-room and kitchen wainscoted. Interior wood-work, finished in hard oil.

COLORS: Clapboards and paneling on front bay, light olive green. Trim, veranda rail, balusters and flooring, all cornices and other mouldings, and the frames of gable panels, dark olive green. Veranda ceiling, oiled. Outside doors and blinds, very dark green. Sashes and brick-work, red. Panels in gables, Tuscan yellow. Wall shingles dipped and brush coated cream color. Roof shingles dipped and brush coated red stain. See colored frontispiece.

ACCOMMODATIONS: The principal rooms and their sizes, closets, etc., are shown by the plans. Cellar under the whole house. Attic floored, but unfinished; space for two rooms and for storage. The plumbing pipes alongside of kitchen chimney cannot freeze and burst. Sliding doors connect dining room and parlor. A large well-arranged pantry connects dining room and kitchen. Two hard wood mantels are included in estimate.

COST: $2,800, † not including range and heater. The estimate is based on ‡ New York prices for materials and labor. In many sections of the country the cost should be less.

Price for working plans, specifications and * license to build, - - - - - - - - - - - - $30.00

Price for †† bill of materials, - - - - - 5.00

Address, THE CO-OPERATIVE BUILDING PLAN ASSOCIATION, Architects, 63 Broadway, New York.

FEASIBLE MODIFICATIONS: Heights of stories, colors, sizes of rooms and kinds of materials may be changed. Cellar may be reduced in size, or omitted. Fireplaces and mantels, a part or all of plumbing, and sliding doors, may be omitted.

The price of working plans, specifications, etc., for a modified design varies according to the alterations required, and will be made known upon application to the Architects.

134

THE CO-OPERATIVE BUILDING PLAN ASSOCIATION, ARCHITECTS, 63 BROADWAY, NEW YORK.

*Shoppell's Modern Houses—*Designs Patented.*

Residence, Design No. 216

PERSPECTIVE.

DESCRIPTION.

For explanation of all symbols (* † etc.) see page 42.

GENERAL DIMENSIONS: Width, 30 ft. 6 in.; depth including veranda, 48 ft. 8 in. Heights of stories, Cellar, 6 ft. 6 in.; first story, 9 ft. 3 in.; second story, 8 ft: 9 in.; attic, 8 ft.

EXTERIOR MATERIALS: Foundations, stone and brick; first story, clapboards; second story, gables and roof, shingles; tower, panels and shingles. Outside blinds to all windows except those of the cellar.

INTERIOR FINISH: Hard white plaster; plaster cornices in hall, parlor and dining room. Soft wood floor and trim. Ash staircase. Panels under hall and dining room windows. Bath-room wainscoted. Interior woodwork finished in hard oil.

COLORS: Clapboards, blinds and sashes, bronze green. Trim, outside doors, veranda floor, and rain conductors, seal brown. Veranda ceiling, chrome yellow. Brick-work, Indian red. Wall shingles dipped and brush coated sienna stain. Roof shingles dipped and brush coated Indian red stain.

ACCOMMODATIONS: The principal rooms and their sizes, closets, etc., are shown by the plans. Cellar under kitchen. Tower room finished in attic. This room makes a pleasant study or smoking room. Bay window in dining room. Back stairway, bath-room and servant's bedroom over kitchen. Fireplace and one hard wood mantel included in estimate.

COST: $2,804, † not including range and heater. The estimate is based on ‡ New York prices for materials and labor. In many sections of the country the cost should be less.

Price for working plans, specifications and * license to build, - - - - - - - - - - - $20.00
Price for †† bill of materials, - - - - - 5.00
Address, THE CO-OPERATIVE BUILDING PLAN ASSOCIATION, Architects, 63 Broadway, New York.

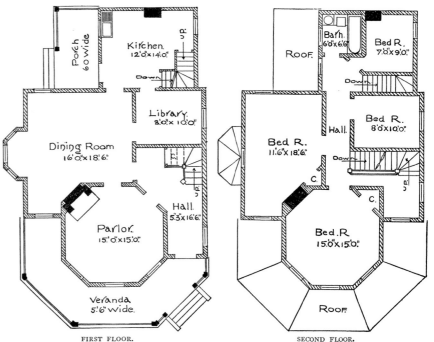

FIRST FLOOR.   SECOND FLOOR.

FEASIBLE MODIFICATIONS: Heights of stories, colors, sizes of rooms and kinds of materials may be changed. Cellar may be extended under whole house. A part or all of the plumbing, and fireplaces and mantels, may be omitted. If heating apparatus be used one chimney will suffice.

135

THE CO-OPERATIVE BUILDING PLAN ASSOCIATION, ARCHITECTS, 63 BROADWAY, NEW YORK.

*Shoppell's Modern Houses—*Designs Patented.*   *Residence, Design No. 535*

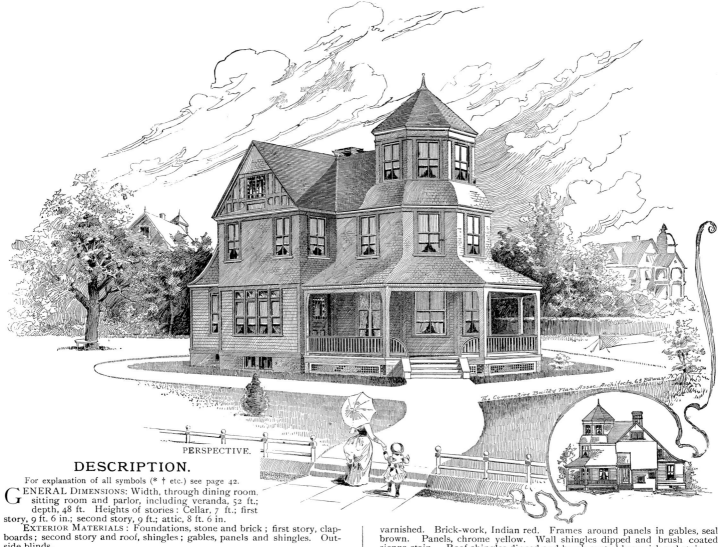

PERSPECTIVE.

DESCRIPTION.

For explanation of all symbols (* † etc.) see page 42.

GENERAL DIMENSIONS: Width, through dining room, sitting room and parlor, including veranda, 52 ft.; depth, 48 ft. Heights of stories: Cellar, 7 ft.; first story, 9 ft. 6 in.; second story, 9 ft.; attic, 8 ft. 6 in.

EXTERIOR MATERIALS: Foundations, stone and brick; first story, clapboards; second story and roof, shingles; gables, panels and shingles. Outside blinds.

INTERIOR FINISH: Hard white plaster; plaster centers in parlor, library and dining room. Soft wood floor, trim and stairs. Panels under windows in parlor and library. Bath-room and kitchen wainscoted. Interior woodwork finished in hard oil.

COLORS: Clapboards, blinds and sashes, bronze green. Trim, outside doors, veranda floor, and rain conductors, seal brown. Veranda ceiling, varnished. Brick-work, Indian red. Frames around panels in gables, seal brown. Panels, chrome yellow. Wall shingles dipped and brush coated sienna stain. Roof shingles dipped and brush coated brownish red stain.

ACCOMMODATIONS: The principal rooms and their sizes, closets, etc., are shown by the plans. Cellar with concrete floor under sitting room and kitchen. Three rooms in attic. Tower makes a good study. Recessed fireplace and mantel in sitting room with seat at sides. Pantry connection between dining room and kitchen shuts off cooking odors. Water-closet is placed in shed at rear of kitchen.

COST: $3,000, † not including mantels, range and heater. The estimate is based on ‡ New York prices for materials and labor. In many sections of the country the cost should be less.

Price for working plans, specifications and * license to build, - $25.00
Price for †† bill of materials, - - - - - - - 10.00

Address, THE CO-OPERATIVE BUILDING PLAN ASSOCIATION, Architects, 63 Broadway, New York.

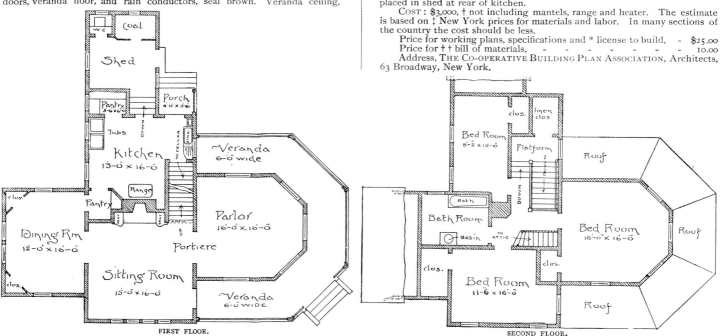

FIRST FLOOR.   SECOND FLOOR.

*Shoppell's Modern Houses—*Designs Patented.* *Cottage, Design No. 530*

PERSPECTIVE.

FIRST FLOOR.

SECOND FLOOR.

DESCRIPTION.

For explanation of all symbols (* † etc.) see page 42.

GENERAL DIMENSIONS: Width, including dining room and staircase bay, 32 ft. 6 in.; depth, 42 ft. 6 in., including veranda and pantry. Heights of stories: Cellar, 6 ft. 6 in.; first story, 9 ft.; second story, 8 ft. (slope of ceiling under roof starts about 6 ft. 3 in. above floor).

EXTERIOR MATERIALS: Foundations, stone; first story, clapboards, second story and roof, shingles; gables, shingles and fan work. Outside blinds to all windows except those of the cellar and attic.

INTERIOR FINISH: Hard white plaster. Soft wood flooring and trim. Ash stairway. Bath-room wainscoted. Interior wood-work finished in hard oil.

COLORS: Clapboards and veranda floor, dark olive drab. Trim, and rain conductors, bronze green. Outside doors and blinds, dark green. Sashes, bright red. Veranda ceiling, varnished. Wall shingles, oiled. Roof shingles left natural.

ACCOMMODATIONS: The principal rooms and their sizes, closets, etc., are shown by the plans. Cellar with concrete floor, under hall; laundry with two tubs under kitchen. One low room finished in attic. Combination front and back stairway economizes space.

COST: $2,600 † not including mantels, range and heater. The estimate is based on ‡ New York prices for materials and labor. In many sections of the country the cost should be less.

Price for working plans, specifications and * license to build, - - - $25.00
Price for †† bill of materials, - 10.00

Address, THE CO-OPERATIVE BUILDING PLAN ASSOCIATION, Architects, 63 Broadway, New York.

FEASIBLE MODIFICATIONS: Heights of stories, colors, sizes of rooms and kinds of materials may be changed. Cellar may be placed under whole house or omitted entirely. Number of fire-places and mantels may be reduced. Kitchen chimney will suffice if house be heated by furnace. A part or all plumbing may be omitted. Side porch may be transferred to rear, under extended roof of pantry.

The price of working plans, specifications, etc., for a modified design varies according to the alterations required, and will be made known upon application to the Architects.

137

Shoppell's Modern Houses—*Designs Patented.   *Cottage, Design No. 576*

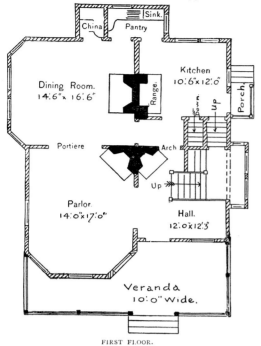

FIRST FLOOR.

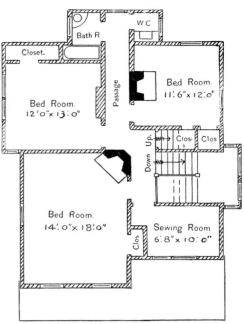

SECOND FLOOR.

DESCRIPTION.

For explanation of all symbols (* † etc.) see page 42.

GENERAL DIMENSIONS: Width, through dining room and kitchen, including side porch, 33 ft.; depth, including veranda and pantry, 42 ft. 6 in. Heights of stories: Cellar, 7 ft.; first story, 9 ft.; second story, 8 ft.; attic, 7 ft.

EXTERIOR MATERIALS AND INTERIOR FINISH same as for Design No. 530, described on opposite page.

COLORS: Clapboards, buff. Trim, outside doors, veranda floor and rain water conductors, dark brown. Blinds and sashes, olive. Veranda ceiling, varnished. Brick-work, unpainted. Wall shingles dipped and brush coated in oil. Roof shingles left the natural color.

ACCOMMODATIONS: The principal rooms and their sizes, closets, etc., are shown by the plans. Cellar under whole house, containing laundry with two tubs. Attic floored and two rooms finished. Combined front and back stairway economizes space. Second story, full height ceilings throughout.

COST: $2,900, † not including mantels, range and heater. The estimate is based on ‡ New York prices for materials and labor. In many sections of the country the cost should be less.

Price for working plans, specifications and * license to build, - - - - - - - - - $25.00
Price for †† bill of materials, - - - - - 5.00

Address, THE CO-OPERATIVE BUILDING PLAN ASSOCIATION, Architects, 63 Broadway, New York.

Cottage, Design No. 577.

The exterior appearance of this design is much like that of No. 530, shown on the opposite page.

DESCRIPTION.

GENERAL DIMENSIONS: Width, including verandas, 42 ft. 5 in.; depth, including verandas, 55 ft. 2 in. Heights of stories: Cellar, 7 ft. 6 in.; first story, 10 ft.; second story, 9 ft.; attic, 7 ft. 6 in.

EXTERIOR MATERIALS: Foundations, stone; first story, clapboards; second story, gables and roofs, shingles. Outside blinds to all except cellar and main stairway windows.

INTERIOR FINISH: Hard white plaster; plaster cornices in halls

and all principal rooms; centers in parlor, dining room and reception room. Flooring and trim throughout, soft wood. Main stairway, ash. Bath-room and kitchen wainscoted. Interior wood-work finished in hard oil.

COLORS: All clapboards, and the body of all panels, dark drab. Trim, outside doors, blinds, rain conductors, paneling and roof finials, dark green. Sashes, seal brown. Veranda floor, dark olive drab. Veranda ceiling, varnished. Brick-work, painted Pompeian red. All shingles dipped and brush coated in Pompeian red paint.

ACCOMMODATIONS: The principal rooms and their sizes, closets, etc., are shown by the plans. Cellar under whole house with inside and outside entrances and concrete floor. Attic floored, but unfinished; space for two rooms. Quaint tower bay on front corner. Four fireplaces and mantels included in estimate. Three laundry tubs on kitchen porch. Wash basin in closet over bath-room.

COST: $3,500, † not including heater and range. The estimate is based on ‡ New York prices for materials and labor. In many sections of the country the cost should be less.

Price for working plans, specifications and * license to build, - - - $30.00.
Price for †† bill of materials, - - - $10.00.

Address, THE CO-OPERATIVE BUILDING PLAN ASSOCIATION, Architects, 63 Broadway, New York.

FEASIBLE MODIFICATIONS: Heights of stories, sizes of rooms, materials and colors may be changed. Bath-room may be placed in second story where linen closet is now shown. One chimney will suffice if heating apparatus be used.

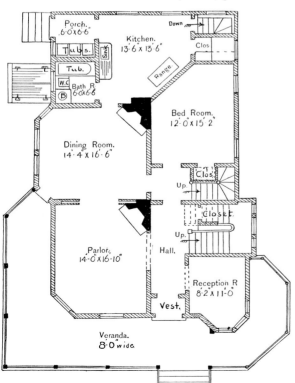

FIRST FLOOR.

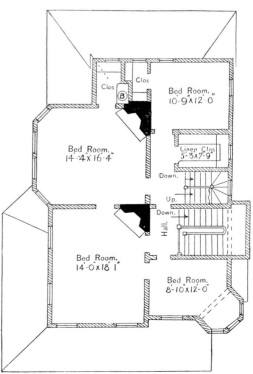

SECOND FLOOR.

138

THE CO-OPERATIVE BUILDING PLAN ASSOCIATION, ARCHITECTS, 63 BROADWAY, NEW YORK.

Shoppell's Modern Houses—*Designs Patented.

Cottage, Design No. 336

PERSPECTIVE.

DESCRIPTION.

For explanation of all symbols (* † etc.) see page 42.

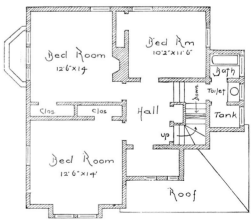

FIRST FLOOR.

SECOND FLOOR.

GENERAL DIMENSIONS: Width over all, 35 ft. 6 in.; depth, 32 ft. Heights of stories: Cellar, 7 ft.; first story, 9 ft.; second story, 8 ft. 6 in.; attic, 7 ft.

EXTERIOR MATERIALS: Foundation, brick; first story, clapboards; second story and roof, shingles; gables, panels and shingles. Outside blinds.

INTERIOR FINISH: Hard white plaster; plaster cornices and centers in parlor, hall and dining room. Soft wood floor and trim. Ash stairway. Panels under parlor and dining room windows. Bath-room and kitchen wainscoted. Interior woodwork finished in hard oil.

COLORS: Clapboards and panels in gables, dark olive drab. Trim, and rain conductors, bronze green. Outside doors and blinds, and the frames of panels in gables, dark green. Sashes, bright red. Veranda floor and ceiling, varnished. Wall shingles dipped and brush coated red stain. Roof shingles, oiled.

ACCOMMODATIONS: The principal rooms and their sizes, closets, etc., are shown by the plans. Cellar with inside and outside entrances and concrete floor, under hall and kitchen. One room and hall in attic. Fireplaces and mantels in parlor, dining room and one bedroom, included in estimate. Water-closet, bath, and wash-basin independent of each other.

COST: $2,938, † not including range and heater. The estimate is based on ‡ New York prices for materials and labor. In many sections of the country the cost should be less.

Price for working plans, specifications and * license to build, - - - - - - - - - - $25.00
Price for † † bill of materials, - - - - - 5.00
Address, THE CO-OPERATIVE BUILDING PLAN ASSOCIATION, Architects, 63 Broadway, New York.

FEASIBLE MODIFICATIONS: Heights of stories, sizes of rooms, colors, and kinds of materials may be changed. Number of fireplaces and mantels may be reduced. Tank shown in second story may be transferred to attic, or omitted where there is a public water supply. The wash-basin in first story may be omitted and the water-closet transferred to tank room. The space thus gained may be re-planned to enlarge kitchen or to form a large pantry.

*Shoppell's Modern Houses—*Designs Patented.*   *Residence, Design No. 478*

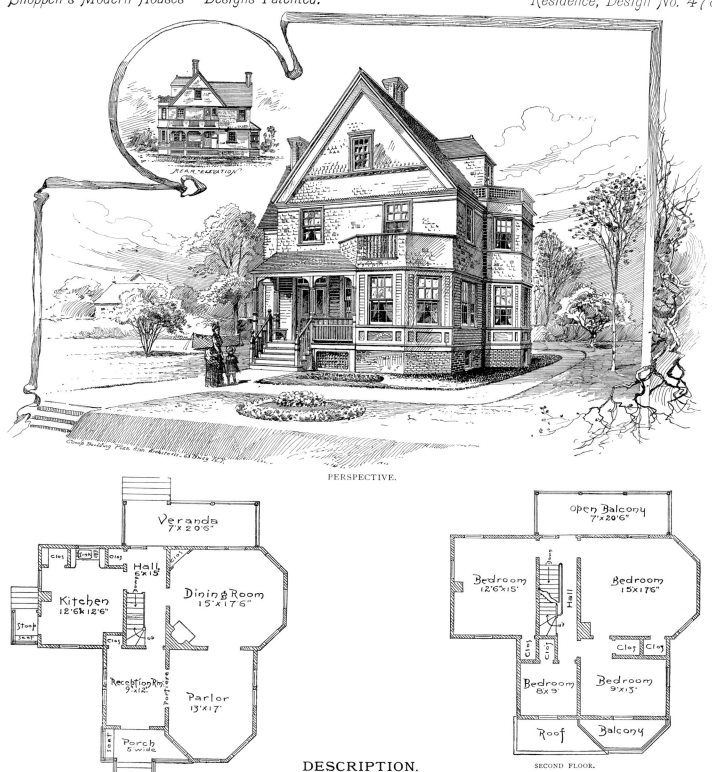

PERSPECTIVE.

FIRST FLOOR.   SECOND FLOOR.

DESCRIPTION.

For explanation of all symbols (* † etc.) see page 42.

GENERAL DIMENSIONS: Width over all, 42 ft.; depth, including rear veranda. 40 ft. 6 in. Heights of stories: Cellar, 6 ft. 6 in.; first story, 9 ft.; second story, 8 ft.

EXTERIOR MATERIALS: Foundation, brick; first story, clapboards; second story, roof and gables, shingles. Outside blinds.

INTERIOR FINISH: Plastering for wall paper. Soft wood flooring and trim. Ash stairway. Interior wood-work finished in hard oil.

COLORS: Clapboards, dark olive drab. Trim, sashes, rain conductors and brick-work, dark red. Outside doors, maroon. Blinds, bronze green. Veranda floor and ceiling, light stone color. Wall shingles dipped and brush coated sienna stain.

ACCOMMODATIONS: The principal rooms, and their sizes, closets, etc., are shown by the plans. Cellar under the whole house, with cemented floor and inside and outside entrances. The stairway is convenient, its position making a back stairway unnecessary. Attic is floored, but unfinished; space for two rooms and storage. One fireplace and mantel included in estimate.

COST: $2,973, † not including range and heater. The estimate is based on ‡ New York prices for materials and labor. In many sections of the country the cost should be less.

Price for working plans, specifications and * license to build, - - - - - - - - - - - - $24.73
Price for †† bill of materials, - - - - - 5.00
Address, THE CO-OPERATIVE BUILDING PLAN ASSOCIATION, Architects, 63 Broadway, New York.

FEASIBLE MODIFICATIONS: Heights of stories, colors, sizes of rooms and kinds of materials may be changed. Cellar may be reduced in size or omitted. Cemented floor may be omitted. Entrance to kitchen may be at rear instead of at side. Front porch may be enlarged. Rear veranda and open balcony may be reduced in size or omitted entirely. Kitchen may be placed at rear to suit narrower lot. Fireplace may be introduced in parlor.

140

THE CO-OPERATIVE BUILDING PLAN ASSOCIATION, ARCHITECTS, 63 BROADWAY, NEW YORK.

*Shoppell's Modern Houses—*Designs Patented.*　　　　　　*Residence, Design No. 637*

PERSPECTIVE.

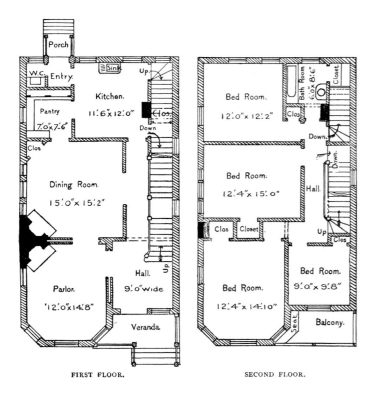

FIRST FLOOR.　　　　　SECOND FLOOR.

DESCRIPTION.

For explanation of all symbols (* † etc.) see page 42.

GENERAL DIMENSIONS: Front, 24 ft. 4 in.; depth, 45 ft. 4 in. Heights of stories: Cellar, 7 ft.; first story, 10 ft.; second story, 9 ft.

EXTERIOR MATERIALS: Foundations, first story and second story, brick; gables, panels and slate; roof, slate.

INTERIOR FINISH: Hard white plaster walls throughout. Plaster cornices and centres in parlor and dining room. All flooring and all trim, white pine. Stairs of ash. Bath-room and kitchen, wainscoted. All wood work finished in hard oil.

COLORS: All brick work, oiled. All trim, outside doors and blinds, and stiles and rails of gable panels, painted dark green. Sashes, Pompeian red. Veranda and balcony floors, dark drab. Veranda and balcony ceilings and gable panels, medium drab.

ACCOMMODATIONS: The principal rooms and their sizes, closets, etc., are shown by the floor plans. There is a cellar under the whole house. The attic is floored but not finished; it affords space for two rooms of good size. W. C. is off the kitchen entry. There is no W. C. in bath-room.

COST: $3000, † not including mantels, range and heater. The estimate is based on ‡ New York prices for materials and labor. In many sections of the country the cost should be less.

Price for working plans, specifications and * license to build, - $30.00
Price for †† bill of materials, - - - - - 10.00

Address, THE CO-OPERATIVE BUILDING PLAN ASSOCIATION, Architects, 63 Broadway, New York.

FEASIBLE MODIFICATIONS: Heights of stories, sizes of rooms, colors, and kinds of materials may be changed. Fire-places and sliding-doors may be omitted. W. C. may be transferred to bath-room. Porch and veranda may be enlarged.

The price of working plans, specifications, etc. for a modified design varies according to the alterations required, and will be made known upon application to the Architects.

141

THE CO-OPERATIVE BUILDING PLAN ASSOCIATION, ARCHITECTS, 63 BROADWAY, NEW YORK.

Shoppell's Modern Houses—*Designs Patented. Residence, Design No. 620

PERSPECTIVE.

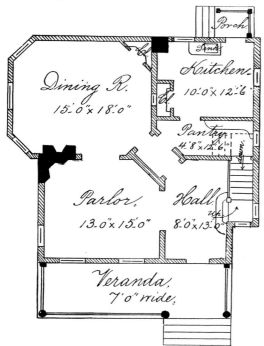

FIRST FLOOR.

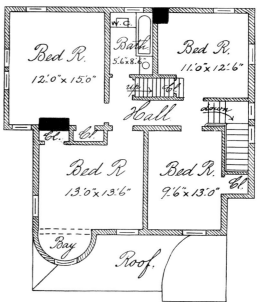

SECOND FLOOR.

DESCRIPTION.

For explanation of all symbols (* † etc.) see page 42.

GENERAL DIMENSIONS: Width through dining room and kitchen, 32 ft.; depth over all, 40 ft. 6 in. Heights of stories: Cellar, 7 ft.; first story, 9 ft. 6 in.; second story, 9 ft.; attic, 8 ft.

EXTERIOR MATERIALS: Foundations, stone and brick; first story, clapboards; second story, gables and roofs, shingles.

INTERIOR FINISH: Hard white plaster, with cornices in hall, parlor and dining room. Soft wood trim throughout, but hard wood stairs. Interior wood-work stained to suit owner, and all finished in hard oil. House piped for gas.

COLORS: Clapboards, and veranda and balcony columns, balusters, floors and ceilings, light seal brown. Trim, veranda rails and all cornices, dark seal brown. All wall shingles stained yellowish red. Roof shingles stained dark brown. Sashes and outside doors, dark green. Brick-work, painted red.

ACCOMMODATIONS: The principal rooms and their sizes, closets, etc., are shown by the plans. Cellar under whole house with inside and outside entrances. Attic floored and two rooms finished. Pantry arrangement prevents kitchen odors pervading house. Dish slide between dining room and kitchen closets. A compact house with a handsome exterior.

COST: $3,000, † not including mantels, range and heater. The estimate is based on ‡ New York prices for materials and labor. In many sections of the country the cost should be less.

Price for working plans, specifications and * license to build, - - - - - - - - - - - $25.00

Price for †† bill of materials, - - - - - 10.00

Address, THE CO-OPERATIVE BUILDING PLAN ASSOCIATION, Architects, 63 Broadway, New York.

FEASIBLE MODIFICATIONS: Heights of stories, sizes of rooms, materials and colors may be changed. Cellar may be reduced in size. Fireplaces and a part or all of plumbing may be omitted.

142

THE CO-OPERATIVE BUILDING PLAN ASSOCIATION, ARCHITECTS, 63 BROADWAY, NEW YORK.

*Shoppell's Modern Houses—*Designs Patented.*   *Residence, Design No. 277*

PERSPECTIVE.

DESCRIPTION.

For explanation of all symbols (* † etc.) see page 42.

GENERAL DIMENSIONS: Width, through dining room and library, 28 ft. 2 in.; depth, 44 ft. 2 in. Heights of stories: Cellar, 7 ft.; first story, 9 ft. 6 in.; second story, 8 ft. 6 in.; attic, 7 ft.

EXTERIOR MATERIALS: Foundation, stone and brick; first story, clapboards; second story, tower and roof, shingles; gables, panels and shingles. Outside blinds.

INTERIOR FINISH: Hard white plaster; plaster cornices and centers in parlor, dining room, library and hall. Soft wood flooring and trim. Ash stairway. Panels under windows in parlor, dining room and library. Bath-room and kitchen wainscoted. Interior wood-work finished in hard oil.

COLORS: Clapboards, dark olive drab. Trim and rain conductors, light olive green. Outside doors, veranda posts, rail, etc., bronze green. Blinds and sashes, dark red. Veranda floor, light stone color. Veranda ceiling, light gray. Wall shingles dipped and brush coated sienna stain. Roof shingles dipped and brush coated grayish brown stain. Tower shingles dipped and brush coated red stain.

ACCOMMODATIONS: The principal rooms and their sizes, closets, etc., are shown by the plans. Cellar under main house. Two rooms in attic with space for another. Fireplaces in parlor, dining room and library.

COST: $3,039, † not including mantels, range and heater: The estimate is based on ‡ New York prices for materials and labor. In many sections of the country the cost should be less.

Price for working plans, specifications and * license to build, - - - - - - - - - - - - $30.00

Price for † † bill of materials, - - - - - 5.00

Address, THE CO-OPERATIVE BUILDING PLAN ASSOCIATION, Architects, 63 Broadway, New York.

FEASIBLE MODIFICATIONS: Heights of stories, colors, sizes of rooms and kinds of materials may be changed. Cellar may be reduced in size or omitted. Fireplaces and mantels may be reduced in number or omitted. If heating apparatus be used rear chimney will suffice. Attic finish may be omitted except flooring. Part or all plumbing may be omitted.

The price of working plans, specifications, etc., for a modified design varies according to the alterations required, and will be made known upon application to the Architects.

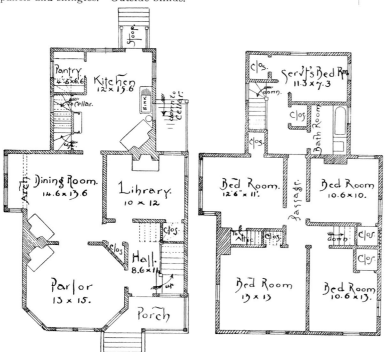

FIRST FLOOR.   SECOND FLOOR.

143

THE CO-OPERATIVE BUILDING PLAN ASSOCIATION, ARCHITECTS, 63 BROADWAY, NEW YORK.

Shoppell's Modern Houses—*Designs Patented.   *Residence, Design No. 152*

DESCRIPTION.

For explanation of all symbols (* † etc.) see page 42.

GENERAL DIMENSIONS: Width, through dining room and kitchen, 34 ft. 6 in.; depth, 42 ft. 10 in. over all. Heights of stories: Cellar, 6 ft. 9 in.; first story, 9 ft. 4 in.; second story, 9 ft..; attic, 7 ft. 6 in.

EXTERIOR MATERIALS: Foundations, stone and brick; first story, clapboards; second story, gables and roof, shingles. Outside blinds.

INTERIOR FINISH: Hard white plaster; plaster cornices in hall, parlor and dining room. Georgia pine flooring in kitchen, bath-room and pantries. Balance of flooring, soft wood. Trim, white pine. Main stairway, ash. Panels under windows in parlor and dining room. Wainscot in bath-room. Interior wood-work finished in hard oil.

COLORS: Clapboards, blinds and sashes, olive green. Trim, and rain conductors, bronze yellow. Outside doors and veranda ceiling, dark green. Veranda floor, drab. Brick-work, Indian red. Wall shingles dipped and brush coated in oil. Roof shingles dipped and brush coated in red stain.

ACCOMMODATIONS: The principal rooms and their sizes, closets, etc., are shown by the plans. Cellar under parlor and hall. No finish in attic except flooring; space for three rooms. Fireplaces and hard wood mantels in parlor and dining room included in estimate. Sliding doors between parlor and dining room. Servant's water-closet off rear porch. Side entrance under main stairs. Five bedrooms and bath-room in second story.

COST: $3,048, † not including range and heater. The estimate is based on ‡ New York prices for materials and labor. In many sections of the country the cost should be less.

Price for working plans, specifications and * license to build, - - - - - - - - - - - - - $30.00
Price for † † bill of materials, - - - - - -   5.00

Address, THE CO-OPERATIVE BUILDING PLAN ASSOCIATION, Architects, 63 Broadway, New York.

FRONT ELEVATION.

FEASIBLE MODIFICATIONS: Heights of stories, colors, sizes of rooms and kinds of materials may be changed. Cellar may be enlarged or omitted. Servants' water-closet and a part or all of the other plumbing may be omitted. Kitchen may be placed where pantry and bedroom are now shown, and present kitchen become a library, sitting room or bedroom. Fireplaces, mantels and sliding doors may be omitted. If heating apparatus be used rear chimney will suffice.

The price of working plans, specifications, etc., for a modified design varies according to the alterations required, and will be made known upon application to the Architects.

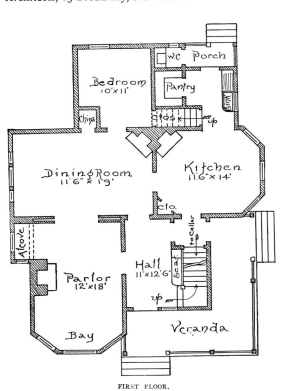

FIRST FLOOR.

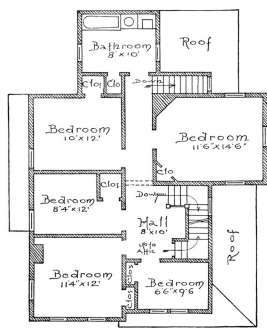

SECOND FLOOR.

144

THE CO-OPERATIVE BUILDING PLAN ASSOCIATION, ARCHITECTS, 63 BROADWAY, NEW YORK.

Shoppell's Modern Houses—*Designs Patented.   *Residence, Design No. 282*

PERSPECTIVE.

DESCRIPTION.

For explanation of all symbols (* † etc.) see page 42.

GENERAL DIMENSIONS: Extreme width, 32 ft.; extreme depth, 51 ft. 6 in. Heights of stories: Cellar, 7 ft.; first story, 10 ft.; second story, 9 ft.; attic 7 ft. 6 in.

EXTERIOR MATERIALS: Foundation, stone and brick; first story, clapboards; second story and roof, shingles; gables, panels and shingles. Outside blinds.

INTERIOR FINISH: Hard white plaster; plaster cornices and centers in hall, parlor, dining and sitting rooms. Soft wood flooring and trim. Ash staircase. Kitchen and bath-room wainscoted. Panels under parlor and dining room windows. Interior wood-work finished in hard oil.

COLORS: Clapboards, light olive drab. Trim, and rain conductors, dark olive drab. Outside doors, dark green. Blinds, light olive green. Sashes, dark red. Veranda floor, yellow stone color. Veranda ceiling, gray. Brick-work, Indian red. Wall shingles dipped and brush coated sienna stain. Roof shingles dipped and brush coated dark red stain.

ACCOMMODATIONS: The principal rooms and their sizes, closets, etc., are shown by the plans. Cellar with inside and outside entrance, under main house. Two rooms and storage space in attic. Fireplaces in dining room and parlor.

COST: $3,070, † not including mantels, range and heater. The estimate is based on ‡ New York prices for materials and labor. In many sections of the country the cost should be less.

Price for working plans, specifications and * license to build, - - - - - - $35.00

Price for † † bill of materials, - - - 5.00

Address, THE CO-OPERATIVE BUILDING PLAN ASSOCIATION, Architects, 63 Broadway, New York.

FEASIBLE MODIFICATIONS: Heights of stories, colors, sizes of rooms and kinds of materials may be changed. Cellar may be enlarged, reduced or omitted. Attic may be floored, but otherwise unfinished. Fireplaces and mantels may be omitted. If heating apparatus be used one chimney between dining room and kitchen will suffice.

The price of working plans, specifications, etc., for a modified design varies according to the alterations required, and will be made known upon application to the Architects.

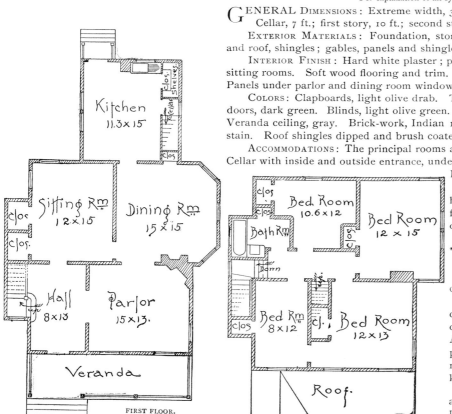

FIRST FLOOR.

SECOND FLOOR.

145

THE CO-OPERATIVE BUILDING PLAN ASSOCIATION, ARCHITECTS, 63 BROADWAY, NEW YORK.

*Shoppell's Modern Houses—*Designs Patented.*   *Residence, Design No. 450*

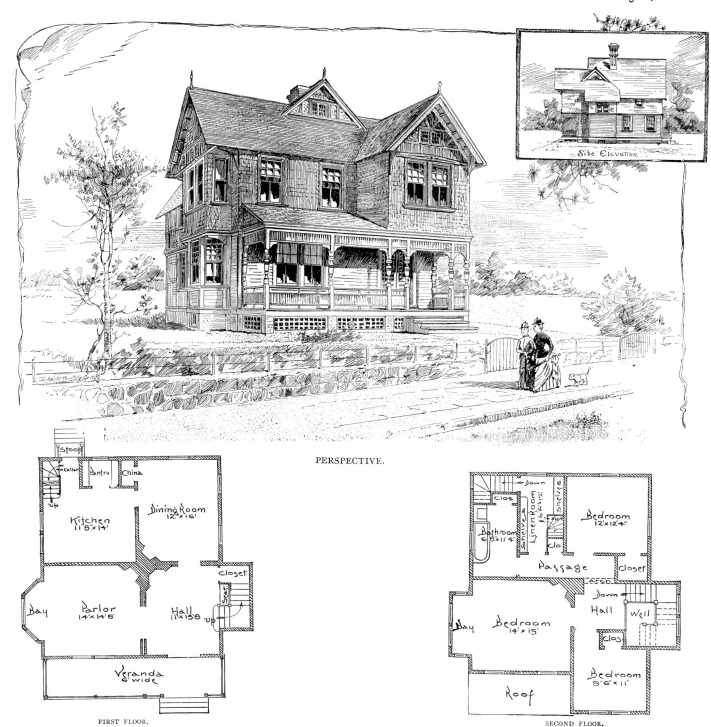

PERSPECTIVE.

FIRST FLOOR.

SECOND FLOOR.

DESCRIPTION.

For explanation of all symbols (* † etc.) see page 42.

GENERAL DIMENSIONS: Extreme width, 35 ft.; depth, including veranda, 37 ft. 6 in. Heights of stories: Cellar, 7 ft.; first story, 9 ft.; second story, 8 ft. 6 in.

EXTERIOR MATERIALS: Foundations, stone; first story, clapboards; second story and roof, shingles; gables, shingles and panels. Outside blinds.

INTERIOR FINISH: Hard white plaster; plaster cornices in hall, parlor and dining room. Yellow pine flooring in hall, dining room, kitchen and pantry; other flooring, soft wood. Trim, white pine. Stairs, ash. Bath-room and kitchen wainscoted. Interior woodwork finished in hard oil.

COLORS: Clapboards, yellow stone color. Trim and veranda floor, yellow drab. Outside doors and blinds, dark green. Sashes, maroon. Veranda ceiling, varnished. Brick-work, Indian red. Wall shingles dipped and brush coated red stain. Roof shingles dipped and brush coated darker red stain.

ACCOMMODATIONS: The principal rooms and their sizes, closets, etc., are shown by the plans. Cellar with concrete floor under the whole house Attic floored, but unfinished; space for two rooms. Sliding doors between hall and parlor and dining room. Coat and hat closet in hall. Handsome staircase with seat. Fireplaces with mantels in hall, parlor, dining room and one bedroom. Hall intended for a reception room.

COST: $3,112, † not including range and heater. The estimate is based on ‡ New York prices for materials and labor. In many sections of the country the cost should be less.

Price for working plans, specifications and * license to build, - - - - - - - - - - - - - $30.00
Price for † † bill of materials, - - - - - - 5.00

Address, THE CO-OPERATIVE BUILDING PLAN ASSOCIATION, Architects, 63 Broadway, New York.

FEASIBLE MODIFICATIONS: Heights of stories, colors, sizes of rooms and kinds of materials may be changed. Cellar may be reduced or omitted. Concrete floor may be omitted. Sliding doors, and any or all fireplaces and mantels may be omitted. By combining pantry and china closet to form butler's pantry, direct communication between kitchen and dining room may be closed. A part or all plumbing may be omitted. If bath-room be omitted and rear stairway re-planned one more good bedroom may be had in second story.

*Shoppell's Modern Houses—*Designs Patented.*   *Cottage, Design No. 206*

PERSPECTIVE.

DESCRIPTION.

For explanation of all symbols (* † etc.) see page 42.

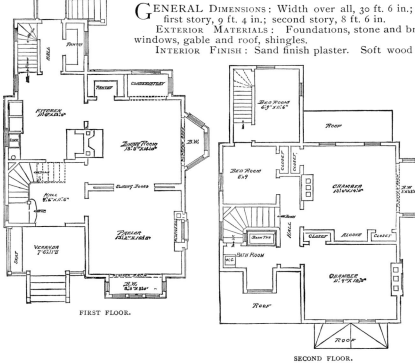

FIRST FLOOR.

SECOND FLOOR.

GENERAL DIMENSIONS: Width over all, 30 ft. 6 in.; depth over all, 46 ft. 6 in. Heights of stories: Cellar, 7 ft.; first story, 9 ft. 4 in.; second story, 8 ft. 6 in.

EXTERIOR MATERIALS: Foundations, stone and brick; first story, clapboards; second story, clapboards; bay windows, gable and roof, shingles.

INTERIOR FINISH: Sand finish plaster. Soft wood flooring and trim. Ash stairway. Kitchen and bath-room wainscoted. Panels under parlor and dining room windows. Interior wood-work finished in hard oil.

COLORS: All clapboards, sashes, and panels of outside doors, light olive green. Trim, bronze green. Cornices and veranda finish, and frames forming panels of outside doors, bronze yellow. Veranda ceiling, medium drab. Brick-work and blinds, Indian red. Roof shingles dipped and brush coated Indian red. Wall shingles dipped and brush coated sienna stain.

ACCOMMODATIONS: The principal rooms and their sizes, closets, etc., are shown by the plans. Cellar under kitchen and dining room, with inside and outside entrances. Attic floored, but unfinished; space for two small rooms. Fireplaces and mantels in dining room and parlor. A novelty of this design is building the front chimney around a stained glass window which shows over the parlor mantel.

COST: $3,131, † not including mantels, range and heater. The estimate is based on ‡ New York prices for materials and labor. In many sections of the country the cost should be less.

Price for working plans, specifications and
* license to build, - - - - - - $25.00
Price for †† bill of materials, - - - - 5.00
Address: THE CO-OPERATIVE BUILDING PLAN ASSOCIATION, Architects, 63 Broadway, New York.

FEASIBLE MODIFICATIONS: Heights of stories, colors, sizes of rooms and kinds of materials may be changed. Cellar may extend under whole house or be omitted.

147

THE CO-OPERATIVE BUILDING PLAN ASSOCIATION, ARCHITECTS, 63 BROADWAY, NEW YORK.

*Shoppell's Modern Houses—*Designs Patented.*   *Residence, Design No. 393*

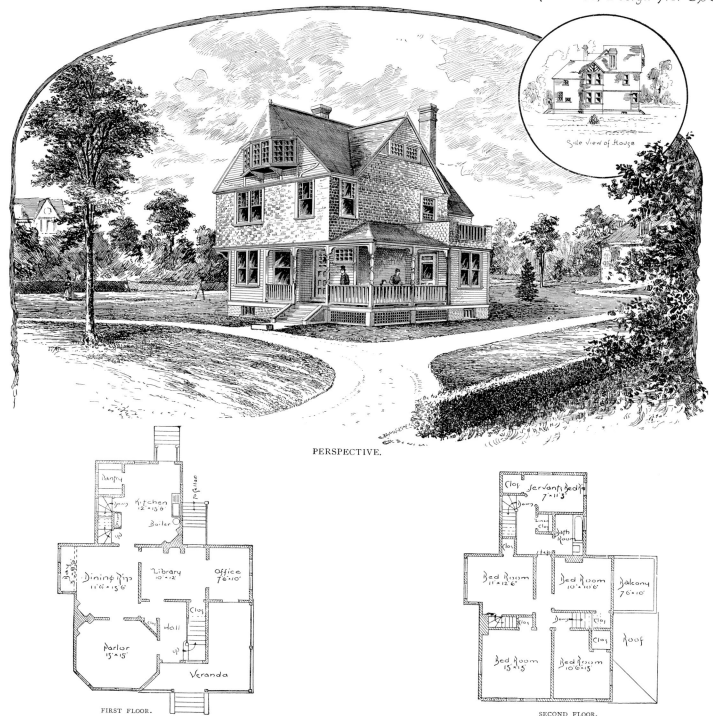

Side View of House

PERSPECTIVE.

FIRST FLOOR.

SECOND FLOOR.

DESCRIPTION.

For explanation of all symbols (* † etc.) see page 42.

GENERAL DIMENSIONS: Width, 36 ft. 2 in.; depth, 44 ft. Heights of stories: Cellar, 7 ft.; first story, 9 ft. 6 in.; second story, 8 ft. 10 in.; attic, 7 ft. 6 in.

EXTERIOR MATERIALS: Foundation, stone and brick; first story, clapboards; second story and roof, shingles; gables, panels and shingles. Outside blinds.

INTERIOR FINISH: Hard white plaster; plaster cornices and centers in parlor, dining room, library and hall. Soft wood flooring and trim. Panels under windows in parlor, dining room and library. Picture molding in principal rooms and hall of first story. Chair rail in dining room and halls. Stairs, ash. Wainscot in bath-room and kitchen. Interior wood-work finished in hard oil.

COLORS: Clapboards, olive drab. Trim, and rain conductors, olive. Blinds and sashes, Pompeian red. Veranda floor, buff. Veranda ceiling, light grayish green. Outside doors, veranda posts and rails, green drab. Wall shingles dipped and brush coated sienna stain. Roof shingles dipped and brush coated walnut stain.

ACCOMMODATIONS: The principal rooms and their sizes, closets,

etc., are shown by the plans. Cellar under main part of house, with outside entrance and concrete floor. Two rooms finished in attic. Good design for a professional man. Fireplaces and mantels in parlor, dining room and library.

COST: $3,198, † not including range and heater. The estimate is based on ‡ New York prices for materials and labor. In many sections of the country the cost should be less.

Price for working plans, specifications and * license to build, - - - - - - - - - - - - $30.00
Price for †† bill of materials, - - - - 5.00

Address, THE CO-OPERATIVE BUILDING PLAN ASSOCIATION, Architects, 63 Broadway, New York.

FEASIBLE MODIFICATIONS: Heights of stories, colors, sizes of rooms and kinds of materials may be changed. The office and library may be combined to form a large dining room, in which case the present dining room should be disconnected from kitchen and be used as library or back parlor, connecting with the parlor by a wider opening. A part or all of plumbing may be omitted.

148

THE CO-OPERATIVE BUILDING PLAN ASSOCIATION, ARCHITECTS, 63 BROADWAY, NEW YORK.

Shoppell's Modern Houses—*Designs Patented.   *Residence, Design No. 578*

PERSPECTIVE.

DESCRIPTION.

For explanation of all symbols (* † etc.) see page 42.

GENERAL DIMENSIONS: Width over all, 31 ft.; depth, 39 ft. 10 in. Heights of stories: Cellar, 6 ft. 8 in.; first story, 9 ft.; second story, 8 ft. 6 in.

EXTERIOR MATERIALS: Foundations, stone; first and second stories, gables and roofs, shingles. Outside blinds to all windows except those of the cellar and attic.

INTERIOR FINISH: Hard white plaster; plaster cornices and centers in parlor, library and dining room. Flooring throughout, white pine. Second story flooring deafened. Bath-room and kitchen wainscoted. Hall, main stairway and front door, antique oak. Interior wood-work finished in hard oil.

COLORS: Trim, outside doors (except front door, which is finished in hard oil), blinds, sashes, and rain conductors, greenish drab. Veranda floor, drab. Veranda ceiling varnished. Wall shingles dipped and brush coated in Tuscan yellow paint. Roof shingles unpainted.

ACCOMMODATIONS: The principal rooms and their sizes, closets, etc., are shown by the plans. Cellar under whole house, with concrete floor. Laundry with two tubs and servant's W. C. in cellar. One room finished in attic. Seven fireplaces in first and second stories.

COST: $3,200, † not including mantels, range and heater. The estimate is based on ‡ New York prices for materials and labor. In many sections of the country the cost should be less.

Price for working plans, specifications and * license to build, - - - - - - $30.00
Price for † † bill of materials, - - - - - 10.00

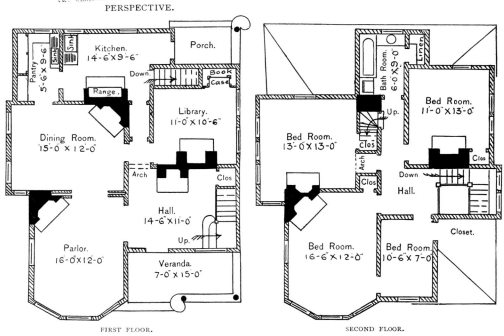

FIRST FLOOR.

SECOND FLOOR.

Address, THE CO-OPERATIVE BUILDING PLAN ASSOCIATION, Architects, 63 Broadway, New York.

FEASIBLE MODIFICATIONS: Heights of stories, sizes of rooms, materials and colors may be changed. Cellar may be reduced in size. Fireplaces, sliding doors, and a part or all of the plumbing may be omitted. If heating apparatus be used one chimney will suffice.

149

THE CO-OPERATIVE BUILDING PLAN ASSOCIATION, ARCHITECTS, 63 BROADWAY, NEW YORK.

Shoppell's Modern Houses—*Designs Patented.

Residence, Design No. 382

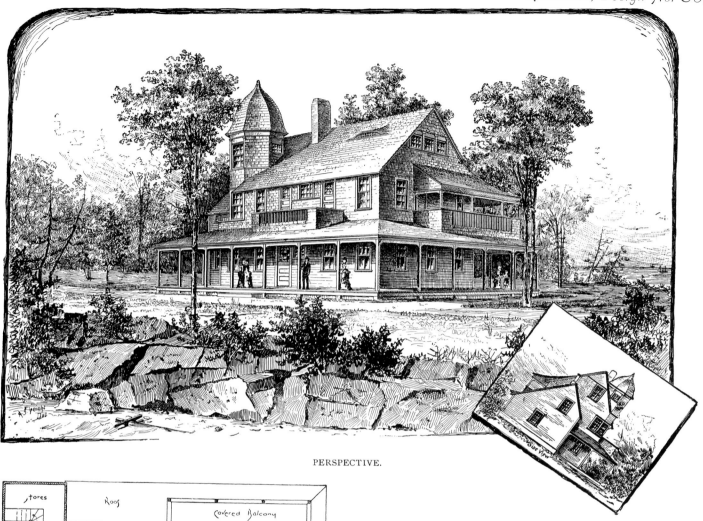

PERSPECTIVE.

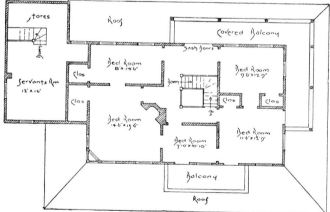

FIRST FLOOR.

SECOND FLOOR.

DESCRIPTION.

For explanation of all symbols (* † etc.) see page 42.

GENERAL DIMENSIONS: Width, 65 ft., including kitchen and veranda; depth, including veranda, 42 ft. Heights of stories: First story, 9 ft. 6 in.; second story, 8 ft.

EXTERIOR MATERIALS: Foundation, stone piers; first story, clapboards; second story, gables and roof, shingles. Outside blinds.

INTERIOR FINISH: Sand finish plaster. Soft wood flooring; yellow pine trim and stairway; all finished in hard oil.

COLORS: Clapboards, and veranda posts and rail, dark olive drab. Trim, and rain conductors, bronze green. Outside doors and blinds, dark green. Sashes, bright red. Veranda floor and ceiling, varnished. Brick-work, Indian red. Wall shingles, oiled. Roof shingles, left natural.

ACCOMMODATIONS: The principal rooms and their sizes, closets, etc., are shown by the plans. No cellar. Attic floored, but unfinished; space for three rooms. Tower entered from attic. Three open fireplaces with hard wood mantels included in estimate.

COST: $3,214, † not including range. The estimate is based on ‡ New York prices for materials and labor. In many sections of the country the cost should be less.

Price for working plans, specifications and * license to build, - - - - - - - - - - - $40.00

Price for †† bill of materials, - - - - - 5.00

Address, THE CO-OPERATIVE BUILDING PLAN ASSOCIATION, Architects, 63 Broadway, New York.

FEASIBLE MODIFICATIONS: Heights of stories, colors, sizes of rooms and kinds of materials may be changed. Tower and balconies may be omitted and extent of veranda reduced. A bath-room with partial or full plumbing may be introduced. Cellar may be built. Kitchen extension may be omitted. Number of fireplaces and mantels may be reduced or omitted.

150

THE CO-OPERATIVE BUILDING PLAN ASSOCIATION ARCHITECTS, 63 BROADWAY, NEW YORK.

*Shoppell's Modern Houses—*Designs Patented.*   *Residence, Design No. 288*

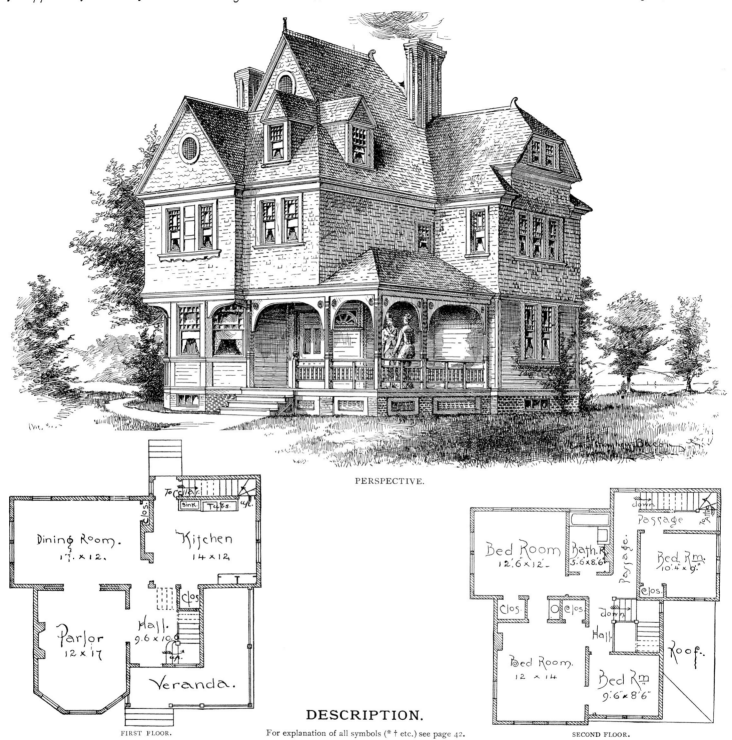

PERSPECTIVE.

FIRST FLOOR.   For explanation of all symbols (* † etc.) see page 42.   SECOND FLOOR.

DESCRIPTION.

GENERAL DIMENSIONS: Extreme width, 34 ft.; depth, 33 ft. 2 in. Heights of stories: Cellar, 7 ft.; first story, 9 ft. 6 in.; second story, 8 ft. 6 in.; attic, 7 ft. 10 in.

EXTERIOR MATERIALS: Foundations, stone and brick; first story, clapboards; second story, gables, dormers and roofs, shingles. Outside blinds to all except cellar and attic windows.

INTERIOR FINISH: Hard white plaster; plaster cornices and centers in parlor, hall and dining room. Soft wood flooring and trim. Ash stairway. Panels under windows in parlor and dining room. Wainscot in kitchen and bath-room. Interior wood-work finished in hard oil.

COLORS: All clapboards, dark olive drab. Trim, sashes, rain conductors, and brick-work, dark red. Outside doors, maroon. Blinds, bronze green. Veranda floor and ceiling, light stone color. Wall shingles dipped and brush coated sienna stain. Roof shingles dipped and brush coated with umber stain.

ACCOMMODATIONS: The principal rooms and their sizes, closets, etc., are shown by the plans. Cellar under whole house. Four bed-rooms in attic. Wash-bowl in the closet between two bedrooms

Open fireplace, and mantel in parlor and range in kitchen, included in estimate.

COST: $3,258, † not including heater. The estimate is based on ‡ New York prices for materials and labor. In many sections of the country the cost should be less.

Price for working plans, specifications and * license to build, - - - - - - - - - $40.00
Price for † † bill of materials, - - - - - 5.00
Address, THE CO-OPERATIVE BUILDING PLAN ASSOCIATION, Architects, 63 Broadway, New York.

FEASIBLE MODIFICATIONS: Heights of stories, colors, sizes of rooms and kinds of materials may be changed. Cellar may be reduced or omitted entirely. Attic may be left unfinished except flooring. Sliding doors, set range, and fireplace and mantel may be omitted. Rear chimney will suffice if house be heated by apparatus. A part or all of the plumbing may be omitted. Kitchen extension may be planned.

The price of working plans, specifications, etc., for a modified design varies according to the alterations required, and will be made known upon application to the Architects.

151

THE CO-OPERATIVE BUILDING PLAN ASSOCIATION, ARCHITECTS, 63 BROADWAY, NEW YORK.

*Shoppell's Modern Houses—*Designs Patented.*

Residence, Design No. 621

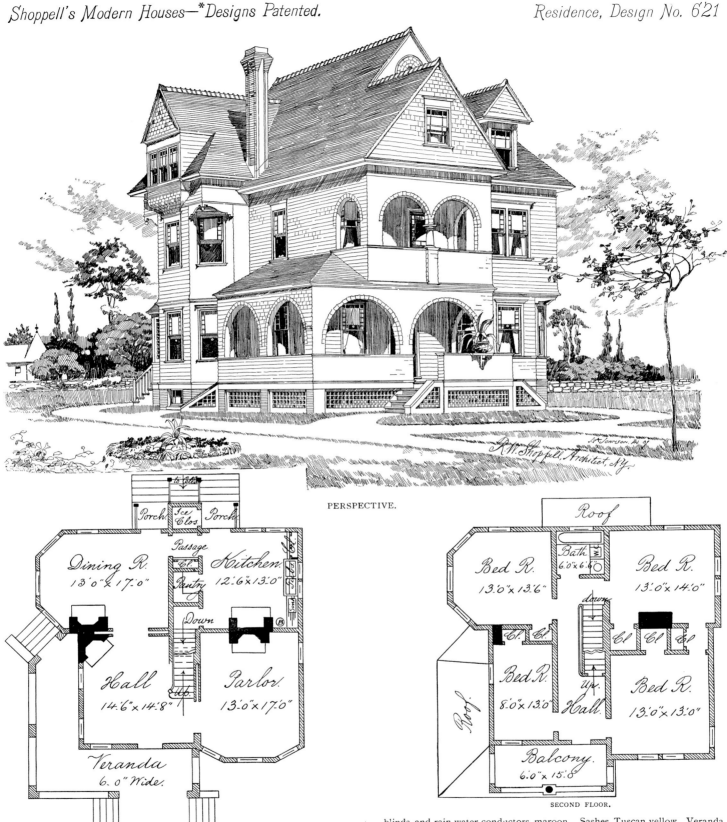

PERSPECTIVE.

FIRST FLOOR.

SECOND FLOOR.

DESCRIPTION.

For explanation of all symbols (* † etc.) see page 42.

GENERAL DIMENSIONS : Width, including veranda, 36 ft.; depth, including veranda and porches, 39 ft. 6 in. Heights of stories : Cellar, 7 ft.; first story, 9 ft. 6 in.; second story, 9 ft.; attic, 8 ft.

EXTERIOR MATERIALS : Foundations, stone and brick; first story, clapboards; second story, gables and dormers, shingles; roof, slate.

INTERIOR FINISH : Hard white plaster. Soft wood trim. Hard wood stairs. All interior wood-work stained to suit owner, and finished in hard oil. Bath-room and kitchen wainscoted. Hall and dining room floored with hard wood, remainder of flooring soft wood.

COLORS : Clapboards, tan color. Trim, seal brown. Outside doors, blinds, and rain water conductors, maroon. Sashes, Tuscan yellow. Veranda floor, brown. Veranda ceiling, buff. Brick-work to be oiled. Ridge roll to be painted in imitation of terra cotta. Wall shingles dipped and brush coated with Tuscan yellow paint.

ACCOMMODATIONS : The principal rooms and their sizes, closets, etc., are shown by the plan. Cellar under the whole house. Two rooms and hall finished in attic.

COST : $3,300 † not including mantels, range and heater. The estimate is based on ‡ New York prices for materials and labor. In many sections of the country the cost should be less.

Price for working plans, specifications and * license to build, - $30.00
Price for † † bill of materials, - - - - - - - - 15.00
Address, THE CO-OPERATIVE BUILDING PLAN ASSOCIATION, Architects, 63 Broadway, New York.

FEASIBLE MODIFICATIONS : Heights of stories, sizes of rooms, materials and colors may be changed. Concrete and hard wood floors may be omitted, Fireplaces and sliding doors may be omitted. A part or all of the plumbing may be omitted. One chimney may be omitted if heating apparatus be used.

152

THE CO-OPERATIVE BUILDING PLAN ASSOCIATION, ARCHITECTS, 63 BROADWAY, NEW YORK.

Shoppell's Modern Houses—*Designs Patented.   *Residence, Design No. 597*

PERSPECTIVE.

DESCRIPTION.

For explanation of all symbols (* † etc.) see page 42.

GENERAL DIMENSIONS : Width, through dining room and sitting room, 34 ft.; depth, including veranda, 51 ft. 6 in. Heights of stories : Cellar, 7 ft.; first story, 9 ft. 6 in.; second story, 8 ft. 10 in.; attic, 7 ft. 6 in.

EXTERIOR MATERIALS : Foundations, stone and brick ; first story, clapboards ; second story and roof, shingles ; gables, paneled and shingled. Bay windows have inside sliding blinds ; all other windows except those of cellar have outside blinds.

INTERIOR FINISH : Hard white plaster throughout; plaster cornices and centers in hall, parlor, sitting and dining rooms. Oak trim in hall and dining room. Georgia pine in second story and white pine in remainder of house. Main stairs, oak. All inside wood-work finished in hard oil.

COLORS : All clapboards, light brown. Trim, water table, corner boards, casings, bands, veranda posts and rails, dark seal brown. Front door finished with hard oil ; all other outside doors and outside blinds painted dark seal brown. Gables, dark buff with dark seal brown panels. Sashes, dark buff. Veranda floors, dark brown. Veranda ceiling finished natural color. Panel work in first and second stories, dark seal brown for framing of panels and light brown for panels. Wall shingles dipped and brush coated buff stain. Roof shingles dipped and brush coated dark brown stain.

ACCOMMODATIONS : The principal rooms and their sizes, closets, etc. are shown by the plans. Cellar with concrete floor under whole house. Laundry tubs in kitchen. Combined front and back stairs economize room. Coat and hat closet in hall. Three hard wood mantels and stained glass in staircase window included in estimate. House piped for gas. Two bedrooms and hall finished in attic. Wash basin in closet under main stairs.

COST : $3,300,† not including range and heater. The estimate is based on ‡ New York prices for materials and labor. In many sections of the country the cost should be less.

Price for working plans, specifications and * license to build, - - - - - - - - - - - - - - - - $35.00
Price for † † bill of materials, - - - - - - - - 10.00

Address, THE CO-OPERATIVE BUILDING PLAN ASSOCIATION, Architects, 63 Broadway, New York.

FIRST FLOOR.   SECOND FLOOR.

FEASIBLE MODIFICATIONS : Heights of stories, sizes of rooms, materials and colors may be changed. Cellar may be reduced in size and concrete floor omitted. Fireplaces, sliding doors, balcony, stained glass, gas piping and a part or all of the plumbing may be omitted. Front chimney may be omitted.

The price of working plans, specifications, etc. for a modified design varies according to the alterations required, and will be made known upon application to the Architects.

153

THE CO-OPERATIVE BUILDING PLAN ASSOCIATION, ARCHITECTS, 63 BROADWAY, NEW YORK.

*Shoppell's Modern Houses—*Designs Patented.*   *Cottage, Design No. 638*

PERSPECTIVE.

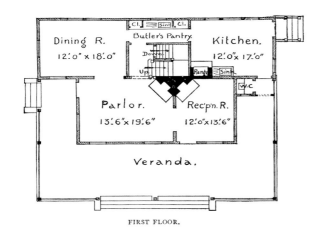

FIRST FLOOR.

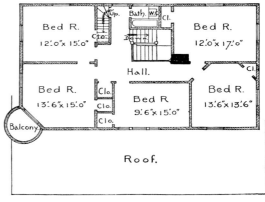

SECOND FLOOR.

DESCRIPTION.

For explanation of all symbols (* † etc.) see page 42.

GENERAL DIMENSIONS: Extreme width, 49 ft.; extreme depth, 39 ft. Heights of stories: Cellar, 7 ft.; first story, 9 ft. 6 in.; second story, 9 ft.

EXTERIOR MATERIALS: Foundations, stone; first story, clapboards; second story, gables and roof, shingles.

INTERIOR FINISH: Hard white plaster throughout. All trim and the stairs soft woods finished in hard oil. Floors of first story, hard wood; remainder of floors, soft wood.

COLORS: All clapboards, all shingles (except roof) and blinds, "Colonial" yellow. All trim and entrance doors, white. Veranda floor and ceiling and all brick work, oiled.

ACCOMMODATIONS: The principal rooms and their sizes, closets, etc. are shown by the floor plans. Beside these there is a cellar under the whole house. No rooms are finished in the attic, but there is space for three if required. Small balcony on attic floor. The location of the stairway is convenient for all parts of the house. A curtain may be drawn between the parlor and stairway hall when servants are using the stairway.

COST: $3300, † not including mantels, range and heater. The estimate is based on ‡ New York prices for materials and labor. In many sections of the country the cost should be less.

Price for working plans, specifications and * license to build, $30.00
Price for †† bill of materials,   -   -   -   -   -   -   10.00

Address, THE CO-OPERATIVE BUILDING PLAN ASSOCIATION, Architects, 63 Broadway, New York.

FEASIBLE MODIFICATIONS: Heights of stories, exterior materials and colors may be changed. Cellar may by reduced in size or omitted. The first floor W. C. (intended for servants), the hard wood floors, all balconies, fire-places and the set range may be omitted. Both ends of the roof may be alike. All of the bed-rooms may be connected by doors.

The price of working plans, specifications, etc. for a modified design varies according to the alterations required, and will be made known upon application to the Architects.

THE CO-OPERATIVE BUILDING PLAN ASSOCIATION, ARCHITECTS, 63 BROADWAY, NEW YORK.

*Shoppell's Modern Houses—*Designs Patented.*   *Residence, Design No. 662*

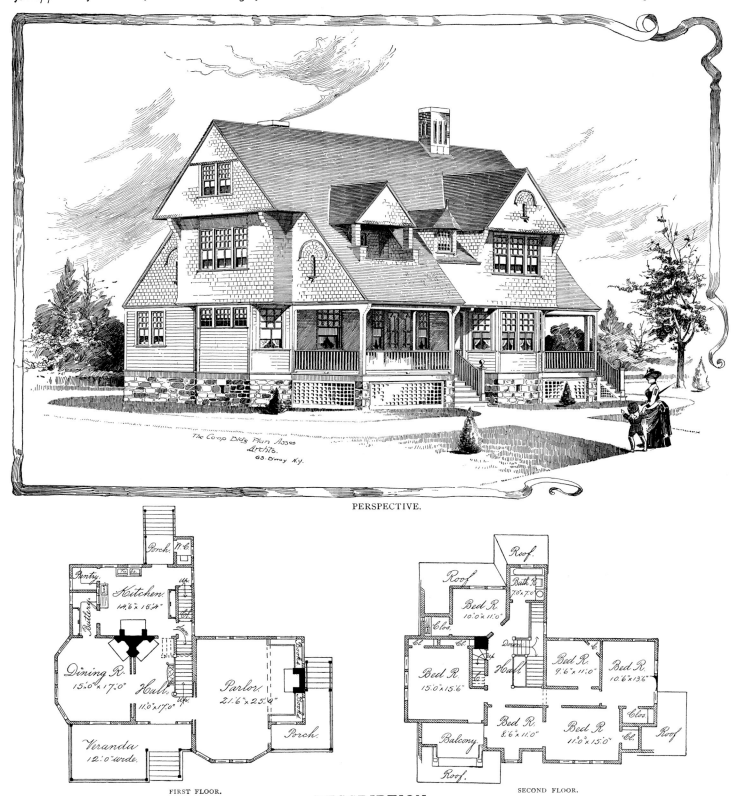

PERSPECTIVE.

FIRST FLOOR.   SECOND FLOOR.

DESCRIPTION.

For explanation of all symbols (* † etc.) see page 42.

GENERAL DIMENSIONS: Width, 55 ft. 6 in., including porch; depth, 45 ft., including veranda. Heights of stories: Cellar, 7 ft.; first story, 9 ft.; second story, 8 ft. 6 in.; attic, 8 ft.

EXTERIOR MATERIALS: Foundations, stone; first story, clapboards; second story and gables, dormers and roofs, shingles.

NOTE.—The parlor chimney comes out of the roof at the extreme right end of ridge instead of where shown on the perspective.

INTERIOR FINISH: Hard white plaster. Plaster centers in hall, parlor and dining room. Double floors in first story, finishing with yellow pine in kitchen portion and oak in remainder. Second story and attic flooring, white pine. Oak trim in dining room, hall and parlor. Main staircase, oak. Panels under windows in hall, parlor and dining room. Bath-room and kitchen wainscoted. Interior wood-work stained to suit owner and finished in hard oil.

COLORS: Clapboards, light drab. Trim and rain conductors, dark drab. Outside doors stained and finished in hard oil. Sashes, dark red. Veranda floor, oiled. Veranda ceiling, varnished. Brick-work, oiled. Wall shingles dipped and brush coated umber stain. Roof shingles left natural color.

ACCOMMODATIONS: The principal rooms and their sizes, closets, etc., are shown by the plans. Cellar under whole house. Two rooms and hall finished in the attic. Space for sideboard under triple high-up windows in dining room. Recess off parlor with bookcases, fireplace and mantel, produces handsome effect.

COST: $4,000, † not including mantels, range and heater. The estimate is based on ‡ New York prices for materials and labor. In many sections of the country the cost should be less.

Price for working plans, specifications and * license to build, - $35.00
Price for †† bill of materials, - - - - - - - 10.00

155

THE CO-OPERATIVE BUILDING PLAN ASSOCIATION, ARCHITECTS, 63 BROADWAY, NEW YORK.

*Shoppell's Modern Houses—*Designs Patented.*   *Residence, Design No. 588*

PERSPECTIVE.

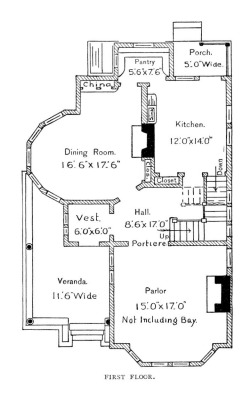

FIRST FLOOR.   SECOND FLOOR.

DESCRIPTION.

For explanation of all symbols (* † etc.) see page 42.

GENERAL DIMENSIONS: Width, through dining room and kitchen, 30 ft.; depth over all, 48 ft. 6 in. Heights of stories: Cellar, 7 ft.; first story, 9 ft. 6 in.; second story, 9 ft.; third story, 8 ft.

EXTERIOR MATERIALS: Foundations, stone; first story, clapboards; second story and gables, dormers, roofs, and veranda enclosure, shingles.

INTERIOR FINISH: Hard white plaster throughout and plaster cornices and centers in hall, parlor and dining room. Trim, yellow pine. Staircase of cherry. Bath-room and kitchen wainscoted. All wood-work finished in hard oil. Flooring in kitchen, pantry and bath-room, yellow pine, and in attic, spruce; elsewhere, white pine.

COLORS: All clapboards, brown. Trim and rain conductors, orange red. Outside doors, blinds and sashes, dark green. Veranda floor, tan color. Veranda ceiling, varnished. Wall shingles dipped in and brush coated with dark red stain.

ACCOMMODATIONS: The principal rooms and their sizes, closets, etc., are shown by the plans. Cellar under whole house. One room

finished in attic and space for one more. Colonial in style and regarded as a very pleasing design.

COST: $3,300, † not including mantels, range and heater. The estimate is based on ‡ New York prices for materials and labor. In many sections of the country the cost should be less.

Price for working plans, specifications and * license to build, - - - - - - - - - - - - - - - - $35.00
Price for ‡ ‡ bill of materials, - - - - - 10.00
Address, THE CO-OPERATIVE BUILDING PLAN ASSOCIATION, Architects, 63 Broadway, New York.

FEASIBLE MODIFICATIONS: Heights of stories, sizes of rooms, materials and colors may be changed. Cellar may be reduced in size. Fireplaces may be omitted. If heating apparatus be used parlor chimney may be omitted. Front door may be placed in vestibule where windows are now shown. Sliding doors may be introduced between parlor and hall.

The price of working plans, specifications, etc., for a modified design varies according to the alterations required, and will be made known upon application to the Architects.

THE CO-OPERATIVE BUILDING PLAN ASSOCIATION, ARCHITECTS, 63 BROADWAY, NEW YORK.

Shoppell's Modern Houses—*Designs Patented.   *Residnce, Design No. 444*

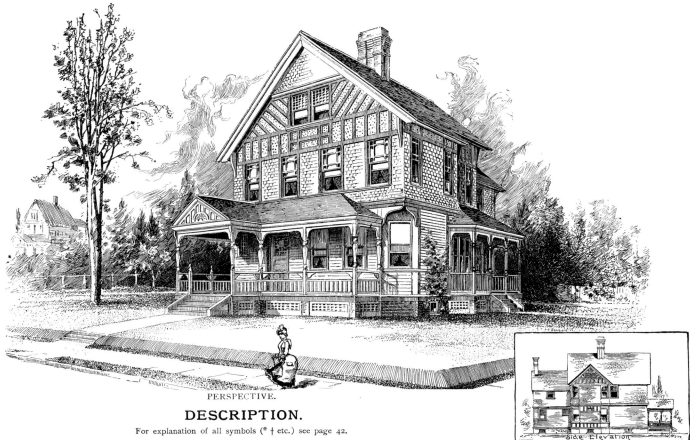

PERSPECTIVE.

DESCRIPTION.

For explanation of all symbols (* † etc.) see page 42.

GENERAL DIMENSIONS : Extreme width, 32 ft.; depth, including veranda, 54 ft. Heights of stories: Cellar, 7 ft.; first story, 9 ft.; second story, 8 ft. 4 in.; attic, 8 ft.

EXTERIOR MATERIALS: Foundations, stone and brick; first story, clapboards; second story and roof, shingles ; gables, panels and shingles. Outside blinds.

INTERIOR FINISH : Hard white plaster. Cellar ceiling plastered one heavy coat. Soft wood flooring and trim. Ash stairs. Wainscot in bath-room. Panels under windows in parlor, library and dining room. Interior wood-work stained to suit owner, finished in hard oil.

COLORS : Clapboards, light brown. Trim, blinds and sashes, dark brown. Outside doors, dark brown with light brown panels. Veranda floor, dark drab. Veranda ceiling, varnished. Rain conductors, dark green. Brick-work, Indian red. Wall shingles dipped and brush coated with umber stain. Roof shingles dipped and brush coated with dark red stain.

ACCOMMODATIONS : The principal rooms and their sizes, closets, etc., are shown by the plans. Cellar with concrete floor under whole house. A bedroom, a trunk-room, and a hallway finished in attic. Furnace pipes from cellar throughout the house, with registers, are included in estimate. Fireplaces with mantels in dining room, hall, parlor, library and one bedroom.

COST : $3,363, † not including range and heater. The estimate is based on ‡ New York prices for materials and labor. In many sections of the country the cost should be less.

Price for working plans, specifications and * license to build, - - $30.00

Price for ‡‡ bill of materials,   5.00

Address, THE CO-OPERATIVE BUILDING PLAN ASSOCIATION, Architects, 63 Broadway, New York.

FEASIBLE MODIFICATIONS : Heights of stories, colors and sizes of rooms and kinds of materials, may be changed. Cellar may be reduced in size and concrete floor may be omitted. A part or all plumbing and any or all fireplaces and mantels may be omitted. Verandas may be reduced, extended or omitted.

The price of working plans, specifications, etc., for a modified design varies according to the alterations required, and will be made known upon application to the Architects.

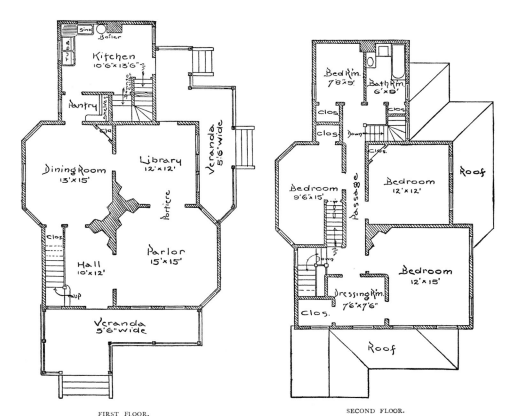

FIRST FLOOR.   SECOND FLOOR.

157

THE CO-OPERATIVE BUILDING PLAN ASSOCIATION, ARCHITECTS, 63 BROADWAY, NEW YORK.

*Shoppell's Modern Houses—*Designs Patented.*   *Residence, Design No. 451*

PERSPECTIVE.

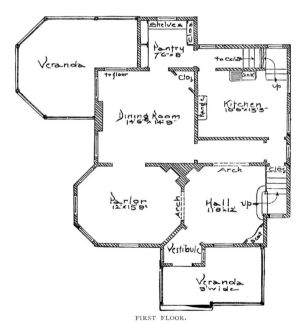

FIRST FLOOR.

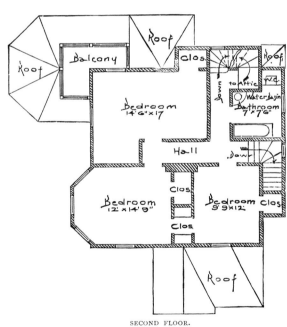

SECOND FLOOR.

DESCRIPTION.

For explanation of all symbols (*† etc.) see page 42.

GENERAL DIMENSIONS: Extreme width, 41 ft. 8 in.; depth, including veranda, 45 ft. Heights of stories: Cellar, 7 ft. 6 in.; first story, 9 ft.; second story, 8 ft. 6 in.

EXTERIOR MATERIALS: Foundations, stone; first story, clapboards; second story, clapboards and shingles; gables and roofs, shingles. Outside blinds.

INTERIOR FINISH: Hard white plaster; plaster cornices and centers in parlor, hall and dining room. Soft wood flooring and trim. Ash stairs. Panels under windows in parlor, hall and dining room. Wainscot in bath-room and kitchen. Interior wood-work finished in hard oil.

COLORS: First story clapboards, yellow stone color. Trim and rain conductors, seal brown. Outside doors, blinds and sashes, veranda balusters, rails, posts and cornices, maroon. Veranda floor, light drab. Veranda ceiling, lilac. Brick-work, Indian red. Wall shingles dipped and brush coated dark red stain. Second story clapboards painted same color as wall shingles. Roof shingles dipped and brush coated very dark red.

ACCOMMODATIONS: The principal rooms and their sizes, closets, etc., are shown by the plans. Cellar under rear veranda, dining room and kitchen, with outside and inside entrances and concrete floor. Three bedrooms finished in attic. Though designed for a hillside location, this design is quite suitable for a level grade.

COST: $3,437, † not including range and heater. The estimate is based on ‡ New York prices for materials and labor. In many sections of the country the cost should be less.

Price for working plans, specifications, and * license to build, - - - - - - - - - - $35.00
Price for †† bill of materials, - - - - - 5.00

Address, THE CO-OPERATIVE BUILDING PLAN ASSOCIATION, Architects, 63 Broadway, New York.

FEASIBLE MODIFICATIONS: Heights of stories, colors, sizes of rooms and kinds of materials may be changed. Cellar may extend under whole house or may be omitted.

158

THE CO-OPERATIVE BUILDING PLAN ASSOCIATION, ARCHITECTS, 63 BROADWAY, NEW YORK.

*Shoppell's Modern Houses—*Designs Patented.*   *Two-Family Residence, No. 437*

PERSPECTIVE.

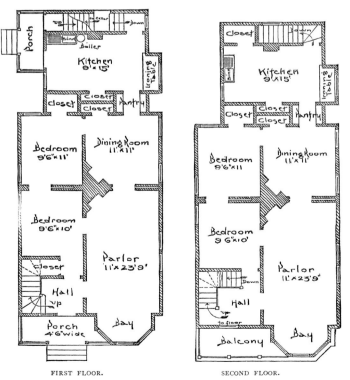

FIRST FLOOR.   SECOND FLOOR.

FEASIBLE MODIFICATIONS: Heights of stories, colors, sizes of rooms and kinds of materials may be changed. Dining rooms may be enlarged at the expense of the parlors. Sliding doors, fireplaces and mantels may be reduced in number or omitted. Front balcony may be omitted. Side entrance and porch to lower kitchen may be omitted. Design may be re-planned for one family.

DESCRIPTION.

For explanation of all symbols (* † etc.) see page 42.

GENERAL DIMENSIONS: Width, 22 ft.; depth over all, 52 ft. 9 in.
    Heights of stories: Cellar, 7 ft.; first story, 9 ft. 6 in.; second story, 9 ft.; attic, 7 ft. 6 in.

EXTERIOR MATERIALS: Foundation, brick; first story, clapboards; second story, clapboards; gables, clapboards and shingles; roof, shingles.

INTERIOR FINISH: Hard white plaster. Plaster cornices and centers in parlors, dining rooms and halls. Soft wood flooring and trim. Ash stairway. Panels under windows in parlors. Kitchens wainscoted. Interior wood-work finished in hard oil.

COLORS: All clapboards, light olive drab. Trim, and rain conductors, light olive green. Outside doors, veranda posts, rails, etc., bronze green. Blinds and sashes, dark red. Veranda floor, yellow stone color. Veranda ceiling, gray. Wall shingles dipped and brush coated sienna stain. Roof shingles dipped and brush coated red stain. Brick-work, red.

ACCOMMODATIONS: The principal rooms and their sizes, closets, etc., are shown by the plans. Cellar under whole house; laundry with stationary tubs, also water-closet, in cellar. Two bedrooms and trunk-room finished in attic. Front and rear stairway. Open fireplaces with mantels in both parlors and dining rooms. Sliding doors between bedrooms and between parlors and dining rooms.

COST: $3,440, † not including range and heater. The estimate is based on ‡ New York prices for materials and labor. In many sections of the country the cost should be less.

Price for working plans, specifications and * license to build, - - - - - - - - - - - $30.00
Price for † ‡ bill of materials, - - - - - 5.00
    Address, THE CO-OPERATIVE BUILDING PLAN ASSOCIATION, Architects, 63 Broadway, New York.

159

THE CO-OPERATIVE BUILDING PLAN ASSOCIATION, ARCHITECTS, 63 BROADWAY, NEW YORK.

*Shoppell's Modern Houses—*Designs Patented.*
Residence, Design No. 406

PERSPECTIVE.

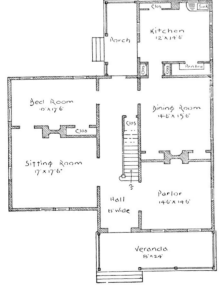

FIRST FLOOR.
For explanation of all symbols (* † etc.) see page 42.
SECOND FLOOR.

DESCRIPTION.

GENERAL DIMENSIONS: Width, 42 ft.; depth, including veranda, 57 ft. 4 in. Heights of stories: First story, 10 ft.; second story, 9 ft.

EXTERIOR MATERIALS: Foundation, brick piers; first story, clapboards; second story, and roof, shingles; gables, panels and shingles. Outside blinds.

INTERIOR FINISH: Hard white plaster; plaster cornices in parlor, hall, sitting and dining rooms. Soft wood flooring and trim. Panels under windows in parlor, sitting and dining rooms. Wainscot in kitchen. Stairs, ash. Interior wood-work finished in hard oil.

COLORS: Clapboards and veranda floor, dark olive drab. Trim, outside doors and blinds, rain conductors, posts of covered balcony and of veranda, bronze green. Sashes, dark red. Veranda ceiling, varnished. Brick-work, Indian red. Wall shingles, dipped and brush coated Venetian red stain. Roof shingles dipped and brush coated dark red stain.

ACCOMMODATIONS: The principal rooms and their sizes, closets, etc., are shown by the plans. No cellar. Attic unfinished, but floored; space for two rooms. Fireplaces and mantels in parlor, dining and sitting rooms, and four bedrooms. Hall extends clear through house. Large balcony at rear may be enclosed with glass or with netting, to suit season.

COST: $3,455, † not including mantels. The estimate is based on ‡ New York prices for materials and labor. In many sections of the country the cost should be less.

Price for working plans, specifications and * license to build, - - - - - - - - - $30.00
Price for † ‡ bill of materials, - - - - - 5.00

Address, THE CO-OPERATIVE BUILDING PLAN ASSOCIATION, Architects, 63 Broadway, New York.

FEASIBLE MODIFICATIONS: Heights of stories, colors, sizes of rooms and kinds of materials may be changed. Cellar may be placed under a part or entire building, with stone or brick walls. Kitchen extension may be carried up two stories. Bath-room with partial or full plumbing may be introduced in first, second or attic story. Front hall in second story may be partitioned for small bedroom or dressing room. Veranda may be extended. Balcony may be omitted, or enclosed to form another bedroom. If heating apparatus be used number of chimneys may be reduced. Fireplaces and mantels may be reduced in number or omitted. Staircase may be placed at rear end of hall with suitable platforms.

The price of working plans, specifications, etc., for a modified design varies according to the alterations required, and will be made known upon application to the Architects.

160

THE CO-OPERATIVE BUILDING PLAN ASSOCIATION, ARCHITECTS, 63 BROADWAY, NEW YORK.

Shoppell's Modern Houses—*Designs Patented.   *Residence, Design No. 348*

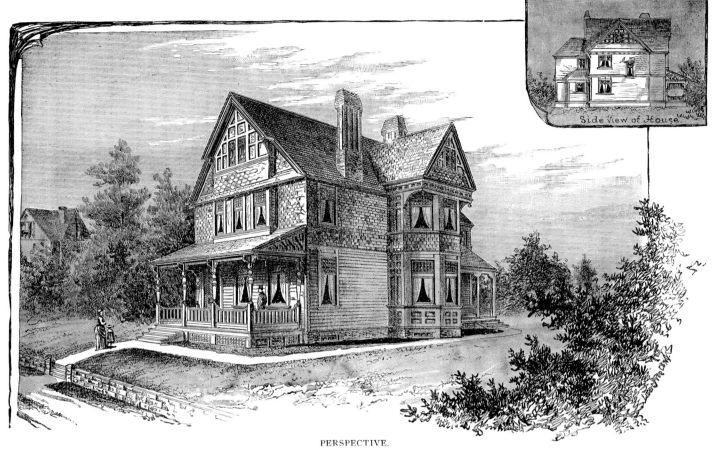

PERSPECTIVE.

DESCRIPTION.

For explanation of all symbols (* † etc.) see page 42.

GENERAL DIMENSIONS: Width, through dining room and library, 32 ft.; depth, including veranda, 50 ft. 6 in. Heights of stories: Cellar, 7 ft.; first story, 9 ft. 8 in.; second story, 8 ft. 10 in.

EXTERIOR MATERIALS: Foundations, stone and brick; first story, clapboards; second story and roof, shingles; gables, panels and shingles. Outside blinds to all windows except those of the cellar and attic.

INTERIOR FINISH: Hard white plaster; plaster cornices and centers in parlor, hall, library and dining room. Soft wood flooring and trim. Panels under windows in parlor, library and dining room. Stairs, ash. Bath-room and kitchen wainscoted. Interior wood-work finished in hard oil.

COLORS: Clapboards, seal brown. Trim, outside doors and blinds, and veranda floor, maroon. Sashes, and rain conductors, dark green. Veranda ceiling, varnished. Brick-work, Indian red. Panels in gables, seal brown; frames around panels, maroon. Wall shingles dipped and brush coated light sienna stain. Roof shingles dipped and brush coated Indian red stain.

ACCOMMODATIONS: The principal rooms and their sizes, closets, etc., are shown by the plans. Cellar under kitchen, dining and sitting rooms; walls extended under whole house. Attic floored, but unfinished; space for three fine rooms. Sliding doors connect parlor, library and dining room. Fireplaces and mantels in library and parlor. Double front door with glazed single vestibule door. Hat and coat closet under main stairs.

COST: $3,497,† not including mantels, range and heater. The estimate is based on ‡ New York prices for materials and labor. In many sections of the country the cost should be less.

Price for working plans, specifications and *license to build, - - - - - $30.00
    Price for † † bill of materials, - - - 5.00

Address, THE CO-OPERATIVE BUILDING PLAN ASSOCIATION, Architects, 63 Broadway, New York.

FEASIBLE MODIFICATIONS: Heights of stories, colors, sizes of rooms and kinds of materials may be changed. Cellar may be reduced in size. Two front bedrooms may be combined, or the smaller form an alcove off the larger. Fireplaces and mantels may be omitted. Rear chimney will suffice if heating apparatus be used. Veranda may be extended at either side.

The price of working plans, specifications, etc., for a modified design varies according to the alterations required, and will be made known upon application to the Architects.

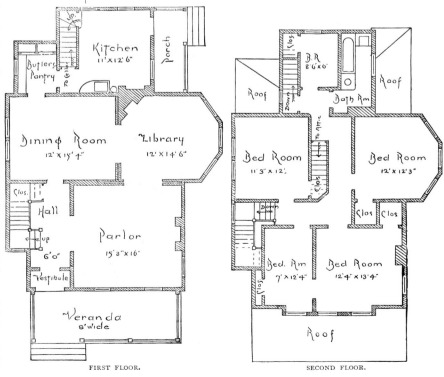

FIRST FLOOR.   SECOND FLOOR.

THE CO-OPERATIVE BUILDING PLAN ASSOCIATION, ARCHITECTS, 63 BROADWAY, NEW YORK.

*Shoppell's Modern Houses—*Designs Patented.* *Residence, Design No. 493*

PERSPECTIVE.

SIDE ELEVATION.

DESCRIPTION.

For explanation of all symbols (* † etc.) see page 42.

GENERAL DIMENSIONS: Width through dining room, 22 ft.; depth, including veranda, 48 ft. Heights of stories: Cellar, 7 ft. 6 in.; first story, 9 ft. 6 in.; second story 9 ft.; attic, 7 ft. 8 in.

EXTERIOR MATERIALS: Foundations, brick; first story, clapboards; second story and roof, shingles; gables, panels and shingles. Outside blinds to all windows except those of the attic.

INTERIOR FINISH: Hard white plaster; plaster cornices and centers in hall, parlor and dining room. Yellow pine flooring in bath-room, laundry and kitchen; soft wood flooring elsewhere. Ash stairway. Panels under windows in parlor and dining room. Bath-room and kitchen wainscoted. Interior wood-work finished in hard oil.

COLORS: Clapboards, bronze green. Trim, and rain conductors, dark olive drab. Outside doors and blinds, olive. Sashes, dark green. Veranda floor and ceiling, oiled. Brick-work, Indian red. Second story wall shingles dipped and brush coated reddish stain. Gable wall shingles dipped and brush coated yellow stain. All roof shingles dipped and brush coated dark red stain.

ACCOMMODATIONS: The principal rooms and their sizes, closets, etc., are shown by the plans. Cellar under whole house with cemented floor and inside and outside entrance. Two good rooms and hall finished in attic, besides space for storage. Alcove for side-board in dining room. Double front door; glazed single vestibule door. Parlor and dining room fireplaces and hard wood mantels included in estimate. House may be built on a 25 foot lot. Laundry with two tubs in cellar.

COST: $3,498, † not including range and heater. The estimate is based on ‡ New York prices for materials and labor. In many sections of the country the cost should be less.

Price for working plans, specifications and * license to build, - - - - - - - - $30.00

Price for † † bill of materials, - - - - - 4.98

Address, THE CO-OPERATIVE BUILDING PLAN ASSOCIATION, Architects, 63 Broadway, New York.

FEASIBLE MODIFICATIONS: Heights of stories, colors, sizes of rooms and kinds of materials may be changed. Cellar may be reduced in size and concrete floor omitted. Sliding doors, either or both fireplaces, and part of or all plumbing, may be omitted. Part of or all attic finish may be omitted.

The price of working plans, specifications, etc., for a modified design varies according to the alterations required, and will be made known upon application to the Architects.

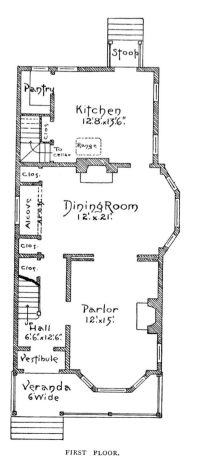

FIRST FLOOR.

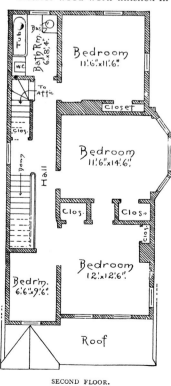

SECOND FLOOR.

THE CO-OPERATIVE BUILDING PLAN ASSOCIATION, ARCHITECTS, 63 BROADWAY, NEW YORK.

*Shoppell's Modern Houses—*Designs Patented.* *Residence, Design No. 601*

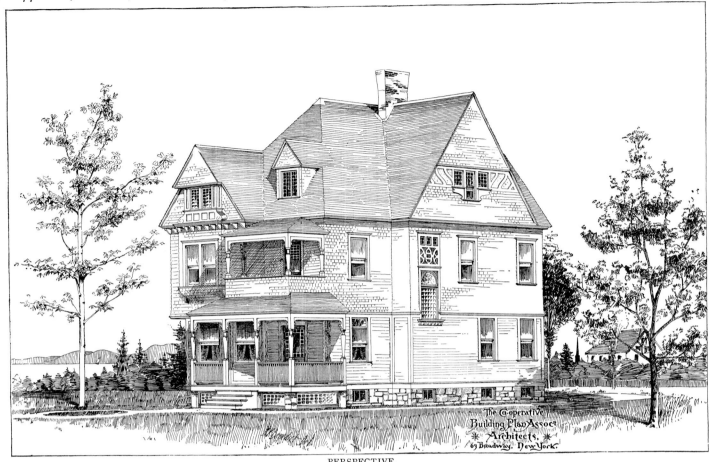

PERSPECTIVE.

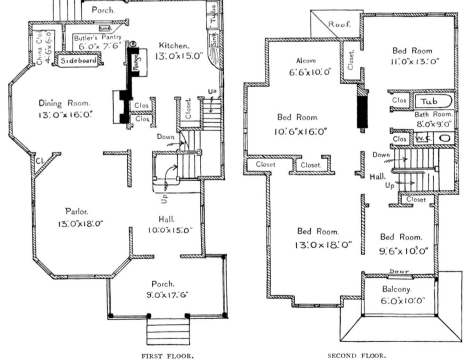

FIRST FLOOR. SECOND FLOOR.

DESCRIPTION.

For explanation of all symbols (* † etc.) see page 42.

GENERAL DIMENSIONS: Width over all, 30 ft. 8 in.; depth, including front porch, 48 ft. 8 in. Heights of stories: Cellar, 7 ft.; first story, 9 ft. 6 in.; second story, 8 ft. 9 in.; attic, 8 ft. 6 in.

EXTERIOR MATERIALS: Foundations, stone; first story, clapboards; second story, roofs and dormers, shingles; gables, shingles and panels. Outside blinds to all except casements, main stairway and cellar windows.

INTERIOR FINISH: Ceilings, hard white plaster; side walls plastered for papering. White pine trim. Hall and staircase of oak. Oak double floor in main hall; yellow pine floor in kitchen, bath-room and pantry; all other floors soft wood. Bath-room and kitchen wainscoted.

COLORS: All clapboards, olive drab. Trim and framing of panels in gables, olive. Front door, hard oil finish; other outside doors, blinds, and rain water conductors, dark red. Sashes, dark green. Body of panels in gables, Tuscan yellow. All shingles dipped and brush coated in dark red stain. Veranda floor and ceiling, oiled.

ACCOMMODATIONS: The principal rooms and their sizes, closets, etc., are shown by the plans. Cellar under whole house. Ample closets. Fireplace in dining-room. Three bedrooms and balcony in attic. Combination front and back stairway economizes space.

FEASIBLE MODIFICATIONS: Heights of ceilings, sizes of rooms, colors and materials may be changed. Balcony may be enclosed with glass or omitted. Cellar and a part or all of plumbing may be omitted.

The price of working plans, specifications, etc., for a modified design varies according to the alterations required, and will be made known upon application to the Architects.

COST: $3,500, † not including mantels, range and heater. The estimate is based on ‡ New York prices for materials and labor. In many sections of the country the cost should be less.

Price for working plans, specifications and * license to build, - - - - - - - - - - $35.00
Price for †† bill of materials, - - - - - 10.00

Address, THE CO-OPERATIVE BUILDING PLAN ASSOCIATION, Architects, 63 Broadway, New York.

163

THE CO-OPERATIVE BUILDING PLAN ASSOCIATION, ARCHITECTS, 63 BROADWAY, NEW YORK.

*Shoppell's Modern Houses—*Designs Patented.*   *Residence, Design No. 622*

PERSPECTIVE.

DESCRIPTION.

For explanation of all symbols (* † etc.) see page 42.

GENERAL DIMENSIONS : Width over all, 30 ft.; depth over all, 50 ft. Heights of stories : Cellar, 7 ft.; first story, 9 ft. 6 in.; second story, 9 ft.; attic, 7 ft. 6 in.

EXTERIOR MATERIALS : Foundations, brick; first story, clapboards; second story, gables and roofs, shingles.

INTERIOR FINISH : Hard plaster for all rooms. Trim and flooring, soft wood. Stairs, hard wood. All interior wood-work finished in hard oil. House piped for gas.

COLORS : All clapboards, light red. All trim, cornices, veranda posts and rails, dark red. Shingles in second story dipped and brush coated with dark yellow stain. Shingles in gables dipped and brush coated with light yellow stain. Roof shingles dipped and brush coated with red stain. Brick-work painted red. Sashes and outside doors painted dark green. Porch floor and ceiling, hard wood, oiled.

ACCOMMODATIONS : The principal rooms and their sizes, closets, etc., are shown by the plans. Cellar, with concrete floor, under whole house, with inside and outside entrances. Laundry with stationary tubs under kitchen. One room finished in attic, with space for one more. Three fireplaces with hard wood mantels included in the estimate.

COST : $3,500, † not including range and heater. The estimate is based on ‡ New York prices for materials and labor. In many sections of the country the cost should be less.

Price for working plans, specifications and * license to build, - - - - $30.00
Price for †† bill of materials, - 15.00
Address, THE CO-OPERATIVE BUILDING PLAN ASSOCIATION, Architects, 63 Broadway, New York.

FEASIBLE MODIFICATIONS : Heights of stories, sizes o_ rooms, colors and materials may be changed. Cellar may be reduced in size. Fireplaces and a part or all of plumbing may be omitted. Sliding doors may be introduced. Front chimney may be omitted if heating apparatus be used. Veranda may be extended.

The price of working plans, specifications, etc., for a modified design varies according to the alterations required, and will be made known upon application to the Architects.

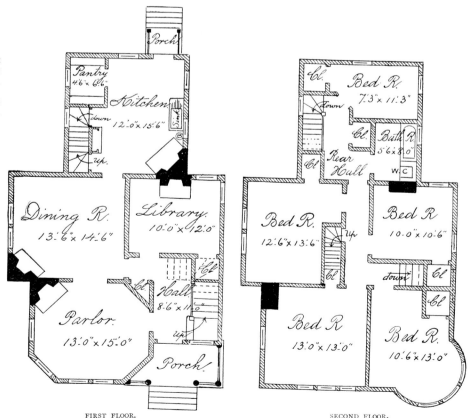

FIRST FLOOR.   SECOND FLOOR.

164

THE CO-OPERATIVE BUILDING PLAN ASSOCIATION ARCHITECTS, 63 BROADWAY, NEW YORK.

*Shoppell's Modern Houses—*Designs Patented.*　　　　　　*Residence, Design No. 623*

PERSPECTIVE.

FIRST FLOOR.　　　　　SECOND FLOOR.

DESCRIPTION.

For explanation of all symbols (* †, etc.) see page 42.

GENERAL DIMENSIONS: Width through dining room and library, 31 ft. 10 in.; depth, including veranda, 48 ft. 9 in. Heights of stories: Cellar, 7 ft.; first story, 9 ft. 6 in.; second story, 9 ft.; attic, 8 ft.

EXTERIOR MATERIALS: Foundations, stone and brick; first story, clapboards; second story, gables and roofs, shingles; Outside blinds to all windows of first and second stories.

INTERIOR FINISH: Hard white plaster. Soft wood trim. Hard wood stairs. Hard wood floor in hall and dining room; all other floors, soft wood. All interior woodwork stained to suit owner and finished in hard oil.

COLORS: All clapboards, veranda and porch columns, and rails and balusters, light green. Trim, cornices, outside blinds, outside rear door, and all sashes, a darker green, Shingling in second story dipped and brush coated in a yellowish red stain. Gable shingles dipped and brush coated in dark yellow stain. Soffit of roof projection, veranda and porch ceilings and floors, light green. Roof shingles dipped and brush coated with red stain. All brick-work painted Venetian red.

ACCOMMODATIONS: The principal rooms and their sizes, closets, etc., are shown by the plans. Cellar under the whole house. Laundry with stationary tubs under kitchen. Two fireplaces and two hard wood mantels included in the estimate. Hall and one large room finished in the attic; space for another room if desired.

COST: $3,500, † not including heater and range. The estimate is based on ‡ New York prices for materials and labor. In many sections of the country the cost should be less.

Price for working plans, specifications, and * license to build, - - - - - - - - - - - - - $30.00
Price for ‡ † bill of materials, - - - - - 15.00
Address, THE CO-OPERATIVE BUILDING PLAN ASSOCIATION, Architects, 63 Broadway, New York.

FEASIBLE MODIFICATIONS: Heights of stories, colors, sizes of rooms, and kinds of materials may be changed. Cellar may be reduced in size. Fireplaces, sliding doors, and a part or all of plumbing, may be omitted. Front chimney may be omitted if heating apparatus be used.

The price of working plans, specifications, etc., for a modified design varies according to the alterations required, and will be made known upon application to the Architects.

165

THE CO-OPERATIVE BUILDING PLAN ASSOCIATION, ARCHITECTS, 63 BROADWAY, NEW YORK.

*Shoppell's Modern Houses—*Designs Patented.*   *Residence, Design No. 640*

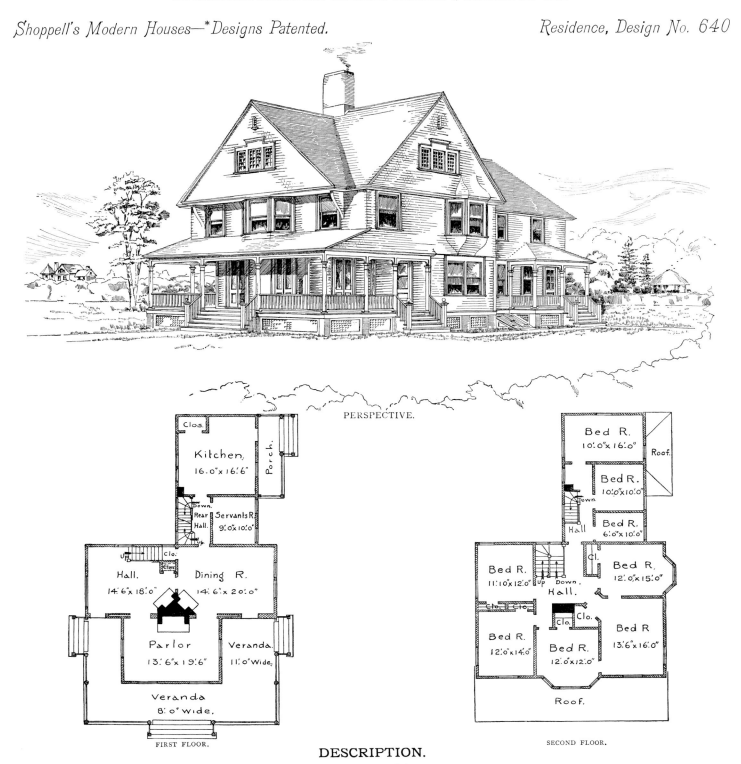

PERSPECTIVE.

FIRST FLOOR.

SECOND FLOOR.

DESCRIPTION.

For explanation of all symbols (* † etc.) see page 42.

GENERAL DIMENSIONS: Width, 40 ft. 6 in.; depth, 65 ft. Heights of stories: Cellar 6 ft. 6 in.; first story, 9 ft.; second story, 8 ft.

EXTERIOR MATERIALS: Foundations, stone walls and piers; first story, clapboards; second story, gables and roofs, shingles.

INTERIOR FINISH: Walls plastered two coats for papering. First and second floors, white pine; attic, spruce. Stairs and trim throughout, white pine. All doors in second story halls have transoms and adjustable lifts. All interior wood work finished in hard oil. Very plain finish throughout.

COLORS: All roof shingles left natural color; all other shingles oiled. All clapboards, outside doors and blinds, painted "Colonial" yellow. Trim and sashes, white. Veranda floor and ceiling, oiled.

ACCOMMODATIONS: The principal rooms and their sizes, closets, etc., are shown by the plans. In addition there is a cellar under the kitchen wing. There are no finished rooms in the attic but there is space for three large rooms or six small rooms. With the large number of bed-rooms on the second floor and the large number possible on the attic floor this is a suitable design for a summer boarding house. The roofs are high, affording cool air spaces over the attic rooms.

COST: $3500, † not including mantels, range and heater. The esti-mate is based on ‡ New York prices for materials and labor. In many sections of the country the cost should be less.

Price for working plans, specifications and * license to build, - $35.00
Price for †† bill of materials,   -   -   -   -   -   -   10.00

Address, THE CO-OPERATIVE BUILDING PLAN ASSOCIATION, Architects, 63 Broadway, New York.

FEASIBLE MODIFICATIONS: Heights of stories, exterior materials and colors may be changed. Sizes of rooms may be enlarged. The 6 ft. x 10 ft. bed-room may be changed to a bath-room. The servants' room may be changed to butler's pantry and closets. The second story bay may be omitted or extended down to dining room. A fire-place may be introduced in front middle bed-room by re-arranging closets. Fire-places, sliding doors and one staircase may be omitted.

The price of working plans, specifications, etc. for a modified design varies according to the alterations required, and will be made known upon application to the Architects.

166

THE CO-OPERATIVE BUILDING PLAN ASSOCIATION, ARCHITECTS, 63 BROADWAY, NEW YORK.

*Shoppell's Modern Houses—*Designs Patented.* *Residnce, Design No. 625*

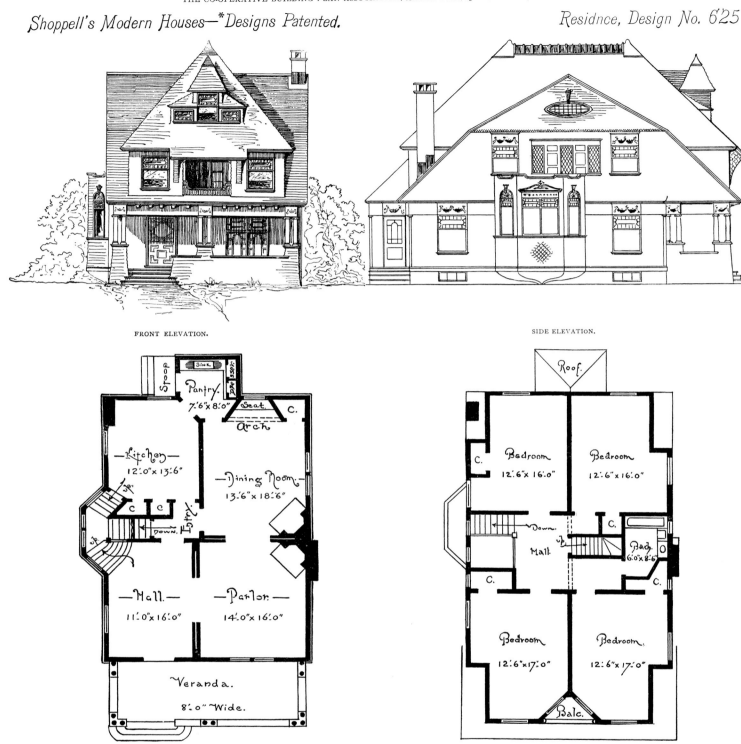

FRONT ELEVATION.

SIDE ELEVATION.

FIRST FLOOR.

SECOND FLOOR.

DESCRIPTION.

For explanation of all symbols (* † etc.) see page 42.

GENERAL DIMENSIONS: Width over all, 31 ft.; depth, including veranda and pantry, 50 ft. 6 in. Heights of stories: Cellar, 7 ft.; first story, 9 ft.; second story, 8 ft.; attic, 8 ft.

EXTERIOR MATERIALS: Foundations, stone; first story, clapboards; second story, gables and roof, shingles.

INTERIOR FINISH: Hard white plaster. Soft wood flooring and trim. Main stairs, ash. Kitchen and bath-room wainscoted. All wood-work stained to suit owner and finished in hard oil. Stained glass in the staircase bay windows. Beveled plate glass in the front door. Inside blinds to all windows of first and second stories except staircase and closet windows. House piped for gas.

COLORS: Clapboards, a pale yellow; shingles on veranda and on second story gables dipped and brush coated Colonial yellow. Trim, veranda columns, all moldings, window and door frames, ornamentation over windows, and porch frieze in first story to be white. Veranda and balcony floors and ceilings, oiled.

ACCOMMODATIONS: The principal rooms and their sizes, closets, etc.,

are shown by the plans. Cellar under whole house. One room and hall finished in attic. Combination front and back stairway economizes room.

COST: $3,500, † not including mantels, range and heater. The estimate is based on ‡ New York prices for materials and labor. In many sections of the country the cost should be less.

Price for working plans, specifications and * license to build, - - - - - . - - - - - - $30.00
Price for †† bill of materials, - - - - - - 15.00

Address, THE CO-OPERATIVE BUILDING PLAN ASSOCIATION, Architects, 63 Broadway, New York.

FEASIBLE MODIFICATIONS: Heights of stories, colors, sizes of rooms and kinds of materials may be changed. Cellar may be reduced in size. Fireplaces, sliding doors, balconies, stained glass, a part or all the plumbing, and attic room, may be omitted. By omitting balcony the front rooms in second story will have square corners; a mullion window should take the place of the balcony.

The price of working plans, specifications, etc., for a modified design varies according to the alterations required, and will be made known upon application to the Architects.

167

THE CO-OPERATIVE BUILDING PLAN ASSOCIATION, ARCHITECTS, 63 BROADWAY, NEW YORK.

*Shoppell's Modern Houses—*Designs Patented.*   *Southern Cottage, Design No. 639*

PERSPECTIVE.

DESCRIPTION.

For explanation of all symbols (* † etc.) see page 42.

GENERAL DIMENSIONS: Width of main house, including veranda, 62 ft.; depth of main house, including veranda, 58 ft. 6 in. Heights of stories: First story, 12 ft.; second story, 9 ft. Width of kitchen annex, 25 ft. 6 in.; depth, 26 ft. 6 in. Height of annex story, 12 ft.

EXTERIOR MATERIALS: Foundations, posts; first story and all gables and dormers, shingles; roof, tin shingles.

INTERIOR FINISH: No plaster; all walls and ceilings are made of narrow, tongued and grooved boards nailed to studding and joists and made smooth to receive, first muslin, and then wall paper. Double flooring in first story with heavy building paper between. All floors and all trim and doors, white pine. Oak stairs. All wood work finished in hard oil.

COLORS: All roof shingles, dark red; all other shingles, cream color. Blinds, veranda, posts, rails and balusters and facia under cornice, cream color. Trim, sashes and rain conductors, dark red. Brick work, veranda floor and ceiling, oiled.

ACCOMMODATIONS: No cellar. Designed for the seashore or a warm climate. The detached kitchen and servants' quarters is placed at any distance from the main house and connected therewith by a covered and latticed passage way. Mason work, which is always expensive, is used as sparingly as possible. The rooms are large and well lighted, and all, except one, face the front. By placing the house properly the prevailing breeze may reach all rooms. The rear hallway leads under the main stairs to the back porch.

COST: $3500 for the main house, † not including mantels or heater; $700 for the kitchen annex, † not including range.

Price for working plans, specifications and * license to build, - - - - $35.00
Price for †† bill of materials, - - - - - - - - - 10.00

Address, THE CO-OPERATIVE BUILDING PLAN ASSOCIATION, Architects, 63 Broadway, New York.

FEASIBLE MODIFICATIONS: Heights of stories, sizes of rooms, materials used and colors, all may be changed. Cellar may be built under whole or part of either building. Interior of house may be plastered. Annex, sliding doors, balcony, and any or all of the fire-places, may be omitted. A kitchen, instead of the annex, may be planned directly at the rear or side of the dining room.

The price of working plans, specifications, etc. for a modified design varies according to the alterations required, and will be made known upon application to the Architects.

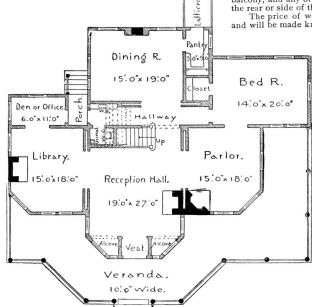

FIRST FLOOR.

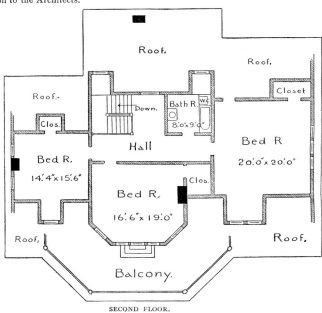

SECOND FLOOR.

168

THE CO-OPERATIVE BUILDING PLAN ASSOCIATION, ARCHITECTS, 63 BROADWAY, NEW YORK.

Shoppell's Modern Houses—*Designs Patented.　　　　*Residence, Design No. 540*

PERSPECTIVE.

DESCRIPTION.

For explanation of all symbols (* † etc.) see page 42.

GENERAL DIMENSIONS: Width, including veranda, 49 ft. 2 in.; depth over all, 49 ft. 4 in. Heights of stories: Cellar, 7 ft.; first story, 9 ft. 6 in.; second story, 9 ft.; attic, 8 ft.

EXTERIOR MATERIALS: Foundation, brick; first story, clapboards; second story and roofs, shingles; gables, panels, fan work and shingles. Outside blinds.

INTERIOR FINISH: Hard white plaster; plaster cornices and centers in reception room, front hall, parlor and dining room. Hard pine flooring in kitchen, hall and bath-room; soft wood flooring elsewhere. Soft wood trim, except hard pine in kitchen. Bath-room and kitchen wainscoted. Interior wood-work stained to suit owner and finished in hard oil.

COLORS: Clapboards, veranda balusters, spindles, and shingles in gables, pale yellow. Trim, outside doors, veranda posts and rails, all cornices, and the frames of all panels, seal brown. Sashes and veranda floor, dark green. Veranda ceiling, oiled. Brick-work, red. Wall shingles in second story dipped and brush coated Tuscan yellow. Roof shingles dipped and brush coated Indian red.

ACCOMMODATIONS: The principal rooms and their sizes, closets, etc., are shown by the plans. Cellar under whole house with inside and outside entrances. One room finished in attic; space for another, besides storage room.

COST: $3,500, † not including mantels, range and heater. The estimate is based on ‡ New York prices for materials and labor. In many sections of the country the cost should be less.

Price for working plans, specifications and * license to build, - $35.00
Price for † † bill of materials, - - - - - - - - 15.00

Address, THE CO-OPERATIVE BUILDING PLAN ASSOCIATION, Architects, 63 Broadway, New York.

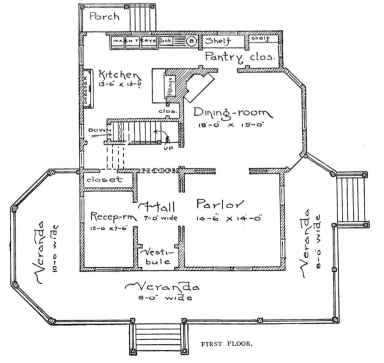

FIRST FLOOR.

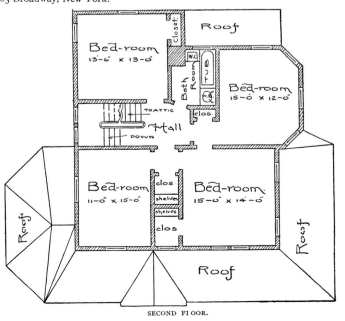

SECOND FLOOR.

Shoppell's Modern Houses—*Designs Patented.   *Residence, Design No. 517*

PERSPECTIVE.

DESCRIPTION.

For explanation of all symbols (* † etc.) see page 42.

GENERAL DIMENSIONS: Extreme width, 32 ft.; depth, including veranda, 51 ft. 8 in. Heights of stories : Cellar, 6 ft. 6 in.; first story, 9 ft.; second story, 8 ft. 3 in.; attic, 7 ft.

EXTERIOR MATERIALS: Foundations, stone and brick; first story, clapboards; second story and roofs, shingles; gables, panels and shingles. Outside blinds to all windows except those of the attic and cellar, and the small windows in first story hall.

INTERIOR FINISH : Hard white plaster ; cellar ceiling one heavy coat ; plaster cornices and centers in hall, parlor, library and dining room. Soft wood flooring and trim. Ash staircase. Bath-room and kitchen wainscoted. Interior wood-work finished in hard oil.

COLORS : Clapboards and panels in gables, seal brown. Frames of panels in gables, trim ; outside doors, blinds and veranda floor, maroon. Sashes, and rain conductors, dark green. Brick-work, Indian red. Wall shingles dipped and brush coated light sienna stain. Roof shingles dipped and brush coated Indian red stain.

ACCOMMODATIONS : The principal rooms and their sizes, closets, etc., are shown by the plans. Cellar under whole house, with inside and outside entrance and cemented floor. Two bedrooms finished in attic, besides ample storage ; space for one more room. Floors of balconies made watertight. Two windows on main staircase filled with stained glass ; front door glazed with beveled plate glass. Fireplaces and mantels in parlor and dining room. Hat and coat closet in front hall.

COST : $3,508, † not including mantels, range and heater. The estimate is based on ‡ New York prices for materials and labor. In many sections of the country the cost should be less.

Price for working plans, specifications
    and * license to build,   -   - $31.00
Price for †† bill of materials,   -   5.00
    Address, THE CO-OPERATIVE BUILDING PLAN ASSOCIATION Architects, 63 Broadway, New York.

FEASIBLE MODIFICATIONS: Heights of stories, colors, sizes of rooms and kinds of materials may be changed. Extent of cellar may be reduced ; cement floor may be omitted. Attic finish, balconies, part or all of plumbing may be omitted. Chimney between dining room and parlor may be moved to outer wall.

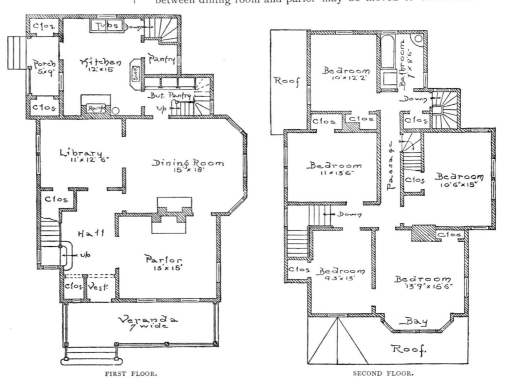

FIRST FLOOR.   SECOND FLOOR.

170

THE CO-OPERATIVE BUILDING PLAN ASSOCIATION, ARCHITECTS, 63 BROADWAY, NEW YORK.

Shoppell's Modern Houses—*Designs Patented.　　　　　*Cottage, Design No. 290*

PERSPECTIVE.

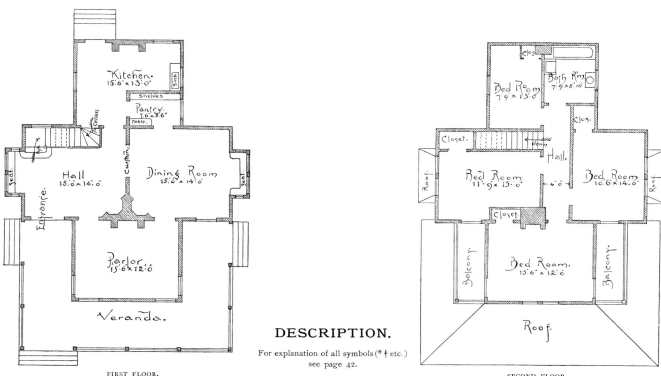

FIRST FLOOR.

SECOND FLOOR.

DESCRIPTION.

For explanation of all symbols (* † etc.)
see page 42.

GENERAL DIMENSIONS: Width over all, 36 ft.; depth, including veranda, 48 ft. 2 in. Heights of stories: Cellar, 7 ft.; first story, 10 ft.; second story, 9 ft.

EXTERIOR MATERIALS: Foundation, brick; first story, clapboards; second story, gables and roof, shingles. Outside blinds.

INTERIOR FINISH: Hard white plaster; plaster cornices in hall, parlor, dining room, and three chambers. Soft wood flooring and trim. Ash stairway. Panels under windows in parlor, hall and dining room. Bathroom and kitchen wainscoted. Interior wood-work finished in hard oil.

COLORS: Clapboards and sashes, olive. Trim, dark green. Outside doors, dark green, with olive panels. Blinds, rain conductors and brickwork, Pompeian red. Veranda floor and ceiling, drab. Underside of roof overhang, medium drab. Panels on sides of brackets and over bay windows,
Pompeian red. Wall shingles dipped and brush coated with reddish stain. Roof shingles dipped and brush coated with Indian red stain.

ACCOMMODATIONS: The principal rooms and their sizes, closets, etc., are shown by the plans. Cellar under kitchen and pantry. Fireplaces with hard wood mantels in hall, parlor, dining room and one bedroom, and kitchen range, included in estimate. Hall designed to be used as sitting room. The attic is floored for storage.

COST: $3,516, † not including heater. The estimate is based on ‡ New York prices for materials and labor. In many sections of the country the cost should be less.

Price for working plans, specifications and * license to build, - $35.00
Price for † † bill of materials, - - - - - - - - 5.00

Address, THE CO-OPERATIVE BUILDING PLAN ASSOCIATION, Architects, 63 Broadway, New York.

171

THE CO-OPERATIVE BUILDING PLAN ASSOCIATION, ARCHITECTS, 63 BROADWAY, NEW YORK.

*Shoppell's Modern Houses—*Designs Patented.*   *Residence, Design No. 349*

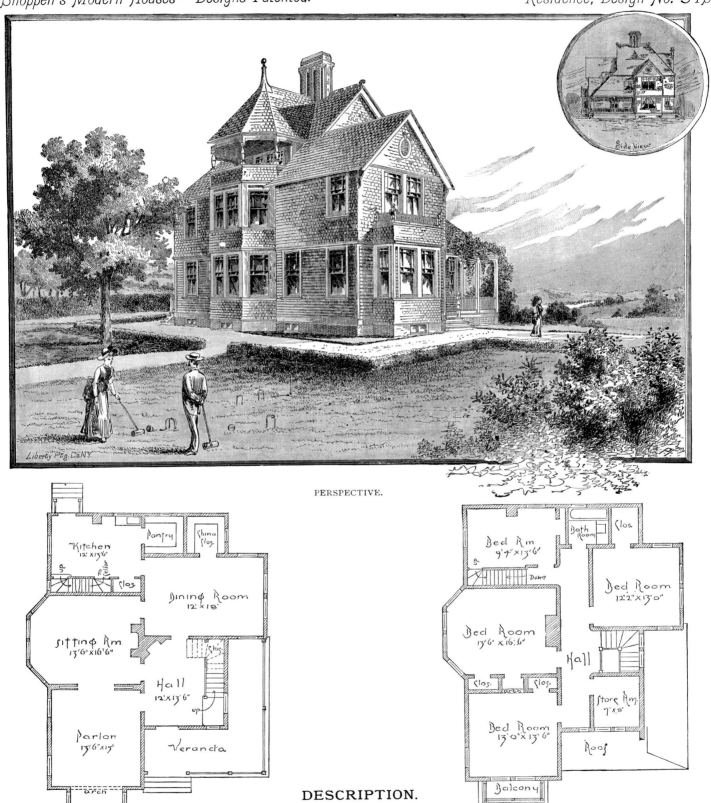

PERSPECTIVE.

Side View

FIRST FLOOR.

SECOND FLOOR.

For explanation of all symbols (* † etc.) see page 42.

DESCRIPTION.

GENERAL DIMENSIONS: Extreme width, 36 ft.; depth, 46 ft. Heights of stories : Cellar, 6 ft. 6 in.; first story, 9 ft. 6 in.; second story, 9 ft.; attic, 8 ft. 6 in.

EXTERIOR MATERIALS: Foundation, brick ; first story, clapboards ; second story, gables and roofs, shingles. Outside blinds.

INTERIOR FINISH: Hard white plaster ; plaster cornices and centers in hall, parlor, sitting and dining rooms. Soft wood flooring and trim. Ash stairs. Panels under windows in parlor, sitting and dining rooms. Bath-room and kitchen wainscoted. Interior wood-work finished in hard oil.

COLORS : Clapboards, light olive drab. Trim, outside doors and rain conductors, bronze green. Blinds and sashes, dark red. Veranda floor, light stone color. Veranda ceiling, lilac. Wall shingles dipped and brush coated sienna stain. Roof shingles dipped and brush coated dark red stain.

ACCOMMODATIONS : The principal rooms and their sizes, closets, etc., are shown by the plans. Cellar under kitchen, sitting room and parlor, with concrete floor. One room finished in attic. Fireplaces in hall and sitting room.

COST : $3,561, † not including mantels, range and heater. The estimate is based on ‡ New York prices for materials and labor. In many sections of the country the cost should be less.

Price for working plans, specifications and * license to build, - - - - - - - - - - - $35.00
Price for † † bill of materials, - - - - - - - - 5.00

Address, THE CO-OPERATIVE BUILDING PLAN ASSOCIATION, Architects, 63 Broadway, New York.

FEASIBLE MODIFICATIONS : Heights of stories, colors, sizes of rooms and kinds of materials may be changed. Cellar may be extended, reduced or omitted. A part or all plumbing may be omitted. If heating apparatus be used one chimney will suffice. By a slight re-arrangement of second story another bedroom may be planned. Direct communication between kitchen and dining room may be closed, and a passage made through pantry. The attic balcony may be omitted, and its space given to attic room.

THE CO-OPERATIVE BUILDING PLAN ASSOCIATION, ARCHITECTS, 63 BROADWAY, NEW YORK.

*Shoppell's Modern Houses—*Designs Patented.* Residence, Design No. 291

PERSPECTIVE.

DESCRIPTION.

For explanation of all symbols (* † etc.) see page 42.

GENERAL DIMENSIONS: Width, including veranda, 37 ft. 8 in.; depth over all, 54 ft. 8 in. Heights of stories: Cellar, 7 ft.; first story, 10 ft.; second story, 9 ft. 6 in.; attic, 7 ft. 8 in.

EXTERIOR MATERIALS: Foundations, stone; first story, clapboards; second story and roof, shingles; gables, panels and shingles. Outside blinds.

INTERIOR FINISH: Hard white plaster; plaster cornices and centers in parlor, library, dining room and hall. Soft wood flooring, doubled in first and second stories. Soft wood trim. Ash stairs. Panels under windows in parlor, library and dining room. Interior wood-work finished in hard oil.

COLORS: Clapboards, blinds and sashes, maroon. Trim, cornices, front doors, veranda floor, and the frames of all paneling, light chocolate. Veranda ceiling, varnished. Lattice work, dark green. Panels and fan work, cream color. Wall shingles dipped and brush coated reddish stain. Roof shingles dipped and brush coated very dark red stain.

ACCOMMODATIONS: The principal rooms and their sizes, closets, etc., are shown by the plans. Cellar, with concrete floor, under whole house. Two bedrooms finished in attic, besides storage space. Fireplace in library, parlor and dining room.

COST: $3,601, † not including mantels, range and heater. The estimate is based on ‡ New York prices for materials and labor. In many sections of the country the cost should be less.

Price for working plans, specifications and * license to build, - - - - - - $35.00

Price for †† bill of materials, - - - 5.00

Address, THE CO-OPERATIVE BUILDING PLAN ASSOCIATION, Architects, 63 Broadway, New York.

FEASIBLE MODIFICATIONS: Heights of stories, colors, sizes of rooms and kinds of materials may be changed. Cellar may be reduced or omitted. Attic finish may be omitted except flooring. If heating apparatus be used number of chimneys may be reduced. Parlor and library may be transposed. A part or all plumbing may be omitted.

The price of working plans, specifications, etc., for a modified design varies according to the alterations required, and will be made known upon application to the Architects.

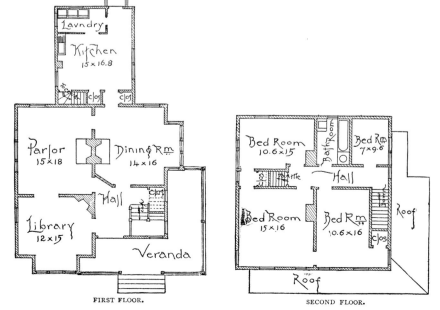

FIRST FLOOR.

SECOND FLOOR.

173

THE CO-OPERATIVE BUILDING PLAN ASSOCIATION, ARCHITECTS, 63 BROADWAY, NEW YORK.

*Shoppell's Modern Houses—*Designs Patented.*   *Residence, Design No. 224*

PERSPECTIVE.

DESCRIPTION.

For explanation of all symbols (* † etc.) see page 42.

GENERAL DIMENSIONS : Width, 36 ft., including veranda ; depth, 49. ft. 6 in. Heights of stories: Cellar, 7 ft.; first story, 9 ft. 6 in.; second story, 9 ft.

EXTERIOR MATERIALS : Foundations, stone ; first story, clapboards; second story and roof, shingles; gables, panels and shingles.

INTERIOR FINISH : Hard white plaster. Soft wood flooring and trim. Ash stairway. Kitchen, wainscoted. All inside wood-work finished in hard oil.

COLORS : Clapboards, olive green. Trim, cornices, veranda posts, rails and balusters, bronze green. Veranda ceiling, yellow stone color. Sashes, Pompeian red. Veranda floor, dark brown. Outside doors, dark green. Roof shingles dipped and brush coated slate color stain. Wall shingles dipped and brush coated reddish stain. Paneling and fan work, Tuscan yellow with bronze green frames.

ACCOMMODATIONS : The principal rooms and their sizes, closets, etc., are shown by the plans. Cellar under whole house, with inside and outside entrances and concrete floor. Attic floored, but unfinished ; space for two rooms and storage room. Open fireplaces with hard wood mantels in hall, parlor and dining room, also kitchen range, included in estimate.

COST : $3,626, † not including heater. The estimate is based on ‡ New York prices for materials and labor. In many sections of the country the cost should be less.

Price for working plans, specifications and * license to build, - - $35.00

Price for † † bill of materials, - 5.00

Address, THE CO-OPERATIVE BUILDING PLAN ASSOCIATION, Architects, 63 Broadway, New York.

FEASIBLE MODIFICATIONS : Heights of stories, colors, sizes of rooms and kinds of materials may be changed. Size of cellar may be reduced and concrete floor omitted. A part or all of plumbing and fireplaces and mantels may be omitted.

The price of working plans, specifications, etc., for a modified design varies according to the alterations required, and will be made known upon application to the Architects.

FIRST FLOOR.   SECOND FLOOR.

174

THE CO-OPERATIVE BUILDING PLAN ASSOCIATION, ARCHITECTS, 63 BROADWAY, NEW YORK.

Shoppell's Modern Houses—*Designs Patented.   *Residence, Design No. 449*

PERSPECTIVE.

DESCRIPTION.

For explanation of all symbols (* † etc.) see page 42.

GENERAL DIMENSIONS: Extreme width, 30 ft. 8 in.; depth, including veranda and porch, 54 ft. 2 in. Heights of stories: Cellar, 7 ft.; first story, 9 ft. 6 in.; second story, 8 ft. 6 in.; attic, 7 ft.

EXTERIOR MATERIALS: Foundations, stone and brick; first story, clapboards; second story, tower and roof, shingles; gables, panels, fan work and shingles. Outside blinds.

INTERIOR FINISH: Hard white plaster; plaster cornices and centers in parlor, dining room, library and hall. Soft wood flooring and trim. Ash stairs. Panels under windows in parlor, dining room and library. Kitchen and bath-room wainscoted. Wood-work finished in hard oil.

COLORS: Clapboards, dark olive drab. Trim and rain conductors, light olive green. Outside doors, bronze green. Blinds and sashes, dark red. Veranda floor, light stone color. Veranda ceiling, light gray. Wall shingles dipped and brush coated with sienna stain. Roof shingles dipped and brush coated with reddish stain.

ACCOMMODATIONS: The principal rooms and their sizes, closets, etc., are shown by the plans. Cellar under main house with inside and outside entrances and concrete floor. Two bedrooms finished in attic. Open fireplaces with hard wood mantels in parlor, library and dining room, also kitchen range, included in estimate.

COST: $3,606, † not including heater. The estimate is based on ‡ New York prices for materials and labor. In many sections of the country the cost should be less.

Price for working plans, specifications and * license to build, - - - - - - - - - - $35.00
Price for † † bill of materials, - - - 5.00

Address, THE CO-OPERATIVE BUILDING PLAN ASSOCIATION, Architects, 63 Broadway, New York.

FEASIBLE MODIFICATIONS: Heights of stories, colors, sizes of rooms and kinds of materials may be changed. Cellar may be reduced in size, and concrete floor omitted. Attic finish may be reduced or omitted. Fireplaces may be omitted. If heating apparatus be used rear chimney will suffice. A part or all of plumbing may be omitted.

The price of working plans, specifications, etc., for a modified design varies according to the alterations required, and will be made known upon application to the Architects.

SECOND FLOOR

FIRST FLOOR.

175

THE CO-OPERATIVE BUILDING PLAN ASSOCIATION, ARCHITECTS, 63 BROADWAY, NEW YORK.

Shoppell's Modern Houses—*Designs Patented.　　　　　　　　*Residence, Design No. 344*

PERSPECTIVE.

DESCRIPTION.

For explanation of all symbols (* † etc.) see page 42.

GENERAL DIMENSIONS : Width over all, 33 ft. 6 in.; depth, including veranda, 50 ft. 6 in. Heights of stories : Cellar, 7 ft.; first story, 9 ft. 3 in.; second story, 8 ft. 9 in.; attic, 8 ft.

EXTERIOR MATERIALS : Foundation, brick ; first story, clapboards ; second story, tower, gables and roof, shingles. Outside blinds to all windows.

INTERIOR FINISH : Hard white plaster ; plaster cornices and centers in parlor, sitting and dining rooms and hall. Soft wood flooring and trim. Ash stairs. Panels under windows in principal rooms of first and second stories. Kitchen and bathroom wainscoted. Interior wood-work finished in hard oil.

COLORS : Clapboards, light olive green. Trim, and rain conductors, bronze green. Outside doors, dark green. Blinds and sashes, dark red. Veranda floor, yellow stone color. Veranda ceiling, light olive drab. Brick-work, red. Veranda posts, rails, balusters, cornices, etc., dark green. Wall shingles dipped and brush coated sienna stain. Roof shingles dipped and brush coated red stain.

ACCOMMODATIONS: The principal rooms and their sizes, closets, etc., are shown by the plans. Cellar under whole house, with concrete floor. Open fireplace in sitting room. Large bedrooms and closets. Back stairway and well-lighted second story hall. Two rooms and hall finished in attic.

COST : $3,628, † not including mantels, range and heater. The estimate is based on ‡ New York prices for materials and labor. In many sections of the country the cost should be less.

Price for working plans, specifications, and * license to build,　-　-　-　$35.00

Price for † † bill of materials,　-　　5.00

Address, THE CO-OPERATIVE BUILDING PLAN ASSOCIATION, Architects, 63 Broadway, New York.

FEASIBLE MODIFICATIONS : Heights of stories, colors, sizes of rooms and kinds of materials may be changed. Cellar may be reduced in size or omitted. Either or both bay windows may be omitted, or they may be extended to second story.

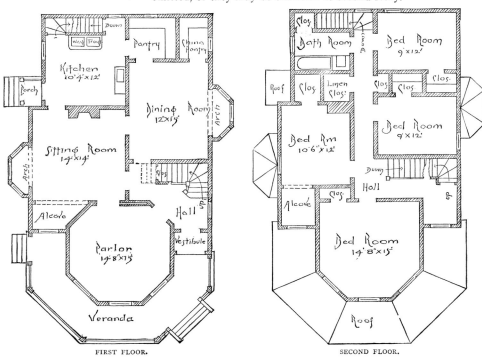

FIRST FLOOR.　　　　　　SECOND FLOOR.

176

THE CO-OPERATIVE BUILDING PLAN ASSOCIATION, ARCHITECTS, 63 BROADWAY, NEW YORK.

*Shoppell's Modern Houses—*Designs Patented.*   *Residence, Design No. 337*

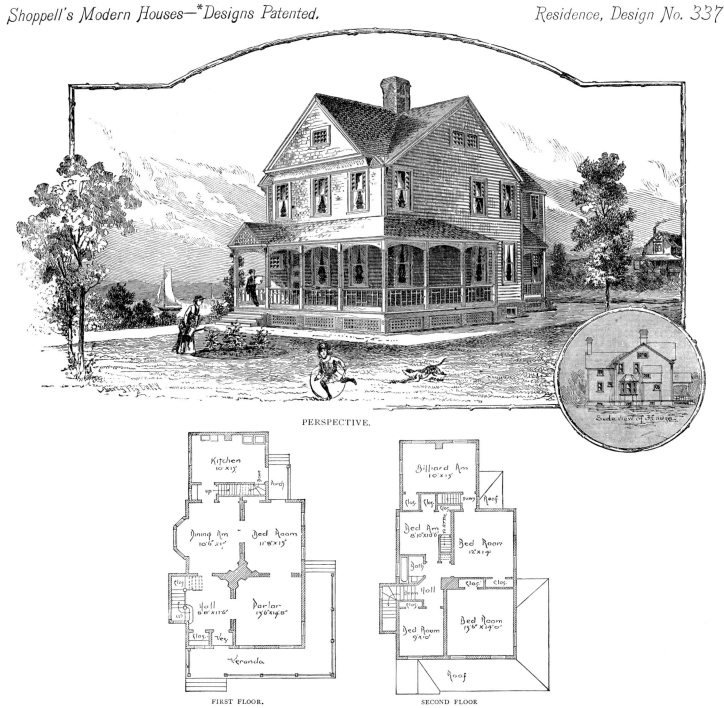

PERSPECTIVE.

FIRST FLOOR.   SECOND FLOOR.

DESCRIPTION.

For explanation of all symbols (* † etc.) see page 42.

GENERAL DIMENSIONS : Width, including veranda and stairway annex, 33 ft. 6 in.; depth, including veranda, 51 ft. 6 in. Heights of stories: Cellar, 6 ft. 6 in.; first story, 10 ft.; second story, 9 ft.

EXTERIOR MATERIALS: Foundations, stone and brick ; first story, clapboards ; second story, clapboards and shingles ; roof, shingles ; gables, shingles and clapboards. Outside blinds.

INTERIOR FINISH : Hard white plaster, with plaster cornices and centers in hall, parlor, dining room and bedroom first story. Soft wood flooring and trim. Ash stairway. Panels under windows in principal rooms of first story. Kitchen and bath-room wainscoted. Interior wood-work finished in hard oil.

COLORS : Clapboards, Oriental drab. Trim, and rain conductors, olive. Outside doors, veranda cornices, posts, rails, etc., bronze green. Blinds and sashes, dark red. Veranda floor, light olive drab. Veranda ceiling, lilac. Wall shingles dipped and brush coated sienna stain. Roof shingles dipped and brush coated dark red stain.

ACCOMMODATIONS : The principal rooms and their sizes, closets, etc., are shown by the plans. Cellar with concrete floor under whole house. Attic floored, but unfinished ; space for two rooms. Four open fireplaces with mantels grouped around central chimney, also kitchen range, included in the estimate. Sliding doors connect all principal rooms of first story. Stationary wash-tubs in kitchen. Back stairway to second story. Billiard room over kitchen.

COST : $3,642, † not including heater. The estimate is based on ‡ New York prices for materials and labor. In many sections of the country the cost should be less.

Price for working plans, specifications and * license to build, - - - - - - - - - - $30.00

Price for †† bill of materials, - - - - 5.00

Address, THE CO-OPERATIVE BUILDING PLAN ASSOCIATION, Architects, 63 Broadway, New York.

FEASIBLE MODIFICATIONS : Heights of stories, colors, sizes of rooms and kinds of materials may be changed. Cellar may be reduced in size or omitted. Any or all fireplaces, a part or all of plumbing, sliding doors and bay window may be omitted. Passage may connect main second story hall with rear extension, wherein bath-room and small bedroom instead of billiard room may be placed. If heating apparatus be used one chimney will suffice.

The price of working plans, specifications, etc., for a modified design varies according to the alterations required, and will be made known upon application to the Architects.

177

THE CO-OPERATIVE BUILDING PLAN ASSOCIATION, ARCHITECTS, 63 BROADWAY, NEW YORK.

*Shoppell's Modern Houses—*Designs Patented.*   *Residence, Design No. 642*

PERSPECTIVE.

DESCRIPTION.

For explanation of all symbols (* † etc.) see page 42

GENERAL DIMENSIONS: Width, 34 ft.; depth, including veranda, 51 ft. 6 in. Heights of stories: Cellar, 7 ft.; first story, 9 ft. 6 in.; second story, 8 ft. 10 in.

EXTERIOR MATERIALS: Foundations, brick; first story, clapboards; second story, gables and roof, shingles.

INTERIOR FINISH: Hard white plaster throughout. Yellow pine floors in kitchen and bath-room; all other floors, white pine. Main staircase, ash. All trim, white pine. Bath-room, kitchen and hall wainscoted. All wood work finished in hard oil. Stained glass window on main stairs. Windows of bays have inside sliding blinds, except the large front window. House piped for gas.

COLORS: All clapboards, veranda and balcony floors, and panels of bay window, painted light brown. Trim, outside doors, blinds and stiles and rails of paneling, maroon. Sashes, ecru. Roof shingles stained mahogany brown; all other shingles stained sienna. Veranda and balcony ceilings varnished, natural color.

ACCOMMODATIONS: The principal rooms and their sizes, closets, etc., are shown by the plans. Cellar under the whole house, part of it being bricked off for a cold storage room. Attic floored but not finished. Space in attic for three rooms. The middle window of the parlor bay is very large; an attractive feature.

COST: $3700, † not including mantels, range and heater. The estimate is based on ‡ New York prices for materials and labor. In many sections of the country the cost should be less.

Price for working plans, specifications and *license to build, - $35.00
Price for †† bill of materials, - - - - - 10.00

Address, THE CO-OPERATIVE BUILDING PLAN ASSOCIATION, Architects, 63 Broadway, New York.

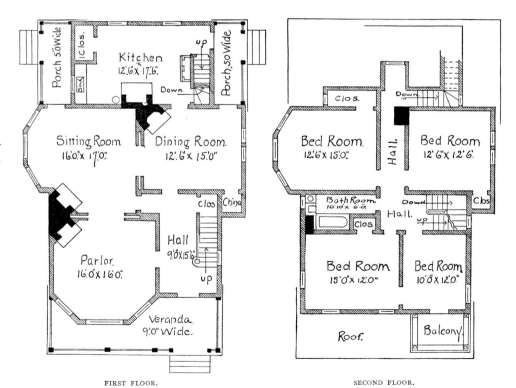

FIRST FLOOR.   SECOND FLOOR.

FEASIBLE MODIFICATIONS: Heights of stories, sizes of rooms, materials and colors, all may be changed. Cellar may be reduced in size. Fireplaces, sliding doors, balcony, stained glass, and a part or all of plumbing, may be omitted. The front chimney may be omitted if a heating apparatus is used.

The price of working plans, specifications, etc. for a modified design varies according to the alterations required, and will be made known upon application to the Architects.

178

THE CO-OPERATIVE BUILDING PLAN ASSOCIATION, ARCHITECTS, 63 BROADWAY, NEW YORK.

Shoppell's Modern Houses—*Designs Patented.   *Residence, Design No. 294*

PERSPECTIVE.

DESCRIPTION.

For explanation of all symbols (* † etc.) see page 42.

GENERAL DIMENSIONS. Width, 37 ft. 7 in. over all; depth, including veranda, 51 ft. 6 in. Heights of stories: Cellar, 6 ft. 6 in.; first story, 9 ft. 6 in.; second story, 8 ft. 6 in.

EXTERIOR MATERIALS: Foundations, stone; first story, clapboards; second story and roof, shingles; gables, panels and shingles. Outside blinds.

INTERIOR FINISH: Hard white plaster; plaster cornices and centers in parlor, dining room, library and hall. Soft wood flooring and trim. Ash stairs. Panels under windows in parlor, dining room and library. Bath-room and kitchen wainscoted. Interior wood-work finished in hard oil.

COLORS: Clapboards, light olive drab. Trim and rain conductors, dark olive drab. Outside doors, dark green. Blinds, light olive green. Sashes, dark red. Veranda floor, yellow stone color. Veranda ceiling, gray. Brick-work, Indian red. Wall shingles dipped and brush coated sienna stain. Roof shingles dipped and brush coated dark red stain.

ACCOMMODATIONS: The principal rooms and their sizes, closets, etc., are shown by the plans. Cellar under the whole house. Open fireplaces and mantels in parlor, dining room and library, also kitchen range, included in estimate. Attic floored, space for three rooms.

COST: $3,850, † not including heater. The estimate is based on ‡ New York prices for materials and labor. In many sections of the country the cost should be less.

Price for working plans, specifications and * license to build, - - - - - - $40.00

Price for † † bill of materials, - - - 10.00

Address, THE CO-OPERATIVE BUILDING PLAN ASSOCIATION, Architects, 63 Broadway, New York.

FEASIBLE MODIFICATIONS: Heights of stories, colors, sizes of rooms and kinds of materials may be changed. Cellar may be reduced in size or omitted. Fireplaces and mantels and a part or all of plumbing may be omitted. Two front bedrooms may be made one.

The price of working plans, specifications, etc., for a modified design varies according to the alterations required, and will be made known upon application to the Architects.

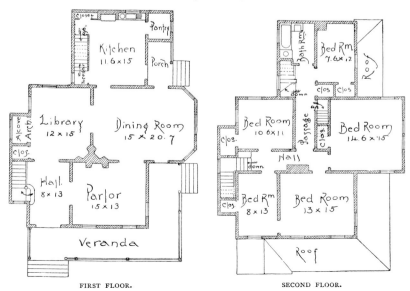

FIRST FLOOR.   SECOND FLOOR.

179

THE CO-OPERATIVE BUILDING PLAN ASSOCIATION, ARCHITECTS, 63 BROADWAY, NEW YORK.

*Shoppell's Modern Houses—*Designs Patented.*

Residence, Design No. 446

PERSPECTIVE.

DESCRIPTION.

For explanation of all symbols (* † etc.) see page 42.

GENERAL DIMENSIONS : Width through dining room and library, 34 ft. 6 in.; depth, including veranda, 52 ft. Heights of stories : Cellar, 6 ft. 6 in.; first story, 9 ft.; second story, 8 ft. 6 in.; attic, 7 ft. 6 in.

EXTERIOR MATERIALS : Foundations, stone and brick ; first story, clapboards ; second story and roof, shingles ; gables, panels and shingles. Outside blinds.

INTERIOR FINISH : Sand finish plaster; plaster cornices and centers in parlor, library, dining room and hall. Soft wood flooring and trim. Ash stairway. Kitchen and bath-room wainscoted. Interior wood-work finished in hard oil.

COLORS : Clapboards and panels in gables, seal brown. Trim, outside doors, blinds, veranda floor and the frames around all panels in gables, maroon. Sashes and rain conductors, dark green. Veranda ceiling, varnished. Large cornice on front, oiled. Wall shingles dipped and brush coated light sienna stain. Roof shingles dipped and brush coated Indian red paint.

ACCOMMODATIONS: The principal rooms and their sizes, closets, etc., are shown by the plans. Cellar under whole house. Two rooms and hall finished in attic, besides storage space. Hall windows glazed with stained glass. Heater pipes and registers provided ready to connect with furnace, and their cost included in the estimate.

COST : $3,866, † not including mantels, range and heater. The estimate is based on ‡ New York prices for materials and labor. In many sections of the country the cost should be less.

Price for working plans, specifications and * license to build, - - - - - - - - $40.00

Price for †† bill of materials, - - - - - 5.00

Address, THE CO-OPERATIVE BUILDING PLAN ASSOCIATION, **Architects, 63 Broadway, New York.**

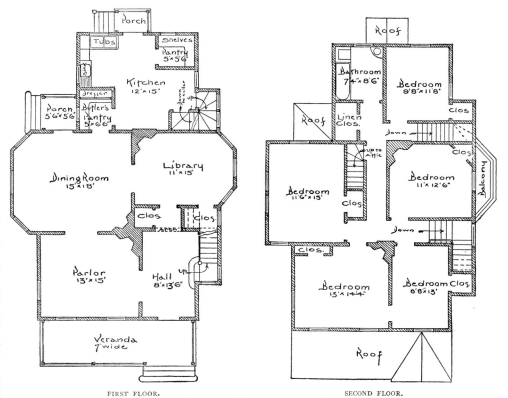

FIRST FLOOR.

SECOND FLOOR.

FEASIBLE MODIFICATIONS : Heights of stories, colors, sizes of rooms and kinds of materials may be changed. Any or all fire-places and mantels and a part or all of plumbing may be omitted.

The price of working plans, specifications, etc., for a modified design varies according to the alterations required, and will be made known upon application to the Architects.

180

THE CO-OPERATIVE BUILDING PLAN ASSOCIATION, ARCHITECTS, 63 BROADWAY, NEW YORK.

*Shoppell's Modern Houses—*Designs Patented.*　　　　　*Residence, Design No. 220A*

PERSPECTIVE.

DESCRIPTION.

For explanation of all symbols (* † etc.) see page 42.

GENERAL DIMENSIONS : Width over all, 54 ft. 7 in.; depth, including veranda and pantry, 53 ft. 2 in. Heights of stories : Cellar, 6 ft. 6 in.; first story, 10 ft.; second story, 9 ft.; attic, 7 ft. 6 in.

EXTERIOR MATERIALS : Foundations, stone and brick ; first story, clapboards ; second story and roof, shingles ; gables, shingles and panels. Outside blinds.

INTERIOR FINISH: Hard white plaster; plaster cornices and centers in hall, parlor and dining room. Soft wood flooring and trim. Ash stairs. Panels under windows in parlor, hall and dining room. Kitchen, bath-room and pantry wainscoted. Interior wood-work finished in hard oil.

COLORS : Clapboards, olive drab. Trim, blinds and rain conductors, bronze green. Outside doors, veranda cornice, posts, etc., dark green. Sashes, bright red. Veranda floor, yellow stone color. Veranda ceiling, cream. Brick-work, Indian red. Wall shingles dipped and brush coated sienna stain Roof shingles dipped and brush coated dark red stain.

ACCOMMODATIONS : The principal rooms and their sizes, closets, etc., are shown by the plans. Cellar under whole house. Two bedrooms and hall finished in attic. Ample veranda and fine porte cochere. Arrangement of rooms very complete and exterior appearance imposing. Three fireplaces and mantels, also kitchen range, included in estimate.

COST ; $3,897, † not including heater. The estimate is based on ‡ New York prices for materials and labor. In many sections of the country the cost should be less.

Price for working plans, specifications and * license to build, - - - - - - - $40.00
Price for †† bill of materials, - - - 10.00

Address, THE CO-OPERATIVE BUILDING PLAN ASSOCIATION, Architects, 63 Broadway, New York.

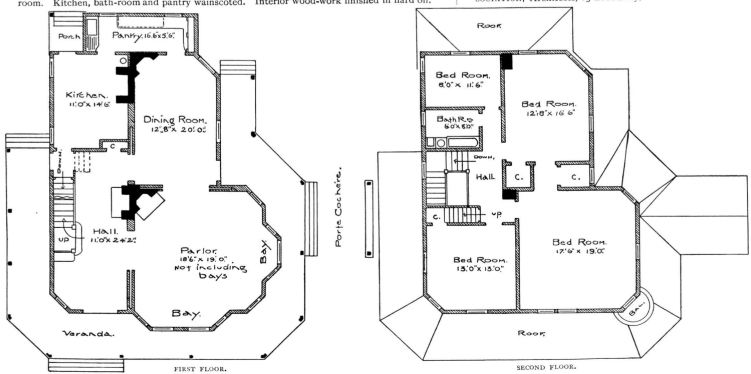

FIRST FLOOR.　　　　　SECOND FLOOR.

181

THE CO-OPERATIVE BUILDING PLAN ASSOCIATION, ARCHITECTS, 63 BROADWAY, NEW YORK.

*Shoppell's Modern Houses—*Designs Patented.*   *Residence, Design No. 390*

Side Elevation.

PERSPECTIVE.

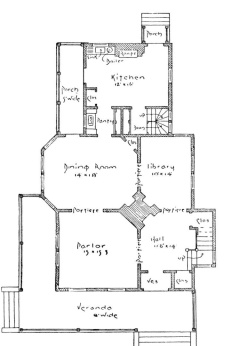

FIRST FLOOR.

DESCRIPTION.

For explanation of all symbols (* † etc.) see page 42.

GENERAL DIMENSIONS : Width over all, 37 ft. 6 in.; depth, including veranda, 56 ft. 6 in. Heights of stories : Cellar, 7 ft.; first story, 10 ft.; second story, 9 ft.

EXTERIOR MATERIALS : Foundations, stone and brick ; first story, clapboards ; second story and roof, shingles ; gables, panels and shingles. Outside blinds.

INTERIOR FINISH : Hard white plaster ; plaster cornices and centers in parlor, library, dining room and hall. Soft wood flooring and trim. Yellow pine stairs. Bath-room and kitchen wainscoted. Interior wood-work finished in hard oil.

COLORS : Clapboards, olive. Trim and rain conductors, dark green. Outside doors and blinds, dark green with olive panels. Sashes, Pompeian red. Brick-work and veranda floor, oiled. Veranda ceiling, dark brown. Wall shingles dipped and brush coated slightly darker stain than natural color of the wood. Roof shingles, oiled.

ACCOMMODATIONS : The principal rooms and their sizes, closets, etc., are shown by the plans. Cellar under whole house. Laundry under kitchen. Heater pipes and registers included in estimate. Attic floored, but unfinished ; space for three rooms. Parlor windows have sliding sashes carried to the floor. Door from dining room to rear porch. Portieres between all principal rooms of first story.

COST : $3,775, † not including mantels, range and heater. The estimate is based on ‡ New York prices for materials and labor. In many sections of the country the cost should be less.

SECOND FLOOR.

Price for working plans, specifications and * license to build, - - - - - - - - - - $40.00

Price for †† bill of materials, - - - - 5.00

Address, THE CO-OPERATIVE BUILDING PLAN ASSOCIATION, Architects, 63 Broadway, New York.

FEASIBLE MODIFICATIONS : Heights of stories, colors, sizes of rooms and kinds of materials may be changed. Laundry tubs may be placed in kitchen. Any or all fireplaces and mantels and a part or all of plumbing may be omitted. Sliding or folding doors may be introduced. Position of attic stairs may be changed.

The price of working plans, specifications, etc., for a modified design varies according to the alterations required, and will be made known upon application to the Architects.

182

THE CO-OPERATIVE BUILDING PLAN ASSOCIATION, ARCHITECTS, 63 BROADWAY, NEW YORK.

Shoppell's Modern Houses—*Designs Patented.   *Residence, Design No. 559*

PHOTOGRAPHIC VIEW.

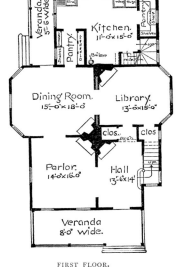

FIRST FLOOR.

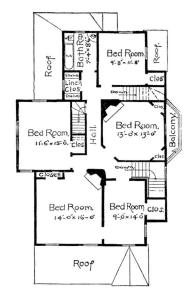

SECOND FLOOR.

DESCRIPTION.

For explanation of all symbols (* † etc.) see page 42.

GENERAL DIMENSIONS: Width through dining room and library, 35 ft.; depth, including veranda, 59 ft. 8 in. Heights of stories: Cellar, 6 ft. 6 in.; first story, 10 ft.; second story, 9 ft.

EXTERIOR MATERIALS: Foundations, stone; first story, clapboards; second story and roof, shingles; gables, panels and shingles. Outside blinds to all except attic and staircase windows.

INTERIOR FINISH: Hard white plaster. Plaster cornices and centers in parlor, hall, dining room and library. Soft wood flooring and trim. Ash staircase. Bath-room and kitchen wainscoted with yellow pine. Interior wood-work finished in hard oil.

COLORS: Clapboards and panels in gables, brown. Trim, outside doors, blinds and veranda floor, maroon. Sashes and rain conductors, dark green. Veranda ceiling, varnished. Brick-work, Indian red. Cement cornice on front, oiled. Frames around panels in gables, buff. Wall shingles dipped and brush coated sienna stain. Roof shingles dipped and brush coated Indian red stain.

ACCOMMODATIONS: The principal rooms and their sizes, closets, etc., are shown by the plans. Cellar, with inside and outside entrance, under whole house. Attic floored, but unfinished; space for three bedrooms, hall and storage. Open fireplaces in hall, parlor, dining room, library and two bedrooms. Sliding doors connect

dining room and library. Door from dining room to rear veranda. Water-closet at rear of kitchen, entered from veranda. Bath-room with W. C. and full plumbing in second story. Stationary tubs, sink and boiler in kitchen. Coat and hat closet in hall.

COST: $3,866, † not including mantels, range and heater. The estimate is based on ‡ New York prices for materials and labor. In many sections of the country the cost should be less.

Price for working plans, specifications and * license to build, - - - - - - - - - - - - $35.00
Price for †† bill of materials, - - - - - 10.00

Address, THE CO-OPERATIVE BUILDING PLAN ASSOCIATION, Architects, 63 Broadway, New York.

FEASIBLE MODIFICATIONS: Heights of stories, colors, sizes of rooms and kinds of materials may be changed. Cellar may be reduced in size or omitted. Any or all fireplaces and mantels and a part or all of plumbing may be omitted. Veranda at side of kitchen may be reduced in size or omitted. Main veranda may be extended. Vestibule may be planned for front hall.

The price of working plans, specifications, etc., for a modified design varies according to the alterations required, and will be made known upon application to the Architects.

Importance of Perfect Working Plans, Specifications, Etc.

THE contract for an important building is never made without drawings (working plans and detail sheets) showing what the form and details of the proposed buildings shall be, and without specifications describing how the work shall be done and the quality of the materials to be used.

For a house of low or moderate cost, however, which should have equally careful attention, the owner is too often content with imperfect drawings and specifications. Sometimes he simply contracts for a duplicate of some other house, not knowing that the contractor can duplicate the appearance without duplicating the value. Sometimes he allows the contractor to make the drawings and specifications, which is far from being the part of wisdom.

The contractor is always apprehensive, with good reason, that the profit "on paper," which seems to be satisfactory, may disappear in labor troubles, delays, mistakes, advance of materials, etc. Occasionally he will ostentatiously show the owner a bit of detail of better quality than the contract calls for as proof that he is building a good house, but all the same he will perform the work just as cheaply as the specifications allow, and he is not to be blamed for it, either, although for every dollar he saves by reason

of incomplete drawings and defective specifications, the owner may be deprived of $10 of value.

Example: If the specifications do not require the sheathing of the structure, why should the contractor spend $40 for sheathing boards and labor, even admitting that the increased strength and warmth of the house may be worth $400 to the owner? The sheathing is all covered up anyway. Or, if the specifications do not call for the sheathing boards to be laid close together, why should not the contractor save $5 worth of boards by following the custom of leaving wide cracks? Or, if the quality of the sheathing paper is not stated, why should he not put on the cheapest, saving $5, perhaps, although dampness will soon make it worthless for the purpose intended.

If the specifications do not call for a double first floor, why should the contractor supply it, although the extra cost is only $3 per "square" (10 feet by 10 feet)?

In the flues, in the plumbing, and in a hundred other things the contractor may save a little by reason of imperfect drawings and specifications, at the expense of a great deal to the owner.

183

THE CO-OPERATIVE BUILDING PLAN ASSOCIATION, ARCHITECTS, 63 BROADWAY, NEW YORK.

Shoppell's Modern Houses—*Designs Patented.

Residence, Design No. 503

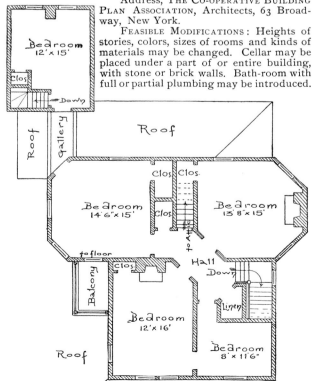

Coop. Building Plan Ass'n
architects
63 B'way NY PERSPECTIVE.

— Side Elevation —

DESCRIPTION.

For explanation of all symbols (* † etc.) see page 42.

GENERAL DIMENSIONS : Width over all, including kitchen, 44 ft. 6 in.; depth, including veranda and kitchen, 66 ft. Heights of stories : First story, 9 ft. 6 in.; second story, 9 ft.; attic, 7 ft. 6 in.

EXTERIOR MATERIALS : Foundation, brick piers; first story, clapboards; second story, gables and roof, shingles. Outside blinds to all windows.

INTERIOR FINISH : Hard white plaster. Soft wood flooring and trim. Ash stairway. Chair rail in dining room and kitchen. Interior wood-work finished in hard oil.

COLORS : Clapboards, medium drab. Trim, outside doors, blinds and rain conductors, light brown. Sashes and brick-work, bright red. Veranda floor and ceiling varnished. Wall shingles dipped and brush coated sienna stain. Roof shingles dipped and brush coated red paint.

ACCOMMODATIONS : The principal rooms and their sizes, closets, etc., are shown by the plans. No cellar. Three rooms in attic. Detached kitchen, with servants' bedroom over same. Large, well-ventilated pantry. Extensive verandas. Fireplaces in principal rooms.

COST : $3,914 † not including mantels, range and heater. The estimate is based on ‡ New York prices for materials and labor. In many sections of the country the cost should be less.

Price for working plans, specifications and * license to build, - - - - - - - $40.00
Price for †† bill of materials, - - - - - - 5.50

Address, THE CO-OPERATIVE BUILDING PLAN ASSOCIATION, Architects, 63 Broadway, New York.

FEASIBLE MODIFICATIONS : Heights of stories, colors, sizes of rooms and kinds of materials may be changed. Cellar may be placed under a part of or entire building, with stone or brick walls. Bath-room with full or partial plumbing may be introduced.

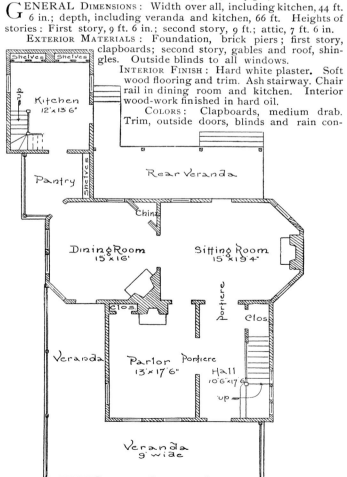

FIRST FLOOR.

SECOND FLOOR.

184

THE CO-OPERATIVE BUILDING PLAN ASSOCIATION, ARCHITECTS, 63 BROADWAY, NEW YORK.

Shoppell's Modern Houses—*Designs Patented.   *Residence, Design No.* 624

PERSPECTIVE

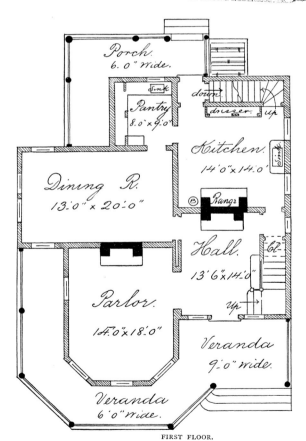

FIRST FLOOR.

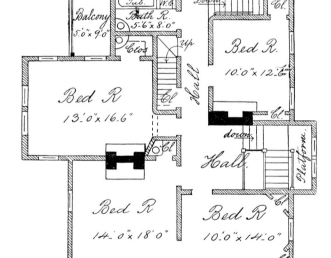

SECOND FLOOR.

DESCRIPTION.

For explanation of all symbols (* † etc.) see page 42.

GENERAL DIMENSIONS: Width through dining room and kitchen, 35 ft. 6 in.; depth, including veranda and porch, 54 ft. Heights of stories: Cellar, 7 ft.; first story, 9 ft.; second story, 8 ft. 6 in.; attic, 8 ft.

EXTERIOR MATERIALS: Foundations, stone; first story, clapboards; second story, gables, and veranda roofs, shingles; main roofs, metallic shingles. Outside blinds to kitchen and pantry windows, inside folding blinds to all other windows in first and second stories.

INTERIOR FINISH: Hard white plaster. Soft wood trim and floors throughout. Hard wood main stairs. Windows in parlor have panels below. All interior wood-work finished in hard oil and stained to imitate hard woods.

COLORS: Clapboards, light golden brown. Trim, veranda posts, rail, etc., brown. Outside doors, blinds, and veranda floor, seal brown. Sashes, dark brown. Wall shingles and veranda and porch roof shingles dipped in yellow stain. Metallic shingles painted dark red.

ACCOMMODATIONS: The principal rooms and their sizes, closets, etc., are shown by the plans. Cellar under whole house, with outside and inside entrances and concrete floor. Wash-bowls in closets of two bedrooms and in bath-room. Five fireplaces with hard wood mantels are included in the estimate. Extensive front and rear verandas. Well lighted halls—no dark corners. Two rooms finished in attic, leaving ample storage space.

COST: $3,900, † not including heater and range. The estimate is based on ‡ New York prices for materials and labor. In many sections of the country the cost should be less.

Price for working plans, specifications and * license to build, - - - - - - - - - - - $35.00

185

THE CO-OPERATIVE BUILDING PLAN ASSOCIATION, ARCHITECTS, 63 BROADWAY, NEW YORK.

*Shoppell's Modern Houses—*Designs Patented.*   *Residence, Design No. 539*

PERSPECTIVE.

DESCRIPTION.

GENERAL DIMENSIONS: Width, including veranda and bay, 39 ft.; depth, including veranda, 54 ft. 6 in. Heights of stories: Cellar, 7 ft.; first story, 9 ft.; second story, 8 ft. 6 in.; attic, 8 ft.

EXTERIOR MATERIALS: Foundations, stone and brick; first story, clapboards; second story and gables, shingles and panels; roof, slate. Outside blinds

INTERIOR FINISH: Hard white plaster ceilings; walls plastered for papering. Plaster cornices and centers in parlor, library, dining room and hall. Soft wood flooring and trim. Ash staircase. Bath-room and kitchen wainscoted. Interior woodwork finished in hard oil.

COLORS: Clapboards and panels, light brown. Trim, outside doors, blinds, rain conductors and frames around all panels, very dark brown. Sashes, red. Veranda floor, brown. Veranda ceiling, varnished. Brickwork, red. Wall shingles dipped and brush coated sienna stain.

ACCOMMODATIONS: The principal rooms and their sizes, closets, etc., are shown by the plans. Cellar under whole house. Laundry under kitchen. Two large rooms, hallway, and storage room in attic.

COST: $4,000, † not including mantels, range and heater. The estimate is based on ‡ New York prices for materials and labor. In many sections of the country the cost should be less.

Price for working plans, specifications and * license to build, $35.00
Price for †† bill of materials, 10.00
Address, THE CO-OPERATIVE BUILDING PLAN ASSOCIATION, Architects, 63 Broadway, New York.

FEASIBLE MODIFICATIONS: Heights of stories, colors, sizes of rooms and kinds of materials may be changed. Laundry tubs may be placed in kitchen instead of in basement. Attic may be re-planned to give eight rooms of fair size. A part or all of plumbing may be omitted.

The price of working plans, specifications, etc., for a modified design varies according to the alterations required, and will be made known upon application to the Architects.

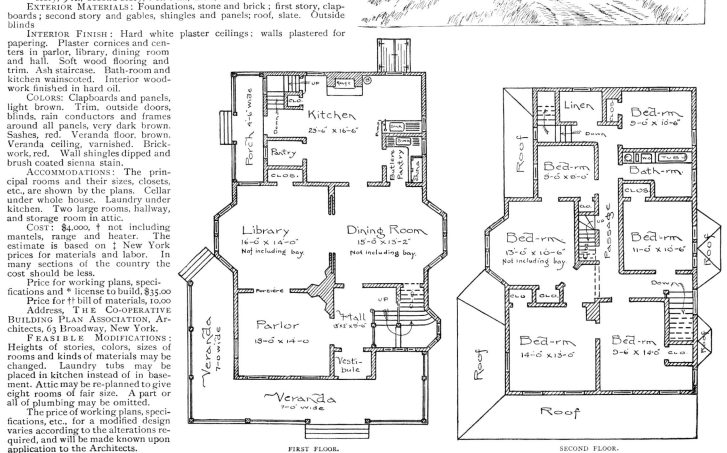

FIRST FLOOR.   SECOND FLOOR.

186

THE CO-OPERATIVE BUILDING PLAN ASSOCIATION, ARCHITECTS, 63 BROADWAY, NEW YORK.

Shoppell's Modern Houses—*Designs Patented.   *Residence, Design No. 641*

PERSPECTIVE.

DESCRIPTION.

For explanation of all symbols (* † etc.) see page 42.

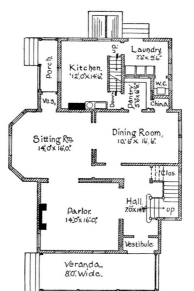

FIRST FLOOR.

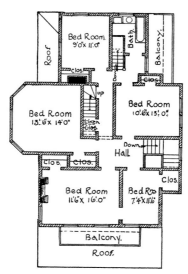

SECOND FLOOR.

GENERAL DIMENSIONS: Width, 34 ft. 6 in.; depth, including veranda, 53 ft. Heights of stories: Cellar, 7 ft.; first story, 9 ft.; second story, 8 ft. 6 in.; attic, 8 ft.

EXTERIOR MATERIALS: Foundations, stone; first story, clapboards and panels; second story and gables, shingles and panels; roofs, shingles.

INTERIOR FINISH: Hard white plaster throughout. Double floors, with paper between, in first and second stories. These floors are carried out between the studding to the sheathing to prevent draughts in the walls. The finishing floor is spruce laid after the plastering is finished. Main stairway, oak. Trim of first story, sycamore; trim of second story and attic, white pine. Bath-room and kitchen, wainscoted. Vestibule door glazed with stained glass. Sycamore and oak finished in hard oil; all other trim painted with tints to suit owner.

COLORS: All clapboards, all panels and veranda floor, buff. All trim, stiles and rails of all panels and rain conductors, cream white. Roof shingles, painted Indian red; all other shingles oiled. Sashes, dark green. Veranda ceiling, varnished.

ACCOMMODATIONS: The principal rooms and their sizes, closets, etc. are shown by the floor plans. There is a cellar under the whole house. Two rooms finished in the attic, where there is space for two more. Unique design of balcony roof. Balconies reached through casement windows. Front attic bed-room may be enlarged for a billiard room.

COST: $4000, † not including mantels, range and heater. The estimate is based on ‡ New York prices for materials and labor. In many sections of the country the cost should be less.

Price for working plans, specifications and * license to build, $40.00
Price for †† bill of materials,   -   -   -   -   -   -   10.00

Address, THE CO-OPERATIVE BUILDING PLAN ASSOCIATION, Architects, 63 Broadway, New York.

FEASIBLE MODIFICATIONS: Heights of stories, sizes of rooms, materials and colors, all may be changed. Balconies, one W. C., vestibule and side porch, sliding doors, exterior paneling, fire-places and stained glass, all or any may be omitted. For all shingles on walls clapboards may be substituted.

The price of working plans, specifications, etc. for a modified design varies according to the alterations required, and will be made known upon application to the Architects.

Shoppell's Modern Houses—*Designs Patented.   *Residence, Design No. 643*

PERSPECTIVE.

DESCRIPTION.

For explanation of all symbols (* † etc.) see page 42.

GENERAL DIMENSIONS: Width, including porte-cochere, 56 ft. 6 in.; depth, including veranda, 63 ft. Heights of stories: Cellar, 8 ft. 6 in.; first story, 9 ft. 6 in.; second story, 9 ft.

EXTERIOR MATERIALS: Foundations, stone; first story, brick veneer; second story, gables and roofs, shingles.

INTERIOR FINISH: Hard white plaster throughout. White pine trim and flooring. Oak staircase.

COLORS: Brick veneer, oiled. Roof shingles, stained red; all other shingles stained sienna. Trim, outside doors and blinds, medium dark green. Sashes, red. Veranda and porch floors and ceilings, oiled.

ACCOMMODATIONS: The principal rooms and their sizes, closets, etc. are shown by the floor plans. Cellar under the whole house. No rooms finished in the attic, but there is space for four rooms of good size. Lavatory with W. C. and wash basin, under main stairs. Ash-pit under parlor fireplace. Laundry tubs in cellar. Convenient side entry. Cosy nook with seats on staircase landing.

COST: $4000, † not including mantels, range and heater. The estimate is based on ‡ New York prices for materials and labor. In many sections of the country the cost should be less.

Price for working plans, specifications and * license to build,   -   -   - $40.00
Price for †† bill of materials, 10.00

Address, THE CO-OPERATIVE BUILDING PLAN ASSOCIATION, Architects, 63 Broadway, N. Y.

FEASIBLE MODIFICATIONS :— Heights of stories, exterior materials, interior finish, sizes of rooms and colors may be changed. Veneered walls may be built solid. Fire-places, ash-pit, sliding doors, lavatory, seat in dining room, porte-cochere and part of veranda may be omitted. Front chimney may be built inside of house line.

The price of working plans, specifications, etc. for a modified design varies according to the alterations required, and will be made known upon application to the Architects.

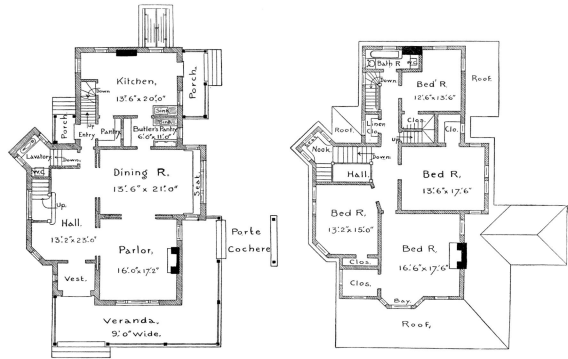

FIRST FLOOR.   SECOND FLOOR.

188

THE CO-OPERATIVE BUILDING PLAN ASSOCIATION, ARCHITECTS, 63 BROADWAY, NEW YORK.

*Shoppell's Modern Houses—*Designs Patented.*   *Residence, Design No. 599*

PERSPECTIVE.

DESCRIPTION.

For explanation of all symbols (* † etc.) see page 42.

GENERAL DIMENSIONS: Width, 39 ft. 6 in., including bay; depth, 43 ft. 6 in., including veranda and porch. Heights of stories: Cellar, 7 ft.; first story, 9 ft. 6 in.; second story, 8 ft. 6 in.; attic, 8 ft.

EXTERIOR MATERIALS: Foundation, brick; first story, clapboards; second story, gables, dormers and roofs, shingles. Outside blinds to all windows except sewing room bay and cellar windows. Windows in sewing room to have inside folding blinds.

INTERIOR FINISH: Hard white plaster. Soft wood trim except in first story hall, which is yellow pine. Hard wood staircase. First story to have hard

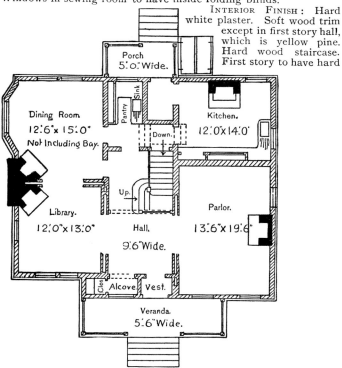

FIRST FLOOR.

wood double floor in hall, library and dining room; two rooms on second floor and studio on third floor to have hard wood border laid to a pattern. All interior wood-work finished in hard oil.

ACCOMMODATIONS: The principal rooms and their sizes, closets, etc., are shown by the plans. Cellar with concrete floor under the whole house, containing three stationary tubs and servants' W. C. Fireplaces with mantels in parlor, library and dining room, included in the estimate. Four bedrooms in attic; one of the attic rooms suitable for a studio.

COST: $4,000, † not including range and heater. The estimate is based on ‡ New York prices for materials and labor.

Price for working plans, specifications, and * license to build, - - - - - - - - - - - - - - - - $40.00
Price for †† bill of materials, - - - - - - - - 10.00

Address, THE CO-OPERATIVE BUILDING PLAN ASSOCIATION, Architects, 63 Broadway, New York.

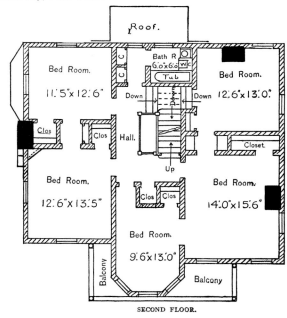

SECOND FLOOR.

189

THE CO-OPERATIVE BUILDING PLAN ASSOCIATION, ARCHITECTS, 63 BROADWAY. NEW YORK.

*Shoppell's Modern Houses—*Designs Patented.*   *Residence, Design No. 644*

PERSPECTIVE.

DESCRIPTION.

For explanation of all symbols (* † etc.) see page 42.

Gᴇɴᴇʀᴀʟ Dɪᴍᴇɴsɪᴏɴs : Width, 36 ft. 4 in.; depth, including veranda, 57 ft. 4 in. Heights of stories : Cellar, 7 ft.; first story, 10 ft.; second story, 9 ft.; attic, 8 ft.

Exᴛᴇʀɪᴏʀ Mᴀᴛᴇʀɪᴀʟs : Foundations, stone; first and second stories, brick; gables, brick and shingles; roofs, slate.

Iɴᴛᴇʀɪᴏʀ Fɪɴɪsʜ : Hard white plaster throughout. Flooring of first and second stories, yellow pine; attic, common flooring. Oak trim in hall and dining room; ash trim in parlor and library; trim elsewhere, yellow pine. Main stairs, oak. Bath-room, wainscoted. The ash trim to be hard finished with a dull gloss; all other trim to be finished in hard oil with a bright gloss.

Cᴏʟᴏʀs : All brick work to be pointed with red mortar and left natural color, after being cleaned with acid. Outer doors, trim and blinds, painted "blue-stone" color. Sashes and rain conductors, dark terra-cotta. Veranda floor, slate color; veranda ceiling, oiled. All shingles, stained sienna.

Aᴄᴄᴏᴍᴍᴏᴅᴀᴛɪᴏɴs : The principal rooms and their sizes, closets, etc., are shown by the floor plans. In addition there is a cellar (with concrete floor) under the whole house (a cistern under the laundry) and one room finished in the attic. The vegetable cellar is separated by a brick wall from the remainder of cellar. An ash-pit in the cellar, under the fire-place. Water tank in the attic, capacity 500 gallons. The triple window on the staircase is glazed with stained glass. The chimney breasts shown in the parlor and dining room are for furnace flues and are not carried above the roof.

Cᴏsᴛ : $4000, † not including mantels, range and heater. The estimate is based on ‡ New York prices for materials and labor. In most sections of the country the cost should be less.

Price for working plans, specifications and * license to build, - $40.00
Price for †† bill of materials, - - - - 10.00

Address, Tʜᴇ Cᴏ-ᴏᴘᴇʀᴀᴛɪᴠᴇ Bᴜɪʟᴅɪɴɢ Pʟᴀɴ Assᴏᴄɪᴀᴛɪᴏɴ, Architects, 63 Broadway, New York.

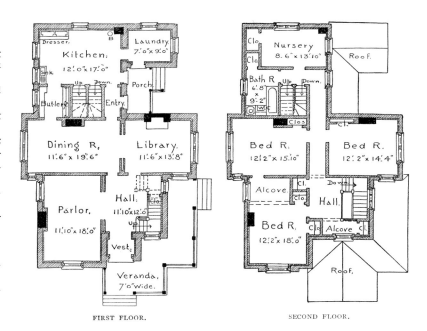

FIRST FLOOR.   SECOND FLOOR.

Fᴇᴀsɪʙʟᴇ Mᴏᴅɪғɪᴄᴀᴛɪᴏɴs : Heights of stories, sizes of rooms, kinds of materials and colors may be changed. A laundry may be placed under kitchen and present laundry omitted. Cistern, ash-pit, sliding doors and fire-place may be omitted. The dining room and the library may be transposed, in which case the door from the butler's pantry should be closed and a new butler's pantry planned to connect with the new dining room.

The price of working plans, specifications, etc. for a modified design varies according to the alterations required, and will be made known upon application to the Architects.

190

THE CO-OPERATIVE BUILDING PLAN ASSOCIATION ARCHITECTS, 63 BROADWAY, NEW YORK.

*Shoppell's Modern Houses—*Designs Patented.*   Residence, Design No. 490

PERSPECTIVE.

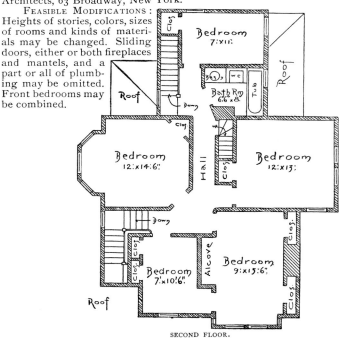

SIDE ELEVATION.

DESCRIPTION.

GENERAL DIMENSIONS: Width through dining and sitting rooms, 35 ft.; depth, including veranda, 50 ft. 6 in. Heights of stories: Cellar, 7 ft.; first story, 10 ft.; second story, 9 ft.; attic, 8 ft.

EXTERIOR MATERIALS: Foundations, stone and brick; first story, clapboards; second story, gables and roof, shingles. Outside blinds.

INTERIOR FINISH: Hard white plaster. Plaster cornices and centers in parlor, library, dining room and hall. Soft wood flooring and trim. Ash stairs. Panels under windows in parlor, library and dining room. Bath-room and kitchen wainscoted. Interior wood-work finished in hard oil.

COLORS: Clapboards, seal brown. Trim, blinds and rain con-

ductors, bronze green. Outside doors and sashes, dark green. Veranda floor, yellow drab. Veranda ceiling, oiled. Brick-work, Indian red. Wall shingles dipped and brush coated yellow stain. Roof shingles dipped and brush coated Indian red.

ACCOMMODATIONS: The principal rooms, and their sizes, closets, etc., are shown by the plans. Cellar under whole house. Open fireplaces and hard wood mantels in sitting room and parlor included in estimate. One room finished in the attic. Inner vestibule door glazed with plate glass.

COST: $4,068, † not including range and heater. The estimate is based on ‡ New York prices for materials and labor. In many sections of the country the cost should be less.

Price for working plans, specifications and * license to build, - - - - - - - - - - - - - $40.00
Price for †† bill of materials, - - - - - 5.00

Address, THE CO-OPERATIVE BUILDING PLAN ASSOCIATION, Architects, 63 Broadway, New York.

FEASIBLE MODIFICATIONS: Heights of stories, colors, sizes of rooms and kinds of materials may be changed. Sliding doors, either or both fireplaces and mantels, and a part or all of plumbing may be omitted. Front bedrooms may be combined.

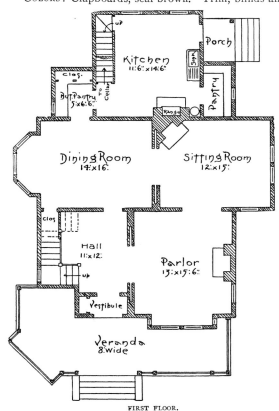

FIRST FLOOR.

SECOND FLOOR.

*Shoppell's Modern Houses—*Designs Patented.* *Residence, Design No. 645*

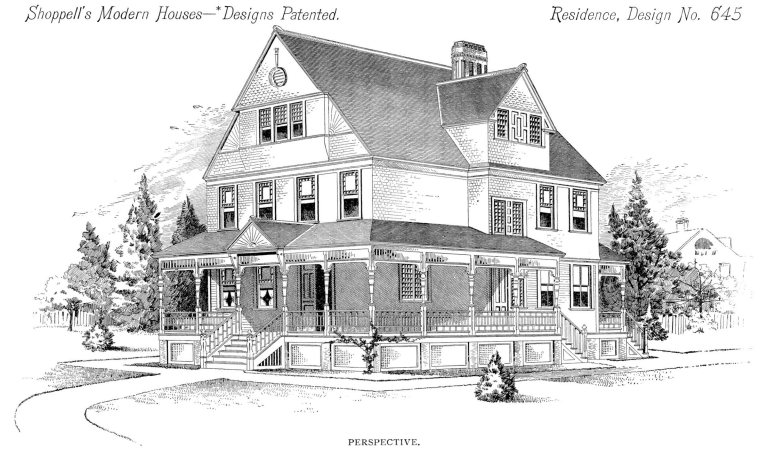

PERSPECTIVE.

DESCRIPTION.

For explanation of all symbols (* † etc.) see page 42.

GENERAL DIMENSIONS: Width, including veranda, 40 ft.; depth including veranda, 55 ft. Heights of stories: Cellar, 7 ft.; first story, 9 ft. 6 in.; second story, 9 ft.; attic, 8 ft.

EXTERIOR MATERIALS: Foundations, brick; first story, clapboards; second story, shingles; gables, panels and shingles; roofs, slate.

INTERIOR FINISH: Hard white plaster throughout. Flooring in dining room, butler's pantry and kitchen, yellow pine; all other flooring, white pine. Trim of first and second stories, white wood (poplar); attic trim, white pine. White wood staircase. Bath-room and kitchen wainscoted. All wood work stained and finished same as hard woods.

COLORS: All clapboards, outside doors and veranda floor, gray. Shingles dipped in dark red stain. Trim and blinds, lead color. Veranda ceiling, oiled. Brick work, Pompeian red.

ACCOMMODATIONS: The principal rooms and their sizes are shown by the plans. There is a cellar under the whole. One finished room in the attic with space for one more and storage room. The ventilated loft keeps the attic cool. Combination front and back stairway. The rear hall and the pantry shut off views and odors from the kitchen. Book closet in sitting room. Stained glass may be introduced in staircase windows and vestibule doors.

COST: $4200, † not including mantels, range and heater. The estimate is based on ‡ New York prices for materials and labor. In many sections of the country the cost should be less.

Price for working plans, specifications and * license to build, - $40.00
Price for †† bill of materials, - - 10.00

Address, THE CO-OPERATIVE BUILDING PLAN ASSOCIATION, Architects, 63 Broadway, New York.

FEASIBLE MODIFICATIONS: Heights of stories, exterior materials and interior finish, sizes of rooms and colors, all can be changed. An additional bedroom with a suitable passage, can be planned over the dining room; the bathroom then would be placed over the pantry. The front and rear halls may be connected by an arch, the dining room door opening into the rear hall; this would "square" the parlor. Sliding doors and the fire-place may be omitted. Fire-places may be introduced in the hall, parlor or library. A part or all of the plumbing may be omitted.

The price of working plans, specifications, etc. for a modified design varies according to the alterations required, and will be made known upon application to the Architects.

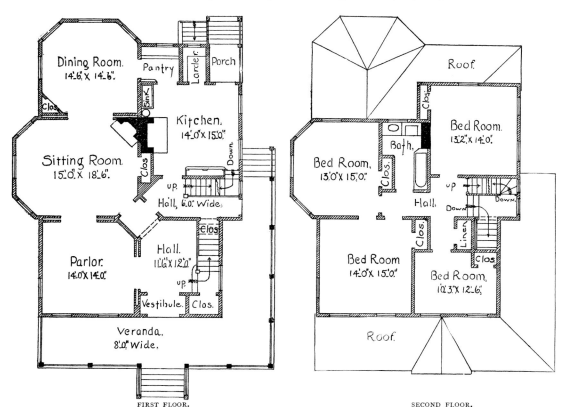

FIRST FLOOR.   SECOND FLOOR.

192

THE CO-OPERATIVE BUILDING PLAN ASSOCIATION, ARCHITECTS, 63 BROADWAY, NEW YORK.

*Shoppell's Modern Houses—*Designs Patented.*

Residence, Design No. 561

PHOTOGRAPHIC VIEW.

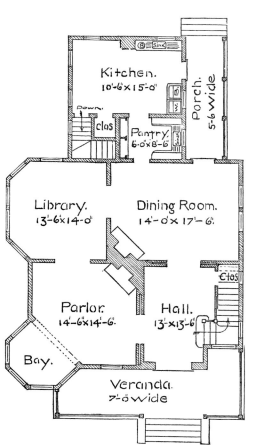

FIRST FLOOR.

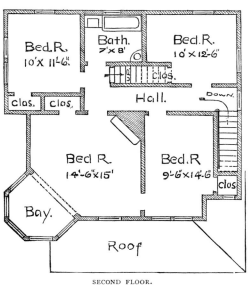

SECOND FLOOR.

DESCRIPTION.

For explanation of all symbols (* † etc.) see page 42.

GENERAL DIMENSIONS: Extreme width, 32 ft. 6 in.; depth, including veranda, 54 ft. Heights of stories: Cellar, 7 ft.; first story, 9 ft. 6 in.; second story, 8 ft. 6 in.; attic, 7 ft. 6 in.

EXTERIOR MATERIALS: Foundations, stone; first story, clapboards; second story, gables and roofs, shingles. Outside blinds.

INTERIOR FINISH: Hard white plaster. Plaster cornices and centers in hall, parlor, dining room and library. Soft wood flooring and trim. Ash staircase. Panels under windows in parlor, dining room and library. Bath-room and kitchen wainscoted. Interior wood-work stained colors to suit owner, and finished in hard oil.

COLORS: Clapboards, light chocolate. Trim, sashes and rain conductors, maroon. Outside doors and blinds, chocolate. Veranda floor, blue stone color. Veranda ceiling finished in hard oil. Brick-work, Indian red. All shingles dipped and brush coated dark terra cotta.

ACCOMMODATIONS: The principal rooms and their sizes, closets, etc., are shown by the plans. Cellar under whole house. One room and storage space in attic. Mantels in dining room, parlor and one bedroom included in estimate. Door from dining room to rear porch.

COST: $4,200, † not including range and heater. The estimate is based on ‡ New York prices for materials and labor. In many sections of the country the cost should be less.

Price for working plans, specifications and * license to build, - $35.00
Price for † † bill of materials, - 10.00

Address, THE CO-OPERATIVE BUILDING PLAN ASSOCIATION, Architects, 63 Broadway, New York.

FEASIBLE MODIFICATIONS: Heights of stories, colors, sizes of rooms and kinds of materials may be changed. Sliding doors, any or all mantels and a part or all of plumbing may be omitted. Side porch may be omitted and window substituted for door from dining room. Kitchen entrance may be at rear instead of at side.

The price of working plans, specifications, etc., for a modified design varies according to the alterations required, and will be made known upon application to the Architects.

193

THE CO-OPERATIVE BUILDING PLAN ASSOCIATION, ARCHITECTS, 63 BROADWAY, NEW YORK.

Shoppell's Modern Houses—*Designs Patented.　　　　　　　*Residence, Design No. 397*

PERSPECTIVE.

DESCRIPTION.

For explanation of all symbols (* † etc.) see page 42.

GENERAL DIMENSIONS: Extreme width, 32 ft. 6 in.; depth, including veranda, 66 ft. 6 in. Heights of stories: Cellar, 7 ft.; first story, 9 ft. 6 in.; second story, 8 ft. 6 in.; attic, 7 ft. 6 in.

Exterior Materials, Interior Finish and Colors same as those of Design No. 561, described on the opposite page.

ACCOMMODATIONS: The principal rooms and their sizes, closets, etc., are shown by the plans. Cellar under whole house. One room and hall finished in attic. Stained Cathedral glass in staircase windows. Open fireplaces and hard wood mantels in parlor and dining room. An earth closet in woodshed. Heater pipes and registers throughout house, included in estimate.

COST: $4,267, † not including mantels, range and heater. The estimate is based on ‡ New York prices for materials and labor. In many sections of the country the cost should be less.

Price for working plans, specifications and * license to build, - - - - $30.00

Price for †† bill of materials, - - 5.00

Address: THE CO-OPERATIVE BUILDING PLAN ASSOCIATION, Architects, 63 Broadway, New York.

FEASIBLE MODIFICATIONS: Heights of stories, colors, sizes of rooms and kinds of materials may be changed. Cellar may be reduced in size. Fireplaces, sliding doors, stained glass and a part or all of plumbing may be omitted. One chimney will suffice if heating apparatus be used. Corner bay may be carried up higher to form a tower.

The price of working plans, specifications, etc., for a modified design varies according to the alterations required, and will be made known upon application to the Architects.

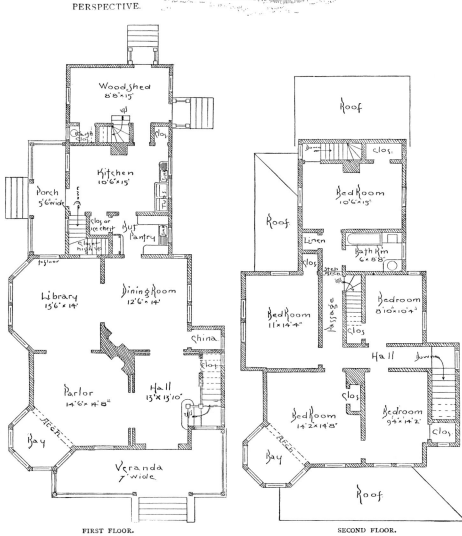

FIRST FLOOR.　　　　　　　SECOND FLOOR.

194

THE CO-OPERATIVE BUILDING PLAN ASSOCIATION, ARCHITECTS, 63 BROADWAY, NEW YORK.

*Shoppell's Modern Houses—*Designs Patented.*

Residence, Design No. 225

PERSPECTIVE.

DESCRIPTION.

For explanation of all symbols (* † etc.) see page 42.

GENERAL DIMENSIONS: Width, through dining room and library, 36 ft. 6 in.; depth, including veranda, 51 ft. Heights of stories: Cellar, 6 ft. 6 in.; first story, 9 ft. 6 in.; second story, 9 ft.; attic, 8 ft. 6 in.

EXTERIOR MATERIALS: Foundations, stone and brick; first story, clapboards; second story, clapboards and shingles; gables and roof, shingles. Outside blinds to all windows except those of the cellar.

INTERIOR FINISH: Hard white plaster; plaster cornices in hall, parlor, dining and sitting rooms, and two bedrooms and hall of second story. Hard pine flooring in front hall and bath-room; all other flooring soft wood. Soft wood trim. Ash stairs. Panels under windows in parlor, dining and sitting rooms. Wainscot in bath-room and kitchen. Interior wood-work stained to suit owner and finished in hard oil.

COLORS: Clapboards, blinds and sashes, olive green. Trim and rain conductors, bronze yellow. Outside doors, dark green. Veranda floor, dark olive drab. Veranda ceiling, light olive drab. Brick-work, Indian red. Wall shingles dipped and brush coated sienna stain. Roof shingles dipped and brush coated reddish stain.

ACCOMMODATIONS: The principal rooms and their sizes, closets, etc., are shown by the plans. Cellar under rear half of house, with outside and inside entrances and concrete floor. Three bedrooms, hall and storage room in attic. Large balcony in second story front. Four fireplaces and hard wood mantels, also kitchen range, included in estimate.

COST: $4,300, † not including heater. The estimate is based on ‡ New York prices for materials and labor. In many sections of the country the cost should be less.

Price for working plans, specifications and * license to build, - - - - - - - - $40.00

Price for † † bill of materials, - - - - - 10.00

Address, THE CO-OPERATIVE BUILDING PLAN ASSOCIATION, Architects, 63 Broadway, New York.

FEASIBLE MODIFICATIONS: Heights of stories, colors, sizes of rooms and kinds of materials may be changed. Cellar may be extended or reduced. Attic may be left unfinished. Sliding doors, fireplaces and mantels, and a part or all of plumbing may be omitted. Front balcony may be enclosed with glass, or, if preferred, may be enclosed to form a bedroom.

The price of working plans, specifications, etc., for a modified design varies according to the alterations required, and will be made known upon application to the Architects.

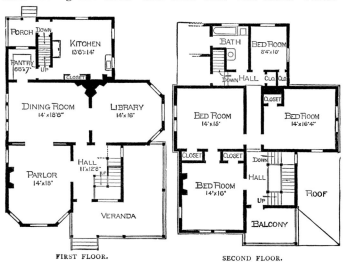

FIRST FLOOR.　　SECOND FLOOR.

THE CO-OPERATIVE BUILDING PLAN ASSOCIATION, ARCHITECTS, 63 BROADWAY, NEW YORK.

Shoppell's Modern Houses—*Designs Patented.   *Residence, Design No. 646*

PERSPECTIVE.

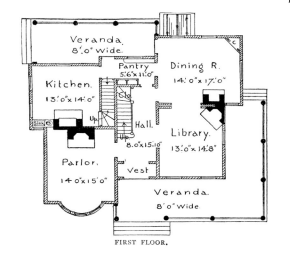

FIRST FLOOR.

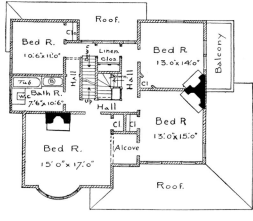

SECOND FLOOR.

DESCRIPTION.

For explanation of all symbols (* † etc.) see page 42.

GENERAL DIMENSIONS: Width, including veranda, 48 ft. 6 in.; depth 41 ft. 6 in. Heights of stories: Cellar 6 ft. 6 in.; first story, 10 ft. 6 in.; second story, 10 ft.; attic, 7 ft. 6 in.

EXTERIOR MATERIALS: Foundations, stone; first story, clapboards; second story, gables and roofs, shingles.

INTERIOR FINISH: Hard white plaster throughout. White pine flooring and trim throughout. Walnut staircase. All wood work finished in hard oil.

COLORS: All clapboards painted tan color; roof shingles painted dark red; all other shingles stained sienna. Sashes, Pompeian red. Trim, outside doors and veranda floor, brown. Brick work cleaned with acid and left natural.

ACCOMMODATIONS: The principal rooms and their sizes, closets, etc., are shown by the plans. In addition there is a cellar under the whole house and there are two rooms (with space for one more) in the attic. A loft over the attic rooms (large enough for storage) keeps the attic rooms cool. The plumbing is quite concentrated—always a good feature.

COST: $4300, † not including mantels, range and heater. The estimate is based on ‡ New York prices for materials and labor. In many sections of the country the cost should be less.

Price for working plans, specifications and * license to build, - $45.00
Price for †† bill of materials, - - - - 10.00

Address, THE CO-OPERATIVE BUILDING PLAN ASSOCIATION, Architects, 63 Broadway, New York.

FEASIBLE MODIFICATIONS: Heights of stories, exterior materials, interior finish, sizes of rooms and colors may be changed. A number of the fire-places and the sliding doors may be omitted. Linen closets may be moved, permitting the stairs to run straight. Alcove and closet space between front bed-rooms may be planned for a small bed-room. May omit balcony and curtail plumbing.

The price of working plans, specifications, etc. for a modified design varies according to the alterations required, and will be made known upon application to the Architects.

196

THE CO-OPERATIVE BUILDING PLAN ASSOCIATION, ARCHITECTS, 63 BROADWAY, NEW YORK.

*Shoppell's Modern Houses—*Designs Patented.*　　　　　　*Residence, Design No. 458*

PERSPECTIVE.

DESCRIPTION.

For explanation of all symbols (* † etc.) see page 42.

GENERAL DIMENSIONS: Extreme width, 31 ft. 8 in.; depth, including veranda, 57 ft. Heights of stories: Cellar, 7 ft.; first story, 9 ft. 6 in.; second story, 9 ft.; attic, 8 ft.

EXTERIOR MATERIALS: Foundations, stone and brick; first and second stories, brick; gables, balconies and roofs, shingles. Outside blinds.

INTERIOR FINISH: Hard white plaster; plaster cornices and centers in hall, parlor, library, dining room and billiard room. Yellow pine floor in kitchen; all other flooring soft wood. Soft wood trim. Ash stairway. Panels under windows in dining room, parlor and library. Wainscoting in kitchen, bath-room and pantry. Interior wood-work finished in hard oil.

COLORS: Brick-work to be washed down with acid and oiled. Trim, outside doors and rain conductors, bronze green. Blinds and sashes, bright red. Veranda floor, dark slate color. Veranda ceiling, lilac. Wall shingles on gables, balconies, dormers, etc., dipped and brush coated terra cotta. Roof shingles, dipped and brush coated dark red stain.

ACCOMMODATIONS: The principal rooms and their sizes, closets, etc., are shown by the plans. Cellar under whole house. Two bedrooms, storeroom and hallway in attic. Sliding doors connect principal rooms in first story. Heater pipes and registers provided in all rooms. Foundations treated with asphalt, to prevent dampness rising through walls. Fireplaces and mantels in hall, parlor, dining room and library.

COST: $4,326, † not including mantels, range and heater. The estimate is based on ‡ New York prices for materials and labor. In many sections of the country the cost should be less.

Price for working plans, specifications and * license to build, - - - - $50.00
Price for †† bill of materials, - - 10.00
Address, THE CO-OPERATIVE BUILDING PLAN ASSOCIATION, Architects, 63 Broadway, New York.

FEASIBLE MODIFICATIONS: Heights of stories, colors, sizes of rooms and kinds of materials may be changed. Attic may be left unfinished. Sliding doors, fireplaces and mantels, and a part or all of plumbing may be omitted. Billiard room may be changed to bedroom. Bath-room may be placed over kitchen. Balcony may be omitted or enclosed.

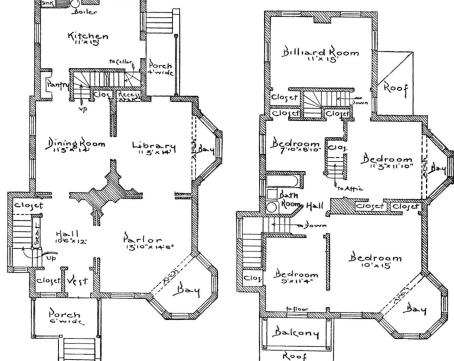

FIRST FLOOR.　　　　　　SECOND FLOOR.

197

THE CO-OPERATIVE BUILDING PLAN ASSOCIATION, ARCHITECTS, 63 BROADWAY, NEW YORK.

*Shoppell's Modern Houses—*Designs Patented.

Residence, Design No. 457

PERSPECTIVE.

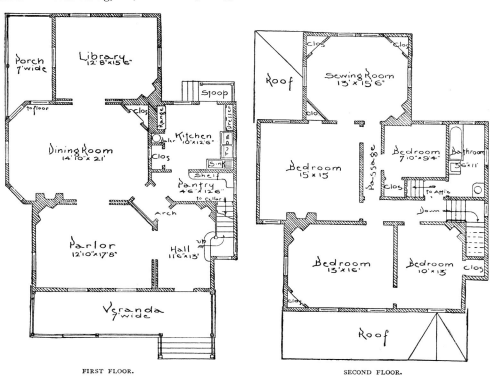

- Side Elevation -

DESCRIPTION.

For explanation of all symbols (* † etc.) see page 42.

GENERAL DIMENSIONS: Width through dining room and kitchen, 35 ft.; depth, including veranda, 50 ft. Heights of stories: Cellar, 6 ft. 6 in.; first story, 9 ft.; second story, 8 ft. 6 in.; attic, 7 ft. 6 in.

EXTERIOR MATERIALS: Foundation, brick; first story, clapboards; second story and roof, shingles; gables, panels and shingles. Outside blinds to all windows.

INTERIOR FINISH: Hard white plaster. Plaster cornices and centers in parlor, hall, library and dining room. Soft wood flooring and trim. Ash stairs. Wainscot in bath-room and kitchen. Interior wood-work stained to suit owner and finished in hard oil.

COLORS: Clapboards and panels in gables, seal brown. Trim, outside doors, blinds, veranda floor, and frames of panels in gables, maroon. Sashes and rain conductors, dark green. Veranda ceiling, varnished. Brick-work, Indian red. Front cement cornice, oiled. Wall shingles dipped and brush coated light sienna stain. Roof shingles dipped and brush coated Indian red.

ACCOMMODATIONS: The principal rooms and their sizes, closets, etc., are shown by the plans. Cellar under whole house, with concrete floor. Two bedrooms finished in attic. Eight fireplaces with mantels, also kitchen range, included in estimate. Sliding doors between all principal rooms on first floor. Kitchen isolated by two doors and a pantry. Dish slide between dining room and kitchen closet. Each room may be heated independently of the others.

COST: $4,352, † not including heater. The estimate is based on ‡ New York prices for materials and labor. In many sections of the country the cost should be less.

Price for working plans, specifications
and * license to build, - - $40.00
Price for † † bill of materials, - 5.00

Address, THE CO-OPERATIVE BUILDING PLAN ASSOCIATION Architects, 63 Broadway, New York.

FEASIBLE MODIFICATIONS: Heights of stories, colors, sizes of rooms and kinds of materials may be changed. Cellar may be reduced in size and concrete floor omitted. Fireplaces, sliding doors, side porch and a part or all of plumbing may be omitted. If heating apparatus be used one chimney will suffice. Size of veranda may be extended or reduced.

The price of working plans, specifications, etc., for a modified design varies according to the alterations required, and will be made known upon application to the Architects.

FIRST FLOOR.

Porch 7' wide

Library 12'8"x15'6"

Stoop

Kitchen 10'x12'6"

Dining Room 14'10"x21'

Clos

Pantry 4'6"x12'6"

Arch

Parlor 12'10"x17'8"

Hall 11'6"x13'

Veranda 7' wide

SECOND FLOOR.

Roof

Clos

Sewing Room 13'x15'6"

Clos

Bedroom 15'x15'

Bedroom 7'10"x9'4"

Bathroom

Clos

to Attic

Down

Bedroom 13'x16'

Bedroom 10'x13'

Clos

Roof

198

THE CO-OPERATIVE BUILDING PLAN ASSOCIATION, ARCHITECTS, 63 BROADWAY, NEW YORK.

Shoppell's Modern Houses—*Designs Patented.

Residence, Design No. 455

PERSPECTIVE.

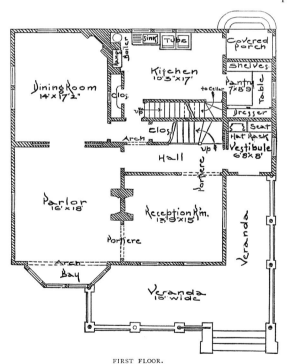

FIRST FLOOR.

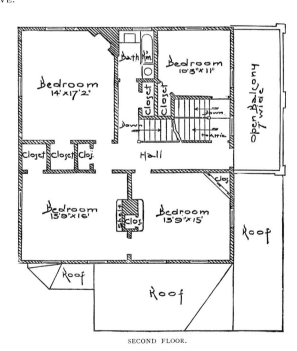

SECOND FLOOR.

DESCRIPTION.

GENERAL DIMENSIONS: Extreme width, 40 ft.; depth, including veranda, 47 ft. 6 in. Heights of stories: Cellar, 6 ft. 8 in.; first story, 9 ft. 4 in.; second story; 9 ft.; attic, 8 ft.

EXTERIOR MATERIALS: Foundation, stone and brick; first story, brick-work up to sills of windows, shingles above sills extending through second story; gables and roof, shingles. Inside blinds to all windows of first and second stories, outside blinds to all other windows.

INTERIOR FINISH: Sand finish plaster; plaster cornices and centers in vestibule, hall, parlor, reception and dining rooms. Soft wood flooring and trim. Ash staircase. Panels under windows in parlor, dining and reception rooms. Chair rail in dining room. Picture molding in principal rooms and hall of first story. Bath-room and kitchen wainscoted. Wood-work in kitchen and scullery grained. Attic finish painted tints to suit owner; other wood-work finished in hard oil, stained to suit owner.

COLORS: Brick-work, red. Trim, outside blinds and rain conductors, light olive green. Outside doors, light olive green with light olive drab panels. Sashes, and veranda ceiling, bright red. Veranda floor, posts and rails, light olive drab. Wall shingles dipped and brush coated sienna stain. Roof shingles dipped and brush coated red.

ACCOMMODATIONS: The principal rooms and their sizes, closets, etc., are shown by the plans. Cellar with concrete floor under whole house. Three large bedrooms with closets finished in attic; large air space above attic floored for storage. Attic rooms of this house are particularly desirable. Four fireplaces and mantels, also kitchen range, are included in estimate. Plumbing is so arranged that freezing of pipes is almost impossible. Back stairway leads directly to attic.

COST: $4,431, † not including heating apparatus. The estimate is based on ‡ New York prices for materials and labor. In many sections of the country the cost should be less.

Price for working plans, specifications and * license to build, - - - - - - - - - - - - - - - $40.00
Price for † † bill of materials, - - - - - - - 10.00

199

THE CO-OPERATIVE BUILDING PLAN ASSOCIATION, ARCHITECTS, 63 BROADWAY, NEW YORK.

Shoppell's Modern Houses—*Designs Patented.　　　　*Cottage, Design No. 456*

PERSPECTIVE.

DESCRIPTION.

For explanation of all symbols (* † etc.) see page 42.

GENERAL DIMENSIONS: Extreme width, 36 ft. 2 in.; extreme depth, 51 ft. 2 in. Heights of stories: Cellar, 6 ft. 6 in.; first story, 10 ft. 4 in.; second story, 9 ft.; attic, 6 ft. 6 in.

EXTERIOR MATERIALS: Foundation, brick walls; first story, clapboards; second story, gables and roof, shingles. Outside blinds.

INTERIOR FINISH: Hard white plaster. Plaster cornices in hall, parlor, dining room and three bedrooms. Soft wood flooring and trim. Ash stairway. Panels under windows in parlor, hall and dining room. Picture molding in principal rooms and hall of first story. Wainscot in kitchen and bath-room. Interior wood-work finished in hard oil.

COLORS: Clapboards and sashes, olive. Trim, dark green. Outside doors, dark green with olive panels. Blinds rain conductors and brick-work, Pompeian red. Veranda floor and ceiling, medium drab. Wall shingles dipped and brush coated in red stain. Roof shingles dipped and brush coated Indian red stain.

ACCOMMODATIONS: The principal rooms and their sizes, closets, etc., are shown by the plans. Cellar under kitchen and hall. Three good rooms in attic. Large hall used as a reception room. Four open fireplaces and hard wood mantels, and kitchen range, included in estimate. A fireplace heater in parlor or dining room will heat two bedrooms.

COST: $4,500, † not including heater. The estimate is based on ‡ New York prices for materials and labor. In many sections of the country the cost should be less.

Price for working plans, specifications and * license to build, - $35.00

Price for †† bill of materials, - - - - - $5.00
Address, THE CO-OPERATIVE BUILDING PLAN ASSOCIATION, Architects, 63 Broadway New York.

FEASIBLE MODIFICATIONS: Heights of stories, colors, sizes of rooms and kinds of materials may be changed. Sliding doors, outside blinds, fireplaces and mantels may be omitted.

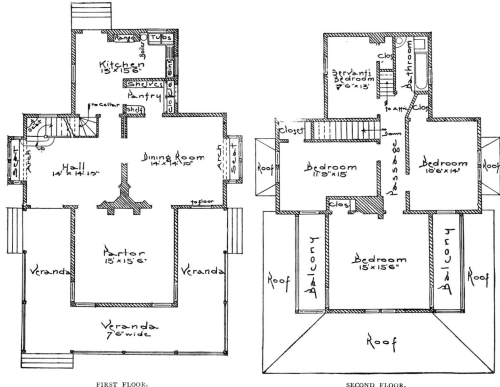

FIRST FLOOR.　　　　SECOND FLOOR.

THE CO-OPERATIVE BUILDING PLAN ASSOCIATION, ARCHITECTS, 63 BROADWAY, NEW YORK.

*Shoppell's Modern Houses—*Designs Patented.*   Residence, Design No. 626

PERSPECTIVE.

FIRST FLOOR.

SECOND FLOOR.

DESCRIPTION.

*For explanation of all symbols (* † etc.) see page 42.*

GENERAL DIMENSIONS : Width over all, 46 ft.; depth, including veranda, 52 ft. Heights of stories: Cellar, 7 ft.; first story, 9 ft.; second story, 8 ft. 6 in.; attic, 7 ft. 6 in.

EXTERIOR MATERIALS : Foundations, stone; first story, clapboards; second story, gables and roof, shingles.

INTERIOR FINISH : Hard white plaster ceilings; walls, two coats plaster for papering. Plaster cornices and centers in library, main hall and dining room. Library, den, lavatory, main hall, vestibule and dining room have double floors of soft woods with broad hard wood borders. Trim, soft woods. Main staircase, hard wood. Bath-room and kitchen wainscoted. Six fireplaces and hard wood mantels included in estimate. All interior wood-work to be finished in hard oil; soft woods stained to suit owner.

COLORS: All clapboards and veranda ceiling, ecru. Trim and rain conductors, olive drab. Outside doors, stained oak and varnished. Blinds, dark green. Sashes, bright red. Veranda floor, seal brown. Brick-work, Venetian red. Wall shingles dipped and brush coated dark sienna. Roof shingles dipped and brush coated with oil.

ACCOMMODATIONS : The principal rooms and their sizes, closets, etc., are shown by the plans. Cellar under all with inside and outside entrances and a concrete floor. Three fine rooms in attic beside ample storage space. Ice-box is so arranged that it may be filled from outside and be used in connection with kitchen, pantry and china closet. Back stairway extends from first story directly to attic.

COST : $4,500, † not including range and heater. The estimate is based on ‡ New York prices for materials and labor. In many sections of the country the cost should be less.

Price for working plans, specifications and * license to build, - - - - - - - - - - $40.00
Price for †† bill of materials, - - - - - - 20.00
Address, THE CO-OPERATIVE BUILDING PLAN ASSOCIATION, Architects, 63 Broadway, New York.

201

THE CO-OPERATIVE BUILDING PLAN ASSOCIATION, ARCHITECTS, 63 BROADWAY, NEW YORK.

Shoppell's Modern Houses—*Designs Patented.   *Residence, Design No. 661*

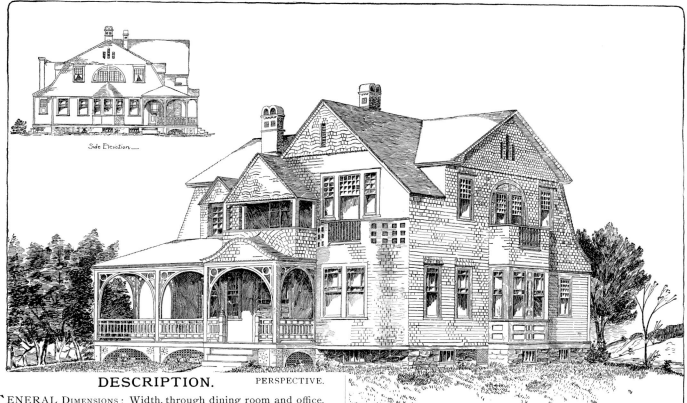

Side Elevation

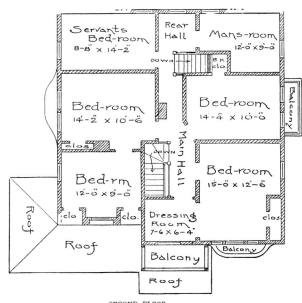

PERSPECTIVE.

The Cooperative Building Plan Ass'n
Architects 63 Broadway N.Y.

DESCRIPTION.

GENERAL DIMENSIONS : Width, through dining room and office, 38 ft.; depth, including veranda, porch and bath-room, 50 ft. Heights of stories : Cellar, 7 ft.: first story, 9 ft. 6 in.: second story, 8 ft. 6 in.

EXTERIOR MATERIALS : Foundations, stone ; first story, clapboards and shingles ; second story, gables and roof, shingles. Outside blinds.

INTERIOR FINISH : Hard white plaster ; plaster cornices and centers in parlor and dining room. Soft wood flooring and trim. Ash staircase. Chair rail in dining room. Wainscot in bath-room and kitchen. Interior wood-work finished in hard oil.

COLORS : Clapboards, light chocolate. Trim, blinds, sashes and rain conductors, maroon. Outside doors, veranda posts, rails, etc., dark chocolate. Veranda floor, brown stone color. Veranda ceiling, buff. Wall shingles dipped and brush coated mahogany stain. Roof shingles dipped and brush coated dark red stain.

ACCOMMODATIONS : The principal rooms and their sizes, closets,

etc., are shown by the plans. Cellar under whole house. Attic floored for storage. Two open fireplaces and mantels included in estimate. Reception room has separate outside entrance. House designed for a physician; office, bedroom, bath-room and front and rear entrance conveniently arranged. Wash-basin in closet of private office.

COST : $4,500, † not including range and heater. The estimate is based on ‡ New York prices for materials and labor. In many sections of the country the cost should be less.

Price for working plans, specifications and * license to build,   - - - - - - - - - - - - - - - $40.00
Price for † † bill of materials,   - - - - - - -   10.00

Address, THE CO-OPERATIVE BUILDING PLAN ASSOCIATION, Architects, 63 Broadway, New York.

FEASIBLE MODIFICATIONS : Heights of stories, colors, sizes of rooms and kinds of materials may be changed. Sliding doors, fireplaces and a part or all plumbing may be omitted. A part or all of veranda may be omitted.

FIRST FLOOR.

SECOND FLOOR.

202

THE CO-OPERATIVE BUILDING PLAN ASSOCIATION, ARCHITECTS, 63 BROADWAY, NEW YORK.

Shoppell's Modern Houses—*Designs Patented   *Residence, Design No. 647*

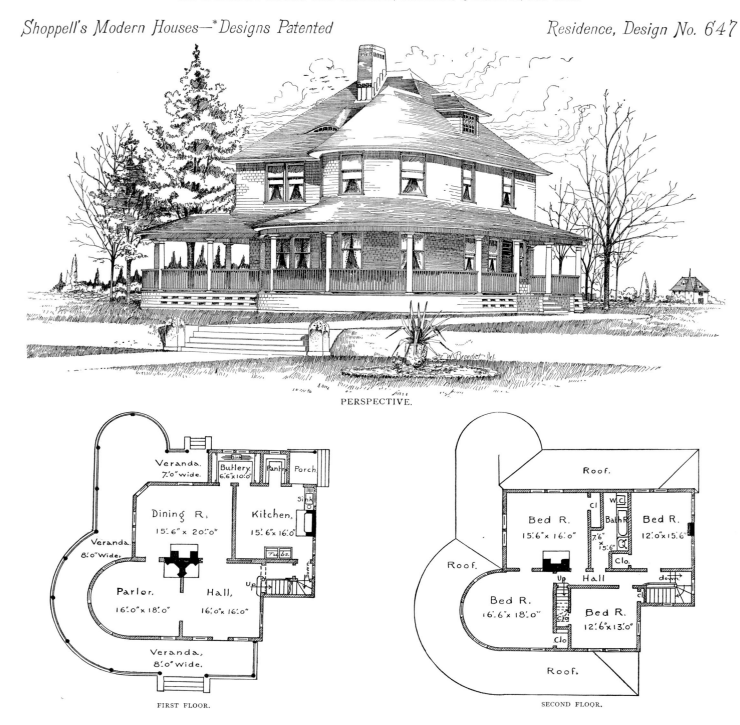

PERSPECTIVE.

FIRST FLOOR.

SECOND FLOOR.

DESCRIPTION.

For explanation of all symbols (* † etc.) see page 42.

GENERAL DIMENSIONS : Width, over all, 54 ft.; depth, over all, 55 ft. 10 in. Heights of stories : Cellar, 7 ft.; first story, 9 ft.; second story, 8 ft. 6 in.; attic, 8 ft.

EXTERIOR MATERIALS : Foundation, brick ; walls of both stories, dormers and veranda base, shingles ; main and dormer roofs, slate ; veranda roof, shingles.

INTERIOR FINISH : Hard white plaster throughout, except cellar ceiling, which is rough plastered. Plaster cornices and centres in hall, parlor and dining room. Floors in first story, hard pine ; in second story, soft wood. Trim throughout soft wood stained and finished as hard wood. Stairway and front door, oak. House piped for gas.

COLORS : All shingles dipped in oil. All trim, also blinds and sashes, painted ivory white. Outside doors finished in hard oil. Veranda floor and ceiling and all brick work, oiled.

ACCOMMODATIONS : The principal rooms and their sizes, closets, etc., are shown by the plans. Beside these there is a cellar (with concrete floor) under the whole house, and there are two rooms and a hall finished in the attic.

COST : $4500, † not including mantels, range and heater. The estimate is based on ‡ New York prices for materials and labor. In many sections of the country the cost should be less.

Price for working plans, specifications and * license to build, - $45.00
Price for †† bill of materials, - - - - 10.00

Address, THE CO-OPERATIVE BUILDING PLAN ASSOCIATION, Architects, 63 Broadway, New York.

FEASIBLE MODIFICATIONS : Heights of stories, kinds of materials and colors may be changed ; size of cellar reduced ; width and length of veranda changed ; attic rooms, bath-room, and sliding doors omitted ; form of parlor and bed-room bays changed from circular to polygonal. Any or all of the fire-places may be omitted.

The price of working plans, specifications, etc. for a modified design varies according to the alterations required, and will be made known upon application to the Architects.

*Shoppell's Modern Houses—*Designs Patented.*   *Residence, Design No. 411*

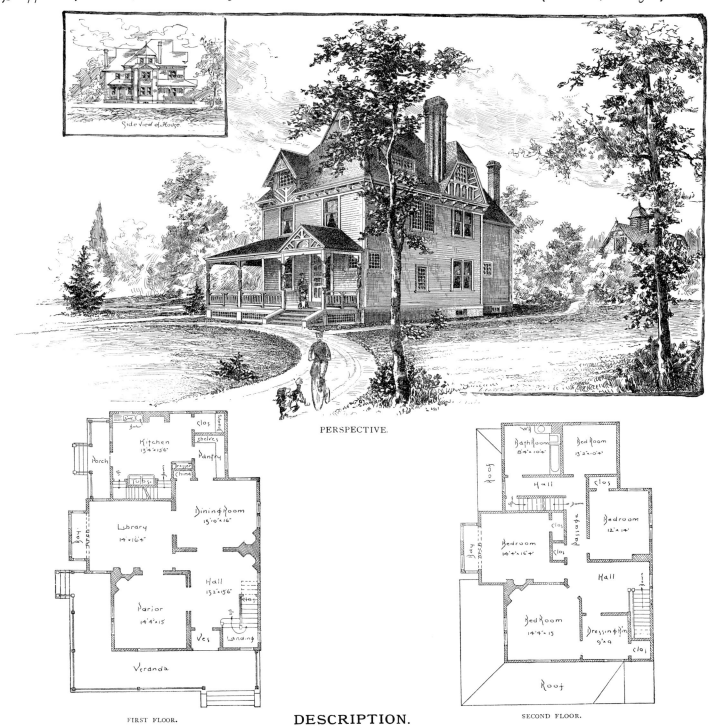

Side View of House.

PERSPECTIVE.

FIRST FLOOR.　SECOND FLOOR.

DESCRIPTION.

For explanation of all symbols (* † etc.) see page 42.

GENERAL DIMENSIONS: Extreme width, 37 ft. 8 in.; depth, including veranda, 57 ft. 8 in. Heights of stories: Cellar, 7 ft.; first story, 9 ft. 4 in.; second story, 8 ft. 4 in.

EXTERIOR MATERIALS: Foundations, stone; first and second stories, clapboards; gables, panels; roof, shingles. Outside blinds.

INTERIOR FINISH: Hard white plaster; plaster cornices and centers in hall (both stories), parlor, library and dining room. Soft wood flooring and trim. Ash stairs. Panels under windows in hall, parlor, library and dining room. Bath-room, pantry and kitchen wainscoted. Interior wood-work finished in hard oil.

COLORS: Clapboards, light olive drab. Trim, dark olive drab. Outside doors, bronze green. Blinds and sashes, maroon. Veranda floor and ceiling, oiled. Rain conductors and veranda finish, olive. Wall shingles dipped and brush coated sienna stain. Roof shingles dipped and brush coated red stain.

ACCOMMODATIONS: The principal rooms and their sizes, closets, etc., are shown by the plans. Cellar under the whole house. Attic unfinished, but floored; space for three rooms and storage. Fireplaces in hall, parlor, library, dining room and two bedrooms.

COST: $4,631, † not including mantels, range and heater. The estimate is based on ‡ New York prices for materials and labor. In many sections of the country the cost should be less.

Price for working plans, specifications and * license to build, - - - - - - - - $50.00
Price for † † bill of materials, - - - - - 10.00

Address, THE CO-OPERATIVE BUILDING PLAN ASSOCIATION, Architects, 63 Broadway, New York.

FEASIBLE MODIFICATIONS: Heights of stories, colors, sizes of rooms and kinds of materials may be changed. Open fireplaces and mantels, sliding doors, a part or all of plumbing, side porches and veranda may be omitted. Kitchen porch may be placed at rear.

The price of working plans, specifications, etc., for a modified design varies according to the alterations required, and will be made known upon application to the Architects.

204

THE CO-OPERATIVE BUILDING PLAN ASSOCIATION, ARCHITECTS, 63 BROADWAY, NEW YORK.

Shoppell's Modern Houses—*Designs Patented.   *Residence, Design No. 563*

PERSPECTIVE.

DESCRIPTION.

For explanation of all symbols (* † etc.) see page 42.

GENERAL DIMENSIONS: Extreme width, 34 ft. 6 in.; depth, including veranda, 55 ft. Heights of stories: Cellar, 7 ft.; first story, 9 ft. 6 in.; second story, 8 ft. 6 in.; attic, 8 ft.

EXTERIOR MATERIALS: Foundations, stone and brick; first and second stories, brick; gables, shingles; roof, slate. Outside blinds.

INTERIOR FINISH: Hard white plaster; plaster cornices and centers in parlor, hall, sitting and dining rooms. Hard pine flooring in pantries and kitchen. Soft wood flooring elsewhere. Soft wood trim. Ash staircase. Panels under windows in parlor, hall, sitting and dining room. Wainscot in bath-room and kitchen. Interior wood-work finished in hard oil.

COLORS: Brick-work cleaned down with acid and neatly pointed. Clapboards of kitchen extension, all blinds and rain conductors, seal brown. Trim and outside doors, dark green. Sashes, maroon. Veranda floors, dark olive drab. Veranda ceiling, light blue. Wall shingles dipped and brush coated terra cotta.

ACCOMMODATIONS: The principal rooms and their sizes, closets, etc., are shown by the plans. Cellar with concrete floor under kitchen. Two rooms and hall in attic. Sliding doors between parlor and sitting room. Open fireplaces in parlor, sitting, dining and one bedroom. Side porch entry to sitting room. Water-closet off kitchen porch. Balcony in second and attic stories.

COST: $4,585, † not including mantels, range and heater. The estimate is based on ‡ New York prices for materials and labor. In many sections of the country the cost should be less.

Price for working plans, specifications
and * license to build, - - - - $50.00
Price for †† bill of materials, - - 10.00

Address, THE CO-OPERATIVE BUILDING PLAN ASSOCIATION, Architects, 63 Broadway, New York.

FEASIBLE MODIFICATIONS: Heights of stories, colors, sizes of rooms and kinds of materials may be changed. Cellar may extend under whole house. Balconies may be enclosed with sliding sashes or may be enclosed to form part of adjoining rooms. Sliding doors, fireplaces and mantels, set range, a part or all of plumbing, and attic finish, may be omitted.

The price of working plans, specifications, etc., for a modified design varies according to the alterations required, and will be made known upon application to the Architects.

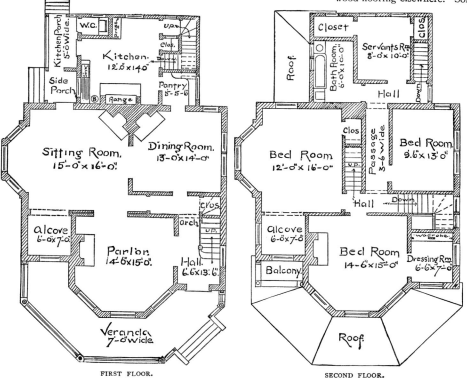

FIRST FLOOR.   SECOND FLOOR.

205

THE CO-OPERATIVE BUILDING PLAN ASSOCIATION, ARCHITECTS, 63 BROADWAY, NEW YORK.

Shoppell's Modern Houses—*Designs Patented. *Residence, Design No. 521*

DESCRIPTION.

The exterior appearance is the same as that of No. 563, shown on opposite age.

GENERAL DIMENSIONS: Width over all, 42 ft. 6 in.; depth, including veranda, 58 ft. 6 in. Heights of stories: Cellar, 7 ft.; first story, 9 ft. 6 in.; second story, 8 ft. 6 in.; attic, 8 ft. 6 in.

EXTERIOR MATERIALS: Foundations, stone; first story of main house, brick; kitchen extension, clapboards; second story, shingles; gables, panels and shingles; roof, slate. All windows in kitchen and pantry and throughout second story have outside blinds.

INTERIOR FINISH: Hard white plaster; plaster cornices and centers in hall, parlor, dining and sitting rooms. Hard pine flooring in bath-room and kitchen; soft wood flooring elsewhere. Soft wood trim. Ash staircase. Panels under windows in first and second stories, main part of house. Bathroom and kitchen wainscoted. Inside sliding blinds in parlor, dining and sitting rooms. Interior wood-work finished in hard oil.

COLORS: All brick-work washed down with acid and oiled. Clapboards, trim, outside doors, blinds and rain conductors, bronze green. Sashes, dark green. Veranda floor and ceiling, oiled. Shingles in gables dipped and brush coated sienna stain; all other wall shingles and roof shingles dipped and brush coated brownish stain.

ACCOMMODATIONS: The principal rooms and their sizes, closets, etc., are shown by the plans. Cellar under whole house, with cemented floor and inside and outside entrance. Handsome staircase with broad landings. Open fireplaces in parlor, dining and sitting room, and two bedrooms. Three rooms, hallway and storeroom finished in attic. Balconies in second and attic story. Large air space over attic rooms floored for storage.

COST: $5,800, † not including mantels, range and heater. The estimate is based on ‡ New York prices for materials and labor. In many sections of the country the cost should be less.

Price for working plans, specifications and * license to build, - - - - - - - - - $48.00
   Price for † † bill of materials, - - - - - 10.00
   Address, THE CO-OPERATIVE BUILDING PLAN ASSOCIATION, Architects, 63 Broadway, New York.

FEASIBLE MODIFICATIONS: Heights of stories, colors, sizes of rooms and kinds of materials may be changed. Cellar may be reduced in size and cemented floor omitted. Open fireplaces and mantels, sliding doors, side bay window, a part or all of plumbing and part or all of attic finish (except flooring) may be omitted.

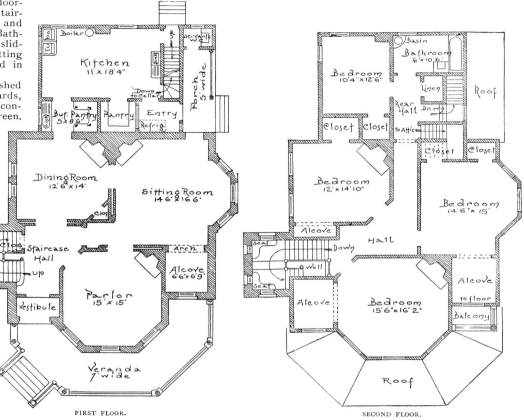

FIRST FLOOR.   SECOND FLOOR.

Residence, Design No. 557.

The exterior appearance is the same as that of No. 563, shown on opposite page.

DESCRIPTION.

For explanation of all symbols (* † etc.) see page 42.

GENERAL DIMENSIONS: Extreme width, 34 ft. 6 in.; depth, including veranda, 48 ft. 10 in. Heights of stories: Cellar, 6 ft. 6 in.; first story, 9 ft. 3 in.; second story, 8 ft. 6 in.; attic, 8 ft.

EXTERIOR MATERIALS: Foundations, stone and brick; first

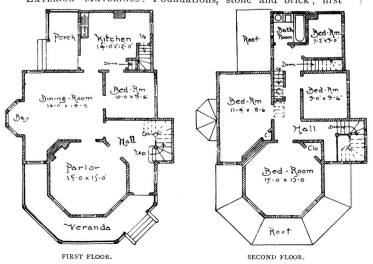

FIRST FLOOR.   SECOND FLOOR.

story, brick veneer; second story and roof, shingles; gables, panels and shingles. Outside blinds.

INTERIOR FINISH: Hard white plaster; plaster cornices in hall, parlor and dining room. Soft wood flooring and trim. Ash staircase. Panels under windows in parlor and dining room. Bathroom wainscoted. Interior wood-work finished in hard oil.

COLORS: Clapboards, blinds and sashes, light seal brown. Trim, outside doors, veranda floor and rain conductors, seal brown. Veranda ceiling, buff. Brick-work, oiled. Wall shingles dipped and brush coated sienna stain. Roof shingles dipped and brush coated Indian red.

ACCOMMODATIONS: The principal rooms and their sizes, closets, etc., are shown by the plans. Cellar under kitchen. Open fireplace in parlor. Extensive veranda. Cosy tower room in attic for study or studio.

COST: $3,000, † not including mantels, range and heater. The estimate is based on ‡ New York prices for materials and labor. In many sections of the country the cost should be less.

Price for working plans, specifications and * license to build, - - - - - - - - - $35.00
   Price for † † bill of materials, - - - - - 10.00
   Address, THE CO-OPERATIVE BUILDING PLAN ASSOCIATION, Architects, 63 Broadway, New York.

FEASIBLE MODIFICATIONS: Heights of stories, colors, sizes of rooms and kinds of materials may be changed. Cellar may be extended or omitted. Two more rooms may be finished in attic. Sliding doors may be introduced. Fireplaces and mantels and a part or all of plumbing may be omitted.

The price of working plans, specifications, etc., for a modified design varies according to the alterations required, and will be made known upon application to the Architects.

206

THE CO-OPERATIVE BUILDING PLAN ASSOCIATION, ARCHITECTS, 63 BROADWAY, NEW YORK.

*Shoppell's Modern Houses—*Designs Patented.*

Residence, Design No. 513

For Description and Specifications
of this Design, see page 207.

PERSPECTIVE.

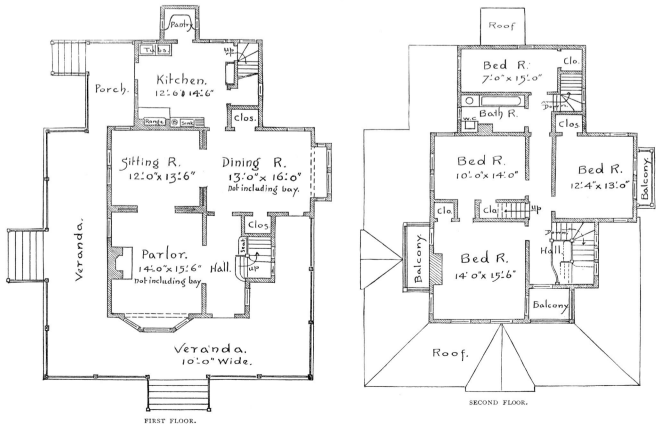

FIRST FLOOR.

SECOND FLOOR.

DESCRIPTION AND SPECIFICATIONS OF DESIGN NUMBER 513

SEE PERSPECTIVE VIEW AND PLANS

SIZE OF STRUCTURE: Front, including veranda, 42 ft. Side, including veranda and refrigerator room, 59 ft., 6 in.

SIZE OF ROOMS: See floor plans.

HEIGHT OF STORIES: First Story, 10 ft.; Second Story, 9 ft.; Attic, 8 ft., 6 in.

MATERIALS: Foundation, brick piers; First Story, clapboarded; Second Story, shingled; Tower, shingled; Gables, shingled and paneled; Roof, slate.

COST: $4,600. See "EXTRAS" on page 77, for other items that may be desirable to include in contract.

SPECIAL FEATURES.—Designed for a seaside house. The veranda is carried around three sides, and is 10 ft. wide. No cellar.

The parlor, sitting-room and dining-room are connected by sliding doors, the hall and parlor by a portiere.

A glass door leads from the dining-room to the side veranda.

Two good rooms are finished in the attic and another can be obtained if desired.

The full specification of material and labor is given below. We may add that the specifications furnished with our working plans are all as complete as this one. Many people, who have had little or no experience in building, think that working plans, details and specifications are unnecessary, and some builders encourage this idea. An examination of this specification, which does not contain a single word that is not needed to insure the proper construction of the house and the use of good materials, must convince such people of the indispensable importance of it.

SPECIFICATION

of Work and Materials required for the erection and completion of a Frame Dwelling for Mr.......to be situated......County of......and State of......in accordance with this Specification and the accompanying Drawings, as furnished by THE CO-OPERATIVE BUILDING PLAN ASSOCIATION, Architects, New York.

GENERAL DESCRIPTION

The building is to be located on the lot in such position as may be designated by the owner or his representative.

GENERAL NOTES AND CONDITIONS

Reference must be made to the Drawings for the above and all other measurements, together with the arrangement of rooms and general finish; the Drawings are to be considered as a part of this Specification, and should correspond in every particular. Should, however, any discrepancy appear between the figures and scale measurements, or between the wording of the Specifications and the coloring or lettering on Drawings, the figures shall in all cases take precedence of scale measurements, and the wording of the Specifications shall take precedence of all.

In case an error becomes apparent to the contractor, which is not explained by reference to the Drawings or Specifications, the same shall be referred to the architects for correction before proceeding with the work.

All materials to be of the best quality of their respective kinds, unless otherwise specified.

The contractor is to give his personal attention to the work, or have a competent foreman in charge; and is to see that all the works are performed in a thorough and workmanlike manner, by skilled mechanics; to furnish all material and labor necessary for the due performance of the work, as hereinafter described; to furnish all necessary implements, scaffolding, cartage, etc; to obtain all necessary permits for obstructing the street, connecting with the sewer, tapping water and gas mains, etc., and pay all necessary fees for same; to be responsible for any damages incurred through violation, on his part or that of his workmen, of village ordinances; construct proper enclosures for the protection of the public during the progress of the work, perfectly re-instate pavements, make good any damage to adjoining premises, and shall hold the owner harmless from any damage or expense incurred through neglect of these conditions; to provide stoves and fuel for heating the house while plastering is being done, during cold weather, hard coal or coke only to be used in same (no wood), and under no circumstances is the heater or range to be used by the workmen; neither are fires to be made in the fire-places, nor any heating apparatus used that will blacken or discolor the walls or other interior finish.

To protect all work properly while the building is in his hands; remove all rubbish and superfluous material from off the premises, and leave all clean and perfect at completion of contract.

No part of the work to be sub-let, unless by the written consent of the owner or his representative.

MASON'S WORK

EXCAVATION

Excavate for the foundation piers 12 inches larger than same all round, 3½ ft. below grade. Fill in around piers after same are above ground and the mortar set; thoroughly tamp the earth and grade from the building 10 feet off, around same.

FOOTINGS

The foundation and chimney piers are to start 3½ ft. below grade. Footings to be full size of excavation, 1 ft. thick, of concrete composed of four parts broken stone and sand to one part cement, well mixed and tamped solid.

PIERS

Build the foundation piers and chimneys of merchantable, hard burned brick, properly bonded, laid close, straight and plumb and well flushed in. Brick to be wetted when laid up in hot dry weather, and kept perfectly dry if laid up in frosty weather. All exterior joints to be neatly pointed where exposed to view, and re-pointed where necessary at completion. Select best brick for facing piers. Chimney flues to be left clean. All brick-work below grade to be laid up in cement mortar.

PIER CAPS

Cap all piers with 3-inch blue-stone, full size of piers.

FIRE-PLACE

Build the fireplace of size and shape shown on Drawings, with proper ledges in throats. Face the breast 8 inches, and the jambs and back of fire-place with Trenton pressed brick laid up in red putty. Turn flat 12-inch arch over fire-place with pressed brick.

KITCHEN FIRE PLACE

Face the piers, and the jambs and back above the range to a height of 5½ ft. with best Trenton pressed brick, laid in red putty. Build in rubbed stone shelf lintel 4x8 inches the full width of breast; hearth to be rubbed stone, 2 feet wide by the length of lintel.

HEARTH

Hearth in parlor to be of black enameled brick bedded in cement and projecting ¼ inch above floor, and to extend to the back of the fire-place.

MORTAR

Use fresh burned lime, best to be found in the market. Thoroughly mix with clean, sharp sand in the proportion of two parts lime to five parts sand. Cement mortar to be made by mixing cement and sand, dry, and adding water to bring it to the proper consistency when ready to use. After the first setting it is not to be tempered up for use again. Use Rosendale brand of cement.

THIMBLES

Build in sheet iron thimbles, 5 inches in diameter, with ventilating covers, in rooms having no fireplaces.

TOPPING OUT

Top out the chimneys above roof with best select stock brick, as shown on Drawings, laid up in cement mortar, joints neatly pointed.

Chimney caps to be blue-stone, in one piece, 3 inches thick axed edges, with flue holes cut to correspond with top of chimney.

TRIMMER ARCHES

Build 4-inch brick trimmer arches for all hearths, and level up with concrete. All arches to be turned on wood centres, which will be furnished by carpenter.

DRAINS

All pipes to be laid below action of frost. All drain pipes to be laid to a uniform grade of not less than ⅜ inch to the foot. All joints in earthen pipes to be made absolutely tight with fresh Portland cement. Furnish and lay a line of 5-inch salt glazed earthen socket-jointed drain pipe, connecting with the iron pipe just under ground, and running thence to the sewer in street.

Fill in all trenches, and tamp thoroughly after pipes are laid.

DRAIN TRAP

About 6 feet from house, in the line of main drain, place an earthen running trap same size as pipe, with hand hole for cleaning. Between the trap and house insert a **T** branch, and carry from same to 12 inches above grade line a 3-inch iron pipe to serve as fresh air inlet, same to be protected by a ventilating cap.

Connect the rain water leaders with main drain by 4-inch earthen pipes. All connections of different lines of pipes to be made with **Y** branches. All joints to be made tight with cement, and to be made clean on the inside.

LATHING AND PLASTERING

All walls, ceilings, partitions and work that is furred off throughout the first, second and attic stories to be lathed with sound, merchantable lath, placed ⅜ inch apart, nailed to each bearing, with joints broken every ten courses. Laths to be placed horizontally, with solid angles; none to pass behind partition framing from one room to another, and to extend to the floor. Where chimneys are set flush in partitions or form a part of studded breast, laths are to extend over the brick-work and be nailed to thin vertical stripping, placed 12 inches apart. Back lath and plaster behind all wainscoting on outer walls.

After the lathing is finished, the floors are to be swept clean and covered ½ inch deep with sand, for protection of floors while plastering is going on; also, if chimneys are to be built after floors are laid, the floors are to be protected by rough boards or sand. Disregard of this precaution will render the contractor liable to damages for stains or injury to floor. Before plastering is commenced, see that the exterior openings are closed with old sash or boards, with one window movable in each room; if weather is warm the openings are to be closed with muslin on movable frames; put up temporary outside doors.

Do all patching, cleaning off, whitening, etc., that may be required, after other workmen, to make the job perfect at completion of contract.

For mortar use plastering lime, fresh burned and thoroughly slacked under water in a slack box, and run off through a wire screen set into the spout of the slack box, into the mortar bed, mixed with clean sharp sand in the proportion of three parts sand to one part lime; to be stacked in the rough two weeks before using. Under no circumstances must the lime be slacked in a heap with sand.

Lime for putty to be run off in same manner and run through a sieve.

All lathing to be covered with a good coat of mortar, having plenty of long cattle hair thoroughly mixed in, and applied with sufficient force to secure strong clinches: this to be well scratched, and covered with a heavy coat of brown mortar (without hair) screeded even and true to the grounds with all angles straight and plumb and brought to an even surface, and good sand finish for tinting.

Attic rooms, all closets, and the rooms in rear extension are to have white plaster finish laid on the first coat, which is not to be scratched.

CARPENTER'S WORK

TIMBER

All timber used in building to be well seasoned, mill sawed, merchantable, and free from imperfections that may impair its durability or strength. Timber to be hemlock, except sills, which are to be spruce, and girts, which are to be yellow pine.

FRAMING

Building to be substantially framed in the most workmanlike manner, to be leveled, squared and plumbed, strongly anchored and strapped where necessary. Frame to be what is known as balloon style, sills halved together at angles, and posts to be tenoned into same. Headers and trimmers carrying more than one tail joist to be doubled, and all joists carrying partitions to be doubled with separators the thickness of the partition to be carried.

Frame around fire-places, well holes, scuttles, etc., with mortise and tenon, and spike thoroughly.

Girts to be let into studding, and floor joists notched over same, and spiked to studding. Where it is necessary to splice sills or plates, perform splicing with a ship lap, or mitre splice. All mouldings to be mitre spliced.

Roofs to be properly framed for all gables, dormers, etc., and brace and tie same thoroughly where necessary, and as shown or directed.

The two outside corners of tower are to be made with two 4 x 6-inch spruce joists spiked together, tenoned into main sill, and running from sill to the ceiling of tower room without splice.

Frame the floor of the upper tower room with joists projecting out to carry balcony, as shown on framing plan.

SIZES OF TIMBER

Sizes of timber to be as follows:

Girders, . . .	6x8 in.	Rafters, . . .	2x6 in.	**VERANDA TIMBER**	
Sills, ...	4x8 in.	1st floor joists, .	3x8 in.	Sills, ...	3x8 in.
Posts, ...	4x6 in.	2d " " .	3x8 in.	Cross sills, . .	3x8 in.
Plates, ...	4x4 in.	3d " " .	2x8 in.	Floor joists, . .	2x8 in.
Studding, . . .	2x4 in.	Collar boards, .	2x6 in.	Plates, ...	4x8 in.
Girts, . . .	1⅛x6 in.	Braces, ...	3x4 in.	Ceiling joists, .	2x6 in.
Valley rafters, .	3x7 in.	Ridgetrees, . .	2x8 in.	Rafters, . . .	2x6 in.

SPACING

1st floor joists to be spaced 16-in. centres.	Collar boards to be spaced 24-in centres.
2d " " " " 16 " "	Rafters " " 24 " "
3d " " " " 16 " "	Outside studding " 16 " "
Partition studding, " 16 " "	

BRIDGING

Each tier of floor joists to be bridged in every span exceeding 8 feet with one row **2x2** inch cross-bridging, nailed with two 10d. nails at each end. Every span exceeding 15 feet to have two rows bridging.

All partitions of first story to have one row of **W** bridging.

PARTITIONS

Principal partitions, where practicable, are to pass through between floor joists and rest directly on the girder or plate of partition underneath. All to be set plumb, and well nailed top and bottom, to have plates not less than 3x4 inches, and in case they do not run through between beams, they are to have sills not less than 2x4 inches.

Studs at all openings to be doubled, also to be doubled at all angles. Form a truss over openings that exceed 3 feet in width. All partitions having no support underneath, to be well trussed.

FURRING

Do all necessary furring about stairs, chimneys, roof, etc., and where called for by the plans.

GROUNDS

Put up ⅞x1¼-inch dry pine grounds to all door and window openings to finish plastering against.

SHEATHING

Cover the entire frame with seasoned ⅞-inch surfaced hemlock boards, laid diagonally and well nailed with 10d. nails.

SHEATHING PAPER

Cover the sheathing, except roof, with one thickness Sackett's No. 1 sheathing paper, well lapped and nailed, and passing under all casings, corner boards, etc. so as to make a tight job.

SIDING

Cover the exterior walls of first story, as shown on drawings, with first quality white pine 6-inch beveled clapboards, laid 4¾ inches to the weather, 1¼-inch lap, securely nailed with 6d. nails properly set. To be well seasoned, joints properly broken, heading joints and all uneven places to be made smooth.

ROOF SHINGLING

Cover the roofs of the entire building and tower with 16-inch first quality shaved white cedar shingles, laid 5½ inches to the weather, well nailed and with joints well broken. Valleys to be left open and to be widest at the bottom.

FLASHING

Flash the valleys and angles of all roofs, and around chimneys, scuttle, skylight, etc., and over door and window heads, with I. C roofing tin in the best manner; build step counter flashings into the joints of brick-work of chimneys, on rake of roof. All the flashings, etc., to be painted both sides with one coat metallic paint before laying, and all to be made tight.

SHINGLING ON SIDE WALLS

Cover the walls of second story main house with alternate courses of round butt and square butt first quality white pine 6-inch dimension shingles, laid 6 inches to the weather, well nailed and with joints properly broken. Enclose sides of tower in similar manner.

Enclose second story of extension, and cover veranda roofs with plain clear pine shingles. Shingle gables and upper part of tower with fancy cut shingles as shown. All shingling except main roof to be dipped in oil stain before laying. See painter's specification.

EXTERIOR FINISH

All exterior trim to be of first common well seasoned white pine, free from large or loose knots; to be planed and smoothed by hand, with clean sharp angles; nail heads "set."

Corner boards and outside casings for doors and windows to be 4½x1¼ inches.

Water table, bands, belts, cornices, eaves, etc., to be made and moulded as per detail drawings. Put up rough bracketing for projecting cornices where necessary.

Enclose between the foundation piers with panels formed with 1 x 5-inch T. & G. white pine and 1¼ x 6-inch frame or rails as shown.

GUTTERS

Form gutters in the cornices of house and verandas as shown; to be lined with I. C. charcoal tin same to be carried well up under the roofing and carried over front edge of gutter and neatly tacked. Grade the gutters properly toward the leaders and put in the necessary tubes for connecting with the leaders.

The tower will not have gutters.

GABLES

The east side gable will be shingled. The front and west side gables will be ceiled vertically with 1x3-inch dressed No. 1 white pine, and have 1x6-inch panel strips planted on as shown.

VERANDA

Cross sills to be strongly secured to the house, floor joists to be framed into them, so that the flooring will run at right angles to house; floor to have an inclination of ⅛ inch to the foot from house.

Flooring to be 1x3 inch white pine, joints laid in lead paint, driven up close, and blind nailed; all joints made smooth. At corners the floor boards are to be stepped together, not mitred. To be finished at edges with rounded nosing and cove moulding.

Steps to be formed of 1¼-inch pine stepstuff with ⅞-inch risers, ⅞-inch strings, nailed to 2-inch carriages. Rail and balusters at side of steps to be same as veranda rail, etc.

Posts to be square, built out of 1¼-inch white pine, tongued together, quarter circle spandrils cut out of the solid and let into posts.

Rail and balusters to be formed as per drawings; top rail, 2½x3½ inches moulded; bottom rail, 2½x3 inches beveled top; balusters, 1¾ inches square, plain; frieze rail, 2¾x2¾ moulded; frieze slats, 1½ inches square, plain. Set solid 6x6-inch chestnut newel posts, chamfered, with turned top, posts to set 5 feet in the ground. Rail to match veranda rail. Veranda balcony and tower ceiling to be formed level with ⅝-inch beaded yellow pine ceiling boards blind nailed; step the ceiling together at the corners or returns, cover the intersections with house and plate, with a small moulding.

BALCONIES

The balconies on front and west side, and over east side bay window, and the open tower, will have floors laid with 1x5-inch T. & G. pine, graded properly to outlet. On this, lay "Standard" roofing, well lapped and joints made with "Standard" cement. To be turned up at least 6 inches on all sides, behind the siding, and all made water tight.

Ceil the inside face of balconies below rail with ⅝ beaded yellow pine ceiling, and form cap and rail, etc., as shown on detail drawings. Turned posts for front balcony and tower to be dry white pine, 6 inches square. Spandrils 2 inches thick.

The large modillions under tower balcony to be built out of six 2-inch planks glued and nailed.

FLOORING

All floors to be made smooth, and left clean at completion.

FIRST STORY floor to be tongued and grooved 1x3-inch dry selected yellow pine, laid with close joints, and well blind nailed.

SECOND STORY floor, except where otherwise specified, to be tongued and grooved 1x4-inch dry white pine, laid as above described.

ATTIC floor to be 1x6-inch second quality white pine.

Set moulded hardwood thresholds to all doorways, and hardwood borders to all hearths.

DOOR FRAMES

All door frames, unless otherwise specified, to be made of seasoned white pine dadoed at heads. All frames for outside doors to be 1¼ inches thick, rabbetted for doors. All interior door frames to be 1 inch thick, to have ½-inch x 2-inch moulded stop planted on face of frame. Door frames to be blocked for locks and butts on both sides.

WINDOW FRAMES

All window frames, unless otherwise specified, to be second quality dry merchantable white pine properly framed together, and of sizes shown on drawings.

CELLAR FRAMES to be made of first quality white pine 1½x6-inch plank, rabbetted for sash, 1½-inch sills, weathered.

SLIDING SASH FRAMES to be made in the usual manner, 1-inch pulley stiles, 1-inch top sills, 1½-inch subsills; to be housed at heads and sills, and to have 1⅛-inch blind stop, parting strips, double cut pockets, stop beads, and steel pinion noiseless pulleys, 2 inches diameter. For thickness of sash, see "Sashes."

The circle head windows in tower attic room, in front hall second story, and over first landing stairway first story hall, are to have frames made of 1¼-inch stuff, rabbetted for sash, which will be hinged to open outward; sills same as for sliding windows.

Frame for oval window in east gable to be made for pivoting sash in centre each side.

Frames for triple window in second story hall to be made for stationary fanlights.

SASHES

All sashes to be made of clear, dry white pine, of size and design shown on drawings; to be moulded, coped and framed together, and all to be smooth, clean and workmanlike in construction.

SLIDING SASH to be double-hung with best hemp sash cord, and solid eye cast iron weights properly balanced; meeting rails to be weather-lipped. All sliding sash in first and second story main rooms and hall to be provided with Ives' patent plain bronze sash locks; other windows to have Ives' patent sash locks, Berlin bronze.

All sashes except the small attic windows to be 1½ inches thick. The latter to be 1¼ inches thick.

The circle head windows in tower attic room, front hall second story, and over first landing stairway, to have sash hung with 2-inch japanned butts, and to fasten with small mortise latch with crank handle. To have deeply undercut drips tongued into the sash.

GLAZING

All glass to be well bedded, tacked in and back puttied.

All first and second story sash, unless otherwise specified, to be glazed with first quality French sheet. In rear extension and attic use third quality French. All glass over 60 united inches to be double thick.

STAINED GLASS

Two sash on east side of hall, first story, and fanlight over three windows, hall second story, to be glazed with stained, rolled cathedral glass, in tints as directed.

BLINDS

Provide and hang to all windows, not otherwise specified below, outside blinds with rolling slats, of best quality dry, white pine, 1¼ inches thick, made smooth, slats to move easily.

Hangers and fasteners to be heavy and substantial, and of approved make. On mullion windows the blinds are to have galvanized iron adjustable fasteners, so that they can be secured at any desired angle.

Front and east side bay windows, hall first and second story and attic windows will not have blinds. Mullion windows will have blinds made in one fold.

INTERIOR TRIM

To be made according to detail drawings, of clear, dry stuff, hand smoothed and to have all stains removed on each work as required for finishing in the natural color; to be well and securely put in place, and nailed with finishing nails; all nail heads to be "set." None of the trim is to be brought into the house or set until the finishing coat of plaster is dry.

Trim throughout, unless otherwise specified, to be clear white pine for finishing natural color or staining.

CASINGS

Door and window casings in first and second stories to be ⅞x5 inches, with base blocks and turned corner blocks; see details.

Casings in closets and attic rooms to be ⅝x3½ inches with moulded edge.

WINDOW FINISH

Casings of all windows to finish on neat stool cap with apron and moulding. Portiere openings to be trimmed same as doors.

BASE

In all finished rooms throughout the house put base or skirting boards of same material as the general finish of rooms, moulded as per detail or as described below; to have carpet strip, and to be coped at the corners.

NOTE.—The height of base given below includes plinth and moulding.

In first story principal rooms and hall base is to be 10 inches high.

In second story to be 9 inches high.

In closets and attic rooms to be 6 inches high, plain board with beveled top.

PICTURE MOULDING

In the principal rooms and hall of first story put a finished hardwood picture moulding placed 12 inches below the ceiling.

CHAIR RAIL

Put a moulded chair rail at a height (to centre of rail) of two feet 10 inches above the floor, on the walls of the dining-room; to be of same wood as the general finish of the room, angles neatly mitred.

STAIRS

To be built as shown on drawings, properly supported on 3x6 carriage timbers spiked in place after stairs are up.

Main staircase to have 1¼-inch treads, ⅞-inch risers, tongued and grooved together, and housed into wall string, and to be wedged, glued and blocked. *Treads* finished with rounded nosings and cove mould under.

Outer string to be 2-inch yellow pine, bracketed and face reeded.

Treads and risers to be yellow pine.

Newels, rail and balusters to be yellow pine.

Principal newel to be 6x6 inches, turned and chamfered, with carved panel.

Other newels to be 5x5 inches, turned and chamfered.

Balusters to be 1¾ inches, square reeded, dovetailed at bottom and dowelled into handrail.

Level rail in second story to be finished against a half newel.

Panel the spandril under stairs down to seat, as shown on detail, with yellow pine rails halved together. Form the seat, front and end to same as shown, of 2-inch yellow pine.

Build the back stairway, as shown, with 1-inch treads and risers, tongued and grooved into each other, rounded nosings, all of white pine. Hang door at bottom and put 4x4-inch square pine post and rail in second story, as shown, 1¼-inch square pine balusters.

BATH-ROOM

Wainscot the walls 4 feet high with ⅝ x 3-inch yellow pine ceiling boards beaded. Cap neatly and cover joint at floor with small quarter round mould.

Bath-tub to be encased with narrow ceiling to match wainscoting. Top to be 1¼-inch cherry, with projecting rounded edges and cove mould under, top to go back to the plaster and wainscoting of wall to be scribed neatly on same.

Enclose water-closet neatly with 1-inch cherry, seat to be framed together, made smooth, and hinged ; flap to be cleated and hinged ; front to be removable.

Build proper support for wash bowl, and enclose underneath slab same as tub ; to have a door hung with brass butts, and spring catch.

All fittings in bath-room and around pipes to be put together with brass screws, and all wood-work to be made smooth with sand paper, and finished the natural color of the wood.

KITCHEN

Walls to be wainscoted 4 feet high with ⅝x3-inch tongued and grooved double beaded yellow pine or ash ceiling boards, on grounds set before lathing ; to have moulded cap, and quarter round at joint with floor. Behind the sink and draining board the wainscoting is to be 2 feet higher than sink. Behind the boiler carry the wainscoting to the ceiling. Provide proper support and grooved draining board (in one piece) for the sink as shown on plans, of ash ; draining board and rim around sink to have rounded edges and all made smooth. Space underneath sink is to be left open.

DRESSER

Build a pine dresser in the kitchen, as shown on plan, 7 feet high, upper part to be 12 inches deep, and to have 3 shelves, enclosed by glazed folding doors, hung on bronzed iron butts, and to have a bolt and 2-inch bronzed spring catch ; lower part to be 20 inches deep, and to have 2 drawers, provided with locks and pulls. Two single paneled doors to lockers below with suitable hardware.

SHELVING

All closets throughout the house to be fitted up with an average of 3 shelves each. All shelves to be inch thick, dry shelving on rabbetted cleats, all according to the directions of the owner or architect. Put up throughout the house, on beaded cleats, 4 dozen tinned "Gem" wire hooks, as directed.

WOOD MANTELS

Provide and set in the parlor and bedroom over same, wood mantels. That in parlor to cost $30, and in bedroom, $20, net.

Chimney breasts to be measured for mantels after the plastering is finished.

DOORS

Furnish and hang all doors throughout, as shown on drawings and as specified. To be of clear selected dry stuff, put together in the most workmanlike manner, and made smooth and clean. All doors are to be blind mortised and tenoned and finished by hand. For sizes and thicknesses of doors see plans.

All doors, unless otherwise specified, to be made of clear, white pine,

Doors in attic and rear extension may be "stock" doors, not blind mortised.

Ordinary ROOM DOORS throughout first and second stories, main house, to be 1½ inches thick, 4 panels, moulded, hung with 3-inch loose pin, light bronzed butts, good, city-made, mortise locks, brass fronts and striking plates and hardwood knobs. In extension and attic hang with 3-inch japanned butts, and put good rim locks and black China knobs, all with brass keys to vary.

NOTE.—Opening between hall and parlor will have no doors, but will be cased same as door openings with plain jambs.

SLIDING DOORS to be 1¾ inches thick, 4 panels, hung with Philadelphia overhead hangers.

Doors to slide smoothly and easily,double sliding doors to have astragal front ; to have mortise lock, with bronzed front, and bronzed flush finger plates, and spring pulls.

FRONT ENTRANCE DOOR and dining-room door to veranda to be 2 inches thick, paneled as shown. To be made of clear, dry, white pine, and to be hung with 4-inch bronzed loose pin butts with ball tips, and to have a 5-inch mortise lock, with night-latch attachment bronze front and striking plate, and three plated keys, and hardwood knobs. To a have a 6-inch Ives' mortise bolt ; upper part of doors to have centre and border lights of plain plate glass put in with wood moulding—no putty.

CLOSET DOORS throughout are to correspond in style with the doors of the rooms in which they are located; to be 1¼ inches thick, moulded one side, butts and furniture to be same as for the room doors.

MISCELLANEOUS

Doors throughout, opening against plaster walls, to have hardwood base knobs, with rubber tips, screwed into base.

Provide all locks, butts, hooks, bolts, etc., of suitable character and finish, that may be necessary to make a perfect and complete job.

Put up 1¼-inch angle beads 5 feet long, with turned tips, on all exposed angles of plastered walls.

WASH-TUBS

Provide and set in kitchen two stationary wash-tubs, constructed of clear dry 1½-inch white pine, housed together at all points in white lead, and nailed tight. To be supported on neat turned legs. Lids to be 1¼ inches thick, cleated at the ends and hinged with 2-inch galvanized iron back flaps.

PIPE CASING

Where water or other pipes pass through rooms place neat pine boards, with beaded edges, for pipes to be fastened to; boards to be varnished.

Where pipes are to be carried horizontally underneath the floor, place boards, with proper incline, between the floor joists to lay pipes on.

TINNER

All tinwork to be thoroughly soldered where necessary. Use I. C. charcoal Terne plate tin, unless otherwise specified; provide and perform all tin flashings, etc., as specified in carpenter work ; paint all tin-work two good coats metallic paint before putting in place.

Line the gutters and valleys with tin, carrying same well up under the roof and over the front of cornice moulding or gutter, where it is to be tacked down smoothly.

LEADERS

Provide and put up where shown on Drawings leaders of I. C. tin to carry rain water from gutter to ground. Those from main roof to be 4 inches diameter; those for veranda and bay window roofs 3 inches diameter; make all branches where necessary, neatly and gracefully. Secure the leaders to the house with galvanized iron holdfasts. Put galvanized iron leader guards over all openings in gutters. Connect leaders with the earthen pipes leading to main drain.

BELL

Provide and put upon neat board, in kitchen, a good 5-inch gong. To be connected with front doorway with steel wire, to work with all necessary cranks. To have an appropriate bell-pull and plate at front door to match front door furniture. Wire to be carried out of sight underneath floor.

FINIAL

Provide and set the wrought and galvanized iron finial and vane on tower as per detail drawings.

PLUMBER

The plumber is to furnish all labor and materials of the best description, as specified below, and make a complete and perfect job. He is to comply with all the rules of the local Board of Health, and should said rules require any deviation from the Specification, he is to make them, accordingly, without extra expense to the owner.

All water service pipes to be put on wood stripping, prepared by carpenter, and secured with hard metal tacks and screws.

No pipes to be run on outside walls unless absolutely necessary, and should it be necessary to run them where there is danger of freezing, they are to be thoroughly packed with mineral wool, or other good non conductor, and encased by the carpenter.

All pipes to be evenly graded so as to drain dry when water is turned off.

All connections of lead pipes to be made with wiped solder joints.

All connections of lead pipes with iron pipes are to be made through brass ferrules, soldered to the lead, and caulked with oakum and lead into the iron hub.

All fixtures are to be trapped with lead **S** trap—of same size as waste pipe—with brass trap screw.

Place safes of 3-lb. sheet lead—edges turned up 2 inches all around—under all fixtures above ground floor.

SOIL PIPE

Connect with the main earthen drain under house, and carry from that point a vertical line of 4-inch cast iron pipe, tarred, with all proper and necessary branches for connection with water closet, waste pipe, etc.; these connections to be made with **Y** branches. Carry soil pipe 30 inches above the roof and leave the end open. Secure the pipe to walls with iron holdfasts. All joints to be caulked with oakum, run with molten lead, and bedded with caulking iron and hammer, care being taken not to crack the hub. This line to be closed at the bottom and subjected to water test. Carry this pipe alongside of kitchen chimney. Carry a line of 2-inch pipe alongside of soil pipe starting at trap of sink, for ventilation of traps—turn into soil pipe above upper fixture. Carry a separate line of 2-inch iron pipe from trap of wash-tubs through roof for ventilation.

WATER SUPPLY

Supply the house with water from main in street through 1-inch AA lead pipe, carried to bath-room, to rise alongside of kitchen chimney. Pipe to be laid below frost and thoroughly protected where it rises to kitchen.

RANGE

To be furnished by owner and set by plumber and connected with water supply and made ready for use.

BOILER

Furnish and set on cast-iron pillar, a 30-gallon galvanized iron boiler, connected with water back of range with ¾-inch AA pipe, and with main supply by ¾-inch A pipe, with ground brass couplings complete.

Boiler to have sediment stop and waste cock at bottom, and finished stop and waste cocks at top to shut off both hot and cold water from upper part of house. Run ½-inch circulation pipe from boiler to wash basin.

SINK

Set in kitchen a 30x18x6-inch galvanized cast-iron sink, with strainer ; supply hot and cold water through ⅝-inch A pipe. Cocks to be brass compression, with flange and thimble, same size as pipes, cold water cock to have hose end. Waste to soil pipe through 2-inch B lead pipe, trapped.

WASH-TUB

Supply with hot and cold water through 1-inch A pipe and ⅝-inch brass flange and thimble compression tray bibbs. Waste through 1½-inch B lead pipe, trapped, and brass sockets, strainer, plug, and chain.

BASINS

Set in bath-room a white overflow wash basin 14 inches in diameter. Supply hot and cold water through ⅝-inch A lead pipe, and ½-inch plated compression basin cocks. To have plated strainer, plug, chain and stay. Waste through 1¼-inch B lead, trapped. Overflow to be ⅝-inch, connected with waste above trap. Basin to have white marble countersunk slab, and marble back 12 inches high, moulded edges.

BATH-TUB

Set a 5 ft. 16 oz. tinned and planished overflow bath-tub. Supply with hot and cold water through ⅝-inch A lead pipe and ⅝-inch plated flange and thimble bath compression bibb cocks. Waste through 1¼-inch B lead pipe, and provide plated strainer, plug, chain and stay. Overflow for bath and for all other fixtures is to be connected with the waste pipe above the trap.

WATER-CLOSET

Fit up in bath-room, in proper working order, a "National" water-closet in one piece, flushed with water from painted cast-iron 3-gallon cistern with Weeden's patent time valve. Trap to be connected with soil pipe in proper manner.

TRAP VENTILATION

Ventilate all traps by 2-inch lead pipe into the ventilation pipe.

GAS PIPING

Pipe the house for gas in thorough and proper manner with best wrought iron gas pipe, leaving all outlets of proper length. No pipe for fixture connections to be less than ⅜-inch, and larger where required for chandeliers. Put all joints together with cement. The whole to be tested and all openings left capped.

Pipe for drop lights in halls first and second stories, parlors, dining-room, kitchen and three bedrooms. Pipes for bracket lights in all other rooms and attic hall.

PAINTER

Provide all materials and perform all labor for the full and proper painting, staining, etc., as specified below; putty all nail holes, etc., smoothly, of both interior and exterior work, after the priming is done; cover all knots, etc., with strong shellac before priming. All paint to be best Atlantic white lead and linseed oil.

EXTERIOR

Paint the exterior wood-work, etc., 3 coats, finishing in the following colors:

Body of the work, first story, light brown.

Trim—including water table, corner boards, casings, cornices, bands, veranda posts, rail, etc., dark brown ; panels in gables, dark brown.

Outside doors, dark brown.

Blinds, dark brown.

Sashes, dark brown.

Veranda, floor, light brown.

Veranda, ceiling, to be twice oiled.

Conductors, dark brown.

Brick-work, Indian red.

NOTE.—Consult the architect for exact colors.

Shingling on side walls to be dipped in an oil stain of burnt sienna. This to include all shingling of second story and tower.

Shingled roofs to be twice oiled.

INTERIOR

All interior wood-work to be thoroughly grain filled with a good wood filler, and finished with two coats hard oil varnish.

Tint the walls and ceilings, in halls and principal rooms first and second stories in tints as directed, with two coats water colors.

210

THE CO-OPERATIVE BUILDING PLAN ASSOCIATION, ARCHITECTS, 63 BROADWAY, NEW YORK.

*Shoppell's Modern Houses—*Designs Patented.*   *Cottage, Design No. 491*

PERSPECTIVE.

DESCRIPTION.

GENERAL DIMENSIONS: Width, including verandas, 54 ft.; depth, including verandas, 39 ft. 6 in. Heights of stories: Cellar, 7 ft. 6 in.; first story, 10 ft.; second story, 9 ft.; attic, 8 ft.

EXTERIOR MATERIALS: Foundation, brick; first and second stories, gables, dormers, balconies and roofs, shingles. Outside blinds.

INTERIOR FINISH: Hard white plaster. Soft wood flooring and trim. Ash stairs. Bath-room and kitchen wainscoted. All interior wood-work finished in hard oil.

COLORS: Shingles in first story dipped and brush coated red stain. All other wall shingles dipped and brush coated sienna stain. Roof shingles dipped and brush coated dark red stain. Trim, outside doors, blinds, veranda floor and ceiling, and rain conductors, seal brown. Brick-work, red.

ACCOMMODATIONS: The principal rooms and their sizes, closets, etc., are shown by the plans. Cellar under whole house. One room finished in attic. Gallery on main stairs with seat; cosy nook under gallery for bookcases and study. Rear stairway ascends to gallery of main stairs. Recessed nook with seats, fireplace and mantel in dining room. Broad lounging seat in dining room. Dotted lines across dining room indicate a casing where a curtain or folding doors may be hung.

COST: $4,640, † not including mantels, range and heater. The estimate is based on ‡ New York prices for materials and labor. In many sections of the country the cost should be less.

Price for working plans, specifications and * license to build, - $41.40
Price for †† bill of materials, - - - - - - - 5.00
Address, THE CO-OPERATIVE BUILDING PLAN ASSOCIATION, Architects, 63 Broadway, New York.

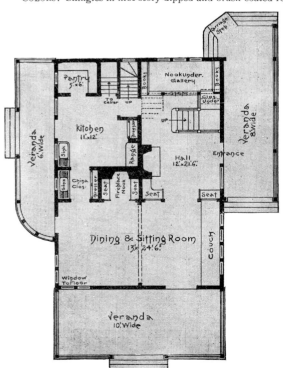

FIRST FLOOR.

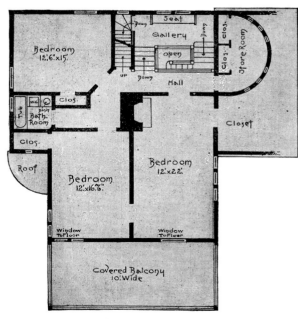

SECOND FLOOR.

211

THE CO-OPERATIVE BUILDING PLAN ASSOCIATION, ARCHITECTS, 63 BROADWAY, NEW YORK.

*Shoppell's Modern Houses—*Designs Patented.*

Residence, Design No. 460

PERSPECTIVE.

DESCRIPTION.

For explanation of all symbols (* † etc.) see page 42.

GENERAL DIMENSIONS : Width over all, 54 ft. 6 in.; depth, including veranda, 65 ft. Heights of stories : Cellar, 6 ft. 6 in.; first story, 10 ft.; second story, 9 ft.; attic, 8 ft.

EXTERIOR MATERIALS : Foundation, brick ; first story, clapboards ; second story, gables, tower and roof, shingles. Outside blinds.

INTERIOR FINISH : Hard white plaster. Double flooring in first story, finishing with yellow pine ; all other flooring soft wood. Soft wood trim. Ash stairs. Wainscot in bath-room, pantry and kitchen. Chair rail in dining room. Interior wood-work finished in hard oil.

COLORS : Clapboards, medium drab. Trim and rain conductors, light olive drab. Outside doors, light olive drab with medium drab panels. Blinds and sashes, maroon. Veranda floor, olive. Veranda ceiling, lilac. Brick-work, Indian red. Wall shingles dipped and brush coated dark terra-cotta stain. Roof shingles dipped and brush coated dark red stain.

ACCOMMODATIONS : The principal rooms and their sizes, closets, etc., are shown by the plans. Cellar under kitchen. Two rooms finished in attic. Two open fireplaces with hard wood mantels, and kitchen range, included in estimate. Large tank in upper part of tower.

COST : $4,750, complete. The estimate is based on ‡ New York prices for materials and labor. In many sections of the country the cost should be less.

Price for working plans, specifications and * license to build, - $50.00
Price for †† bill of materials, - - - - - - - 10.00

Address, THE CO-OPERATIVE BUILDING PLAN ASSOCIATION, Architects, 63 Broadway, New York.

FEASIBLE MODIFICATIONS : Heights of stories, colors, sizes of rooms and kinds of materials may be changed. Cellar may extend under whole house. Attic may remain unfinished. Attic tank may be omitted if house be supplied by water from main in street. Open fireplaces and mantels and a part or all of plumbing may be omitted. Veranda may be reduced in width and extent

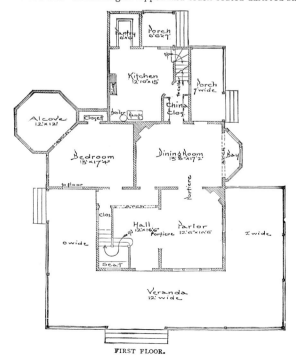

FIRST FLOOR.

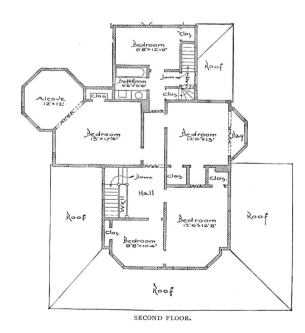

SECOND FLOOR.

Shoppell's Modern Houses—*Designs Patented.   *Residence, Design No. 381*

PERSPECTIVE.

DESCRIPTION.

For explanation of all symbols (* † etc.) see page 42.

GENERAL DIMENSIONS: Width, including veranda, 32 ft. 6 in.; depth, including veranda and porch, 61 ft. Heights of stories: Cellar, 7 ft.; first story, 10 ft.; second story, 9 ft.; attic, 8 ft.

EXTERIOR MATERIALS: Foundations, stone; first and second stories, clapboards; gables, panels and shingles: roof, slate. Outside blinds.

INTERIOR FINISH: Hard white plaster. Plaster cornices and centers in parlor, library, dining room and main hall of first and second stories. Chestnut flooring and trim in main halls of first and second stories. All other flooring and trim soft wood. Stairs, chestnut. Wainscot in bath-room. Interior wood-work finished in hard oil.

COLORS: All clapboards, French olive. Trim and rain conductors, bronze green. Outside doors, French olive, except front and vestibule doors, which are to be varnished. Blinds and sashes, Pompeian red. Veranda floor, oiled. Veranda ceiling, dark red. Brick-work, oiled.

ACCOMMODATIONS: The principal rooms and their sizes, closets, etc., are shown by the plans. Cellar under kitchen, library and dining room. Large hall with handsome staircase. Sliding doors connect rooms and hall of first story. Piping and registers for furnace heat are provided. Open fireplaces and mantels in library, dining room and parlor, and set range in kitchen, included in estimate. Three good bedrooms and storage space in attic. Side entrance to front hall.

COST: $4,752, † not including heating apparatus. The estimate is based on ‡ New York prices for materials and labor. In many sections of the country the cost should be less.

Price for working plans, specifications and * license to build, - - $40.00
Price for † † bill of materials, - 5.00
Address, THE CO-OPERATIVE BUILDING PLAN ASSOCIATION, Architects, 63 Broadway, New York.

FEASIBLE MODIFICATIONS: Heights of stories, colors, sizes of rooms and kinds of materials may be changed. Cellar may be enlarged or reduced. Sliding doors, open fireplaces and mantels, set range, a part or all of plumbing, and all hard wood finish, may be omitted.

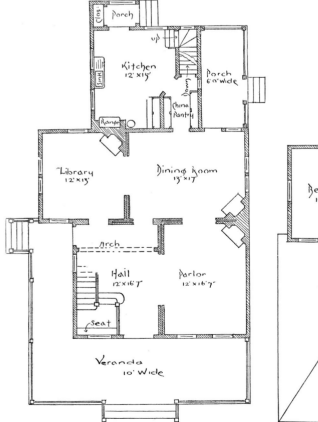

FIRST FLOOR.

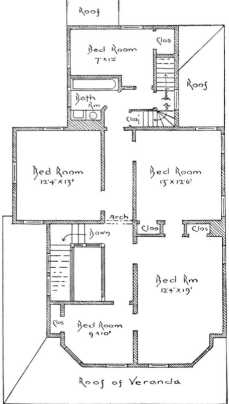

SECOND FLOOR.

213

THE CO-OPERATIVE BUILDING PLAN ASSOCIATION, ARCHITECTS, 63 BROADWAY, NEW YORK.

*Shoppell's Modern Houses—*Designs Patented.*   *Residence, Design No. 459.*

Side Elevation

PERSPECTIVE.

DESCRIPTION.

For explanation of all symbols (* † etc.) see page 42.

GENERAL DIMENSIONS : Extreme width, including veranda, 36 ft. 2 in.; depth, including veranda, 48 ft. Heights of stories : Cellar, 7 ft.; first story, 9 ft. 6 in.; second story, 9 ft.; attic, 8 ft.

EXTERIOR MATERIALS: Foundations, stone ; first story, clapboards ; second story, gables and roof, shingles. Outside blinds to all windows except those of the cellar.

INTERIOR FINISH : Hard white plaster ; plaster cornices and centers in main hall (first and second story) and parlor, library and dining room. Hard pine flooring in laundry, pantry, china closet, water closet and kitchen ; remainder of flooring, soft wood. Ash trim in first story, soft wood trim in remainder. Ash staircase. Panels under windows in library, parlor and dining room. Wainscot in bath-room, laundry, pantry, china closet and kitchen. Interior wood-work finished in hard oil, except attic, which is painted colors to suit owner.

COLORS : All clapboards and panels in gables, olive drab. Trim, blinds, rain conductors and frames of gable panels, olive green. Outside doors, dark green with olive green panels. Sashes, dark red. Veranda floor and ceiling varnished. Wall shingles oiled and stained a little darker than natural color of wood. Roof shingles dipped and brush coated in red stain.

ACCOMMODATIONS : The principal rooms and their sizes, closets, etc., are shown by the plans. Cellar, with concrete floor and inside and outside entrance, under whole house. Three bedrooms finished in attic. Laundry under kitchen. Sliding doors connect principal rooms of first story. Four open fireplaces and hard wood mantels, and set range, included in estimate. Balconies in second and attic story.

COST: $4,865, † not including heater. The estimate is based on ‡ New York prices for materials and labor. In many sections of the country the cost should be less.

Price for working plans, specifications and * license to build, - $55.00
Price for † † bill of materials,   10.00
Address, THE CO-OPERATIVE BUILDING PLAN ASSOCIATION, Architects, 63 Broadway, New York.

FEASIBLE MODIFICATIONS: Heights of stories, colors, sizes of rooms and kinds of materials may be changed. Cellar may be reduced in size and concrete floor omitted. Attic finish, open fireplaces and mantels, sliding doors, set range and a part or all of plumbing may be omitted. Sewing room may be somewhat enlarged by a slight re-arrangement to serve as a small bedroom. Front balcony may be omitted. Attic balcony may be enclosed with glass or may be re-arranged to form part of adjoining room.

The price of working plans, specifications, etc., for a modified design varies according to the alterations required, and will be made known upon application to the Architects.

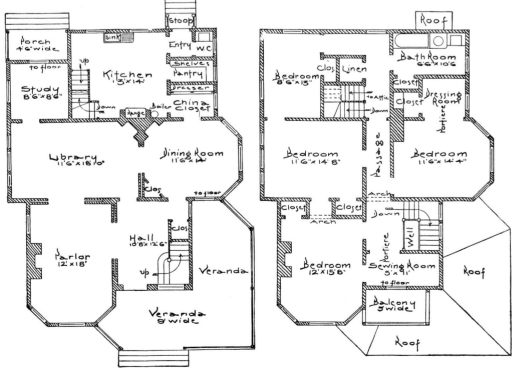

FIRST FLOOR.   SECOND FLOOR.

214

THE CO-OPERATIVE BUILDING PLAN ASSOCIATION, ARCHITECTS, 63 BROADWAY, NEW YORK.

*Shoppell's Modern Houses—*Designs Patented.*

Residence, Design No. 300

PERSPECTIVE.

DESCRIPTION.

For explanation of all symbols (* † etc.) see page 42.

GENERAL DIMENSIONS: Width through dining room and library, including bay, 38 ft.; depth, including veranda, 56 ft. 6 in. Heights of stories: Cellar, 7 ft.; first story, 9 ft. 4 in.; second story, 8 ft. 4 in.; attic, 8 ft.

EXTERIOR MATERIALS: Foundations, stone and brick; first and second stories, clapboards; gables, panels and shingles; roof, shingles. Outside blinds.

INTERIOR FINISH: Hard white plaster. Plaster cornices and centers in parlor, dining room, library, main hall (first and second story), and two bedrooms. Soft wood flooring and trim. Ash stairs. Panels under windows in hall, parlor, library and dining room. Bath-room, pantry, laundry and kitchen wainscoted. Interior wood-work finished in hard oil. Laundry wood-work painted.

COLORS: All clapboards, light olive drab. Trim, dark olive drab. Outside doors, bronze green. Blinds and sashes, maroon. Veranda floor and ceiling, oiled. Rain conductors, olive. Walls shingles dipped and brush coated sienna stain. Roof shingles dipped and brush coated red stain.

ACCOMMODATIONS: The principal rooms and their sizes, closets, etc., are shown by the plans. Cellar with inside and outside entrances and concrete floor under whole house. Laundry with two tubs in basement. Two rooms and store-room in attic. Fireplaces and hard wood mantels in parlor, library, dining room and front bedroom, and set range in kitchen, included in estimate.

COST: $4,871, † not including heater. The estimate is based on ‡ New York prices for materials and labor. In many sections of the country the cost should be less.

Price for working plans, specifications and * license to build, - - - - - - - - - $50.00
Price for † † bill of materials, - - - 10.00
Address, THE CO-OPERATIVE BUILDING PLAN ASSOCIATION, Architects, 63 Broadway, New York.

FEASIBLE MODIFICATIONS: Heights of stories, colors, sizes of rooms and kinds of materials may be changed. Cellar may be reduced in size and concrete floor omitted. Laundry may be omitted and tubs placed in kitchen. Sliding doors, fireplaces and mantels, set range, a part or all of plumbing and a portion of veranda may be omitted. Attic may be floored, but unfinished.

The price of working plans, specifications, etc., for a modified design varies according to the alterations required, and will be made known upon application to the Architects.

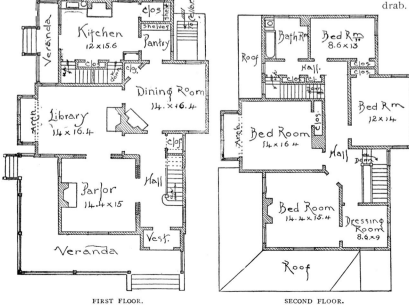

FIRST FLOOR.　　　SECOND FLOOR.

215

THE CO-OPERATIVE BUILDING PLAN ASSOCIATION, ARCHITECTS, 63 BROADWAY, NEW YORK.

Shoppell's Modern Houses—*Designs Patented. *Residence, Design No. 356*

PERSPECTIVE.

DESCRIPTION.

GENERAL DIMENSIONS: Width through dining and sitting rooms, including bay, 37 ft. 6 in.; depth, including veranda, 54 ft. 6 in. Heights of stories: Cellar, 7 ft.; first story, 9 ft. 6 in.; second story, 9 ft.; attic, 8 ft.

EXTERIOR MATERIALS: Foundations, stone; first and second stories, clapboards; gables, panels and shingles; roof, shingles. Outside blinds.

INTERIOR FINISH: Hard white plaster. Plaster cornices and centers in hall, parlor, dining and sitting rooms. Hard pine floors in entry, pantry, laundry and kitchen; soft wood floors with hard wood borders in hall, parlor, dining and sitting room; all other flooring soft wood. First story flooring double with paper between. Trim of first story, main part, cherry; all other trim soft wood. Panels under windows in all principal rooms of first and second story. Kitchen and bath-room wainscoted. Stairs, ash. Interior wood-work finished in hard oil, stained to suit owner.

COLORS: All clapboards, yellow stone color. Trim and rain conductors, seal brown. Outside doors, blinds and sashes, maroon. Veranda floor and ceiling, oiled. Brick-work, dark red. Wall shingles dipped and brush coated dark red stain. Roof shingles dipped and brush coated in a darker red stain.

ACCOMMODATIONS: The principal rooms and their sizes, closets, etc., are shown by the plans. Cellar under whole house, contains laundry with two tubs, and has inside and outside entrance and concrete floor. Open fireplaces with mantels in dining and sitting room included in estimate. Three rooms in attic.

COST: $4,892, † not including range and heater. The estimate is based on ‡ New York prices for materials and labor. In many sections of the country the cost should be less.

Price for working plans, specifications and * license to build, $50.00

Price for † † bill of materials, 10.00

Address, THE CO-OPERATIVE BUILDING PLAN ASSOCIATION, Architects, 63 Broadway, New York.

FEASIBLE MODIFICATIONS: Heights of stories, colors, sizes of rooms and kinds of materials may be changed. Entry to kitchen may be at rear instead of at side. Balcony, part of the veranda, sliding doors, fireplaces and mantels may be omitted.

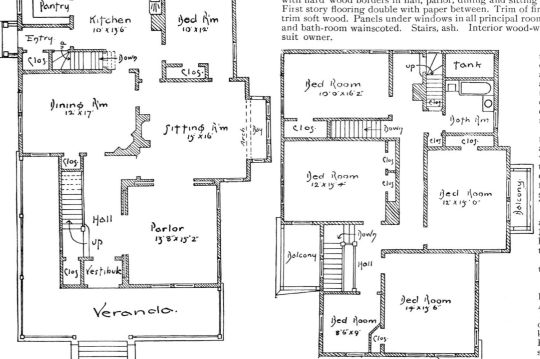

FIRST FLOOR.   SECOND FLOOR.

216

THE CO-OPERATIVE BUILDING PLAN ASSOCIATION, ARCHITECTS, 63 BROADWAY, NEW YORK.

*Shoppell's Modern Houses—*Designs Patented.*   *Residence, Design No. 479*

PERSPECTIVE.

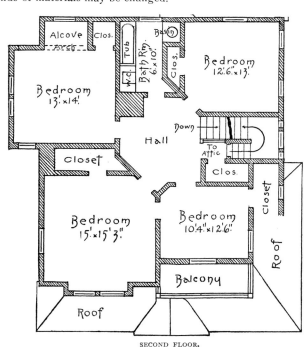

SIDE ELEVATION.

DESCRIPTION.

GENERAL DIMENSIONS : Width over all, 40 ft.; depth, including veranda and rear porch, 48 ft. Heights of stories: Cellar, 7 ft.; first story, 10 ft.; second story, 9 ft. 6 in.; attic, 8 ft.

EXTERIOR MATERIALS : Foundations, stone and brick ; first story, clapboards; second story, clapboards and shingles; gables, panels and shingles; roof, slate. Outside blinds.

INTERIOR FINISH : Hard white plaster ceilings and sand finish for walls ; plaster cornices and centers in parlor, dining room and halls of first and second stories. Yellow pine flooring in hall, pantry, kitchen and bath-room ; all other flooring, soft wood. Hall and staircase finished in oak; all other trim, soft wood. Panels under windows in parlor, hall, dining room and three bedrooms. Bath-room and kitchen wainscoted. All interior wood-work finished in hard oil.

ACCOMMODATIONS : The principal rooms and their sizes, closets, etc., are shown by the plans. Cellar under whole house. Three rooms finished in attic. Open fireplaces and hard wood mantels in parlor and dining room included in estimate. Fine hall and staircase; cosy nook with seat. Combination front and back stairway economizes space. Laundry tubs in kitchen.

COST : $4,963, † not including range and heater. The estimate is based on ‡ New York prices for materials and labor. In many sections of the country the cost should be less.

Price for working plans, specifications and * license to build, - - - - - - - - - - - - - - - $44.63
Price for † † bill of materials, - - - - - - - - - 5.00

Address, THE CO-OPERATIVE BUILDING PLAN ASSOCIATION, Architects, 63 Broadway, New York.

FEASIBLE MODIFICATIONS: Heights of stories, sizes of rooms and kinds of materials may be changed.

FIRST FLOOR.

SECOND FLOOR.

217

THE CO-OPERATIVE BUILDING PLAN ASSOCIATION, ARCHITECTS, 63 BROADWAY NEW YORK.

*Shoppell's Modern Houses—*Designs Patented.*   *Residence, Design No. 362*

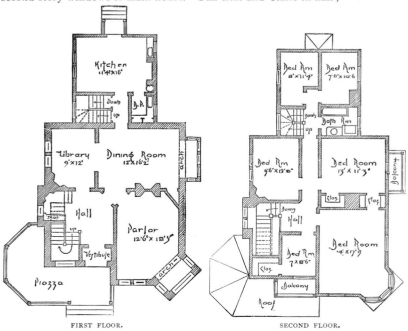

Side View of House.

PERSPECTIVE.

DESCRIPTION.

For explanation of all symbols (* † etc.) see page 42.

GENERAL DIMENSIONS: Extreme width, 39 ft. 6 in.; depth, including veranda, 55 ft. Heights of stories: Cellar, 7 ft.; first story, 10 ft.; second story, 9 ft.

EXTERIOR MATERIALS: Foundation and first story, brick; extension, first story, clapboards; second story and roof, shingles; gables, panels. Outside blinds to all windows of kitchen extension.

INTERIOR FINISH: Hard white plaster; plaster cornices in hall, parlor, dining room and library. Hard pine floor in kitchen, butler's pantry and bath-room. Inside sliding blinds to first and second story windows of main house. Oak trim and stairs in hall; soft wood trim elsewhere. Panels under windows in parlor, dining room and library. Wainscot in bath-room and kitchen. All interior wood-work finished in hard oil and stained as follows: Parlor, cherry; dining room, walnut; library, mahogany.

COLORS: Clapboards, sashes and rain conductors, red. Trim, outside doors and outside blinds, very dark green. Veranda floor, varnished. Veranda ceiling, oiled. Panels, reddish yellow with very dark green frames. Wall shingles dipped and brush coated sienna stain. Roof shingles dipped and brush coated slate color stain.

ACCOMMODATIONS: The principal rooms and their sizes, closets, etc., are shown by the plans. Cellar with concrete floor under whole house. Attic floored, but unfinished; space for four rooms. Open fireplaces in hall, parlor, dining room, library and one bedroom. Nook under main stairs with seat, fireplace and window. Deep bays in parlor and dining room. Rear stairway extends from first story to attic.

COST: $5,000, † not including mantels, range and heater. The estimate is based on ‡ New York prices for materials and labor. In many sections of the country the cost should be less.

Price for working plans, specifications and *
license to build, - - - - - - $50.00
Price for † † bill of materials, - - - 10.00

Address, THE CO-OPERATIVE BUILDING PLAN ASSOCIATION, Architects, 63 Broadway, New York.

FEASIBLE MODIFICATIONS: Heights of stories, colors, sizes of rooms and kinds of materials may be changed. Cellar may be reduced in size and concrete floor omitted. Fireplaces and mantels, part of the piazza, the balcony, dining room bay, and a part or all of plumbing, may be omitted. Tower in attic may be enclosed.

The price of working plans, specifications, etc., for a modified design varies according to the alterations required, and will be made known upon application to the Architects.

FIRST FLOOR.   SECOND FLOOR.

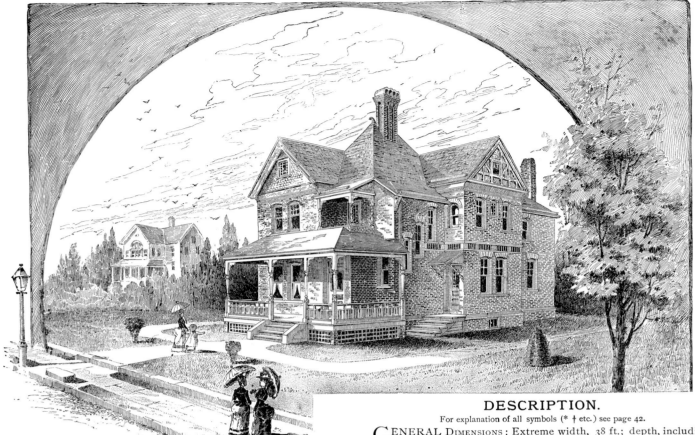

218

THE CO-OPERATIVE BUILDING PLAN ASSOCIATION, ARCHITECTS, 63 BROADWAY, NEW YORK.

*Shoppell's Modern Houses—*Designs Patented.*   *Residence, Design No. 407*

PERSPECTIVE.

FIRST FLOOR.   SECOND FLOOR.

DESCRIPTION.

For explanation of all symbols (* † etc.) see page 42.

GENERAL DIMENSIONS: Extreme width, 38 ft.; depth, including veranda, 64 ft. Heights of stories: Cellar, 7 ft.; first story, 10 ft.; second story, 9 ft.

EXTERIOR MATERIALS: Foundations, stone and brick; first and second stories, brick; gables, shingles and panels; roof, slate. Solid shutters on cellar windows; blinds elsewhere.

INTERIOR FINISH: Hard white plaster; plaster cornices in hall, parlor, sitting and dining room. Hard pine flooring in first and second story. Ash trim in hall, parlor and sitting room; black walnut in dining room; all other trim throughout, soft wood. Staircase, ash. Panels under windows in parlor, sitting and dining rooms. Kitchen and bath-room wainscoted. Chair rail in dining room. Front entrance doors, hard wood. Interior wood-work finished in hard oil.

COLORS: Brick-work washed down with acid at completion, and oiled. Trim, bronze green. Outside doors and sashes, dark green. Blinds, rain conductors and cresting, maroon. Veranda floor, light brown. Veranda ceiling, oiled. Gable shingles, oiled. Frames of panels in gable, dark green, with light brown panels.

ACCOMMODATIONS: The principal rooms and their sizes, closets, etc., are shown by the floor plans. Cellar under kitchen, sitting and dining rooms. Attic unfinished. Exterior brick walls have air space between brick-work and plastering.

COST: $5,084, † not including mantels, range and heater. The estimate is based on ‡ New York prices for materials and labor. In many sections of the country the cost should be less.

Price for working plans, specifications and * license to build, $70.00
Price for ‡‡ bill of materials,   15.00

Address, THE CO-OPERATIVE BUILDING PLAN ASSOCIATION, Architects, 63 Broadway, New York.

FEASIBLE MODIFICATIONS: Heights of stories, colors, sizes of rooms and kinds of materials may be changed. Cellar may extend under whole house. Three rooms may be finished in attic. Balconies and part or all of plumbing may be omitted.

219

THE CO-OPERATIVE BUILDING PLAN ASSOCIATION, ARCHITECTS, 63 BROADWAY, NEW YORK.

Shoppell's Modern Houses—*Designs Patented.　　　　　　　　*Residence, Design No. 462*

PERSPECTIVE.

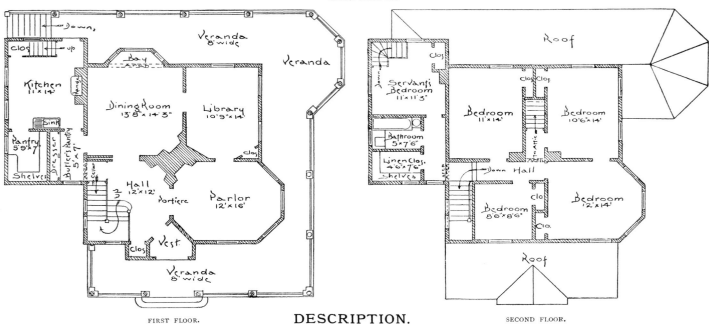

FIRST FLOOR.　　　　SECOND FLOOR.

DESCRIPTION.

GENERAL DIMENSIONS: Width over all, 50 ft.; depth, including verandas, 43 ft. 6 in. Heights of stories: Cellar, 6 ft. 6 in.; first story, 9 ft. 6 in.; second story, 8 ft. 6 in.

EXTERIOR MATERIALS: Foundations, stone; first story, clapboards; second story, gables, and veranda roofs, shingles; main roof, slate. Outside blinds to all windows except those of the staircase, attic and cellar.

INTERIOR FINISH: Sand finish plaster. Cellar ceiling plastered one heavy coat. Ash floor in first story with an under-flooring of soft wood; hard pine floor in attic; soft wood floors elsewhere. Soft wood trim. Ash staircase. Panels under windows in parlor, dining room and library. Kitchen and bath-room wainscoted. Interior wood-work finished in hard oil.

COLORS: Clapboards, bronze green. Trim, blinds, sashes and rain conductors, dark red. Outside doors, dark red with bronze green panels. Veranda floor, dark olive drab. Veranda ceiling, lilac. Brick-work, Indian red. Wall shingles, dipped and brush coated red; roof shingles a darker red.

ACCOMMODATIONS: The principal rooms and their sizes, closets, etc., are shown by the plans. Cellar under whole house. Laundry under kitchen. Attic plastered and finished as a large playroom; space for three or four bedrooms instead, if preferred. Heater pipes and registers in all rooms. All sides of the house equally presentable. Open fireplaces and mantels in hall, parlor and dining room, and set range in kitchen, included in estimate.

COST: $5,081, † not including heater. The estimate is based on ‡ New York prices for materials and labor. In many sections of the country the cost should be less.

Price for working plans, specifications and * license to build, - - - - - - - - $55.00

Price for †† bill of materials, - - - - - - 10.00

Address, THE CO-OPERATIVE BUILDING PLAN ASSOCIATION, Architects, 63 Broadway, New York.

FEASIBLE MODIFICATIONS: Heights of stories, colors, sizes of rooms and kinds of materials may be changed. Laundry tubs may be placed in kitchen. Foundation may be planned for a level grade.

THE CO-OPERATIVE BUILDING PLAN ASSOCIATION, ARCHITECTS, 63 BROADWAY, NEW YORK.

Shoppell's Modern Houses—*Designs Patented.

Residence, Design No. 223

PERSPECTIVE.

DESCRIPTION.

For explanation of all symbols (* † etc.) see page 42.

GENERAL DIMENSIONS: Width through parlor and sitting room, including bay, 41 ft.; depth, including porch, 60 ft. 4 in. Heights of stories · Cellar 7 ft.; first story, 10 ft.; second story, 9 ft.; attic, 8 ft.

EXTERIOR MATERIALS: Foundations, stone; first story, clapboards; second story and gables, shingles; roof, slate. Outside blinds to all windows except those of the cellar and attic, the bay window and second story corner windows.

INTERIOR FINISH: Hard white plaster. (Cellar ceiling plastered one heavy coat). Plaster cornices and centers in hall, parlor, sitting and dining rooms. Soft wood flooring and trim. Ash staircase. Inside Venetian blinds in parlor bay and for the corner windows in second story. Panels under windows in parlor, sitting, dining and bedroom first story. Wainscot in kitchen and bath-room. Chair rail in dining room. Interior wood-work finished in hard oil. Vestibule door glazed with heavy plate glass.

COLORS: Clapboards and rain conductors, olive. Trim, light brown. Outside doors and blinds, dark green. Sashes, dark red. Veranda floor and ceiling varnished. Iron cresting and finials on roof, olive green. Wall shingles, oiled.

ACCOMMODATIONS: The principal rooms and their sizes, closets, etc., are shown by the plans. Cellar with concrete floor under whole house. Three rooms and storage space in attic. Covered balcony over entrance. Four open fireplaces and hard wood mantels, and kitchen range, included in estimate. Sliding doors connect sitting and dining room. This house was built in central Pennsylvania for $3,200, including gas fixtures and heater.

COST: $5,200, † not including heater. The estimate is based on ‡ New York prices for materials and labor. In many sections of the country the cost should be less.

Price for working plans, specifications and * license to build, - - - - - - - $60.00
Price for † † bill of materials, - - - - 10.00

Address, THE CO-OPERATIVE BUILDING PLAN ASSOCIATION, Architects, 63 Broadway, New York.

FEASIBLE MODIFICATIONS: Heights of stories, colors, sizes of rooms and kinds of materials may be changed. Cellar may be reduced in size and concrete floor omitted. Attic may be left unfinished. Bath-room may be planned to adjoin the bedroom over kitchen. Main hall may be extended clear through, in both stories. Balcony may be omitted. Veranda may be extended or reduced. Open fireplaces and mantels, a part or all of plumbing, and the sliding doors, may be omitted. If heating apparatus be used two chimneys will suffice.

The price of working plans, specifications, etc., for a modified design varies according to the alterations required, and will be made known upon application to the Architects.

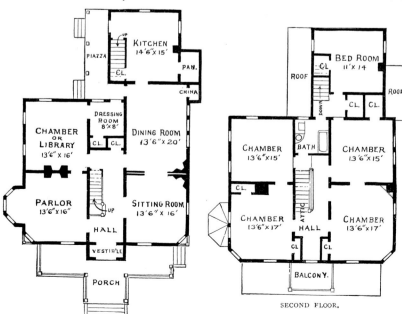

FIRST FLOOR.

SECOND FLOOR.

THE CO-OPERATIVE BUILDING PLAN ASSOCIATION, ARCHITECTS, 63 BROADWAY, NEW YORK.

Shoppell's Modern Houses—*Designs Patented.   *Design No. 354*

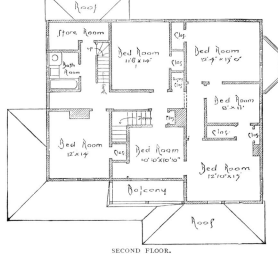

PERSPECTIVE.

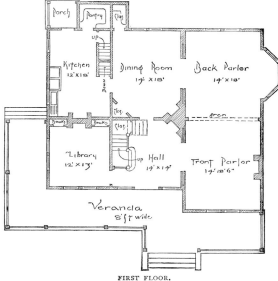

FIRST FLOOR.

SECOND FLOOR.

DESCRIPTION.

GENERAL DIMENSIONS: Extreme width, including bay and veranda, 54 ft. 10 in.; depth, including veranda and pantry, 51 ft. 6 in. Heights of stories: Cellar 7 ft.; first story, 10 ft.; second story, 9 ft.; attic, 8 ft. 6 in.

EXTERIOR MATERIALS: Foundations, stone; first story, clapboards; second story, clapboards and shingles; tower and gables, shingles and panels; roof, shingles. Outside blinds.

INTERIOR FINISH: Hard white plaster; plaster cornices and centers in parlor, dining room, library and hall. Hard pine flooring in bath-room, pantry and kitchen; soft wood flooring elsewhere. Soft wood trim. Ash stairs. Panels under windows in parlor, hall, dining room and library. Wainscoting in pantry, bath-room and kitchen. Interior wood-work finished in hard oil.

COLORS: Clapboards, yellow stone color. Trim and rain conductors, seal brown. Outside doors, blinds, sashes, veranda and balcony posts, rails, etc., maroon. Veranda floor, light drab. Veranda ceiling, lilac. Brick-work, Indian red. All shingles dipped and brush coated red stain.

ACCOMMODATIONS: The principal rooms and their sizes, closets, etc., are shown by the plans. Cellar with concrete floor under kitchen and dining room. Two rooms finished in attic. Open fireplaces in hall, parlor, dining room and library. Laundry tubs in kitchen.

COST $5,288 † not including mantels, range and heater. The estimate is based on ‡ New York prices for materials and labor. In many sections of the country the cost should be less.

Price for working plans, specifications and * license to build, - $65.00
Price for † † bill of materials, - - - - - - - - 10.00
Address, THE CO-OPERATIVE BUILDING PLAN ASSOCIATION, Architects, 63 Broadway, New York.

FEASIBLE MODIFICATIONS: Heights of stories, colors, sizes of rooms and kinds of materials may be changed. Cellar may extend under whole building, or be omitted entirely. Any or all fireplaces and mantels, sliding doors, bay window, balcony, and part or all of plumbing, may be omitted.

THE CO-OPERATIVE BUILDING PLAN ASSOCIATION, ARCHITECTS, 63 BROADWAY, NEW YORK.

*Shoppell's Modern Houses—*Designs Patented.* *Residence, Design No. 412*

DESCRIPTION.   PERSPECTIVE.

For explanation of all symbols (* † etc.) see page 42.

GENERAL DIMENSIONS : Width, including veranda, 53 ft.; depth, including veranda, 55 ft. Heights of stories : Cellar, 7 ft.; first story, 10 ft.; second story, 9 ft.; attic, 8 ft.

EXTERIOR MATERIALS : Foundation, brick; first story, clapboards; second story and roof, shingles; gables and dormers, panels and shingles. Outside blinds.

INTERIOR FINISH : Hard white plaster. Plaster cornices and centers in parlor, dining room and main hall. Pine flooring in first story with soft wood under-flooring ; soft wood flooring for second story and attic. Soft wood trim. Laundry and bath-room wainscoted. Chair rail in dining room and kitchen. Ash stairs. All interior wood-work finished in hard oil.

COLORS : Clapboards, light olive green. Trim and rain conductors, dark green. Outside doors, dark green with light olive green panels. Blinds and sashes, Pompeian red. Veranda floor and ceiling and all brick-work oiled. Wall shingles dipped and brush coated in oil, stained slightly darker than natural color of wood. Roof shingles oiled.

ACCOMMODATIONS : The principal rooms and their sizes, closets,

etc., are shown by the plans. Cellar under the kitchen and front hall. Three rooms finished in attic. Heat piping and register provided. Two open fireplaces with mantels and kitchen range included in estimate. Kitchen thoroughly isolated, preventing odors from entering body of the house.

COST : $5,325, † not including heater. The estimate is based on ‡ New York prices for materials and labor. In many sections of the country the cost should be less.

Price for working plans, specifications and * license to build, - - - - - - - - - - - - $55.00
Price for † † bill of materials, - - - - - 10.00

Address, THE CO-OPERATIVE BUILDING PLAN ASSOCIATION, Architects, 63 Broadway, New York.

FEASIBLE MODIFICATIONS : Heights of stories, colors, sizes of rooms and kinds of materials may be changed. May extend or omit cellar. Heat pipes and registers, attic finish, a part or all of plumbing, either or both fireplaces, and much of veranda, may be omitted.

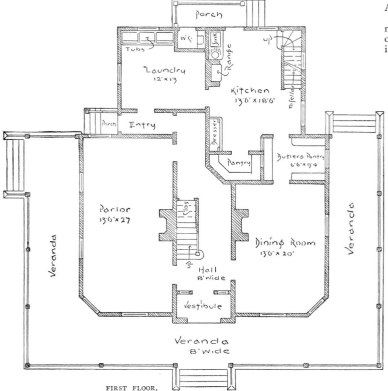

FIRST FLOOR.

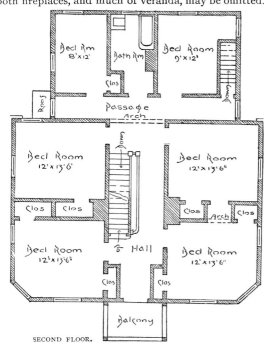

SECOND FLOOR.

223

THE CO-OPERATIVE BUILDING PLAN ASSOCIATION, ARCHITECTS, 63 BROADWAY, NEW YORK.

Shoppell's Modern Houses—*Designs Patented. *Residence, Design No. 461*

PERSPECTIVE.

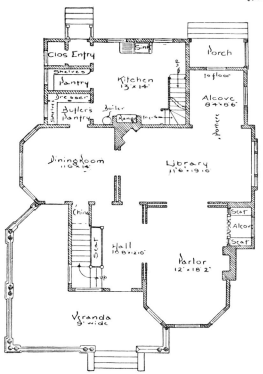

FIRST FLOOR.

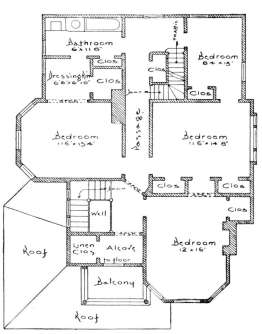

SECOND FLOOR.

DESCRIPTION.

GENERAL DIMENSIONS: Width over all, 37 ft. 8 in.; depth over all, 48 ft. 4 in. Heights of stories: Cellar, 7 ft.; first story, 9 ft. 6 in.; second story, 9 ft.; attic, 8 ft.

EXTERIOR MATERIALS: Foundations, stone; first story, clapboards; second story and gables, shingles; main roof, slate; veranda roof, shingles, Outside blinds.

INTERIOR FINISH: Hard white plaster; plaster cornices and centers in parlor, dining room, alcove, library and front bedroom. Hard pine floor in laundry. Soft wood flooring throughout the house. Soft wood trim. Ash staircase. Panels under windows in parlor, dining room, library and alcove. Chair rail in dining room. Wainscot in bath-room and kitchen. Interior wood-work finished in hard oil.

COLORS: All clapboards, light chocolate. Trim, sashes and rain conductors, maroon. Outside doors, maroon with light chocolate panels. Blinds, chocolate. Veranda floor and ceiling, oiled. Brick-work, terra cotta color. Wall shingles dipped and brush coated in dark terra cotta paint. Veranda roof shingles dipped and brush coated dark red.

ACCOMMODATIONS: The principal rooms and their sizes, closets, etc., are shown by the plans. Cellar under whole house. Laundry with three tubs under kitchen. Large billiard room, bedroom and storeroom in attic. Heater pipes and registers provided throughout house. Three open fireplaces and hardwood mantels, also set range in kitchen, included in estimate. Dutch door from dining room to front veranda.

COST: $5,330, † not including heater. The estimate is based on ‡ New York prices for materials and labor. In many sections of the country the cost should be less.

Price for working plans, specifications and * license to build, - $55.00
Price for †† bill of materials, - - - - - - - - - 10.00
Address, THE CO-OPERATIVE BUILDING PLAN ASSOCIATION, Architects, 63 Broadway, New York.

FEASIBLE MODIFICATIONS: Heights of stories, colors, sizes of rooms and kinds of materials may be changed. Tubs may be placed in kitchen and laundry omitted. Alcove may be partitioned off from library, to serve as laundry or servant's room. Any or all sliding doors, fireplaces and mantels, attic rooms, part or all of plumbing and either or both balconies may be omitted. Alcove and linen closet may be slightly enlarged to form bedroom.

224

THE CO-OPERATIVE BUILDING PLAN ASSOCIATION, ARCHITECTS, 63 BROADWAY, NEW YORK.

*Shoppell's Modern Houses—*Designs Patented.*

Residence, Design No. 649

PERSPECTIVE.

DESCRIPTION.

For explanation of all symbols (* † etc.) see page 42.

GENERAL DIMENSIONS: Front width, over all, 49 ft. 6 in.; depth including veranda, 49 ft. Heights of stories: Cellar, 7 ft.; first story, 10 ft.; second story, 9 ft. 6 in.; attic, 8 ft.

EXTERIOR MATERIALS: Foundations, brick; first and second stories, clapboards; gables and veranda roof, shingles; main roof, slate with terra-cotta cresting.

INTERIOR FINISH: Hard white plaster throughout. Double floor in first story. All floors are spruce, intended to be carpeted. Main stairs, oak. Oak trim in lower hall; all other trim, white pine. Picture moulding in first story. Oak wainscot in hall and up stairway; ash wainscot in bath-room; yellow pine wainscot in kitchen and butler's pantry. Front door, oak. House piped throughout for gas. All interior wood work finished in hard oil.

COLORS: Clapboards of first story, olive; clapboards of second story, drab. Trim, such as corner boards, water table, casings, etc., dark brownish red. Outside doors (except front door which is finished in hard oil), also blinds, dark brownish red. Sashes, bright red. Veranda floors, dark red; veranda ceiling, drab. Gable shingles dipped in Indian red stain; veranda roof shingles dipped in red stain.

ACCOMMODATIONS: The principal rooms and their sizes, closets, etc. are shown by the plans. In addition there is a cellar and laundry (3 set tubs) with concrete floors under the whole house, and there are two bed-rooms finished in the attic. Ventilating grate and recess for sideboard in dining room. An ornamental arch separates the main hall from the staircase hall. The side entrance is convenient to staircase. A well lighted and ventilated linen closet of good size off the bath-room. Store closets large enough to hold barrels off butlery. Servants' W. C. off kitchen porch.

COST: $5500, † not including mantels, range and heater. Estimate is

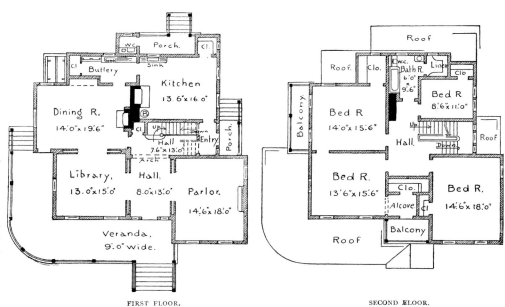

FIRST FLOOR.

SECOND FLOOR.

based on ‡ New York prices for materials and labor. In many sections of the country the cost should be less.

Price for working plans, specifications and * license to build, - $55.00
Price for †† bill of materials, - - - - - - 10.00
Address, THE CO-OPERATIVE BUILDING PLAN ASSOCIATION, Architects, 63 Broadway, New York.

FEASIBLE MODIFICATIONS: Heights of stories, colors, sizes of rooms and kinds of materials, may be changed. Balconies may be omitted with little or no injury to the exterior appearance. In the second story a small room may be planned where the closets, alcove and balcony are shown, still leaving closets for the adjoining bed-rooms.

The price of working plans, specifications, etc. for a modified design varies according to the alterations required, and will be made known upon application to the Architects.

THE CO-OPERATIVE BUILDING PLAN ASSOCIATION, ARCHITECTS, 63 BROADWAY, NEW YORK.

*Shoppell's Modern Houses—*Designs Patented.*   *Residence, Design No. 650*

PERSPECTIVE.

DESCRIPTION.

For explanation of all symbols (* † etc.) see page 42.

GENERAL DIMENSIONS : Front width, over all, 80 ft. 6 in.; depth including wing, 63 ft. 8 in. Heights of stories: Cellar, 7 ft. 6 in.; first story, 9 ft. 6 in.; second story, 9 ft.

EXTERIOR MATERIALS : Foundations, stone and brick; first story, clapboards; second story, shingles ; gables, panels and shingles ; roof, shingles.

INTERIOR FINISH : Hard white plaster throughout. Flooring, trim and stairways, all white pine. All interior wood work finished in hard oil.

COLORS : All clapboards, doors, blinds, and gable panels, painted pale yellow. All shingles, stained silver. All trim, white. Brick work cleaned with acid and left natural.

ACCOMMODATIONS : The principal rooms and their sizes, closets, etc., are shown by the plans. There is a cellar, with concrete floor, under the whole house. Two rooms in attic—space for four more. A part of veranda is left uncovered to afford good light for the hall and reception room.

This is a large, comfortable house, imposing in appearance, and of very moderate cost.

COST : $5500, † not including mantels, range and heater. The estimate is based on ‡ New York prices for materials and labor. In many sections of the country the cost should be less.

Price of working plans, specifications and *license to build, - $55.00
Price for †† bill of materials, - 10.00

Address, THE CO-OPERATIVE BUILDING PLAN ASSOCIATION, Architects, 63 Broadway, New York.

FEASIBLE MODIFICATIONS : Heights of stories, exterior materials, interior finish and colors, may be changed. Conservatory, parlor chimney, all fire-places, part of veranda, the covered balcony and the bays, may be omitted. Library and reception room may be connected by doors or they may be made one room. The parlor, library, and reception room may be combined to make one large room.

The price of working plans, specifications, etc. for a modified design varies according to the alterations required, and will be made known upon application to the Architects.

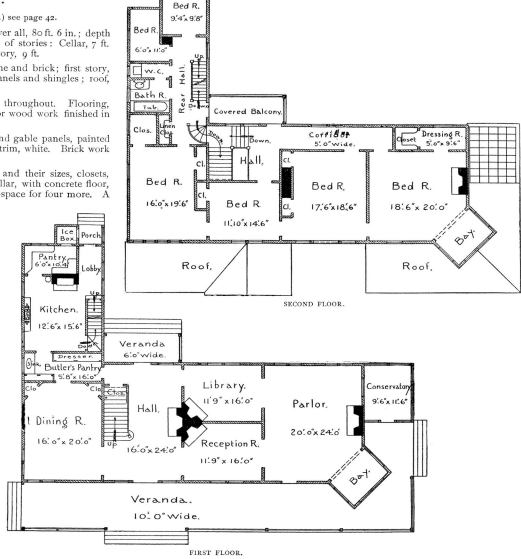

SECOND FLOOR.

FIRST FLOOR.

Shoppell's Modern Houses—*Designs Patented.   *Residence, Design No. 586*

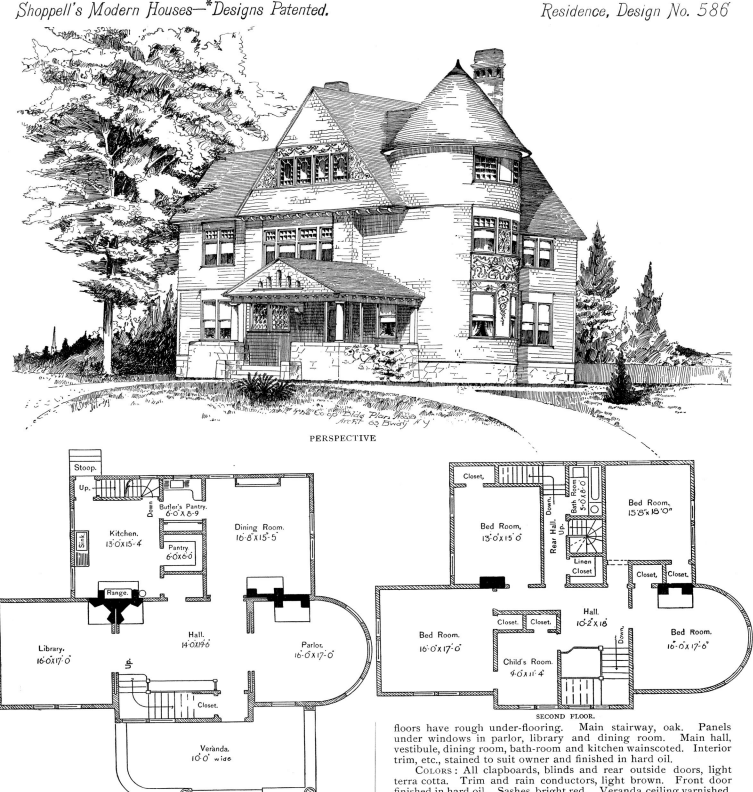

PERSPECTIVE

FIRST FLOOR.

SECOND FLOOR.

DESCRIPTION.

For explanation of all symbols (* † etc.) see page 42.

GENERAL DIMENSIONS : Width, through library, hall and parlor, 56 ft. 6 in.; depth, including veranda, 46 ft. 8 in. Heights of stories : Cellar, 7 ft.; first story, 10 ft.; second story, 9 ft.; attic, 8 ft. 6 in.

EXTERIOR MATERIALS : Foundations, stone ; first story, clapboards and shingles ; second story, gables, tower and roof, shingles.

INTERIOR FINISH : Plastering, hard white, with cornices and centers in hall, parlor, dining room and library. Trim in hall and dining room, oak ; remainder of trim, soft woods. Flooring, oak in hall, vestibule and dining room ; yellow pine in laundry, kitchen and butler's pantry ; all other floors white pine. Hard wood

floors have rough under-flooring. Main stairway, oak. Panels under windows in parlor, library and dining room. Main hall, vestibule, dining room, bath-room and kitchen wainscoted. Interior trim, etc., stained to suit owner and finished in hard oil.

COLORS : All clapboards, blinds and rear outside doors, light terra cotta. Trim and rain conductors, light brown. Front door finished in hard oil. Sashes, bright red. Veranda ceiling varnished. Veranda floor and all brick-work oiled. Wall shingles dipped and brush coated reddish stain. Roof shingles dipped and brush coated dark terra cotta stain.

ACCOMMODATIONS : The principal rooms and their sizes, closets, etc., are shown by the plans. Cellar under whole house. Three bedrooms and storage room finished in attic. Colonial design.

COST : $5,500, † not including mantels, range and heater. The estimate is based on ‡ New York prices for materials and labor. In many sections of the country the cost should be less.

Price for working plans, specifications and * license to
build, - - - - - - - - - $55.00
Price for †† bill of materials, - - - - 15.00
Address, THE CO-OPERATIVE BUILDING PLAN ASSOCIATION, Architects, 63 Broadway, New York.

FEASIBLE MODIFICATIONS : Heights of stories, sizes of rooms, materials and colors may be changed. Cellar may be reduced in size. Veranda may be extended indefinitely.

*Shoppell's Modern Houses—*Designs Patented.*   *Residence, Design No. 648*

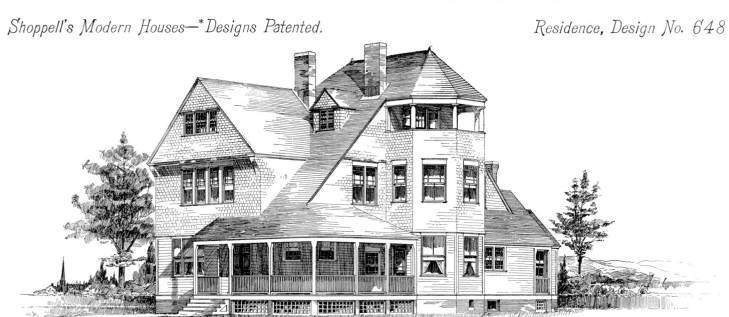

PERSPECTIVE.

DESCRIPTION.

For explanation of all symbols (* † etc.) see page 42.

GENERAL DIMENSIONS : Width, 46 ft.; depth, 73 ft. 6 in. Heights of stories: Cellar, 6 ft. 6 in.; first story, 11 ft.; second story, 10 ft. 6 in.

EXTERIOR MATERIALS : Foundations, stone; first story, clapboards; second story, roof and gables, shingles.

INTERIOR FINISH : Hard white plaster throughout. Plaster cornices and centres in hall, parlor, dining room and sitting room. Hard wood floors (ash and walnut alternate boards) in vestibule and hall; remainder of floors white pine, except the attic floor which is spruce. Trim of vestibule and hall, ash and walnut; all other trim, white pine. Staircase : string, treads and risers, ash; newels, rails and balusters, walnut. Hall, bath-room and kitchen, wainscoted. Front doors, ash with walnut mouldings. All wood work finished in hard oil.

COLORS : Clapboards and blinds, light drab. Shingles of side walls and gables, oiled. Roof shingles left natural. Sashes, Pompeian red. Veranda floors and ceilings and brick work, oiled.

ACCOMMODATIONS : The principal rooms and their sizes, closets, etc., are shown by the plans. In addition there is a cellar under the kitchen and pantries, and in the attic there are two bed-rooms, a large hall, a balcony, a tank room and a storage room. Hall through the house and kitchen isolated, as preferred in the South.

COST : $5500, † not including mantels, range and heater. Estimate is based on ‡ New York prices for materials and labor. In many sections of the country the cost should be less.

Price for working plans, specifications and * license to build, - $55.00
Price for †† bill of materials, - - - - - 10.00

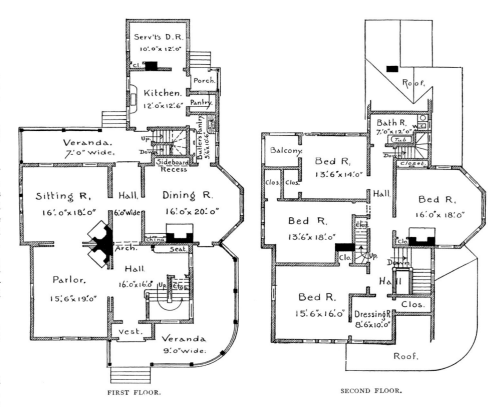

FIRST FLOOR.   SECOND FLOOR.

Address, THE CO-OPERATIVE BUILDING PLAN ASSOCIATION, Architects, 63 Broadway, New York.

FEASIBLE MODIFICATIONS : Heights of stories, exterior materials and colors may be changed. Cellar may be enlarged. Balconies may be enclosed. Servants' dining room may be used as a summer kitchen or a laundry, or it may be omitted. Number of fire-places may be reduced.

The price of working plans, specifications, etc. for a modified design varies according to the alterations required, and will be made known upon application to the Architects.

*Shoppell's Modern Houses—*Designs Patented.*   *Residence, Design No. 569*

PHOTOGRAPHIC VIEW.

DESCRIPTION.

GENERAL DIMENSIONS: Width, 36 ft. 6 in. over all; depth, including veranda, 56 ft. Heights of stories: Cellar, 7 ft.; first story, 9 ft. 6 in.; second story, 9 ft.; attic, 8 ft.

EXTERIOR MATERIALS: Foundations, stone and brick; first story, clapboards; second story and roof, shingles; tower and gables, panels and shingles. Outside blinds.

INTERIOR FINISH: Hard white plaster. Plaster cornices and centers in parlor, dining and sitting room, library, hall of first story, and front bedrooms and hall of second story. Quartered oak flooring in hall, first story; ash flooring in dining-room; yellow pine in kitchen; alternate walnut and cherry floor in bath-room; remainder of flooring soft wood. Cherry trim in parlor, sitting and dining rooms; ash in hall; yellow pine in kitchen; soft wood elsewhere. Oak stairway. Panels under windows in parlor, library, sitting and dining rooms. Wainscot in bath-room and kitchen. Interior wood-work finished in hard oil.

COLORS: Clapboards, olive green. Trim and rain conductors, dark olive drab. Outside doors, bronze green. Blinds, olive. Sashes, Pompeian red. Veranda floor and gable panels, Tuscan yellow. Veranda ceiling, Oriental drab. Brick-work, bright red. Wall shingles of second story dipped and brush coated brownish stain. Gable shingles dipped and brush coated sienna stain. Roof shingles dipped and brush coated red stain.

ACCOMMODATIONS: The principal rooms and their sizes, closets, etc., are shown by the plans. Cellar under whole house. Laundry, with three tubs and servants' water-closet, in basement. Four rooms finished in attic. Four open fireplaces and mantels included in estimate. Sliding doors connect hall and parlor and library and dining room. Alcove with seats under main staircase.

COST: $5,500, † not including range and heater. The estimate is based on ‡ New York prices for materials and labor. In many sections of the country the cost should be less.

Price for working plans, specifications and * license to build, - $50.00
Price for †† bill of materials, - - - - - - - 10.00

Address THE CO-OPERATIVE BUILDING PLAN ASSOCIATION, Architects, 63 Broadway, New York.

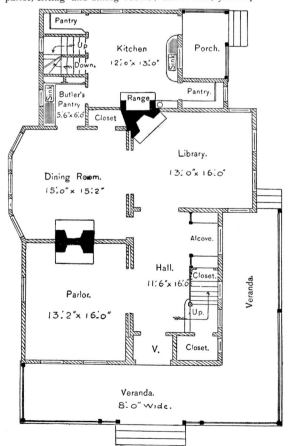

FIRST FLOOR.

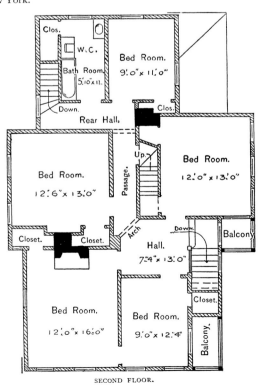

SECOND FLOOR.

THE CO-OPERATIVE BUILDING PLAN ASSOCIATION, ARCHITECTS, 63 BROADWAY, NEW YORK.

Shoppell's Modern Houses—*Designs Patented.

Residence, Design No. 602

PERSPECTIVE.

DESCRIPTION.

For explanation of all symbols (* † e c.) see page 42.

GENERAL DIMENSIONS: Width, 38 ft. 6 in., including veranda; depth, including veranda, 62 ft. Heights of stories: Cellar, 6 ft. 6 in.; first story, 9 ft. 6 in.; second story, 9 ft.

EXTERIOR MATERIALS: Foundations, stone and brick; first story, clapboards; second story, gables and roofs, shingles. Outside blinds to all windows except those of cellar and the casement sashes.

INTERIOR FINISH: Hard white plaster finish; cornices and centers in hall, parlor, library and dining room. Trim, white pine. Main staircase, ash. Tile hearths in hall and library; rubbed slate in dining and bedrooms. Soft wood flooring throughout. Bath-room and kitchen wainscoted. All interior wood-work finished in hard oil.

COLORS: All clapboards, yellow. Trim, veranda posts, spindle work and balusters, Tuscan yellow. Outside doors, blinds, rain water conductors, brick-work, cresting and finials, dark Tuscan yellow. Sashes, dark green. Veranda floor and ceiling varnished. Wall shingles dipped and brush coated sienna stain. Roof shingles dipped and brush coated mahogany stain.

ACCOMMODATIONS: The principal rooms and their sizes, closets, etc., are shown by the plans. Cellar under the kitchen only, with outside and inside entrances. Four fireplaces with their mantels are included in the estimate. Attic is floored but not otherwise finished; space for four rooms.

COST: $5,500, † not including range and heater. The estimate is based on ‡ New York prices for materials and labor. In many sections of the country the cost should be less.

Price for working plans, specifications and * license to build, - $55.00
Price for †† bill of materials, - 15.00

Address, THE CO-OPERATIVE BUILDING PLAN ASSOCIATION, Architects, 63 Broadway, New York.

FEASIBLE MODIFICATIONS: Heights of ceilings, sizes of rooms, kinds of materials and colors may be changed. Cellar may be enlarged. First story may be brick or stone. Open veranda may be enclosed with glass or its space added to attic room. If heating apparatus be used rear chimney will suffice. The laundry extension may be omitted and tubs placed in cellar.

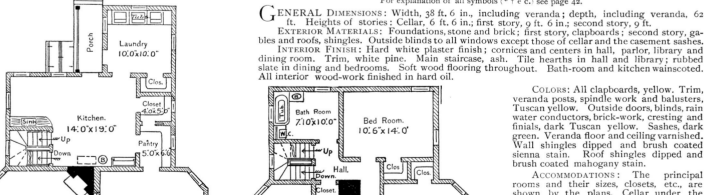

FIRST FLOOR.

SECOND FLOOR.

230

THE CO-OPERATIVE BUILDING PLAN ASSOCIATION, ARCHITECTS, 63 BROADWAY, NEW YORK.

Shoppell's Modern Houses—*Designs Patented.   *Residence, Design No. 504*

PERSPECTIVE.

DESCRIPTION.

For explanation of all symbols (* † etc.) see page 42.

GENERAL DIMENSIONS : Width, through dining and sitting rooms, 37 ft. 6 in.; depth, including veranda, 50 ft. 10 in.   Heights of stories : Cellar, 7 ft.; first story, 9 ft. 6 in.; second story, 9 ft.

EXTERIOR MATERIALS : Foundations, stone and brick; first story, clapboards; second story, clapboards, panels and shingles; gables, panels and shingles ; roof, slate.   Outside blinds to all windows except those of the parlor, hall, sitting and dining room.

INTERIOR FINISH : Hard white plaster.   Plaster cornices and centers in hall, parlor, dining and sitting room.   Soft wood flooring and trim.   Ash stairs.   Inside folding blinds in hall, parlor, sitting and dining room.   Wainscot in butler's pantry, bath-room and kitchen.   Interior wood-work finished in hard oil.

COLORS : Clapboards and veranda floor, medium drab.   Trim, outside doors, blinds and rain conductors, olive.   Sashes and all brick-work, Pompeian red.   Veranda ceiling, varnished.   All panels, medium drab with olive frames.   All shingles dipped and brush coated red stain.

ACCOMMODATIONS : The principal rooms and their sizes, closets, etc., are shown by the plans.   Cellar under whole house.   Laundry under kitchen. Attic floored, but unfinished; space for three rooms and storage.   Fireplace, seat and window under the main stairway.   Six open fireplaces and hard wood mantels included in estimate.   Wash-basins and hot and cold water supply in bedrooms over parlor and sitting room.

COST: $5,537, † not including range and heater.   The estimate is based on ‡ New York prices for materials and labor.   In many sections of the country the cost should be less.

Price for working plans, specifications and * license to build,   - $45.37
Price for ‡ ‡ bill of materials,   -   -   -   -   -   -   -   -   10.00

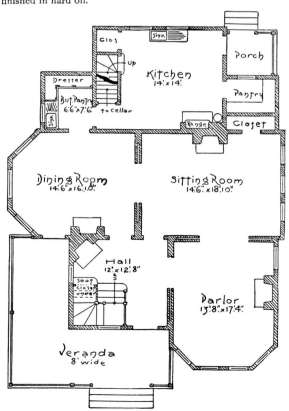

FIRST FLOOR.

SECOND FLOOR.

ESTIMATE OF MATERIALS AND LABOR FOR DESIGN NUMBER 504

BUILDERS and owners always question the accuracy of the estimates made by architects. This is not surprising, because, generally, the architect simply guesses at the cost or bases a short calculation on the cubic contents of the house or the square feet of its floors.

The value of the designs in this publication is greatly enhanced by the careful and painstaking estimates that are made to arrive at the costs. The detailed estimate printed below is given as a specimen of the way the estimating is done for each design.

The Asterisk (*) prefixed to a line denotes that materials and labor are both included.

	Quan.	Price.	Cost.
MASON'S MATERIALS.			
EXCAVATION.			
Excavating for cellar, etc.......cub. yds.	342	$ .25	$85.50
STONEWORK.			
*Rubble work in foundations.....cub. ft.	1,800	.16	288.00
Stone sills for cellar door 2½"x18"..lin. ft.	3	.35	1.05
" " " " windows 2½"x 8".....lin. ft.	28	.25	7.00
Stone lintel for kitchen fireplace, 2½"x16"....... "	6	.50	3.00
Stone caps for chimneys 2½ ins. thick.......sq. ft.	15½	.65	10.07
Stone steps for cellar area, 2"x10".lin. ft.	29	.25	7.25
" coping for cellar area, 2"x 10"....... "	10	.25	2.50
BRICKWORK, ETC.			
*Hard brick in walls, piers, etc.......per M laid	4,500	15.00	67.50
*Hard brick in chimney (above first tier floor joists)......... "	18,000	15.00	270.00
Tile hearths in 7 rooms.............sq. ft.	48	1.00	48.00
Stove pipe thimbles and covers..........	2	.25	.50
CONCRETING.			
*Cellar bottom 3 ins. thick...sq. yds. laid	140	.40	56.00
PLASTERING.			
*3 coat work in 1st and 2d stories.sq. yds.	8.20	.30	246.00
*2 " " " 1st, 2d and attic stories....... "	545	.25	136.25
*1 coat work in cellar and laundry....... "	159	.20	31.80
*Cornice in 1st story, 6"x8".........lin. ft.	229	.25	57.25
*Centre-pieces, 20"..........	4	2.50	10.00
*Brackets or trusses..........	4	.75	3.00
*Whitewashing cellar walls and laundry.......sq. yds.	396	.02	7.92
Total for Mason's Materials.......	......	......	$1338.59
CARPENTER'S MATERIALS.			
16 Pieces for sleepers, 3"x4"x14', chestnut....... ft. B.M.	324	.03	$9.72
1 Piece for girders, 6"x8"x23' 92 "			
1 " " " 6"x8"x20' 80 "			
1 " " " 6"x8"x13' 52 "			
1 " " " 6"x8"x7' 28 "			
1 " " sills, 4"x7"x19'.... 44 "			
7 " " " 4"x7"x16'.... 261 "			
3 " " " 4"x7"x14'.... 98 "			
12 " " floor joists, 2"x10" x18'....... 360 "			
66 Pieces for floor joists, 2"x 10"x16'.......1760 "			
72 Pieces for floor joists, 2"x 10"x15'.......1800 "			
16 Pieces for floor joists, 2"x 10"x13'....... 347 "			
16 Pieces for floor joists, 2"x 8"x20'....... 426 "			
18 Pieces for floor joists, 2"x 8"x18'....... 432 "			
34 Pieces for floor joists, 2"x 8"x16'....... 725 "			
16 Pieces for floor joists, 2"x 8"x13'....... 277 "			
15 Pieces for corner posts, 4" x6"x21'....... 630 "			
310 Pieces studding 2"x4"x22'..4547 "			
80 " " 2"x4"x18'.. 960 "			
150 Lin. ft. for girts, 1"x6".... 75 "			
285 " " plates, 4"x4"... 380 "			
38 Pieces for rafters, 2"x6"x 24'....... 912 "			
18 Pieces for rafters, 2"x6"x 18'....... 324 "			
16 Pieces for rafters, 2"x6"x 14'....... 224 "			
38 Pieces for rafters, 2"x6"x 12'....... 456 "			
2 Pieces for valley rafters, 3"x8"x21'....... 84 "			
2 Pieces for valley rafters, 3"x8"x18'....... 72 "			
2 Pieces for ridges, 2"x8"x 18'....... 48 "			
2 Pieces for ridges, 2"x8"x 16'....... 43 "			
36 Pieces for collar beams, 1" x6"x16'....... 288 "			
Lin. ft. for veranda sills, 4"x 8"x109'....... 291 "			
Lin. ft. for plates, 4"x6"x95' .. 190 "			
Lin. ft. for floor joists, 2"x8"x 136'....... 181 "			
18 Pieces for ceiling, 2"x3"x 18'....... 162 "			
36 Pieces for rafters, 2"x4"x 10'....... 240 "			
	16,889	15.00	253.34
LUMBER, &C.			
Bridging, 1¼"x3".......lin. ft.	700	.01	7.00
Furring, 1"x2"....... "	300	.00½	1.50
Grounds for casing, 1"x1"....... "	1,200	.00¼	3.00
Sheathing for side walls.....4300 ft. B.M.			
" " roofs..........2700 "			
	7,000	16.00	112.00
Carried forward.......	......	......	$386.56

	Quan.	Price.	Cost.
Brought forward.......	......	......	$386.56
Sheathing paper.......sq. ft.	4,100	$.00¼	10.25
Clapboards.......ft. B.M.	1,500	30.00	45.00
Plank for cellar coal bins, 2 in. matched....... "	600	.02½	15.00
Ceiling, T. and G. dressed....... "	525	.03	15.75
Shingles for side walls, dimension.......per M.	10,000	5.00	50.00
Shingles for roofs....... "	1,800	3.50	6.30
Flooring, 2 stories, 1"x4", white pine.......3300 ft. B.M.			
Flooring, attic and laundry, 1"x6".......1650 "			
	4 950	30.00	148.50
Flooring for veranda, 1"x4", yellow pine....... "	·500	.03½	17.50
FINISHING WORK OUTSIDE.			
Ridge roll 2"x2".......lin. ft.	67	.02⅖	1.61
Lumber for finish, gutters, etc., 1"....... 900 ft. B.M.			
Lumber for panels, etc., matched, 1"x3".......1600 "			
Lumber for finish, 1¼".......1300 "			
" " " 2"....... 320 "			
" " balcony posts, 6" 144 "			
	4,264	.03½	149.24
Mouldings for cornice, 1½"x5¼"....lin. ft.	560	.04⅗	25.76
" " " 1¼"x2½".... "	255	.01¾	4.46
" " frieze, 2"x4"....... "	115	.04⅘	5.52
" " " 1¼"x2¾"..... "	15	.02	.30
" " " 1¼"x2"....... "	115	.01½	1.72
" " belts, 1¼"x4¼"....... "	181	.03⅕	5.79
" " sill course, 1"x2".... "	270	.01⅕	3.24
" " cove, ¾"....... "	250	.00½	1.25
Patent roofing for balcony floors...sq. ft.	154	.03	4.62
Turned spindles for balcony frieze 2"x 18 in.......	36	.10	3.60
Brackets for gables, 6"x6"x4".......	15	.15	2.25
" " frieze, 11"x13"x5".......	6	.50	3.00
" " dormer, 8"x27"x4".......	2	.75	1.50
Carved panels, window cap and circular casings.......			15.00
Ramps for balcony, 2"x9".......	8	.50	4.00
Bracket for front bay, 45"x54"x4".......	1		4.50
VERANDA AND PORCH.			
Cornice moulding, 1¼"x7".......lin. ft.	53	.05¼	2.78
Cove moulding....... "	300	00½	1.50
Brackets, 8"x10"x2".......	16	.10	1.60
" 4"x12"x4".......	2	.20	.40
Posts, 6"x6"x9' turned.......	9	2.50	22.50
Hand rail, 3"x4".......lin. ft.	57	.07⅕	4.10
Bottom rail, 3"x3"....... "	57	.05⅖	3.08
Ramps for hand rail.......	14	.60	8.40
Balusters and spindles....... 30 ft. B.M.			
Steps, yellow pine, 1¼-in..... 53 "			
Risers, facia and boxing, 1-in. 200 "			
3 posts for porch, 6-in....... 54 "			
	337	.03	10.11
Lattice under sills, halved.......sq. ft.	53	.05	2.65
Lattice panel enclosing porch, halved....... "	36	.15	5.40
SASHES.			
Pair sash for 1st story, 3'x6'x1½".......	3	2.65	7.95
" " " " 2'8"x6'x1½".......	2	2.50	5.00
" " " " 2'6"x6'x1½".......	6	2.35	14.10
Single sash for dining-room, 4'x2'4"x1½", stained glass.......	1		7.50
Single sash for hall, 3'x2'8"x1½", stained glass.......	1		6.00
Single sash for kitchen dpt., 2'6"x3'6"x1¼"	2	1.15	2.30
Pair " " " " 3'x5'6"x1½"..	2	2.30	4.60
" " " 2d story, 4'x5'6"x1½".......	1		3.30
" " " " 3'x5'6"x1½".......	7	2.30	16.10
" " " " 3'x5'x1½".......	2	2.25	4.50
" " " casement, 4'x6'6"x1½"....	1		4.00
" " " " 3'6"x6'6"x1½"..	1		3.70
Single " " " 2'6"x3'6"x1½"..	2	1.22	2.44
" " " " 10"x2'8"x1¼"...	2	1.00	2.00
" " " attic, 2'x3'4"x1¼".......	1		.95
" " " " 2'4"x2'4"x1¼".......	1		.85
Pair " " " 3'x4'x1¼".......	2	1.80	3.60
" " " " 2'8"x4'x1¼".......	1		1.40
Single " " gable, 1'6x"1'6"x1¼", circular.......	1		1.00
Single sash for gable, 2'x2'x1¼", circular.......	2	1.50	3.00
Single sash for cellar, 3'x1'8"x1¼".......	8	.80	6.40
" " " " 2'x1'8"x1¼".......	1		.55
" " " balcony, 7'8"x3'6"x1½"....	1		4.10
" " " " 4'x3'6"x1½".......	1		2.10
" " " " 2'4"x3'6"x1½"....	2	1.25	2.50
" " " " 7'8"x1'10"x1¼"...	1		2.30
" " " " 4'x1'10"x1¼".....	1		1.20
" " " " 2'4"x1'10"x1¼"...	2	.80	1.60
BLINDS.			
NOTE.—Sash sizes are given. Outside blinds to be ⅜" narrower and 1" longer. All 1¼" thick.			
Pair outside slat blinds for 1st story, 3'x 5'6".......	2	1.45	2.90
Pair outside slat blinds for 2d story, 4'x5' 6".......	1		1.90
Pair outside slat blinds for 2d story, 3'x5' 6".......	7	1.45	10.15
Pair outside slat blinds for 2d story, 3'x5'	2	1.37	2.74
" " " " " " " 2'6"x 3'6".......	1		.93
Pair outside slat blinds for 2d story, 3'6"x 6'6".......	1		1.71
Carried forward.......	......	......	$1130.11

	Quan.	Price.	Cost.
Brought forward.......	......	......	$1130.11
Pair inside blinds for 1st story, 3'x6'.......	3	$3.20	9.60
" " " " " 2'6"x6'....	6	3.20	19.20
" " " " " 2'8"x6'....	2	3.20	6.40
LUMBER FOR WINDOW FRAMES.			
Pulley stiles and heads, 1"....260 ft. B.M.			
Sills and blind stops, 1".......125 "			
Sub-sills, 2".......215 "			
Casements, 1¼"....... 50 "			
Plank for cellar frames, 1½"..135 "			
	785	.03	23.55
Parting strips.......lin. ft.	520	.00⅗	3.12
Stop beads....... "	520	.00⅗	3.12
INSIDE WINDOW AND DOOR TRIM.			
Moulded stool caps, 1¼"x3".......lin. ft.	112	.02⅖	2.69
" aprons, 1¼"x2"....... "	112	.01½	1.68
" casings, 1"x4¼"....... "	1,100	.02½	27.50
Back band for casings, 1¼"x2".... "	1,200	.01½	18.00
Moulded casings, 1"x4½"....... "	220	.02½	5.50
" " 1"x3½"....... "	325	.02⅖	7.80
Corner blocks, 4¼"x4¼", turned.......	132	.06	7.92
Paneled backs.......	11	1.50	16.50
Paneling under dining-room window.......sq. ft.	14	.35	4.90
DOORS.			
Front door, glazed, 3'4"x7'6"x1¾".......	1		15.00
Outside " for dining room 3'x7'6"x1¾"....	1		8.50
Pair sliding doors, 5 panels 6'8"x8'x1¾"...	1		17.00
" " " 5 " 5'8"x8'x1¾"...	1		14.00
" " " 5 " 4'4"x8'x1¾"...	1		12.60
Doors, 5 panels, 1st story, 2'10"x7'4"x1½".	3	3.34	10.02
" 5 " closet, 2'6"x7'4"x1¼".....	1		2.61
" 5 " kitchen, 2'8"x6'10"x1½"..	1		2.92
" 5 " " 2'6"x6'10"x1½"..	1		2.78
" 5 " " 2'6"x6'10"x1¼"..	1		2.27
" 5 " " 2'4"x6'10"x1¼"..	2	2.17	4.34
" 5 " 2d story, 2'8"x6'10"x1½"..	7	2.92	20.44
" 5 " closets, 2'6"x6'10"x1¼"....	5	2.27	11.35
" 5 " " 2'4"x6'10"x1¼"...	2	2.17	4.34
" 5 " " 2'x6'10"x1¼".....	1		1.92
" 4 " attic, 2'6"x6'8"x1¼".......	3	2.23	6.69
" 4 " cellar, 2'10"x6'6"x1¼".....	1		2.39
" 4 " " 2'6"x6'6"x1¼".....	1		2.14
Glazed door, cellar, 2'8"x6'6"x1½".......	1		3.76
LUMBER FOR DOOR JAMBS.			
Jambs for outside doors, 1½"..112 ft. B.M.			
" " ordinary doors, 1".210 "			
	322	.05	16.10
Lin. ft. moulded door stops, ½"x2".......	450	.01	4.50
" " " saddles, ⅝"x4"....	110	.02	2.20
STAIRS—FIRST STORY TO ATTIC.			
Material and labor complete.......			150.00
BACK STAIRS.			
Strings, treads, risers, etc.......	175	.03	5.25
CELLAR STAIRS.			
Treads and strings....... 90 ft. B.M.			
Risers and enclosing....... 150 "			
	240	.03	7.20
BASE OR SKIRTING.			
Moulded shoe, 1¼"x3" for 1st story.lin. ft.	120	.02	2.40
" " 1¼"x2" " 2d " "	240	.01½	3.60
cap, 1½"x2", for both stories "	360	.01⅘	6.48
Plinth, 1"x5", for both stories.. 160 ft. B.M.			
Base, 1"x6", for closets....... 97 "			
	257	.03½	8.99
*WOOD MANTELS.			
Mantels for parlor sitting and dining rooms.......	3	35.00	105.00
Mantel for hall.......	1		30.00
" " bedrooms.......	3	10.00	30.00
WAINSCOTING, ETC.			
Ceiling strips in kitchen, ⅝"x3", white pine.......ft. B.M.	300	.03	9.00
Ceiling strips in bath-room ⅝"x3" cherry....... "	175	.05	8.75
Capping, 1¼"x2", cherry.......lin. ft.	32	.02½	.80
" 1¼"x2", pine....... "	64	.01½	.96
Floor Moulding....... "	100	.01	1.00
Bath tub top cherry 1 in....... 9 ft. B.M.			
Water closet, seat, flap, back and sides.......15 "			
	24	.06	1.44
DRESSER.			
Glazed doors for front size about 12x48 in.	5	.60	3.00
Pine lumber.......ft. B.M.	140	.04	5.60
Mouldings 4 in.......lin. ft.	12	.02⅖	.29
Drawer pulls.......	12	.03	.36
THREE WASH TRAYS.			
Fronts, backs, bottoms and partitions, 1½ in. plank.......100 sq. ft.			
Top and lids, 1¼ in. stuff.......13 "			
	113	.04	4.52
Supports, turned legs.......	4	.10	.40
MISCELLANEOUS.			
Angle beads.......lin. ft.	90	.01½	1.35
Cellar hatchway....... 45 ft. B.M.			
Shelving, etc....... 215 "			
	260	.03	7.80
Drip boards for sinks, ash.......ft. B.M.	13	.06	.78
Legs for sinks, turned.......	4	.15	.60
Total for Carpenter's Materials.......	......	......	$1851.03
HARDWARE.			
Common nails.......lbs.	1,500	.03	$45.00
Finishing nails....... "	200	.05	10.00
Brads and screws.......			11.00
Pair bronze butts, 4"x4", for dutch doors	4	2.25	9.00
Carried forward.......	......	......	$75.00

ESTIMATE OF DESIGN NUMBER 504—Continued.

	Quan.	Price.	Cost.
Brought forward			$75.00
Pair bronzed butts, 3½"x3½", for other doors	29	$ .55	15.95
Pair bronzed butts, 3"x3", for French window	4	.42	1.68
Pair bronzed butts, 2½"x2½", for casement and cellar windows	13	.36	4.68
Pair brass butts, 2"x2" for bath-room and dresser, etc	10	.04	.40
Pair strap hinges for cellarway	2	.10	.20
Front door locks	2	1.50	3.00
Sliding door locks	3	1.00	3.00
4-in. mortise door locks	13	.35	4.55
3½-in. rim door locks	16	.25	4.00
French window locks	2	.50	1.00
" " bolts	4	.15	.60
Pair front door knobs, wood	2	.35	.70
" door knobs, wood	4	.35	1.40
" " mineral	25	.10	2.50
Small knobs for cupboards, etc	12	.03	.36
Sets sliding door flush furniture and stop	3	2.00	6.00
Brass rail for sliding doors	35	.10	3.50
Sets slot sheaves for sliding doors	3	1.40	4.20
Flush bolts for front doors	6	.50	3.00
Barrel bolts, 6-in	4	.10	.40
" " 4-in	18	.08	1.44
Sash fasteners	28	.20	5.60
" weights...lbs	672	.01½	8.06
" cord...lbs	15	.30	4.50
" pulleys	112	.02½	2.80
Cupboard catches	12	.06	.72
Clothes hooks	72	.02	1.44
Base knobs	24	.08	1.92
Pair hinges for outside blinds	28	.10	2.80
Sets fastenings for outside blinds	14	.03	.42
Inside blind hardware, 11 fastenings, sets complete	11	.50	5.50
Pot hooks	12	.02	.24
Bell pull and gong	1		3.00
Total for Hardware			$174.56
*TINNING.			
Gutter and valley linings...lin. ft	203	.10	$20.30
Flashings... "	50	.15	7.50
Carried forward			$27.80

	Quan.	Price.	Cost.
Brought forward			$27.80
3-in. leaders... "	139	$ .12	16.68
2-in. "	36	.08	2.88
Total for Tinner's Materials (including labor)			$47.36
*SLATING.			
Sq. ft. roof slating	2,373	.08	$189.84
" roofing paper or felt	2,373	.00½	11.86
Zinc flashing...lin. ft.	165	.15	24.75
Hip and ridge covering zinc "	115	.10	11.50
Total for Slating (including labor)			$237.95
PLUMBING.			
Lin. ft., 4-in. cast iron pipe	40	.18	$ 7.20
" 2-in. "	90	.12	10.80
Lead pipe for water and waste service...lbs.	1,580	.06	94.80
Lead traps	7	.75	5.25
Finished brass cocks	8	.75	6.00
Rough stop cocks	1		.60
Plated bath cocks	2	1.50	3.00
" basin "	6	1.00	6.00
" butler's pantry cocks	2	2.00	4.00
Sets brass strainer, plug and chain	3	.50	1.50
Sets plated strainer, plug and chain and stay	4	.75	3.00
Sink in kitchen, galv. iron	1		2.50
Sink in butler's pantry, galv. iron	1		2.50
Kitchen boiler and standard, couplings, etc., complete, galv. iron, 40 gall	1		14.00
Marbled overflow basin	3	1.50	4.50
Marble slab, back and sides...sq. ft.	31	.80	24.80
Bath tub, 16 oz. copper	1		14.00
Water closet, porcelain, with cistern, etc	1		25.00
Lead safes...lbs.	111	.06	6.66
Gas pipe, varying sizes	400	.04½	18.00
Drops and fittings...lbs.	25	.13	3.25
Labor, plumbers, gas fitters and helpers			100.00
Total for Plumber's Materials & Labor			$357.36

	Quan.	Price.	Cost.
*PAINTING.			
856 Sq. yds. to paint 3 times, exterior work=	2,568	$ .07	$179.76
Sq. yds. to stain shingling	150	.07	10.50
28 Sq. yds. to paint 2 times brickwork=	56	.07	3.92
44 Sq. yds. to oil 2 times, ceiling=	88	.05	4.40
Sq. yds. to stain and finish in hard oil inside	575	.20	115.00
Lbs. putty	73	.03	2.19
Total of Painter's Materials (including Labor)			$315.77
CARPENTER'S LABOR.			
Framing, raising and enclosing, exterior trimming, making and setting frames in exterior walls			635.00
Laying floors, setting minor partitions and grounds for plastering			115.00
Finishing veranda porch and balconies			75.00
Setting inside trim, hanging sash, doors and blinds, fixing hardware, and all carpenter's inside work not included above			390.00
Total Carpenter's Labor			$1215.00

RECAPITULATION.

Mason's materials and labor	$1,338.59
Carpenter's materials	1,851.03
Hardware	174.56
Tinning—Materials and labor	47.36
Slating— " " "	237.95
Plumbing— " " "	357.36
Painting— " " "	315.77
Carpenter's labor	1,215.00
Cost of House	$5,537.62
Add cost of Working Plans, Specifications, &c., 1 per cent	$55.37
Add extras (if any)	

ABOUT HEATING AND VENTILATING

IN the August number of this publication Mr. Wingate contributed many valuable hints on these subjects, describing particularly the proper management of stoves. However long a magazine article may be, there will be many things left unwritten, as these subjects would require a volume to present them fully. As health and comfort depend on proper heating and ventilating, we feel that they cannot be discussed too often.

Proper ventilation goes with heating necessarily. The air in the rooms must be kept in circulation and renewed constantly. There is no better ventilator than an open fireplace, with a fire. This will carry away the colder air lying near the floor, and keep the purer and warmer upper air circulating. Even though there is no fire in the fireplace there will be enough draught up the chimney to be of great aid in ventilating and keeping an equable temperature.

If there be no fireplace in the room there should be a register in the wall near the floor, connected with a flue in the chimney or with a tin pipe going up to the top of the house and through the roof. A register near the ceiling is desirable also, in order that the room may be cooled, when too warm, without creating draughts. The room will be much cooler in summer if such escape is provided for the hot air. The opening of windows or doors, in cold weather, to cool a room is a fruitful source of colds.

The ventilation of closets is something which is rarely done, even in costly and well built dwellings. Yet it can be done at trifling expense by means of an ordinary tin heater pipe carried to the roof or to some ventilating flue, and having its aperture near the ceiling of the closet. Closets are generally hot, stuffy and ill-smelling. A tin pipe of six inches diameter costs about twelve cents per foot; the trouble of placing it does not amount to anything worth speaking of. Pantries, or closets where eatables are stored, and the bath room particularly, should be provided with such ventilators.

Heaters or furnaces placed in the cellar are now generally used for heating the house in cold weather, fireplaces alone being insufficient. These can be commended and in fact present the best solution of the heating problem, if they are of proper construction and are set and managed carefully. The cheap heaters are made principally of cast iron; this is objectionable because when heated to a high degree cast iron will allow carbonic oxide to pass through it. This deadly gas, passing from the fire chamber into the air chamber vitiates the air supplying the rooms with heat. The heater should have a steel radiator, through which no gases will pass. It should have a supply of fresh air from outside of the house, conveyed through a tight wood box carried along the cellar ceiling.

Any system of heating which does not supply constantly fresh warm air, is objectionable. Particular care should be taken to have the cellar warm and well ventilated. To this end it is well to have a flue in one of the chimneys, opening near the cellar floor, for ventilating the cellar. This will help also to keep the cellar air dry as the air carried away by the flue will be replaced by fresh air, drawn in from outside. There should be a number of large windows, particularly on the South or warmest side.

An excellent automatic appliance is manufactured to regulate the temperature in a house and keep it at one point.

THE KITCHEN AND SERVANTS' HALL

The space allowed for the kitchen should be ample, but it should be divided up into a Mixing Pantry and a Cook Room. In the former, away from the heat, all the food should be prepared for cooking; in the latter the actual cooking should be done. The reason is evident, it confines the heat to one small room, which need not be hotter because it is smaller than the usual kitchen. Another room of fair size should join the kitchen—a Servants' Hall, where the servants can dine, sit and receive their company. This room may contain the ironing table and even, perhaps, the laundry tubs, but its particular purpose should be to provide for the comfort of the servants.

When the walls of the rooms are to be papered, or tinted in flat color, it is better not to put on the common hard or plaster Paris, finish. The second or brown coat, if brought to an even surface will give an excellent ground for either tinting or paper.

If the intention is to tint the walls there should be a little cement in the mortar to make it set harder, so that it will not be easily injured by anything that may be brought in contact with it.

The omission of the white coat effects a saving of from five to ten cents per square yard.

The recent great advancement in electric science seems to indicate that at a not far distant date electricity will largely supersede gas and oil for illuminating purposes. For this reason it is wise, when building a house for residence, to put in wires which may be used for electric lighting at a future time. The expense of putting them in when building is trifling. They should follow the lines of the gas pipes.

233

THE CO-OPERATIVE BUILDING PLAN ASSOCIATION, ARCHITECTS, 63 BROADWAY, NEW YORK.

*Shoppell's Modern Houses—*Designs Patented.*   *Store and Office Building, Design No. 604*

DESCRIPTION.

For explanation of all symbols (* † etc.) see page 42.

GENERAL DIMENSIONS: Front, 33 ft.; depth over all, 44 ft. 8 in. Heights of stories: Cellar, 7 ft. 2 in.; first story, 11 ft.; second story, 9 ft. 6 in.; third story, 9 ft.

EXTERIOR MATERIALS: Foundations, brick; first, second and third stories, brick, stone and iron; roof, tin. Show windows and all front entrance doors glazed with French plate glass; all other windows with double thick sheet glass. All rear windows provided with solid shutters.

INTERIOR FINISH: Hard white plaster and white wood trim throughout. Interior wood-work stained to suit owner and finished in hard oil. All flooring hard wood. Stairways and front entrance doors, oak. Building piped for gas. k

COLORS: Stone-work of front and brick-wor_ of rear cleaned at completion with acid. Wood work of store fronts and the wood-work of entrances to basement and second story painted dark green. Galvanized iron work in first and second stories, main cornice, and ornamental iron work surmounting front to be painted seal brown. All panels and other sunken work, light brown; all raised work, dark brown. Transoms in first story and all other sashes throughout the building painted Pompeian red. Iron railings of entrances to basement and second story painted black and picked out sparingly with gilding.

ACCOMMODATIONS: The principal rooms and their sizes, vaults, etc., are shown by the plans. Basement or cellar extends under the entire building. Brick-work of vaults extends from foundation up, and is double, with ventilated air space. Show windows are large and attractive. Bay windows in second and third stories add to the appearance of the front and increase the sizes of rooms. Two hard wood mantels are included in the estimate. All the main offices may be heated by stoves. Water-closets placed in basement and second story serve all tenants. Third story has the same general arrangement as the second, except that the private offices are omitted, the space thus gained being equally divided among the other rooms.

COST: $6,000, † not including heating apparatus. The estimate is based on ‡ New York prices for materials and labor. In many sections of the country the cost should be less.

Price for working plans, specifications and * license to build, - - - - $60.00
Price for †† bill of materials, - - 15.00

Address, THE CO-OPERATIVE BUILDING PLAN ASSOCIATION, Architects, 63 Broadway, New York.

FEASIBLE MODIFICATIONS: Heights of ceilings, sizes of rooms, colors and materials may be changed. Fireplaces may be omitted, and if heated by steam or hot water the number of chimneys may be reduced. The offices may be rearranged. Vaults and front entrances to basement may be omitted.

FRONT ELEVATION.

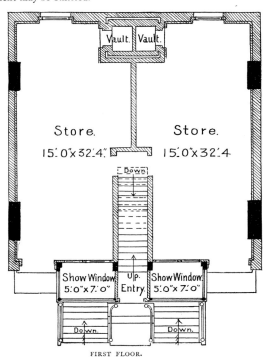

FIRST FLOOR.

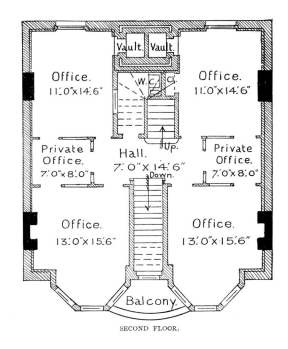

SECOND FLOOR.

Shoppell's Modern Houses—*Designs Patented. Residence, Design No. 653

PERSPECTIVE.

DESCRIPTION.

For explanation of all symbols (* † etc.) see page 42.

GENERAL DIMENSIONS: Width, 41 ft. 10 in.; depth, 56 ft. Heights of stories: Cellar, 7 ft.; first story, 10 ft. 6 in.; second story, 10 ft.

EXTERIOR MATERIALS: Foundations, stone; first story, clapboards; second story, clapboards and shingles; roof, shingles.

INTERIOR FINISH: Two-coat plaster for wall paper throughout. Plaster cornices in parlor, sitting room, dining room and main hall. Yellow pine flooring in kitchen, rear halls, pantry and bath-room; all other flooring of first and second stories, white pine; attic flooring, spruce. Walnut trim in parlor and main hall; remainder of main house, oak trim and walnut mouldings. All rooms, etc., both stories, of the kitchen extension, yellow pine trim. The main stairs have ash treads and risers, and oak newels, rails and balusters. Front and vestibule doors, oak. Bath-room and kitchen wainscoted. All interior wood work finished in hard oil.

COLORS: Clapboards of first story, and all gable panels and shingles, dark olive drab. Trim, rain conductors, and bars of panels, chocolate. Outside doors finished natural color and varnished. Blinds, dark green. Sashes, Pompeian red. Brick work, Venetian red. Veranda floor and ceiling, oiled. Clapboards and shingles of second story painted Indian red. Roof shingles dipped in yellowish red stain.

ACCOMMODATIONS: The principal rooms and their sizes, closets, etc., are shown by the plans. Cellar, with concrete floor, under the kitchen extension. Attic is floored but not finished—space for four rooms. Dining room, kitchen, rear hall and laundry have independent outside entrances.

COST: $6000, †not including mantels, range and heater. The estimate is based on ‡New York prices for materials and labor. In many sections of the country the cost should be less.

Price for working plans, specifications and *license
    to build, - - - - - - - - $60.00
Price for †† bill of materials, - - - - - 15.00

Address, THE CO-OPERATIVE BUILDING PLAN ASSOCIATION, Architects, 63 Broadway, New York.

FEASIBLE MODIFICATIONS: Heights of stories, sizes of rooms, materials and colors, all may be changed. Cellar may be extended under whole house. By a slight re-arrangement a small bed-room may be planned at front of second story, or one of the present bed-rooms may be enlarged.

The price of working plans, specifications, etc. for a modified design varies according to the alterations required, and will be made known upon application to the Architects.

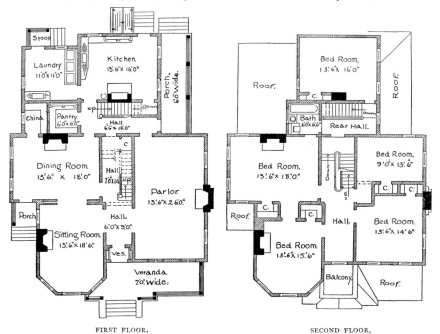

FIRST FLOOR.   SECOND FLOOR.

235

THE CO-OPERATIVE BUILDING PLAN ASSOCIATION, ARCHITECTS, 63 BROADWAY, NEW YORK.

Shoppell's Modern Houses—*Designs Patented.　　　　　　　*Residence, Design No. 651*

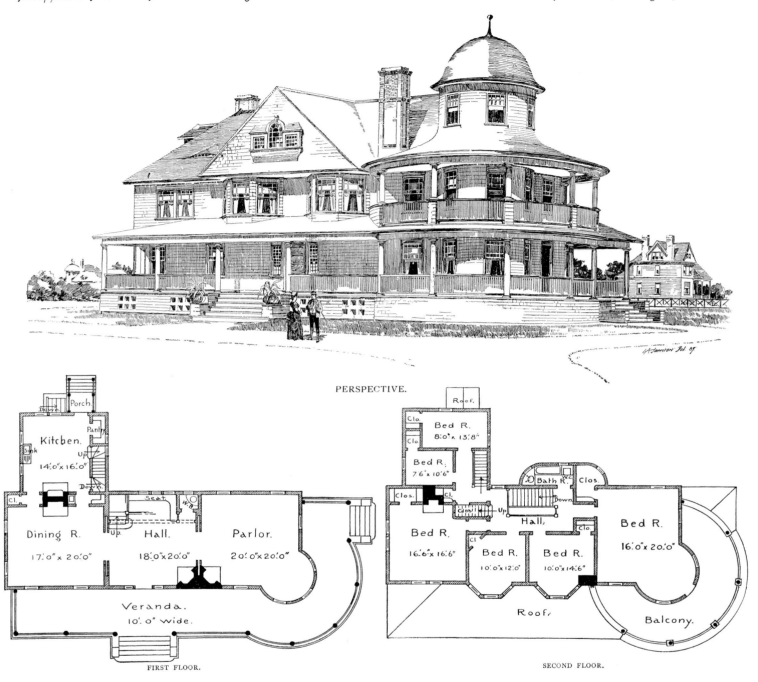

PERSPECTIVE.

FIRST FLOOR.

SECOND FLOOR.

DESCRIPTION.

For explanation of all symbols (* † etc.) see page 42.

GENERAL DIMENSIONS: Front width, over all, 71 ft.; depth, 47 ft. 6 in. Heights of stories: Cellar, 6 ft. 6 in.; first story, 10 ft.; second story, 9 ft.; attic, 8 ft.

EXTERIOR MATERIALS: Foundation, brick; first story, clapboards; second story, gables, tower and roof, shingles. All windows to have outside blinds except those of the cellar and bath-room and those at back of main hall.

INTERIOR FINISH: Walls and ceiling of dining room covered with matting. Walls of hall covered with hard wood. Ceilings of hall and parlor show open timber work. All other walls and ceilings finished with two coats of plaster. Cellar ceiling has one rough coat whitewashed. Double floors in first and second stories. Floors of kitchen, bath-room and hall (first story) of hard pine; all other floors, soft pine. Trim of kitchen and hall (first story) yellow pine; trim elsewhere, soft woods. Main stairs and seat in hall, yellow pine. Walls of kitchen and bath-room, wainscoted. All interior wood work finished in hard oil.

COLORS: All clapboards and blinds Colonial yellow. Trim and sashes, white. Veranda floor and ceiling, brick work and all shingling, oiled.

ACCOMMODATIONS: The principal rooms and their sizes, closets, etc. are shown by the plans. Besides these there is a cellar extending under the kitchen and part of dining room, and there are three rooms and a hall in the attic.

COST: $6000, † not including mantels, range and heater. The estimate is based on ‡ New York prices for materials and labor. In many sections of the country the cost should be less.

Price for working plans, specifications and * license to-build, - $60.00
Price for †† bill of materials, - - - - - 15.00

Address, THE CO-OPERATIVE BUILDING PLAN ASSOCIATION, Architects, 63 Broadway, New York.

FEASIBLE MODIFICATIONS: Heights of stories and colors may be changed. Tower and balcony may be omitted and the extent of veranda reduced. Parlor and hall fire-places and chimney may be omitted. Bath-room may be moved to the smaller rear bed-room. Attic finish may be omitted. All walls and ceilings may be plastered. Woods for interior finish may be changed. Cellar may be enlarged.

The price of working plans, specifications, etc. for a modified design varies according to the alterations required, and will be made known upon application to the Architects.

236

THE CO-OPERATIVE BUILDING PLAN ASSOCIATION, ARCHITECTS, 63 BROADWAY, NEW YORK.

*Shoppell's Modern Houses—*Designs Patented.*   *Cottage, Design No. 541*

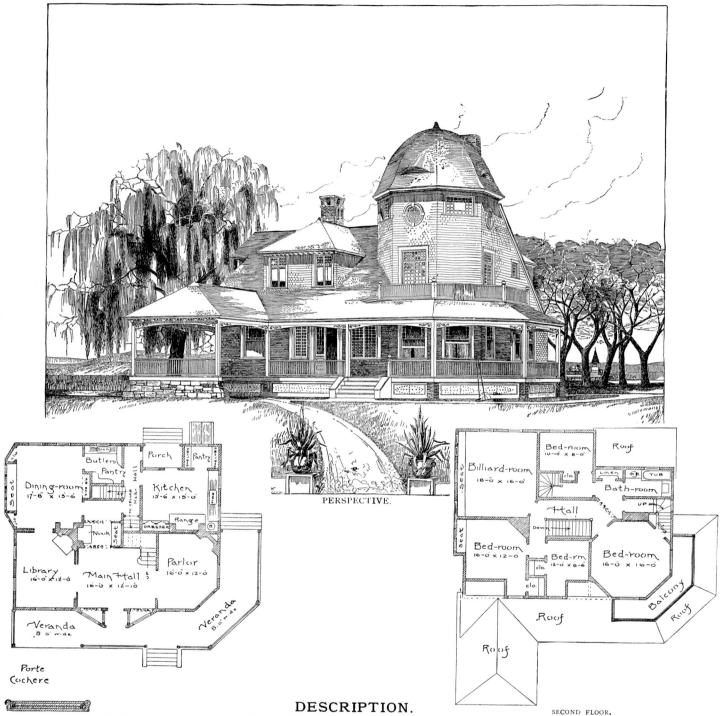

PERSPECTIVE.

FIRST FLOOR.

SECOND FLOOR.

DESCRIPTION.

For explanation of all symbols (* † etc.) see page 42.

GENERAL DIMENSIONS: Extreme width, including veranda and dining room bay, 52 ft. 4 in.; depth, including veranda, 43 ft. 6 in. Heights of stories: Cellar, 7 ft.; first story, 10 ft.; second story, 9 ft.; attic, 8 ft. 6 in.

EXTERIOR MATERIALS: Foundations, stone and brick; first and second stories and roof, shingles. Outside blinds.

INTERIOR FINISH: Plastered for papering. Double floors in first story and billiard room, finishing with oak; all other floors soft wood. Cherry trim in hall, parlor and library; oak in dining room; remainder of the house in soft wood, trim stained to suit owner. All wood-work finished in hard oil. Staircase, cherry. wainscot in bath-room and kitchen. Front and vestibule doors, cherry.

COLORS: All wall shingles dipped and brush coated light yellow. Trim, cornices, veranda posts, rails and balusters, white. Front doors finished in hard oil; other outside doors and blinds, white with yellow panels and slats. Sashes, dark red. Veranda floor and ceiling oiled. Brick-work painted red. Roof shingles dipped and brush coated silver stain.

ACCOMMODATIONS: The principal rooms and their sizes, closets, etc., are shown by the plans. Cellar under whole house. Studio in

tower. Air space over second story floored for storage. Laundry and servant's water-closet in basement. Seat and fireplace nook under main stairs. Fireplaces in parlor, hall, library and dining room.

COST: $6,000, † not including mantels, range and heater. The estimate is based on ‡ New York prices for materials and labor. In many sections of the country the cost should be less.

Price for working plans, specifications and * license to build, - - - - - - - - - - - - - $60.00
Price for † † bill of materials, - - - - - 15.00
Address, THE CO-OPERATIVE BUILDING PLAN ASSOCIATION, Architects, 63 Broadway, New York.

FEASIBLE MODIFICATIONS: Heights of stories, colors, sizes of rooms and kinds of materials may be changed. Cellar may be reduced in size and concrete floor omitted. A number of fireplaces and mantels, sliding doors, part or all of plumbing, balcony, porte-cochere and part of veranda may be omitted.

The price of working plans, specifications, etc., for a modified design varies according to the alterations required, and will be made known upon application to the Architects.

237

THE CO-OPERATIVE BUILDING PLAN ASSOCIATION, ARCHITECTS, 63 BROADWAY, NEW YORK.

*Shoppell's Modern Houses—*Designs Patented.*   *Residence, Design No. 603*

PERSPECTIVE.

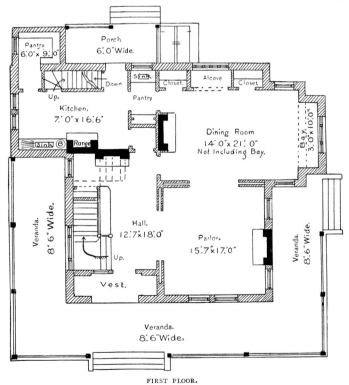

FIRST FLOOR.

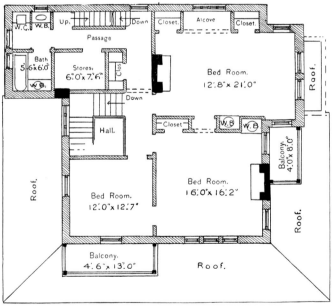

SECOND FLOOR.

DESCRIPTION.

For explanation of all symbols (* † etc.) see page 42.

GENERAL DIMENSIONS: Width, including veranda, 48 ft.; depth, including veranda and porch, 51 ft. 6 in. Heights of stories: Cellar, 7 ft. 6 in.; first story, 12 ft.; second story, 11 ft.

EXTERIOR MATERIALS: Foundations, stone and brick; first and second stories, brick. Veranda, balconies, attic story and roof, shingles.

INTERIOR FINISH: Hard white plaster throughout; plaster cornices and centers in parlor, dining room, halls, vestibule and three principal bedrooms. Trim throughout, white wood. Main stairway, oak. Five hard wood mantels included in estimate. All interior wood-work finished in hard oil.

ACCOMMODATIONS: The principal rooms and their sizes, closets, etc., are shown by the plans. Cellar under dining room and kitchen. Alcove in dining room for sideboard. Seat in hall and closet under main stairs.

COST: $6,000, † not including range and heater. The estimate is based on ‡ New York prices for materials and labor. In many sections of the country the cost should be less.

Price for working plans, specifications, and * license to build, - - - - - - - - - - - - - $60.00
Price for † † bill of materials, - - - - - - 15.00

Address, THE CO-OPERATIVE BUILDING PLAN ASSOCIATION, Architects, 63 Broadway New York.

FEASIBLE MODIFICATIONS: Heights of ceilings, sizes of rooms, kinds of material and colors may be changed. Balconies may be omitted. Size of veranda may be reduced. Cellar may extend under whole house. A part or all of the plumbing may be omitted. That part of second story over kitchen may be re-arranged to give another bedroom and still retain the bath-room. Number of mantels and fireplaces may be reduced.

238

THE CO-OPERATIVE BUILDING PLAN ASSOCIATION, ARCHITECTS, 63 BROADWAY, NEW YORK.

*Shoppell's Modern Houses—*Designs Patented.*   *Residence, Design No.* 355

PERSPECTIVE.

DESCRIPTION.

For explanation of all symbols (* † etc.) see page 42.

GENERAL DIMENSIONS: Extreme width, including verandas, 66 ft.; depth, including veranda, 56 ft. Heights of stories: Cellar, 7 ft.; first story, 10 ft. 6 in.; second story, 9 ft. 6 in.; attic, 8 ft. 6 in.

EXTERIOR MATERIALS: Foundation, brick; first story, clapboards; second story, gables, dormers and roofs, shingles. Outside blinds to all windows except those of the attic and dining room.

INTERIOR FINISH: Hard white plaster; plaster cornices and centers in hall, parlor, study, dining and sitting rooms. Soft wood flooring and trim. Ash staircase. Inside Venetian hard wood blinds in dining room. Panels under windows in hall, parlor, dining and sitting rooms and study. Bath-room and kitchen wainscoted. Interior wood-work finished in hard oil.

COLORS: All clapboards, yellow stone color. Trim, seal brown. Outside doors, blinds, sashes, rain conductors, veranda and balcony posts, rails, balusters, etc., maroon. Veranda floor, gray. Veranda ceiling, cream color. Wall shingles dipped and brush coated sienna stain. Roof shingles dipped and brush coated dark red stain.

ACCOMMODATIONS: The principal rooms and their sizes, closets, etc., are shown by the plans. Cellar under whole house. Two rooms and ample storage space in attic. Verandas 9 feet wide. Five open fireplaces and mantels, and kitchen range, included in estimate. Sliding doors connect parlor and hall.

COST: $6,107, † not including heater. The estimate is based on ‡ New York prices for materials and labor. In many sections of the country the cost should be less.

Price for working plans, specifications and * license to build, - - - - - - - - - - $50.00
Price for †† bill of materials, - - - - - 10.00
Address, THE CO-OPERATIVE BUILDING PLAN ASSOCIATION, Architects, 63 Broadway, New York.

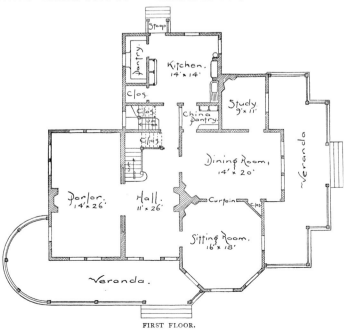

FIRST FLOOR.

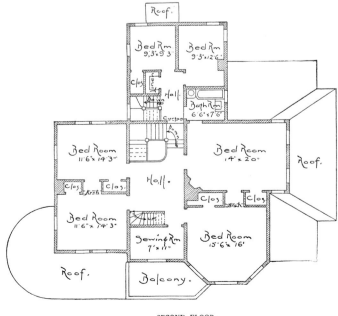

SECOND FLOOR.

Shoppell's Modern Houses—*Designs Patented.   *Residence, Design No. 359*

PERSPECTIVE.

DESCRIPTION.

For explanation of all symbols (* † etc.) see page 42.

GENERAL DIMENSIONS: Extreme width, including veranda, 37 ft.; depth, including veranda, 48 ft. 6 in. Heights of stories: Cellar, 7 ft.; first story, 9 ft. 6 in.; second story, 9 ft.; attic, 8 ft.

EXTERIOR MATERIALS: Foundations, stone; first story, stone and clapboards; second story, brick and shingles; gables, panels and shingles; balconies, shingles; roofs, slate. Blinds to all windows except those of the cellar and attic.

INTERIOR FINISH: Hard white plaster. Plaster cornices in main hall of both stories, parlor, library, dining room and front bedroom. Soft wood flooring and trim. Ash stairs. Panels under windows in parlor, dining room and library. Wainscot in kitchen lobby, china closet, bath-room and kitchen. Interior wood-work finished in hard oil.

COLORS: All stone and brick-work cleaned down with acid. Brick-work oiled. Clapboards, chocolate. Trim, outside doors, blinds and sashes, maroon. Veranda floor oiled. Veranda ceiling varnished. Rain conductors, dark green. All shingles oiled.

ACCOMMODATIONS: The principal rooms and their sizes, closets, etc., are shown by the plans. Cellar under whole house. Laundry under kitchen. Three rooms finished in attic. Four open fireplaces with mantels, also kitchen range, included in estimate. Sliding doors connect principal rooms and hall. Servant's water-closet off kitchen entry. China closet connects kitchen and dining room. Hat and coat closet under main stairs. Sewing room in second story.

COST: $6,286, † not including heater. The estimate is based on ‡ New York prices for materials and labor. In many sections of the country the cost should be less.

Price for working plans, specifications and * license to build, - $65.00
Price for †† bill of materials, 10.00

Address, THE CO-OPERATIVE BUILDING PLAN ASSOCIATION, Architects, 63 Broadway, New York.

FEASIBLE MODIFICATIONS; Heights of stories, colors, sizes of rooms and kinds of materials may be changed. Size of cellar may be reduced. Balconies may be enclosed or omitted. Any or all fireplaces and mantels, part or all of plumbing, and sliding doors, may be omitted. Dressing room may be enlarged to form small bedroom. Water-closet may be retained in second story, and bath-room placed in attic.

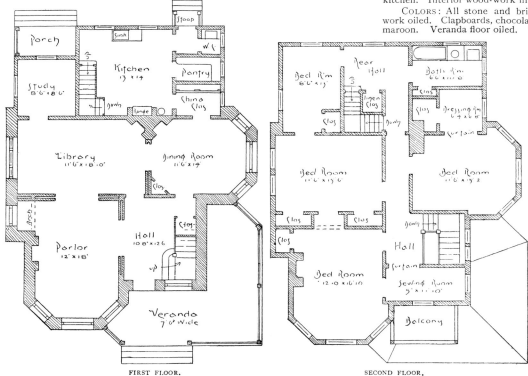

FIRST FLOOR.   SECOND FLOOR.

240

THE CO-OPERATIVE BUILDING PLAN ASSOCIATION, ARCHITECTS, 63 BROADWAY, NEW YORK.

Shoppell's Modern Houses—*Designs Patented.   *Residence, Design No. 506*

PERSPECTIVE.

Side Elevation.

DESCRIPTION.

For explanation of all symbols (* † etc.) see page 42.

GENERAL DIMENSIONS: Width, 43 ft.; depth, including veranda, 64 ft. Heights of stories: Cellar, 7 ft. 6 in.; first story, 11 ft.; second story, 10 ft.; attic, 8 ft. 6 in.

EXTERIOR MATERIALS: Foundations, stone; first story, clapboards; second story, shingles and clapboards; gables, panels; roof, shingles. Outside blinds to all windows except those of the cellar, attic, main staircase, parlor, dining room and library.

INTERIOR FINISH: Hard white plaster; plaster cornices and centers in parlor, dining room, library, vestibule and halls, and three bedrooms. Double floor in first story, finishing with hard pine in butler's pantry, bath-room and kitchen; finishing floor elsewhere, soft wood. Soft wood trim. Ash stairs. Panels under windows in parlor, library and dining room. Wainscot in bath-room and kitchen. Interior wood-work finished in hard oil.

COLORS: Clapboards, very light drab. Trim, light chocolate. Outside doors, maroon with chocolate panels. Blinds, sashes and rain conductors, maroon. Veranda floor, cream color. Veranda ceiling oiled. All shingles dipped and brush coated reddish stain.

ACCOMMODATIONS: The principal rooms and their sizes, closets, etc., are shown by the plans. Cellar under the whole house. Five bedrooms and trunk room in attic. Sliding doors connect hall and principal rooms of first story. Five open fireplaces, with hard wood mantels and set range in kitchen, included in estimate.

COST: $6,353, † not including heater. The estimate is based on ‡ New York prices for materials and labor. In many sections of the country the cost should be less.

Price for working plans, specifications
and * license to build,   -   -   -   - $52.00
Price for † † bill of materials,   -   -   10.00

Address, THE CO-OPERATIVE BUILDING PLAN ASSOCIATION, Architects, 63 Broadway, New York.

FEASIBLE MODIFICATIONS: Heights of stories, colors, sizes of rooms and kinds of materials may be changed. Part or all of plumbing, any or all fireplaces and mantels, and sliding doors, may be omitted. Veranda may be extended indefinitely.

The price of working plans, specifications, etc., for a modified design varies according to the alterations required, and will be made known upon application to the Architects.

FIRST FLOOR.   SECOND FLOOR

241

THE CO-OPERATIVE BUILDING PLAN ASSOCIATION, ARCHITECTS, 63 BROADWAY, NEW YORK.

*Shoppell's Modern Houses—*Designs Patented.*   *Residence, Design No. 654*

PERSPECTIVE.

DESCRIPTION.

For explanation of all symbols (* † etc.) see page 42.

GENERAL DIMENSIONS: Width, including veranda, 39 ft. 9 in.; depth, including veranda, 62 ft. 6 in. Heights of stories: Cellar, 7 ft.; first story, 10 ft.; second story, main house, 9 ft.; extension, 8 ft.

EXTERIOR MATERIALS: Foundations, stone; first and second stories and rear gable, brick veneer; side gable and roofs, shingles.

INTERIOR FINISH: Hard white plaster throughout. Oak flooring and trim in reception hall, yellow pine in dining room, and all other flooring and trim, white pine. Oak stairway. Oak ceiling, imitating open timber work in reception hall. Dining room, reception hall and stairway, bath-room, kitchen, butler's and other pantry and store-room, are all wainscoted to match trim. All soft woods painted, grained and varnished. All hard wood trim finished in hard oil. All hard wood floors polished.

COLORS: All brick work cleaned with acid. All roof shingles dipped in a blue-stone shade of paint. Trim, rain conductors and blinds, painted bronze green. Sashes and window frames, maroon. Veranda floors, dark olive drab; veranda ceilings, blue-stone shade.

ACCOMMODATIONS: The principal rooms and their sizes, closets, etc. are shown by the plans. There is a cellar with concrete floor, under the whole house. The attic is floored but not finished; there is space for four rooms and storage. Hinged sash windows opening upon verandas from parlor, dining room and library. Scullery and laundry combined. Stained glass in hall windows.

COST: $6500, † not including mantels, range and heater. The estimate is based on ‡ New York prices for materials and labor. In many sections of the country the cost should be less.

Price for working plans, specifications and * license
to build. - - - - - - $65.00
Price for †† bill of materials, - - - - 15.00

Address, THE CO-OPERATIVE BUILDING PLAN ASSOCIATION, Architects, 63 Broadway, New York.

FEASIBLE MODIFICATIONS: Heights of stories, sizes of rooms, exterior materials, interior finish and colors may all be changed. Fireplaces, sliding doors, stained glass and seats in halls may be omitted. Laundry may be placed in cellar. Dining room and library may be transposed, re-planning butler's pantry to suit. Another bed-room may be planned on the second floor where the dressing room and sewing room are shown.

The price of working plans, specifications, etc. for a modified design varies according to the alterations required, and will be made known upon application to the Architects.

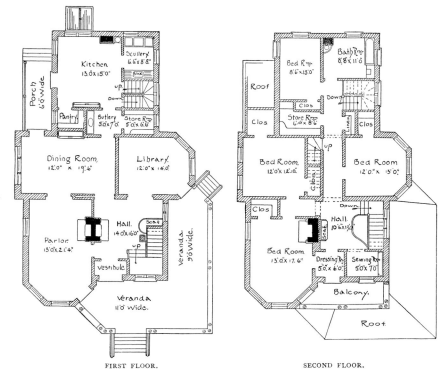

FIRST FLOOR.   SECOND FLOOR.

THE CO-OPERATIVE BUILDING PLAN ASSOCIATION, ARCHITECTS, 63 BROADWAY, NEW YORK.

Shoppell's Modern Houses—*Designs Patented.　　　　　*Residence, Design No. 562*

PERSPECTIVE.

DESCRIPTION.

For explanation of all symbols (* † etc.) see page 42.

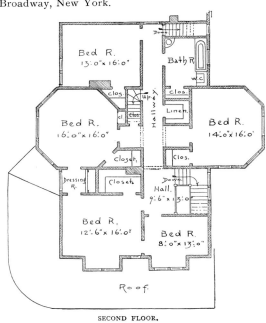

GENERAL DIMENSIONS: Width over all, 51 ft. 6 in.; depth, including veranda, 70 ft. 6 in. Heights of stories: Cellar, 6 ft. 6 in.; first story, 9 ft. 6 in.; second story, 9 ft.; attic, 7 ft. 6 in.

EXTERIOR MATERIALS: Foundations, stone; first story, clapboards; second story, tower, gables and roof, shingles. Outside blinds.

INTERIOR FINISH: Hard white plaster; plaster cornices and centers in parlor, dining and sitting room and octagonal bedroom. Hard pine flooring in kitchen, laundry, pantries and bath-room; soft wood flooring in all other rooms. Oak trim in first story hall; yellow pine trim in laundry, pantries, kitchen and bath-room; all other trim, soft wood, stained to suit owner. Chair rail in dining room. Staircase, oak. Wainscot in bath-room and kitchen. Front and vestibule doors, oak. Interior wood-work finished in hard oil.

ACCOMMODATIONS: The principal rooms and their sizes, closets, etc., are shown by the plans. Cellar under rear part of house, with inside and outside entrances and concrete floor. One room and hall in attic. Open fireplaces in parlor and sitting room. Large closets throughout house.

COST: $6,500, † not including mantels, range and heater. The estimate is based on ‡ New York prices for materials and labor. In many sections of the country the cost should be less.

Price for working plans, specifications and * license to build, - - - - - - - - - - - - $45.00
Price for † † bill of materials, - - - - - - 15.00

Address, THE CO-OPERATIVE BUILDING PLAN ASSOCIATION, Architects, 63 Broadway, New York.

FIRST FLOOR.

SECOND FLOOR.

243

THE CO-OPERATIVE BUILDING PLAN ASSOCIATION, ARCHITECTS, 63 BROADWAY, NEW YORK.

*Shoppell's Modern Houses—*Designs Patented.*   *Residence, Design No. 564*

PHOTOGRAPHIC VIEW.

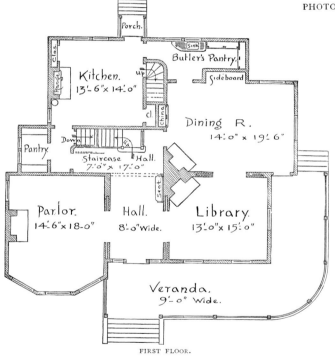

FIRST FLOOR.

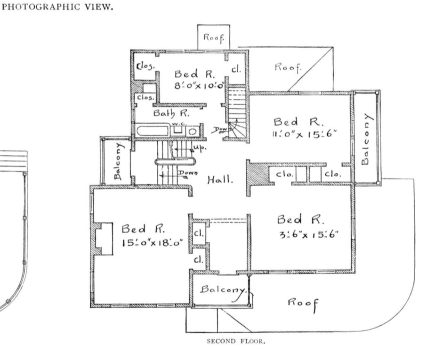

SECOND FLOOR.

DESCRIPTION.

GENERAL DIMENSIONS: Width, including veranda, 49 ft. 6 in.; depth, including veranda, 44 ft. 6 in. Heights of stories: Cellar, 7 ft.; first story, 9 ft. 6 in.; second story, 9 ft.; attic, 8 ft. 6 in.

EXTERIOR MATERIALS: Foundation, stone and brick; first story, clapboards; second story, gables, dormers and roof, shingles. Cellar windows have solid shutters; outside blinds to all other windows.

INTERIOR FINISH: Hard white plaster; plaster cornices and centers in parlor, library, dining room and hall. Hard pine flooring in first story and bath-room; soft wood flooring elsewhere. Cherry trim in parlor; ash trim in hall and library; oak trim in dining room; soft wood trim elsewhere. Ash staircase. Interior wood-work finished in hard oil. Panels under windows in parlor, library and dining room. Picture molding in principal rooms and hall of first story. Chair rail in dining room. Wainscot in bath-room and kitchen.

COLORS: All clapboards, light brown. Trim and rain conductors, brown. Front doors finished in hard oil; other outside doors and blinds, and veranda floor, dark brown. Sashes, dark green. Veranda ceiling varnished. Wall shingles dipped and brush coated golden brown. Roof shingles dipped and brush coated dark red stain.

ACCOMMODATIONS: The principal rooms and their sizes, closets, etc., are shown by the plans. Cellar under whole house. One room and hall finished in attic. Four open fireplaces with mantels, and range in kitchen, included in estimate. Sliding doors connect parlor, hall, library and dining room. Handsome staircase in semi-detached hall.

COST: $6,500, † not including heater. The estimate is based on ‡ New York prices for materials and labor. In many sections of the country the cost should be less.

Price for working plans, specifications and * license to build, - - - - - - - - - $75.00

Price for † † bill of materials, - - - - - - 15.00

Address, THE CO-OPERATIVE BUILDING PLAN ASSOCIATION, Architects, 63 Broadway, New York.

FEASIBLE MODIFICATIONS: Heights of stories, colors, sizes of rooms and kinds of materials may be changed. Attic may be left unfinished. Sliding doors, open fireplaces and mantels, set range, balconies and a part or all of plumbing may be omitted. The balcony over front entrance may be enclosed with glass, or another bedroom may be planned to occupy balcony space and a part of the hall.

244

THE CO-OPERATIVE BUILDING PLAN ASSOCIATION, ARCHITECTS, 63 BROADWAY, NEW YORK.

*Shoppell's Modern Houses—*Designs Patented.*   *Residence, Design No. 507*

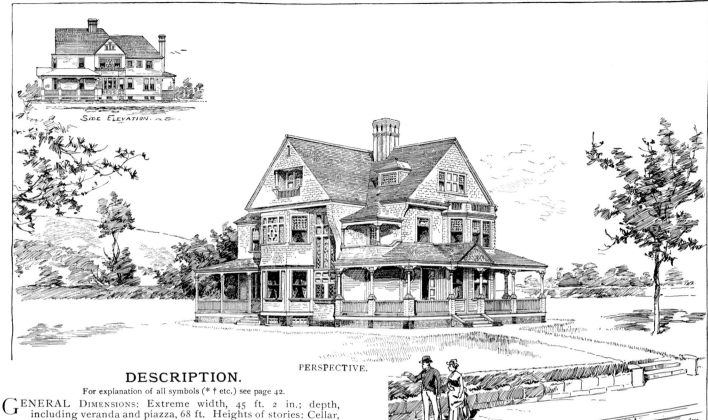

SIDE ELEVATION.

PERSPECTIVE.

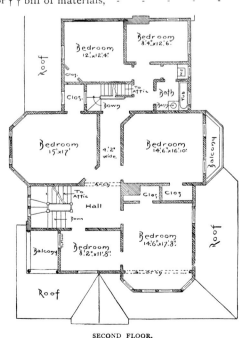

DESCRIPTION.

For explanation of all symbols (* † etc.) see page 42.

GENERAL DIMENSIONS: Extreme width, 45 ft. 2 in.; depth, including veranda and piazza, 68 ft. Heights of stories: Cellar, 7 ft. 6 in.; first story, 10 ft.; second story, 9 ft. 6 in.; attic, 8 ft.

EXTERIOR MATERIALS: Foundations, stone; first story, clapboards; second story, gables, dormers and roof, shingles. Outside blinds.

INTERIOR FINISH: Hard white plaster. Plaster cornices and centers in parlor, hall, sitting and dining room. Yellow pine flooring in bath-room, butler's pantry and kitchen; all other floors single and soft wood. Trim, soft wood. Stairs, ash. Panels under windows in parlor, sitting and dining room. Picture molding in principal rooms of first story. Chair rail in dining and sitting room. Wainscot in bath-room and kitchen. Interior wood-work finished in hard oil.

COLORS: Clapboards, seal brown. Trim, outside blinds, sashes and rain conductors, maroon. Outside doors, dark green. Veranda floor and ceiling, oiled. Brick-work, Indian red. Wall shingles, dipped and brush coated brownish stain. Gable shingles dipped and brush coated dark red stain. Roof shingles dipped and brush coated Indian red.

ACCOMMODATIONS: The principal rooms and their sizes, closets, etc., are shown by the plans. Cellar under whole house, with inside and outside entrance and concrete floor. Hall and two rooms in attic. Four open fireplaces and six mantels, also set range in kitchen, included in estimate. Large hall. Handsome staircase, with office under same large enough for desk. Hat and coat closet in hall.

COST: $6,615, † not including heater. The estimate is based on ‡ New York prices for materials and labor. In many sections of the country the cost should be less.

Price for working plans, specifications and * license to build, - - - - - - - - - - - - - $58.00
Price for † † bill of materials, - - - - - - 10.00

Piazza 7 wide

Piazza 7 wide

Dresser

Kitchen 12'4"x23'

Sink

Lobby

Down up

Clos. Clos.

Pantry

Sitting Room 14'6"x21'2"

Dining Room 14'6"x20'

up

Office 5'6"x9'

Down

Hall 11'8"x12'8"

Parlor 14'x20'8"

Veranda 8 wide

Clos. Vestibule

Veranda 9 wide

FIRST FLOOR.

Roof

Bedroom 12'x12'4"

Bedroom 8'4"x12'6"

Clos.

Clos. Clos.

To Attic Bath Tub

Down

Bedroom 15'x17'

4'2" wide

Bedroom 14'6"x16'10"

Balcony

To Attic Hall

Clos. Clos.

Down

Balcony

Bedroom 8'2"x11'8"

Bedroom 14'6"x17'8"

Roof

Roof

SECOND FLOOR.

THE CO-OPERATIVE BUILDING PLAN ASSOCIATION, ARCHITECTS, 63 BROADWAY, NEW YORK.

*Shoppell's Modern Houses—*Designs Patented.*   *Double House, Design No. 488*

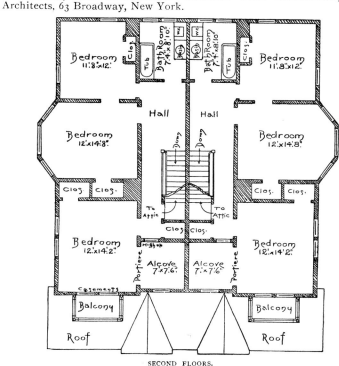

PERSPECTIVE.

DESCRIPTION.

For explanation of all symbols (* † etc.) see page 42.

GENERAL DIMENSIONS: Width through dining rooms, 45 ft. 10 in.; depth, including veranda and stoop, 55 ft. 2 in. Heights of stories: Cellar, 7 ft.; first story, 9 ft. 6 in.; second story, 8 ft. 6 in.; attic, 8 ft.

EXTERIOR MATERIALS: Foundations, stone; first story, clapboards; second story and roof, shingles; gables, panels and shingles. Outside blinds.

INTERIOR FINISH: Hard white plaster. Plaster centers in parlors, dining rooms and halls of first story and two bedrooms in each second story. Soft wood flooring, trim and stairs. Inside Venetian blinds in bay windows of parlors. Bath-rooms wainscoted. All interior wood-work finished in hard oil stained colors to suit owner.

COLORS: All clapboards, seal brown. Trim, outside doors, blinds and veranda floor, maroon. Sashes and rain conductors, bronze green. Brick-work, Indian red. Gable panels, seal brown with maroon frames. Wall shingles dipped and brush coated sienna stain. Roof shingles dipped and brush coated Indian red.

ACCOMMODATIONS: The principal rooms and their sizes, closets, etc., are shown by the plans. Cellar under whole building. Three rooms in each attic; over each attic a large loft in which other rooms may be finished. Fireplaces and mantels in each parlor included in estimate.

COST: $6,767, † not including heater and range. The estimate is based on ‡ New York prices for materials and labor.

Price for working plans, specifications and * license to build, - - - - - - - - - $70.00
Price for † † bill of materials, - - - - - 10.00
Address, THE CO-OPERATIVE BUILDING PLAN ASSOCIATION, Architects, 63 Broadway, New York.

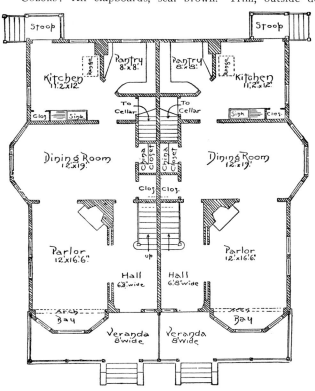

FIRST FLOORS.

SECOND FLOORS.

246

THE CO-OPERATIVE BUILDING PLAN ASSOCIATION, ARCHITECTS, 63 BROADWAY, NEW YORK.

*Shoppell's Modern Houses—*Designs Patented.*

Residence, Design No. 600

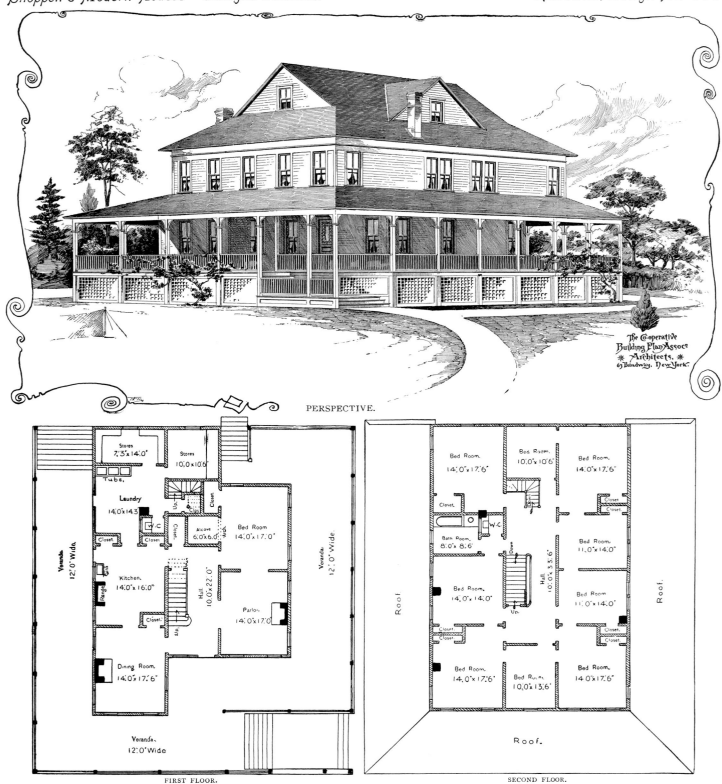

PERSPECTIVE.

FIRST FLOOR.

SECOND FLOOR.

DESCRIPTION.

For explanation of all symbols (* † etc.) see page 42.

GENERAL DIMENSIONS: Width, 64 ft., including verandas; depth, 71 ft. 6 in., including veranda. Heights of stories: Cellar, 7 ft.; first story, 10 ft.; second story, 9 ft.

EXTERIOR MATERIALS: Foundation, brick; first and second stories, clapboards; roofs, tin. Outside blinds to all windows.

INTERIOR FINISH: Hard white plaster. White pine trim and flooring. Main staircase, ash. All finished in hard oil. Bath-room and kitchen wainscoted.

COLORS: Clapboards, trim, outside doors, sashes, veranda floor and rain conductors, white. Blinds, green. Veranda ceiling, blue. Roofs, dark red.

ACCOMMODATIONS: The principal rooms and their sizes, closets, etc., are shown by the plans. Cellar, 13 ft. x 40 ft. under kitchen portion; remainder of house on brick piers. Fireplaces in parlor and dining room. Very wide and ample verandas. Attic floored, but unfinished; space for five or six rooms.

COST: $6,800, † not including mantels, range and heater. The estimate is based on ‡ New York prices for materials and labor. In many sections of the country the cost should be less.

Price for working plans, specifications and * license to build, - - - - - - - - - - - $70.00
Price for †† bill of materials, - - - - - - - 15.00
Address, THE CO-OPERATIVE BUILDING PLAN ASSOCIATION, Architects, 63 Broadway, New York.

FEASIBLE MODIFICATIONS: Heights of stories, sizes of rooms and kinds of materials and colors may be changed. First story may be brick. Cellar may be extended under the whole house with brick or stone walls, or may be omitted entirely. Laundry may be placed where storeroom is now shown, and kitchen and dining room enlarged. Laundry and servants' W. C. may be placed in the cellar. A part or all of the plumbing may be omitted. Wainscoting and fireplaces may be omitted. If heating apparatus be used one chimney will suffice.

The price of working plans, specifications, etc., for a modified design varies according to the alterations required, and will be made known upon application to the Architects.

Shoppell's Modern Houses—*Designs Patented.   *Residence, Design No. 605*

SIDE ELEVATION.

DESCRIPTION.

For explanation of all symbols (* † etc.) see page 42.

GENERAL DIMENSIONS: Width, 47 ft.; extreme depth, 63 ft. Heights of stories: Cellar, 7 ft.; first story, 11 ft.; second story, 9 ft; attic, 8 ft.

EXTERIOR MATERIALS: Foundations, stone and brick; first and second stories, clapboards; roofs and dormers, shingles.

INTERIOR FINISH: Oak floor in main hall and oak staircase from first to attic story. Soft wood trim throughout, finished in hard oil natural colors or painted white. All walls and ceilings, hard white plaster. Plaster cornices and centers in hall, parlor, dining and sitting rooms and library. Outside blinds to all windows. Panels under windows of first story. Hall, vestibule, bath-room and kitchen, wainscoted.

COLORS: All clapboards, trim, sashes, portico and porch ceilings and rain water leaders, white. Front doors, grain filled and finished in hard oil; other outside doors painted white. Blinds, Colonial yellow. Portico and porch floors, and all brick-work, oiled. Roof shingles left natural. Dormer shingles painted white.

ACCOMMODATIONS: The principal rooms and their sizes, closets, etc., are shown by the plans. Cellar under main house; laundry and servants' W. C. under kitchen. Three bedrooms and storage room finished in attic. Regarded as a pure example of the best Colonial style.

COST: $7,000, † not including mantels, range and heater. The estimate is based on ‡ New York prices for materials and labor. In many sections of the country the cost should be less.

Price for working plans, specifications and * license to build, - $70.00
Price for †† bill of materials, - - - - - - - 20.00
Address, THE CO-OPERATIVE BUILDING PLAN ASSOCIATION, Architects, 63 Broadway, New York.

FEASIBLE MODIFICATIONS: Heights of stories, sizes of rooms, kinds of materials and colors may be changed.

FRONT ELEVATION.

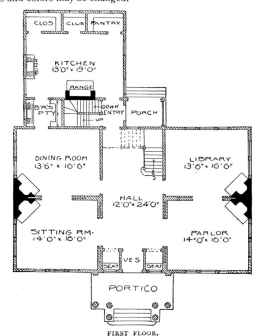

FIRST FLOOR.

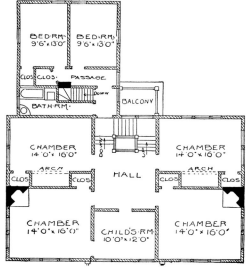

SECOND FLOOR.

*Shoppell's Modern Houses—*Designs Patented.*   *Residence, Design No. 417*

PERSPECTIVE.

DESCRIPTION.

GENERAL DIMENSIONS: Extreme width, 47 ft. 2 in.; depth, including veranda, 62 ft. Heights of stories: Cellar, 7 ft. 6 in.; first story, 10 ft. 6 in.; second story, 10 ft.; attic, 8 ft. 6 in.

EXTERIOR MATERIALS: Foundations, stone; first story, brick; second story and gables, shingles; roof, slate. Outside blinds to all windows.

INTERIOR FINISH: Hard white plaster. Plaster cornices and centers in main hall, first and second stories, parlor, dining and sitting rooms. Soft wood flooring. Soft wood trim, except as follows: main hall and dining room, oak; parlor, cherry; sitting room, ash. Main stairs, oak. Panels under windows in parlor, sitting and dining rooms. Wainscot in bath-room. Interior wood-work finished in hard oil.

COLORS: Brick-work oiled. Trim, blinds and rain conductors, dark green. Front doors finished in hard oil. Sashes, Pompeian red. Veranda floor and ceiling and wall shingles oiled.

ACCOMMODATIONS: The principal rooms and their sizes, closets, etc., are shown by the plans. Cellar under whole house. Laundry under kitchen. Three rooms in attic. Four open fireplaces and five wood mantels, also kitchen range, included in estimate. Clothes chute from second story to laundry.

COST: $7,010, † not including heater. The estimate is based on ‡ New York prices for materials and labor.

Price for working plans, specifications and * license to build, - $85.00
Price for †† bill of materials, - - - - - - - 10.00

Address, THE CO-OPERATIVE BUILDING PLAN ASSOCIATION, Architects, 63 Broadway, New York.

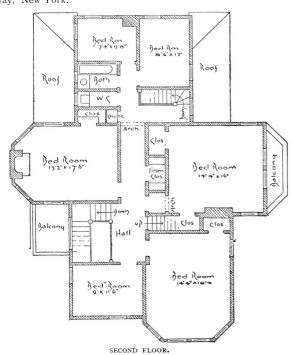
Side View of House.

FIRST FLOOR.

SECOND FLOOR.

Shoppell's Modern Houses—*Designs Patented.   *Residence, Design No. 309*

PERSPECTIVE.

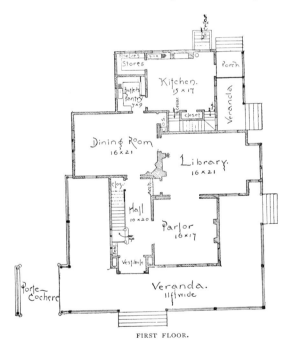

FIRST FLOOR.

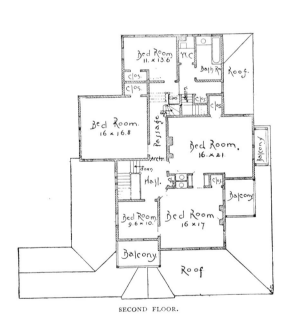

SECOND FLOOR.

DESCRIPTION.

For explanation of all symbols (* † etc.) see page 42.

GENERAL DIMENSIONS: Width over all, 49 ft. 4 in.; depth, including veranda, 66 ft. 8 in. Heights of stories: Cellar, 7 ft.; first story, 11 ft.; second story 10 ft.; attic, 8 ft. 6 in.

EXTERIOR MATERIALS: Foundation, brick; first story, clapboards; second story, shingles; roof, slate; gables, panels and shingles. Outside blinds.

INTERIOR FINISH: Hard white plaster; plaster cornices and centers in parlor, library, dining room and hall. First floor double, finished with hard pine; all other flooring, soft wood. Trim, soft wood. Stairs, ash. Panels under windows in parlor, library and dining room. Stained Cathedral glass in staircase windows. Chair rail in dining room. Wainscot in bath-room, billiard room and kitchen. Interior wood-work finished in hard oil.

COLORS: Clapboards and balusters of veranda and balcony, olive. Trim and rain water conductors, dark olive drab. Outside doors and blinds, light olive green. Front doors finished in hard oil. Sashes, dark red. Veranda floor and ceiling, oiled. Brick-work, Pompeian red. Wall shingles dipped and brush coated brown stain. Gable shingles dipped and brush coated sienna stain.

ACCOMMODATIONS: The principal rooms and their sizes, closets, etc., are shown by the plans. Cellar under whole house. Two bedrooms and billiard room in attic. Wash bowls in two bedrooms. Sliding doors connect principal rooms of first story. Five open fireplaces with wood mantels, also kitchen range, included in estimate.

COST: $7,500, † not incuding heater. The estimate is based on ‡ New York prices for materials and labor. In many sections of the country the cost should be less.

Price for working plans, specifications and * license to build, - - - - - - - - - - - - - - $100.00
Price for †† bill of materials, - - - - - 25.00

Address, THE CO-OPERATIVE BUILDING PLAN ASSOCIATION, Architects, 63 Broadway, New York.

FEASIBLE MODIFICATIONS: Heights of stories, colors, sizes of rooms and kinds of materials may be changed. Sliding doors, any or all fireplaces, porte-cochere, balconies, a part of the veranda and part or all of plumbing may be omitted. The balconies may be enclosed with sliding sashes or may be planned as part of adjoining bedrooms.

The price of working plans, specifications, etc., for a modified design varies according to the alterations required, and will be made known upon application to the Architects.

250

THE CO-OPERATIVE BUILDING PLAN ASSOCIATION, ARCHITECTS, 63 BROADWAY, NEW YORK.

*Shoppell's Modern Houses—*Designs Patented.*   *Residence, Design No. 608*

PERSPECTIVE.

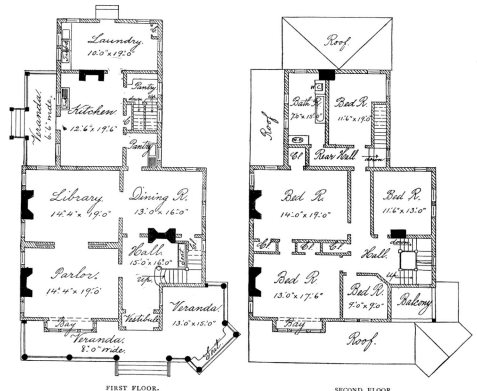

FIRST FLOOR.   SECOND FLOOR.

DESCRIPTION.

For explanation of all symbols (* † etc.) see page 42.

GENERAL DIMENSIONS: Width, including veranda, 42 ft. 8 in.; depth, including veranda, 72 ft. 6 in. Heights of stories: Cellar, 7 ft. 6 in.; first story, 10 ft. 6 in.; second story, 9 ft. 6 in.; attic, 8 ft. 6 in.

EXTERIOR MATERIALS: Foundations, stone and brick; first story, clapboards; second story, shingles; gables are paneled, bracketed and shingled; roof, slate.

INTERIOR FINISH: Hard wood main staircase. Three coat hard white plaster throughout; plaster cornices and centers in parlor, library, dining room and hall. Hard wood trim in halls (both stories), parlor, library and dining room; other rooms throughout trimmed with soft woods of handsome design. Halls wainscoted with hard wood. Hard wood floors throughout first story. All wood-work finished in hard oil. House piped for gas, and wired for electric bells from front door to kitchen and from front second story and attic halls to kitchen. All large window panes plate glass.

COLORS: All clapboards, light yellow. Trim, cornices, veranda, and balcony posts, rails, balusters, gable brackets, and framing of panels, white. Second story shingles dipped in and brush coated with yellowish red stain. Shingles in gables and veranda pediment, panels in gables, and cheeks of dormers painted light yellow. Slate on roof oiled. Brick-work of foundation and veranda piers painted red. Brick-work of chimneys painted yellow. Cresting and finials painted red. Veranda floors and ceilings oiled. All sashes, dark green.

ACCOMMODATIONS: The principal rooms and their sizes, closets, etc., are shown by the plans. Cellar under the whole house. Three rooms and hall finished in attic, beside ample storage room. Fireplaces in parlor, library, dining room, hall and two bedrooms of second story. Handsome stairway and seat in hall. Tile floor in vestibule.

FEASIBLE MODIFICATIONS: Heights of stories, sizes of rooms and kind of materials may be changed. First story may be brick or stone. Small front bedroom may be connected with larger bedroom and serve as a dressing room. The number of fireplaces and chimneys may be reduced if heating apparatus be used. One chimney will suffice. Gas piping, a portion or all of plumbing, electric bells, and all hard wood may be omitted.

COST: $7,500, † not including mantels, range and heater. The estimate is based on ‡ New York prices for materials and labor. In many sections of the country the cost should be less.

Price for working plans, specifications and * license to build, - $75.00
Price for †† bill of materials, - - - - - - - - - 35.00

Address, THE CO-OPERATIVE BUILDING PLAN ASSOCIATION, Architects, 63 Broadway, New York.

251

THE CO-OPERATIVE BUILDING PLAN ASSOCIATION, ARCHITECTS, 63 BROADWAY, NEW YORK.

*Shoppell's Modern Houses—*Designs Patented.*   *Residence, Design No. 583*

PERSPECTIVE.

DESCRIPTION.

For explanation of all symbols (* † etc.) see page 42.

GENERAL DIMENSIONS: Width through dining room, 43 ft. 10 in., including veranda; depth, 71 ft., including veranda. Heights of stories: Cellar, 7 ft. 6 in.; first story, 10 ft.; second story, 9 ft.; attic, 8 ft.

EXTERIOR MATERIALS: Foundation, stone and brick; first story, clapboards; second story and roof, shingles; gables, panels and shingles. Outside blinds to all windows except those of the attic and cellar.

INTERIOR FINISH: Hard white plaster; plaster cornices and centers in parlor, dining room, sitting room, library, first and second story halls and bed-rooms over dining room and parlor. Flooring to be oak in first story hall, ash in dining room, yellow pine in kitchen, alternate walnut and cherry in bath-room, and white pine elsewhere. Stained glass in vestibule door and in the window opening on balcony. Trim to be cherry in parlor, ash in sitting and dining rooms, oak in hall, yellow pine in kitchen and remainder soft woods. Panels under windows in parlor, dining and sitting rooms, and library. Chair rail in dining room. Main stairway oak. Bath-room and kitchen wainscoted. All wood-work finished in hard oil. Mantels included in estimate.

COLORS: Clapboards, olive green. Trim and rain conductors, dark olive drab. Outside doors, bronze green. Blinds, olive. Sashes, Pompeian red. Veranda floor and plaster work on gables, Tuscan yellow. Veranda ceiling, Oriental drab. Brick-work, bright red. Wall shingles dipped and brush coated brown stain. Gable shingles dipped and brush coated sienna stain. Roof shingles dipped and brush coated dark red stain.

ACCOMMODATIONS: The principal rooms and their sizes, closets, etc., are shown by the plans. Cellar under whole house. Two rooms and hallway finished in attic. Seven fireplaces in first and second stories. Extensive veranda.

COST: 7,500, † not including range and heater. The estimate is based on ‡ New York prices for materials and labor. In many sections of the country the cost should be less.

Price for working plans, specifications and * license to build, - $75.00
Price for †† bill of materials, - - - - - - - - - 15.00
Address, THE CO-OPERATIVE BUILDING PLAN ASSOCIATION, Architects, 63 Broadway, New York.

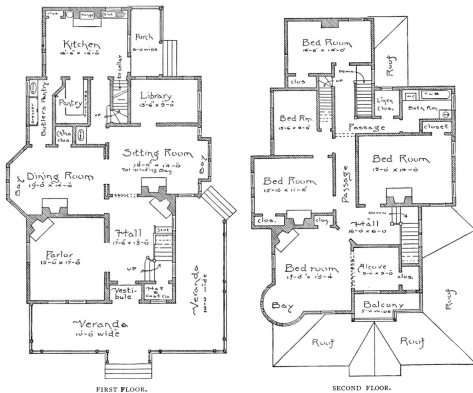

FIRST FLOOR.   SECOND FLOOR.

FEASIBLE MODIFICATIONS: Heights of stories, sizes of rooms, materials and colors may be changed. Cellar may be reduced in size. Fireplaces, sliding doors, balcony, stained glass and a part or all of the plumbing may be omitted. Fewer chimneys will be required if heating apparatus be used. Dining room and parlor may be connected by a wide opening if fireplaces are re-arranged. Veranda may be reduced or extended.

252

THE CO-OPERATIVE BUILDING PLAN ASSOCIATION, ARCHITECTS, 63 BROADWAY, NEW YORK.

*Shoppell's Modern Houses—*Designs Patented.*   *Residence, Design No. 414*

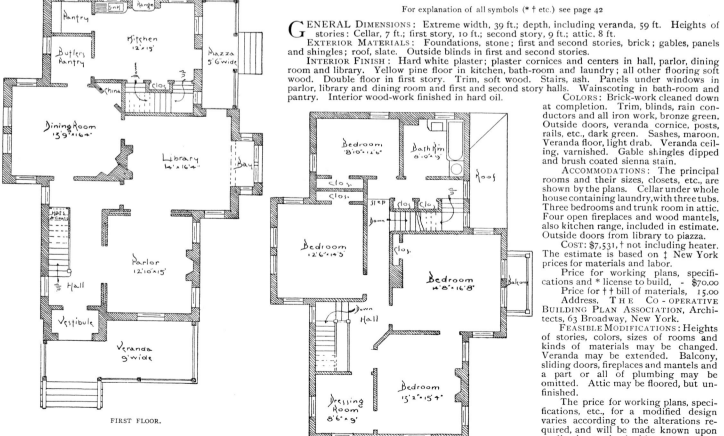

Side Elevation

PERSPECTIVE.

FIRST FLOOR.

SECOND FLOOR.

DESCRIPTION

For explanation of all symbols (* † etc.) see page 42

GENERAL DIMENSIONS: Extreme width, 39 ft.; depth, including veranda, 59 ft. Heights of stories: Cellar, 7 ft.; first story, 10 ft.; second story, 9 ft.; attic, 8 ft.

EXTERIOR MATERIALS: Foundations, stone; first and second stories, brick; gables, panels and shingles; roof, slate. Outside blinds in first and second stories.

INTERIOR FINISH: Hard white plaster; plaster cornices and centers in hall, parlor, dining room and library. Yellow pine floor in kitchen, bath-room and laundry; all other flooring soft wood. Double floor in first story. Trim, soft wood. Stairs, ash. Panels under windows in parlor, library and dining room and first and second story halls. Wainscoting in bath-room and pantry. Interior wood-work finished in hard oil.

COLORS: Brick-work cleaned down at completion. Trim, blinds, rain conductors and all iron work, bronze green. Outside doors, veranda cornice, posts, rails, etc., dark green. Sashes, maroon. Veranda floor, light drab. Veranda ceiling, varnished. Gable shingles dipped and brush coated sienna stain.

ACCOMMODATIONS: The principal rooms and their sizes, closets, etc., are shown by the plans. Cellar under whole house containing laundry, with three tubs. Three bedrooms and trunk room in attic. Four open fireplaces and wood mantels, also kitchen range, included in estimate. Outside doors from library to piazza.

COST: $7,531, † not including heater. The estimate is based on ‡ New York prices for materials and labor.

Price for working plans, specifications and * license to build, - $70.00
Price for † † bill of materials, 15.00

Address, THE CO-OPERATIVE BUILDING PLAN ASSOCIATION, Architects, 63 Broadway, New York.

FEASIBLE MODIFICATIONS: Heights of stories, colors, sizes of rooms and kinds of materials may be changed. Veranda may be extended. Balcony, sliding doors, fireplaces and mantels and a part or all of plumbing may be omitted. Attic may be floored, but unfinished.

The price for working plans, specifications, etc., for a modified design varies according to the alterations required, and will be made known upon application to the Architects.

THE CO-OPERATIVE BUILDING PLAN ASSOCIATION, ARCHITECTS, 63 BROADWAY, NEW YORK.

Shoppell's Modern Houses—*Designs Patented.   *Residence, Design No. 498*

PERSPECTIVE.

DESCRIPTION.

For explanation of all symbols (* † etc.) see page 42.

GENERAL DIMENSIONS: Width over all, 44 ft. 8 in.; depth, including veranda, 75 ft. 4 in. Heights of stories: Cellar, 7 ft. 6 in.; first story, 10 ft.; second story, 9 ft.; attic, 8 ft.

EXTERIOR MATERIALS: Foundation, brick; first story, clapboards; second story, gables and roof, shingles. Outside blinds to all windows.

INTERIOR FINISH: Hard white plaster; plaster cornices and centers in parlor, library, dining room, and main hall first and second stories, and two bedrooms. Oak floor in hall and dining room; all other flooring soft wood. Oak trim in hall and dining room; soft wood trim elsewhere. Oak staircase. Panels under windows in hall, parlor, dining room and library. Chair rail in dining room. Wainscoting in bath-room. Front and vestibule doors, oak. Interior wood-work finished in hard oil, except in kitchen and laundry, where paint is used.

COLORS: Clapboards, dark drab. Trim and rain conductors, light olive green. Outside doors and blinds, light olive green with dark drab panels. Sashes, red. Veranda floor, light lead color. Veranda ceiling, blue. Brick-work, oiled. Wall shingles dipped and brush coated light drab. Roof shingles dipped and brush coated dark red.

ACCOMMODATIONS: The principal rooms and their sizes, closets, etc., are shown by the plans. Cellar under whole house. Three bedrooms, hall and store-room in attic. Six open fireplaces, six mantels, and kitchen range, included in estimate. Laundry (with two tubs) may be used as summer kitchen. Handsome staircase. Electric bells and annunciators in dining room, library and two front bedrooms, also for front door.

COST: $7,592, † not including heater. The estimate is based on ‡ New York prices for materials and labor. In many sections of the country the cost should be less.

Price for working plans, specifications and * license to build, - - - - - - - $65.00
Price for † † bill of materials, - - - - 10.00

Address, THE CO-OPERATIVE BUILDING PLAN ASSOCIATION, Architects, 63 Broadway, New York.

FEASIBLE MODIFICATIONS: Heights of stories, colors, sizes of rooms and kinds of materials may be changed. Any or all sliding doors, fireplaces and mantels, electric bells, part or all of plumbing, laundry at rear, and kitchen side porch, may be omitted. Balconies may be planned to enlarge adjoining bedroom, or may be enclosed with sliding sashes. Veranda may be reduced or extended. Attic may be left unfinished.

The price of working plans, specifications, etc., for a modified design varies according to the alterations required, and will be made known upon application to the Architects.

FIRST FLOOR.

SECOND FLOOR.

254

THE CO-OPERATIVE BUILDING PLAN ASSOCIATION, ARCHITECTS, 63 BROADWAY, NEW YORK.

Shoppell's Modern Houses—*Designs Patented.   *Residence, Design No. 471*

PERSPECTIVE.

DESCRIPTION.

For explanation of all symbols (* † etc.) see page 42.

GENERAL DIMENSIONS: Extreme width, 62 ft. 6 in.; depth, including veranda, 78 ft. 8 in. Heights of stories: First story, 10 ft. 6 in.; second story, 9 ft. 6 in.; attic, 8 ft.

EXTERIOR MATERIALS: Foundation, piers; first story, clapboards; second story, gables and roofs, shingles. Outside blinds to all windows except those of parlor, library, dining and drawing room.

INTERIOR FINISH: Hard white plaster; plaster cornices and centers in parlor, library and dining room. Hard pine flooring in hall, dining room, kitchen and servants' hall; soft wood flooring elsewhere. Red baywood trim in first and second stories, except in kitchen and pantry, where soft wood is used. Ceiling of hall and dining room paneled to imitate open timber work. Panels under windows in parlor, main halls, library and dining room. Wainscoting in kitchen and bath-room. Stairs, baywood. Interior wood-work finished in hard oil.

ACCOMMODATIONS: The principal rooms and their sizes, closets, etc., are shown by the plans. No cellar. Billiard room, hall, two bedrooms and tank room in attic. Hall 10 feet wide runs through house from front to rear, with very handsome recessed staircase. Sliding doors connect hall, parlor, library and dining room. Open fireplaces in parlor, dining room, sitting room, library and three bedrooms. Two bath-rooms in second story, and two independent water-closets.

COST: $8,405, † not including mantels, range and heater. The estimate is based on ‡ New York prices for materials and labor.

Price for working plans, specifications and * license to build, - - - - - - - - - - - $100.00
Price for † † bill of materials, - - - - - 25.00

Address, THE CO-OPERATIVE BUILDING PLAN ASSOCIATION, Architects, 63 Broadway, New York.

FIRST FLOOR.

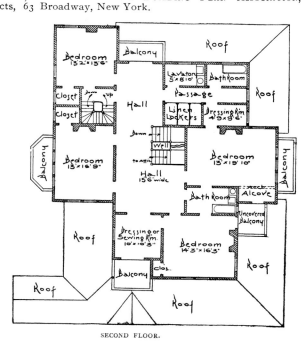

SECOND FLOOR.

255

THE CO-OPERATIVE BUILDING PLAN ASSOCIATION, ARCHITECTS, 63 BROADWAY, NEW YORK.

*Shoppell's Modern Houses—*Designs Patented.*   *Residence, Design No. 655*

PERSPECTIVE.

DESCRIPTION.

For explanation of all symbols (* † etc.) see page 42

GENERAL DIMENSIONS: Extreme front, 97 ft. 8 in.; depth, 39 ft. 6 in. Heights of stories: Cellar, 7 ft.; first story, 9 ft.; second story, 8 ft. 6 in.; attic, 8 ft. In kitchen extension the height of both first and second stories is 8 ft.

EXTERIOR MATERIALS: Foundations, brick; first story, main part brick, kitchen extension, clapboards; second story and gables, shingles; main roof, slate; roof of "lean to" to kitchen, shingles.

INTERIOR FINISH: Ceilings of vestibule and all rooms of first story (except kitchen) are finished with open timber panels; all other ceilings finished with hard white plaster. Walls of dining room and reception room are sand finished; all other walls finished with hard white plaster. Cellar ceiling rough plastered. Plaster cornices in reception and dining rooms. Flooring of first and second stories, hard wood; attic floor, soft wood. Main staircase and front doors, oak. Library, hall, bath-room and kitchen are wainscoted. Trim of vestibule, hall, library and dining room, oak; all other trim, soft woods. All interior wood work finished in hard oil.

COLORS: All blinds and the clapboards on kitchen first story, "Colonial" yellow. All shingles dipped in oil. Trim and sashes, white. Veranda floor and ceiling, oiled.

ACCOMMODATIONS: The principal rooms and their sizes, closets, etc., are shown by the plans. Beside these there is a cellar under the whole house except kitchen part, and there are two bed-rooms, a store room and a hall finished in the attic.

COST: $8000, † not including mantels, range and heater. The estimate is based on ‡ New York prices for materials and labor. In many sections of the country the cost should be less.

Price for working plans, specifications and * license to build, $80.00
Price for †† bill of materials, - - - - - - 20.00

Address, THE CO-OPERATIVE BUILDING PLAN ASSOCIATION, Architects, 63 Broadway, New York.

FEASIBLE MODIFICATIONS: Heights of ceilings, sizes of rooms and colors may be changed. Foundations may be stone. First story may be brick or frame. Open veranda may be covered or omitted. Balcony may be omitted and space given to bed-rooms. Paneled ceilings, wainscoting, attic rooms, fire-place in second story, and dining room chimney, any or all of these features may be omitted. Soft woods may be used throughout. Shingles may be used for the roof in place of slate.

The price for working plans, specifications, etc. for a modified design varies according to the extent of the alterations required, and will be made known upon application to the Architects.

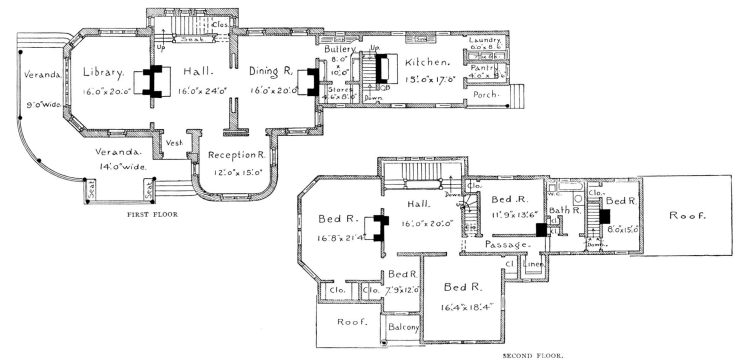

FIRST FLOOR.

SECOND FLOOR.

256

THE CO-OPERATIVE BUILDING PLAN ASSOCIATION, ARCHITECTS, 63 BROADWAY, NEW YORK.

*Shoppell's Modern Houses—*Designs Patented.*

Residence, Design No. 485

PERSPECTIVE.

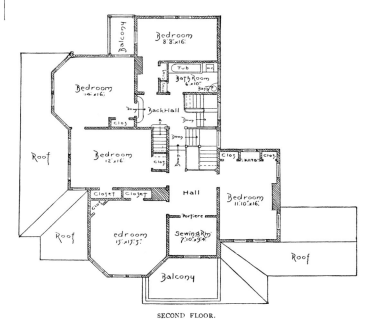

Side Elevation

DESCRIPTION.

For explanation of all symbols (* † etc.) see page 42.

GENERAL DIMENSIONS: Width over all, 67 ft.; depth, including veranda, 59 ft. Heights of stories: Cellar, 8 ft. 6 in.; first story, 10 ft.; second story, 9 ft. 6 in.; attic, 8 ft. 6 in.

EXTERIOR MATERIALS: Foundation, brick; first story, clapboards; second story and roof, shingles; gables, panels and shingles. Outside window blinds in kitchen extension.

INTERIOR FINISH: Hard white plaster. Plaster cornices and centers in parlor, hall, library, sitting and dining room. Soft wood flooring and trim. Ash stairway. Inside folding window blinds in first and second stories, except in kitchen extension. Panels under windows and picture molding on walls in principal rooms and hall of first story. Kitchen and bath-room wainscoted. Interior wood-work finished in hard oil.

COLORS: Clapboards, light olive drab. Trim and rain conductors, bronze green. Outside doors and blinds, bronze green with light olive drab panels. Sashes, buff. Veranda floor and ceiling, Pompeian red. Brick-work oiled. Wall shingles dipped and brush coated bright red. Roof shingles dipped and brush coated darker red.

ACCOMMODATIONS: The principal rooms and their sizes, closets, etc., are shown by the plans. Cellar with cemented floor under whole house. Four bedrooms and two store-rooms in attic. Five open fireplaces and mantels included in estimate. Wash-basin under main staircase at rear of main hall. Porte-cochère and extensive verandas and balconies. Large air space over attic rooms.

COST: $8,264, † not including range and heater. The estimate is based on ‡ New York prices for materials and labor. In many sections of the country the cost should be less.

Price for working plans, specifications and * license to build, - $72.00
Price for †† bill of materials, - - - - - - 10.00
Address, THE CO-OPERATIVE BUILDING PLAN ASSOCIATION, Architects, 63 Broadway, New York.

FEASIBLE MODIFICATIONS: Heights of stories, colors, sizes of rooms and kinds of materials may be changed. Any or all attic rooms, part or all of plumbing, sliding doors, open fireplaces and mantels, porte-cochère, second story balconies and much of the veranda may be omitted. Attic balcony may be enclosed with sliding sashes or may be planned as a room.

The price of working plans, specifications, etc., for a modified design varies according to the alterations required, and will be made known upon application to the Architects.

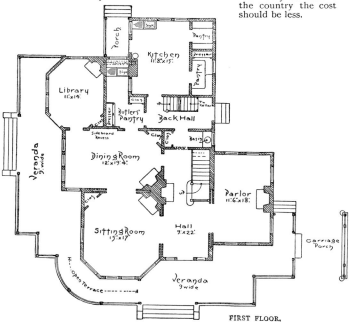

FIRST FLOOR.

SECOND FLOOR.

257

THE CO-OPERATIVE BUILDING PLAN ASSOCIATION, ARCHITECTS, 63 BROADWAY, NEW YORK.

Shoppell's Modern Houses—*Designs Patented.   *Residence, Design No. 486*

The exterior appearance of this design is the same as that of No. 485, shown on opposite page.

DESCRIPTION.

For explanation of all symbols (* † etc.) see page 42.

GENERAL DIMENSIONS: Width over all, 65 ft. 4 in.; depth, including veranda, 56 ft. Heights of stories: first story, 11 ft.; second story, 10 ft.; attic, 9 ft.

EXTERIOR MATERIALS: Foundation, brick walls; first story, clapboards; second story and roof, shingles; gables, panels and shingles. Outside blinds to all windows.

INTERIOR FINISH: Hard white plaster; hall and dining room have wood ceilings. Plaster cornices and centers in parlor, sitting room and study. Hard pine flooring throughout. Oak trim in hall and dining room; yellow pine trim elsewhere. Panels under windows in first story, except in kitchen. Kitchen, rear hall and bath-room wainscoted. Main staircase, oak. Interior wood-work finished in hard oil.

COLORS: Clapboards, dark olive drab. Trim, outside doors, blinds and rain conductors, bronze green. Sashes, and brick-work, Pompeian red. Veranda floor and ceiling oiled. All shingles dipped and brush coated in red stain.

ACCOMMODATIONS: The principal rooms and their sizes, closets, etc., are shown by the plans. No cellar. Two bedrooms and hall in attic. Seven open fireplaces and mantels included in estimate. Sliding doors between parlor and hall. Stained glass in front door.

COST: $7,617, † not including range. The estimate is based on ‡ New York prices for materials and labor.

Price for working plans, specifications and * license to build, $66.00
Price for † † bill of materials,   -   -   -   -   -   -   10.00

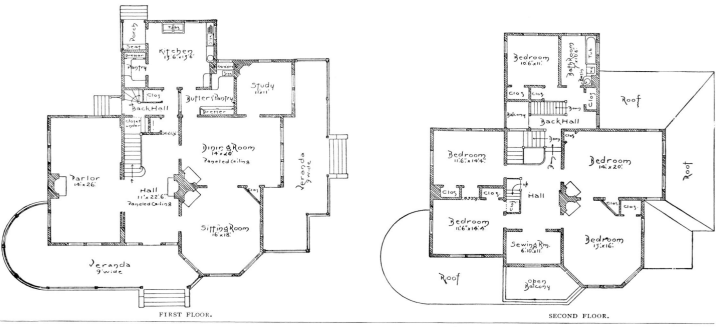

FIRST FLOOR.   SECOND FLOOR.

Residence, Design No. 487.

The exterior appearance is much the same as that of No. 485, shown on the opposite page.

DESCRIPTION.

GENERAL DIMENSIONS: Extreme width, 72 ft.; depth, including veranda, 73 ft. Heights of stories: Cellar, 7 ft.; first story, 10 ft. 6 in.; second story, 9 ft. 6 in.; attic, 8 ft.

EXTERIOR MATERIALS: Foundation, stone and brick; first story, clapboards; second story and roof, shingles; gables, panels and shingles. Outside blinds.

INTERIOR FINISH: Hard white plaster; plaster cornices and centers in parlor, library and nursery. Double floors in first and second stories, finishing with yellow pine; soft wood floors elsewhere. Soft wood trim. Oak stairs. Inside Venetian blinds in dining room. Panels under windows in parlor, hall, nursery, sitting and dining room. Chair rail in nursery. Wainscot in kitchen. Hall and dining room ceilings paneled with wood. Laundry and attic wood-work painted colors to suit owner. All other interior wood-work finished in hard oil, stained to suit owner.

ACCOMMODATIONS: The principal rooms and their sizes, closets, etc., are shown by the plans. Cellar under kitchen, pantry and halls. Four bedrooms and hallway in attic. Seven open fireplaces with mantels included in estimate.

COST: $8,714, † not including range and heater. The estimate is based on ‡ New York prices for materials and labor.

Price for working plans, specifications and * license to build,   - $77.00
Price for † † bill of materials,   -   -   -   -   -   -   -   10.00

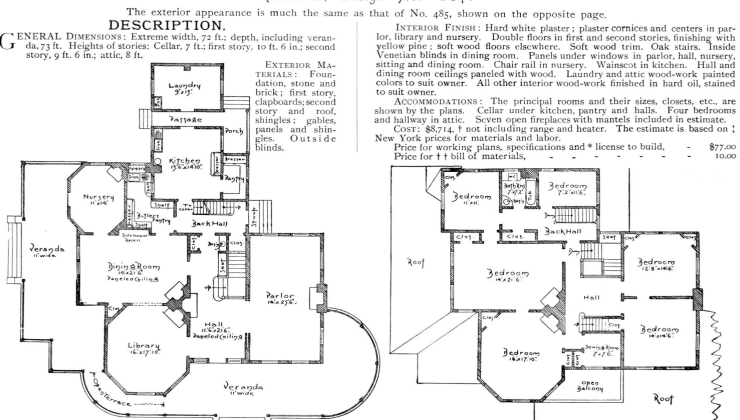

FIRST FLOOR.   SECOND FLOOR.

258

THE CO-OPERATIVE BUILDING PLAN ASSOCIATION ARCHITECTS, 63 BROADWAY NEW YORK.

*Shoppell's Modern Houses—*Designs Patented.*   *Residence Design No. 416*

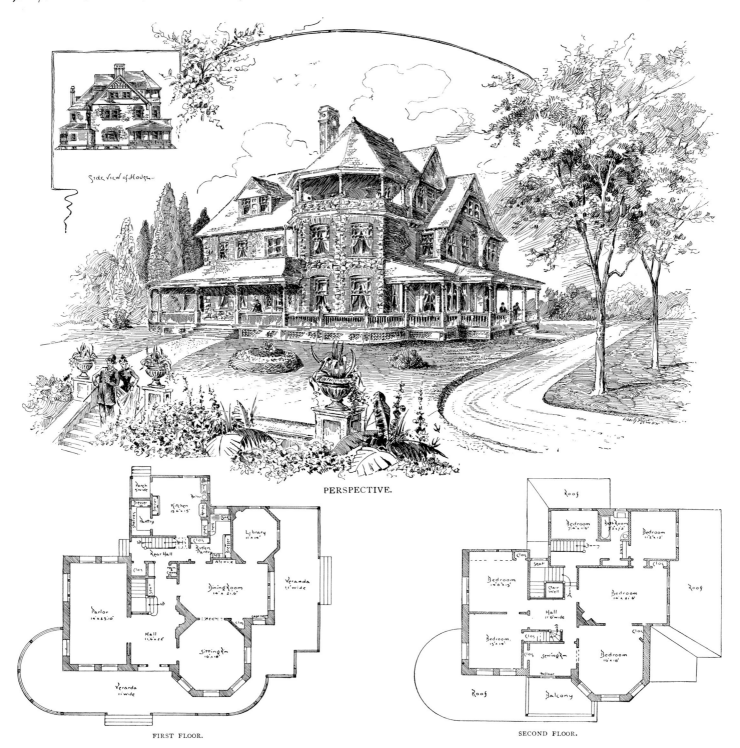

Side view of House.

PERSPECTIVE.

FIRST FLOOR.

SECOND FLOOR.

DESCRIPTION.

For explanation of all symbols (* † etc.) see page 42.

GENERAL DIMENSIONS: Extreme width, 74 ft.; depth, including veranda, 61 ft. Heights of stories: Cellar, 7 ft.; first story, 10 ft. 6 in.; second story, 9 ft. 6 in.; attic, 8 ft. 6 in.

EXTERIOR MATERIALS: Foundation, stone; first story, main part, stone; rear extension, clapboards. Second story, main part, stone; rear extension, shingles. Gables, panels and shingles; roof, shingles. Outside blinds to all windows except those of the parlor, dining and sitting room.

INTERIOR FINISH: Hard white plaster; plaster cornices and centers in parlor, sitting and dining room, and library. Soft wood flooring and trim. Inside blinds in parlor, dining and sitting room. Main stairs, oak. Panels under windows in parlor, sitting and dining room. Wainscot in butler's pantry, kitchen and bath-room. Chair rail in dining room. Interior wood-work finished in hard oil.

COLORS: Stone and brick-work cleaned down at completion. Clapboards, dark olive drab. Trim, light brown. Outside doors, dark green. Sashes, black. Veranda floor oiled. Veranda ceiling varnished. Rain conductors, buff. Wall shingles dipped and brush coated in oil. Roof shingles left natural.

ACCOMMODATIONS: The principal rooms and their sizes, closets, etc., are shown by the plans. Cellar under whole house. Three bedrooms and store-room in attic. If stone be dark colored, red brick should be used for trimming around all windows and for chimneys; if stone be light colored, buff brick should be used. Second story balcony provided with standards for awning. Three fireplaces and mantels, also kitchen range, included in estimate. Large open balcony in attic.

COST: $9,749, † not including heater. The estimate is based on ‡ New York prices for materials and labor. In many sections of the country the cost should be less.

Price for working plans, specifications and * license to build, - - - - - - - - - - - - - - - $85.00
Price for †† bill of materials, - - - - - - 15.00

Address, THE CO-OPERATIVE BUILDING PLAN ASSOCIATION, Architects, 63 Broadway, New York.

THE CO-OPERATIVE BUILDING PLAN ASSOCIATION, ARCHITECTS, 63 BROADWAY, NEW YORK.

*Shoppell's Modern Houses—*Designs Patented.*   *Residence, Design No. 656*

PERSPECTIVE.

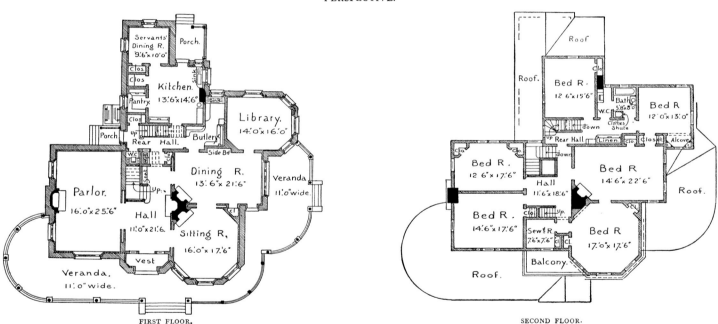

FIRST FLOOR.   SECOND FLOOR.

DESCRIPTION.

For explanation of all symbols (* † etc.) see page 42.

GENERAL DIMENSIONS: Front width, over all, 75 ft. 6 in.; depth, over all, 71 ft. 4 in. Heights of stories: Cellar, 7 ft.; first story, 10 ft. 6 in.; second story, 9 ft. 6 in.; attic, 8 ft.

EXTERIOR MATERIALS: Foundations, stone; first story, stone (quarry or rock-faced); second story and gables, shingles; roofs, slate.

INTERIOR FINISH: Hard white plaster throughout. Plaster cornices and centres in parlor, sitting room, library, and in two bed-rooms. Main hall and dining room panel wainscoted and ceilings of same paneled. Trim throughout to be poplar, except in kitchen, laundry and pantries, where it is to be white pine. Main staircase and front entrance door, oak. A picture moulding in main rooms and halls of first and second stories.

COLORS: Trim, such as casings, cornices, etc., bronze. Outside doors, blinds and lattice, dark green. Sashes, bright red. Shingles on side walls and gables, dipped in red stain. Brick work of chimneys, etc., oiled.

ACCOMMODATIONS: The principal rooms and their sizes, closets, etc., are shown by the plans. Beside these there is a cellar (with concrete floor) under the whole house, and there are five rooms, a fine balcony and two hallways in the attic. Two rooms in the attic may be combined to make a billiard-room. The cellar has a laundry (three tubs), a servants' W.C., a store room, and ash-pits connected by flues with all fire-places.

Tiled floor in vestibule. W.C., lavatory and hat closet convenient to both front and rear halls. Linen closet and slop sink in second story rear hall; also a soiled clothes shute. W.C. and bath-room detached.

COST: $10,000, †not including mantels, range and heater. The estimate is based on ‡New York prices for materials and labor. In many sections of the country the cost should be less.

Price for working plans, specifications and *license to build, - $100.00
Price for ††bill of materials, - - - - - - 25.00

Address, THE CO-OPERATIVE BUILDING PLAN ASSOCIATION, Architects, 63 Broadway, New York.

FEASIBLE MODIFICATIONS: The heights of stories and colors may be changed. The attic rooms may be entirely re-arranged or omitted. The first story may be brick or frame. The bed-rooms over parlor may be united to make one large room. The servants' dining room may be omitted or it may be used as a laundry in place of having the laundry in the basement. The paneled ceilings, the wainscoting, tiling and ash-pits may be omitted. Shingles or other materials may be used for roofs.

The price for working plans, specifications, etc. for a modified design varies according to the extent of the alterations required, and will be made known upon application to the Architects.

260

THE CO-OPERATIVE BUILDING PLAN ASSOCIATION, ARCHITECTS, 63 BROADWAY, NEW YORK.

Shoppell's Modern Houses—*Designs Patented.　　　　　　　*Residence, Design No. 627*

PERSPECTIVE.

DESCRIPTION.

For explanation of all symbols (* † etc.) see page 42.

GENERAL DIMENSIONS: Width through parlor and hall, including verandas, 53 ft.; depth, including veranda and pantry, 75 ft. 6 in. Heights of stories: Cellar, 7 ft.; first story, 10 ft.; second story, 9 ft.; third story, 9 ft.

EXTERIOR MATERIALS: Foundations, stone; first story, clapboards; second story, shingles; roof, slate. Outside blinds to all windows except those of the library and bedroom over hall, which have inside blinds.

INTERIOR FINISH: All walls throughout the house finished with adamant plaster. Cornices and centers in hall, library, parlor and dining room. Hall and bath-room wainscoted, Picture molding in principal rooms and hall of first story. Trim of hall and dining room, oak; remainder of trim, whitewood stained and finished in hard oil, imitating hard woods. Oak floor in hall and parlor. Yellow pine floor in kitchen, laundry, pantry, and butler's pantry; remainder of flooring white pine. Entire first story double-floored. Main staircase, oak.

COLORS: All clapboards, olive. Trim, bronze green. Front outside doors finished in hard oil. Other outside doors and blinds painted olive. Sashes, Pompeian red. Veranda floor oiled. Veranda and balcony ceilings varnished. Brick-work oiled. Shingles dipped and brush coated with reddish stain.

ACCOMMODATIONS: The principal rooms and their sizes, closets, etc., are shown by the plans. Cellar under whole house. Four rooms and storage space in attic. The high roof makes attic rooms as desirable as any others.

COST: $8,500, † not including mantels, range and heater. The estimate is based on ‡ New York prices for materials and labor. In many sections of the country the cost should be less.

Price for working plans, specifications and * license to build, - $85.00
Price for †† bill of materials, - - - - - - - 40.00

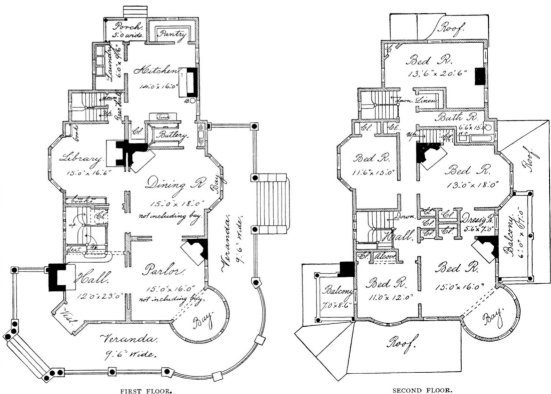

FIRST FLOOR.　　　　　　　SECOND FLOOR.

Address, THE CO-OPERATIVE BUILDING PLAN ASSOCIATION, Architects, 63 Broadway, New York.

FEASIBLE MODIFICATIONS: Heights of stories, colors, sizes of rooms and kinds of materials may be changed. Tower and balconies may be omitted. Extent of veranda may be reduced. Number of chimneys may be reduced. Fireplaces and sliding doors may be omitted wholly or in part. Attic may be left unfinished.

The price of working plans, specifications, etc., for a modified design varies according to the alterations required, and will be made known upon application to the Architects.

261

THE CO-OPERATIVE BUILDING PLAN ASSOCIATION, ARCHITECTS, 63 BROADWAY, NEW YORK.

Shoppell's Modern Houses—*Designs Patented.*   *Residence, Design No. 606*

PERSPECTIVE.

DESCRIPTION.

For explanation of all symbols(*† etc) see page 42.

GENERAL DIMENSIONS: Width, including veranda and dining room chimney, 51 ft. 8 in.; depth, including veranda and porch, 72 ft. Heights of stories: Cellar, 7 ft.; first story, 9 ft. 6 in.; second story, 9 ft; attic, 8 ft.

EXTERIOR MATERIALS: Foundations, stone; first story, clapboards; second story, gables and roofs, shingles.

INTERIOR FINISH: Entire house plastered for paper; plaster cornices in parlor, four bedrooms, and second story hall. Main stairway through all stories, and trim of first story, oak; second story trim, white wood stained to imitate hard wood; third story, yellow pine. House wired for electric bells and piped for gas. Hall ceiling open timbers, paneling between; dining room ceiling paneled flat. Hard wood inside Venetian blinds to windows in parlor, dining room, halls, and bedrooms over parlor and dining room. Outside blinds to all other windows. All interior woodwork finished in hard oil.

COLORS: Clapboards and veranda and balcony posts, light green. Trim, gable brackets, all cornices, veranda lattice work, rails and balusters, dark green. Shingles of second story, terra cotta stain. Gable shingles and panels, Tuscan yellow stain. Carved work over front entrance, terra cotta color. All brick-work Venetian red. Roof, dark red. Front doors are oak finished in natural color and hard oiled; all other outside doors painted dark green with light green panels. Sashes, Pompeian red. Veranda floor and ceiling, yellow pine, oiled.

ACCOMMODATIONS: The principal rooms and their sizes, closets, etc., are shown by the floor plans. Cellar under whole house contains servants' bath-room and W. C. A billiard room, hallway and two bedrooms finished in attic. Both stairways extend to attic. Sideboard recess in dining room.

COST: $8,500, † not including mantels, range and heater. The estimate is based on ‡ New York prices for materials and labor. In many sections of the country the cost should be less.

Price for working plans, specifications and * license to build,   - $85.00
Price for †† bill of materials,   -   -   -   -   -   -   20.00

FIRST FLOOR.

Porch. 5' 0" Wide.
Wash Tubs
Pantry
Closet
Kitchen 14'.2" x 22'.4"
Sink
Sink
Butler's Pantry 7'.0" x 22'.4"
Up
Down
Closet
Dining Room 16'.0" x 24'.6"
Hall. 17'.0" x 43'.6"
Up
Parlor, 16'.0" x 18'.0"
Alcove. 4'.0" x 6'.0"
Veranda
Veranda. 12'.0" Wide.

SECOND FLOOR.

Roof.
Bath Room 6'.0" x 12'.10"
Alcove. 5'.6" x 6'.6"
W. C.
Tub.
Bed Room. 13'.6" x 14'.0"
Rear Hall.
Down
Bed Room, 11'.0" x 17'.0"
Dressing Room 7'.0" x 8'.6"
Closet
Closet
Rear Hall
Linen Closet
Hall. 14'.0" x 20'.0"
Bed Room. 16'.0" x 20'.4"
Trunks. 6'.0" x 7'.0"
Down
Up
Passage.
Roof.
Bed Room. 16'.0" x 18'.4"
Bed Room. 12'.4" x 15'.10"
Roof.
Balcony. 5'.0" x 10'.0"
Roof.

Address, THE CO-OPERATIVE BUILDING PLAN ASSOCIATION, Architects, 63 Broadway, New York.

FEASIBLE MODIFICATIONS: Sizes of rooms, heights of stories, colors, and kinds of materials may be changed. Paneled ceilings, wainscoting, inside blinds, and some of the fireplaces may be omitted. A part or all of plumbing may be omitted. Balconies may be enclosed with glass. The portion of main hall back of stairway may be partitioned off to form a library or sitting room, still leaving a large, handsome hallway.

262

THE CO-OPERATIVE BUILDING PLAN ASSOCIATION, ARCHITECTS, 63 BROADWAY, NEW YORK.

Shoppell's Modern Houses—*Designs Patented.　　　　　*Residence, Design No. 585*

PERSPECTIVE.

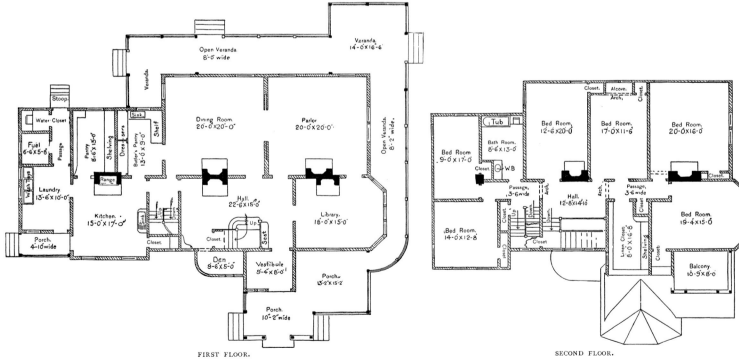

FIRST FLOOR.　　　　　SECOND FLOOR.

DESCRIPTION.

For explanation of all symbols (* † etc.) see page 42.

GENERAL DIMENSIONS: Width, 79 ft.; depth, 69 ft., including verandas. Heights of stories: Cellar, 7 ft. 6 in.; first story, 10 ft.; second story, 9 ft. 6 in.; attic, 9 ft.

EXTERIOR MATERIALS: Foundation, brick; first story, clapboards; second story, gables, dormers and roofs, shingles.

INTERIOR FINISH: Hard white plaster. Maple flooring in kitchen and butler's pantry. Yellow pine flooring in hall, den and vestibule. All other flooring soft woods. Yellow pine trim in hall, den and vestibule; remainder of house trimmed with white pine. Halls in first and second stories, kitchen and bath-room wainscoted. Main stairway, ash. Interior wood-work finished in hard oil. Front doors yellow pine, finished in hard oil.

COLORS: Clapboards, light olive drab. Trim and rain conductors, bronze green. All outside doors, except front door, and all veranda posts, rails and balusters, dark green. Blinds and sashes, maroon. Veranda floors and ceiling, oiled. Wall shingles dipped and and brush coated sienna stain. Roof shingles dipped and brush coated dark red stain.

ACCOMMODATIONS: The principal rooms and their sizes, closets, etc., are shown by the plans. Cellar under hall, parlor, library and dining room, with inside and outside entrances and concrete floor. Three fine rooms and hall finished in attic. Extensive veranda with portions left uncovered to admit ample light to first story. Six fireplaces. Large hall with handsome staircase. Ample pantries and closets. Loft over attic rooms floored for storage.

COST: $8,500, † not including mantels, range and heater. The estimate is based on ‡ New York prices for materials and labor. In many sections of the country the cost should be less.

Price for working plans, specifications and * license to build,　-　-　-　-　-　-　-　-　-　-　-　$85.00

Price for †† bill of materials,　-　-　-　-　-　-　15.00

263

THE CO-OPERATIVE BUILDING PLAN ASSOCIATION, ARCHITECTS, 63 BROADWAY, NEW YORK.

*Shoppell's Modern Houses—*Designs Patented.*   *Residence, Design No. 418*

PERSPECTIVE.

DESCRIPTION.

For explanation of all symbols (* † etc.) see page 42.

GENERAL DIMENSIONS: Extreme width, 47 ft. 6 in.; depth over all, 68 ft. Heights of stories: Cellar, 7 ft.; first story, 12 ft.; second story, 10 ft.; attic, 8 ft.

EXTERIOR MATERIALS: Foundation, stone; first and second stories, brick; gables, panels and shingles; roof, slate. Outside blinds.

INTERIOR FINISH: Hard white plaster; plaster cornices and centers in parlor, dining and sitting room, library and front hall, and in hall and three principal bedrooms of second story. Double floor in first story, finishing with hard pine; soft wood floors elsewhere. Soft wood trim. Oak stairs. Stained glass in main staircase arched window, colors to be approved by owner. Panels under windows in parlor, dining and sitting room and library. Picture molding in principal rooms and hall of first story. Chair rail in dining room. Wainscot in bath-room and kitchen. Interior wood-work finished in hard oil.

COLORS: Brick-work cleaned down at completion and oiled. Trim, rain conductors and outside blinds, bronze green. Outside doors, dark green. Veranda floor, light drab. Veranda ceiling varnished. Sashes, dark red.

ACCOMMODATIONS: The principal rooms and their sizes, closets, etc., are shown by the plans. Cellar under half the house, with inside and outside entrance, concrete floor and laundry with three tubs. Open fireplaces in hall, parlor, dining and sitting room, and one bedroom. Three rooms in attic. Wide verandas. Large hall and handsome staircase. High ceilings.

FIRST FLOOR.

SECOND FLOOR.

COST: $9,000, † not including mantels, range and heater. The estimate is based on ‡ New York prices for materials and labor. In many sections of the country the cost should be less.

Price for working plans, specifications and * license to build, - $125.00

Price for †† bill of materials, - - - - - - 25.00

Address, THE CO-OPERATIVE BUILDING PLAN ASSOCIATION, Architects, 63 Broadway, New York.

FEASIBLE MODIFICATIONS: Heights of stories, colors, sizes of rooms and kinds of materials may be changed. Cellar may be enlarged or omitted. Attic finish, any or all fireplaces, and mantels, sliding doors, part or all of plumbing, and open balconies, may be omitted. Front bedroom may be enlarged at expense of hall.

The price of working plans, specifications, etc., for a modified design varies according to the alterations required, and will be made known upon application to the Architects.

264

THE CO-OPERATIVE BUILDING PLAN ASSOCIATION, ARCHITECTS, 63 BROADWAY, NEW YORK.

*Shoppell's Modern Houses—*Designs Patented.*   *Residence, Design No. 542*

SIDE-ELEVATION

PERSPECTIVE.

DESCRIPTION.

GENERAL DIMENSIONS: Extreme width, 39 ft. 8 in.; depth, including rear veranda, 62 ft. 4 in. Heights of stories: Cellar, 7 ft.; first story, 10 ft. 6 in.; second story, 9 ft. 6 in.; attic, 7 ft. 8 in.

EXTERIOR MATERIALS: Foundations, stone; first and second stories, brick; gables and bay window, panels and shingles; roof, slate. Outside blinds to all windows except those of the parlor and bay.

INTERIOR FINISH: Hard white plaster; plaster cornices and centers in parlor, dining room and hall. Ceiling of parlor paneled in plaster. Hard pine flooring in first story. Soft wood flooring elsewhere. Double flooring in first story. Oak trim in hall and library; cherry trim stained mahogany in parlor; soft wood trim elsewhere. Main staircase, oak. Inside folding blinds in parlor; inside Venetian blinds in dining room and library windows. Panels under windows in parlor, library and dining room. Chair rail in dining room. Wainscot in bath-room and kitchen. Interior wood-work finished in hard oil.

COLORS: All brick-work cleaned down at completion. Trim and rain conductors, chocolate. Outside doors, light brown. Blinds, Pompeian red. Sashes, cherry red. Veranda floor and ceiling oiled. Wall shingles on bays dipped and brush coated butternut brown stain. Shingles in gables dipped and brush coated terra cotta stain.

ACCOMMODATIONS: The principal rooms and their sizes, closets, etc., are shown by the plans. Cellar under the whole house, with inside and outside entrance and concrete floor. Five bedrooms in attic. Laundry with three tubs in basement. Fireplaces and mantels in library and dining room, also a mantel in parlor and set range in kitchen, included in estimate. Sliding doors between hall, parlor, library and dining room.

COST $9,000 † not including heater. The estimate is based on ‡ New York prices for materials and labor. In many sections of the country the cost should be less.

Price for working plans, specifications and * license to build, - $80.00
Price for †† bill of materials, - - - - - - - 20.00
Address, THE CO-OPERATIVE BUILDING PLAN ASSOCIATION, Architects, 63 Broadway, New York.

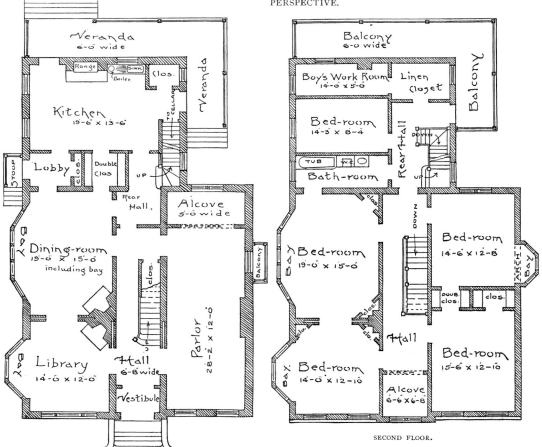

FIRST FLOOR.

SECOND FLOOR.

FEASIBLE MODIFICATIONS: Heights of stories, colors, sizes of rooms and kinds of materials may be changed. Cellar may be reduced in size and concrete floor omitted. Rear bedroom may be enlarged by including boy's work room. Rear veranda may be reduced in size and balcony omitted. Veranda may be placed across the front and at either side. Small bedroom may be planned with the space of linen closet and a part of rear hall. Fireplaces and mantels, sliding doors, attic finish and a part or all plumbing may be omitted.

265

THE CO-OPERATIVE BUILDING PLAN ASSOCIATION, ARCHITECTS, 63 BROADWAY, NEW YORK.

*Shoppell's Modern Houses—*Designs Patented.*   *Residence, Design No. 480*

PERSPECTIVE.

DESCRIPTION.

For explanation of all symbols (* † etc.) see page 42.

GENERAL DIMENSIONS : Width over all, 44 ft.; depth, including veranda, 69 ft. Heights of stories : Cellar, 7 ft.; first story, 10 ft.; second story 9 ft.; attic, 8 ft. 6 in.

EXTERIOR MATERIALS : Foundation, first story, and main part of second story, stone; rear part of second story, shingles; gables, panels and shingles; veranda and laundry roofs, shingles; main roof, red slate. Outside blinds to windows of first and second stories and kitchen extension.

INTERIOR FINISH : Hard white plaster; plaster cornices and centers in hall, parlor, dining room and library, and in hall and three bedrooms of second story. Soft wood flooring ; parlor trim, cherry ; library trim, butternut ; dining room and hall trim, oak. All other trim, soft wood. Oak staircase. Panels under windows in first and second story main rooms. Picture molding in principal rooms and halls. Wainscot in bath-room and kitchen. Front doors, oak. Interior wood-work finished in hard oil.

COLORS : Stone and brick-work cleaned down with acid at completion of work. Brick-work painted Indian red. Trim and rain conductors, bronze green. Rear outside doors, dark olive drab. Front entrance doors to hall and library finished in hard oil. Sashes, dark green. Veranda floor and ceiling, oiled. Roof shingles dipped and brush coated Indian red.

ACCOMMODATIONS : The principal rooms and their sizes, closets, etc., are shown by the plans. Cellar under all but laundry. Three bedrooms, and bath-room for servants, in attic. Separate boiler for hot water in laundry. Seven open fireplaces and mantels included in estimate. Sliding doors between dining room, parlor and library, and between two principal bedrooms of second story.

COST: $9,880, † not including range and heater. The estimate is based on ‡ New York prices for materials and labor. In many sections of the country the cost should be less.

Price for working plans, specifications and
* license to build, - - - - - - $88.80
   Price for †† bill of materials, - - - 10.00

Address, THE CO-OPERATIVE BUILDING PLAN ASSOCIATION, Architects, 63 Broadway, New York.

FEASIBLE MODIFICATIONS : Heights of stories, colors, sizes of rooms and kinds of materials may be changed. Front veranda may be reduced in size. Side entrance to library may be omitted. Sliding doors, open fireplaces and mantels, part or all of plumbing, and any or all attic rooms, may be omitted. Laundry may be omitted and tubs placed in kitchen or in basement.

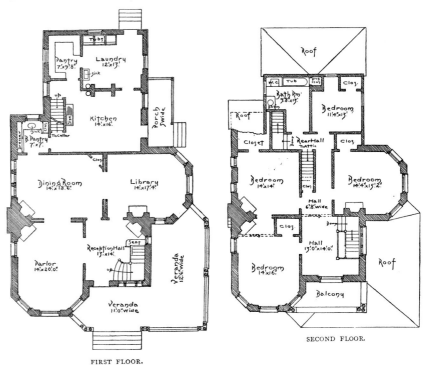

FIRST FLOOR.

SECOND FLOOR.

THE CO-OPERATIVE BUILDING PLAN ASSOCIATION, ARCHITECTS, 63 BROADWAY, NEW YORK.

*Shoppell's Modern Houses—*Designs Patented.*   Residence, Design No. 524A

PERSPECTIVE.

DESCRIPTION.

GENERAL DIMENSIONS: Width, 44 ft. 10 in.; depth, including front veranda, 60 ft. 4 in. Heights of stories: Cellar, 7 ft. 6 in.; first story, 11 ft.; second story, 10 ft.; attic, 9 ft.

EXTERIOR MATERIALS: Foundations and first story, stone; second story, brick; gables, shingles and panels; roof, slate. Outside blinds.

INTERIOR FINISH: Hard white plaster; plaster cornices and centers in parlor, library, dining and sitting room, and main halls first and second stories. Double flooring in first story; hall and passage finished with parquetry flooring. Hard pine flooring in kitchen. Maple and oak, alternate strips, in bath-room. Soft wood flooring elsewhere. Trim in hall and passage first story, sycamore; dining room, ash; bath-room, chestnut; all other trim soft wood. Panels under windows in principal rooms first and second stories. Wainscot in bath-room and kitchen. Interior wood-work finished in hard oil.

COLORS: All stone and brick-work cleaned down at completion. Trim and rain conductors, dark bronze green. Outside doors and blinds, light bronze green. Sashes in stonework, Pompeian red; and in brick-work, dark olive green. Veranda floor and ceiling oiled. Wall shingles dipped and brush coated dark red stain. Panels in gables, Pompeian red. Veranda roof shingles dipped and brush coated dark red stain.

ACCOMMODATIONS: The principal rooms and their sizes, closets, etc., are shown by the plans. Cellar under whole house. Laundry, with three stationary tubs and servants' water-closet, in basement. Seven open fireplaces and mantels, and set range, included in estimate. Sliding doors connect principal rooms of first floor. Six bedrooms on second floor and two on attic floor.

COST: $9,000, † not including heater. The estimate is based on ‡ New York prices for materials and labor.

FIRST FLOOR.

SECOND FLOOR.

Price for working plans, specifications and * license to build, - - - - - - - - - - - - $100.00
Price for †† bill of materials, - - - - - - - - 25.00
Address THE CO-OPERATIVE BUILDING PLAN ASSOCIATION, Architects, 63 Broadway, New York.

FEASIBLE MODIFICATIONS: Heights of stories, colors, sizes of rooms and kinds of materials may be changed. Cellar may be reduced and concrete floor omitted. Attic rooms, any or all fireplaces and mantels, sliding doors, part or all of plumbing, balconies, and part of veranda, may be omitted.

267

THE CO-OPERATIVE BUILDING PLAN ASSOCIATION, ARCHITECTS, 63 BROADWAY, NEW YORK.

*Shoppell's Modern Houses—*Designs Patented.*   *Residence, Design No. 582*

PERSPECTIVE.

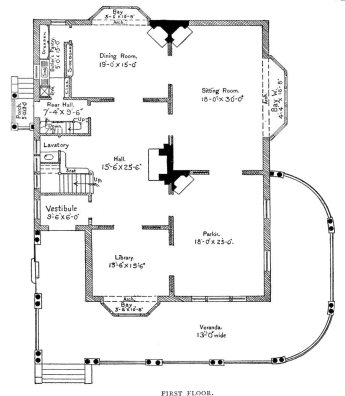

FIRST FLOOR.

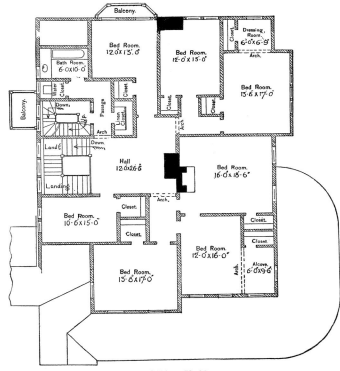

SECOND FLOOR.

DESCRIPTION.

For explanation of all symbols (* † etc.) see page 42.

GENERAL DIMENSIONS: Width, including veranda and porte-cochere, 72 ft. 4 in.; depth, including veranda and dining room bay, 73 ft. 10 in. Heights of stories: Cellar, 9 ft.; first story, 11 ft. 6 in.; second story, 9 ft.; attic, 8 ft. 7 in.

EXTERIOR MATERIALS: Foundations, stone; first story, brick; second story, gables, dormers and roofs, shingles.

INTERIOR FINISH: Hard white plaster and plaster cornices and centers in main hall, dining and sitting rooms, parlor and library; cornices only in vestibule and main hall and in all rooms of second story. Double floors in first and second stories, finishing with butternut in hall and vestibule. Interior trim, main hall and vestibule butternut; remainder of house white pine. Wainscot in hall, vestibule, bath-room and kitchen. Panels under windows in library, sitting and dining rooms, parlor and vestibule. Main stairway butternut. Open timber ceiling in hall. All interior wood-work finished in hard oil.

COLORS: All brick-work, oiled. Body wood-work of bay windows first story, light drab. Trim and rain conductors, dark drab. Front door finished in hard oil. Other outside doors and blinds, light drab. Sashes, Pompeian red. Veranda floor oiled. Veranda ceiling varnished. Wall shingles dipped and brush coated umber stain. Roof shingles dipped and brush coated silver stain.

ACCOMMODATIONS: The principal rooms and their sizes, closets, etc., are shown by the plans. Cellar under whole house, a part of it being used for cisterns, laundry, servants' W. C., kitchen and pantries. Four rooms and hallway finished in attic. Loft over attic floored for storage. Dumb waiter from basement to first story. Five fireplaces and mantels included in estimate. House piped for gas.

COST: $12,000, † not including range and heating apparatus. The estimate is based on ‡ New York prices for materials and labor. In many sections of the country the cost should be less.

Price for working plans, specifications and * license to build, - - - - - - - - - - - $100.00
Price for †† bill of materials, - - - - - - - 25.00

THE CO-OPERATIVE BUILDING PLAN ASSOCIATION, ARCHITECTS, 63 BROADWAY, NEW YORK.

Shoppell's Modern Houses—*Designs Patented.   *Residence, Design No. 419*

PERSPECTIVE.

DESCRIPTION.

For explanation of all symbols (* † etc.) see page 42.

GENERAL DIMENSIONS : Width over all, 60 ft.; depth, including veranda, 74 ft. 6 in. Heights of stories: Cellar, 8 ft.; first story, 10 ft.; second story, 9 ft. 6 in.; attic, 9 ft.

EXTERIOR MATERIALS: Foundation and first story, stone; second story and veranda roof, shingles ; gables, panels and shingles ; roof, slate. Outside blinds to all windows.

INTERIOR FINISH : Hard white plaster. Double flooring in first story. Yellow pine floor in rear hall, pantries, kitchen and bath-room; hall floor, quartered oak ; soft wood flooring elsewhere. Hall trim, oak ; other trim, soft wood. Panels under windows of main rooms in first and second story. Main staircase, oak. Wainscot in bath-room and kitchen. Interior wood-work finished in hard oil.

COLORS : Stone and brick-work to be cleaned down. Brickwork painted Pompeian red. Trim and rain conductors, dark olive drab. Front door finished in hard oil ; other outside doors, blinds, and panels in gables, painted olive. Sashes, Pompeian red. Veranda floor and ceiling, oiled. Wall shingles dipped and brush coated red stain. Gable shingles dipped and brush coated light sienna stain. Veranda roof shingles dipped and brush coated slate color.

ACCOMMODATIONS : The principal rooms and their sizes, closets, etc., are shown by the plans. Cellar under whole house. Laundry with three tubs, also servants' water-closet, in basement. Five rooms in attic. Eight open fireplaces with wood mantels, also set range in kitchen, included in estimate. Stationary wash-bowls, hot and cold water, in two dressing rooms. Six bedrooms in second story. Sliding doors connect all principal rooms of first story. Passages connect front and rear hall in both stories. Open balcony in attic. All fireplaces supplied with flues leading to ash-pits in cellar. Dish slide between kitchen and butler's pantry.

COST : $12,200, † not including heater. The estimate is based on ‡ New York prices for materials and labor. In many sections of the country the cost should be less.

Price for working plans, specifications and * license to build, - - - - - - - - - - - - $125.00
Price for † † bill of materials, - - - - - 25.00

Address, THE CO-OPERATIVE BUILDING PLAN ASSOCIATION Architects, 63 Broadway, New York.

FEASIBLE MODIFICATIONS : Heights of stories, colors, sizes of rooms and kinds of materials may be changed. Laundry tubs may be placed in kitchen. Attic rooms, part or all of plumbing, any or all fireplaces, mantels, sliding doors and open balcony may be omitted. Veranda may be reduced. Tower may be omitted. Open balcony may be planned as part of a room.

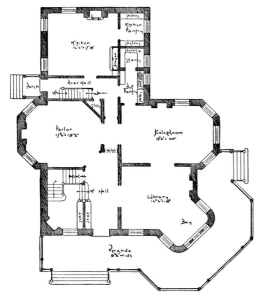

FIRST FLOOR.

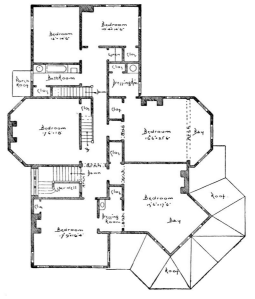

SECOND FLOOR.

THE CO-OPERATIVE BUILDING PLAN ASSOCIATION, ARCHITECTS, 63 BROADWAY, NEW YORK.

Shoppell's Modern Houses—*Designs Patented.*   *Residence, Design No. 544*

PERSPECTIVE.

DESCRIPTION.

For explanation of all symbols (* † etc.) see page 42.

GENERAL DIMENSIONS: Width through dining and sitting rooms, 47 ft.; depth, including veranda and porch, 75 ft. 8 in. Heights of stories: Cellar, 8 ft.; first story, 11 ft. 6 in.; second story, 10 ft.; attic, 8 ft.

EXTERIOR MATERIALS: Foundations, stone; first and second stories, brick; gables, tiles; roof, slate. Outside blinds to all windows except those of the dining and sitting room.

INTERIOR FINISH: Hard white plaster; plaster cornices and centers in hall, parlor, dining and sitting rooms. Double floors in first and second stories, finishing with soft woods except in main hall, where the finishing floor is oak, and in kitchen and laundry, where it is maple. Trim in main hall, first and second story, alcove and dining room, quartered oak; in parlor and bath-room, cherry; in sitting room, red mahogany; in front bedroom and sewing room, butternut; in north bedroom, bird's-eye maple; in large bed-room, sycamore; in basement and attic, white pine; all other trim, Georgia pine. Main staircase, oak. Interior wood-work finished in hard oil. Wainscot in bath-room and main hall, dining and sitting room, second story hall and kitchen.

COLORS: All stone and brick-work cleaned down at completion. Brick-work, oiled. Trim, rear outside doors, veranda posts, railing, cornices, and frames of all panel work, dark green. All ornamental or plain panels, Tuscan yellow. Veranda floor and ceiling, oiled.

ACCOMMODATIONS: The principal rooms and their sizes, closets, etc., are shown by the plans. Cellar under whole house. Four bedrooms, storage and trunk rooms in attic. Laundry with set tubs, servants' bath-room and water-closet, also store-closet in basement. Six open fireplaces and mantels included in estimate. Wash-basin and toilet-closet under main staircase. Square hall with staircase of elegant design. Sliding doors connect principal rooms and hall of first story. Large pantries and ice room. Rear stairs from cellar to attic.

COST: $15,000, † not including range and heater. The estimate is based on ‡ New York prices for materials and labor. In many sections of the country the cost should be less.

Price for working plans, specifications and * license to build, - - - $150.00
Price for †† bill of materials, - 30.00

Address, THE CO-OPERATIVE BUILDING PLAN ASSOCIATION, Architects, 63 Broadway, New York.

FEASIBLE MODIFICATIONS: Heights of stories, colors, sizes of rooms and kinds of materials, may be changed. Any or all open fireplaces, mantels, sliding doors, a part of veranda, and part or all of plumbing, may be omitted. Open balconies may be enclosed with sliding sashes or planned to form part of adjoining rooms.

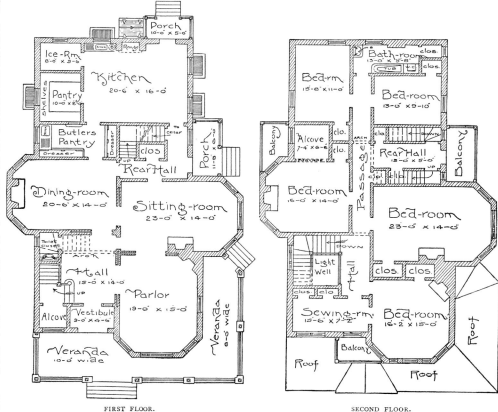

FIRST FLOOR.   SECOND FLOOR.

270

THE CO-OPERATIVE BUILDING PLAN ASSOCIATION, ARCHITECTS, 63 BROADWAY, NEW YORK.

*Shoppell's Modern Houses—*Designs Patented.*   *Residence, Design No. 366A*

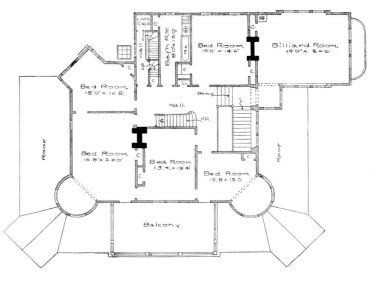

Side View of House.

PERSPECTIVE.

DESCRIPTION.

For explanation of all symbols (* † etc.) see page 42.

GENERAL DIMENSIONS: Width over all, 91 ft.; depth, including veranda, 78 ft. Heights of stories: Cellar, 8 ft.; first story, 12 ft.; second story, 10 ft.; attic, 8 ft. 6 in.

EXTERIOR MATERIALS: Foundations, stone; first story, stone and clapboards; second story, shingles; gables, panels and shingles; roof, tile.

INTERIOR FINISH: Hard white plaster. Plaster cornices and centers in parlor, dining room and three bedrooms of second story. Soft wood flooring and trim. Inside Venetian blinds in dining room, parlor, main hall, and all bedrooms and billiard room. Soft wood staircase. Wainscot in main halls, including main staircase, dining and billiard room, bath-room and kitchen. Ceiling of main hall first story, and of billiard room, paneled with wood. Interior wood-work finished in hard oil, stained to suit owner.

COLORS: Clapboards painted color to match stone-work. Trim of first story, bronze green; trim above first story, light brown. Outside doors and all panels under windows, dark green. Blinds, light brown. Sashes, Pompeian red. Veranda floor, and all brick-work, oiled. Veranda ceiling, varnished. All paneling in gables, etc., dark brown with light brown framing. Wall shingles oiled.

ACCOMMODATIONS: The principal rooms and their sizes, closets, etc., are shown by the plans. Cellar under whole house. Laundry and servants' hall in basement. Two guest and two servants' bedrooms in attic. Very large hall, handsome staircase, and stained glass window. Open fireplaces in hall, parlor, dining room, billiard room and three bedrooms. Lavatory with water-closet and wash-bowl off rear hall. Stationary wash-bowl in billiard room.

COST: $15,000, † not including mantels, range and heater. The estimate is based on ‡ New York prices for materials and labor. In many sections of the country the cost should be less.

Price for working plans, specifications and * license to build, - $125.00
Price for †† bill of materials, - - - - - - - - - 50.00

Address, THE CO-OPERATIVE BUILDING PLAN ASSOCIATION, Architects, 63 Broadway, New York.

FEASIBLE MODIFICATIONS; Heights of stories, colors, sizes of rooms and kinds of materials may be changed. Porte-cochere and billiard room may be omitted. Veranda may be reduced and either or both towers omitted. Attic tower may be enclosed with sliding sash. Sliding doors, fireplaces and mantels, part or all of plumbing, attic rooms, and second story open balconies, may be omitted.

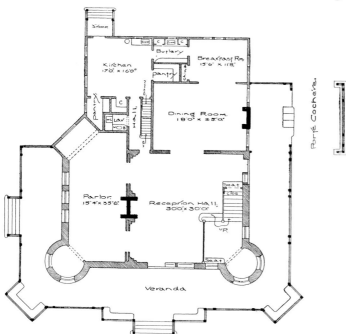

FIRST FLOOR.

SECOND FLOOR.

271

THE CO-OPERATIVE BUILDING PLAN ASSOCIATION, ARCHITECTS, 63 BROADWAY, NEW YORK.

*Shoppell's Modern Houses—*Designs Patented.*

Residence, Design No. 420

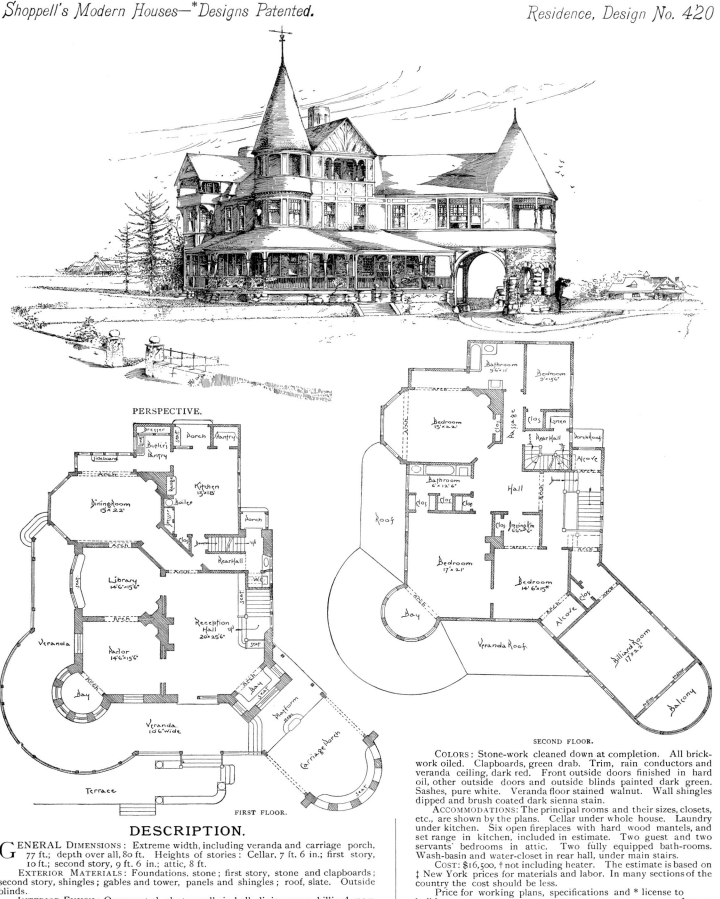

PERSPECTIVE.

FIRST FLOOR.

SECOND FLOOR.

DESCRIPTION.

GENERAL DIMENSIONS: Extreme width, including veranda and carriage porch, 77 ft.; depth over all, 80 ft. Heights of stories: Cellar, 7 ft. 6 in.; first story, 10 ft.; second story, 9 ft. 6 in.; attic, 8 ft.

EXTERIOR MATERIALS: Foundations, stone; first story, stone and clapboards; second story, shingles; gables and tower, panels and shingles; roof, slate. Outside blinds.

INTERIOR FINISH: Ornamented plaster walls in hall, dining room, billiard room and front bedroom. All plaster to be sand finish. Ash flooring with rough diagonal under-flooring in first story. Hard pine flooring in second story. All other flooring soft wood. Oak trim in hall and dining room; cherry in reception room and library; soft wood elsewhere. Panels under windows in hall, library, reception and dining room. Main staircase, oak. Paneled ceilings in hall, dining and billiard room. Wainscot in bath-room and kitchen. Lincrusta Walton dado in dining room, main hall (both stories), main stairway and billiard room. Interior wood-work stained to suit owner and finished in hard oil.

COLORS: Stone-work cleaned down at completion. All brick-work oiled. Clapboards, green drab. Trim, rain conductors and veranda ceiling, dark red. Front outside doors finished in hard oil, other outside doors and outside blinds painted dark green. Sashes, pure white. Veranda floor stained walnut. Wall shingles dipped and brush coated dark sienna stain.

ACCOMMODATIONS: The principal rooms and their sizes, closets, etc., are shown by the plans. Cellar under whole house. Laundry under kitchen. Six open fireplaces with hard wood mantels, and set range in kitchen, included in estimate. Two guest and two servants' bedrooms in attic. Two fully equipped bath-rooms. Wash-basin and water-closet in rear hall, under main stairs.

COST: $16,500, † not including heater. The estimate is based on ‡ New York prices for materials and labor. In many sections of the country the cost should be less.

Price for working plans, specifications and * license to build, - - - - - - - - - - - $150.00
Price for †† bill of materials, - - - - - - 50.00
Address, THE CO-OPERATIVE BUILDING PLAN ASSOCIATION, Architects, 63 Broadway, New York.

FEASIBLE MODIFICATIONS: Heights of stories, colors, sizes of rooms and kinds of materials may be changed. Carriage porch and billiard room may be omitted. Open balconies may be closed. Tower, sliding doors, fireplaces, mantels, part or all of attic finish, part or all of plumbing, and hard wood, may be omitted.

272

THE CO-OPERATIVE BUILDING PLAN ASSOCIATION, ARCHITECTS, 63 BROADWAY, NEW YORK.

Shoppell's Modern Houses—*Designs Patented.   *Row of Dwellings, Design No. 268*

PERSPECTIVE.

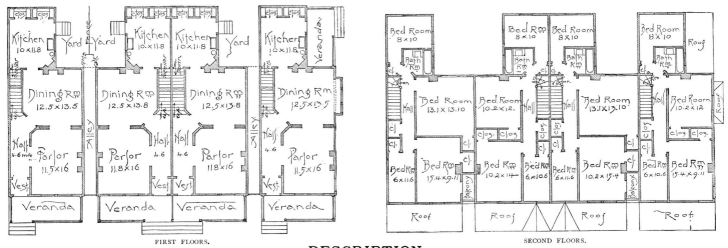

FIRST FLOORS.   SECOND FLOORS.

DESCRIPTION.

For explanation of all symbols (* † etc.) see page 42.

GENERAL DIMENSIONS: Extreme width, 76 ft. 6 in.; depth, including verandas, 50 ft. Heights of stories: Cellar, 7 ft.; first story, 10 ft.; second story, 9 ft. 6 in.

EXTERIOR MATERIALS: Foundations, stone; first story, clapboards; second story, clapboards and shingles; roof, tin. Outside blinds to all windows except those of the cellar.

INTERIOR FINISH: Hard white plaster; plaster cornices and centers in halls, parlors and dining rooms. Soft wood flooring and trim. Ash staircase. Chair rail in dining rooms. Bath-rooms and kitchens wainscoted. Interior wood-work finished in hard oil.

COLORS: All clapboards, dark brown. Trim, outside doors, blinds and rain conductors, dark green. Sashes, maroon. Veranda floor, bronze green. Veranda ceiling, light drab. Brick-work, Indian red. Shingles dipped and brush coated reddish stain. Roof painted red.

ACCOMMODATIONS: The principal rooms and their sizes, closets, etc., are shown by the plans. Cellars under all with outside and inside cellar entrance to each house. Two open fireplaces and two

mantels for each house, also kitchen range, included in estimate. Sliding doors connect parlors and dining rooms. Bath-rooms with water-closets and bath tubs. Sink and boiler in kitchens. Joint alleyways to rear yards.

COST: $7,820 for four dwellings, † not including heaters. The estimate is based on ‡ New York prices for materials and labor In many sections of the country the cost should be less.

Price for working plans, specifications and * license to build, - - - - - - - - - - - - - $25.00
Price for † † bill of materials, - - - - - - 5.00

Address, THE CO-OPERATIVE BUILDING PLAN ASSOCIATION, Architects, 63 Broadway, New York.

FEASIBLE MODIFICATIONS: Heights of stories, colors, sizes of rooms and kinds of materials may be changed. Cellars may be reduced in size or omitted. Fireplaces and mantels, sliding doors, and part or all of plumbing, may be omitted. Verandas may be reduced in size. Gable or mansard roofs may be added, providing an attic or full third story.

273

THE CO-OPERATIVE BUILDING PLAN ASSOCIATION, ARCHITECTS, 63 BROADWAY, NEW YORK.

Shoppell's Modern Houses—*Designs Patented.　　　　　　　*Double Cottage, Design No. 179*

FRONT ELEVATION.

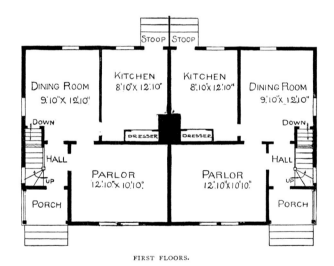

FIRST FLOORS.

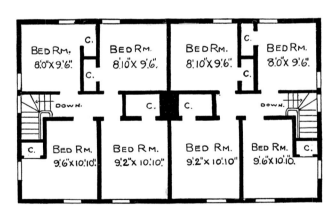

SECOND FLOORS.

DESCRIPTION.

For explanation of all symbols (* † etc.) see page 42.

GENERAL DIMENSIONS : Width, 39 ft. 6 in.; depth, 25 ft. Heights of stories : Cellar, 7 ft.; first story, 8 ft. 6 in.; second story, 8 ft.

EXTERIOR MATERIALS : Foundations, stone; first story, clapboards ; second story and roof, shingles ; gables, panels.

INTERIOR FINISH : Hard white plaster ; plaster cornices in halls, parlors and dining rooms. Soft wood flooring and trim. Ash staircases. Interior wood-work finished in hard oil.

COLORS : Clapboards, veranda floor and ceiling, olive. Trim, cornices, blinds and sashes, dark brown. Panels in gables and second story, dark green with dark red frames. Outside doors, dark green. Brick-work, Indian red. All shingles dipped and brush coated red stain.

ACCOMMODATIONS : The principal rooms and their sizes, closets, etc., are shown by the plans. Cellar under each house. Attics suitable for storage. Porches widely separated. Central chimney serves for both houses.

COST : $2,325. The estimate is based on ‡ New York prices for materials and labor. In many sections of the country the cost should be less.

Price for working plans, specifications and * license to build,　-　-　-　-　-　-　-　-　-　-　-　$25.00
Price for † † bill of materials,　-　-　-　-　-　5.00

Address, THE CO-OPERATIVE BUILDING PLAN ASSOCIATION, Architects, 63 Broadway, New York.

FEASIBLE MODIFICATIONS : Heights of stories, colors, sizes of rooms and kinds of materials may be changed. Cellar may be reduced in size or omitted. Bath-rooms with partial or full plumbing may be introduced. Sliding doors, open fireplaces and mantels may be added. A one or two story extension may be added at rear.

The price of working plans, specifications, etc., for a modified design varies according to the alterations required, and will be made known upon application to the Architects.

274

THE CO-OPERATIVE BUILDING PLAN ASSOCIATION, ARCHITECTS, 63 BROADWAY, NEW YORK.

Shoppell's Modern Houses—*Designs Patented.　　　*Double Cottage, Design No. 553*

PERSPECTIVE.

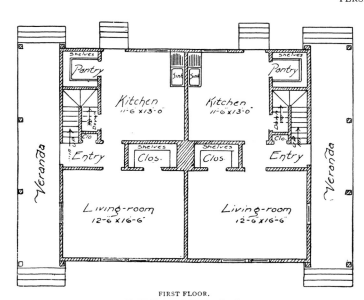

FIRST FLOOR.

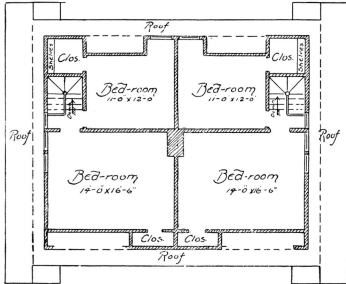

SECOND FLOOR.

DESCRIPTION.

For explanation of all symbols (* † etc.) see page 42.

GENERAL DIMENSIONS: Extreme width, 46 ft.; depth, 31 ft. Heights of stories: Cellar, 6 ft. 6 in.; first story, 8 ft. 6 in.; second story, 8 ft.

EXTERIOR MATERIALS: Foundation, stone; first story, clapboards; second story, gables and roof, shingles. Outside blinds to first and second story windows.

INTERIOR FINISH: Hard white plaster. Soft wood flooring, trim and stairways. Interior wood-work painted tints to suit owner.

COLORS: Clapboards, light brown. Trim, veranda posts and all cornices, seal brown. Second story shingles dipped and brush coated light brown. Gable shingles over second story windows dipped and brush coated Tuscan yellow. Roof shingles dipped and brush coated red stain.

ACCOMMODATIONS: The principal rooms and their sizes, closets, etc., are shown by the plans. Cellar under whole structure. No attic—air space floored for storage. A central chimney serves both houses. Extensive verandas. Large pantries.

COST: $2,500. The estimate is based on ‡ New York prices for materials and labor. In many sections of the country the cost should be less.

Price for working plans, specifications and * license to build, - - - - - - - - - - - $20.00
Price for † † bill of materials, - - - - 10.00
Address, THE CO-OPERATIVE BUILDING PLAN ASSOCIATION, Architects, 63 Broadway, New York.

FEASIBLE MODIFICATIONS: Heights of stories, colors, sizes of rooms and kinds of materials may be changed. Cellars may be reduced in size or omitted. Verandas may be greatly reduced.

The price of working plans, specifications, etc., for a modified design varies according to the alterations required, and will be made known upon application to the Architects.

275

THE CO-OPERATIVE BUILDING PLAN ASSOCIATION, ARCHITECTS, 63 BROADWAY, NEW YORK.

*Shoppell's Modern Houses—*Designs Patented.*   *Two-Family Cottage, Design No. 545*

PERSPECTIVE.

DESCRIPTION.

For explanation of all symbols (* † etc.) see page 42.

GENERAL DIMENSIONS: Width, 24 ft. 2 in.; depth, including veranda and porches, 34 ft. 9 in. Heights of stories: First story, 9 ft.; second story, 8 ft. 4 in.

EXTERIOR MATERIALS: Foundation, posts; first and second stories, clapboards; gables and roof, shingles. Outside blinds.

INTERIOR FINISH: Tinted two coat plastering. Soft wood flooring and trim. Hard pine staircase. Interior wood-work finished in hard oil. Living rooms wainscoted.

COLORS: All clapboards, dark drab. Trim, veranda floor, and steps, bronze green. Outside doors, bronze green with dark red panels. Blinds, sashes and rain conductors, dark red. Veranda ceiling, oiled. All shingles dipped and brush coated dark red stain.

ACCOMMODATIONS: The principal rooms and their sizes, closets, etc., are shown by the plans. Coal bins, oil barrels, and earth closets, for each family. Sinks and pumps in living room closets. No cellar nor attic. Air space over second story floored. House designed to be used by one or two families. Front entrances combine to present the appearance of one entrance only.

COST: $1,700. The estimate is based on ‡ New York prices for materials and labor. In many sections of the country the cost should be less.

Price for working plans, specifications and * license to build, - - - - - - - - - - - $10.00

Price for †† bill of materials, - - - - 5.00

Address: THE CO-OPERATIVE BUILDING PLAN ASSOCIATION, Architects, 63 Broadway, New York.

FEASIBLE MODIFICATIONS: Heights of stories, colors, sizes of rooms and kinds of materials may be changed. Cellar may be

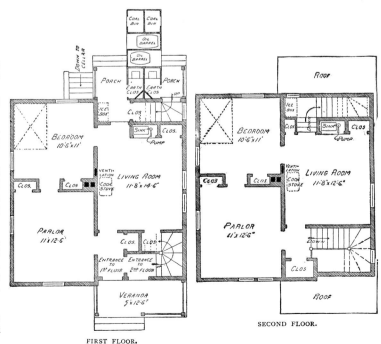

FIRST FLOOR.

SECOND FLOOR.

placed under a part or whole. Bath-rooms with partial or full plumbing may be planned. Earth closets and rear sheds may be omitted. Sliding doors, open fireplaces and mantels, may be introduced.

The price of working plans, specifications, etc., for a modified design varies according to the alterations required, and will be made known upon application to the Architects.

276

THE CO-OPERATIVE BUILDING PLAN ASSOCIATION, ARCHITECTS, 63 BROADWAY, NEW YORK.

*Shoppell's Modern Houses—*Designs Patented.*   *Two-Family House, Design No. 439*

PERSPECTIVE.

DESCRIPTION.

For explanation of all symbols * † etc.) see page 42.

GENERAL DIMENSIONS: Extreme width, 25 ft.; extreme depth, 63 ft. Heights of stories: Cellar, 6 ft. 6 in.; first story, 10 ft.; second story, 9 ft.

EXTERIOR MATERIALS: Foundation, brick walls; first story, clapboards; second story, roof and gables, shingles. Outside blinds to windows of first and second story.

INTERIOR FINISH: Hard white plaster. Soft wood flooring, trim and stairs; all finished in hard oil.

COLORS: Clapboards and all paneling, light red. Trim, outside doors and blinds, dark red. All shingles dipped and brush coated moss green stain.

ACCOMMODATIONS: The principal rooms and their sizes, closets, etc., are shown by the plans. Separate entrance for each family. Designed for one small and one large family. Bath-rooms for each. Three attic rooms in connection with the larger apartments. Cellar under whole house, with inside and front outside entrances. Five open fireplaces with mantels.

COST: $3,000, † not including mantels, ranges and heaters. The estimate is based on ‡ New York prices for materials and labor. In many sections of the country the cost should be less.

Price for working plans, specifications and * license to build,   - - $35.00

Price for † † bill of materials, - - - - - - - - - - - - 5.00

Address, THE CO-OPERATIVE BUILDING PLAN ASSOCIATION, Architects, 63 Broadway, New York.

FEASIBLE MODIFICATIONS: Heights of stories, colors, sizes of rooms and kinds of materials may be changed. Attic finish, part or all of plumbing, sliding doors, open fireplaces and mantels, and a part or all of the cellar may be omitted. House may be used by one family, the smaller portion being admirably adapted for physician's use.

The price of working plans, specifications, etc., for a modified design varies according to the alterations required, and will be made known upon application to the Architects.

FIRST FLOOR.

SECOND FLOOR.

THE CO-OPERATIVE BUILDING PLAN ASSOCIATION, ARCHITECTS, 63 BROADWAY, NEW YORK..

Shoppell's Modern Houses—*Designs Patented.　　　　　*Double Residence, Design No. 394*

PERSPECTIVE.

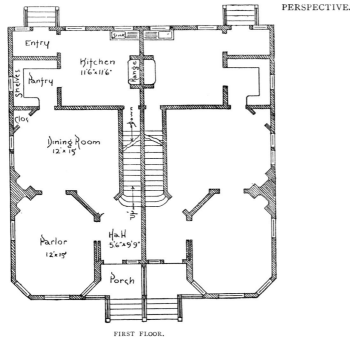

FIRST FLOOR.

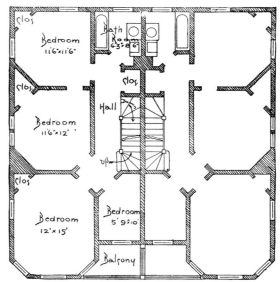

SECOND FLOOR.

DESCRIPTION.

GENERAL DIMENSIONS: Width, 38 ft.; depth, 40 ft. 7 in. Heights of stories: Cellar, 7 ft.; first story, 10 ft.; second story, 9 ft.; attic, 8 ft.

EXTERIOR MATERIALS: Foundations, stone; first story, clapboards; second story and roof, shingles; gables, panels and shingles.

INTERIOR FINISH: Hard white plaster. Plaster cornices and centers in first story halls, parlors and dining rooms. Soft wood flooring and trim. Ash staircases. Panels under windows in first story halls, parlors and dining rooms. Chair rails in dining rooms. Wainscot in bath-rooms and kitchens. Interior wood-work stained to suit owner, and finished in hard oil.

COLORS: All clapboards, seal brown. Trim, outside doors, blinds and sashes, maroon. Veranda floor and rain conductors, dark green. Veranda ceiling varnished. Panels in gables, seal brown with maroon framing. Wall shingles dipped and brush coated light sienna stain. Roof shingles dipped and brush coated Indian red stain.

ACCOMMODATIONS: The principal rooms and their sizes, closets, etc., are shown by the plans. Cellar under whole of each house. Three rooms in each attic. Open fireplaces in parlors and dining rooms.

COST: $4,510, † not including mantels, ranges and heaters. The estimate is based on ‡ New York prices for materials and labor. In many sections of the country the cost should be less.

Price for working plans, specifications and * license to build, - $50.00
Price for † † bill of materials, - - - - - - - - 10.00

Address, THE CO-OPERATIVE BUILDING PLAN ASSOCIATION, Architects, 63 Broadway, New York.

FEASIBLE MODIFICATIONS: Heights of stories, colors, sizes of rooms and kinds of materials may be changed. Cellars may be reduced in size. Attic finish, part or all of plumbing, sliding doors, open fireplaces, mantels and set ranges, may be omitted.

The price of working plans, specifications, etc., for a modified design varies according to the alterations required, and will be made known upon application to the Architects.

*Shoppell's Modern Houses—*Designs Patented.*   *Double Residence, Design No. 441*

FRONT ELEVATION.

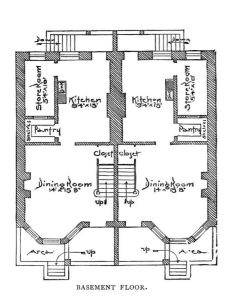

BASEMENT FLOOR.

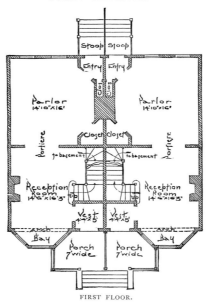

FIRST FLOOR.

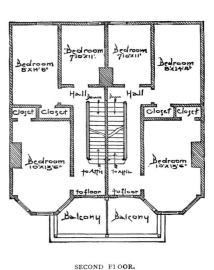

SECOND FLOOR.

DESCRIPTION.

For explanation of all symbols (* † etc.) see page 42.

GENERAL DIMENSIONS: Width, 34 ft.; depth, including front porch, 39 ft. Heights of stories: Cellar, 8 ft.; first story, 9 ft. 6 in.; second story, 8 ft. 6 in.

EXTERIOR MATERIALS: Foundations, stone and brick; first story, clapboards; second story, clapboards and shingles; gables and roofs, shingles. Outside blinds.

INTERIOR FINISH: Hard white plaster; plaster cornices in reception halls, parlors and vestibules. Soft wood flooring and trim. Cherry stairways. Wainscot in kitchens. Interior woodwork finished in hard oil.

COLORS: Clapboards, light olive green. Trim and rain conductors, dark green. Outside doors, dark green with light olive green panels. Blinds and sashes, Pompeian red. Porch floors and ceilings oiled. Wall shingles dipped and brush coated in oil, stained slightly darker than natural color of wood. Roof shingles left natural.

ACCOMMODATIONS: The principal rooms and their sizes, closets, etc., are shown by the plans. Attics floored, but unfinished; space for two large rooms in each. All rooms get light from front or rear. Any number of houses may be built in a row. Open fireplaces and mantels in dining and reception rooms included in estimate.

COST: $4,048, † not including heaters and ranges. The estimate is based on ‡ New York prices for materials and labor. In many sections of the country the cost should be less.

Price for working plans, specifications, and * license to build, - - - - - - - - - - - - - $40.00
Price for †† bill of materials, - - - - - 10.00

Address, THE CO-OPERATIVE BUILDING PLAN ASSOCIATION, Architects, 63 Broadway, New York.

FEASIBLE MODIFICATIONS: Heights of stories, colors, sizes of rooms and kinds of materials may be changed. Sub-cellar may be placed under kitchens and dining rooms. An extension may be planned at rear, providing for kitchens and dining rooms in first story. Open fireplaces and mantels and open balconies may be omitted. Bath-rooms with partial or full plumbing may be introduced.

279

THE CO-OPERATIVE BUILDING PLAN ASSOCIATION, ARCHITECTS, 63 BROADWAY, NEW YORK.

Shoppell's Modern Houses—*Designs Patented.   *Double House, Design No. 652*

PERSPECTIVE.

DESCRIPTION.

For explanation of all symbols (* † etc.) see page 42.

GENERAL DIMENSIONS: Width, including porches, 43 ft. 6 in.; depth, including outside cellar stairways, 56 ft. Heights of stories: Cellar, 7 ft. 6 in.; first story, 9 ft. 6 in.; second story, 9 ft.; attic, 7 ft. 6 in.

EXTERIOR MATERIALS: Foundations, brick; first story, clapboards; second story, clapboards and shingles; gables, dormers and roofs, shingles; deck roof, tin.

INTERIOR FINISH: Two coats of plaster for wall paper throughout. Plaster cornices in parlors, main halls and dining rooms. Flooring of first stories, white pine; of second stories and attics, spruce. Trim, white pine. Stairways, ash. Bathrooms and kitchens, wainscoted. All interior wood work hard oil finished.

COLORS: Clapboards of first stories, porch ceilings and panels of outside doors painted yellow stone color. Clapboards and shingles of second stories and shingles of dormers painted Colonial yellow. Trim, stiles and rails of outside doors and outside blinds, dark yellow. Sashes, dark green. Roof shingles and porch floors, light brown. Brick work, Venetian red.

ACCOMMODATIONS: The principal rooms and their sizes, closets, etc. are shown by the plans. There is a cellar, with concrete floor and fuel bins, under the whole of each house. No rooms finished in the attic, but there is space for three in each house. Skylights over stairways. All plumbing is so concentrated that one set of supply and waste pipes will answer for both houses, but independent pipes are recommended as preferable. Both houses piped for gas.

COST: For both houses, $5500 † not including mantels, ranges and heaters. The estimate is based on ‡ New York prices for materials and labor. In many sections of the country the cost should be less.

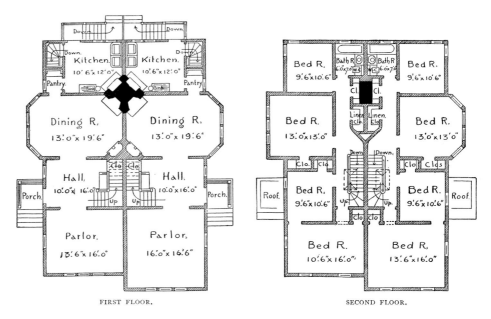

FIRST FLOOR.   SECOND FLOOR.

Price for working plans, specifications and * license to build, - $55.00
Price for †† bill of materials, - - - - - 15.00

Address, THE CO-OPERATIVE BUILDING PLAN ASSOCIATION, Architects, 63 Broadway, New York.

FEASIBLE MODIFICATIONS: Heights of stories, sizes of rooms, materials and colors may be changed. Cornices, centres, gas-pipes and fire-places may be omitted. Fire-places may be introduced in parlors and bed-rooms over.

The price of working plans, specifications, etc. for a modified design varies according to the alterations required, and will be made known upon application to the Architects.

280

THE CO-OPERATIVE BUILDING PLAN ASSOCIATION, ARCHITECTS, 63 BROADWAY, NEW YORK.

*Shoppell's Modern Houses—*Designs Patented.*   *Double Residence, Design No. 497*

SIDE ELEVATION

PERSPECTIVE.

DESCRIPTION.

For explanation of all symbols (* † etc.) see page 42.

GENERAL DIMENSIONS: Width over all, 52 ft. 10 in.; depth over all, 48 ft. Heights of stories: Cellar, 6 ft. 10 in.; first story, 10 ft.; second story, 9 ft.

EXTERIOR MATERIALS: Foundations, stone and brick; first story, clapboards; second story and roof, shingles; gables, panels and shingles. Outside blinds.

INTERIOR FINISH: Hard white plaster. Hard pine flooring in halls, pantries and kitchens. Soft wood flooring elsewhere. Soft wood trim. Ash staircases. Wainscoting in kitchens, pantries and bath-rooms. Chair rails in dining rooms. Interior wood-work finished in hard oil.

COLORS: Clapboards, seal brown. Trim, outside doors, blinds and veranda floor, maroon. Sashes and rain conductors, dark green. Veranda ceiling varnished. Brick-work, Indian red. Gable panels, seal brown with maroon framing. Wall shingles dipped and brush coated light sienna stain. Roof shingles dipped and brush coated Indian red.

ACCOMMODATIONS: The principal rooms and their sizes, closets, etc., are shown by the plans. Cellar under whole of each house, with cemented floors and outside and inside entrances. Attics floored, but unfinished; space for three rooms in each. Designed for double house with the appearance of single one. Five open fireplaces and mantels included in estimate.

COST: $6,704, † not including ranges and heaters. The cost of the larger house is $3,674, and of the smaller house, $3,030. The estimate is based on ‡ New York prices for materials and labor. In many sections of the country the cost should be less.

Price for working plans, specifications and * license to build, - - - - - - - - - - - $57.00
Price for †† bill of materials, - - - - - 10.00
Address, THE CO-OPERATIVE BUILDING PLAN ASSOCIATION, Architects, 63 Broadway, New York.

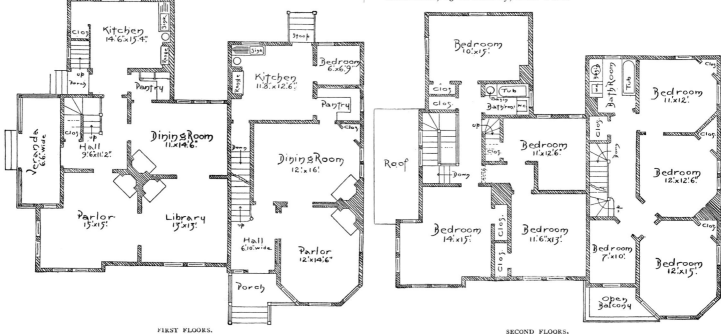

FIRST FLOORS.   SECOND FLOORS.

THE CO-OPERATIVE BUILDING PLAN ASSOCIATION, ARCHITECTS, 63 BROADWAY, NEW YORK.

Shoppell's Modern Houses—*Designs Patented.   *Double Residence, Design No. 303*

PERSPECTIVE.

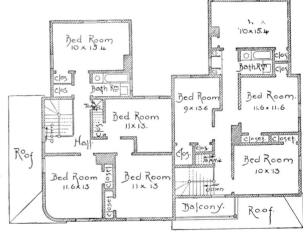

FIRST FLOORS.

SECOND FLOORS.

DESCRIPTION.

For explanation of all symbols (*† etc.) see page 42.

GENERAL DIMENSIONS: Width over all, 58 ft.; depth, 47 ft. 6 in. Heights of stories: Cellar, 7 ft.; first story, 9 ft.; second story, 8 ft.

EXTERIOR MATERIALS: Foundation, stone and brick; first story, clapboards; second story and roof, shingles; gables, panels and shingles. Outside blinds.

INTERIOR FINISH: Hard white plaster. Hard pine flooring in pantries, halls and kitchens; soft wood flooring elsewhere. Soft wood trim. Ash staircases. Wainscot in kitchens, pantries and bath-rooms. Interior wood-work finished in hard oil.

COLORS: Clapboards, seal brown. Trim, outside doors, blinds and veranda floor, maroon. Sashes and rain conductors, dark green. Veranda ceilings, varnished. Brick-work, Indian red. Gable panels, seal brown with maroon framing. Wall shingles dipped and brush coated light sienna stain. Roof shingles dipped and brush coated Indian red.

ACCOMMODATIONS: The principal rooms and their sizes, closets, etc., are shown by the plans. Cellar under whole house with outside and inside entrances and concrete floors. Attics floored, but unfinished; space for three rooms in each. Each house is separate and complete, but the exterior has the appearance of one house. Open fireplaces in parlors, libraries and dining rooms.

COST: $5,628, † not including mantels, ranges and heaters. The estimate is based on ‡ New York prices for materials and labor. In many sections of the country the cost should be less.

Price for working plans, specifications and * license to build, - - - - - - - - - - - - - $75.00
Price for †† bill of materials, - - - - - - - 15.00

Address, THE CO-OPERATIVE BUILDING PLAN ASSOCIATION, Architects, 63 Broadway, New York.

FEASIBLE MODIFICATIONS: Heights of stories, colors, sizes of rooms and kinds of materials may be changed. Cellars may be reduced in size and concrete floors omitted. Open balcony, fireplaces and mantels, and a part or all of plumbing may be omitted.

282

THE CO-OPERATIVE BUILDING PLAN ASSOCIATION, ARCHITECTS, 63 BROADWAY, NEW YORK.

*Shoppell's Modern Houses—*Designs Patented.* *Hotel, Design No. 607*

DESIGN·OF·HOTEL·
THE·NEWPORT·COTTAGE·CO.
The Co-operative Building Plan Assoc'n Architects, New York.

PERSPECTIVE VIEW.

DESCRIPTION.

For explanation of all symbols (* † etc.) see page 42.

GENERAL DIMENSIONS: Front, 150 ft., not including porte-cochere or veranda; depth, 100 ft., not including veranda. Heights of stories: Cellar, 8 ft. 6 in.; first story, dining room, 15 ft.; elsewhere, 12 ft.; second story, 10 ft.; third and fourth stories, 9 ft.

EXTERIOR MATERIALS: Foundations, stone; first story, clapboards; second and third stories, tower, gables, dormers and roofs, shingles.

INTERIOR FINISH: Hard white plaster. Rotunda, parlor, dining room and corridor floored with hard wood. Trim in rotunda, parlor and dining room to be hard wood, elsewhere soft wood stained to suit owner, and oiled. Main staircase through all stories and front entrance doors, hard wood. Picture molding in rotunda, parlor and dining room.

COLORS: All clapboards, light red. Trim, veranda and balcony rails and balusters, dark red. All shingles on walls of second and third stories, gables, dormers and tower walls, dipped and brush coated cream color. Roof shingles dipped and brush coated terra cotta. Sashes, dark green. All ornamental carved work and veranda and balcony posts painted cream color.

ACCOMMODATIONS: The principal rooms and their sizes, closets, etc., are shown by the plans. There is a cellar under the whole building, with concrete floor and high ceiling. A number of the bedrooms have private baths. There are toilet rooms at convenient points

throughout the building. An elevator shaft is provided near main entrance, running up in the tower. The tower forms an imposing feature of the design, and provides room for distribution tanks for water supply. The stairways are so placed as to afford ready egress in case of fire. Dining room is entirely free from posts and has a good serving pantry conveniently connected with the kitchen pantry by dumb waiters and stairs. Cellar contains kitchen, laundry, furnace and coal rooms, billiard and bar-rooms, wine cellar, refrigerators, servants' W. C. and bath-rooms, barber shop, baggage room, steward's room, etc. Servants' sleeping quarters in the attic. Building heated by steam throughout.

COST: $45,000, † not including mantels, ranges, heating apparatus and elevator. The estimate is based on ‡ New York prices for materials and labor. In many sections of the country the cost should be less.

Price for working plans, specifications and * license to build will be made known upon application.

Price for †† bill of materials will be made known upon application.

Address, THE CO-OPERATIVE BUILDING PLAN ASSOCIATION, Architects, 63 Broadway, New York.

283

THE CO-OPERATIVE BUILDING PLAN ASSOCIATION, ARCHITECTS, 63 BROADWAY, NEW YORK.

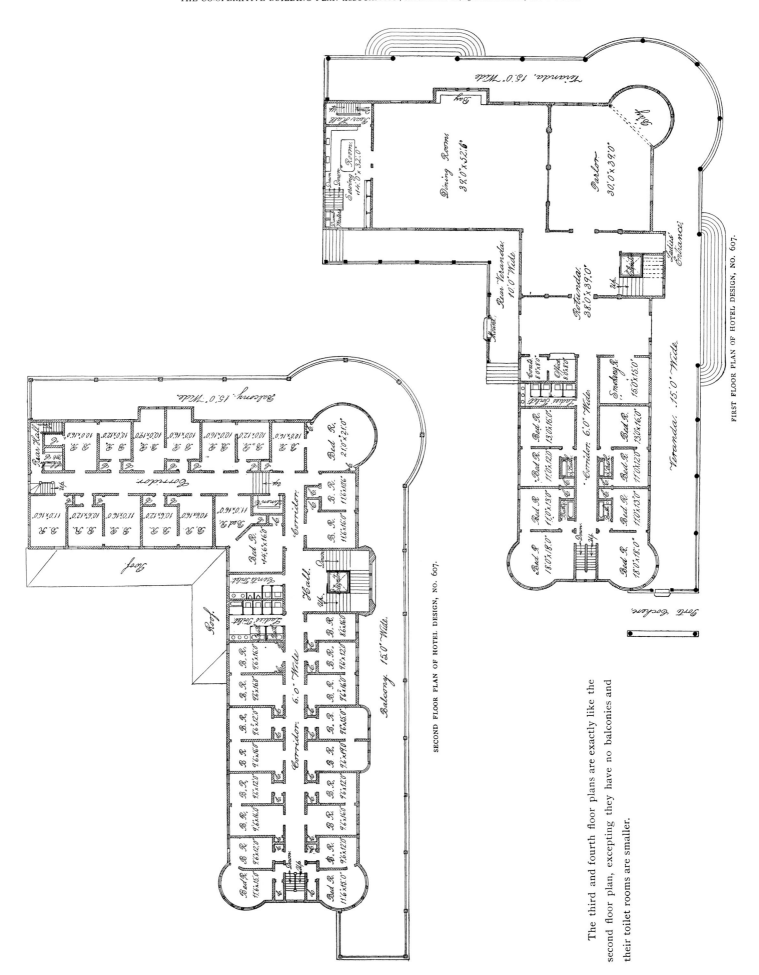

FIRST FLOOR PLAN OF HOTEL DESIGN, NO. 607.

SECOND FLOOR PLAN OF HOTEL DESIGN, NO. 607.

The third and fourth floor plans are exactly like the second floor plan, excepting they have no balconies and their toilet rooms are smaller.

284

THE CO-OPERATIVE BUILDING PLAN ASSOCIATION, ARCHITECTS, 63 BROADWAY, NEW YORK.

*Shoppell's Modern Houses—*Designs Patented.* *Library or Club House, Design No. 657*

PERSPECTIVE.

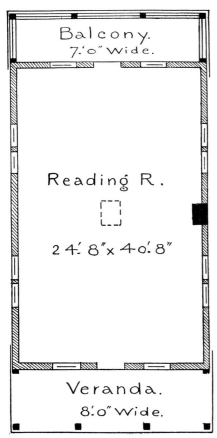

PLAN.

DESCRIPTION.

For explanation of all symbols (* † etc.) see page 42.

GENERAL DIMENSIONS: Width, 26 ft.; depth, including veranda and balcony, 57 ft. Height of story, 12 ft.

EXTERIOR MATERIALS: Foundations, stone; first story, gables and roof, shingles.

INTERIOR FINISH: Flooring, hard pine; trim, soft wood. Tinted plaster, sand finished, for walls and ceilings.

COLORS: Wall and gable shingles dipped in mahogany stain. Roof shingles dipped in reddish brown stain. All trim and outside doors, painted Pompeian red. Sashes, dark green. Veranda and balcony floors, blue-stone color; veranda and balcony ceilings, lilac.

ACCOMMODATIONS: The first story is one large room. The attic is floored but no rooms are finished. No cellar. Designed for a library, but is well suited for a club.

COST: $1800. The estimate is based on ‡ New York prices for materials and labor. In many sections of the country the cost should be less.

Price for working plans, specifications and * license to build, - - - - $20.00
Price for †† bill of materials, - - - - - - - - - - 10.00

Address, THE CO-OPERATIVE BUILDING PLAN ASSOCIATION, Architects, 63 Broadway, New York.

FEASIBLE MODIFICATIONS: Height of story, general dimensions, materials and colors may be changed. Foundations may be brick walls or piers or wood posts. Plastering and inside trim may be omitted.

The price for working plans, specifications, etc. for a modified design varies according to the extent of the alterations required, and will be made known upon application to the Architects.

285

THE CO-OPERATIVE BUILDING PLAN ASSOCIATION, ARCHITECTS, 63 BROADWAY, NEW YORK.

Shoppell's Modern Houses—*Designs Patented.　　　　　　　　*Club House, Design No. 658*

PERSPECTIVE.

DESCRIPTION.

For explanation of all symbols (* † etc.) see page 42.

GENERAL DIMENSIONS: Width, 62 ft.; depth, 49 ft. Height of story, 14 ft.

EXTERIOR MATERIALS: Foundation, stone piers; first story, clapboards; bays and walls from belt course to roof, shingles; dormers and roof, shingles.

INTERIOR FINISH: No plastering—the entire first story is ceiled with narrow boards of yellow pine. Flooring of first story, maple; of attic, white pine. Stairs and trim throughout, yellow pine. All interior wood work oiled.

COLORS: All clapboards and panels of outside doors, olive. All trim, and stiles and rails of outside doors, dark green. Sashes and rain conductors, dark red. Veranda floors and soffits of overhanging eaves, medium drab. Veranda ceiling, oiled. All roof shingles stained Indian red; all wall shingles dipped in red metallic paint.

ACCOMMODATIONS: All the rooms are shown by the floor plan. No cellar. The attic is floored. No attic rooms are finished, but there is space for two rooms and a hall. Folding doors or portieres may be used to separate the parlors from the hall. Ornamental trusses, showing in the hall, support the attic floor and roof, leaving the whole of the first floor unobstructed by posts. Windows at rear have hinged sashes to serve as doors to the rear veranda. The windows showing above veranda roof are pivoted, to be used for ventilating; they are glazed with stained glass.

COST: $2000. The estimate is based on ‡ New York prices for materials and labor. In many sections of the country the cost should be less.

Price for working plans, specifications and * license to build, - $20.00
Price for †† bill of materials, - - - - - - 10.00

Address, THE CO-OPERATIVE BUILDING PLAN ASSOCIATION, Architects, 63 Broadway, New York.

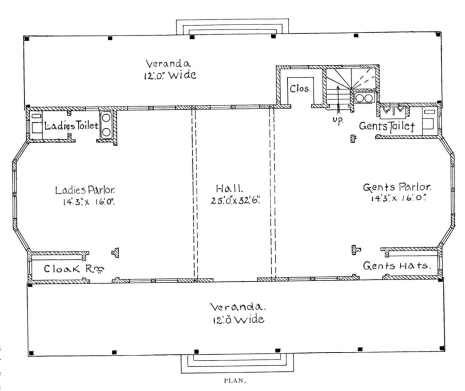

PLAN.

FEASIBLE MODIFICATIONS: Height of story, materials, size and colors may be changed. Cellar and chimney and fire-place may be built. Rear veranda and all plumbing may be omitted. Toilet rooms may be planned for the attic, leaving the first floor as one large room.

The price of working plans, specifications, etc. for a modified design varies according to the extent of the alterations required, and will be made known upon application to the Architects.

THE CO-OPERATIVE BUILDING PLAN ASSOCIATION, ARCHITECTS, 63 BROADWAY, NEW YORK.

Shoppell's Modern Houses—*Designs Patented.

Casino, Design No. 616

PERSPECTIVE.

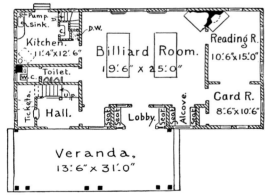

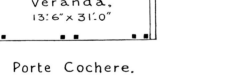

Porte Cochere.

FIRST FLOOR.

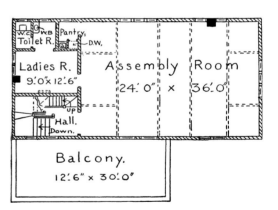

SECOND FLOOR.

DESCRIPTION.

For explanation of all symbols (* † etc.) see page 42.

GENERAL DIMENSIONS: Width, 50 ft.; depth, including veranda, 38 ft. 6 in. Heights of stories: Cellar, 6 ft. 6 in.; first story, 9 ft.; second story, 14 ft. 6 in.

EXTERIOR MATERIALS: Foundation, posts; first and second stories, gables, dormers and roofs, shingles. Outside blinds to all windows of first and second stories.

INTERIOR FINISH: Walls of first and second stories wainscoted with hard wood; remainder of walls as well as all ceilings covered with plaster board. In second story the roof timbers and trussing are dressed and oil finished natural color. All floors hard wood. All trim soft wood. Main stairs hard wood. All interior wood-work finished in hard oil.

COLORS: Shingles in first and second stories, gables, cheeks of dormers, and sides of tower and second story balcony, Colonial yellow. Trim, sashes, doors and blinds, red. Veranda floor and ceiling, and tower ceiling, oiled. Roof shingles stained silver. Awning and flag poles, white. Brick-work painted dark red.

ACCOMMODATIONS: The principal rooms and their sizes, closets, etc., are shown by the plans. A small cellar under kitchen. Designed for a social club and well adapted for lectures, private theatricals, parties, etc. Dumb waiter from kitchen to assembly room pantry. Toilet rooms for both sexes.

COST: $3,500, † not including mantels, heater and range. The estimate is based on ‡ New York prices for materials and labor. In many sections of the country the cost should be less.

Price for working plans, specifications and * license to build, - $30.00
Price for † † bill of materials, - - - - - - - 15.00

Address, THE CO-OPERATIVE BUILDING PLAN ASSOCIATION, Architects, 63 Broadway, New York.

FEASIBLE MODIFICATIONS: Heights of stories, sizes of rooms, colors and materials may be changed. Cellar may be enlarged. Fireplaces and a part or all of plumbing may be omitted. One chimney may be omitted if heating apparatus be used. Sliding doors may be introduced between billiard, reading and card rooms.

The price of working plans, specifications, etc., for a modified design varies according to the alterations required, and will be made known upon application to the Architects.

THE CO-OPERATIVE BUILDING PLAN ASSOCIATION, ARCHITECTS, 63 BROADWAY, NEW YORK.

Shoppell's Modern Houses—*Designs Patented.　　　　　　　　　　　*Chapel, Design No. 617*

PERSPECTIVE.

DESCRIPTION.

For explanation of all symbols (* † etc.) see page 42.

GENERAL DIMENSIONS : Width, including tower, 43 ft. 2 in; depth, 46 ft 2 in. Heights of stories : Cellar, 8 ft.; auditorium, 22 ft.

EXTERIOR MATERIALS : Foundations, stone; first story, clapboards and shingles ; gables, tower and roofs, shingles.

INTERIOR FINISH : Walls and ceilings plastered hard white finish. Cornice extends around entire auditorium. Trim, floor and staircase are soft woods. Pews and other furniture are not included in the estimate. Building piped for gas and heating. Interior wood-work stained and finished like hard wood.

COLORS : Clapboards, brown. Trim and outside doors, dark green. Sashes and rain conductors, Pompeian red. Ceilings of porch and tower oiled. Wall shingles stained dark brown. Roof shingles painted dark red

ACCOMMODATIONS : The principal rooms and their sizes, etc., are shown by the plans. Cellar under the whole building, with ceiling high enough to be used as a Sunday-school room. Windows are large, and well adapted for stained glass memorials.

COST : $3,500, † not including heating apparatus. The estimate is based on ‡ New York prices for materials and labor. In many sections of the country the cost should be less.

Price for working plans, specifications and * license to build, - $30.00
Price for † † bill of materials, - - - - - - - 15.00

Address, THE CO-OPERATIVE BUILDING PLAN ASSOCIATION, Architects, 63 Broadway, New York.

FEASIBLE MODIFICATIONS : Heights of stories, sizes of rooms, materials and colors may be changed. Cellar may be reduced in size or omitted. Tower may be enclosed to form belfry or it may be omitted entirely. The ceilings may be finished in hard wood and timber of roof allowed to show. The platform and the chancel may be planned for any denomination.

The price of working plans, specifications, etc., for a modified design varies according to the alterations required, and will be made known upon application to the Architects.

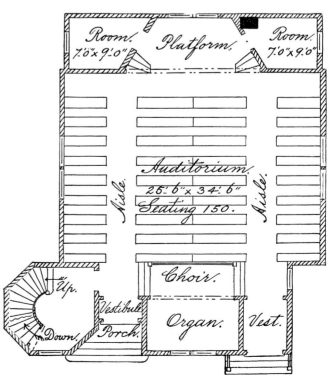

FLOOR PLAN.

288

THE CO-OPERATIVE BUILDING PLAN ASSOCIATION, ARCHITECTS, 63 BROADWAY, NEW YORK.

*Shoppell's Modern Houses—*Designs Patented.*

School House, Design No. 659

PERSPECTIVE.

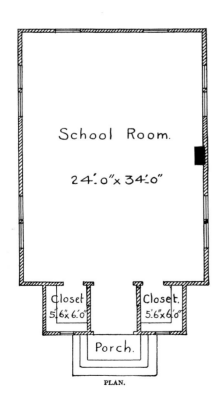

School Room.

24′.0″ x 34′.0″

Closet.
5′.6″x 6′.0″

Closet.
5′.6″x 6′.0″

Porch.

PLAN.

The price of working plans, specifications, etc., for a modified design varies according to the alterations required, and will be made known upon application to the Architects.

DESCRIPTION.

For explanation of all symbols (* † etc.) see page 42.

GENERAL DIMENSIONS: Width, 25 ft.; depth, including closets, 41 ft. 6 in. Height of first story, 12 ft.

EXTERIOR MATERIALS: Foundation, brick piers; first story, clapboards and shingles; belfry, dormers and roofs, shingles.

INTERIOR FINISH: Hard white plaster. Soft wood flooring and trim, finished in hard oil.

COLORS: Clapboards, Colonial yellow. Trim and outside doors, dark bottle green. Sashes and rain conductors, liver red. Porch and steps, seal brown. Wall shingles dipped and brush coated yellow stain. Roof shingles left natural color.

ACCOMMODATIONS: The principal room, size, closets, etc., are shown by the floor plan. Closets for children's coats and hats opening into school-room on either side of vestibule. Loft floored for storage of books, etc.; space for small class-room or laboratory, if desired.

COST: $1,500. The estimate is based on ‡ New York prices for materials and labor. In many sections of the country the cost should be less.

Price for working plans, specifications and * license to build, - - - - - - - - - - $15.00

Price for †† bill of materials, - - - - - 10.00

Address: THE CO-OPERATIVE BUILDING PLAN ASSOCIATION, Architects, 63 Broadway, New York.

FEASIBLE MODIFICATIONS: Height of story, colors, size, and kinds of materials may be changed. Cellar may be introduced under whole building. Design is suitable for a small chapel or hall, and for that use the attic floor may be omitted and ceiling of auditorium carried up to roof. Belfry may be omitted. Fireplace may be introduced.

*Snoppell's Modern Houses—*Designs Patented.* *Boat House, Design No. 660*

PERSPECTIVE.

DESCRIPTION.

For explanation of all symbols (* † etc.) see page 42.

GENERAL DIMENSIONS: Width, 20 ft.; depth, including balcony, 49 ft. Heights of stories: First story, 9 ft.; second story, 8 ft. 6 in.

EXTERIOR MATERIALS: Foundation, posts; first story, clapboards; second story and roof, shingles; gables, panels and shingles.

INTERIOR FINISH: Interior frame-work planed and finished with varnish. Soft wood flooring throughout.

COLORS: Clapboards and panels in doors and gables, cream color. Trim, balcony and platform rails, posts and balusters, and the frames of all paneling in gables and doors, brownish red. Wall shingles dipped and brush coated yellow stain. Roof shingles dipped and brush coated silver stain. Sashes, bright red. Flagstaffs, oiled natural color. Flooring of platform, balcony and porch, oiled. Ceilings of platform and balcony varnished. Foundation posts, etc., dark red.

ACCOMMODATIONS: General arrangement shown by the floor plans. First story intended for storage, cleaning of boats, etc. Second story devoted to store-room, toilet-room and assembly hall.

COST: $1,000. The estimate is based on ‡ New York prices for materials and labor. In many sections of the country the cost should be less.

Price for working plans, specifications and * license to build, - - - - - - - - - - - - - $15.00

Price for † † bill of materials, - - - - - - 10.00

Address, THE CO-OPERATIVE BUILDING PLAN ASSOCIATION Architects, 63 Broadway, New York.

FEASIBLE MODIFICATIONS: Balcony and all finish in second story, and a part or all of the plumbing, may be omitted. On a high bank the building may be placed on brick or stone foundations, and boat-room placed in basement; first story would then be used as reception hall, and second story for lockers, etc.

The price of working plans, specifications, etc., for a modified design varies according to the alterations required, and will be made known upon application to the Architects.

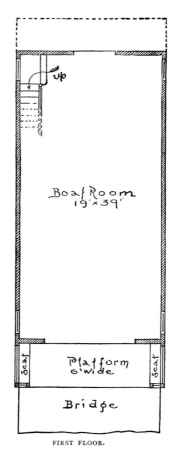

FIRST FLOOR.

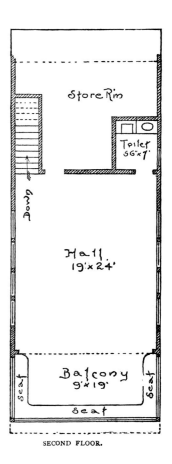

SECOND FLOOR.

290

THE CO-OPERATIVE BUILDING PLAN ASSOCIATION, ARCHITECTS, 63 BROADWAY, NEW YORK.

*Shoppell's Modern Houses—*Designs Patented.* *Stable, Design No. 473*

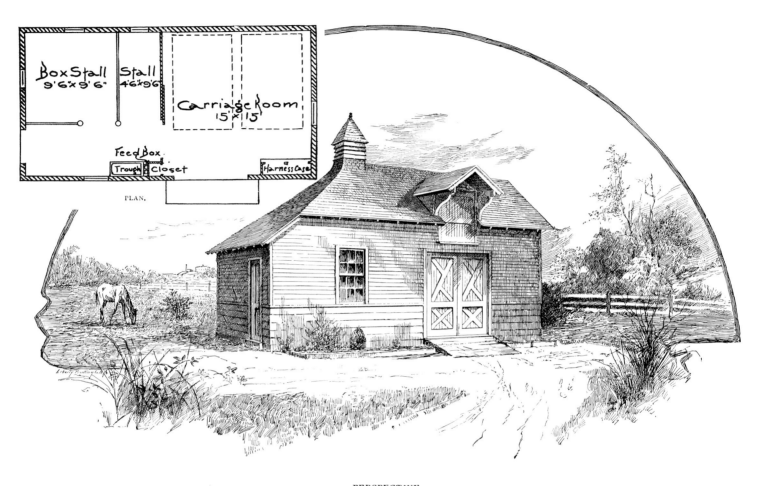

PERSPECTIVE.

DESCRIPTION.

For explanation of all symbols (* † etc.) see page 42.

GENERAL DIMENSIONS: Width, 30 ft.; depth, 16 ft. Height of story, 8 ft. 8 in.

EXTERIOR MATERIALS: Foundations, stone; first story, clapboards; roof, shingles.

INTERIOR FINISH: Soft wood flooring. Mangers and stalls, hard pine. Harness case and partition between carriage room and stable, soft wood. Interior unpainted.

COLORS: Wide lower clapboards, dark red; other clapboards, light brown. Trim, cornices, etc., seal brown. Outside doors, seal brown with light brown panels. Sashes, dark green. Roof shingles dipped and brush coated red stain.

ACCOMMODATIONS: Stalls, closets, etc., are shown by the plan. Hay loft (reached by a step-ladder) has two grain bins provided with galvanized iron tubes leading to feed boxes in stable; also ample space for hay storage. Space for two carriages and two horses. Sliding door connects stable and carriage room.

COST: $454. The estimate is based on ‡ New York prices for materials and labor. In many sections of the country the cost should be less.

Price for working plans, specifications and * license to build, - - - - - - - - - - $12.00

Price for † † bill of materials, - - - - - 3.00

Address, THE CO-OPERATIVE BUILDING PLAN ASSOCIATION, Architects, 63 Broadway, New York.

FEASIBLE MODIFICATIONS: Height of story, colors, sizes of rooms and kinds of materials may be changed. Roof ridge may be continued to stable end and terminate as a gable, same as at carriage room end. Box stall may be divided, forming two single stalls. Grain bins and galvanized iron tubes may be omitted. Roof finial may be omitted.

The price of working plans, specifications, etc., for a modified design varies according to the alterations required, and will be made known upon application to the Architects.

291

THE CO-OPERATIVE BUILDING PLAN ASSOCIATION, ARCHITECTS, 63 BROADWAY, NEW YORK.

*Shoppell's Modern Houses—*Designs Patented.*　　　　　　　　　　　*Stable, Design No. 489.*

FRONT ELEVATION.

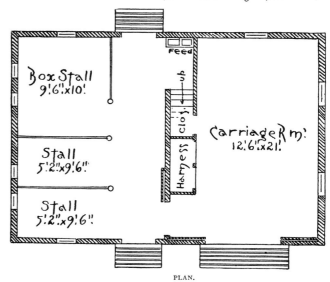

PLAN.

DESCRIPTION.

For explanation of all symbols (* † etc.) see page 42.

GENERAL DIMENSIONS : Width, 31 ft. 6 in.; depth, 22 ft. Heights of stories : First story, 9 ft. 4 in.; second story, 6 ft. 6 in.

EXTERIOR MATERIALS : Foundation, posts ; first story, clapboards ; second story, roofs and gables, shingles.

INTERIOR FINISH : Soft wood flooring throughout ; removable top flooring in stalls. Soft wood trim and stairway. Hay chute, stalls, mangers, feed bins and spouts, soft wood. Stall posts, hard wood. Stall posts oiled. Remainder of interior wood-work left unfinished.

COLORS : Clapboards, light chocolate. Trim and rain conductors, dark chocolate. Outside doors, maroon, with dark chocolate panels. Sashes, maroon. Wall shingles dipped and brush coated sienna stain. Roof shingles dipped and brush coated dark red.

ACCOMMODATIONS : Stalls, closets, etc., are shown by the plan. Stableman's room partitioned off in second story. Feed bins in second story provided with chutes to point shown on floor plan. Sliding door connects stable with carriage room.

COST : $916. The estimate is based on ‡ New York prices for materials and labor. In many sections of the country the cost should be less.

Price for working plans, specifications and * license to
build, - - - - - - - - - - - $12.00
Price for †† bill of materials, - - - - - - 3.00
Address, THE CO-OPERATIVE BUILDING PLAN ASSOCIATION, Architects, 63 Broadway, New York.

FEASIBLE MODIFICATIONS : Heights of stories, colors, sizes of rooms and kinds of materials may be changed. A root cellar may be placed under part of building. Stableman's room may be omitted. A ladder to reach attic in place of stairway would enlarge both stable and carriage room. Box stall may be planned in place of two single stalls. The main roof ridge may be continued out to form gables, and thus enlarge second story.

The price of working plans, specifications, etc., for a modified design varies according to the alterations required, and will be made known upon application to the Architects.

Stable, Design No. 589.

DESCRIPTION.

GENERAL DIMENSIONS : Width, 24 ft.; depth, 30 ft. Heights of stories : First story, 10 ft.; second story, 9 ft. 6 in.

EXTERIOR MATERIALS : Foundation, posts ; first story, clapboards ; second story, gables and roofs, shingles.

INTERIOR FINISH : Flooring first story, 2-inch hemlock plank ; second story, good quality tongued and grooved pine boarding. Both sides of partition between carriage room and stalls ceiled with narrow tongued and grooved pine boards. One of the front sliding doors has a hinged panel to serve as a single door. The stalls have neatly turned chestnut posts.

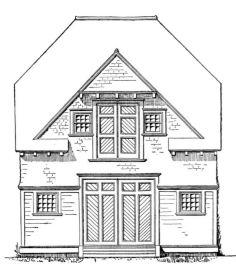

FRONT ELEVATION.

COLORS : Clapboards, light brown. Trim, dark brown. Outside doors, panels light brown ; framing of panels, dark brown. Sashes, Pompeian red. Wall shingles dipped and brush coated sienna stain. Roof shingles dipped and brush coated Indian red.

ACCOMMODATIONS : The principal rooms, stalls, etc., are shown by the floor plan. No cellar. Second story is an open mow. Wickets at the heads of stalls through which feed may be passed without entering stalls. Suitable beam and hook in front gable to hoist bales, etc., to mow. Room for three carriages. Ample space in mow for storage of sleighs.

COST : $600, † not including stalls, feed bins, etc. The estimate is based on ‡ New York prices for materials and labor. In many sections of the country the cost should be less.

Price for working plans, specifications and * license to build, - - $15.00
Price for †† bill of materials, - 5.00
Address, THE CO-OPERATIVE BUILDING PLAN ASSOCIATION, Architects, 63 Broadway, New York.

FEASIBLE MODIFICATIONS : Heights of stories, sizes of rooms, colors and materials may be changed. Cellar may be placed under a part of or whole building. Feed-bins may be placed in second story, with proper chutes leading to first story. Tool room and man's bedroom may be placed in second story. Two of the stalls may be combined to form a large box stall.

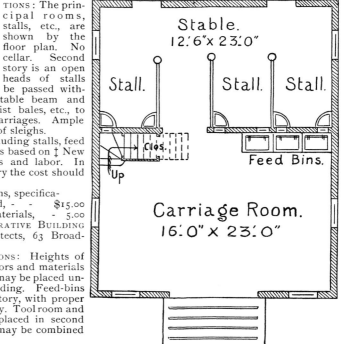

PLAN.

*Shoppell's Modern Houses—*Designs Patented.*   *Stable, Design No. 421*

PERSPECTIVE.

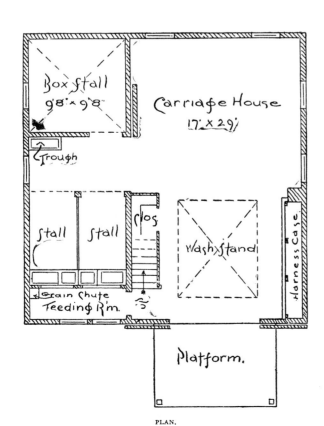

PLAN.

DESCRIPTION.

For explanation of all symbols (* † etc.) see page 42.

GENERAL DIMENSIONS: Width, 28 ft.; depth, 30 ft. Heights of stories: First story, 10 ft.; second story, 7 ft. 6 in.

EXTERIOR MATERIALS: Foundations, stone; first story, clapboards; second story and roof, shingles; gables, panels and shingles.

INTERIOR FINISH: Soft wood flooring throughout, carriage house to have double floor and stable to have heavy plank floor; stalls to have supplementary floor of hard wood strips with space between. Stable and feeding room wainscoted with rough boards to a height of 4 ft. 6 in., and ceiled above that with smooth hard pine. Stall posts and divisions, hard pine. Carriage room covered on sides and ceiling with soft wood ceiling boards. Stable and feeding room covered with yellow pine. The rooms in second story plastered hard white. Trim in second story rooms, soft wood painted colors to suit owner. Walls and ceilings, and all other wood-work of first story, to be filled and varnished.

COLORS: Clapboards, gray stone color. Wall shingles dipped and brush coated dark sienna stain. Trim and doors, olive green. Sashes and platform ceiling, dark red. Roof shingles left natural. Brick-work, red.

ACCOMMODATIONS: Stalls, closets, etc., are shown by the plans. Two rooms finished in second story, besides storage space for hay, etc. Ventilator showing above roof is connected with stable ceiling. Sliding doors between carriage room and stable. Feed bins located in second story and connected with feeding room by chutes.

COST: $1,236. The estimate is based on ‡ New York prices for materials and labor. In many sections of the country the cost should be less.

Price for working plans, specifications and * license to build, - - - - - - - - - - - $15.00
Price for †† bill of materials, - - - - - - 5.00

Address, THE CO-OPERATIVE BUILDING PLAN ASSOCIATION, Architects, 63 Broadway, New York.

FEASIBLE MODIFICATIONS: Heights of stories, colors, sizes of rooms and kinds of materials may be changed. A root cellar may be placed under part of the building. Side entrance may be placed in stable. Box stall may be planned from two single stalls. Feeding room may be omitted, giving more space for stalls. Ladder may be substituted for stairway and more space gained for carriage room. Chimney and second story rooms may be omitted.

The price of working plans, specifications, etc., for a modified design varies according to the alterations required, and will be made known upon application to the Architects.

293

THE CO-OPERATIVE BUILDING PLAN ASSOCIATION, ARCHITECTS, 63 BROADWAY, NEW YORK.

*Shoppell's Modern Houses—*Designs Patented.*   *Stable, Design No. 369.*

PERSPECTIVE.

DESCRIPTION.

For explanation of all symbols (* † etc.) see page 42.

GENERAL DIMENSIONS : Width, including manure pit, 41 ft. 6 in.; depth, 29 ft. Heights of stories : First story, 10 ft.; second story, 8 ft.

EXTERIOR MATERIALS : Foundations, stone; first story, stable part brick, carriage house part clapboards and shingles; second story and gables, panels and shingles; roof, shingles.

INTERIOR FINISH : Inside of exposed brick walls and the rooms in second story, plastered hard white finish. Soft wood flooring, trim and stairs. Hard wood stall posts, soft wood partitions; hard wood caps, mangers and troughs. Soft wood harness closets. Interior wood-work, including all exposed studding and under side of second story flooring, oiled.

COLORS : Brick-work cleaned down and oiled. Clapboards painted light red to correspond with brick-work. Trim, cornices, brackets, finials and ventilating slats, dark red. Outside doors, dark red with light red panels. Sashes, dark green. Weather vane, black with gilt letters, arrow and finial. All wall shingles dipped and brush coated Tuscan yellow. Roof shingles dipped and brush coated dark brown.

ACCOMMODATIONS: Stalls, rooms, closets, etc., shown by the floor plan. Manure pit placed conveniently near the stable and well ventilated above roof. Washing stand connected with the drain. Under the main ventilator is a hoistway for taking up bales, bags, etc. Coachman's room in second story, heated by a register connected with harness room stove. Harness and carriage rooms well separated from stable to avoid effects of gases upon varnish. Vehicles can enter at either side.

COST : $1,458. The estimate is based on ‡ New York prices for materials and labor. In many sections of the country the cost should be less.

Price for working plans, specifications and * license to build, - - - - - - - - - - - $25.00
Price for † † bill of materials, - - - - - 5.00

Address, THE CO-OPERATIVE BUILDING PLAN ASSOCIATION, Architects, 63 Broadway, New York.

FEASIBLE MODIFICATIONS : Heights of stories, colors, sizes of rooms and kinds of materials may be changed. Attic finish may be omitted. Vertical ladder may take the place of attic stairs. Two extra stalls may be planned where box stall and stairs are now shown. Doors may be placed where gates are shown.

The price of working plans, specifications, etc., for a modified design varies according to the alterations required, and will be made known upon application to the Architects.

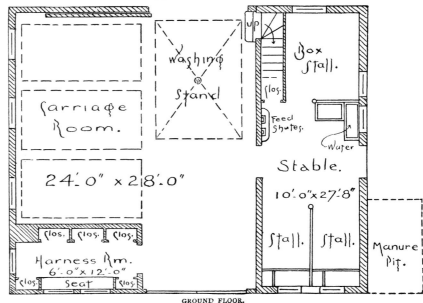

GROUND FLOOR.

294

THE CO-OPERATIVE BUILDING PLAN ASSOCIATION, ARCHITECTS, 63 BROADWAY, NEW YORK.

*Shoppell's Modern Houses—*Designs Patented.* *Stable, Design No. 310*

FRONT ELEVATION.

DESCRIPTION.

For explanation of all symbols (* † etc.) see page 42.

GENERAL DIMENSIONS: Width, 40 ft.; depth, 24 ft. Height of first story, 10 ft.; second story extends to rafters.

EXTERIOR MATERIALS: Foundations, stone; first and second stories, clapboards; roof, shingles.

INTERIOR FINISH: Soft wood flooring, with portable slat floor in stalls. Interior trim and stairs, soft wood. Hard wood stall posts; soft wood partitions; hard wood mangers and feeding troughs. Stall posts, oiled; remainder of interior left unpainted.

COLORS: All clapboards, light chocolate. Trim and rain conductors, dark chocolate. Outside doors, maroon with dark chocolate panels. Sashes, maroon. Wall shingles dipped and brush coated sienna stain. Roof shingles dipped and brush coated dark red stain.

ACCOMMODATIONS: Rooms, stalls, closets, etc., are shown by the plans. Store-room and man's bedroom in second story; feed bins in hay loft with chutes convenient to feeding passage. Harness and other closet under stairway. Sliding doors between stable and carriage room, also sliding entrance doors with overhead wheels and track. Hay chute from loft to feed passage. Stalls for four horses and a large carriage room.

COST: $1,575. The estimate is based on ‡ New York prices for materials and labor. In many sections of the country the cost should be less.

Price for working plans, specifications and * license to build, - - - - - - $15.00

Price for † † bill of materials, - - - 5.00

Address, THE CO-OPERATIVE BUILDING PLAN ASSOCIATION, Architects, 63 Broadway, New York.

FEASIBLE MODIFICATIONS: Heights of stories, colors, sizes of rooms and kinds of materials may be changed. Feeding passage, finished rooms in second story, and roof ventilator, may be omitted. Box stall may be planned in place of two single stalls. Ladder to loft may be planned in place of staircase. Doorway may be placed at rear of stable passage, same as at front. Roof ridge may be extended and terminate in large gables at ends, giving more space in second story.

The price of working plans, specifications, etc., for a modified design varies according to the alterations required, and will be made known upon application to the Architects.

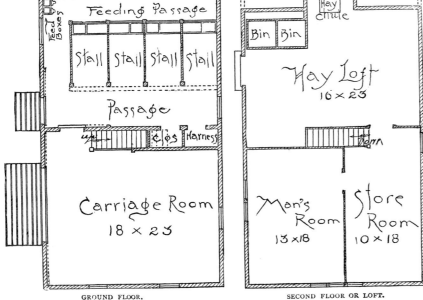

GROUND FLOOR. SECOND FLOOR OR LOFT.

295

THE CO OPERATIVE BUILDING PLAN ASSOCIATION, ARCHITECTS, 63 BROADWAY, NEW YORK.

Shoppell's Modern Houses—*Designs Patented.   *Stable, Design No. 311*

PERSPECTIVE.

DESCRIPTION.

For explanation of all symbols (* † etc.) see page 42.

GENERAL DIMENSIONS : Width, 39 ft. 6 in.; depth, 36 ft. Heights of stories : First story, 11 ft.; second story (man's room), 7 ft. 6 in.

EXTERIOR MATERIALS: Foundations, stone; first story, clapboards; second story and roof, shingles.

INTERIOR FINISH : Man's room finished with two coat plaster and whitewashed. Soft wood flooring; top slat flooring with space between in stalls. Harness room ceiled with yellow pine. Interior wood-work finished in hard oil, natural color.

COLORS : Clapboards and stall blinds, dark drab. Trim and rain conductors, dark green. Outside doors, dark green with dark drab panels. Sashes, dark red. Washing stand ceiling finished in hard oil. Brick-work and all wall shingles oiled. Roof shingles dipped and brush coated red stain.

ACCOMMODATIONS : Rooms, stalls, closets, etc., are shown by the floor plan. Man's room in second story heated by flue which passes up from harness room. Stall accommodations for four horses ; room for three or four carriages.

COST : $1,930. The estimate is based on ‡ New York prices for materials and labor. In many sections of the country the cost should be less.

Price for working plans, specifications and * license to build, - - - - - - - - - $25.00

Price for † † bill of materials, - - - - - 5.00

Address, THE CO-OPERATIVE BUILDING PLAN ASSOCIATION, Architects, 63 Broadway, New York.

FEASIBLE MODIFICATIONS : Heights of stories, colors, sizes of rooms and kinds of materials may be changed. Man's room, cemented washing stand and roof ventilator, may be omitted. Box stall may be planned for two single stalls. Entrance to carriage room may be directly at the front.

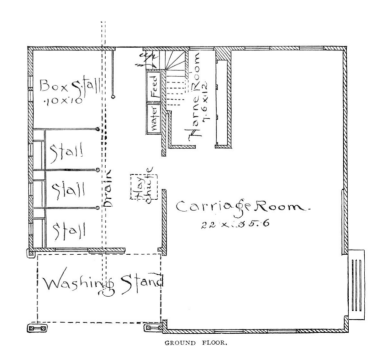

GROUND FLOOR.

The price of working plans, specifications, etc., for a modified design varies according to the alterations required, and will be made known upon application to the Architects.

296

THE CO-OPERATIVE BUILDING PLAN ASSOCIATION, ARCHITECTS, 63 BROADWAY, NEW YORK.

*Shoppell's Modern Houses—*Designs Patented.*   *Stable. Design No. 477*

PERSPECTIVE.

REAR ELEVATION.

DESCRIPTION.

For explanation of all symbols (* † etc.) see page 42.

GENERAL DIMENSIONS: Width, 52 ft.; depth, 35 ft. 6 in. Heights of stories: First story, 10 ft.; second story (man's room), 7 ft. 6 in.

EXTERIOR MATERIALS: Foundation, brick; first story, clapboards; second story, gables and roof, shingles.

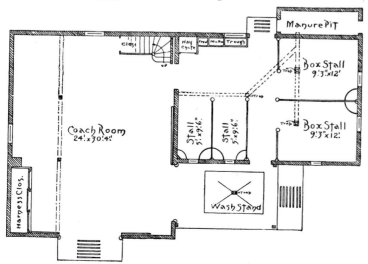

GROUND PLAN.

INTERIOR FINISH: Man's room plastered two coats. Flooring soft wood with slat top flooring in stalls. Entire first story wainscoted with hard pine; in the coach room above the wainscoting the walls are ceiled with hard pine. The entire first story ceiling is covered with hard pine. Man's room trimmed with soft wood. All interior wood-work finished in hard oil.

COLORS: Clapboards, sashes and brick-work, Pompeian red. Trim and rain conductors, dark green. Outside doors, dark green with light olive green panels. Porch, and washing stand ceiling, light olive green. Wall shingles dipped and brush coated Pompeian red. Roof shingles left natural.

ACCOMMODATIONS: Stalls, coach room, etc., are shown by the plan. Man's room second story, also storage space for hay and feed, with chutes for sending hay and feed to first story. Two box and two single stalls properly drained to manure pit. Washing stand is out of the way of carriage entrance. Dwarf tower for tank and wind-mill. Sliding doors in coach room. All wood-work in stalls exposed to "cribbing" are protected by metal.

COST: $2,330, † not including tank and wind-mill. The estimate is based on ‡ New York prices for materials and labor. In many sections of the country the cost should be less.

Price for working plans, specifications, and * license to build, - - - - - - - - - - - $20.00

Price for † † bill of materials, - - - - - - - 3.30

Address, THE CO-OPERATIVE BUILDING PLAN ASSOCIATION, Architects, 63 Broadway, New York.

FEASIBLE MODIFICATIONS: Heights of stories, colors, sizes of rooms and kinds of materials may be changed. Man's room, washing stand, manure pit, tank tower and wind-mill may be omitted. Box stalls may be planned for four single stalls.

The price of working plans, specifications, etc., for a modified design varies according to the alterations required, and will be made known upon application to the Architects.

297

THE CO-OPERATIVE BUILDING PLAN ASSOCIATION, ARCHITECTS, 63 BROADWAY, NEW YORK.

*Shoppell's Modern Houses—*Designs Patented.*   *Stable, Design No. 475*

PERSPECTIVE.

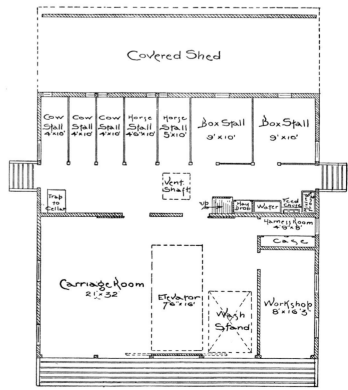

Side Elevation.

DESCRIPTION.

For explanation of all symbols (* † etc.) see page 42.

GENERAL DIMENSIONS: Width, 41 ft. 6 in.; depth, 52 ft., including rear shed. Heights of stories: Cellar, 6 ft. 6 in.; first story, 10 ft.

EXTERIOR MATERIALS: Foundations, stone; first story, clapboards; second story, tower, gables and roof, shingles.

INTERIOR FINISH: Soft wood floor. Hard pine trim in first story, soft wood finish in second story. Soft wood wainscoting in carriage and harness rooms, and workshop. Hard pine posts for stalls; soft wood partitions. All interior wood-work oiled.

COLORS: Clapboards, seal brown. Trim and outside doors, maroon. Sashes and rain conductors, dark green. Gable panels, seal brown with maroon frames. Wall shingles dipped and brush coated light sienna stain. Roof shingles dipped and brush coated Indian red.

ACCOMMODATIONS: The principal rooms, stalls, closets, etc., are shown by the plan. Root cellar with stone walls under part of the carriage room. Vehicle elevator from carriage room to loft. Cart and implement shed at rear. Open loft for storage of hay, grain, vehicles, etc. Harness room, workshop and washing stand convenient to carriage room. Vent shaft in stable ceiling is carried up to top of tower, the roof of which forms a ventilator. Feed chutes from second story to first story.

COST: $2,510. The estimate is based on ‡ New York prices for materials and labor. In many sections of the country the cost should be less.

Price for working plans, specifications and * license to build, - - - - - - - $25.00
Price for † † bill of materials, - - - - - 5.00
Address, THE CO-OPERATIVE BUILDING PLAN ASSOCIATION, Architects, 63 Broadway, New York.

FEASIBLE MODIFICATIONS: Heights of stories, colors, sizes of rooms and kinds of materials may be changed. Cellar may be omitted. A tank may be placed in tower. Man's room may be planned for second story. Workshop may be placed in second story, thus enlarging carriage room. Box stalls may be planned for single stalls. Cow stalls may be widened for horse stalls. Covered shed at rear may be omitted or enclosed to form additional stable room. Elevator and washing stand may be omitted.

GROUND FLOOR.

THE CO-OPERATIVE BUILDING PLAN ASSOCIATION, ARCHITECTS, 63 BROADWAY, NEW YORK.

*Shoppell's Modern Houses—*Designs Patented.*   *Stable, Design No. 510*

PERSPECTIVE.

DESCRIPTION.

For explanation of all symbols (* † etc.) see page 42.

GENERAL DIMENSIONS: Width, including shed, 66 ft. 8 in.; depth, 37 ft. 2 in. Height of first story, 10 ft.

EXTERIOR MATERIALS: Foundations, stone; first story, clapboards; second story, gables and roof, shingles.

INTERIOR FINISH: Soft wood floors; top flooring in stalls laid with incline to gutters. Trim of first story, hard pine; soft wood trim in man's room. Interior wood-work finished in hard oil.

COLORS: Clapboards, sashes and brick-work, Pompeian red. Trim and rain conductors, dark green. Outside doors, dark green with light olive green panels. Porch floor, dark red. Porch ceiling, light olive green. Wall shingles dipped and brush coated Pompeian red. Roof shingles left natural.

ACCOMMODATIONS: The principal rooms and their sizes, closets, stalls, etc., are shown by the floor plan. One room finished in second story for stable man. Washing stand placed out of the way of carriage entrance. Water-closet at rear of carriage room. Feed passage at head of stalls. Shed for visitors' vehicles. Well ventilated manure pit convenient to stable.

COST: $2,609. The estimate is based on ‡ New York prices for materials and labor. In many sections of the country the cost should be less.

Price for working plans, specifications and * license to build, - - - - - - - - - - - $21.09
Price for †† bill of materials, - - - - - - 5.00

Address, THE CO-OPERATIVE BUILDING PLAN ASSOCIATION, Architects, 63 Broadway, New York.

FEASIBLE MODIFICATIONS: Height of story, colors, sizes of rooms and kinds of materials may be changed. Washing stand, water closet, man's room, shed, manure pit and harness room may be omitted. Box stalls may be planned for single stalls. Staircase from second story may be omitted and a ladder substituted, thus enlarging carriage room.

The price of working plans, specifications, etc., for a modified design varies according to the alterations required, and will be made known upon application to the Architects.

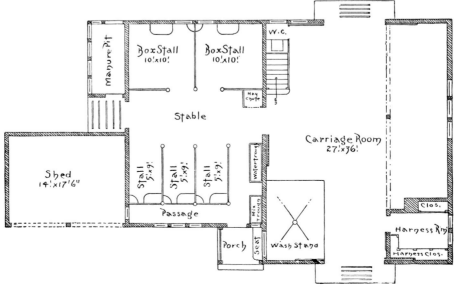

GROUND PLAN.

299

THE CO-OPERATIVE BUILDING PLAN ASSOCIATION, ARCHITECTS, 63 BROADWAY, NEW YORK.

*Shoppell's Modern Houses—*Designs Patented.*   *Stable, Design No. 422*

PERSPECTIVE.

DESCRIPTION.

For explanation of all symbols (* † etc.) see page 42.

GENERAL DIMENSIONS : Width over all, 64 ft. 8 in.; depth, 41 ft. 2 in. Heights of stories : First story, 10 ft.; second story (man's room), 8 ft.

EXTERIOR MATERIALS : Foundations, stone; first story, clapboards ; second story and gables, shingles ; roof, slate.

INTERIOR FINISH : Man's room and closet plastered two coats. Soft wood flooring ; top flooring in stalls inclined to drain. First story wainscoted, and walls and ceilings covered with hard pine boards. All interior wood-work finished in hard oil.

COLORS : Clapboards, sashes and brick-work, Pompeian red. Trim and rain conductors, dark green. Outside doors, dark green with light olive green panels. Porch floor, dark red. Porch ceiling, light olive green. Wall shingles dipped and brush coated Pompeian red.

ACCOMMODATIONS : The principal rooms, closets, stalls, etc., are shown by the floor plans. Man's room partitioned off in second story over harness room, may be heated by a stove in harness room. Water-closet at rear of carriage room. Washing stand at side of carriage room entrance. Well ventilated manure pit convenient to stable. Shed at side of stable. Feeding passage at heads of single stalls.

COST : $2,772. The estimate is based on ‡ New York prices for materials and labor. In many sections of the country the cost should be less.

Price for working plans, specifications and * license to build, - - - - - - - - - - - $30.00
Price for † † bill of materials, - - - - - - 5.00

Address, THE CO-OPERATIVE BUILDING PLAN ASSOCIATION, Architects, 63 Broadway, New York.

FEASIBLE MODIFICATIONS : Heights of stories, colors, sizes of rooms and kinds of materials may be changed. Second story balcony, harness room bay window, washing stand, shed, manure pit, water-closet and man's room, may be omitted. Single stalls may be planned in place of box stalls.

The price of working plans, specifications, etc., for a modified design varies according to the alterations required, and will be made known upon application to the Architects.

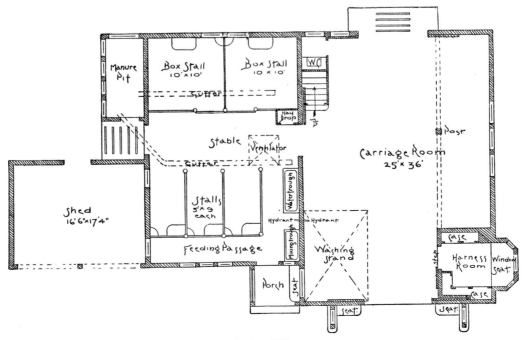

GROUND PLAN.

300

THE CO-OPERATIVE BUILDING PLAN ASSOCIATION, ARCHITECTS, 63 BROADWAY, NEW YORK.

Shoppell's Modern Houses—*Designs Patented.   *Stable, Design No. 476*

SIDE ELEVATION.

PERSPECTIVE.

DESCRIPTION.

For explanation of all symbols (* † etc.) see page 42.

GENERAL DIMENSIONS: Width, 48 ft.; depth, 41 ft. 4 in. Height of first story, 11 ft.

EXTERIOR MATERIALS: Foundations, stone; first story, brick; second story and gables, shingles; roof, slate.

INTERIOR FINISH: Two coat plaster in rooms of stable men. Double floor in first story, top flooring of hard pine. Flooring in second story hard pine with smooth surface laid to form ceiling for first story. Slat floor in stalls with proper slope to gutters. Carriage room wainscoted with hard pine. Inside of brick walls pointed with red mortar. Second story floor joists smooth, hard pine. Interior wood-work oiled. Carriage entrance doors hard pine.

COLORS: All brick-work cleaned down at completion and oiled. All wall shingles dipped and brush coated red stain. Porch posts, all cornices and other moldings, window and door frames, dark green. Carriage house doors oiled, all other doors painted dark green with light green panels. Sashes, red. Porch ceiling oiled.

ACCOMMODATIONS: The principal rooms and their sizes, closets, stalls, etc., are shown by the floor plans. In the carriage house a storage room is shut off by slide doors; carriages not in constant use may be kept there away from dust and dirt. Two rooms for stable men in second story, besides three grain bins and ample storage space for hay, etc. Water-closet in first story.

COST: $3,039. The estimate is based on † New York prices for materials and labor. In many sections of the country the cost should be less.

Price for working plans, specifications and * license to build, - - - - - - - - - - - - $30.00
Price for †† bill of materials, - - - - - 5.00

FEASIBLE MODIFICATIONS: Height of story, colors, sizes of rooms and kinds of materials may be changed. Stable man's room, carriage wash, water-closet, sliding doors and storage room, may be omitted. Harness room may be turned to open into carriage room. Single stalls may be planned in place of box stalls. Entrance to carriage room may be directly at front instead of at side. Chimney and feed bins may be omitted. Harness room may be reduced in size. Ladder may be substituted for stairway.

The price of working plans, specifications, etc., for a modified design varies according to the alterations required, and will be made known upon application to the Architects.

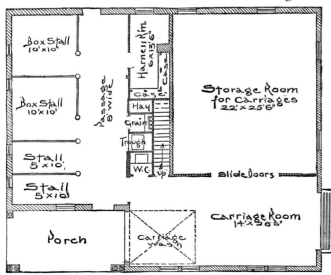

GROUND FLOOR.

SECOND FLOOR.